Praise for *Comparing Religions*

"Jeffrey Kripal provides a thoughtful and compelling discussion of key themes, ideas, and challenges that ground the study of religion across traditions and geographies. It is a layered and textured treatment that will capture the imagination and engage students from start to finish. This important and timely text is not to be missed."

Anthony B. Pinn,
author of *Introducing African American Religion*

"*Comparing Religions* is a lucid, entertaining, and even fun introduction to the comparative study of religion. It will be effective with its target audience, young people and the undergraduate classroom, because, while they must wrestle with the way scholars deconstruct and reduce to social or evolutionary functions such phenomena, Kripal never loses sight of the experiences and meanings of those transformed by, engaged in, and mobilized through it. There is no better single volume to entice students into the fraught and fascinating study of religion."

Bron Taylor,
author of *Dark Green Religion: Nature Spirituality and the Planetary Future*
and editor of *The Encyclopedia of Religion and Nature*

"Kripal is at his very best in this exceptional introduction to the study of religion. After a self-reflexive journey through the religious realms of myth, ritual, nature, science, sex, charisma, soul, salvation, and the imagination and its paranormal powers, we are guided to put it all back together with an eye to religious tolerance, freedom, and pluralism. This book is the red pill. Ingest it and you will be enlightened."

April D. DeConick,
Rice University

"Armed with an extensive array of case studies and a richly diverse portfolio of illustrations, Kripal not only provides a lucid survey of the "facts" of the world's religions but also inspires us to embrace the fundamentally transcendent nature of the religious experience in all of its manifestations, both ordinary and uncanny, and to confront the inherent challenges of studying religion in a responsibly comparative manner. *Comparing Religions* is a masterly example of how a book intended for the classroom can be an invigorating stimulus toward new ways of thinking about a phenomenon that pervades every aspect of our world."

Sarah Iles Johnston,
The Ohio State University

"This book offers the most original and provocative recasting of the comparative study of religion in decades, and it's aimed just where we need this rethinking the most—the classroom. Other textbooks tend to work with a checklist of subjects as they summon the major religions serially to the stage. Kripal starts instead with the mystery of the comparative act itself, allowing that to determine what he brings forward for our attention. So it's charisma, sex, the paranormal, and "soul practices" more than it's Hinduism, Buddhism, and Islam. Kripal recognizes the comparativist in each of us and urges us to take it seriously. The result is deep and wide, and excitingly open minded."

John Stratton Hawley,
Barnard College, Columbia University

COMPARING RELIGIONS

Coming to Terms

Jeffrey J. Kripal

with Ata Anzali, Andrea R. Jain, and Erin Prophet

The Reader (2011), digital artwork by Rob Beschizza for BoingBoing and Jeffrey J. Kripal, "Psi-Fi: Popular Culture and the Paranormal."

WILEY Blackwell

Library of Congress Cataloging-in-Publication data is available for this book.

ISBN 9781118774878 (hardback); ISBN 9781405184588 (paperback)

A catalogue record for this book is available from the British Library.

Cover image: Jaume Plensa, *Mirror*, 2011. Painted stainless steel / 377 × 243 × 245 cm each. Collection: Rice University, Houston, Texas, USA, photographed by Jenna L. Kripal. © DACS 2013
Cover design by Simon Levy Associates

Set in 10/13pt Minion by SPi Publisher Services, Pondicherry, India
Printed and bound in Malaysia by Vivar Printing Sdn Bhd

3   2016

God Appears & God is Light
To those poor Souls who dwell in Night,
But does a Human Form Display
To those who dwell in Realms of day.

William Blake, "Auguries of Innocence"

Be then, within yourself, a receptacle for the forms of all beliefs, for God is too vast and too great to be confined to one belief to the exclusion of another, for indeed He says, "Wheresoever ye turn, there is the Face of God."

Ibn 'Arabi, *Bezels of Wisdom*

About the website

This book has a companion website containing a range of resources for instructors, students, and other readers. The features include:

- a set of simple guidelines for doing responsible comparison
- a set of brief summaries of the standard world religion systems
- suggestions for further reading
- an annotated bibliography of explicitly comparative works
- glossary
- sample syllabus and teaching ideas

and a range of other materials.

These resources can be accessed at www.wiley.com/go/kripal.

Contents

An Important Note to the Instructor
Or Why You Should (or Should Not) Teach This Text

Truly speaking, it is not instruction, but provocation that I can receive from another soul.
Ralph Waldo Emerson, Divinity School Address, 15 July 1838

Education is not the filling of a pail, but the lighting of a fire.
William Butler Yeats

This is a book that focuses on the histories, nuances, promises, and costs of different comparative practices and their potential importance for our contemporary world, not on the content of the religions themselves. It is about exactly what it announces in its subtitle: "coming to terms" with the comparative method itself. This means understanding the comparative method's ancient roots in the religions themselves and, above all, in radical, often heterodox mystical forms of experience and expression. It means understanding the method's paradoxical structures and simultaneous challenges to *both* rationalist reductionism *and* dogmatic religious belief: understanding them "beyond reason" in one case and "beyond belief" in the other. It means refusing to demean and dismiss the comparative enterprise with perfectly true half-truths and a historical consciousness that can see no further back than a few hundred years. It means recognizing comparison everywhere, from the polytheistic logic of ancient Egyptian, Greek, and Roman religions, through the Indian poet Kabir and his radical singing beyond Hindu and Muslim identity, to Darwin's *Origin of Species* and the most basic cognitive structures of the human brain, as mapped

in modern neuroscience. But, above all, this "coming to terms" means acknowledging and working through the very real existential costs (cultural, emotional, religious, familial, and moral) that a disciplined comparative practice demands of anyone who dares take up its call.

Obviously, then, this is not a "world religions" textbook of the kind that goes through each major religion, treats all of them as more or less closed systems of practice and thought, and leaves them mostly unchallenged at the end. I am by no means against such an approach, and I recognize that it can serve all sorts of important remedial purposes. I must confess to a deeper disquiet, though; for I have come to see, with many a colleague (maybe you), that the standard "world religions" approach tends to leave most of the interesting questions and all of the most difficult ones unasked, much less answered. It can also, all too easily, leave unchallenged traditional forms of religious identity and their identity politics, which has played such a central role in real-world conflict. In the language of the historian of religions Charles Long, what I have grown most concerned about is the way in which our academic discipline has helped produce a whole series of *significations*, that is, signs that are much too certain of themselves and that, moreover, hide or suppress their own constructed nature.[1] Students can walk away from such a classroom confirmed in their convictions that they are indeed an eternal this or that, instead of a human being born into a particular cultural context and taking on a particular social and religious identity that is itself largely determined by previous historical processes, cultural debates, institutions, and violences.

This insight into the constructed nature of all types of social and religious identity can be quite disturbing. Or quite liberating. If, after all, we can take apart these social constructions, we can also put them back together again, in new and more adequate forms.

This taking apart and putting back together is what the present book is all about. Its basic premise is that a truly effective pedagogy needs to identify the existential costs of the modern study of religion and then deal with them openly and positively. Put more directly, this text asks us, as both teachers and students, to own up to the radicalism of what we are actually doing in the study of religion. Just as importantly, it asks us to hope for *far more* from the study of religion than we are accustomed to hoping. It warns and celebrates.

Comparing Religions attempts to accomplish this double goal through a modal initiatory structure. The book is divided into three distinct parts: (1) a first part of three chapters in which we historically locate the comparative practices discussed here and ask the students to define their worldviews as they prepare to take up their own comparative practices; (2) a middle or "liminal" part of six chapters in which we guide the student/reader through a series of comparative acts that are meant to be illustrative but by no means exhaustive; and (3) a final part of three chapters in which we ask the student/readers to "come back" to their own beliefs and convictions and to restate them in the light of the comparative acts in which they have engaged over the last few months. The entire book, in short, is organized around the naming, questioning, and revisioning of

the religious or secular identities of the students themselves.

There are five things to emphasize here.

1   The first and most important thing to say is that *the textual initiation, like any initiation, is not for everyone and so requires an initial taking of responsibility and a moral assent on the part of the student or reader.* That is to say, the student needs to be told, up front and immediately, that the existential risks are very real here and that what follows may well feel like an ordeal or trial, even as it points toward a potential transformation at the end.

2   The second thing to emphasize is that *the basic spirit and intent of the book is positive and constructive, not negative and deconstructive.* The text certainly embraces, celebrates, and practices a whole spectrum of reductive and deconstructionist methods (there is plenty here to provoke just about anyone, including the secularist and materialist), but it does not leave the student hanging in the end, without anything positive or hopeful to take away. It does not deconstruct "religion" down into a depressing mush. Rather the book is explicitly designed to help the student engage the critical study of religion in its full force and then emerge from this engagement with a positive and constructive outlook on how to re-read religion.

3   The third thing to emphasize is that, *in both structure and conversational tone, the text is focused on the individual reader.* So, for example, in the third and final part we offer the students a number of options, leaving it to the individual to choose one (or two or three) of these. The goal, obviously, is not to reach the "correct" answer (the comparative study of religion is not a standardized multiple-answer test), but to arrive at a new level of reflexivity and awareness about how religious worldviews function, how they come to be (and come not to be), and how they work in relation to other worldviews.

4   Fourthly, *the book privileges structure over content.* The initiatory or tripartite structure has one major,

and perhaps surprising, implication: in some real sense, it does not matter what you teach in the middle section of the course. What does matter is that you provide the students with enough "confusion" and "difference" here in order to challenge (and thereby sharpen, deepen, or broaden) their specific worldviews and assumptions about sameness, *whatever* those happen to be. Put a bit differently, in the end it does not matter so much what that confusion or difference is, only that the matter is sufficiently confusing and different.

Toward this end, we have provided a set of chapters on six robust comparative themes, many of which we hope you find useful. But you should feel no pressure to use all of them, and you, of course, should feel free to substitute your own. I would also strongly encourage you to provide sets of lectures on at least three different religious traditions at this "liminal" point in the course. The book, in other words, is explicitly designed to work in tandem with an expert: that is, with you. So play to your strengths here. I did.

The flipside is that I am keenly aware of what I do not know, which is really everything other than the few things I do know. Accordingly, I approached the five years it took to write this text with a sensibility that bounced back and forth somewhere between humility, moral despair, and professional terror. Which is all to say that I am all too aware of the text's shortcomings and limitations, particularly with respect to content and cultural reach. I am especially aware of the book's slim treatment of indigenous and tribal religions. I ask you, then, to read and use these pages not as a vain attempt to cover everything, but as one colleague's sincere effort to capture something of the fire that first brought so many of us to the field in the first place. I am mostly after that fire, not after the different pieces of wood that feed it.

5   Fifthly and finally, *the book privileges the extraordinary and the uncanny over the ordinary and the common.* This is probably its primary originality (and offense). I am, after all, hyper-aware that colleagues have argued, and continue to argue, for the

exactly opposite approach, namely that we need to get away from the religious as the fantastic, as the weird, as the strange. We should not be exoticizing religion. We should be normalizing it. J. Z. Smith's eloquent plea, in *Imagining Religion* (1982), for studying religion in the ordinary rather than in the exotic—in "what we see in Europe every day" rather than in those things "which excite horror and make men stare"—is perhaps the most famous example of this position: a position that he captured again, perhaps humorously, in the title of his third collection of essays, *Drudgery Divine* (1990).[2]

Like many, I consider Smith to be a pillar of the field, and I understand and respect this commitment to the ordinary, particularly if one is more sociologically inclined. The statistical and demographic methods of sociology, after all, flatten out and finally erase the anomalous: they turn the divine into the drudgery of Smith's book title. But I happen to think that this normalizing and flattening out of the sacred is largely a function of *what we have chosen to take off the table.* That is, it is a function of what we have chosen to focus on and what we have refused to look at seriously. If we put other things on the table again (as this text clearly does), the field looks very different and, I dare say, much more attractive and exciting to an eighteen-year-old (not to mention this fifty-year-old).

Let me lay my cards on the same table: because I work in comparative mystical literature, a literature that features some of the most extreme experiences on record, I have come to conclude that actual historical human encounters with the sacred *are* uncanny, *are* fantastic, indeed they are often so strange that we cannot possibly exaggerate this weirddom. I even have a personal rule, which I developed out of my ethnographic experiences with individuals who have known such encounters up close and personal: the more one discovers about these kinds of events, the weirder they get. Put differently, such histories become *more* improbable, not less, the more we know about them. I am thus skeptical of models of religion that focus on the normal, on the everyday, and on the ways these events are domesticated, rationalized, and institutionalized. All that, too, is "religion"— of course. Maybe it is most of religion. But, if we *only* focus on these social processes, we will get a very flat view of religion, which is exactly what we have today in much of the field.

I also have a deeper concern here, namely that normalizing scholarship on "ordinary" religion is part of this same domestication, rationalization, and erasure of the sacred. It is as if we can study everything about religion, except what makes it fiercely religious. And then we are told that there is nothing essentially or really religious about religion, which of course is true if we have just erased all of the weird stuff with our methods and philosophical assumptions. If we have taken everything off the table that can challenge our own reigning materialisms, relativisms, and constructivisms, then everything will look like more evidence for materialism, relativism, and constructivism. Which is where we are at the moment.

I am always humorously reminded of a classic sci-fi movie at this point in my long-standing argument with the field. Our present materialist and historicist models have rendered human nature something like the protoganist Scott Carey in the film *The Incredible Shrinking Man* (1957). With every passing decade, that human nature is getting tinier and tinier and less and less significant. In a few more years we'll just blip out of existence, like poor Scott at the end of the film, reduced to nothing more than cognitive modules, replicating strings of DNA, quantum-sensitive microtubules in the synapses of the brain, or whatever. Either that, or these same methods will simply kill us off. Indeed, at this point, we are constantly reminded of the "death of the subject" and told repeatedly that we are basically walking corpses with computers on top—in effect, technological zombies or moist robots. We are in the fantastically ridiculous situation where conscious intellectuals are telling us that consciousness does not really exist as such, that there is nothing to it except cognitive grids, software loops, and warm brain matter. If this were not so patently absurd, it would be very funny.

Why do we want to be so incredibly small? And why do we allow these present philosophical assumptions—and they *are* assumptions—to erase entire swaths of the history of religions, which give powerful witness to the exact opposite, namely that human nature is immense, that mind is not brain, that consciousness is not cognition, and that there is something fundamentally transcendent about, well, us? This does *not* mean that we should then deny or ignore the everyday, the institutional politics, the violences, the daily rituals, the emotions and sensibilities of piety, the visual art and material culture, the demographics, "what we see in Europe every day." Of course not. Why do we have to keep playing ping-pong here? Back and forth. Back and forth. As if we could not simply do both and move on. This, anyway, is the conclusion of the present text: "*Do both.*" Which, of course, is precisely what the field *as a whole*, as a "big tent," has been doing all along.

At the end of the day, however, I have not written this text for our own internal professional debates. I have written it for young people with little or no exposure to what we do and why. I am talking to, chatting with, joking with, provoking them. I would ask, then, that you judge the book and its sometimes admittedly eccentric choices by the total effect these pages have on your students, and not by the measure of whether it fits into this or that professional consensus.

It probably does not, by the way. That was the whole point in writing it.

Notes

1 Charles H. Long, *Significations: Signs, Symbols, and Images in the Interpretation of Religion* (Philadelphia, PA: Fortress Press, 1986).
2 J. Z. Smith, *Imagining Religion: From Babylon to Jonestown* (Chicago, IL: University of Chicago Press, 1982), xii.

A Comment on the Cover Image and the Paintings

Both the cover image and the paintings that announce each chapter are expressions of the vibrant art scene of my campus and home city: Rice University in Houston, Texas.

The cover features the sculpture *Mirror* of the Spanish artist Jaume Plensa. This piece was installed at the center of the campus of Rice University in the spring of 2012, while I was finishing this textbook. Happily, it embodies in striking ways the core practices of the following pages. The two seated figures peacefully face each other, mirroring each other with literally "open" fronts (one can often see children playing inside them). They are also entirely open to the environment: the light, wind, and weather move effortlessly through them, *are* them. Each of their immense bodies, moreover, is constituted entirely of letters from the world's languages (and hence religions), as if to suggest the potentialities inherent in the human form. I imagine these two figures as giant "comparative bodies" that have attained their present magnificence through the radical openness, reflexive mirroring, and spirited diversity that is comparative practice.

The paintings that open each new part and chapter are all by the Houston surrealist artist Lynn Randolph. Lynn and I met a few years ago, after she had read some of my work on erotic mystical literature and detected deep resonances between what she was trying to do on the canvas and what I was trying to do on the page. After I encountered her stunning paintings, I could not agree more. Like the religious imagination at its best, Lynn's paintings are ambiguous, paradoxical, open to multiple meanings, fierce in their honesty and criticism, gorgeous in their bodies, and, above all, magically capable of pushing their viewers into a direct vision, an intuited sense, or at least a gut suspicion that the real is not what we think it is. At all. With Lynn's help, I will be attempting something similar in the pages that follow through the brush strokes, some of them quite surreal, of my words. We paint together here.

Illustrations

Acknowledgments

I would most like to thank Rebecca Harkin, my editor at Wiley-Blackwell. I still remember the day when I received an e-mail from her, in the spring of 2008, asking me to consider proposing a textbook for Wiley-Blackwell on the subject of comparing world religions. I responded that I could not see myself writing another world religions textbook. She artfully responded that she was not asking me to write a world religions textbook; she was asking me to propose something different. Rebecca caught my attention, and then about five years of my teaching and writing life. She has been an ideal editor, guiding, prodding, and supporting the project from beginning to end. Rebecca also employed some most careful and insightful anonymous readers of the manuscript at different stages, who responded to the project with enthusiasm, care, and constructive criticism. I have tried my very best to take their suggestions and criticisms to heart, even when I occasionally disagreed with them, in some cases profoundly.

I am also in debt to Rice University's Humanities Research Center in the persons of Vice Provost Caroline Levander (the former director of the Center), Carolyn Adams, Dr. Melissa Bailar, Lauren Kleinschmidt, and, most recently, Director and Professor Farès El-Dahdah. The Center has supported this project through multiple channels, including a Mellon-funded seminar on the history and practice of comparativism and a semester-long teaching leave. As has my dean, Dean Nicolas Shumway, who has done more than anyone to support my work and welfare in these middle years. I am extremely grateful.

I must also thank my co-writers. I wrote this textbook after teaching the aforementioned Mellon Seminar, and then, again in the spirit of the Mellon Foundation's desire to encourage collaborative research, with the help of four of my advanced graduate students: Michael Adair-Kriz, Ata Anzali, Andrea Jain, and Erin Prophet. This, by the way, is why the voice of the text alternates, consciously and intentionally, between the "I" and the "we" (I have consciously used "I" in those places where I want to make it clear that what is being said reflects my own positions and approaches, which, of course, are not always those of my co-writers). Michael is an anthropologist and Mormon who wrote his dissertation on graffiti art and gay identity in Chile. He eventually had to leave the project for other academic commitments, but he was, and is, an important conversation partner. Ata is a historian of religions teaching at Middlebury College and working on Sufi traditions of the Islamic world, especially in Iran, from a comparative perspective. Andrea is a scholar of Indian religions teaching at Indiana University-Purdue University Indianapolis who shares a dual

Jain and Protestant parentage and is presently finishing her first book on the constructions of yoga in contemporary consumer culture. My fourth co-writer, Erin Prophet, is presently studying with me here at Rice as an expert on new religious movements in the USA, partly out of deep and abiding intellectual interests, partly because she grew up in one. Obviously, comparison is much more than an abstract intellectual exercise for this team. It is who we are.

Another key contributor to the textbook is Lynn Randolph, a gifted surrealist artist here in Houston who initially contacted me after reading some of my work. Lynn's paintings and person grace the following pages and, I hope, provide the work with a striking and consistent aesthetics that will be difficult to forget. The truth is that I have always thought of my own work as an intellectual and literary expression of the surreal and that I wanted to be an artist in my youth, so this was an especially happy collaboration for me. Lynn's late husband, Bill, also needs to be recognized here, as his image and his body play key roles in the openings of Chapters 9 and 12.

There were also colleagues who "test-ran" the textbook at different institutions: the New Testament critic and scholar of early Christianity Brent Landau of the University of Oklahoma; the classicist Roshan Abraham of Washington University; and the historian of Christianity and philosopher of religion Chad Pevateaux of St. Mary's College, Maryland. The feedback we received from these colleagues and their students was invaluable.

I would thus like to thank all those who helped me out in specific areas of expertise. In alphabetical order, they were: Egil Asprem on the history of science and psychical research; Harald Atmanspacher on C. G. Jung and Wolfgang Pauli; William Barnard and David Presti on ayahuasca shamanism; Elias Bongmba on African religions; Bernadette J. Brooten on slavery in the monotheisms; Kelly Bulkeley on religion and cognitive science; Nathan Carlin and Elliot Berger on Protestantism and the King James Bible; Francis X. Clooney, SJ, on comparative theology; April DeConick

on the New Testament and early Christianity; Robert Erlewine on monotheism and religious tolerance; Lawrence Foster on Mother Ann and the early Shaker community; Claire Fanger on the history and structure of magic; Michael Grosso on the flying Catholic Saint Joseph of Copertino; David Haberman on the ecological movement and deep ecology; Wouter Hanegraaff on the history and interpretation of western esotericism, and especially on its influence on the academic study of religion; George Hansen on the paranormal and the social sciences; John Stratton Hawley on Hindu devotionalism; Jess Hollenback on the imagination and the symbol; David Hufford and Whitley Strieber on supernatural assault traditions; Mary Keller on possession studies; Louis Komjathy on Daoism; Daniel Levine on nature and religion; Gurinder Singh Mann on Sikh history; Dennis McKenna on psychoactive sacred plants; Richard Miller on liberalism; Brother Gregory Perron, OSB, on comparative theology; Anthony Pinn on African American thought and black theology; Dinesh Sharma on Hinduism; Robert Sharf on the category of experience; Frederick Smith on a note concerning Indo-European linguistics; Richard Smith on China and the *Yijing*; Rob Swigart on human prehistory; Ann Taves on religion, cognitive science, and evolutionary psychology; Bron Taylor on nature and religion; Ross Tieken on nature and religion; Jeff Wamsley on the Mothman and for a really cool drawing; and Elliot Wolfson on the Kabbalah and the paradoxical nature of the symbol.

I am not the first to imagine structuring an intro-level course around a tripartite initiatory structure inspired by the work of Victor Turner (soon to be explained). Indeed I happily borrowed the idea from my colleague Bryan Rennie, who proposed it to me at Westminster College some time around 1995 or so, after which I taught our introductory course there with this same "Turner" technique throughout the second half of the 1990s. I first described this pedagogy in a paper for a conference at the University of Notre Dame organized by James Boyd White under the auspices of the Erasmus Institute in 2000. This paper was later published as "Liminal Pedagogy: The

Liberal Arts and the Transforming Ritual of Religious Studies," in *How Should We Talk About Religion? Perspectives, Contexts, Particularities*, edited by James Boyd White (South Bend, IN: University of Notre Dame Press, 2006). At least one other scholar has practiced something similar within the textbook genre: Gary Kessler in his *Studying Religion: An Introduction through Cases* (New York: McGraw-Hill, 2002), through his elegant categories of Preliminaries, Liminaries, and Postliminaries. I very much want to acknowledge that confirming resonance, even if I did not become aware of it until I had conceived and written much of the present text.

Finally, a collegial request. I have read and written enough books to know that there is no such thing as a perfect book. I at least have never read or written one, and I doubt very much that anyone else has either. We have done our very best to check our facts (when there are facts to check), share sections with experts for feedback, and more or less do everything in our power to ensure as clean a textbook as possible. I am absolutely certain that we have failed. And so I sincerely hope that you will send me any errata that you happen to find via the website that Wiley-Blackwell has so kindly set up around this project.

This is one of the many things that I love about comparison: it is a collegial project through and through, which relies on the intellectual labors of others. Without those colleagues and their labor, there can be no comparison. Comparison is *us*, or it is nothing at all.

Jeffrey J. Kripal
Houston, Texas
15 April 2013

Listen to the Amniotic Cosmos—Once Upon a Time again (1991), by Lynn Randolph. Diptych, left panel, 36″ × 28″.

PART I

Prehistory, Preparation, and Perspective

In these first three chapters we will be concerned about one and only one matter: locating and defining our own perspectives, that is, the "places" from which we are comparing religions.

In Chapter 1 we will sketch out a few of the innumerable comparative practices of the ancient world, since we do not want to leave the impression that comparison is somehow unique to the modern world. In Chapter 2 we will locate the professional study of religion itself: when it arose, where it came from, how it works or "thinks," and what its most basic values are. In Chapter 3, after offering some working definitions and assumptions, we will ask you to think about your own most basic assumptions, define your present worldview, and "place yourself" in terms of the perennial questions that the religions attempt to answer: where we came from, where we are going, what we are, what the purpose of life is, and, finally, what happens to us when we die.

This is a very important exercise, because, as the textbook progresses into Part II, you will find yourself working with a whole host of stories, practices, and truth claims that you will no doubt compare to your own. You cannot do this, of course, unless you know at least something about your own beliefs, values, and assumptions about the world. It is perfectly fine, of course, not to know, or to be uncertain of these. If you are conscious and clear about your uncertainty or about not knowing, that too is a form of knowledge. Indeed, some would say that this is the best knowledge of all; that this kind of humility, uncertainty, and openness is the beginning of wisdom.

Comparing Religions: Coming to Terms, First Edition. Jeffrey J. Kripal, Ata Anzali, Andrea R. Jain, and Erin Prophet.
© 2014 Jeffrey J. Kripal. Published 2014 by John Wiley & Sons, Ltd.

Introduction
Beginnings

I started out my career thinking that people are basically people, and that their cultural and religious differences are minor or superficial. Now I think that people are mostly different, and that their similarities are minor or superficial.

A colleague in the study of Buddhism
and the psychology of religion

There are no others.

Ramana Maharshi (twentieth-century
Hindu spiritual teacher)

The professional study of religion is a rare bird in most people's lives. It is not often seen. Religion, for example, is almost never studied in high school in a country like the US. Religions may well be safely *described* there in, say, a world history course, but they are never critically compared or analyzed. As a consequence, few of the undergraduates who come to my particular university each fall consider majoring in the study of religion, and most of them think that our department is here to meet someone's religious needs or affirm some very particular set of beliefs. They also assume that a religious studies major is "soft," as opposed to the sciences, which are "hard."

The truth is that the study of religion aligns itself with no particular religion and is in fact deeply suspicious of any and all absolute truth claims. This does not mean, however, that the field as a whole is against religion. The discipline is neither pro-religious nor anti-religious (although, as we shall repeatedly see, its comparative terms arose out of very particular religious contexts and its basic methods are clearly incompatible with particular types of religiosity). There is, moreover, nothing "easy" or "soft" about what we do. One of my former students put it best: she felt each day as she left class that her tennis shoes had just burst into flames, that she had just stepped onto some very dangerous, but very exciting ground. And why not? As Margaret M. Mitchell has captured it so well, when we are talking about religion deeply, we are essentially playing with fire. Scholars of religion play with this fire for a living, and we teach others how to do this too, hopefully without getting burnt.[1]

Some of us get burnt anyway.

Which is all to say that scholars of religion are not here to justify or confirm anyone's religious assumptions. We are here to interrogate them. We are here to

Comparing Religions: Coming to Terms, First Edition. Jeffrey J. Kripal, Ata Anzali, Andrea R. Jain, and Erin Prophet.
© 2014 Jeffrey J. Kripal. Published 2014 by John Wiley & Sons, Ltd.

think critically about religious systems the same way political scientists think about political institutions, sociologists think about social systems, anthropologists think about cultures, or literary critics think about literature. Indeed, we use *all* of these to do our own work, for religions are always and everywhere also political, social, cultural, and textual phenomena. You might say that we are radically interdisciplinary. I prefer to think of us as intellectually promiscuous.

I wrote this textbook together with my three co-authors for two reasons. I will, by the way, do my best to make it clear when I am writing strictly in my own voice; you will thus notice a common shift between "I" and "we" in the textbook.

The first conviction out of which I wrote this textbook is that the critical study of religion is the most relevant, the most exciting and dangerous (hence the flaming tennis shoes metaphor), and the most radical intellectual study presently pursued in the colleges and universities of the modern world. The so-called "hard" sciences in fact do the easy stuff: they study things that can be measured, that can be controlled, that can be predicted. We do the truly hard stuff: we study things that cannot be measured, that cannot be controlled, that are fiercely alive, and that are ultimately about the "hardest" of all humanistic and scientific problems: the nature of consciousness itself.

More specifically, it is the methods of the humanities, and particularly those of historiography (the recovery, writing, and analysis of history), that represent the greatest challenge to religious claims.[2] Religious claims, after all, routinely claim to be exempt from history as such, that is, they claim that their scriptures and doctrines are eternal, when in fact good historical scholarship can always show that, whatever else they may or may not point toward, *all* religious expressions—including (and especially) scriptural texts—are also products of human labor, human agency, and human history. Religious texts and beliefs may or may not "fall from the sky," as we say, but they always, always fall through human beings.

The second conviction out of which I wrote this textbook is that the future hinges largely on how future generations, including (and especially) *your* generation, critically compare across cultural, religious, and social divisions.

I am not exaggerating either point. You are about to be introduced to an intellectual practice and to a body of knowledge that leave few unmoved. What you encounter will almost certainly excite you, scare you, or infuriate you. It will also very likely change you and, with you, the world. If you are not ready to be changed and challenged to your very core, put down this textbook and read no further. As David Weddle once put it with respect to his own comparative study of miracles: "Like every serious book, this one is also out to get you."[3]

Consider yourself forewarned.

•••

Before we begin, it is important that you understand the most basic nature of this textbook's central focus: **comparison**. What is comparison anyway? Most simply, comparison is the intellectual act of negotiating **sameness** and **difference** in a set of observations. More complexly, this act of negotiating sameness and difference leads to the recognition of *patterns* and to a subsequent *classification* of what has been observed. Most complexly, these classifications in turn lead to a *theory* about the deep underlying structures that produce these particular patterns, that is, to a model of what might lie behind them. There are at least four stages, then, implied in that single word "comparison": (1) the negotiation of sameness/difference in a set of observations; (2) the identification of patterns in that data set; (3) the construction of a classificatory scheme that organizes these patterns into some meaningful whole; and (4) a theory to explain the patterns one sees.

Comparison lies at the root of some of the simplest acts of perception and thinking. It also lies at the root of some of the most stunning and successful achievements of human thought.

Take Darwin's idea of natural selection, for example, which has since morphed into the achievements of evolutionary biology, the discovery of DNA, and the mapping of the human genome. Darwin's original discovery involved no complicated mathematical formulas or computers. Rather he used the exact same methods that the comparative study of religion employs. He traveled a great deal. He compared this wing in this place to that wing in that place, this limb to that limb, this beak to that bill, and so on, until he recognized patterns, classified them into larger wholes, speculatively mapped them through long stretches of time, and eventually arrived at his model of natural selection. Darwin, in short, was a comparativist through and through.

It is not just Darwin, though. Everyone compares. If you think, you compare. If tomorrow you somehow lost the ability to compare and classify, you would not be able to think or organize your world of experience. Go ahead. Look at some object in the immediate environment in which you are reading this book. If you can step back and watch how you instinctively classify and identify this object, you will notice that what you are really doing is comparing the object and its characteristics to other objects and their characteristics until you can give the object a reliable label within a particular scheme or worldview.

Something like this: "I see an object on a desk across the library reading room. It's red, round, about the size of a fist. It looks like a rubber ball of some kind." I get up from my chair and walk across the reading room, closer, closer. "No, no, I take that back. It has a stem coming out of one end, and it's too shiny under this light to be rubber. It's an apple." I come closer still. I pick it up, feel it, smell it. "No, it's not an apple after all. It's a wax apple, perhaps for some kind of art project. I now see drawing tools on the table around it."

There were mistakes made here, a few perceptual illusions to work through, but they were all eventually corrected until an accurate identification could be made through closer inspection and an understanding of the cultural context of the object, in this case a college art project. Simple stuff. Right?

But what if we are now comparing *subjects* instead of objects, worlds made of *meaning* instead of things made of matter? If you think about human beings, about the seeming infinity of human cultures they have created, and the common human nature that they all share (any infant can be raised in any human culture and successfully learn the language and customs as its own), you will end up comparing in an especially obvious—and especially fraught—way. For one thing, you *are* a human being (you were not a wax apple), so in some sense *you are comparing yourself*—a weird, paradoxical exercise from the start.

This "looking into the mirror" of humanity, however, is further fraught by a very specific tension or balance, which we might define most simply as a both–and. Let us refer to the two poles of this both–and with two of the terms of our opening definition of comparison above; let us refer to them as sameness and difference. We are all, after all, so very similar (the shared human nature of our universal infant). And we are all so very different (the virtual infinity of human cultures of our mature experience). There are religious traditions that emphasize this human sameness. Indeed, many of our most impressive and noble modern values—like human rights, civil liberties, and racial and gender equity—flow out of notions of sameness and equality. Sometimes sameness is justice.

There are also religious traditions, and whole bodies of contemporary critical theory, however, that emphasize the differences, the "absolutely unique" aspects of being human in this or that local context. These traditions and bodies of critical theory not only generally produce better and more detailed scholarship. They are also advanced for key moral reasons. After all, we know all too well how political, social, and religious systems are very good at squashing difference, persecuting minorities, even killing whole peoples who do not fit into some universal notion of what a human being is or should be. Sometimes sameness is deadly.

So any responsible and ethical comparative practice must balance this human sameness and this human difference, see moral value in both, and—most importantly—be ready to be critical of either pole. Hence it is significant that the colleague in the psychology of Buddhism who opened this

Introduction has since mellowed on his conclusion about everyone being so different (they are also similar), and the quotation from the Hindu sage took place in a conversation—that is, in a social space defined by two different persons (in this social sense there are indeed others). This is the most basic truth, the "both–and" or "yes, but" through which all responsible comparison works, including (and especially) the comparative study of religion. That, anyway, is the fundamental claim and lesson of the textbook you hold in your hands.

At times we will veer so far into the difference side of things that you will think we have landed on Mars (we may even spot a few Martians). At other times we will veer so far into the sameness side of things that you will think we have somehow slipped inside your own body and mind. But we will always return to an insistence on the both–and, on the difference *and* the sameness. The Martians may indeed be coming, but it turns out that they look a lot like us.

As I have already pointed out, the stakes are certainly high enough (with comparison now, not with the Martian invasion). It is no doubt an exaggeration, but an instructive one, to suggest that most of our world's social, political, and religious conflicts depend on a fundamental failure to hold that both–and in balance, that is, to suggest that they arise, at least partly, from our inability to look into the mirror of history and culture and compare one another in subtle and sophisticated ways (as opposed to just seeing our own faces, or the faces of demons, terrorists, or unbelievers). More specifically, many of our most dangerous global problems arise from individuals, groups, or whole political systems trying to suppress or erase one or the other pole of this species-wide spectrum of sameness and difference.

It's a depressingly familiar logic. We must all be the same, believe the same things, worship the same invisible deity, think the same thoughts, eat the same things, dress the same way, perform the same rituals, hold the same moral values, have the same color of skin, feel the same sexual desires, and so on. Or, conversely, we must be completely different, so different in fact that "they" are no longer anything like "us,"

and so "we" can kill "them," or at least pass laws and policies to make their lives sufficiently miserable. But we, of course, are not all the same. Nor are we completely different. Nor will we ever be either.

Ever.

Religions are especially obvious subjects to compare because they themselves treat universal human questions (the origin and structure of the world, the meaning of life, the proper uses of sexuality, the boundaries of self and community, morality, suffering, and death), but they come up with very different responses to these same universal experiences. In other words, it is simply not true that all religions teach the same things. Not even close. Moreover, religious traditions have arisen from within (and most often against) previous religious traditions, and so religions are generally keenly aware of the ways their responses to life are similar to and different from the responses of other religions, especially the religions from which they themselves arose. Put simply, *religions compare and are themselves products of comparison.*

Sometimes religions compare in sophisticated and subtle ways. Sometimes religions compare in simplistic and dangerous ways. Sometimes religions deny comparison altogether, as if their values and teachings were "incomparable." Watch out for this. Watch out for anything that claims it is incomparable.

Still, the religious systems that seek to protect themselves from the comparative project do so out of a perfectly accurate insight: there are real costs and risks involved in comparing religions. We will return to these soon enough. For now, it is enough to point out that there is also real excitement and promise in the comparative project. After all, if many of our social and political problems lie in our failure to compare one another in a sufficiently radical way, the long-lasting resolution of these problems may well lie in our learning to compare ourselves better. The problem and the promise, in other words, are both functions of the same (really quite different) comparative practices.

But there is another reason for enthusiasm here. That reason comes down to a whole complex of deep and powerful human responses to what we might call, for lack of a better expression, the realm of the sacred (we will define that expression in due time). Such a realm has inspired terror, intolerance, and violence. It has also inspired beauty, justice, order, fascination, and awe. Religions are some of the most stunning, uncanny, fantastic, baffling, outrageous, sophisticated, weird, complex, and meaningful products that human beings have created in response to … well, we don't really know what. *Comparing Religions* is about those human responses, which we know quite a bit about, to the realm of the sacred, which we know little about. More specifically, it is about the human religious imagination and its cultural expressions, expressions that we can study the same way in which we study any other cultural product, for instance a political system, a work of art or literature, a piece of architecture, or a language. As for the realm of the sacred itself, well, we will never quite get to that, not at least in these pages. We cannot get to that for one blazingly simple reason: the sacred is not a thing or an object, although it may very well be expressed through things and objects.

I know that this is confusing. Let us return, then, to our analogy of looking into the mirror of human nature. It is one thing to look into the mirror of comparison and examine the expressions of the sacred—as myth and ritual, as artifact and text, as community and institution. It is quite another to step or fall through that mirror and reappear on the other side, like Alice in Wonderland. There are people who have claimed to have done just that, with similarly mind-bending results. I have spent most of my life reading these "mystics," writing about them, sometimes even meeting and talking to them. All that I write in the following pages is informed by those textual and personal encounters. But I will make no such claims here. At the very end, I will suggest what it might look like to be on the other side of the mirror, but we will never really step through. Our goals are more humble.

Still, it is worth admitting up front and immediately that we are already on paradoxical ground, claiming to study that which we cannot know from this side of what we can know, acknowledging both the terror and the beauty of the subject, poised as it is between the problems and the promises of our own future, with the whole world hanging in the balance.

How on earth did we get here?

Notes

1   Margaret M. Mitchell, "Playing with Fire: The Task of the Divinity School." *Criterion* 48.2 (2011), 2–7.
2   I am indebted to Wouter Hanegraaff for this particular line of thought, but the same insight can be found in other scholars, Bruce Lincoln foremost among them.
3   David L. Weddle, *Miracles: Wonder and Meaning in World Religions* (New York: New York University Press, 2010), 4.

El mano poderoso (1990), by Lynn Randolph, 58″ × 46″.

1

Comparative Practices in Global History
If Horses Had Hands

The Scriptures contain many things which never came to pass, interwoven with the history, and he must be dull indeed who does not of his own accord observe that much which the Scriptures represent as having happened never actually occurred.
Church Father Origen (third century CE), *On First Principles*, as quoted in
David Friedrich Strauss, *The Life of Jesus Critically Examined*

God is neither Hindu nor Muslim.
Guru Nanak

Comparing Religions: Coming to Terms, First Edition. Jeffrey J. Kripal, Ata Anzali, Andrea R. Jain, and Erin Prophet.
© 2014 Jeffrey J. Kripal. Published 2014 by John Wiley & Sons, Ltd.

Like all human practices, comparing religions has a history. Rooted, as we shall see, in forms of thought that were originally Christian and Jewish, it gradually separated from those religious traditions over the last two hundred years until it became its own unique and largely independent thing. Its definitive birth occurred in the Protestant, mostly German universities of Europe in the beginning of the nineteenth century, with a few particularly brave professors who were reading the Bible carefully and noticing all sorts of contradictions and repeated stories, rather like Origen in our opening epigraph (much more on this in Chapter 2).

Birth is one thing, however, and development or maturation is quite another. Many of the field's most generative and radical thinkers have been secular (non-religious) Jewish intellectuals living in Christian societies. As we shall repeatedly see, the "outsider" usually sees things more clearly. In the last decades a number of major theorists have emerged from around the globe, often with rich multicultural backgrounds and educations. If one used to read mostly European names for much of the twentieth century (Durkheim, Eliade, Feuerbach, Freud, Marx, Otto, and Weber, for example), one reads more and more Asian, African, and Middle Eastern names today

(Appiah, Asad, Kakar, Obeyesekere, and Said, for example).

In terms of pure numbers, institutional homes, and publishing houses, however, the centers of the field today remain primarily in the USA and Europe. There is a reason for this. Whether of Christian or Jewish origin, whether practiced in the Americas, Europe, the Middle East, Asia, Africa, or Australia, the study of religion as a broad-based institution established and carried in centers of higher learning in literally thousands of classrooms every day is a historical product and reflection of modern Western civilization, of its secular values, and of its broad vision of a liberal or "free" society.

The Comparative Practices of Polytheism

Which is not to say at all that comparative practices around that human activity we now call "religion" are unique to the modern world. They are not. Indeed such forms of thought go back as far as we can see in the written historical record. Martin Riesbrodt describes this ancient human ability to recognize religious activity and the religions this way:

> In all ages people have distinguished interaction with superhuman powers from other forms of action. In different times and cultures, religious actors and institutions have seen each other as similar, no matter whether this perception was expressed in competition and polemics or in cooperation, assimilation, and identification. In addition, all rulers of religious pluralistic empires—the Achaemenids, the Sassanians, the Romans, the T'ang, Ming, or Qing dynasties, the Japanese emperors, the Fatimids, or the Mughal dynasty—have pursued a politics of religion.[1]

In short, human beings, communities, and political powers have been "comparing religions" more or less effortlessly for a very long time. They've had to. Which is not to say that all of these comparative practices worked in the same way or, much less, came to the same conclusions. They did not.

From the Mysteries to the Mystical

We will be looking at a broad spectrum of comparative practices and conclusions as we proceed. One such comparative style–which bears a particularly close relationship to the comparative practices of some of the modern intellectuals who, as we shall see in Chapter 2, created the discipline of "comparative religion"—can be found among individuals whom we have come to call mystics. Since we will be returning to this theme of a resonance between comparativism and mysticism at different points in the textbook, it seems appropriate to begin with it here.

The language of the "mystical" stretches back to the ancient Greek mysteries, a set of special rituals that were believed to bestow immortality on those who partook of them. Their details were successfully shrouded from history as a result of the imposition of strict vows of silence and secrecy. Hence the Greek initiate was known as a *mustēs*—literally someone who keeps silent or "shut" (this is the origin of the modern word "mystic"). Hence also the adjective *mustikos*—"secret," and later on "mystical."

We do not really like the clumsy modern noun "mysticism." We will employ it from time to time, because our sources do, but we much prefer adjectival forms like the **mystical** (as in the French *la mystique*, with all the scholarship on it). Such expressions are part of a comparativist language that scholars use to refer back to, and compare, all those traditions within the general history of religions that emphasize some "hidden" or "secret" communion, connection, even complete identity, between human nature and the "really Real," however these two are conceived. Precisely because of this experienced unity or identity, mystical traditions generally emphasize sameness and downplay difference. Indeed, the most radical forms of mystical thought deny difference altogether, insisting that cultural, religious, and ethnic differences are entirely surface matters and that deep down we all share, we all *are*, the same Reality.

The Axial Age

This transcending of local differences in the name of some shared or deeper sameness has a history too. Most of the doctrines that surround these types of claims can be traced no further back than the middle of the first millennium BCE. Following the German psychiatrist and philosopher Karl Jaspers, this general period of global history is sometimes called the **Axial Age**, since civilizations around the world, seemingly without clear contact, turned in new directions during these centuries, as if around a shared global–spiritual axis. The Axial Age may have emerged from the rise of urbanization, social stratification, and the disillusionments of city life. It may also have arisen from the specialization and leisure of new priestly and scribal elites, or from altered states of mind of individual forest sages and trance prophets. Or, perhaps most likely of all, it may have emerged from all of these factors working together. Whatever the causes, something appears to have "clicked" around the globe.

Karen Armstrong summarizes Jaspers's thesis in her usual, clear way:

> From about 900 to 200 BCE, in four distinct regions, the great world traditions that have continued to nourish humanity came into being: Confucianism and Daoism in China; Hinduism and Buddhism in India; monotheism in Israel; and philosophical rationalism in Greece. This was the period of the Buddha, Socrates, Confucius, and Jeremiah, the mystics of the Upanishads, Mencius, and Euripides. During this period of intense creativity, spiritual and philosophical geniuses pioneered an entirely new kind of human experience.[2]

What was this new experience? Put one way, we might say that the Axial Age turned particular individuals "in" to produce new forms of self-consciousness that were not simply social or communal but could now reflect back on society in a critical and distant fashion. For the first time, human beings began to "step outside themselves" in significant numbers. They no longer completely equated their experiences of consciousness with their cultures. As a result, some

individuals could now extend their view of the human being beyond their local tribe, city, or even empire. They could think universally instead of only locally. They could think of sameness as well as of difference. In short, they discovered comparativism.

Early Projection Theory

Comparativist thinking, of course, is not always based on religious experiences. Indeed, more often it is based on keen observation, careful classification, and rational analysis. The results here are very different. Difference now tends to subsume sameness. One of the earliest, and certainly one of the most striking examples of this kind of rational comparison occurs in the ancient Greek writer Xenophanes of Colophon (c. 570–475 BCE). Xenophanes left us the following lines on what we today call **anthropomorphism**, that is, the universal tendency of human beings to imagine their deities in human (*anthropos*) form (*morphē*), and more especially in the forms of their own ethnicities and physical features:

> If oxen, or lions, or horses had hands like men, they too,
> If they could fashion pictures, or statues they could hew,
> They would shape in their own image each face and form divine—
> Horses' gods like horses, like kine the gods of kine.
> "Snub-nosed are the Immortals, and black," the Ethiops say;
> But "No," the Thracians answer, "red-haired, with eyes of grey."[3]

Early Diffusion Theory

Perhaps a little later, the Greek fifth-century historian Herodotus took the comparative practice one step further when he argued that much of Greek culture and religious practice (including his own) was indebted to the earlier practices and beliefs of the Egyptians. He also "compared" (really identified) the Greek gods with their Egyptian counterparts in a way that supported what we would today call a **diffusion theory**—that is, the idea that a religious complex in one place came from another place and that religious ideas and practices in general tend to "spread out" through migration, trade, war, empire, and other human activities that involve travel.[4] Later Roman authors would similarly "compare" or identify their own Roman deities with the earlier Greek ones, hence the Greek Zeus became the Roman Jupiter, the Greek Hermes became the Roman Mercury, and so on.

Polytheism as Cross-Cultural Understanding

It was in this way that **polytheism**—the belief in many deities—functioned as an implicit form of comparative practice. How? In the polytheistic imagination it is not only the case that the gods of one culture can be translated into those of another. There is also an underlying assumption that it is perfectly natural, and hence acceptable, that different peoples will worship different deities. Polytheism thus effectively relativizes religious practice and assumes that no practice or belief of this nature should be imposed on another people or community. It is not, of course, the case that polytheistic cultures have not engaged in cross-cultural violences of various sorts, including invasion and empire. They most certainly have. But these have generally not been motivated by or articulated through explicit religious reasons (such as conversion or salvation).

The scholar of ancient Egypt Jan Assmann traces this polytheistic logic all the way back to the beginning of written history, to Mesopotamia in the third millennium BCE, from which it would have spread throughout the ancient Near East in the second millennium BCE. In doing so, he suggests that the polytheistic comparative practice was based on three separate notions or principles: (1) *name* (the local name of the deity in Egyptian, Greek, Latin, and so on); (2) *shape* (what the deity looked like or how it was imagined); and (3) *function* (what natural or cosmic process the deity was believed to control or look over). Whereas the names and shapes differed dramatically from context to context, the functions were relatively stable. It was in this

way that ancient polytheistic practices could effectively balance difference (1 and 2) and sameness (3). Here is how Assmann puts the matter:

> The polytheistic religions overcame the primitive ethnocentrism of tribal religions by distinguishing several deities by name, shape, and function. The names are, of course, different in different cultures, because the languages are different. The shapes of the gods and the forms of worship may also differ significantly. But the functions are strikingly similar … The different peoples worshipped different gods, but nobody contested the reality of foreign gods and the legitimacy of foreign forms of worship.[5]

Assmann can thus speak of polytheism as a kind of "intercultural translatability." What he means by this is that the logic of polytheism allowed peoples to understand and even appreciate the deities and rituals of other peoples by "translating" them into their own languages and customs. Today we might frame this as a kind of cross-cultural understanding. In any case, the gods could be compared, because they served very similar functions. This was their sameness.

Euhemerism

There were other ways of explaining why there were so many gods. One of these would become connected to the figure of Euhemerus (c. 330–260 BCE). Euhemerus advanced the theory that the gods had originally been human beings who were worshipped in their own lives for their accomplishments and later, after their deaths, were divinized as local gods. This was a very solid thesis in a Mediterranean world where Egyptian pharaohs had been worshipped as gods on earth for millennia, the Macedonian King Alexander the Great (356–223 BCE) had *just* been divinized, and living Roman emperors would soon be worshipped as gods by their subjects. This idea of gods as exaggerated human beings is still very much with us in numerous forms and is called, after its apparent creator, **Euhemerism**.

Figure 1.1   Giant stone statue portraying the Egyptian pharaoh Ramses II (c. thirteenth century BCE) as Osiris (the god of the afterlife). Abu Simbel temple, Egypt. Photographed by Andrew Holt. © Andrew Holt/Getty Images.

The Nonlocal Self

Before we leave the ancient polytheistic world, we might also mention the Egyptian-born Greek philosopher Plotinus (c. 205–270 CE). After studying for 11 years with a mysterious teacher in Alexandria, Egypt, Plotinus became convinced that he needed to learn more about Persian and Indian philosophy.[6] This may have been because he saw profound similarities between his own early experiences of a transcendent and immortal "Mind" (*nous*) as the knower of "the One" (*to hen*) beyond all multiplicity and the Indian doctrines of the immortal "Self" (*atman*) as the

knower of the cosmic ground of all being (*brahman*). They certainly look alike.[7]

Plotinus was hardly the first to locate wisdom in the East. Intellectuals of his culture had long and commonly done the same. This ancient comparativist conviction has been called **Platonic orientalism**, on account of (1) its reverence for the philosophy of Plato as a kind of divine revelation; and (2) its location of earlier expressions of this divine revelation in "the orient" or "the East." As we shall have numerous occasions to see, this ancient location of a special wisdom "in the East" has been an extremely consistent conviction throughout western history.

The scholar who coined the expression, John Walbridge, did so in order to name the "science of lights" of a twelfth-century Muslim mystic named Suhrawardi (1155–1191), who venerated the sages of Egypt, Persia, India, and China and emphasized direct experience and a photic "illumination" (that is, the experience of an actual if non-ordinary light, *phōs*) over abstract thinking, rational speculation, and literal belief. The true philosopher, Suhrawardi declared, teaches out of these experiences of divine radiance through evocative symbols, which are actual refractions and reflections of the mystical light.[8]

Whether it was because of his experiences of Mind or out of this comparativist conviction in the wisdom of the East (or both), Plotinus hitched a ride with the Roman army on its way to march on the Persians and the Indians. The army was beat back and Plotinus never got to study with the Persians or the Indians. Still, the apparent desire of the philosopher to understand more deeply his own experiences in the mirror of not one, but two foreign cultures is a remarkable early example of the comparativist spirit.

The case of Plotinus points toward a most interesting pattern within the general history of religions that is seldom mentioned, probably because it violates how religion is supposed to work. Human beings, it turns out, sometimes have life-changing experiences that cannot be fit into their own local categories and social contexts (which is how this is supposed to work), but that fit well within the categories of a "foreign" culture. For the sake of more examples to come, let us call this comparativist pattern the **nonlocal self**. The self is "nonlocal" here in the simple sense that its deepest experiences can find few or no resources in the culture in which it was born. Here comparison ceases to be an abstract exercise and becomes a quest for the truth of one's own deepest self, which is reflected and refracted most accurately elsewhere.

Hence Plotinus on his way to Persia and India.

Cosmotheism and Evolutionary Monotheism

Figures like Plotinus should alert us to the fact that ancient peoples often asked (and answered) very serious questions about why there were so many religions and how they were related to one another, even at great distances. They should alert us to the fact that ancient peoples were "comparing religions." These peoples were thus constantly balancing sameness and difference and translating the latter into the former. Accordingly, polytheisms around the ancient world (Egypt, Greece, Rome, Persia, and India—all come to mind) often developed into extremely sophisticated forms of monotheism as well. Jan Assmann calls this phenomenon **evolutionary monotheism**, since these forms of monotheism "evolved" or developed out of earlier polytheisms. He also calls them forms of **cosmotheism**.[9]

The last term, which was originally coined from the Greek in 1782, refers to any model of the divine that understands the physical universe (*kosmos*) to be an actual manifestation of a god or God (*theos*) and—just as importantly—commonly understands the local or multiple deities as a kind of interface between the physical universe and this hidden animating force: in short, this is a kind of poly-mono-theism. The key, though, is this: the world is not separate from the ultimate god or God in it. The physical universe *is* a god.

As in other theological visions, there is a spectrum here, and the different colors of the spectrum blend in and out of one another. Modern thinkers have latched onto particular bandwidths and provided yet

more names. In some forms of cosmotheism, God is the universe and the universe is God, and nothing is—as it were—left over. These forms are referred to as **pantheism**, literally "everything-[is]-God-ism." In other forms the cosmic God is the universe, but this God also overflows or transcends the universe. The cosmos, as it is commonly put, is "God's body." Scholars sometimes refer to these models as forms of **panentheism**, literally "all-in-God-ism."

Wherever we ourselves choose to locate the models on this spectrum, it is clear that something like cosmotheism had major repercussions for how comparison was carried out in the ancient world. Assman, for example, uses the myths and metaphors of cosmotheism to explain how ancient peoples often understood their own religious images and symbols as *both* revealing *and* concealing the truth of divinity at the same time. Just as the god both is the world and is not (just) the world, so too images and symbols reveal this cosmic divinity even as they fail to encompass or fully explain it. The gods are an interface or medium, not the final truth. Every revealing is thus, by necessity, also a concealing.[10] This is a sophisticated comparative practice, to be sure, and it should warn us away, immediately and firmly, from any naïve framing of polytheism as the simple worship of many gods. It should also remind us that even polytheistic cultures sometimes find a form of monotheism that can balance sameness and difference to be a fuller and deeper truth than a simple polytheism that can express only difference. Sometimes polytheism *is* monotheism of another sort.

Theory as "Vision Trip"

The implicit linking of philosophy and travel in the story of Plotinus bears witness to the roots of the Greek term *theōria* ("spectacle," "contemplation"), from which we get our own modern "theory." Figures like the Greek philosopher Plato used the term to mean something like "cosmic vision" or the direct knowing of divine truths, beyond mere opinion: in short, it had the exact opposite value of what many people mean today when they quip, "it's just a theory."

It was not just a theory in ancient Greece. The word *theōria* originally referred to the practice of state pilgrimage, in which a person called a *theōros* ("seer") would travel to another city to witness religious spectacles or to consult an oracle. The seer could do this officially, on behalf of his own city, or personally, for his own private needs. In the former case, which probably became a model for Greek philosophers like Plato, the key was the entire process of (1) leaving home; (2) witnessing divine things on a journey abroad; and then (3) returning to one's own city in order to report on the witnessed spectacle.

The return was not just a return, however, for the seer was inevitably transformed by the spectacular journey. As Andrea Wilson Nightingale explains, "he thus 'returns' as a sort of stranger to his own kind, bringing radical alterity [otherness or strangeness] into the city … he possesses a divine perspective that is foreign to the ordinary man."[11] To put it in our own terms now (and this is most important), *the concept of "theory" originated in the triple process of departure from one's own culture, comparative envisioning of other people's religious spectacles abroad, and return home—often to a certain confusion, isolation, or even rejection—to report on what was seen.*

Thomas Tweed has summarized the matter in a three-word sound bite, very much worth memorizing at the beginning of our own journey together: "theory is travel."[12] This makes more than a little sense, since a person generally does not, and usually cannot, question (that is, theorize) his or her own society and beliefs until he or she physically leaves that culture and encounters a very different one. Only then can a person realize, often with something of a shock, that there are many ways to be a human being and that none of them is obviously or necessarily superior to the others. Travel has become a kind of embodied comparative practice, and the theorist or seer has become a stranger to his or her own community.

For us, the lesson is clear enough: if you want to become a real thinker and a real comparativist, you must leave home in every sense of that term. Come back, for sure. But you really must leave first. So go.

The Comparative Practices of Monotheism: Early Judaism

During the Axial Age, the polytheism of the ancient Near East was definitively interrupted and, eventually, effectively cancelled in many places by the rise of **monotheism**: the belief in one deity, almost always imagined as male, that is, as a god. The rise of monotheism is generally connected with the ancient religion of the Israelites.

Ancient Israelite religion is the source tradition out of which the later monotheisms of Judaism and Christianity emerged. It was this ancient Israelite culture that broke with the mythical imagination of the ancient world, which tended to think in terms of cycles, and began to imagine its god as acting in material history and in linear time. God became the Lord of history, and history itself came to be experienced as an expression of the will and intentions of the divine. It was the ancient Israelites, again, who claimed a particular covenant or "contractual agreement" with the single God and thus articulated a theology of election—in other words the religious notion that a particular people (in this case, the Israelites) is called by God to give witness, to "the nations," to the existence of the one God and to his ethical intentions for all of humanity, eventually conceived of, in the Jewish imagination, as a single community under a single God. And it was ancient Israelite culture that developed, through its ecstatic and visionary prophets, a tradition of moral critique and social justice and later, through its scholar-teachers or rabbis, extremely sophisticated techniques for interpreting its own scriptural texts. It was this learned rabbinic culture that eventually created what we now think of as Judaism.

The Modern Birth of "Monotheism"

With the biblical religion of the ancient Israelites, however, we plunge already into a whole series of historical and comparative dilemmas. To begin with, the word "monotheism" was not invented until the eighteenth century. It is found nowhere, for example, in the Jewish or Christian scriptures (a **scripture** is any set of texts that is considered revealed or sacred by a community). It appears nowhere in the Jewish scripture, the Torah (this is a Hebrew word derived from the same root as the verb "to instruct" or "to give advice" such as a teacher gives to a student or a parent a child). Nor is it found anywhere in the Bible (from the Greek *biblion*, "book"—namely the books, *biblia*, that make up the Christian scriptures). When we use a term like monotheism, then, we are speaking of *our* modern worldviews more than of any ancient worldview.

God(s)

Consider this. Even if this one god is capitalized in English as "God," it is important to understand that there is no capitalization practice in Hebrew, the language of the Torah. To make matters more complicated still, one of the oldest Hebrew terms for "God" is *elohim*, which is in fact plural and means "the gods." That is right: one of the most ancient words for "god" in the Bible actually means "the gods." The single English capital letter "G," then, carries a whole set of religious assumptions, all of which revolve around the idea that "God" is different from "the gods" or "(a) god." In short, it is important that you understand that that single English capitalized letter is itself a comparative practice and is imbued with all sorts of assumptions. It is designed to emphasize difference, to set apart and distinguish the capitalized "God" from all those lower-case "gods."

The Monotheistic Distinction

Assmann has called this insistence on absolute difference, on God against the gods, the "monotheistic distinction"—"distinction" here as in "what sets apart" or "makes different." If cosmotheism was an "evolutionary monotheism" that affirmed all the gods as ultimately One, the monotheistic distinction was a **"revolutionary monotheism"** that broke with the

earlier systems and insisted that all other gods must be rejected.

Such a revolutionary monotheism did not begin with Moses or, for that matter, with the Torah. Historically speaking, this kind of monotheism is clearly attested for the first time in connection with the Egyptian Pharaoh Akhenaten, also known as Pharaoh Amenophis IV, who dramatically enforced a monotheistic religion around the sun god Aten in the fourteenth century BCE, well before there was any Torah or Judaism. Akhenaten's was a most radical break with all that came before in Egyptian religion, which was robustly polytheistic. Indeed, Akhenaten's new religion was *so* different and *so* incongruous that after his death this religion was cancelled, his name was removed from the lists of kings, and artistic representations of him were defaced.

Centuries later another revolutionary monotheism would resurface in the same part of the world and would become connected to another Egyptian name: Moses. It was this remembered Moses who played the central role in what would become the Jewish story of being saved or liberated from polytheistic Egypt—which came to represent, in this same monotheistic imagination, everything that was wrong, everything that was to be rejected as "pagan" or "idolatrous." This absolute distinction between the one God of Israel and the polytheistic corruptions of Egypt is what Assmann means by the "monotheistic distinction." The ancient Israelites had been chosen or "elected" to become "witness" of the one true God. Jews were to be set apart from all of the other surrounding peoples and cultures, which they came to call "gentiles"—that is, peoples and nations who are not part of the Israelite community.

This same distinction would have an immeasurable impact on the future of religion not just in the ancient Near East, but around the world up to this very day. It is as central to the histories of Christianity and Islam as it is to the histories of Judaism, even though, as we shall soon see, Christianity and Islam took this distinction further with their explicit policies of conquest and conversion. It would also have a major impact on the comparative imagination. No longer could other people's deities be translated into the conceptions of one's own monotheistic community. It was no longer a matter of your sun god and my sun god doing the same solar work under different names and cultural shapes. Now it was all a matter of "true religion" and "false religion." Compromise was out. A new form of human difference had appeared.

Indeed, Assmann has argued that the whole concept of "religion" is itself a construction of monotheism, since, before monotheism, no one would have spoken or thought like that; no one would have thought of "true" and "false" religions. He puts it this way:

> The distinction I am concerned with … is the distinction between true and false religion that underlies more specific distinctions such as Jews and Gentiles, Christians and pagans, Muslims and unbelievers. Once the distinction is drawn, there is no end of reentries or subdistinctions. We start with Christians and pagans and end up with Catholics and Protestants, Calvinists and Lutherans, Socinians and Latitudinarians, and a thousand more similar denominations and subdenominations. Cultural or intellectual distinctions such as these construct a universe that is not only full of meaning, identity, and orientation, but also full of conflict, intolerance, and violence.[13]

Monotheism, then, is not just another religion. It is a "counter-religion," as it is poised against every other religion. Indeed "it rejects and repudiates everything that went before." And so, "whereas polytheism … rendered different cultures mutually transparent and compatible, the new counter-religion blocked intercultural translatability. False gods cannot be translated."[14] They can only be denied. Or destroyed.

Because of this, the subsequent Jewish, Christian, and Muslim attitudes toward other religions were more or less intolerant on a narrative, structural, or logical plane, and sometimes coercive, or even violent, on an economic, social, and political plane. Again, this is not to claim, of course, that polytheistic religions and peoples were perfectly tolerant or did not engage in cross-cultural violences. They were

not; and they did. It is to observe that a new, powerful logic and language of religious intolerance had appeared on the scene.

The Gods and Early Israelite Intolerance

Generally speaking, the Hebrew texts of the Torah do not deny the existence of other gods. Quite the contrary, they assume their existence. The Hebrew prophets certainly saw the local gods and goddesses as dangerous competitors. One of the common biblical ways to express Israel's relationship to its god and to his competitors was through the language of sexuality. In the words of some of the prophets (particularly Hosea and Isaiah), the community of Israel was understood to be the "wife" or "bride" of God. Hence any commerce with these other deities was labeled "adultery." One prophet, Hosea, was even married to a prostitute and used this relationship to act out or prophesy about Israel's unfaithful "whoring" with other nations and deities.

This sense of difference went far beyond the metaphorical language of sexual jealousy and adultery, however. Israel was encouraged to destroy the people, the children, even the livestock that made up the surrounding Canaanite cultures. Here are some sample passages from the Hebrew scriptural texts:

> Whoever sacrifices to any god, other than the LORD alone, shall be devoted to destruction. (Exodus 22.20)

> you shall not bow down to their gods, or worship them, or follow their practices, but you shall utterly demolish them and break their pillars in pieces. (Exodus 23.24)

> you shall drive out all the inhabitants of the land from before you, destroy all their figured stones, destroy all their cast images, and demolish all their high places. You shall take possession of the land and settle in it, for I have given you the land to possess. (Numbers 33.52–53)

"Intolerant" seems much too tame a word to describe this biblical god, at least as we have him described and represented in passages like these.

Qualifications

But we have to be very careful here, and for at least four reasons.

1 First, we must be both humble about what we know about the ancient world and suspicious of what the ancient texts tell us. To take only one example, there simply is no archaeological or anthropological evidence that any kind of military invasion or conquest of Palestine ever occurred along the lines called for and described in such passages (as we will repeatedly emphasize, scriptural texts cannot be read as accurate historical reports). What did happen must remain in the realm of speculation. One possible scenario is that the "Israelites" were originally semi-nomads who settled in the highlands by the thirteenth century BCE and came into conflict with the political authorities of the lowlands, that is, the Egyptians and Canaanites. As the centuries ticked by and the political authority of the Egyptians and Canaanites waned, these different highland tribes consolidated, took on their own political and religious identity (which, like all identities, they invented), and adopted a variety of practices and identity markers, like circumcision and the avoidance of pork, probably because their main enemies, the Philistines, did not circumcise and ate copious amounts of pork.[15] Whether this or some other scenario is accurate, one consensus remains strong: the Hebrew stories were originally designed to fuse a political and a religious identity. They were not a collection of accurate histories of "what really happened."

2 Second, no religious tradition can be identified with its scriptural texts: religions are much more than their texts, however sacred these are held to be. Rituals, cultural customs, social institutions, artistic representations, and countless invisible acts of piety and prayer are just as important, if not more. Moreover, scriptural traditions are often filled with teachings, prohibitions, and exhortations that are, quite simply, impossible to follow for any but the most devout and extreme. If the truth be told, the religious life of the vast majority of people is as much about politely ignoring particular scriptural texts as it is about acting them out. We will return to this idea in Chapter 10, when we will see that the modern virtue of "tolerance" is largely about *not* acting on one's religious convictions.

3 Third, most religions, especially Judaism, have developed sophisticated ways of reading scriptural texts that qualify, or even deny, their own most troubling passages. Much of Jewish history is a history of minority communities engaging in sophisticated innovation, critical compromise, and learned refashioning of the tradition through legal and rabbinic scholarship and, much later, through modern Jewish philosophy. The ancient rabbis often accomplished this innovation through the distinction between an oral and a written Torah. This distinction was based on the idea that the Hebrew text of the Torah (the "written Torah") needed to be constantly interpreted by living scholars and that these interpretations constituted a second "oral Torah," perhaps not of equal authority, but nevertheless of great importance and practical implications.

This idea was in turn based on the principle that the Torah does not mean just one thing but is rather infinitely meaningful, and hence always capable of revealing more of the divine truth. Since no single interpretation can exhaust the Torah's revelation, it naturally follows that the Torah can and should be interpreted anew, in each generation and for each community. This sensibility was expressed powerfully by Rabbi Moshe Hayyim Luzzatto, an eighteenth-century writer who went so far as to claim that "all the roots of the souls of Israel are in the Torah, so that they are six-hundred-thousand interpretations of the Torah, which are apportioned to the six-hundred-thousand souls of Israel."[16] In short, there are as many appropriate interpretations of the Jewish scriptures as there are Jews.

4 Fourth, there are other Torah passages that present a different sort of deity, one not entirely obsessed with preserving the ritual purity of Israel vis-à-vis its

Figure 1.2   *A Difficult Passage of the Talmud*, by Isaac Snowman. © Bettmann/Corbis.

surrounding cultures. In these, we find prophets witnessing against the social and economic injustices of poverty and political oppression and proclaiming a kind of universal salvation through the chosen nation of Israel and its promised restoration. The prophetic traditions of Amos, Hosea, and Isaiah are most remarkable examples of such visions of social and economic justice poised against the rich and powerful. The book of Isaiah is probably the clearest example of a developing religious universalism in the Torah.

Still, the texts of the Torah as such never really reach what we would consider tolerance in the very modern sense of that term—that is, an equal respect for other traditions. We cannot be anachronistic here. Religious tolerance and an accurate comparativism are *our* concerns and values, not those of the Torah. Bottom line? The ancient biblical record is, at best, profoundly ambiguous on questions of cross-cultural understanding and fair comparison, at least as we understand these two

kinds of values and practices today, in our globalizing world. In truth, in these early texts there was little of either.

The Comparative Practices of Monotheism: Early Christianity

In the first few centuries of the Common Era, the early Christian communities, which in the beginning were Jewish communities, came to believe in what they would call a "new covenant" with God, which was now believed to surpass and complete the "old covenant" of the Torah. Hence the eventual Christian expressions New Testament and Old Testament ("testament" simply comes from *testamentum*, "will, testament," the noun used in the Latin translation to render the earlier Hebrew category of "covenant"). This new contract revolved around the belief that a Jewish rabbi named Jesus (Hebrew Yeshua, or Joshua) was the "anointed" one (*messiah* in Hebrew, *Christos* in Greek)—that is, the one chosen to re-establish the reign of God or, as Jesus himself appears to have expressed it (mostly through parable or enigmatic story), "the kingdom of heaven." This same Jewish rabbi was eventually executed by the Roman authorities as a rabble-rouser and criminal—he was sent to the electric chair of the time: a gory public crucifixion.

Biblical scholars have debated endlessly how Jesus understood his own relationship with God. They are hardly alone. We know that early Christians fought for centuries over the same question. Some early Christians considered Jesus to be a great man, a prophet perhaps, but nothing more. Others regarded him as a pure god whose humanity and sufferings were an illusion. Others still took him for an eternal savior figure who had descended from the heavens into the material world to enlighten and awaken the divine spark in individuals and so rescue them from the clutches of a corrupt, even demonic social and religious order. Finally, others—and these are the people who eventually won these early cultural wars—considered him to be literally the son of God, namely a son born of a virgin, who had suffered and died on a cross as a sacrifice for the sins of the world and was resurrected by God on the third day.

In short, Christianity developed the most astonishing claim that God had taken on human nature—had been "enfleshed"—in Jesus of Nazareth. Jesus, in this winning view, was both fully human *and* fully divine. As the much later Nicene Creed put the matter (in Greek philosophical terms), he was of the "same substance" (*homoousios*) as God himself. Jesus was God. And he was a human being.

On "Old" and "New" as Comparative Terms

As they fought over who Jesus was, the early followers of Jesus were also faced with how to articulate their relationship with the parent religion—an emerging Judaism. Over the course of a century or so, they would accomplish this with the help of the already mentioned expressions "Old Testament" and "New Testament." These are examples of what scholars call

polemics or **apologetics**: religious categories that are designed to criticize, subordinate, or argue against another religious worldview (hence they are "polemical"), even as they establish the superior truths of one's own religious worldview (hence they are "apologetic"). Having these features, the "testament" expressions are designed to argue that the Greek Christian texts of the "*New* Testament" complete or fulfill the Hebrew Jewish texts or "*Old* Testament." To put it a bit more bluntly, the claim embedded in them is that Christianity has inherited the mantle of Israel and is now the true spiritual Israel, as it were.

Historical accuracy and religious polemics and apologetics, however, are two very different matters. Accordingly, many biblical scholars no longer use the phrase (or title) Old Testament except when they are explicitly treating Christian materials or readings, and then they do it always with a clear explanation of how this phrase has been used to privilege Christianity over Judaism.

Canon Formation

The development of the Christian "New Testament" and the Christian renaming of the Jewish Torah as the "Old Testament" are also examples of what scholars call **canon formation**. The word "canon" comes from a Greek term that originally referred to a measuring plumb line used by ancient carpenters to assure a straight line. It was later adopted by Christian theologians and bishops to name the set of texts that were held to be revealed, sacred, and authoritatively "straight," in contrast to the "crooked" ones that were held to have human authorship and hence to fall outside the realm of true revelation. Related here are the nouns **orthodoxy** (literally "straight teaching") and **heterodoxy** (literally "other/different teaching," but here something like "wrong teaching").

The important thing to keep in mind is that a canon is *relative to a particular religious tradition*. What is "canonical" or "revealed" for one religious tradition is often only partially true or, worse yet, destructive or just plain silly for another. Often, however, one canon does not simply dismiss or demean a previous parent canon: it *includes* it, if always at a lower level, within its own canon. So the Christian canon absorbed and changed the meaning of the Jewish canon in the second century CE, when it developed its notions of the "Old" and "New" Testaments. Then the Islamic tradition absorbed and changed the meaning of both "the Torah" and "the Gospels" in the seventh and eighth centuries, when it argued that Islam includes and corrects these earlier revelations in the perfect and final revelation that is the Quran. *Muslims* were now God's true elect. Same move. Different religion.

Christian Theology

With respect to the formation of the Christian canon and its particular comparative approaches to other religions and peoples, things developed slowly. Christian comparative practices were pioneered by a group of Greek and Latin intellectuals who came to be called "the Church Fathers." These were highly educated church leaders, monks, scholars, and bishops writing from the second to the fifth century who developed the diverse stories and teachings of the New Testament into a coherent system or theology. A **theology** is a rational explanation (*logos*) of God (*theos*). The term is generally used to describe the attempt of human reason to explain and systematize divine revelation for a particular faith community.

Today theology is usually associated with Christianity, but its terminology is actually pre-Christian. *Theologia* ("discourse on the divine") and cognates had been already familiar since Plato; for Aristotle it was crucial—he identified it either with metaphysics or with its highest and "divine" part, first philosophy (see Book 5 of his *Metaphysics*). A very influential Church Father, Augustine of Hippo (354–430 CE), would cite an earlier Roman pagan author, Varro, on the three different types of theology or "talking about the gods": that pertaining to the nature of reality (which was the concern of philosophers); that pertaining to political or civil matters (which was the concern of priests); and that concerning myths or tales of the fabulous (which was the concern

of poets).[17] In short, talking about the gods in philosophical, political, and poetic terms was another comparative practice that appears to have been first invented by the ancient Greeks and Romans.

Some type of theology was, of course, always practiced *implicitly* in the mythologies, ritual hymns, processions, and prayers of different cultures, all of which implied or assumed particular understandings of the deities that they worshiped. But it was probably not until (roughly) the time of the Greeks, Romans, and Christians that systematic theology proper developed. We might, then, distinguish, with Assmann, between **implicit theology**, which every religious system has practiced, and **explicit theology**, which only some have. We might also distinguish, for our own purposes, between implicit and explicit comparative practices, which inevitably flow from these same implicit and explicit theologies.

In any case, it was through the extensive writings of the Church Fathers that Christianity came to adopt a whole set of new doctrines or "teachings," such as the trinity (the **doctrine** that God is three persons in one substance or nature), the incarnation (the doctrine that God took flesh and became human in Jesus of Nazareth), original sin (the doctrine that all human beings are born with an ancestral moral fault inherited from humanity's first parents, Adam and Eve), and *theōsis*, "divinization" (the doctrine, much more developed in the eastern Greek and Russian Orthodox traditions, that God became man so that man might become God). None of these terms appears anywhere in the biblical texts. Many of them were finally crystallized in the famous Nicene Creed, which was not composed and finalized until 325 CE at the Council of Nicaea, almost three hundred years after the life and teachings of Jesus of Nazareth.

The Gods and Early Christian Intolerance

With respect to other religions, early Christianity did something that early Judaism never could: it carried out the intolerant aspects of biblical monotheism and enshrined them in institutional structures and political practices. It could do this because, in the first decades of the fourth century, the Christian communities aligned themselves with the incredible power and reach of the Roman Empire (or, perhaps more accurately, the Roman Empire aligned itself with the expanding reach and organizational power of the Christian churches). In the centuries that followed, the Christian church would align itself with the developing European monarchies, and eventually with nation-states as well. Due to this political–religious fusion with major political powers and to its own effective administrative structure, the Christian church could now carry out the kinds of religious intolerance and political persecution that the Israelite legal writers and prophets had envisioned and written about but could seldom, if ever, carry through. Islam, as we shall see, followed the example of Christianity here, not that of Judaism.

Assmann has put it this way: whereas the monotheistic distinction of Judaism was directed "inwards" and resulted in a separation from the Other (as in other cultures and nations), the monotheistic distinction of Christianity and that of Islam were directed "outwards" and resulted in religious, political, and military projects aiming to convert or vanquish the Other.[18] Judaism separated itself from other cultures and religions: its method was *segregation*. Christianity and Islam attempted to change other cultures and religions into images of themselves: their methods were *conversion* and *conquest*.

The latter strategies can be seen in the various comparative practices of the early Christian communities, including those enshrined in language through the use of notions such as pagans, demons, and heretics.

The Pagans   One of the most general and long-lasting comparative practices that the early Christians developed involved the use of a single, potent word: **pagan**. To simplify a rather difficult matter, the word originally referred to inhabitants of the countryside (or people who lived in villages or small county districts, *pagoi*). Since Christianity was largely an urban phenomenon—that is, since it had the most success in cities, where it took deep root through administrative structures modeled after those of the Roman Empire

(hence *Roman* Catholicism)—it was in the countryside that its reach was weakest; it was there that the traditional polytheistic practices of Roman religion survived longest. For the Church Fathers, then, the "pagans" were quite literally the "country folk," the uneducated and uncivilized: in contemporary polemical terms, the "hicks" who had not yet embraced the true religion and divine light of Christianity.

The same category was later expanded to refer to any non-Christian religion. "Pagan" thus came to function in ways not dissimilar to the Jewish "gentile." If gentile meant "anyone who is not Jewish," pagan came to mean "anyone who is not Christian." There were multiple comparative nuances here, however. Ancient Christian writers, for example, would not describe Jewish people as pagans, since they were perfectly aware that the Christian revelation emerged from the Jewish revelation. Ancient Jewish writers, however, would and did refer to Christians as gentiles, since the revelation of the Torah was in no way indebted to the Christian "New Testament," which they did not recognize as a revelation at all.

The Demons   The Church Fathers also wrote and spoke of the gods of other people's religions in rather negative terms. Under their pen foreign gods, and especially the Roman gods and goddesses, were more or less equated (and more rather than less) with foreign *daimones*—that is, simply put, with un-Christian spirits or "demons." These were to be battled against and exorcised by the faithful as if they were diseases or mental illnesses—which, in turn, were also understood to be symptoms of demonic possession.

The Heretics   Perhaps the most dangerous of all, though, were those religious Others "inside the family," that is, the countless Christians whose faith and practice did not meet the standards of those in power and authority. These erring members of the Christian community or "family" were the **heretics**: individuals who, instead of submitting to the authority of the bishops, willingly chose to believe something else. The term *heresy* comes from the Greek *hairesis*, which means "choice," "opinion," and also "sect" or "school of thought"; we could say—quite anachronistically but not at all inaccurately—that *hairesis* is, more or less, what we mean today by "religious freedom." We might, then, also say that heresy was originally understood as freely chosen beliefs, as opposed to authoritative ones to which one submits.

Like demon talk, heresy talk was suffused with what we might call today "immunological" associations. If, after all, the "disease" or "poison" of a particular heresy was allowed to spread, it would eventually "infect" the entire "body" of the church. It had to be stopped. It had to be stamped out. Augustine was especially influential here. He would develop a justification for the use of state violence against heretical Christians as just such an "immunological" response.

Arguments of this kind would turn out to be immensely influential in later Christian history. Thousands of individuals would be burned at the stake, imprisoned, or otherwise harassed and tortured in the later history of Christianity for their freely chosen beliefs or "heresies." And this is before we even get to something like the crusades—those politically organized campaigns and pitched battles, usually around Jerusalem, in the tenth through the twelfth centuries, during which thousands of Christians and Muslims lost their lives, partly for being "heretics" and "infidels," that is, for having the wrong set of beliefs. Things other than right belief were at stake too, of course—like wealth, treasure, power, and land; but it was belief and religious identity that marked the battle lines and the bodies that fell.

Christians in the Eyes of Others

Roman intellectuals, of course, had their own comparative take on early Christians. Not that they understood them. They were particularly baffled by the Christians' refusal to give proper reverence and worship to the gods, which, in their mind, was an important part of being a good and decent Roman citizen. It appeared to them that the Christians were in fact "atheists." They were atheists because they denied the existence of the gods and refused to participate in the state religion of Rome, which involved worshipping the emperor. It was this last element that resulted in the persecution of Christians by some of the Roman emperors.

Qualifications

As with ancient Israelite religion and early Judaism, we must be careful here about overly simplifying ancient Christianity. We might briefly mention five points.

1   *Inclusive New Testament Passages*   As with the universal God of Isaiah, the New Testament is studded with passages expressing a certain conditional, implicit, or limited universalism. Probably the most famous passage appears in Paul's letter to the Galatians: "There is no longer Jew or Greek, there is no longer slave or free, there is no longer male and female; for all of you are one in Christ Jesus" (Galatians 3.28). It is also worth pointing out here that at least one Church Father, a most remarkable scholar named Origen (185–254 CE), probably preached a form of universal salvation, that is, the doctrine that eventually all men and women would be saved. This teaching was later declared heretical—too much sameness.

2   *The Mystical Element of the New Testament*   It is also worth pointing out that various strands of Jewish mysticism played a major role in the early development and definition of Christianity, and in fact they are very much part of the New Testament. Paul's description of being taken up "to the third heaven" (2 Cor 12.2), for example, is almost certainly an expression of this Jewish mystical element, as was his famous blinding conversion on the road to Damascus via a conscious lightform that he experienced as the resurrected Messiah of his own Jewish faith (Acts 9.3–19; 22.6–21; 26.12–18). These mystical elements of the New Testament were long ago pointed out by the African missionary and pioneering biblical critic Albert Schweitzer in his classic *The Mysticism of Paul the Apostle* (1931). They have since been renewed and expanded by contemporary scholars like Marcus Borg, April DeConick, Elaine Pagels, and Alan Segal.

3   *Ancient Diversity*   Along similar lines, it must also be remembered that both early Judaism and Christianity were mind-bogglingly diverse. *Historically speaking, there simply is no such thing as the first, or the original, Judaism or Christianity.* There were only Judaisms and Christianities. And many of them were open to all sorts of currents of religious thought and practice, from Greek, Roman, and Egyptian astrology and magical practice to the nuanced teachings and ritual practices of various "pagan" philosophies.

The influence of those intellectuals who, one way or another, considered themselves Plato's followers during these first few centuries of the Common Era (they are often called Middle Platonists and Neoplatonists) was immense and long lasting. Indeed many have argued that it is **Neoplatonism** that provided the philosophical base for much of the later histories of Jewish, Christian, *and* Islamic mysticism. This same influence became coded in an anxious question, originally asked by the Church Father Tertullian: "What does Athens have to do with Jerusalem?" That is, what can the religion of the one God learn from the pagan philosophers?

A great deal, as it turned out.

4   *Divine Seeds of the* Logos   Take, for example, the early Christian concept of "seeds of the Word" (*logoi spermatikoi*, literally "spermatic words" or "words endowed with the power of seeds")—that is, seeds of the Logos. This the early Christian intellectuals borrowed directly from Greek philosophical thought. *Logos* is an especially rich Greek term; it had been used, among others, by a group of ancient Greek philosophers called "Stoics" (that is, the philosophers of the Porch, Stoa, in Athens), who employed it to speak and write of a kind of cosmic Mind, intelligent energy, or "fire" behind or within the universe. Some early Christians, no doubt aware of these earlier Stoic meanings, applied the same term to Christ in the beginning of the Gospel of John: "In the beginning was the Word …" "Seeds of the Word," then, meant "seeds of Christ." These Christ seeds, some Church Fathers suggested, were scattered among the world's peoples before the actual birth of Christ, particularly among the Greeks and Jews. Such peoples could thus be considered proto-Christians, even if they themselves were not aware of this.

This agricultural metaphor of seeds of Christ scattered throughout the pre-Christian world allowed the Church Fathers to accomplish three things: (1) it allowed them to answer the common accusation that, because Christianity was new, it could not possibly be true (it was commonly assumed that, for something to be true, it must be ancient); (2) it allowed them to explain the obvious similarities between Christianity and the earlier non-Christian religions (for example, the shared themes of the dying and rising god, of the gods becoming humans, of divine–human births, of the importance of sacrifice, and so on); and (3) it allowed them to assert the superiority of Christianity over the earlier pagan religions and philosophies, however similar they looked. The image of the seed, after all, implies *both* hiddenness (so Christ could be detected in traditions where he was not at all obvious, where he was still "underground," so to speak) *and* a developmental understanding, as the seed eventually grows up into a mature plant. Just as (to use Aristotelian language) the "purpose" of the seed is the mature plant, which looks very different from the seed, so the purpose of the pagan religions was the coming of Christ and Christianity, which looks very different from the earlier pagan religions. Sameness and difference, connection and break, precedent and development were thus all acknowledged and negotiated by and through the symbolism of the seed.

5   *"Knowing" Comparisons*   Then there were the **gnostics**—the "knowers." These were Christian communities whose emphasis on personal mystical knowing (*gnōsis*) did not sit well with the bishops' views. As one would expect, these gnostic Christians (and they *were* Christians), with their strong emphasis on the mystical element of religion, often practiced particularly radical and dramatic forms of comparison. One of the most striking examples is the caustic phrase "not as Moses said": it occurs in the second-century scriptural text *The Secret Book of John*, where it is used as an angry critique of ancient biblical literalism and its divinization, according to the gnostics, of the violent and cruel creator-god who repeatedly appears in the Hebrew scriptures. In short, for the gnostic Christians, the God featured in the

Figure 1.3   *Adoration of the Magi* (1423), by Gentile da Vabriano. Galleria dei Uffizi, Florence, Italy. © Corbis.

Hebrew Bible was not the real God but a fake or lower God. The true God, they concluded, could not possibly behave so badly. It simply cannot be "as Moses said."

One of the most remarkable examples of such gnostic comparisons is *The Revelation of the Magi*, an early Christian text about a traveling orb of light that is said to have appeared to the *magoi*—magicians or astrologers—in the Gospel of Matthew (these astrologer-magicians are often safely described in English translations as "wise men"). In this text at least, the astrologers are in fact members of an ancient religious order in a far eastern land called "Shir" (probably China), where the luminous entity appears to them in a cave, concentrates its form into a "small and humble" humanoid, and leads them to travel to Bethlehem, where in another cave the lightform is "born" as Mary and Joseph's son, now as an infant but still glowing radiantly. Note, again, the theme of wisdom coming from the East.

New Testament scholar Brent Landau concludes his study of this text with what he considers the most remarkable aspect of the revelation, namely that, "instead of seeing non-Christian religions as products of human vanity or demonic inspiration, as most ancient Christians did, the *Revelation of the Magi* sees potentially all revelation as coming from Christ himself." Indeed the star-child never actually identifies himself as Christ to the traveling magicians and makes startling statements like this one: "I am everywhere, because I am a ray of light whose light has shone … in the entire world and in every land by unspeakable mysteries."[19]

We should not, of course, make too much of this single text, but it does show quite dramatically that liberal acts of comparison, and even a certain universalism, were not only possible but practiced within some forms of early Christianity.

The Comparative Practices of Monotheism: Early Islam

Islam, a religion that emerged in the seventh century, is the only "world religion" to have named itself. All others were named by outsiders. In the case of Buddhism, Christianity, Daoism, Hinduism, and Judaism, for example, the original adjectival appellations (Buddhist, Christian, and so on) and eventually the abstract names ending in -ism (in modern languages like English) were given by outsiders. One might expect, then, that the Islamic traditions would have a particularly keen and particularly ancient practice of thinking abstractly and comparatively about "religion."

And one would be correct.

The Arabic Comparative Category of *din* or "Religion"

Much of this ancient comparative practice revolves around the central Arabic term *din*. The term *din* was in use well before the rise of Islam. It was evident, for example, both in the Persian and Semitic cultures of the Mesopotamian world and beyond. In its middle Persian form *den*, it was used extensively in a variety of ways, including one that can well be translated as "religion." For example, we find the phrases *weh-den*, "the good religion," and *mazdesn den*, "the religion of Mazda worship," in Zoroastrian texts. For Manicheans, too, *den* denoted true or right "religion," that is, the Manichaean community.[20]

Zoroastrianism and Manichaeism   A bit of background is in order here. Zoroastrianism and Manichaeism are among the most ancient "world religions" that flourished throughout the ancient world. Both are commonly understood to be Iranian religions, meaning that both developed in conversation with or in the context of ancient Persian civilization. The most central tenant of both religions was a worldview in which the moral forces of good and evil, of truth and falsehood were seen to be both real and locked in an eternal struggle. We call this an "ethical dualism." Sometimes the force of evil was understood to be a function of human choices or inspirations. At other times, it appears to have been understood as having an independent existence, or existences, of its own. These were not quite traditional monotheisms, then, since they sometimes recognized the independent existence of a separate and quite real counterforce in the world.

Having said that, it must also be observed that the traditional monotheisms (Judaism, Christianity, and Islam) have never quite been traditional monotheisms either, as they too have recognized such forces and have never been able really to explain the presence of evil. If there is only one all-powerful God, what is that "other God," traditionally called Satan or the Devil, doing there? If God is good and so powerful, why is there evil in the world? Zoroastrianism and Manichaeism had a clear answer: because there *is* evil in the world.

Traditionally, the figure of Zoroaster is credited with the founding of Zoroastrianism, which focuses on the worship of the good God of all light and truth, Ahura Mazda, the "Wise Lord" who created the universe. The founder's name is based on an ancient Greek version of it: *Zoroastres*. He has also been called "Zarathustra," mostly in European contexts, and "Zarathushtra." Hence many believers today call themselves "Zarathushtis," that is, followers of Zarathushtra, or, alternatively, they describe themselves as "Mazdaean" or "Mazdayasni," the latter ancient expression meaning "Mazda-worshipping."[21]

Scholars have not been able to pin down even an approximately reliable date for Zoroaster. Arguments have been advanced that place him anywhere from the thirteenth to the sixth century BCE, the majority of scholars favoring dates around 1000 BCE.[22] We know virtually nothing about him or what he preached outside of what we have in a body of sacred literature written by Zoroastrian priests a full two thousand years later, that is, around 1000 CE. This was after the fall of the Sassanian Empire (third to seventh century CE) to the Arab invaders who introduced Islam to the same region.

Unlike Zoroastrianism, which rose to political prominence as the national religion of Persia during the Sassanian Empire, Manichaeism became a persecuted minority religion early in its history. Its founding figure, a prophet named Mani, lived in the third century CE and hailed from Persia. His religion shared some fundamental elements with Zoroastrianism, including its dualism, which he took further still. Although Manichaeism was suppressed in the central lands of ancient Iran under Zoroastrianism, it flourished in Central Asia, Africa, and Europe before finally going extinct.

The important point for us is not the origins or content of these two ancient religions, but the fact that, in both Zoroastrian and Manichaean use, the term *den* referred to a privileged and unique set of beliefs and practices, which were held to constitute the true religion. What we have here, in short, is another version of Assman's "monotheistic distinction." Hence no plural form of the noun *den* is used. In the same uncompromising spirit, Kartir, the official Zoroastrian high priest of the Persian emperor in the third century CE, proudly boasts of his accomplishments in this royal inscription:[23]

> And in kingdom after kingdom and place after place ... great dignity came to the religion of Mazda worship ...

and Yahudis (Jews), Sramans (Buddhists), Brahmins (Hindus), Christians ... and Zandiks (Manichaeans) in the empire were smitten. Idols were destroyed and the dens of the demons were obliterated and turned into thrones and seats for the gods.

If you thought our earlier discussion of God/gods was complex, consider this: the Latin word for "god" (*deus*), the Zoroastrian word for "demon" (*dev*) here, and the Indian Sanskrit word for "god" (*deva*) are all derived from the same root of a verb "to shine." As the Zoroastrian and Sanskrit uses make very clear, one culture's gods are often another's demons. That, too, reflects a comparative practice—from our modern academic perspective, a bad one.

"Religion" in the Quran   Four centuries later, the Quran (the sacred scripture of Islam) will adopt the same language, using *din* as a term more or less interchangeable with Islam: "The *din* before God is Islam" (3: 19). Once again, no plural forms are used.

To complicate the picture somewhat, the Quran also makes a gesture toward universalism by depicting the multiplicity of beliefs evident in the world as part of the divine plan. Even here, though, there appears to be a real limit to just how "other" or "different" the religious Other can be:

> Indeed, the faithful [Muslims] and those who are Jews or Christians or Sabaeans—those [among them] who believed in God and the Last Day and performed righteous deeds—will have their reward with their Lord, and no fear will there be concerning them, nor will they grieve. (Quran 2: 62)

This relative religious tolerance, paired with the rapid rise of Islam into a regional and then a global colonial power, made it easier for Muslims to move toward a more inclusive understanding of *din*. Although Islam retained its position as "the most complete" religion, many other systems of belief were now understood and categorized as genuine religions. Such a situation, we might note, stands in contrast to the medieval Christian usage of the term *religio*, which was not treated as a generic category for different systems of belief and practice until the early sixteenth century, when the era of exploration was taking off, literally and metaphorically, and European colonialism was just around the corner.[24]

People of Religion and People of Opinion   Muslim comparative practices were shaped by the Quran, which was itself partly a product of the cultural dynamics of the same Near Eastern world that gave birth to Judaism and Christianity. One could well argue that the same region also gave birth to the very idea of the "holy book" as a central and indispensible element of an authentic religion. Such a trend culminates in the Quran, a text which, for the first time in the general history of religions, self-consciously refers to itself as "the Book" (*al-kitab*) and introduces the comparative category of the "people of the Book" (*ahl al-kitab*) to refer to the Abrahamic lineage of religions, that is, to Judaism, Christianity, and Islam—a bold move of classification and comparison, to be sure.

Hence, in matters of belief, the Muslim scholar of religion Abu al-Fath Muhammad al-Shahrastani (1086–1153) divides people into two groups: (1) those who rely upon revelation rather than opinion and possess a revealed book; he calls them "people of religion," a category that includes Muslims, Christians, and Jews, as well as Zoroastrians and Manicheans; and (2) followers of Indian thought and of the Greek philosophies, Sabaeans, pagans, and others, who depend on their own opinions and reason rather than on revelation or a sacred book; he calls these "people of opinion."

It is easy to recognize the limitations of such division when it comes to a fair comparative practice in the modern world. We might just as well translate "people of religion" and "people of opinion" as "people like us" and "people not like us." But the important fact remains that Muslim scholars were indeed classifying and "comparing religions" in the medieval period. Such practices, moreover, were not merely abstract scholarly entertainments. Rather some Muslim authorities treated (and in some ways still

treat) their subjects on the basis of opinions generated by these practices and passed into Islamic law. For example, people of religion enjoy certain rights because they fall into the legal and Quranic category of "people of the Book" (*ahl al-kitab*), whereas the second group, "people of opinion," otherwise categorized as "idolators" or "infidels" (*kuffar*), face (at least in theory) the stark choice of either converting to Islam or being persecuted under Muslim rule. Note again how "opinion" is framed negatively in the ancient monotheistic imagination, be it Christian or Muslim.

The Gods and Early Islamic Intolerance

It must be admitted that early Islam, like early Judaism and Christianity, was not generally tolerant of other religions.

Jihad   One obvious example of such intolerance is the Quranic concept of jihad, that is, the "struggle" to be waged against the infidel or non-believer, which, of course, only makes sense if the basic binary believer/unbeliever is in place. The injunction for "struggle" was later spiritualized, and jihad was often understood as an interior battle—a battle that one waged within one's own soul against temptation and non-belief—but the historical fact remains: jihad was originally a military and physically violent practice.

It should not surprise us, then, that the Quran is peppered with passages very similar to those of the Jewish Torah on not tolerating the unbelievers or pagans, indeed on killing them:

> But when the forbidden months are past, then fight and slay the Pagans wherever ye find them, and seize them, beleaguer them, and lie in wait for them in every stratagem (of war); but if they repent, and establish regular prayers and practice regular charity, then open the way for them: for Allah is Oft-forgiving, Most Merciful. (Quran 7.5)

> O ye who believe! fight the unbelievers who gird you about, and let them find firmness in you: and know that Allah is with those who fear Him. (Quran 7.123)

Figure 1.4   The Masjid al-Haram or "Sacred Mosque" surrounding the Kaba in Mecca, Saudi Arabia. © Nabeel Turner/ Getty Images.

The Destruction of the Idols   Similar forms of intolerance of other gods were expressed in the attitude of the Prophet Muhammad and the Quran toward the indigenous polytheistic religions of Arabia. The pre-Islamic sacred cubical of the Kaba in Mecca, for example, was the most important religious site and a major pilgrimage destination before the dawn of Islam. It hosted hundreds of sacred images of various local tribal deities. One of Muhammad's most iconic acts in his triumphant return to Mecca after twenty years of exile was his destruction of these "idols," held inside and around the Kaba.

We are reminded here of the same monotheistic impulse in ancient Israelite religion, with its texts on God's commandment to destroy physically Canaanite images and shrines. Later, in the course of the early rapid expansion of Islam, pagan tribes all over the Arabian Peninsula were given the choice of either converting to the new religion or having their property confiscated, their wives and children enslaved, and their men killed.

The Poll Tax   Also important here is the common Islamic practice of demanding a special "poll tax" from adherents of recognized religions, that is, Christianity, Judaism, and Zoroastrianism (the "people of the Book" again), in return for peace and protection:

> Fight those who believe not in Allah nor the Last Day, nor hold that forbidden which hath been forbidden by Allah and His Messenger, nor acknowledge the religion of Truth, among the People of the Book, until they pay the *Jizya* (poll tax) with willing submission, and feel themselves subdued. (Quran 7.29)

Qualifications

As with the ancient Torah texts and the early Christian forms of intolerance, we need to exercise real caution here. Again, in a spirit of fairness and balance, let us mention four points to qualify our observations immediately above.

1 *Inclusive Quranic Passages and Contextual Interpretive Principles* First, it is important to note that Muslim scholars have often insisted on broad limitations to Quranic interpretation, particularly when it comes to the application of the more extreme injunctions. They have had to reconcile the militant tone of the verses expressing intolerance with that of many other verses in which toleration, compromise, and peace are the message. Consider this verse, which immediately follows the first jihad passage quoted above:

> And if any one of the pagans seeks your protection, then grant him protection so that he may hear the words of God. Then deliver him to his place of safety. That is because they are a people who do not know. (9.6)

Moreover, very much like modern biblical scholars, who consistently demonstrate how biblical passages must be read in their original historical contexts before they can be properly applied to any contemporary situation, early Muslim scholars argued that each Quranic verse needs to be understood and interpreted in association with the specific historical circumstance in response to which it was originally revealed to the Prophet. Such circumstantial contexts

were gathered by Muslim scholars in separate books that eventually came to be known as a genre, under the description of *Asbab al-Nuzul* ("Occasions of Revelation").

2 *Empire and Diversity* Another major force that worked to qualify Islamic intolerance toward other religions was the Islamic Empire. Islamic colonialism would push Muslim intellectuals into new territory, both intellectual and literal. As Muslim elites encountered the unbelievable religious diversity of the Muslim-ruled lands, from Spain and West Africa to Central China and Malaysia, they often found it difficult, if not actually impossible, to adhere to this simple polemical or legal distinction between the people of the Book and the people of opinion.

Consider, for example, what happened to Islam after Muslims conquered much of north India and ruled it for half a millennium as a colonial power. The polytheistic outlook of much Hindu religiosity is anathema to Muslim belief. Moreover, the Hindu beliefs in multiple deities and in re-incarnation fly in the face of the two basic principles of Muslim faith: monotheism (signaled by the first Muslim "pillar of faith," namely the declaration that "there is no God but God, and Muhammad is His messenger"); and the belief in the last judgment and in a single afterlife. There was, it seems, no way to categorize Hindus as people of the Book. Hindus and Muslims clearly believed incompatible things.

And yet practical concerns regarding the situation on the ground often prevailed over these religious concerns. Hence there is evidence that, shortly after the conquest of India, some Muslim authorities came to recognize Hindus as a "people of the Book" and so subject to both Muslim protection and to the attached poll tax.[25] Hindus, after all, have their own sacred Book: the Veda.

3 *The Sabaean Umbrella* Another comparative strategy that protected minorities from open persecution was recourse to "Sabaeanism," a category that, as we noted above, was introduced by the Quran itself. The ambiguity of this category, perhaps consciously

left so by the Prophet, made it the perfect shelter for several non-monotheistic minority groups. Examples include the Mandaeans (the only surviving group of gnostics currently living in southeast Iraq and in southwest Iran) and various star-worshiping religions in the ancient town of Harran. In the light of the positive context in which Quran speaks about the Sabaeans, it was not difficult for Muslim rulers and their jurists to grant these communities protection as a people of the Book.

Edward Browne's entertaining, yet generally accurate, re-creation of how this actually happened to the pagans of Harran deserves to be quoted at length here:

> When the Caliph al-Ma'mun passed through the district of Harran on his last campaign against the Byzantines, he remarked amongst the people who came out to meet him and wish him God-speed certain persons of strange and unfamiliar appearance, wearing their hair extremely long, and clad in tightly-fitting coats (*qabā*). Al-Ma'mun, astonished at their appearance, inquired who and what they were, to which they replied, "Harranians." Being further questioned, they said that they were neither Christians, Jews, nor Magians; while to the Caliph's inquiry "whether they had a Holy Book or a Prophet," they returned "a confused reply." Convinced at last that they were heathens ("Zindiqs and worshippers of idols"), the Caliph ordered them, under pain of death, either to embrace Islam, or to adopt "one of the religions which God Almighty has mentioned in His Book," giving them respite for their decision till his return from the war. Terrified by these threats, the Harranians cut their long hair and discarded their peculiar garments, while many became Christians or Muhammadans; but a small remnant would not forsake their own religion, and were greatly perplexed and troubled until a Muhammadan jurist offered, for a consideration, to show them a way out of their difficulty. So they brought him much fine gold from their treasuries, and he counseled them to call themselves Sabaeans when al-Ma'mun returned to question them, since the Sabaeans were mentioned in the Quran, yet, since little was known of them, the change of name would involve no change of beliefs or customs.[26]

4   *The Mystical Element in Islam*   But perhaps the inclusive and tolerant spirit of Islam is nowhere more evident than in Sufism. A Sufi is a Muslim mystic, that is, a religious aspirant or saint who witnesses some profound union with God or the unity of God through such acts as meditation, retreats, and the ritual chanting of the names of God sometimes accompanied by music, poetry, and dance. Not all Sufis have been tolerant of non-Muslim religions, but many have been (this is one of the reasons modern-day Muslim fundamentalists generally despise Sufi communities and shrines). Sufis have often functioned as Islam's premier "border creatives," that is, as effective translators and synthesizers of Islamic and non-Islamic religious forms.

The great Persian poet Shams-al-din Muhammad Hafez (1320–1398) was such a Muslim mystic. His *divan*, a collection of lyric poems, sits beside the Quran in many Muslim homes. It contains lines like these ones:

> Love is a church where all religions meet;
> Islam, or Christ, or Tavern, it is one;
> Thy face of every system is the sun—
> O Sun that shines in the Beloved's street.
> Where Love is there's no need of convent bell,
> And holy living needs no holy frocks;
> Time ticks not to your monastery clocks;
> Where goodness is there God must be as well.[27]

Once again, it is the mystics of a religion who are often the most radical comparative thinkers.

"World Religions" Textbooks of the Islamic World

It is also well worth mentioning that, during the classical period of Islamic civilization (roughly, from the late ninth century to the fifteenth century), a number of Muslim scholars succeeded in introducing what are probably the earliest texts on "world religions" known in the West.

The eleventh-century theologian Abu al-Ma'ali, for example, wrote the first Persian text that we would today recognize as just such a study. He decided that the term *din* was not a proper category when it came to discussing different systems of belief and practice. He chose instead to use the more neutral word *madhhab*, that is, "way" or "path." This might seem a minor lexical change, but it was in fact a significant departure from the earlier comparative practice, which slotted communities into one of just two categories: people of the Book and people of opinion. There could now be, after all, many ways or paths—not just two types of religion, true and false.

Similarly, Shahrastani published his masterpiece *Religions and Sects* at roughly the same time. This work not only provided its readers with a balanced view of different sects within Islam, but addressed Buddhist, Hindu, Zoroastrian, Manichaean, Christian, and Jewish beliefs and practices in a remarkably open spirit. Even more importantly, this text was widely read. Indeed the work became so popular among Muslims that Persian and Turkish translations were commissioned in the medieval period. These were subsequently used throughout the Islamic world, from India to Asia Minor.

The Comparative Practices of Asia: Hinduism

The "world religions" are traditionally divided into those of "the West" (Judaism, Christianity, and Islam) and those of "the East" (Hinduism, Buddhism, Jainism, Sikhism, Daoism, Confucianism, and Shintoism). However reasonable and helpful such a classification may be, there are multiple problems with it, including the simple fact that "western" religions like Judaism, Christianity, and Islam are found throughout Asian cultures, and that "eastern" religions like Sikhism are clearly indebted to "western" religions like Islam and are also now found throughout western cultures. With centuries, really millennia, of immigration, trade, and now instant global communication, expressions like "the West" and "the East" are understood to be increasingly dubious, if not actually misleading.

Still, there is some truth to the traditional observation that the Asian religions generally work through worldviews, beliefs, and philosophies that are fundamentally different from those found in western monotheisms. Not surprisingly, their comparative practices have differed in fundamental ways as well. The Asian attitudes toward other religions have generally been seen as more tolerant. Such a view has good reasons too, even if it is no longer entirely convincing.

The cultures and religions of India, for example, where diversity of every sort has long been the norm, have an especially rich history of comparative practices. Not surprisingly, the same subcontinent has also produced a number of major world religions, including Hinduism, Buddhism, Jainism, Sikhism, and numerous Indian forms of Islam and Christianity. For the sake of space, we will have to be much more brief and selective here.

Cosmotheism in the Vedas and Upanishads

With respect to ancient Hinduism, explicitly comparative insights already appear in the ancient Sanskrit texts of India's earliest scriptures, traditionally known as the Vedas. "The Lord is one, though his names are many," sings the *Rig Veda* (c. 1500–1000 BCE). Already we can see a clear and classic balancing of sameness ("The Lord is one") and difference ("though his names are many"). We can also see an ancient polytheism evolving, as Assmann would say, into a robust cosmotheism, with its usually attending comparative practices and eventual conclusion that the gods are all One.

Similar cosmic convictions and implicit comparative practices can be found throughout the rich histories of Hinduism, but perhaps they are nowhere more clear than in the teachings of the Hindu saint Ramakrishna (1836–1886). In Ramakrishna we find explicit and multiple declarations such as "She herself has become everything," or "He himself has become everything"—that is, God/dess *is* the physical universe, and more.[28] And he was not being metaphorical here. In one of his visions, the saint saw that the Goddess Kali *was* the walls and floor of the sacred temple, even the cat that wandered through the temple grounds: everything was vibrating with and as her "energy" or "power" (*shakti*). At other times, the saint shifted his religious register and likened all deities, persons, and things to freezing and melting icebergs or temporary waves on the surface of a single Ocean of Conscious Light. This was the famous *brahman* of the Advaita ("nondual") Vedanta tradition. Ramakrishna also taught that all religions lead to the same goal. Indeed, he even turned this teaching into a practiced "comparative mysticism" by serially adopting the rituals and teachings of different religious "paths," which he experienced as all leading to the same blissful *brahman*. Note the liberal language of "paths" or "ways" again.

Ramakrishna's cosmotheism and comparative practices were advanced in a British colonial context in which they worked as a powerful response to Christian missionary claims that Hinduism was simple polytheism or, worse yet, "idolatry." In short, Ramakrishna's inclusive comparativism was a critical response to colonial comparative practices and worked to undermine the latter's exclusive religious logic.

Such Hindu comparative practices can hardly be explained by British colonialism, though. Such teachings are in fact ancient in India and can be traced at least as far back as the Upanishads ("Secret Teachings"), which were developed around the middle of the first millennium BCE, right in the middle of Jaspers's Axial Age. Also part of the Vedic tradition, these writings are often considered the "end" or "culmination" (-*anta*) of the Vedic revelation (*Veda*)—hence the aforementioned expression, "Vedanta."

These foundational texts have been variously interpreted in Indian history, and so it would be a serious mistake to identify any one of these interpretations as the correct one; but one constant theme has been the distinction between the surface ego or social self (*ahamkara*, literally the "I-maker") and the deeper human spirit or cosmic Self (*atman*). This distinction is an important one, as it became the basis of a Hindu comparative practice of great power and persuasion. In this model, religious difference and multiplicity are explained as a function of the social self, which, of course, is socialized in radically different ways, whereas the deeper dynamics of religious sameness are explained as a function of the shared and universal cosmic Self, which is generally understood to be immortal and unchanging, or at least quite other than the temporary social self. Hence Ramakrishna's teachings about the surface waves of selves on the deeper Ocean of Light; or ancient secret teachings like this one: "May the gods abandon him who thinks the gods dwell anywhere other than in the Self."[29] The gods are real, but they are not as real as the Self, of which they are temporary projections or local manifestations.

Comparisons in Stone

Such comparative practices, of course, were not just functions of secret texts. Nor were they the sole product of elite intellectuals or recognized saints. They were also commonly and publicly exercised, in ritual and in stone. Many of the Hindu temples, for example, display in striking form a most remarkable comparative practice: numerous gods and goddesses share the same sacred space, as each is understood to be a part of a larger cosmic vision or sacred whole. A comparative practice like this, of course, is an implicit one, that is, the sculptors and temple builders were not setting out consciously to "compare religions." They nevertheless did.

The Caste System and Early Hindu Intolerance

As with the three monotheistic religions, such liberal and inclusive practices have by no means been the whole story of Hinduism. There also have been some fundamental Indian social structures that emphasize difference, social hierarchy, discrimination, and what we would today recognize as religiously based intolerance.

The Foreigner Consider the traditional abhorrence of the *mleccha* (the barbaric "foreigner"), the classical prohibition against "crossing the black waters" (that is, of leaving the subcontinent of South Asia), and, behind and beneath all of this, the caste

Figure 1.5   Hindu pantheon (c. 1985–1997). Sri Murugan Temple near Hampi, India. © Bennett Dean/Eye Ubiquitous/ Corbis.

system that renders entire communities permanently marginalized by declaring them "polluting." For much of Indian history (the situation radically changed in the modern period), to leave Bharat or what is today called India was equivalent to losing one's caste—for what could "caste" mean in a foreign culture that did not recognize it?—which was in turn tantamount to a kind of social and personal destruction. Here travel was openly recognized for what it in fact often is: the dissolution of one's cultural certainties and social self.

The Crushed   Related here is the very difficult subject of Hinduism's historical treatment of millions of people whom it came to call "untouchables," so named because orthodox Hindus will not literally touch them lest they become polluted or rendered ritually impure by such contact. Untouchable people, of course, have a very different perspective on this daily social fact of life in India. From their own perspective,

they are not "untouchable" at all. They are "Dalits." They are "the Crushed."

Hierarchical Inclusions   The truth is that ancient or classical Hinduism was not so much "tolerant" in the modern sense of that word, as it was "hierarchical" in the ancient or medieval sense. That is, before the modern period, Hinduism has generally handled religious and social difference not by accepting the religious or social other as a free citizen within an open liberal society of equals (*no* culture attempted this until the modern period), but by including the religious other within its own caste mentality, always at a lower or subordinate level. One could certainly argue today that this kind of hierarchical inclusion is preferable to the biblical and Quranic strategies of actively suppressing or converting the religious other into oneself, but one can hardly argue that this strategy meets all the modern moral standards of religious pluralism.

The Mystical Element of Hinduism

It was, once again, the poets and mystics who mounted the most radical challenges to these sorts of hierarchical subordinations of other individuals and whole communities. One of the most remarkable of these poets and mystics was the fifteenth-century poet-weaver Kabir. Kabir attempted to move his listeners out of the religious ideas that made both normative Hindu social discrimination and Muslim religious discrimination possible. More particularly, he taught of a God beyond all Hindu, Muslim, ritual, and caste differences, and he did so within an implicit, accessible, effective, and beautiful comparative practice: he *sang*.

Here, for example, is Kabir going after the pundits or learned scholars of conservative Hinduism, their claimed authority to interpret the sacred scriptures (the Vedas and Puranas), and their violent animal sacrifices. Kabir insists that the true God (whom he called "Ram," a common Hindu name for God) cannot be known through words, scriptures, and sacrificial killings. He can only be known through love:

Pundit, how can you be so dumb?
You're going to drown, along with all your kin,
    unless you start speaking of Ram.

Vedas, Puranas—why read them?
    It's like loading an ass with sandalwood!
Unless you catch on and learn how Ram's name goes,
    how will you reach the end of the road?

You slaughter living beings and call it religion:
    Hey brother, what would irreligion be?
"Great Saint"—that's how you love to greet each other:
    Who[m] then would you call a murderer?

And here is the same poet going after the Muslims, their circumcisions, their gender discriminations, and their reliance on another holy book:

Hey, Qazi [an Islamic judge],
    What's that book you're preaching from?
And reading, reading—how many days?
    Still you haven't mastered one word.

Drunk with power, you want to grab me;
    Then comes the circumcision.
        Brother, what can I say?—
If God had wanted to make me a Muslim,
    why didn't he make the incision?
You cut away the foreskin, and then you have
a Muslim;
    so what about your women?
        What are they?
Women, so they say, are only half-formed men;
    I guess they must stay Hindus to the end.
Hindus, Muslims—where did they come from?
    Who got them started down this road?
Search inside, search your heart and look:
    Who made the heavens come to be?
Fool,
    Throw away that book, and sing of Ram.
        What you're doing has nothing to do with him.[30]

It would be difficult to find more dramatic criticisms of religious identity *anywhere* in the modern study of religion. What scholar has spoken like this? What academic has sung? And certainly no form of scholarship can approach the popularity and cultural influence of a people's poet like Kabir. He "compared religions" to transcend religion. And the people loved him for it.

The Comparative Practices of Asia: Sikhism

Somewhere around this same time, a man who came to be known as Guru Nanak (1469–1539)—literally "Teacher Nanak"—came on the scene and established a community among Hindus, Muslims, and Jains. Guru Nanak or Baba Nanak ("Father Nanak") proclaimed a God who united all human beings, in a bold new monotheistic vision that insisted on the equality of all and on the welfare and protection of the poor and the downtrodden. And so was eventually born a new religion, which we have come to call Sikhism (so named after the word "Sikh," probably originally "bearer of divine wisdom or teachings [*sikhia*]," but eventually "disciple").

speak until he ecstatically uttered lines like these: "There is neither Hindu nor Muslim, so whose path shall I follow?" and "God is neither Hindu nor Muslim." Another implicit act of comparison, and of the most dramatic sort.

Revelation as Comparison

The stunning revelation that began with a denial of religious identity became—through centuries of conversion, community building, ritual practice, and anxious defense on the part of the Sikh community before repeated military oppositions—its own strongly marked religious identity, which now represents itself with a symbol consisting of swords. This is an especially complex history, whose details and debates we have neither the space nor the competence to describe here. Only one subject will concern us now: Sikh comparative practices.

As in most premodern religions, the comparative practices of early Sikhism were largely implicit rather than explicit. Guru Nanak's reported declaration that "there is neither Hindu nor Muslim" was precisely such an implicit comparative practice, in this case one that privileged the universal sameness of the human spirit over the superficial differences of religious and social identity.

But it is also clear that Nanak was in effect "comparing" the new religious revelation he had received to the established religious communities of his own place and time. With respect to his own Hindu society, he acknowledged the reality of reincarnation or rebirth, for example, but he strongly opposed both Hindu polytheism and the religiously based caste system. With respect to Islamic society, he followed Muslim theology on many points, particularly the unity and primacy of God as Lord and Creator, but he was deeply critical of the excesses and corruptions of Islamic political practices. With respect to the Jain communities in his midst, he unequivocally denied the atheism of Jain teachings.

Such "comparisons," of course, were not advanced for the sake of any academic or intellectual project, nor did they develop from any purely rational

Figure 1.6 *Guru Nanak*, by Amarjit Singh. © INTERFOTO/Amarjit Singh/Mary Evans.

The Dissolution of Religious Identity

Nanak was born into an upper-caste, land-owning Hindu family in a region that was largely Muslim at this point in space and time. Islam had been practiced in the area for almost eight centuries, that is, from the early eighth century CE on. Somewhere around the year 1500, Nanak had a powerful religious vision, which he described as one of "being taken to the divine court." This vision appears to have involved both a revelation into the true nature of God and a profound personal sense of being called to a divine mission. In one version of this initiatory vision, the Sikh tradition has it that, after receiving his revelation while bathing in a river, Nanak could not be found for three days. When he finally reappeared, he could not processes or logical arguments. They were rather direct outcomes or implications of the divine revelation that he believed he had received at the divine court. Revelation *was* comparison.

The Comparative Practices of Asia: Confucianism, Daoism, and Buddhism in China

Traditional Chinese Ethnocentrism

China, like India, is famously plural and diverse. And famously ethnocentric, even literally so. Indeed the most common indigenous name for China is not "China" (that word appears to have come from the Indian Sanskrit word *cina*, pronounced "cheena"). What the ancient and medieval people of China actually called their culture and land was "the Middle Kingdom." In short, they thought of themselves as living in the center of the world. In their view, every other culture, and thus every other people, lived on the margins, outside the middle.

Even within this so-called Middle Kingdom, however, Chinese culture has generally been dramatically pluralistic, defined in large measure by the weaving together of three separate streams of social and religious thought: those deriving from the teachings of the Chinese scholar-sage and political theorist Confucius, of the Chinese nature mystic Lao-Tzi, and of the north Indian teacher and religious founder Gautama Buddha. Confucius and Lao-Tzi were indigenous to ancient China.[31] Buddhism was an import from South Asia. Buddhism arose around the fifth century BCE in northern India and probably did not reach China until somewhere around the turn of the Common Era, through traveling monks and texts; but these were effectively assimilated and absorbed into Chinese culture in the ensuing centuries by many means, including through extensive translation activities, until they became as "Chinese" as the political philosophy and familial pieties of Confucius or the Way of Lao-Tzi.

The Three Ways

What is relevant about all of this for our present purposes is the fact that early medieval Chinese scholars engaged in ways of writing and talking about these different traditions that were not so different from the ways early modern European scholars wrote comparatively about "religions," or even—eventually—about "world religions."[32] The Chinese, of course, did not use the Latin-based term "religion." Rather they commonly spoke and wrote about "ways" or "practices" (much like Abu al-Ma'ali in his eleventh-century Persian textbook on world religions, or Ramakrishna countering British Christian colonialists in the nineteenth).

The most common category was Dao, which means simply "way" or "path." This was yet another riff on the universal motif of travel, journey, and path. Thus, while the later European scholars would make up various -isms to name the religions—like Taoism (or Daoism), Buddhism, and Confucianism—the medieval Chinese comparativists spoke of *wuwei dadao* or "the Great Way of Intentionless Action," *fodao* or "the Way of Buddha," and *qingyue dadao* or "the Great Way of the Pure Contract."[33] This is sometimes called the "Three Teachings" (*Sanjiao*) tradition. It was especially prominent in the middle of the Ming dynasty (1368–1644).

Unsurprisingly, different scholars writing on the various "ways" often sought to establish the superiority of a particular "way" over the others. For instance, one scholar used the category of Dao to argue that the Ways of the Buddha and Confucius ultimately share a common source, the true Way of Laozi: "Now the three Ways are but different branches extending from the same root. … These three Ways are equally methods of the Most High Lord Lao, though they differ in their teachings and transformative effects. All three find their source in the true Way."[34] Thus, in our own terms now, Daoism becomes the sameness that the surface differences of Confucianism and Buddhism ultimately point toward. This was a fairly easy argument to make, given the language being employed. The "Dao" of Daoism, after all, means the Way, so it would have been quite natural to think of different religions as different "ways," *and* to privilege the Way (that is, the Dao) over the other ways.

It was not all about this kind of one-up-manship, though. Chinese scholars also had a fundamental comparative insight, namely that often it was quite impossible to understand the true shape and nuances of a particular religious tradition without comparing it to another. That is to say, sometimes the "inside" of a religion can only be fathomed by looking at it from the "outside." So, for example, one Ming scholar, Yuan Zongdao (1560–1600), went so far as to write that "we can understand Confucianism for the first time only after we have studied Chan [Buddhism]."[35] This is a most remarkable observation and could easily be put in the mouths of any number of contemporary comparativists. Chinese intellectuals, not unlike their Indian counterparts, were "comparing religions" on their own terms and in their own, well, *ways*.

Colonialism and Comparison on the Horizon

Such comparisons in the mirror of the Other would only quicken in China with the appearance of European missionary activity, which was effectively initiated by the Italian Jesuit missionary Matteo Ricci (1552–1610). European missionaries and colonialists would now bring new forms of European religion, knowledge, and technology to China, which in turn challenged traditional forms of knowledge and catalyzed a whole series of new ways of thinking among the Chinese—including, eventually, new comparative practices. Similar cross-cultural encounters would be catalyzed in India and Hinduism as well, primarily in the nineteenth century around the global center of Calcutta and the colonial and missionary activity of the British Empire, as we shall see in greater detail in our next chapter.

The Tough Questions

1 If you are religious and believe in some sort of deity, does the god you worship look like you? If your tradition forbids making images of the deity, do you nevertheless tend to think of this god in human terms? If so, why? Would it be emotionally possible for you to worship or care about a deity who was *completely* non-human, who looked, say, like an insect or a crab? How about a bacterium?

2 Are the ancient Christian concept of "heresy" and the Islamic category of "people of opinion" really so different from what we today recognize and *value* as religious freedom? What has changed? Are ancient notions of religious orthodoxy and modern notions of human rights compatible?

3 The way we talk matters, and matters a great deal. How would our societies differ if we abandoned the language of "religions" and adopted the language of "paths" or "ways"?

Notes

1 Martin Riesbrodt, *The Promise of Salvation: A Theory of Religion* (Chicago: University of Chicago Press, 2010), xii.

2 Karen Armstrong, *The Great Transformation: The Beginning of Our Religious Traditions* (New York: Anchor, 2007), xvi.

3 Quoted in Eric J. Sharpe, *Comparative Religion: A History* (La Salle, IL: Open Court, 1986), 3.

4 Sharpe, *Comparative Religion*, 4.

5 Jan Assmann, *Moses the Egyptian: The Memory of Egypt in Western Monotheism* (Cambridge, MA: Harvard University Press, 1997), 3.

6 Porphyry, *The Life of Plotinus*, 3.7–21.

7 Frits Staal, *Advaita and Neoplatonism* (Madras, India: University of Madras, 1961).

8   John Walbridge, *The Wisdom of the Mystic East: Suhrawardi and Platonic Orientalism* (Albany: State University of New York Press, 2001).

9   Jan Assmann, *Of God and Gods: Egypt, Israel, and the Rise of Monotheism* (Madison: University of Wisconsin Press, 2008), 70–75.

10   Assmann, *Of God and Gods*, 70–72.

11   Andrea Wilson Nightingale, *Spectacles of Truth in Classical Greek Philosophy: Theoria in Its Cultural Context* (Cambridge: Cambridge University Press, 2004), 5.

12   Thomas A. Tweed, *Crossing and Dwelling: A Theory of Religion* (Cambridge, MA: Harvard University Press, 2006), 13.

13   Assmann, *Moses the Egyptian*, 1.

14   Assmann, *Moses the Egyptian*, 3.

15   Avraham Faust, *Israel's Ethnogenesis: Settlement, Interaction, Expansion and Resistance* (London: Equinox, 2006).

16   Quoted in Jonathan Garb, *Shamanic Trance in Modern Kabbalah* (Chicago, IL: University of Chicago Press, 2011), 41.

17   Varro in Augustine, as used by Assmann, *Of God and Gods*, 20–21.

18   Jan Assmann, *The Price of Monotheism*, trans. Robert Savage (Stanford, CA: Stanford University Press, 2009), 19, 117.

19   Brent Landau, *Revelation of the Magi: The Lost Tale of the Wise Men's Journey to Bethlehem* (New York: HarperOne, 2010), 90–91.

20   Mary Boyce, *A Word-List of Manichaean Middle Persian and Parthian* (Tehran and Liège: Bibliothèque Pahlavi, Acta Iranica 9a, 1977), 38.

21   Jenny Rose, *Zoroastrianism: A Guide for the Perplexed* (London: Continuum, 2011).

22   William W. Malandra, "Zoroastrianism I: Historical Review," *Encyclopædia Iranica*, July 20, 2005, http://www.iranicaonline.org/articles/zoroastrianism-i-historical-review (accessed August 1, 2013).

23   D. N. MacKenzie, "Kerdir's Inscriptions." In *The Sasanian Rock Reliefs at Naqsh-i Rustam: Naqsh-I Rustam 6, The Triumph of Shapur I*, edited by G. Hermann, D. N. Mackenzie, and R. Howell (Berlin: Dietrich Reimer, Iranische Denkmäler 13, 1989), 35–78.

24   Jonathan Z. Smith, "Religion, Religions, Religious." In *Critical Terms for Religious Studies*, ed. Mark C. Taylor (Chicago, IL: University of Chicago Press, 1998), 269–270.

25   J. Burton-Page, "Hindū." In *Encyclopaedia of Islam* (2nd edn., Brill Online, 2012). Reference, Harvard University, July 6, 2012, http://referenceworks.brillonline.com/entries/encyclopaedia-of-islam-2/hindu-SIM_2884 (accessed August 1, 2013). Seyyed Hossein Nasr, *Sufi Essays.* (London: G. Allen and Unwin, 1972), 139.

26   Edward Granville Browne, *A Literary History of Persia: From the Earliest Times until Firdawsi*, vol. 1 (London: T. F. Unwin, 1902), 302–303.

27   Epigraph to Eric Maroney, *Religious Syncretism* (London: SCM Press, 2006).

28   Bengali (the language the saint spoke) does not distinguish gender in its pronouns, nor does Hinduism identify divinity with a single gender: masculine, feminine, and neuter forms are all commonly found. Hence the shifting genders here.

29   *Brihadaranyaka Upanishad* 2.4.6.

30   John Stratton Hawley and Mark Juergensmeyer, *Songs of the Saints of India* (Delhi: Oxford University Press, 2004), 51–52.

31   There is considerable debate as to whether or not Lao-Tzi was a historical figure or a legendary one.

32   I am relying here on Robert Ford Campany, "On the Very Idea of Religions (In the Modern West and in Early Medieval China)." *History of Religions* 42: 4 (May 2003): 287–319.

33   Campany, "On the Very Idea of Religions," 303.

34   Quoted in Campany, "On the Very Idea of Religions," 304.

35   Quoted in Richard J. Smith, *Fathoming the Cosmos and Ordering the World: The* Yijing *(I-Ching, or Classic of Changes) and Its Evolution in China* (Charlottesville: University of Virginia Press, 2008), 165–166.

Eagle Pneuma (2003), by Lynn Randolph, 36″ × 48″.

2

Western Origins and History of the Modern Practice

From the Bible to Buddhism

The human rises up to heaven and takes its measure and knows what is in its heights and its depths … and—greater than all of this—he comes to be on high without leaving earth behind, so enormous is his range. Therefore, we must dare to say that the human on earth is a mortal god but that god in heaven is an immortal human.

Discourse of Hermes Trismegistus, *The Key*, in Brian P. Copenhaver, *Hermetica: The Greek* Corpus Hermeticum *and the Latin* Asclepius

All great truths begin as heresy.

Commonly attributed to Aldous Huxley

Comparing Religions: Coming to Terms, First Edition. Jeffrey J. Kripal, Ata Anzali, Andrea R. Jain, and Erin Prophet.
© 2014 Jeffrey J. Kripal. Published 2014 by John Wiley & Sons, Ltd.

So everyone and every religion compares, and they have all been doing it for a very long time. Indeed every religion *is* a form of comparison, constantly negotiating self and other, sameness and difference. What sets apart the modern comparative study of religion from all of the premodern practices is the scope of its institutionalization—that is, the fact that it now exists in so many colleges, universities, and publishing houses. At no point in human history have so many people been able to spend their entire working lives thinking, writing, and teaching about these matters. The question remains, then: Why did the field emerge where and when it did?

There are many ways to answer such a question, of course. There were in fact countless influences and cross-influences, and in the end it is quite arbitrary how far back we choose to trace the currents that flowed together to form the modern comparative study of religion. For the sake of simplicity, let us imagine this history as a kind of river, restrict ourselves to the last five hundred years or so, and—again, quite arbitrarily—separate that stream story into three navigable segments: (1) a deep upstream, in fifteenth- through eighteenth-century Europe;

(2) a mid-upstream, in the biblical scholarship of the nineteenth century and, again, in Europe; and (3) a near upstream, in the second half of the nineteenth century and throughout the twentieth, now focusing our attention primarily on the scene in the USA.

Deep Upstream: Mystical Humanists, Protesters, Rationalists, and Romantics

In terms of the deep upstream, we can identify at least four different currents: Renaissance humanism, the Protestant Reformation, the Enlightenment, and the romantic movement.

The Italian Renaissance

The fourteenth and fifteenth centuries saw the efflorescence of something we now call Renaissance humanism, an intellectual movement centered in Italy that valued scholarship, language study, the arts, and particularly ancient Greek and Latin literature.

Some of these scholars were especially drawn to a set of newly translated texts of or about Plato; to a collection of Greek fragments about an oracular poem that was believed to be of Babylonian origin—the so-called *Chaldaean Oracles*; and to a collection of dialogues that an Italian scholar named Marsilio Ficino (1433–1499) translated into Latin as *The Book about the Power and Wisdom of God*, also known simply as *Pimander* (1471). The meaning of this strange word, "Pimander," is debated by scholars, but the word itself is probably derived originally from an Egyptian phrase designating some attribute of God as "mind" (perhaps something like "cosmic mind" or the "mind of God").

Hermetism   These texts were believed to have been written by an ancient human wizard named Hermes Trismegestus—"Hermes the Thrice Great." Hermes is a complex character. Literally. The Renaissance humanists believed that he was an actual historical figure from the deep Egyptian past, but scholars today are of one mind: he was a literary fiction representing the religious fusion of different ancient cultures, particularly the Egyptian, the Greek, and the Roman. As ancient Greeks and Romans encountered Egyptian culture in the early centuries of the Common Era, particularly around the city of Alexandria, the Greek god Hermes—the god of communications between the human world and the divine, of middle spaces, of dreams, death, and doorways—merged with the Egyptian god of language, Thoth, and morphed into Hermes Trismegestus. It is this Hermes that featured in Ficino's translation, where he enlightens a disciple about the secrets of the soul, God, and the cosmos.

Although there were many nuances and complexities here, the most basic claim of Ficino and his Italian colleagues has been summed up by Wouter Hanegraaff as a claim about the existence of an "**ancient wisdom narrative**."[1] This narrative located a long line of inspired teachers, who had passed on revealed truths from generation to generation. Some models identified Egypt as the earliest source. Others

identified Moses. Still others looked to the East, to Persia (in the figure of Zoroaster) and India, as we have already noted. This last model—a model of what we have identified in Chapter 1 as Platonic orientalism—was most evident to the Renaissance humanists in the figures of the three magician-astrologers who had come "from the East" (Persia) to pay homage to the Christ child. This is because the humanists generally read this trip as an expression of ancient eastern wisdom finding its final consummation and fullest expression in Christianity.

There were two basic versions of the ancient wisdom narrative. One was referred to as *prisca theologia* ("ancient theology"). This tale of ancient wisdom tended to understand that wisdom had once been revealed but now was more or less forgotten, or at least heavily corrupted. "Ancient wisdom" boiled down to a few central ideas: (1) the key to salvation is a direct experience of the soul's immortality and identity with the divine; (2) this human immortality is accomplished through the acquisition of a spiritual body of light; and (3) the human being is a reflection and embodiment of the heavenly realms— "as above, so below," as the Hermetic thinkers often put it.

The second version or model was referred to as *philosophia perennis* ("perennial philosophy"). This ancient wisdom narrative understood wisdom to be not more or less forgotten and confined to the past, but rather available to the gifted wise man in any age. This was a philosophy that recurred "perennially," from age to age, like a "perennial flower" that comes up each spring. This second model, which is ultimately conservative (since nothing new is ever discovered), goes back to a Vatican librarian named Agostino Steuco. In 1540 Steuco wrote about universal religious truth, which he traced through the world's religious traditions all the way back to antiquity and Hermes again. Steuco, a very close friend of the pope, intended his "perennial philosophy" as a philosophical defense of Roman Catholicism in the middle of the Protestant Reformation. In his view, it was the Catholic Church that had preserved and passed on this "perennial philosophy" from the ancient philosophers through the birth of Christianity to Steuco's own tense present.

Historical scholarship would not be kind to such historical visions, as it was eventually proven, in 1614 by a scholar named Isaac Causabon, that an ancient Hermes could not have possibly written the texts gathered in the Corpus Hermeticum, as these were clearly a product of much later centuries, well after the birth of Christianity.

The Birth of Humanism   Assumptions aside, then, the "humanists," as these Renaissance scholars called themselves, were not all secular or non-religious thinkers. Quite the contrary, some of them were avid students of western mysticism and magic. What made such students "humanists," then, was not their rejection of mystical and magical phenomena, but rather their intuition that events of this sort are, ultimately, expressions of human nature, which they understood to be a kind of mirror that reflects the deepest secrets of both the universe and the divine.

These were also men who deeply valued scholarship and the interpretation of ancient texts but rejected the dry, logical, hyper-rational methods of scholastic philosophy. Scholasticism was a particular type of thinking, developed in the *scholae* ("schools") of Europe: these were essentially monastic institutions that would eventually give birth to the first universities (from the medieval Latin *schola* we got our own words "school" and "scholar"). For the humanists, *how* one said something was as important as *what* one said. Humanists were particularly interested in writing beautiful Greek and Latin, which they believed was the most effective means for exploring and expressing profound philosophical truths.

The Divine Human   Perhaps no one captured this bright new spirit better than the Italian prodigy Pico della Mirandola (1463–1494). It was Pico who wrote one of the era's most famous essays, his "Oration on the Dignity of Man" (1486), when he was just twenty-three years old. Here the young humanist wrote of the unimaginable powers of human nature, which he suggested resides in a third space, between the natural and the supernatural world. Positioned this way between the natural and the divine, human nature is capable of endlessly creating and re-creating itself anew. Here is how Pico put it:

> At last, the Master Creator … took man, this creature of indeterminate image, set him in the middle of the world, and said to him: "We have given you, Adam, no fixed seat or form of your own, no talent peculiar to you alone. This we have done so that whatever seat, whatever form, whatever talent you may judge desirable, these same may you have and possess according to your desire and judgment. Once defined, the nature of all other beings is constrained within the laws We have prescribed for them. But you, constrained by no limits, may determine your nature for yourself, according to your own free will, in whose hands We have placed you. We have set you at the centre of the world so that from there you may more easily gaze upon whatever it contains. We have made you neither of heaven nor of earth, neither mortal nor immortal, so that you may, as the free and extraordinary shaper of yourself, fashion yourself in whatever form you prefer. It will be in your power to degenerate into the lower forms of life, which are brutish. Alternatively, you shall have the power, in accordance with the judgment of your soul, to be reborn into the higher orders, those that are divine."[2]

In modern terms that are not Pico's, we might say that the dignity of the human being resides in the fact that human nature is defined by freedom and creativity rather than by pure instinct and simple biology; that the human being can transform itself through thought, language, art, and culture; that there is no single way to be human; and, most radically of all, that to be human is to be potentially divine.

This is hardly where things ended up, though. Although the first half of the century was still celebrating Renaissance thinkers like Augostino Steuco

Figure 2.1   Portrait of Giovanni Pico Della Mirandola (seventeenth century), anonymous. Galleria degli Uffizi, Florence, Italy. Photographed by Stefano Bianchetti. © Stefano Bianchetti/Corbis.

for envisioning a "perennial philosophy" right at the heart of the church, the same century ended with Italy's early astronomer, cosmologist, and esoteric visionary, the Dominican friar Giordano Bruno (1548–1600), burned at the stake in a Roman market square by order of the Inquisition. The authorities dumped Bruno's ashes in the Tiber and put all of his books on the Index, a list of forbidden books that was kept by the church. Among Bruno's blasphemies was his conviction that the universe is populated by countless other intelligent beings living in other worlds (which called into question the scope of the work of Christ on this one). Bruno's comparative vision, in short, was not just a global one. It was also a cosmic one. His universe and his comparative table were immense beyond measure.

The Protestant Reformation

The Italian Renaissance was an elite phenomenon of scholars and their wealthy patrons. The Protestant Reformation that soon followed, although inspired and led largely by scholars as well, quickly became a populist movement of incredible reach and historical influence. "Protestant Reformation" is the name given to that two-century time period in European history—very roughly the sixteenth and seventeenth centuries—when numerous scholars, monks, priests, and activists began to "protest" what they perceived to be the political abuses and religious falsehoods of the Roman Catholic Church, an institution that until then had been dominant in European history for well over a thousand years.

The reformers honed in on a series of established ritual systems and devotional practices (like the veneration of saints, the ritual mediation of priests, and the devotional use of images and statues) that they believed were rooted in custom and superstition instead of scripture. In their minds, if it wasn't in the Bible, it wasn't any good. Hence one of the reformers' most important rallying cries was *sola scriptura*: "Only the Scripture!"

These were fighting words. Why? Because the church had long held that religious truth could only be known through the Bible read in the light of tradition and of authoritative church teachings. Like Judaism and Islam, Roman Catholicism possessed a rich and sophisticated view of its scriptures, which it read and understood through long-established ritual practices, interpretive techniques, and philosophical assumptions. Very generally speaking, there were two sources of religious truth, not one: scripture and tradition. And neither could be properly understood without the other.

The church had a point. After all, it was the tradition that produced the Bible; the Bible did not produce the tradition. Or, better yet, it was the tradition that produced the Bible, which in turn informed and inspired the later tradition, which in turn informed how the Bible was understood, and so on. Historically speaking, it was clearly a both–and, not an either–or.

Figure 2.2   *Luther and the Heroes of the Reformation* (1874), hand-colored lithograph by H. Schile. © Corbis.

Crimes of Translation   The church went further, though. It had also reserved the interpretation of the Bible to its learned priests and scholars. Indeed the church had gone so far as to prohibit any translation of the Latin Bible, which it considered to be authoritative (despite the fact that it itself was a translation of the original Hebrew and Greek texts). Latin was only accessible to intellectuals and church leaders. What the church was really prohibiting here, then, was a translation of the Bible into any vernacular language, that is, into any language the people spoke in their day-to-day lives and so could understand for themselves, without the guidance of a church authority. Today, in a world flooded with translated and paraphrased Bibles of every imaginable sort, it is difficult for most people to understand just what was at stake in these prohibitions.

Just about everything, from the church's perspective. Consider the case of the Oxford scholar, reformer, and theologian John Wycliffe (c. 1324–1384). Wycliffe was one of the first to try to translate the Latin Bible into the language of the people, in his case English. He also happened to believe that the church should not hold political power but should be poor, like the early Christians (the church was easily the wealthiest landowner in Europe at this time). Such views were not well received. Three decades after his death, at the command of Pope Martin V, Wycliffe's remains were dug up, burned, and thrown in a river, to humiliate his memory and to terrorize his followers.

Other reformers and translators were not so lucky: their bodies were burned while they were still alive. Consider the "father of the English Bible," William Tyndale (1492–1536). Tyndale published an English translation of the New Testament in 1526. After being forced into exile, he translated some more and continued his provocations by publishing an English version of the Old Testament in 1530, after which he was betrayed to the authorities, thrown into prison, put on trial for heresy, and subsequently strangled and burned at the stake on October 6, 1536. Later reformers, like the German monk Martin Luther (1483–1546) and the French theologian John Calvin (1509–1564), died natural deaths, mostly because early state systems had begun to break away from Rome's control and could provide them with what was in effect political asylum and state protection.

Comparing Scriptures and Their Translation Histories   To put this European phenomenon in some comparative perspective, consider the history of the vernacular translations of the Quran. Arabic, from the very beginning of Islam, was considered to be a sacred language. The Quran was Kalamullah, that is, "the Speech of God." God spoke in Arabic. Because of this belief, it was impossible to render the Speech of God, which was considered to be the last prophetic message from heaven, into any other language—merely human as they all were. Still, new converts soon began to translate the Quran into their own vernaculars. The first of these translations was in Persian, perhaps some time in the tenth century.[3]

This surprisingly early translation can be partly explained by the fact that Islamic societies lacked a single central organizational structure that could command the kind of control that the Roman Catholic Church enjoyed. And yet it is also true that Arabic, unlike Latin, has preserved its sacred status.

This is reflected in the fact that almost every vernacular translation is printed side by side with the original Arabic. The message is clear: the translation is *not* what God said; it is simply a human approximation of what God said. One result of this attitude is that, although the Quran was eventually available to a broad audience in a number of languages, the right to interpret it and hence to determine its meaning remained the exclusive right of a group of elite legal and religious scholars who mastered the original Arabic language.

The Priesthood of All Believers   Looked at in the long view now, the Protestant Reformation, we might say, effectively "loosened" the grip of a single normative religious system on western culture and so allowed other religious possibilities to form. The individual believer now had a personal relationship with the Bible, and so he or she could come to his or her own interpretive conclusions—in effect, his or her own religious worldview. This was an example, to invoke the Protestant language, of the priesthood of all believers. Everyone was, in effect, his or her own priest or channel to God. Almost. As the Protestant traditions developed, they too, of course, fostered their own "correct" readings and normative ritual practices, even their own authoritative translations of the Bible.

All that protesting hardly stopped there: others protested against the first Protestants. And then others protested against those protesting the original Protestants, and so on, until there were hundreds, then thousands, then tens of thousands of individual churches and traditions, all claiming to preach the true meaning of the Bible. One can thus drive around a modern American city like Houston, Texas or Chicago, Illinois and see not dozens, but literally hundreds of different churches, all claiming to possess the correct reading of the Bible. This, of course, is exactly what the Roman Catholic Church feared and why it had refused to translate the Bible into the languages of the people. It turns out that the church was right, at least about the social and religious effects of these translations.

The Foundations of Freedom and Fundamentalism
The results of all of this, like most major historical developments, were complex. Intellectually speaking, we might say that the Protestant Reformation laid the groundwork for independent thinking, biblical scholarship, and, eventually, the critical study of religion and the modern concept of religious freedom— certainly *not* what the reformers intended. We might also say that, to the extent that the reformers sought to deny the crucial importance of historical development and tradition and to return to some imagined "golden age" of a pristine and original Christianity, they laid the foundation for what we today call **fundamentalism**.

Briefly, fundamentalism is a category that describes a modern way of being religious that relies on highly selective literalist readings of a scriptural text, which is in turn considered infallible or inerrant ("without error"), in order to return to what is imagined to be the original and pristine "fundamentals" of the faith. Within Christianity, these notions developed into their present forms in the nineteenth and early twentieth centuries. Despite claims to the contrary, they are not ancient and would have been quite foreign to most Christians living before the nineteenth century. Their historical foundations lie in the Protestant Reformation.

In the light of historical scholarship and comparison, we can easily see that there never was any single beginning of Christianity (or of any other religion); that the historical origins of a faith are always extremely complex and conflicted and never pristine or simple; and that there certainly has never been, and never can be, a single and final reading of a scriptural text. There can only be *readings* of scripture, each performed in different historical periods, by different communities of readers, and from different perspectives.

To take a single and ridiculously simple example, consider Jesus' two well-known teachings on poverty and wealth:

> Blessed are you who are poor, for yours is the kingdom of God. (Luke 6.20)

> Indeed, it is easier for a camel to go through the eye of a needle than for someone who is rich to enter the kingdom of God. (Luke 18.25)

To put it mildly, these two passages tend to be read (or not read) very differently by economically depressed and economically privileged communities, that is, by the poor and the rich. John Wycliffe, for example, certainly read these in a different light from the Roman papacy. Even many of the early Christians apparently could not quite accept what Jesus had said, so they changed Luke's "Blessed are you who are poor" to "Blessed are the poor in spirit" in the Gospel of Matthew (5.3). That changes *a lot*. Much later, medieval Christians would go so far as to invent a tradition that claimed that there was once a physical gate somewhere in Jerusalem called "the eye of the needle," through which one could barely (but could) squeeze a camel, and that this is what Jesus was referring to in this difficult passage. There is not the slightest evidence that such a gate existed in Jesus' day. It was in these ways that the original "hard saying" of Jesus in the Gospel of Luke was tamed, domesticated, and ultimately denied by later communities and their reading practices, even within the gospels themselves.

Enlightenment Reason

The humanists may have been onto something when they argued that there is not one way to be a human being; but, according to Enlightenment thought (which appeared in eighteenth-century France, England, Germany, and America), there was only one sure and safe way to guarantee that human beings would arrive at real and reliable truths about the world: human reason.

The historical background is crucial here, since that background was largely defined by the fact that Europe in the seventeenth century was a veritable bloodbath. Protestants killed Catholics and Catholics killed Protestants by the thousands, as individual states and regions chose sides and Europe became a checkerboard of religious intolerance and religious difference. The horrific degree and extent of the religious wars were sickening. As a result the churches, and especially their leaders, lost much of their

Figure 2.3 *Declaration of the Rights of Man and Citizen* (1789), French painting. © The Gallery Collection/Corbis.

authority in the eyes of thinking human beings. The Enlightenment followed, partly as a broad-based movement to wake up Europe out of its long religious nightmare. Enough was enough.

Dare to Know! In England the Enlightenment found its most eloquent voice in the thoughts of the Scottish philosopher David Hume (1711–1776); in France, in the satirist Voltaire (1694–1778); in

America, in the pamphleteerist and provocateur Thomas Paine (1737–1809); and in Germany (really Prussia), in the philosopher Immanuel Kant (1724–1804). It was Kant, though, who most famously defined the movement, in his little essay "Was ist Erklärung?" ("What Is Enlightenment?"). So what is it? Here is Kant:

> Enlightenment is man's emergence from his self-incurred immaturity. Immaturity is the inability to use one's own understanding without the guidance of another. This immaturity is self-incurred if its cause is not lack of understanding, but lack of resolution and courage to use it without the guidance of another. The motto of enlightenment is therefore: *Sapere aude!* Have courage to use your own understanding![4]

More literally: "Dare to know!" Kant was very clear on who traditionally guides thought and therefore keeps us immature: religious and political authorities—or "dogmas and formulas," as he put it. It is these that one must break away from if one truly wants to think for oneself and be enlightened. Other Enlightenment thinkers would target all those mystical texts and esoteric traditions that the Renaissance humanists so loved. The ancient wisdom narratives now became little more than a collection of superstitions. These were no longer histories of wisdom. They were "histories of stupidity."[5]

Deism   There is no way to overestimate the profound influence such thinkers had on western thought. But this kind of "pure reason" also came with a heavy price, particularly as Enlightenment reason aligned itself more and more with the acts of measurement, number, and a mechanistic view of the natural world. With only reason to go by now, the universe came to be seen as a great machine and God became a kind of impersonal cosmic clock-maker, a cold technician who had put all the pieces together, wound the thing up, and then left it to itself. We can now know God only through these mechanical laws of nature. **Deism** was the name for this kind of

natural theology (*deus*, remember, is the Latin for "God").

A **natural theology** is a way of thinking about God that relies on the study of the natural world as a sign or expression of God's nature, wisdom, and intentions. Medieval Christianity had located two sources of revelation: the Book of Scripture (that is, the Bible) and the Book of Nature. Natural theologies like deism read and emphasized the latter. Early modern deists certainly recognized the existence of a creator in the exquisite handiwork of the creation; but they also made this creator irrelevant to the present workings of the universe, and especially to human affairs. Gone was the personal, loving, threatening God of the Bible, who guides and guards human history and suffers along with humanity. In the view of the deists anyway, we were on our own now—which, of course, was not so different from saying that we had been enlightened.

And soon, of course, it would be seen that one did not really need this distant God at all in order to predict and manipulate the workings of the great machine of nature. God had become superfluous. "I had no need of that hypothesis," as the French mathematician Pierre-Simon Laplace (1749–1827) famously quipped when he was asked about the place of God in his mechanistic and mechanical theories. The birth of modern science was just around the corner.

The Romantic Reversal

Not everyone was taken with all those machine metaphors and that clock talk. In the late fifteenth century the Italian humanists had rebelled against what they regarded as the dry and deadening "scholastic" logic of medieval universities. Similarly, in the late eighteenth century many thinkers, poets, and artists began to find the rationalized, mechanical world created by the Enlightenment hard and heartless. Such a vision seemed to fall far short of the richness and beauty of human experience and, particularly, of poetic, artistic, religious, and visionary experience. The romantic movement was thus born across Europe as a kind of response to all that pure and predominant reason.

It would be a serious mistake, however, to assume that romantic thinkers were against reason, or that they wanted to return to some kind of simple faith. They wanted no such thing, as they knew that this was now impossible. They certainly wanted to celebrate the poetic and visionary dimensions of the human being, but they recognized that these were not "out there" in the sky, but rather "in here" in the human being. In many ways, their views on religion were even more radical than those of the Enlightenment thinkers. After all, whereas the Enlightenment figures generally denied revelation and hence separated themselves from such claims altogether, the romantic thinkers negated and affirmed *at the same time*—and thus they stayed close to—what they conceived of as the very wellsprings of revelation and poetry: the human imagination.

Probably no one saw and expressed this double move better than the English poet, artist, and channeling seer William Blake (1757–1827). Blake appears on the scene at the end of the eighteenth century, just after the French and the American Revolution, both of which were key inspirations for him. Like many mystics and poets before him, Blake was a most radical comparativist. One of his first texts was titled *All Religions Are One* (1788). Its seventh and final principle encoded the classic both–and structure of comparative thought: "As all men are alike (tho' infinitely various)." It also expressed the even more radical view that the real origin—or what he called the One of all Religions—is not some particular deity or philosophical idea, but "the true Man … being the Poetic Genius." In short, it is human nature that lies behind it all.

Projection Theory   Here is Blake again, a few years later, on the origin of religion in the human imagination—in his wicked satire of piety and religion, *The Marriage of Heaven and Hell* (1793): "Choosing forms of worship from poetic tales. And at length

they pronouncd that the Gods had ordered such things. Thus men forgot that All deities reside in the human breast."[6] Today we (rather boringly) call this conviction that all deities are really expressions of human nature **projection theory**. According to this model the gods are "projected," like a movie, out of the human brain and its fantastic ability to tell itself stories or myths, which are all, of course, ultimately illusions.

The Romantic Reversal   Blake and his fellow romantics were up to something similar, but also fundamentally different. The divine may be a projection of the human, but the human is also really and truly "divine." God is indeed made in the image of man, but man is also made in the image of God. It's a circle. Or a mirror. We might call this turn or "flip" of Enlightenment reason the **romantic reversal**. As a single example of how this romantic reversal worked, consider that wonderful bit of conversation that an aging Blake had with his old friend Crabb Robinson in December of 1825, not long before the latter died. "On my asking in what light he viewed the great question concerning the Divinity of Jesus Christ," Robinson reported, "he said; '*He is the only God.*' But then he added—'And so am I and so are you.'"[7]

Note the flip here: the literal version of a particular belief is seemingly affirmed ("He is the only God"), but it is then refashioned as a poetic or romantic truth that can be universalized—generalized to all human beings—in a way that clearly violates the same belief's normal or common meaning ("And so am I and so are you"). In effect, religious beliefs are reduced to human scale, much as they were in the Enlightenment; but then human nature is raised to astonishing heights and understood to be basically limitless. This was Blake's "true Man."

Idealism   Blake was only one voice at this time, and a voice largely ignored during his own life. Much more prominent among the romantics were English poets like Samuel Taylor Coleridge (1772–1834) and William Wordsworth (1770–1850) and German idealists like the poet Novalis (1772–1801) or the great philosophers G. W. F. Hegel (1770–1831), Arthur Schopenhauer (1788–1860), and F. W. J. Schelling (1775–1874).

Idealism is a philosophical position that privileges mind as the ultimate nature of reality. Drawing on ancient mystical notions of emanation and return, or involution and evolution (the idea that the universe emerges or "emanates" from, and eventually "returns" to, the divine), romantic idealists, particularly in Germany, wrote about the natural tendency of the cosmos to "unfold" its own implicit consciousness or divine mind. Schelling could thus write that "history is an epic composed in the mind of God" and proclaim that the God who is "involved" in the universe manifests himself as the God who "evolves" out of the universe.[8]

No idealist, however, was more influential than G. W. F. Hegel. Hegel developed a complex philosophy that asserted that a universal mind or spirit (*Geist*) is being increasingly revealed and actualized through the history of human civilization, mythology, religion, society, and, finally and most fully, philosophy (his own system being the final stage of this actualization). There is not one but multiple "forms of consciousness" (*Gestalten des Bewusstseins*) in human history, and later forms are more highly developed than earlier forms.

Mid-Upstream: "Not as Moses Said," or the Biblical Beginnings of Critical Theory

As we have already seen, critical insights into the interpretation of the Bible did not originate in the modern period. They go back, way back. We saw this in Chapter 1, through examples like Origen's observations about the silliness of literal readings and the early Christian gnostics' cutting phrase "not as Moses said." As in the ancient period, so too in the modern: it all began with Moses.

The Five Books Compared

Traditionally, both the Jewish and the Christian traditions had long insisted that Moses had written the first five books of the Bible, and this despite the fact that these books never make such a claim for themselves. In the Jewish tradition these five books possess a pre-eminent authority, as the essence of the Torah. Many of the most famous and most beloved Bible stories come from these first five "Mosaic" books, as do most of the purity codes and ritual laws that define much conservative Jewish life and fundamentalist Christian belief around sexual morality to this day.

Contradictions and Doubles   Then came the problems. As Jewish and Christian readers carefully read these shared scriptural texts, they observed more and more contradictions. They began to ask questions. Biblical scholar Richard Elliot Friedman explains what happened:

> People observed contradictions in the text. It would report events in a particular order, and later it would say that those same events happened in a different order. It would say that there are two of something, and elsewhere it would say that there were fourteen of that same thing. It would say that the Moabites did something, and later it would say that it was the Midianites who did it. It would describe Moses as going to a Tabernacle in a chapter before Moses builds the Tabernacle. People also noticed that the Five Books of Moses included things that Moses could not have known or was not likely to have said. The text, after all, gave an account of Moses' death. It also said that Moses was the humblest man on earth; and normally one would not expect the humblest man on earth to point out that he is the humblest man on earth.[9]

"To This Day" and "Across the Jordan."   Then there were the two seemingly innocent phrases "to this day" and "across the Jordan." Thomas Hobbes, the great British political philosopher, pointed out as early as the seventeenth century that the biblical phrase "to

this day" could obviously not be from the hand of Moses, since it refers to a situation contemporary to the writer, not to a past one from Moses' own time.

Just a few years after Hobbes made this simple observation, a French Calvinist named Isaac de la Peyrère began pounding on the final nail in the coffin of Mosaic authorship. Calvinism is a Protestant branch of Christianity that originated with the French theologian-reformer John Calvin (1509–1564) and became especially influential in the history of American religion. De la Peyrère honed in on the very first verse of Deuteronomy: "These are the words that Moses spoke to all Israel across the Jordan …"

Friedman explains what was at stake here:

> The problem with the phrase "across the Jordan" is that it refers to someone who is on the other side of the Jordan river from the writer. The verse thus appears to be the words of someone in Israel, west of the Jordan, referring to what Moses did on the east side of the Jordan. Moses himself was never supposed to have been in Israel in his life.[10]

In short, we have a supposedly inerrant scriptural text *both* asserting that Moses never made it to the promised land on the west side of the Jordan river *and* having the writer of Deuteronomy presumably write from that same west side. The result? "De la Peyrère's book was banned and burned. He was arrested and informed that in order to be released he would have to become Catholic and recant his views to the Pope."

Friedman explains what happened next: "He did."

Numerous other bannings, burnings, and threats occurred throughout early modern European history. When the great Dutch Jewish philosopher Benedict Spinoza (1632–1677), for example, made a similar argument using different texts, his work was condemned by Catholics and Protestants alike. He had already been excommunicated from the Jewish community for other offensive ideas. Thirty-seven edicts were issued against his book, and his life was threatened. When a French Catholic priest named

Richard Simon offered a much milder version of a similar thesis, suggesting that Moses wrote most of the first five books of the Bible but inspired additions followed, he was expelled from his religious order. Forty Protestant refutations ensued, and only six copies of the thirteen hundred originally printed survived the angry fires that followed. When Simon's book was translated into English, moreover, the translator fared little better. A contemporary scholar named Edward Gray explained with a wry sense of humor what happened next: the translator "repudiated the opinions he had held in common with Simon … in 1688, probably before his release from the tower."[11]

From the Towers to the Universities And so the study of the Bible began, amid censoring flames and tower prisons. But the texts were the texts, and they simply made no literal sense any longer as the products of a single hand, much less that of Moses. As the seventeenth century turned into the eighteenth and the eighteenth turned into the nineteenth, more and more scholars were realizing that the books in the fire and the men in towers and dungeons were right after all. Most of the action was now taking place in the Protestant universities of Germany.

The conclusions followed fast and furious. No, Moses did not write the first five books of the Bible. There were in fact numerous authors and sources. Eventually it was believed that there were four major textual traditions, each with its own distinct concerns and theology. And then there was the redactor or editor of all these sources, that is, the person (or persons) who had cut and pasted all of these diverse traditions and stories together.

The Four Gospels Compared

It was not long, of course, before similar methods were being used and similar conclusions were being reached with respect to the New Testament. One of the pioneers was a remarkable junior lecturer at Germany's Tübingen University by the name of David Friedrich Strauss.

The Fired Professor and the Evolutionary Mystic   In 1835 Strauss published *The Life of Jesus Critically Examined*. Strauss was inspired by the German idealists whom we met above. He also leaned strongly toward pantheism or cosmotheism, now with a most modern development. By 1872 Strauss had abandoned Christianity altogether: "we must acknowledge that we are no longer Christians … although we may still have a religion—the religion of cosmic evolution."[12] Darwin had made his mark already, and Strauss had moved to a new kind of evolutionary mysticism that would come more and more to the fore as the nineteenth century turned into the twentieth and the twentieth turned into the twenty-first.

But all of this went *way* over the heads of the faithful public, and what Strauss really became famous (or infamous) for was his very convincing demonstrations that the four gospels did not agree and that, precisely because of this, they could not be read as straight or simple history. Strauss effectively demolished the literalist readings of the New Testament and put them out of court for future biblical scholarship.

For Strauss, the Christian belief that Jesus was the Son of God is a myth, but one that expresses the deeper truth that the human race as a whole is divine: "Is not the idea of the unity of the divine and human natures a real one in a far higher sense, when I regard the whole race of mankind as its realization, than when I single out one man [Jesus] as such a realization?"[13] Here we can hear echoes of Pico, Blake, and the romantic reversal again. In order to make sufficient room for this positive thesis, however, Strauss had to negate a number of traditional beliefs, including those about the resurrection ("there is nothing to the entire story")[14] and the miracle stories.

The result? Strauss` was fired. When a liberal government in Zürich tried four years later to offer him a professorship (the man was obviously brilliant), "the people rebelled, the government fell, and the young offender was pensioned off before he arrived."[15] The name "David Friedrich Strauss" had become anathema. Three times this name came up for positions. The third time it was accepted, but only until a public outcry forced a referendum in which the populace voted to revoke Strauss' professorship by a margin of 39,225 to 1,048.[16]

When it comes to the study of religion, and particularly to the historical interpretation of scriptural texts, however, the religiously conservative public is always wrong. Really wrong. Hence most of Strauss' negative points, for which he lost his career (he would have likely lost his life in an earlier era), are generally taken for granted today in biblical scholarship. In the end, as two recent biblical scholars have put it, much of his critical analysis was simply "unanswerable."[17]

The Historical Jesus and the Christ of Light   And that was just the beginning. It went on. The apostle Paul was a Jewish rabbi (his Hebrew name was Saul) who never met the **historical Jesus**—the historical figure of Jesus of Nazareth, who was crucified by the Romans; but he composed many of the key ideas that would come to define Christianity after a visionary encounter with a super-being of divine light, whom he experienced as the resurrected **Christ of faith**. As we have seen in Chapter 1, "Christ" renders in Greek the Hebrew notion of a "messiah" or "annointed one" (*christos*): it was a religious title, not a proper name, and it came to be associated with the historical Jesus. "Jesus Christ," then, did not originally designate a man named Jesus, whose (last) name was Christ. It meant Jesus, who is the *christos* or the messiah. His Hebrew name wasn't "Jesus" either, by the way. That is simply an English approximation of the Greek approximation of his Hebrew name, which was closer to "Yeshua."

Biblical Scholarship Is Comparative Scholarship   We have collapsed and grossly simplified many decades of technical scholarship here, but the point, we hope, is clear. The study of religion began in earnest not with a bitter skeptic or a disillusioned believer, but with careful and honest Jewish and Christian readings of the Bible, often at great personal risk and cost. And, ironically, it was *precisely* the literal text that created most of the problems and thereby generated the field of the critical study of religion. It is also worth underlining that much of this careful reading was *comparative* reading, which worked through the simple process of comparing this passage with that passage, this gospel with that gospel, this Hebrew practice with that Canaanite practice, and so on. Such comparative acts demonstrated once and for all that the Bible is not what the traditions had claimed it was.

The Golden Rule of Comparativism   Nor, of course, is any other scripture of any other religion. What we now call the **historical–critical method**—that is, a way of reading a religious text by contextualizing it as the historical product of a particular time and place—can be applied to any scriptural text, with varying degrees of success. It is worth observing, though, and then underlining: before the modern study of religion extended itself and applied its critical and comparative methods to the world's religions and their scriptural texts, it practiced the same on its own. There is *no* scriptural text more studied and analyzed in the professional study of religion than the Bible. As a whole, then, the comparative study of religion has followed, from its very beginning until this day, its own version of the "golden rule": apply the very same methods to your own tradition that you would apply to those of others. And, preferably, do this first and most fully.

The Quran and Historical Criticism

Take, for example, the historical–critical study of the Quran. Ernest Renan (1823–1892) once famously observed that Islam "was born in the full light of history." Still, as European scholars started applying the historical–critical method to the early Islamic materials after they had done the same with the biblical materials, this "full light" of history quickly turned into a thick fog, through which historians have tried to find their way out with little success ever since. Part of the problem is that there exists not a single piece of Islamic writing that can be dated with any certainty to the seventh century other than the Quran. The earliest biography of Muhammad, for example, was compiled almost a full century after his death. Moreover, external sources (that is, non-Muslims writing about the early Islamic movement) are virtually non-existent, and the Quran itself provides us with few clues about the life of the Prophet.

The scarcity of reliable sources for the early formative period of Islam has resulted in radically different scenarios about how Muhammad started his mission and how the early Muslim community developed. Fred Donner, for example, has recently suggested that the early believers did not think of themselves as followers of a distinct religion vis-à-vis Judaism and Christianity. In this model, the boundaries of Muhammad's nascent religious community were much more fluid, allowing for some Christians and Jews to be considered among the "believers."[18] Donner's thesis may or may not be eventually established as consensus among historians. That is not the point. The point is that, once one boards the ship of critical scholarship, there is no saying where one might end up, as we see over and over again in the historical–critical study of the Bible. Like Columbus, one might set off for India and land in America, as it were.

Literary and humanistic approaches to the Quran have not only been undertaken by European and American scholars, of course. The latter half of the twentieth century witnessed the rise of a nascent yet influential critical tradition in some parts of the Islamic world, particularly in Egypt, Pakistan, Syria, and Iran. The Egyptian literary critic Nasr Hamed Abu Zayd (d. 2009), for example, proposed that the Quran needs to be analyzed under the same rules and theories of literary studies as any other text. Furthermore, he suggested, the Quran needs to be understood not merely as a "fixed text" but also as a historical "discourse," that is, as a process that developed in dialogue with several groups of people before it was finally fixed in its present form. For Abu Zayd, the only way to bring the Quran into a meaningful conversation with the modern situation is to understand the original dialectical nature of its discourse and to refuse to "fix" that discourse by tying it to the specific conversations that happened fourteen hundred years ago with communities now long gone.

Like his European counterparts, Abu Zayd had to pay a high price for his innovative views. He was forced to leave his home country after being declared an "infidel" by some jurists and receiving death threats.

Just Upstream: Colonialism and the Modern Births of Spirituality and Fundamentalism

It was also in the nineteenth century that intellectuals began to realize that there was not one but many scriptures, that every religion had its own revelation, and that each of these possessed its own genius and integrity (if also its own fictions and absurdities). This was the birth of the modern comparative study of religion.

Precedents

Of course, there were precedents to this realization, including an astonishing eighteenth-century collection of some 250 engravings on *The Religious Ceremonies and Customs of All the Peoples of the World* published in Amsterdam between 1723 and 1737. Also of note here is Hannah Adams (1755–1831), a self-educated New England woman living near Boston who, despite the rampant sexism of her time, managed to write a generous volume with one of those delightful early modern titles: *Alphabetical Compendium of the Various Sects Which Have Appeared from the Beginning of the Christian Era to the Present Day* (1784). The title eventually morphed into *A Dictionary of All Religions* (1817). Adams was the first American woman to make a living by the pen. Significantly, she wrote her comparative dictionary largely because she was so annoyed with the arrogant and demeaning approaches to non-Christian religions by the Christian clergy.

Max Müller and the Divine Humanity

The most dramatic expression of this new "revelation of revelations" was an Oxford professor of Sanskrit named Friedrich Max Müller (1823–1900). Müller is

often called, and with good reason, the father of the comparative study of religion.

There are many reasons for such a title. One of them was Müller's strong emphasis on language study, translation work, and the philosophy and history of language in general. It was Müller who gave the young field one of its first memorable one-liners: "He who knows one knows none." Müller had in fact borrowed the sound bite from **linguistics**, where it meant more or less the same thing. (Linguistics is the study of languages under all their aspects, including from a comparativist perspective; and historical and comparative linguistics dominated the field in the nineteenth century.) The message was a relatively simple one: if you really want to understand how "language" or "religion" works, as opposed to the language or religion you just happen to speak and adhere to because of the accident of your birth, you must study many languages or religions *together*. Only then will patterns emerge and a broader, truly adequate theory or universal grammar arise.

Müller's legacy is also tied to his massive *Sacred Books of the East* translation series. This project, which he championed and edited until he died, eventually ran to fifty volumes, published between 1879 and 1910. "Sacred Books" was here a kind of stand-in for what Müller would call the "Bibles of humanity," whereas "the East" functioned as a kind of catch-all for what we today call the Middle East, South Asia, and East Asia, India and China playing central roles. Basically Müller was out to show that there is not one, but many "Bibles." He worked closely with one of his Oxford colleagues, a man named James Legge, who handled the Chinese Confucian and Daoist texts for the series. Significantly, he was not allowed to print the Old and New Testaments in his series, because of the offense this would give to Christian readers.[19]

Müller's many Christian readers were often offended anyway by his writings, which they variously described as "subversive," "infidel," "blasphemous," and a form of "atheism under the guise of pantheism."[20] Forms of pantheism they often were. Sort of. Answering his critics in a late book, *Theosophy or Psychological Religion*, the Oxford don quoted one of his favorite

German authors, the great medieval Christian mystic Meister Eckhart: "though all things are dynamically in God, God is actually not in all things."[21] In other words, God is in all things, but all things do not exhaust God, who overflows and transcends the physical universe. This was, in short, what we encountered in Chapter 1 as cosmotheism or panentheism.

Such patently mystical leanings were clearly related to Müller's Sanskrit studies, and in particular to his 1879 translation of Hinduism's most revered mystical texts, the Upanishads. For the rest of his life, Müller would maintain a deep appreciation for Advaita Vedanta, a particular interpretation of the Hindu scriptures that emphasizes the "non-dual" (*a-dvaita*) identity of the deepest core of the human Self (*atman*) and the cosmic essence of all there is (*brahman*). Translated into Müller's own Protestant Christian mystical code, the *atman* or Self was "the Infinite in man," whose final destiny and future religion were what the professor called, perhaps most shockingly of all, a "divine humanity."[22]

The general history of religions, for Müller, was a gradual enfolding of this divine humanity, a series of partial revelations, always in the imperfect and clouded codes of culture. Hence expressions like "Father," "sonship," "child of God," and the "Son of God" were all metaphors for him, not literal truths. They were pointers toward this deeper divine humanity that we all already share, that we already are. In short, Müller had performed another version of the romantic reversal: religious language referred to human nature, which at its deepest core is divine. He spent his last years, in his own words, "thoroughly at home with my friends, the so-called mystics."[23] Once again—and here, please note, it happened through a central founding figure of the field—a comparative practice led to an explicitly mystical sensibility.

Darwin the Comparativist

There were many influences on this "science of religion," as Müller insisted on calling the novel field (few humanists would be comfortable with such an expression today), including influences from the new sciences themselves, especially geology and Darwinian biology.

The implications of these sciences were devastating for traditional or literal Christian belief. Both the creation story in the opening of Genesis, which the seventeenth-century Anglican Bishop James Ussher had famously put at 4004 BCE (on Sunday, October 23, as it would be determined later), and the story of Adam and Eve looked downright silly after the nineteenth-century advances of geology, which pushed the clock back millions of years. And that was before the appearance of Darwin's *The Origin of Species* (1859): this book started a long intellectual process—which now takes the shape of evolutionary biology, human genomics, and genetic anthropology—that would eventually show beyond a shadow of rational doubt that human beings have evolved from earlier hominids.

Some, like Strauss, would reshape Darwin's vision into a new "religion of cosmic evolution." Others would react with rejection and denial, in order to preserve the doctrinal content and literalist readings of their present religions. Still others would seek some middle ground, some examples of which we will encounter later, in Chapter 5.

Such responses, it should be pointed out, were (and are) by no means restricted to Christian communities. The same range of responses can easily be found in Hinduism, for example. There they include various natural theologies that find a divine intelligence behind the design of the universe; the explicitly evolutionary mysticism of a figure like Sri Aurobindo (1872–1950), who envisioned the earth as evolving "from man to Superman"; various attempts to re-read the "ten avatars" (that is, the ten incarnations of God that seem to progress from fish to mammal to human forms) and the doctrines of *karma* and reincarnation through an evolutionary lens; and various outright condemnations of evolutionary biology.[24]

Colonialism, Christian Mission, and Modernity

The other major influence on the origins of the comparative study of religion in the nineteenth century was European, and especially British, colonialism.

The Age of Colonialism   Beginning in the seventeenth century (the chartering of the East India Company on December 31, 1600, is sometimes seen as the beginning of the colonial period), European states sought to control more and more of the globe economically, and soon culturally and politically. To do this, however, they also had to understand something of the cultures they wished to control. Scholarship was encouraged and financially supported not for its own sake, but for the sake of empire.

Although the business instincts of the East India Company originally resisted the idea, the colonial administrators eventually supported, and then even encouraged the Christian missionaries who followed in their steps and waves. The comparative practices of the Christian missions ranged from the most sophisticated forms of cultural translation and adaptation (Catholic Jesuits like Francis Xavier leading the way) to the grossest forms of religious arrogance and ethnocentrism. The latter especially produced countless sermons and pamphlets about the "primitives," "heathens," and "idol worshippers" in need of Christian salvation. Centuries of scholarship, religious encounter, debate, tragedy, violence, and an occasional luminous opening followed, until the colonial period came to a close around 1950: by then most of the colonies had won, or were about to win, their independence.

Postcolonial Complexities   So wide-ranging and so influential was this colonial period that many intellectuals continue to speak of our own age not as something else, but as postcolonial. That is to say, we may be living in an era "after colonialism," but we have hardly escaped or exhausted the effects of colonialism on global history and on the innermost workings of our own psyches, bodies, and cultures. We are colonized (or colonizing) still. From the shape of state borders in the Middle East and South Asia (drawn largely by colonial administrators), through our simplistic stereotypes about "the West" and "the East," to the global distribution of carbon pollution, global warming, and climate change, we are still suffering, thinking, warring, and now polluting our

way through the lasting effects of those three and a half centuries (1600–1950).

The long-range effects of all this on the study of religion were decidedly mixed. On the negative side, some of the methods developed during this period displayed subtle and gross forms of colonial intent and cultural superiority, particularly those that adopted a simplistic evolutionary model in order to show how religion began among "primitive" cultures, evolved through various forms of polytheism, and eventually found its zenith in monotheism. The problem was that the monotheistic zenith of religious evolution always seemed to look more than a little like the particular branch of Christianity to which the comparativist just happened to belong: Lutheran scholars found Lutheranism at the evolutionary summit, Catholic scholars found Catholicism, and so on. In short, the "one God" to which all religions pointed turned out, on closer look, to be "my God."

That was just a bit suspicious.

On the positive side, the colonial period had the opposite effect of opening up intellectuals everywhere, from London and Boston to Calcutta and Hong Kong, to entirely new ideas and philosophies. Indeed, the effects Asian religious and philosophical traditions had on western intellectuals were so great that one scholar, Raymond Schwab, has written of an "oriental Renaissance" whose impact on western culture was every bit as great, and probably greater, than that of the Italian Renaissance.

The Modern Distinction   Having said that, there is no doubt that the effects of western ideas on the African, Middle Eastern, and Asian publics were immeasurably more consequential. These ideas (and the technologies behind them) resulted in billions of individuals eventually converting to modernist beliefs and values. Granted, these were not passive cultures or uninterested elites. Although the balance of military power was tilted strongly in the direction of European empire, this was by no means a one-way street. African, Middle Eastern, and Asian peoples were enthusiastically embracing western ideas—particularly in science and technology—and integrating them into their cultures and lives. They were also reforming, adjusting, and effectively changing their religious traditions in significant ways, partly in response to the criticisms of the Christian missionaries. The end result was that very few Muslims, Hindus, Buddhists, or Confucians were converted to Christianity by the missionaries, but virtually every colonized culture was in some sense converted to western science, technology, and what we now call "modernity."[25]

By **modernity** we generally mean the last two centuries, as this period had increasingly been defined by industrialization, capitalism, a faith in science, technology, progress, and, perhaps above all, a profound sense of a *break* with the past. In this last respect, as many have observed, modernity is deeply indebted to monotheism—which, as we have seen, created a very similar break, cut, or distinction from all that came before it. On this reading at least, modernity is a kind of monotheism in a secular key.

It would be tempting, then, to split what the colonial powers and the Christian missionaries intended—making money and "saving souls"—from what they actually ended up helping to catalyze: the creation of a shared global modernity. But this splitting is not possible historically, since the colonial era was one planetary process with vast, untold numbers of influences passing back and forth between the different cultural actors and institutions involved. Historically speaking, then, there is no simple way to "pull out" this religious or philosophical influence from that scientific or technological influence. It's all one mega-event.

American Metaphysical Religion

These colonial encounters also had some surprising religious effects. One of them was a new (really very old) openness to "the East" and a certain globalizing spirituality, which began to take different forms in Europe and the USA in the middle of the nineteenth century.

The new "orient" was not so much a reflection of the self-understandings of Asian and Middle Eastern peoples, nor was it the old Platonic orientalism of the Greeks, Romans, and the Renaissance humanists. Rather it was a translation, really a transformation, of various Asian ideas and practices as they entered Euro-American individualist idioms and democratic values. Some scholars have seen this historical process as an unfortunate and essentially colonizing "appropriation" of other people's cultures.[26] Other scholars have seen it as an inevitable and in fact very old "combinative" strategy of western, and especially American, culture.

In the spirit of the latter, the historian of American religions Catherine Albanese has written of a "metaphysical Asia." By such a phrase she does not mean to refer to any place on a map. She means to signal the ways in which Asian religious ideas and practices entered and enriched a very old strand of American religion—**metaphysical religion.**[27] The adjective "metaphysical" means "beyond the physical." Here the term acts as an umbrella for those alternative currents of American history that are normally marginalized or neglected by historians. Albanese outlines four central themes within metaphysical religion: (1) an emphasis on mind as a form of transcendent consciousness; (2) magical thinking and experience; (3) a strong emphasis on "energy" as a defining religious metaphor; and (4) a practical concern with physical and psychological healing as a type of this-worldly salvation.

Transcendentalism Foremost among the early exponents of American metaphysical religion was Ralph Waldo Emerson (1803–1882). Emerson helped found transcendentalism, a movement that locates divinity in nature and in the democratically shared spirit of the human being, sometimes called "the Over-Soul." This expression was an American riff on the European romantics and German idealists and their notions of an absolute spirit or mind (*Geist*). Indeed, in some sense, American transcendentalism was romanticism in new American garb. To put the matter in an anachronistic way, the transcendentalists created America's first "spiritual but not religious" movement.

One of cornerstones of this foundation was what many take to be Emerson's own mystical experience,

"Standing on the bare ground, — my head bathed by the blithe air, & uplifted into infinite space, — all mean egotism vanishes. I become a transparent Eyeball."

Nature, p. 13.

Figure 2.4   Emerson's experience of himself as an egoless "transparent eyeball" (1837–1839), humorous drawing by Christopher Pearse Cranch.

which he described in his most famous essay, entitled simply "Nature" (1836). Here is the passage:

> In the woods, we return to reason and faith. … Standing on the bare ground—my head bathed by the blithe air, and uplifted into infinite space—all mean egotism vanishes. I become a transparent eye-ball. I am nothing. I see all. The currents of the Universal Being circulate through me; I am part or particle of God.[28]

Emerson would also write of the human being as a "god in ruins." Two years after "Nature," in 1838, he

would take up another word to name his metaphysical project: "mysticism."

At about this same time Emerson delivered his famous Divinity School Address. On July 15, 1838 he spoke to just six graduating students, their families, and the faculty. In that classic reversal of the romantic spirit, Emerson simultaneously denied the unique divinity of Christ and affirmed the divinity of the "infinite soul" as he celebrated the personal revelations of contemporary religious experience (like his own "transparent eye-ball," we might imagine). He called on his listeners to "live with the privilege of the immeasurable mind" and to refuse the temptation of traditional authority. He encouraged them to move beyond "historical Christianity," an institution whose singular divinization of Jesus as the only divine human being and whose idolatrous reliance on the Bible as somehow final and complete he found particularly odious. More positively, what he wanted was a democratic, individualized form of spirituality, which is open to everyone in the here and now. The goal of the religious life for Emerson was not Christianity, but something deeper still: "They call it Christianity. I call it consciousness."

Within a few weeks of the Divinity School Address, the Boston press was filled with vehement attacks on the author. Charges of impious offense, atheism, insult, and blasphemy flew. Emerson would be banned from Harvard for twenty-five years (again, he would have been killed or consigned to "the tower" in an earlier century). Emerson's response? He resigned from his ministry, took up the lecture circuit, and became one of America's most important literary, intellectual, and religious figures.

Spiritualism   Another major movement within American metaphysical religion that would come to play a significant role in the early study of religion was spiritualism. This involved the practice of communicating with the dead through gifted mediums, in people's homes and—in a much more controversial setting—on stage. Although the practice of speaking to spirits via possession and mediumship was widespread among the African religions and peoples who had been forcefully brought over in the slave trade and was also already known in communities like the Quakers, spiritualism did not really come into vogue in the USA until after 1848, when three sisters in Hydesville, New York, claimed to be communicating, through a series of knockings, with a dead peddler buried in their basement.

That was a match thrown in a dry barn—the dry barn being a country about to be shredded by a brutal civil war that would kill hundreds of thousands of people. The practice of communicating with the dead quickly spread throughout the States, hopped the Atlantic, took root in Europe, and then, largely through a French spiritualist named Allen Kardec, hopped back over the Atlantic to Brazil. Amid all their talking to the dead, spiritualists were also advancing some of the most radical and progressive social agendas, especially around gender and sexuality. To the extent that spiritualism spoke through such mediums, it spoke through what Mary Keller has eloquently called "possessed bodies," whose remarkable powers were both admired and reviled.[29] Significantly, most of these possessed bodies were female. The religious leaders, who were all men, were often not at all happy about this.

The Birth of "Spirituality"　The concept of spirituality, as it is commonly used today, is historically related to, but also quite different from, spiritualism. Before the nineteenth century, "spiritual" and "spirituality" generally referred to the non-physical realm or to hymn books (hence the slightly later mid-nineteenth-century expression "negro spirituals"). The new use of the old word seems to have been originally incubated in Emerson's transcendentalism before it bloomed in the ecstatic poetry of the American poet-prophet Walt Whitman (1819–1892), especially in his remarkable *Leaves of Grass* (1855), which is often seen as the first truly great American poem.

By 1871, when Whitman's *Democratic Vistas* had appeared, we are on totally different ground. Hence Whitman can write "that only in the perfect uncontamination and solitariness of individuality may the

spirituality of religion come forth at all." "Spirituality" was now directly linked to "individuality," that is, to a single person rather than to a community or religious tradition. The poet could also declare that "all religions" are "but temporary journeys."[30] All are replaceable.

Put a bit differently, within this new, modern way of speaking about religion there were two basic ways of relating to religious authority: if one related to religious authority as something that comes *from without*—from, say, a revealed scripture or an authoritative tradition—then one was being "religious"; if, on the other hand, one could be inspired and taught by these scriptures and traditions but finally related to religious authority as something that comes *from within*, then one was being "spiritual." We might define **spirituality**, then, as a modern orientation to religion that locates religious authority within, as opposed to outside, the individual. Spirituality in this sense, we might also note, is logically "combinative" in Albanese's sense, since the individual is free to pick and choose whatever works for him or her.

Whitman's devoted readers treated such shocking ideas like religious revelations and his *Leaves of Grass* as a kind of new American Bible. They were perfectly serious. So was Whitman:

> We consider the bibles and religions divine. … I do
> not say they are not divine,
> I say they have all grown out of you and may grow
> out of you still,
> It is not they who give the life. … it is you who give
> the life;
> Leaves are not more shed from the trees or trees
> from the earth than they are shed out of you.[31]

At Whitman's funeral passages from Jesus, the Buddha, and Confucius were all read. Once again it was a mystic and a poet who expressed one of the era's most radical ways of "comparing religions."

Theosophy　There were other streams of influence. A very powerful one was theosophy, a broad-based movement born in New York City in 1875 that came to revolve around the revelations of a Russian-born woman named Madame Blavatsky. Much like the ancient wisdom narratives, theosophy turned to "the East" as the ultimate source of spiritual wisdom, first in the form of Egypt (the answer of the Italian Renaissance) and then of India (the answer of Blavatsky's own colonial era). Blavatsky's two major works, *Isis Unveiled* (1877) and *The Secret Doctrine* (1888), mark these two highly idealized versions of the orient.

The mission and self-understanding of theosophy morphed over the years, as the phenomenon spread from America to England to India, but the following three goals capture something of the general spirit. Theosophy is a movement that intends (1) to help form the "brotherhood of man"; (2) to encourage the comparative study of religion, philosophy, and science; and (3) to study the unexplained laws of nature and the powers latent in man, that is, what we would call today psychical or paranormal powers. The linking of a universal humanity, the comparative study of religion, and the study of psychical abilities were very much a reflection of the period, but they were also extremely successful in their early effects. For a time at least, theosophy was a popular, undisciplined form of comparativism that became a kind of global sensation (Max Müller despised it).

It is not too difficult to see why this happened. Theosophists certainly were not shy about their claims. They spoke and wrote constantly of "Mahatmas." These were "Great Souls" or spiritual Masters living somewhere, or so the theosophists claimed, in Tibet. They also spoke of astonishing psychical powers and abilities (some of which were clearly faked) and of new occult revelations; so did particularly Blavatsky in her massive two-volume *The Secret Doctrine*, which set out an elaborate anti-Darwinian mythology of humanity evolving spiritually and physically through various cosmic ages. Much of it read like bold science fiction, although it claimed to be perfectly true.

The theosophists' politics was no less ambitious. They helped inspire independence movements in Ceylon (now Sri Lanka) and India. It was a most remarkable theosophist and "white Buddhist" by the name of Colonel Olcott, for example, who designed the new Sri Lankan flag and wrote a Buddhist catechism that helped reform and systematize Buddhist practice and self-identity on the island.[32] It was another theosophist, Annie Besant, who helped lead the independence movement in India for a time, at one point even becoming president of the Indian National Congress (she was also an early labor and women's rights activist and began her political career by scandalizing her British compatriots for helping to publish a book that defended birth control). The early worldview of theosophy, then, was at once a universal humanism, a global occultism, and a radical anti-colonial politics.

The Spiritual and the Secular   How do we make sense of this today? Few have made more sense of the global reach of these developments than the Dutch anthropologist Peter van der Veer. He has argued that the spiritual "as a modern category emerged in the second half of the nineteenth century as part of the Great Transformation [of modernity]. As such it is part of nineteenth-century globalization, a thoroughgoing political, economic, and cultural integration of the world."[33] In van der Veer's view, the spiritual and the secular are, in effect, born together. This is one reason why they both are critical of institutional religion.

The concept of spirituality, however, extends its reach much further than the concept of the secular in that it is *also* poised against materialism, modern capitalism, and colonialism. Indeed, it is precisely within the context of spiritualism, spirituality, and radical mystical movements like the Theosophical Society that, in van der Veer's words again, an "anti-colonial universalism was born."[34] There is an obvious ethical dimension here as well, since "an embracing, vague term like 'spirituality' has been adopted precisely to make peaceful communication between different conceptual universes possible."[35] We are reminded of Assman's polytheism as "intercultural translatability."

William James and the Early Psychology of Religion

This development of "the spiritual" was also aided from another direction: modern psychology, particularly in the figure of the Harvard philosopher and psychologist William James (1842–1910). James, whom we will meet many times, is easily one of America's most important and original thinkers. He also happens to be one of the chief inspirations of the modern comparative study of religion, particularly in its psychological modes and in its emphasis on mysticism. In his classic *The Varieties of Religious Experience* (1902), a comparative project if ever there was one, he effectively showed how the religious experiences of crisis, conversion, and ecstasy could be understood through the workings of the human psyche.

Marx and the Opiate of the People

There were other, very different readings of religion afoot, and few—if any—were more convincing and more influential than that of Karl Marx (1818–1883). Marx, inspired by Hegel's proto-evolutionary view of history, had advanced his own theory of history, whereby different socio-economic arrangements and the movement of "capital" (very simply, how things are produced and sold toward the creation of wealth and the stratification of society into classes) determine different forms of human consciousness, which in turn determine different socio-economic practices, which in turn determine different forms of consciousness, and so on. Marx called his model "dialectical materialism," but eventually it became better known as **Marxism**.

Marxism was "dialectical" to the extent that it argued that human consciousness and economic activity make each other up, that they cannot be separated, that there is a constant "back and forth" between how people labor and exchange goods and how they are aware of the world and understand their own place in it. It was a form of **materialism** to the extent that it expressed the philosophical position that matter is the primary or most basic existent.

For Marx, religion is essentially a form of **false consciousness**, which is to say that it is an illusion that encourages people to focus on non-existent fantasies (like "heaven" or "salvation") and thereby prevents them from tending to the real structures, material and economic, that keep them oppressed and poor. Here is Marx in one of his most famous passages:

> Religion is the sigh of the oppressed creature, the heart of a heartless world and the soul of soulless conditions. It is the opium of the people. The abolition of religion as the illusory happiness of the people is a demand for their real happiness. To call on them to give up their illusions about their condition is to call on them to give up a condition that requires illusions. The criticism of religion is, therefore, in embryo, the criticism of that vale of tears of which religion is the halo.[36]

Religion, in other words, is a drug, a kind of tranquilizer that keeps economically and socially oppressed classes oppressed; convinces them that their plight in a particular society is "natural," inevitable, the way things are, ordained by God, the gods, *karma*, and so on. Not so, Marx argued. The first critical step toward liberation from social oppression is a critical understanding of religion as social oppression posing as divine truth. In short, religion is not the ultimate truth. It is the ultimate trick. And it is, finally, a trick of the rich played on the poor.

The Two World Wars and the End of Optimism

The twentieth century was launched with a vibrant faith in science and progress and with a clear sense of a fundamental break with the past—all hallmarks of what we now call modernity. Those dreams were quickly shattered, however, by the utter devastation of two world wars, both centered in Europe: World War I (1914–1918) and World War II (1939–1945). The former took more than fifteen million lives, the latter over seventy million. World War II, catalyzed by the Nazi Party in Germany, took on explicitly religious dimensions and was driven by a type of racism—directed mostly at Jewish people, but also at Poles, Slavs, Ukranians, Soviet prisoners of war, Roma (gypsies), Jehovah Witnesses (for refusing to defer to the power of the state and its symbols), homosexuals, and dissenting Protestant and Catholic clergy.

The Nazi labor camps, gas chambers, and human ovens were without precedent in their murderous efficiency. The actual numbers are impossible to count, but most sources put the total at around ten to eleven million people, approximately six million of whom were Jews. This unimaginable event became known as the **Holocaust** or, in Hebrew, the **Shoah**. Jewish peoples avoid the former term, because it comes from the theology of sacrifice—"holocaust" derives from a Greek adjective, *holok-autos* ("burnt whole"), that applied in a type sacrifice where the victim was burnt (*kaiein*) or consumed in entirety (*holōs*)—and implies that this catastrophic event had some purpose or religious meaning, that the event was a kind of human sacrifice. Evil now took on a new meaning and a new reality in the modern world. Religiously speaking, the reality of the Jewish Holocaust also put into serious doubt the notion of a just God—indeed, for some, the existence of a God at all.

It now became very difficult, if not actually impossible, to believe in the inevitability of moral progress. And technology and science looked more than a little like the monster of Mary Shelly's novel *Frankenstein* (1818), that is, like a self-created nightmare poised to kill its own creator. World War II, after all, ended on the eastern front with the United States dropping two atomic bombs on two heavily populated Japanese cities, Hiroshima and Nagasaki. Hundreds of thousands of people were immediately vaporized, melted, or heavily radiated. Countless cancers followed. Soon a "cold war" between the Soviet Union and the American and European Allies would follow, a war whose basic logic revolved around the stockpiling of tens of thousands of nuclear warheads and of very plausible visions of the end of the world as we know it. Human civilization and the global ecosystem were, quite literally, pushed to the brink.

Fundamentalism and the Study of Religion

In the early twentieth century, the professional study of religion became the target of a broad-based, profoundly anti-intellectual movement that would come to play a major role in the later part of the twentieth century and now in the twenty-first: fundamentalism. There are, of course, many possible points of origin here, one of which, the Protestant Reformation, we have already briefly visited. A closer one was the populist movement that found expression between 1910 and 1916 through the publication of a series of essays and books called "The Fundamentals." Emerging from what is often called the fundamentalist–modernist controversy, these books were aimed at restoring those aspects of Christian belief that had been shown to be historically questionable by the biblical scholars and liberal theologians of the universities—"fundamentals" like the inerrancy of the Bible, the virgin birth, the miracles, and the bodily resurrection of Christ.

In short, *fundamentalism as a broad-based modern western movement was born in part as a rejection of the critical study of religion, and especially of the professional study of the Bible.* The comparative term "fundamentalism"—which came into broad use as a scholarly term in the 1980s and 1990s, when it was catalyzed and sharpened by the "Fundamentalism Project" of Martin Marty and Scott Appleby at the University of Chicago—is now used to describe similar ultra-conservative, and sometimes violent religious movements around the globe. Different fundamentalist movements, of course, have different origin points and nuances, but their basic logics are strikingly similar: return to a presumed "golden age" in the religious past; read the scriptures literally (but also very selectively, while ignoring the broader tradition and its commentarial nuances); reject aspects of modern science that cannot be fit into these literalist readings; demonize intellectuals (or, in the case of the Middle East and South Asia, "the West"); resist gender equity and the civil rights of sexual minorities; and—above all—control the bodies and minds of women.

The Immediate Wake: Counterculture, Consciousness, Context, and Cosmopolitanism

As the twentieth century progressed, immigration to a country like the USA continued at a snail's pace, mostly because of legal restrictions designed to keep the culture ethnically homogenous, but it picked up significantly after 1965, when these restrictions were lifted. America would now become a more and more plural society. Similar patterns would play out in Europe as well. Between 1960 and 1973, for example, there was large-scale immigration into Europe, especially into Britain and France, which made entry relatively open for citizens of their former colonies.

The New Critical Categories: Race, Gender, and Class

In the USA, the 1960s also witnessed the birth of the civil rights movement, the women's movement, the sexual revolution, the gay rights movement, and the counterculture, all of which would have profound and lasting effects on the professional study of religion. **Race**, **class**, and **gender** would soon become the three central comparative categories of the field. Each would be applied to literally thousands of religious figures, institutions, texts, and practices, more often than not with provocative effects.

1 Critical practices around *race* (the assumed identity of a person or group, largely constructed, on the basis of skin color or physical features) were developments of the civil rights movement and its trenchant analyses of systematic racism in American society.
2 Critical practices around *gender* (the modal model of what it means to be a man, woman, or some third gender in a particular culture or subculture) were developments stemming from Freud's psychoanalysis, the women's movement, and an influential French philosopher named Michel Foucault, who emphasized the fluidity of all human sexualities and the manner in which

the medical profession, broad social forces, and intellectual practices attempt to pathologize, discipline, and control these sexualities through countless implicit and explicit means.
3 Critical practices around *class* (the place of an individual or group in a hierarchical social system, usually determined by birth, wealth, education, and status) went back to Marxist criticism and the sociology of religion.

Wherever one wishes to trace their origins, however, these three categories added up to what amounts to an unanswerable critique of religion in almost every conceivable form. Hence notions of salvation that required obedience and submission to a society dominated by white people and an escapist attitude toward social change ("just endure your sufferings and wait for your heavenly reward") were largely abandoned by black intellectuals and activists. Religious institutions were examined closely for the way they attracted (or repelled) particular classes of society and for the way they aligned themselves to very particular political platforms and interest groups. And every detail of religion was examined for how it inevitably privileges men and disempowers women, always, of course, "in the name of God," or the Bible, or the Quran, or the Hindu *dharma*, or the ancestors, or whatever.

The Counterculture and the Primacy of Consciousness

The counterculture's psychedelia and its fascination with occult ideas of all kinds would also shape the field, in more subtle but nevertheless important ways. As one popular French book of the time had it, this was *Le Matin des magiciens* (Louis Pauwels and Jacques Bergier, 1960): this was "the morning of the magicians."

This magical morning brought many things, including a famous focus us on **altered states of consciousness** (ASC). This particular expression was brought into popular use in 1969, when the American parapsychologist Charles Tart published his edited volume of the same title, at the height of the counterculture. Tart pointed out in his influential Introduction that, unlike countless other societies, where trance and possession are highly valued and common, western secular society produces adults who are vastly deficient in these areas. Hence, whereas an ancient Indian language like Sanskrit produces "about 20 nouns" for "consciousness" and "mind," American English only possesses a few. Tart's philosophical and comparative point here was both on target and prescient. Indeed he was more correct than he imagined, as the Sanskrit technical terms for different states of mind number not a few dozen, but many *hundreds*. The cover of the first edition featured a line drawing of a meditating Zen Buddhist monk and squiggly representations of three types of brain waves.

The American historian Theodore Roszak brought the term "counterculture" into popular use around 1968. In his own framing, the **counterculture** was a youth movement dedicated to the primacy and transformations of consciousness, which would in turn, it was believed, revolutionize society. In Roszak's view, the counterculture was "counter" precisely to the extent that it privileged consciousness over culture and not culture over consciousness.[37] As such, it was a romantic movement through and through. Hence Roszak's focus on poets like the Buddhist Allen Ginsberg and the common countercultural invocation of William Blake.

In other words, something like the American counterculture (there were in fact numerous countercultures in the Americas, Australia, and Europe) was not only about demonstrating against the deadly war in Vietnam or the racial injustices of American society. Nor could it be equated with the Marxist radicalism of places like the University of California in Berkeley. It was certainly about all of those things; but it was also more. On a religious level, it was fundamentally about the transformation of consciousness, even about creating a new kind of human being. Hence the "hippies" of San Francisco sometimes referred to themselves as "mutants" and spoke (and sung) of a new, dawning era of cosmic change—the Age of Aquarius.

The Counterculture and the Asian Religions

Partly, no doubt, because their own dominant cultures had been defined by Christian and Jewish values and beliefs, the American and European youth cultures turned to Asia, and especially to some idealized and romantic forms of Buddhism, Hinduism, and Daoism that were available to them at the time. This, of course, was not an entirely new move, but there *was* something genuinely new here. For one thing, it was during this same period that many European and American youth did precisely what Plotinus could not do and Emerson, Whitman, and even Müller did not do: they travelled to India or other parts of Asia to study the religions and philosophies of "the East."

Perhaps the most culturally influential example of such a "visionary trip" eastward was that of a megaband—the Beatles. In 1968, after the spiritual conversion of band-member George Harrison to a form of devotional Hinduism, the Fab Four travelled to the ashram of Maharishi Mahesh Yogi, an influential teacher of "transcendental meditation" (TM). The trip was a media sensation. No doubt largely because of it, *Life* magazine decided that 1968 was "the Year of the Guru." One could have predicted as much. The year before, the Beatles had released their *Sergeant Pepper's Lonely Hearts Club Band*. The iconic album cover featured not one, not two, but four Indian spiritual teachers (Mahatma Gandhi, Sri Yukteswar, Sri Lahiri Mahasaya, and Sri Paramahansa Yogananda), the novelist and psychedelic writer Aldous Huxley (whom we will meet many times below), and the British ceremonial and sex magician Aleister Crowley. Morning of the magicians, indeed.

There was another important change afoot, which involved the direction of cultural exchange. For those countercultural participants who did not or could not go to Asia, Asia now came to them. Traditionally, Indian spiritual teachers had relied on secret transmission through the traditional guru–disciple relationship in places isolated from the general populace, such as the Indian monastic centers called ashrams.

Figure 2.5   The Beatles' *Sgt. Pepper's Lonely Hearts Club Band*, album cover (1967). Pictorial Press Ltd/Alamy.

Now they, and their East Asian counterparts, began to actively construct, package, and market their teachings to the public in urban locations throughout the world. In effect they went global and became missionaries of Hinduism, Buddhism, and Daoism.

In addition to increased immigration from Asia and these new globalizing spiritual teachers, industrializing and publishing processes facilitated the distribution of religious knowledge at a rate never seen before in history: doctrines that were once secret teachings passed on orally, from guru to disciple, now appeared in cheap paperback editions that could be purchased by anyone. This increase in access to what once constituted elite teachings, combined with

the decreasing stigma around choosing one's own religious worldview rather than simply inheriting that of one's parents and accepting it, resulted in a competitive marketplace where Asian ideas and practices became viable choices for the individual consumer.

Hindu Yoga and Tantra   The influence of specific Hindu traditions, for example, on European and American culture was very real and much deeper than is generally recognized. Since a charismatic Bengali guru named Swami Vivekananda (who had corresponded with Max Müller and met with William James) had brought a reformed, philosophical Hinduism to

America during the World's Parliament of Religions in 1893 in Chicago at the World Columbian Exposition, numerous Hindu teachers followed, each bringing a different type of tradition and, often, a different kind of yoga practice. Americans themselves took up the practices as their own and became yoga teachers in turn, sometimes with wildly eccentric, colorful, and censored results. Significantly, two of the first American yoga teachers, Pierre Bernard and Ida C. Craddock, were most attracted to explicitly Tantric forms of yoga and philosophy.[38] This American fascination with Tantra was a clear but isolated pattern in the first half of the century. It would become the dominant pattern in the second half and the subtext of much of the counterculture.

Tantra is another comparative category. Co-created by Asian and western scholars in the nineteenth and twentieth centuries, it generally refers to esoteric forms of Asian religions (Hindu, Buddhist, Jain, and Daoist) that, like other varieties of mysticism, emphasize the unity—or even identity—of divine nature and human nature, particularly as this human divinity is manifested in the energies of the human body, which, with the right yogic techniques, are understood to function as a kind of portal into other dimensions of consciousness and reality. Sexual energies, symbols, and rituals are key in many Hindu, Buddhist, and Daoist forms of Tantric yoga. These Tantric traditions on the one hand and the American–British countercultures on the other resonated strongly with each other because they shared a comparative base in the human sexual body and because Tantric ideas and images were repeatedly employed to guide and express psychedelic trips, but perhaps mostly because the Tantric traditions had themselves long functioned as the "countercultures" of Asia: in effect, counterculture was resonating with counterculture here. Figures like Bernard and Craddock, or the later 1960s youth culture, then, were hardly seeing the Asian religions in their orthodox or traditional forms. They were looking into a (quite real) set of cultural mirrors and seeing reflections of themselves. It was themselves, for sure, and yet it was also something other and more.

Buddhism and the Beats   Chinese Daoism was also a player in the counterculture, partly through the central Chinese icon of the Dao ("Way") as a complementary union of *yin* and *yang*; partly through different translations of *Tao Te Ching* (*The Way and Its Power*), which emphasized a kind of letting-go and union with the natural processes of nature; and partly through a growing enthusiasm around the martial arts. But, as the decades ticked by, it was different forms of Buddhism that came more and more to the fore, both in the public culture and within the academic study of religion.

Why Buddhism? Part of the answer is that Hinduism is integrally related to caste, and caste is simply unanswerable in European and American contexts that are dedicated, ideally at least, to social equality and freedom. Caste, whatever else it may be (it has become something close to "ethnicity" in modern India), is clearly about social inequality. This is why, to this day, one can easily find, say, African American Buddhists (by one count, some 30,000 since the 1990s, mostly in the Soka Gakkai tradition),[39] but virtually no African American Hindus. In essence, caste looks too much like racism. Buddhism, on the other hand, rejected caste early on and hence was much more palatable in this respect to European and American youth, especially those of color.

There were other forces at work, though. One was Tantra again, since one of the most popular of the Buddhist traditions was also the most Tantric: Tibetan Buddhism. Another was a collective of gifted writers in the 1950s and 1960s, in England and the States, which embraced Buddhism as the next big thing. Alan Watts, the British writer who moved to the States and became the bard of Zen Buddhism in America and the teacher of Beat poets like Jack Kerouac and Allen Ginsberg, was especially influential. It was figures like Watts, Kerouac, and Ginsberg that laid much of the literary foundation for the counterculture. But not without much struggle and suffering. Kerouac died young, of alcoholism, and Ginsberg's famous poem *Howl* was the object of intense censorship campaigns and court battles fought around its alleged obscenity.

To this day, one can find a distant, muted echo of this prominence of Buddhism and its professionalization within "comparative religion" by simply walking into any mega-bookstore and going to the "comparative religion" shelf or section. You will see ten shelves of Buddhist books to every shelf of Hindu books and to every half a shelf of Daoist books (and good luck with finding Confucianism or Jainism, much less Shintoism). Whatever happened in the global countercultures, it was Buddhism that emerged as the dominant force within the western reception of the Asian religions.

The Departments Are Founded

Not accidentally, it was also in the countercultural 1960s that the comparative study of religion came to the fore in the States through the creation of the American Academy of Religion—that was in 1964—and of numerous new departments of "religious studies." It would not be long now before some of the young people involved in the earliest stages of countercultural movements went to graduate school and became professors of Buddhism, Hinduism, and Daoism themselves. The impact of all this on the comparative study of religion was profound. With only a little exaggeration, we could well suggest that, in the context of the USA now, *it was counterculture, not colonialism, that most immediately catalyzed, energized, and supported the comparative study of religion.* What was once an enterprise dedicated almost exclusively to the Bible and Christianity now became a robustly comparative discipline focused on "world religions" or "comparative religion."

The New Perennialism

This new comparative spirit in turn brought with it a new type of **perennialism**. We have already had occasion to see that this comparativist way of thinking can be traced back, in the West, to the implicit Platonic orientalism of the Gospel of Matthew, Islamic mystics like Suhrawardi, the humanists of the Italian Renaissance (where the word was originally coined), and, much more recently, the American transcendentalists.

The new perennialism of the counterculture was historically related to all these traditions, but it was doing very different work. This new perennialism, after all, was not a claim about a single ancient wisdom narrative. It was about the "world religions" now. And it was celebrating Hindu, Buddhist, and Islamic ideas in ways that were simply unprecedented. Indeed, if one dug down deep enough in the countercultural perennialism, one usually found some modern revisioning of the Hindu nondual philosophy of Advaita Vedanta or, in other cases, some modern revisioning of Sufism—best recognized today in the poetic popularity of the Persian poet Rumi.

Historically speaking, the new perennialism was deeply indebted to the novelist Aldous Huxley, whose *The Perennial Philosophy* (1944) was widely read and celebrated throughout these decades (hence his privileged place on the Beatles' album cover). Huxley was steeped in Hindu and Buddhist literature and was fascinated by psychical phenomena, partly through his friendship with a famous Irish medium named Eileen Garrett. His definition of the perennial philosophy went like this:

> PHILOSOPHIA PERENNIS … the metaphysic that recognizes a divine Reality substantial to the world of things and lives and minds; the psychology that finds in the soul something similar to, or even identical with, divine Reality; the ethic that places man's final end in the knowledge of the immanent and transcendent Ground of all being—the thing is immemorial and universal.[40]

We will meet Huxley again.

Constructivism and Fundamentalism Counter the Counterculture

Affirming the unity, or even similarity, of the world's religions was still a very radical thing to do in the 1940s and 1950s. When Huston Smith published his influential *The Religions of Man* (1958), this was a pioneering and provocative thing to do. By the 1980s and 1990s, this was no longer the case. The intervening decades saw a reaction to the perennialist countercultural thinking on at least three fronts: a religious front, a political front, and an intellectual front. If the counterculture had countered culture through an attempted return to consciousness, the countered culture was about to have its revenge. A series of whiplash effects followed.

On the political and religious fronts, various fundamentalist movements rose to power and aligned themselves with conservative political forces around the world to counter what they perceived to be the spiritual nihilism and moral relativism of western society. These groups were horrified by the counterculture and its sexual, social, and psychedelic excesses, and they adamantly rejected the idea that all religions might reflect and refract a shared human truth.

On the intellectual front, scholars of religion reacted against the obvious excesses of perennialist claims and began to stress the local languages, contexts, and nuances of religious doctrine, ritual, and community. This had been the case in Europe for some time, and now it was increasingly becoming the case in the States. Contextualism and constructivism became the new academic standard-bearers.

Contextualism is the position that all human behavior and experience are best explained and interpreted through (and in) their local linguistic, cultural, and political contexts. **Constructivism** is the related position that all forms of human experience, including religious experience, are best understood as "constructed" through these same local contexts and social processes. Both approaches are extremely skeptical of any universalizing claims with respect to religious experience. Truth is not found. Truth is constructed by human beings, in particular historical contexts, for particular agendas. There are no universal truths, except the universal truth that human experience is always contextual and constructed, which contextualists and constructivists generally fail to see as a universalizing, absolute truth claim.

For all of these reasons, universalism and perennialism now appeared to be dead. The comparative poles had flipped. The earlier perennialist conviction about sameness was now replaced by the later contextualist and fundamentalist convictions about difference. On the contextualist side, this emphasis on difference made for much better scholarship; for scholarship flourishes on local nuance and detail, and the new perennialists had clearly overstated their case. On the fundamentalist side, this emphasis on difference worked to deny, even harass and threaten, scholarship on religion, as it asserted local ethnic and religious identities over the legitimacy of human reason and critical thought. From both sides, however, the countercultural primacy of consciousness over culture became deeply suspect.

Cosmopolitanism on the Horizon

The present textbook is at once a positive response to these recent developments and an attempted revision and disciplining of some of the historically deeper mystical, Renaissance humanist, romantic, and countercultural streams that we have traced above.

It is also in line with the new optimism advanced by such intellectuals as Kwame Anthony Appiah, a Ghana-born, British-trained intellectual who has called for a positive cosmopolitanism to replace our past divisive histories. Such a cosmopolitanism moves away from the "clash of civilizations" of both the conservative intellectual and the religious fundamentalist and emphasizes instead what all human beings so obviously share—a desire for equality, justice, flourishing, and human rights.[41] This cosmopolitan spirit of justice and human rights will become especially apparent in Chapters 6 and 10.

Of course, we will not seek to return the pendulum back to some kind of naïve perennialism, as if all religions really are saying the same thing. They are not. Nor do we seek to deny history, or the immeasurably powerful roles that local culture plays in human experience. But neither will we accept the propositions that everything about the human being is constructed and contextual, that there are no common, even universal, grounds from which to make responsible comparisons across space and time. In short, the present textbook is about the both–and, about consciousness *and* culture, about sameness *and* difference.

It is also about that old wizard Hermes, that tricky god of interpretation, translation, doorways, death, and every other transitional space "in between," to which we now turn.

1 What do you make of the fact that the critical study of religion began "in the towers and dungeons"? Or that, to this day, scholars from a variety of disciplines are harassed and threatened in various ways all around the world, often by religious authorities and communities? For a contemporary sampling, see http://scholarsatrisk.nyu.edu/

2 As a way of thinking about our postcolonial context, consider that many individuals, even nation-states, assume that they can learn, practice, and purchase western science and technology without absorbing any of the core cultural values, philosophical influences, and industrial and corporate structures that originally produced and still support and drive that science and technology. In short, they assume that they can embrace science and technology without becoming "western" or "modern." Comment.

3 What would change about how we think of ourselves and organize our societies if we gradually abandoned the labels of religion and moved to the language of "mind" or "consciousness"? To follow Emerson: "They call it Christianity (or Judaism, or Islam, or Hinduism, or Buddhism). I call it consciousness." What is wrong with this?

Notes

1 Wouter J. Hanegraaff, *Esotericism and the Academy: Rejected Knowledge in Western Culture* (Cambridge: Cambridge University Press, 2012).

2 Pico Della Mirandola, *Oration on the Dignity of Man*, edited by Francesco Borghesi, Michael Papio, and Massimo Riva (Cambridge: Cambridge University Press, 2012), 116–117.

3 Travis Zadeh, *The Vernacular Qur'an: Translation and the Rise of Persian Exegesis* (New York: Oxford University Press, 2012).

4 Quoted in Russell T. McCutcheon, ed., *The Insider–Outsider Problem: A Reader* (London: Cassell, 1999), 130.

5 Hanegraaff, *Esotericism and the Academy*, 136.

6 William Blake, *The Marriage of Heaven and Hell*, with an introduction and commentary by Geoffrey Keynes (Oxford: Oxford University Press, 1975), plate 11.

7 G. E. Bentley, *Blake Records* (Oxford: Oxford University Press, 1969), 310.

8 M. H. Abrams, *Natural Supernaturalism: Tradition and Revolution in Romantic Literature* (New York: W. W. Norton, 1971), 223, 269, 186.

9 Richard Elliot Friedman, *Who Wrote the Bible?* (New York: Harper and Row, 1987), 17–18.

10 Friedman, *Who Wrote the Bible?* 20.

11 Friedman, *Who Wrote the Bible?* 21.

12 Peter C. Hodgson, "Editor's Introduction." In David Friedrich Strauss, *The Life of Jesus Critically Examined* (Ramsey, NJ: Sigler Press, 1994), xlv.

13 David Friedrich Strauss, *The Life of Jesus Critically Examined* (Ramsey, NJ: Sigler Press, 1994), 779–780.

14 Hodgson, "Introduction," xx.

15 Robert Morgan with John Barton, *Biblical Interpretation* (New York: Oxford University Press, 1988), 44.

16   Hodgson, "Introduction," xxxvi.

17   Morgan with Barton, *Biblical Interpretation*, 47.

18   Fred M. Donner, *Muhammad and the Believers at the Origins of Islam* (Cambridge: Belknap Press of Harvard University Press, 2010).

19   Lourens van den Bosch, *Friederich Max Müller: A Life Devoted to the Humanities* (Leiden: Brill, 2002), 118.

20   van den Bosch, *Friederich Max Müller*, 151–152.

21   Quoted in van den Bosch, *Friederich Max Müller*, 153.

22   van den Bosch, *Friederich Max Müller*, 154.

23   Quoted in van den Bosch, *Friederich Max Müller*, 159.

24   For a nuanced study of the Hindu case, see C. Mackenzie Brown, *Hindu Perspectives on Evolution: Darwin, Dharma, and Design* (London: Routledge, 2012).

25   Peter van der Veer, *Conversion to Modernities: The Globalization of Christianity* (New York: Routledge, 1996).

26   See Richard King, *Orientalism and Religion: The Mystic East: Post-Colonial Theory, India, and "The Mystic East"* (London: Routledge, 1999).

27   Catherine Albanese, *A Republic of Mind and Spirit: A Cultural History of American Metaphysical Religion* (New Haven, CT: Yale University Press, 2006).

28   "Nature." In Ralph Waldo Emerson, *The Annotated Emerson*, edited by David Mikics, with a Foreword by Philip Lopate (Cambridge, MA: Harvard University Press, 2012), 32–33.

29   Mary Keller, *The Hammer and the Flute: Women, Power, and Spirit Possession* (Baltimore, MD: The Johns Hopkins University Press, 2005).

30   I am relying here on the genealogies of "spirituality" in Leigh Eric Schmidt, *Restless Souls: The Making of American Spirituality* (New York: Harper Collins, 2005); and on Michael Robertson, *Worshipping Walt: The Whitman Disciples* (Princeton, NJ: Princeton University Press, 2008).

31   Walt Whitman, *Leaves of Grass: The First Edition 1855*, edited with an introduction by Malcolm Cowley (New York: Barnes and Noble, 1997), lines 77–82.

32   Stephen Prothero, *The White Buddhist: The Asian Odyssey of Henry Steel Olcott* (Bloomington: University of Indiana Press, 2010).

33   Peter van der Veer, *The Modern Spirit of Asia: The Spiritual and the Secular in China and India* (Princeton, NJ: Princeton University Press, 2014), 36.

34   van der Veer, *The Modern Spirit of Asia*, 38.

35   van der Veer, *The Modern Spirit of Asia*, 45.

36   Karl Marx, *Critique of Hegel's Philosophy of Right*, edited with an Introduction and Notes by Joseph O'Malley (Cambridge: Cambridge University Press, 1982), 131.

37   Theodore Roszak, *The Making of a Counter Culture: Reflections on the Technocratic Society and Its Youthful Opposition* (New York: Anchor Books, 1969).

38   Robert Love, *The Great Oom: The Improbable Birth of Yoga in America* (New York: Viking, 2010); and Leigh Eric Schmidt, *Heaven's Bride: The Unprintable Life of Ida C. Craddock, American Mystic, Scholar, Sexologist, Martyr, and Madwoman* (New York: Basic Books, 2010).

39   Anthony B. Pinn, *The African American Religious Experience in America* (Westport, Connecticut: Greenwood Press, 2006), ch. 4.

40   Aldous Huxley, *The Perennial Philosophy* (Cleveland: Meridian Books, 1962), iv.

41   Kwame Anthony Appiah, *Cosmopolitanism: Ethics in a World of Strangers* (New York: W. W. Norton, 2007).

The Shepherdess (1989), by Lynn Randolph, 46″ × 58″.

3

The Skill of Reflexivity and Some Key Categories

The Terms of Our Time Travel

Do not trust those who analyze magic. They are usually magicians in search of revenge.
Bruno Latour, quoted in opening of Randall Styers, *Making Magic: Religion, Magic, and Science in the Modern World*

Our talent for division, for seeing the parts, is of staggering importance—second only to our capacity to transcend it, in order to see the whole.
Iain McGilchrist, *The Master and his Emissary: The Divided Brain and the Making of the Western World*

Ours is an incredible story. As far as anyone can tell, we're the only system on the planet so complex that we've thrown ourselves headlong into the game of deciphering our own programming language. Imagine that your desktop computer began to control its own peripheral devices, removed its own cover, and pointed its webcam at its own circuitry. That's us.
David Eagleman, *Incognito: The Secret Lives of the Brain*

Comparing Religions: Coming to Terms, First Edition. Jeffrey J. Kripal, Ata Anzali, Andrea R. Jain, and Erin Prophet.
© 2014 Jeffrey J. Kripal. Published 2014 by John Wiley & Sons, Ltd.

We have just treated the histories of some of the pre-modern comparative practices of global history (in Chapter 1) and the recent history of the emergence of the critical study of religion in the modern West (in Chapter 2). Which is to say that we have *located*, and thus *become aware of*, the historical and cultural perspectives from which we will be imagining and thinking. We are not claiming some perfect "bird's eye view" here, then, some objective perspective over and above every other previous culture and era. We, too, are products of our place and time. Which is all to say that we write and think within an *historical consciousness*, that is, within a form of mind that is keenly aware of how it is shaped, sighted, and blinded by its particular space–time location and all that has led up to this particular perspective, place, or position.

Having said that, it is also the case that, true to our earlier analysis of "theory as travel," we are flying or traveling in these pages through both space and time. How exactly are we doing this? For all their wise insistence on the local and the particular (that is, on difference), and for all of their profound reflections on how different social practices and historical contexts produce different types of awareness and experience, historians also assume human sameness. They must. The discipline of history, after all, implies, indeed *demands* that a form of mind, say, in the second decade of the twenty-first century can to some extent understand a form of mind crystallized in a text or an artifact from a previous century, or even from a former millennium. If this were not so, history would be impossible, and we would all be locked down tight into our own present subjectivities.

We take all of this for granted when reading history, but it is an excessively weird claim and a most fantastic accomplishment.

There is no getting around it: historians are time travelers. We fly.

What we are really talking about here is the historical and anthropological imagination, that most remarkable function of mind that allows us to re-imagine whole worlds of meaning from the past (or from the present of another culture). What we will be about in the present chapter is a description and analysis of the basic terms of this imagination, which are also the basic terms of our own time travel. Here too we are "coming to terms," if now in a more literal sense of that expression.

By "terms of our time travel" we mean three things:

- We mean the actual words that are employed, as in "the terms used by historians and anthropologists."
- We also mean the details, complexities, potential failures, and implicit understandings of these same categories, as in "the terms of a contract" (and indeed much of what follows will be about humility, that is, about trying to distinguish between what we are probably projecting and what we may actually be seeing on these time trips).
- And, finally, we mean to signal the manner in which many of these technical terms are in fact related to one another, often as seeming opposites (for example, "religion" and "secularism") along a single shared spectrum of meaning and reference. "Term" here means terminus, that is, an "end point" of a single shared field of reference.

These, then, are the terms of our time travel …

The History of Religions

By "**history of religions**" we mean two things, both of which we will invoke (and have already invoked) at different places in the textbook. In some places we will use the expression to refer to the full historical sweep of humanity's religious experience, from prehistory to the present day (and here we will add the adjective "**general**"). In other places we will use the expression to refer to a particular lineage within the professional study of religion that emphasizes the comparison of religious forms across space and time.

The Parts and the Whole

The history of religions, as a school of thought now, insists that, to understand the nature of religion, one must approach the historical material as both a collection of individual parts (difference) and a single, species-wide whole (sameness). Put succinctly, *the individual parts can only be understood through the larger whole, and the larger whole can only be understood through its individual parts*. This way of putting it may seem obvious to some readers, but it is in fact a hotly contested claim in some corners of the professional study of religion, which have recently insisted that religion can only be understood and so should only be studied in terms of its local historical contexts and meanings. There are *only* parts and partial perspectives in this latter position. It's all difference.

We are sensitive to these critiques and have done our best to integrate them into our own comparative practices, but this is not, in the end, the position or perspective of the present textbook. This is a textbook on how to compare, and so we are highlighting authors who have celebrated and practiced comparison, not condemned it as impossible or suspect.

Making Magic on the Table of Comparison

As we noted early on, the comparative method works in four basic stages: (1) collection and description; (2) classification and the naming of patterns; and (3) comparison toward (4) some sort of general theory of religion. Historical scholarship, textual translation, and detailed studies of individual societies are all absolutely central here (the collection/description stage), but so are the working theories that implicitly organize these otherwise chaotic historical data (the classification and comparison stages) and the philosophical implications to which they all inevitably point (the theorizing stage).

The historian of religions understands acutely that any general interpretation of religion is never a simple or innocent function of "religion" in general, *but of* which *data are selected and of* how *they are organized and classified on the comparativist's table.* Theories about what religion is and how it works emerge gradually from the organization of vast amounts of data, but these theories also precede and largely determine the data collection and their organization. The data themselves do not and cannot speak of such theories. *We do,* by how we choose to organize and interpret it all. In some sense, then, it is the theory, whether conscious or not, that produces the data, not the other way around. And everything comes down to what we choose to put on the table of comparison—and hence to take seriously—and what we choose to take off that table—and hence not to take seriously.[1]

This is the point of our opening epigraph from Bruno Latour and Randall Styles. Latour is observing that long cultural projects around coining, debating, defining, and rejecting particular terms (which is what the present chapter is all about) are essentially magical battles. They are magical battles because those who enter them recognize the astonishing power of words. They recognize that a word—a "spelling"—is also a "spell." They understand that technical terms are imaginative acts that end up, over generations, creating new worldviews and new possibilities (and new impossibilities, I would add). Those who analyze "magic," for example, have almost always done so in an attempt to explain away these phenomena, to cast a curse on them as "irrational" or "superstitious" (today the magical word invoked to make it all disappear is "anecdotal"). In Latour's terms, they have sought revenge on a set of common human experiences that were once acknowledged by virtually all human cultures but now are demeaned and denied by intellectual elites. In Styles's terms, modern scholars have been in the business of "making magic" to conjure away magic.[2]

But the table can always be flipped. We can also "make magic" to conjure magic, that is, we can

acknowledge and attempt to understand in new comparative terms the eerie super-strangeness that people experience and report on a daily basis even today (and we will do just this in Chapter 8). We can put "magic" back on the table as something positive and absolutely central to our practice of comparing religions. But the bottom line is this: *whatever* we decide, whatever terms we use, with those same terms we are asserting and defending a very particular worldview and set of convictions. We are making magic.

Comparison Can Shift the Meaning of a Religious Event

It is really impossible to emphasize how important such working principles are for what follows, since particular religious events, experiences, institutions, or practices can "mean" one thing in their local historical terms and something quite different when placed on the table of comparison, with its very different terms. *There is also a magic in comparison itself.*

Take, as a simple example, the phenomenon of the "miraculous cure," which, of course, is part of the broader class of "miracles." In their original historical contexts, miracles are inevitably taken to be irruptions into ordinary reality that function as "signs" of the holiness of a saint, the power of a local deity or pilgrimage site, and suchlike. In essence, they are meant to increase and undergird faith. But here is the catch: once all of these local healings and sacred spaces are collected, classified, and recontextualized on the comparativist's table, we can see easily that Hindu or Christian saints trigger such cures as commonly as Buddhist saints, Muslim Sufi shrines, or Amazonian shamans do; or that Chinese or Mexican pilgrimage places work as well as French or English ones.

Indeed, we can even notice that we have reports of UFO encounters in North America triggering spontaneous cures and, in a most bizarre twist, one famous European apparition of the Virgin Mary that triggered cures and looked very much like a UFO encounter. I am thinking here of the famous "miracle of the sun" on October 13, 1917, in Fatima, Portugal, which was witnessed by tens of thousands of people. During the event, which was predicted with precision by three child visionaries months before it happened, the sun turned into a spinning "silver disc," shooting "fireworks" and "zig zagging" as it appeared to threaten to fall to earth—all behaviors that strongly resemble the spinning discs and "falling leaf" landing pattern of the numerous UFO sightings that would come later in the same century.

Sometimes comparison just gets you into trouble.

Clearly, then, the meaning of a "miracle" can shift, and shift dramatically, within a comparativist perspective. This new whole in turn allows us to speculate about how these events really work (as opposed to how the individual believers believe that they work). After all, if Catholic saints, Amazonian shamans, Sufi saints, and UFO encounters all catalyze spontaneous cures, how can one possibly say that the healing miracles of one's own tradition "prove" the exclusive truth of one's very particular faith? If we take these seriously, must we not search for some deeper, more global explanation here?

One can, of course, still claim that the miracle establishes the efficacy and power of one's own local religious tradition; but one can hardly claim that *only* a particular faith can result in miracles. The actual historical data rather suggest that some other global process—be it social, psychological, psychosomatic, or spiritual (or all four)—is at work in these local cases. In short, *collection, classification, and comparison allow us to theorize about deeper dynamics and patterns that may not be shared by any single religious tradition being studied and that, in fact, go directly against local exclusive truth claims.*

Put a bit differently, the comparativist who knows that miraculous cures occur in all sorts of religious belief systems may well find it impossible to believe in any of these particular belief systems (for, taken together, they clearly contradict each other), but he or she may well recognize that these local beliefs really do work in their particular contexts and that reports of miracles in all religions actually bolster their plausibility as common human experiences. One is left, then, in the paradoxical position of believing nothing and everything at the same time. Or, if you prefer, one is left in the strange position of not believing in beliefs but believing in belief.

Such a position may well seem paradoxical to you at the moment. Try to sit and be comfortable with that seeming, as radical comparative thinking often displays some version of what we will call the **both–and**. There are many versions of this both–and, and each works a bit differently, so we do not want to define it too narrowly at this point. As we shall repeatedly see, the both–and is one of the surest markers of rich and nuanced comparative thinking. I will address the apparent paradox head-on in Chapter 12 and attempt to resolve it through the anatomy of your brain. But that is a long ways away.

Perspective as Focusing Distortion

Defining one's perspective is a very important part of any responsible comparative practice. There is no such thing as pure objectivity or complete neutrality in the study of religion. Every perspective is a particular one. Which is not at all to say that every perspective is as reliable, accurate, and productive as any other. Nor is such a claim meant to suggest that every perspective is simply focusing or simply distorting. It is much more complicated than that.

As a useful analogy, consider the optics involved in a pair of glasses and a microscope. A pair of glasses can focus sight, but only if its lenses are sufficiently and precisely "distorted" to correct and counter the distorted vision of the curves of the cornea. Here distortion is also focus and vision. It all depends on the particular eyeballs over which the glasses are placed. Similarly, a microscope allows us to see things that are otherwise completely invisible to the naked eye, *but only by shutting out and making invisible everything else.* It is all about focus and scale. Which is all to say that we must acknowledge that every perspective will bring some things into sharp focus and will make others entirely invisible, and that these two processes of focus and erasure are not at all incompatible.

The Principle of Extremity

The "microscope" of our own comparative practices might be called the **principle of extremity**. Pioneered by scholars of religion like William James, that principle argues that we will best understand the deepest dynamics of religious experience by focusing on the most extreme and extraordinary instances; that, in short, the extreme and extraordinary focus and magnify dynamics and patterns that are otherwise invisible in the more "normal" or ordinary range of religious experience.

To borrow from the novelist Aldous Huxley an analogy to which we will return, we might observe that we can only understand that water is a combination of two gases once we expose water to the extraordinary conditions of extreme heat. Only by "traumatizing" the water does it split into hydrogen and oxygen, which we can then trace and measure with special instruments and methods. But—and this is the key point—to the ordinary eye, to the commonsense perspective of people *all over the world*, the claim that liquid water is really two gases glued together by completely invisible forces is completely unbelievable.

It is nevertheless true.

So too with our comparative methods. Again and again, we will focus on the extraordinary and the extreme in order to intuit and speculate about the deeper dynamics and patterns of religious experience and reach tentative conclusions that the believer, of whatever religion, may well not share. We will never reach the certainty of, say, the chemical composition of water, but we will reach some plausible conclusions that will convince some, maybe many, though never all.

So those are our assumptions and perspectives: the parts and the whole of the history of religions; the shifted meanings on the table of comparison; perspective as focused distortion or distorted focus; and the principle of extremity.

It is now time also to become aware of *your* perspective, your pair of glasses. It is time for the individual reader to define his or her worldview and so prepare for the comparative exercises that will follow in Part II. Unlike our previous two chapters, this one is not about the past and someone else. It works toward the present and you. Most of all, it is about the question of whether you are ready for what follows, ready to leave home for a while and witness foreign spectacles along the space–time continuum.

Here are three stories that might help you answer that question.

Patterns of Initiation

The Vision Quest

Scene One: the autobiography of John Fire Lame Deer, a medicine man of the Lakota Sioux nation, as anthologized in a textbook on comparative religious autobiographies. At sixteen, the boy who was about to become a man was left naked on a hilltop for four days and four nights, in a hole, with no water and no food. It was his first *hamblechia* ("vision-seeking"). The boy may have had no food and water, but he was provided with other special objects, including a star blanket that his grandmother had made for him, a sacred pipe with tobacco, and a gourd rattle containing little fossils that ants collect and forty pieces of his grandmother's flesh, which she had carefully cut from her own arm with a razor blade for this purpose.

He prayed to Wakan Tanka, the Great Spirit. He wanted to be a *yuwipi*, a "medicine man," like his ancestors. He wanted to be a healer. Night came. He sensed the presence of the ancestors. He listened to the animal cries and to the wind.[3]

> Suddenly I felt an overwhelming presence. Down there with me in my cramped hole was a big bird. … I felt feathers or a wing touching my back and head. This feeling was so overwhelming that it was just too much for me. I trembled and my bones turned to ice.

The boy began to weep.

But, gradually, he began to understand that the bird cry was speaking to him. He heard a "human voice too, strange and high-pitched, a voice that could not come from an ordinary, living being." And then this: "All at once I was way up there with the birds. … I could look down even on the stars, and the moon was close to my left side." He was then told his destiny. He would be a medicine man some day. "We are the fowl people, the winged ones, the eagles and the owls. We are a nation and you shall be our brother." He was instructed never to kill any of these birds. They would be his totem, that is, his guiding spirits. The boy was also instructed to come to this same hill to learn about herbs and how to heal people. "A man's life is short," the winged ones said. "Make yours a worthy one."

The boy appears to have been in some sort of waking dreamscape. "I was asleep, yet wide awake," as he put it. He then had a vision of his great-grandfather, a chief named Lame Deer, who appeared to him with blood dripping from his chest, where he had been shot in his own earthly life by a white soldier.

> We Sioux believe that there is something within us that controls us, something like a second person almost. We call it *nagi*, what other people might call soul, spirit, or essence. One can't see it, feel it, or taste it, but that time on the hill—and only that once—I knew it was there inside of me. Then I felt the power surge through me like a flood. I cannot describe it, but it filled all of me. Now I knew for sure that I would become a *wicasa wakan*, a medicine man.

Later the boy felt a hand on his shoulder. It was old man Chest, who had brought him to this hill and had now come for him after four days and four nights. The elder told him that he would help him interpret his visions, but that he, the boy, would not understand for a long time what had happened to him in the vision pit. He also told him that he was no longer a boy. He was a man, and his name was Lame Deer.

The Purple Pill

Scene Two: part fiction, part fact. I am teaching a course for which I have assigned a standard collection of essays on the study of spiritual teachers in a particular religious tradition. In one of these essays there is a single footnote abstractly referencing the literature on some sexual scandals involving a particular spiritual teacher. I never mentioned such matters during class. A student approaches me after class, obviously quite distraught by that single footnote, which she had stumbled upon the night before. Her family, it turns out, was devoted to this same spiritual teacher.

She had never seriously considered such matters, probably because she had never heard about the scandals. Now she has. She asks me for advice. I do the best I can. I tell her that there is indeed a substantial literature on these issues: sacred power and sexuality are deeply linked in the general history of religions, and not just in this single tradition. I explain to her that I do not know much about this particular case, but that it fits into a much larger pattern in the literature, which only confirms her deepest anxieties. I offer the open door of my office as a source of future support and processing, should she decide to go in this direction for her research paper.

"Oh," she replies immediately, "this is just like *The Matrix*. You are offering me the red or the blue pill, aren't you?"

I am stunned by the depth of her insight and the appropriateness of the metaphor. Here, of course, the student was referring to the famous early scene in the film where the figure of Morpheus offers Neo a choice of two pills: red or blue. If he chooses the red one, Neo will awaken to a kind of terrifying enlightenment and see, clearly and for the first time, the illusory nature of the virtual world that he now takes for granted as real. If, however, he chooses the blue pill, he will remain asleep, deluded by the Matrix, but happy and secure in his little dream-like life.

"Yes," I reply, now as Morpheus, "I suppose I am. It is up to you. I cannot make this choice for you. You must decide for yourself."

The student approached me again a few weeks later. She had decided to take the blue pill. Except that I could tell, much later in the course, that she was different. "You took the red pill, didn't you?" I asked.

She smiled.

This is how it usually is: a bit of the blue, a bit of the red, and a purple classroom. Can you see the purple yet?

Plato's Cave

Scene Three: we are now in Athens, Greece, in the early fourth century BCE and at the birth of western "philosophy"—literally "the love of wisdom" (*philosophia*). Plato describes what it means to be such a lover of wisdom in his memorable allegory of the cave, which he relates in his political–metaphysical dialogue *The Republic*. Plato was the founder of the Academy in Athens (around 387 BCE), perhaps the best origin point for our modern universities and colleges.

"Plato's Cave," as the allegory has come to be called, tells the story of the common lot of humanity and how we routinely mistake our sensory perceptions for the true nature of reality. Socrates (the main character in Plato's dialogues) describes a group of individuals chained to a cave floor who cannot look back and are made to watch crude shadow shows on the cave wall. These are created by the prison-keepers passing objects in front of a fire at the very back of the cave—essentially, we can imagine this as an ancient movie theater. Plato then describes one of the prisoners breaking free and climbing up out of the cave to the open air and brilliant sun outside. At first blinded, he quickly adjusts and sees, for the first time, the true nature of reality, beautiful and shining. He returns to what we might call "the Cave of Consensus" in order to tell his fellow prisoners about what dazzles above, well outside their dull perceptions. They reject him as crazy, as a dreamer, as a threat to their own sense of how things are. But the truth is the truth, and the visionary can never be tricked again by the banal, boring shadows on the cave wall. He has had a vision (*theōria*). He has seen the Light (see Figure 3.1).

Figure 3.1 *Plato's Cave* (2007), by Ken Stout, oil on panel, 12″ × 16″.

The Humanities: Consciousness Studying Consciousness

What do these three stories have in common? They are all about the necessity of leaving or questioning one's social world in order to find one's place in it. Quest and question merge here. The comparative study of religion can work very much like these three stories. How?

The Skill of Reflexivity

Reflexivity is the most basic and the most important skill that one needs in order to study and compare religions well. What is it? Most simply put, **reflexivity** is the intellectual ability or spiritual capacity to step out of oneself and one's society and reflect critically on *how* one is thinking, or, much more likely, how one is not thinking but *being thought* by one's culture, religion, place, and time. Reflexivity is the human ability to think about thinking, reflect on reflection (the metaphor of the mirror again), become aware of awareness, and so free consciousness from the ruts of society and ego.

This skill is the key to everything that follows. Reflexivity is the leaving of the Cave of Consensus. Reflexivity is, as David Eagleman has it in our opening epigraph, the human biocomputer becoming aware of its own programming and taking control of it. Reflexivity is the red pill.

Will you take it?

Reflexivity is also the key to judging between adequate and inadequate comparative practices. Like any learned skill, there are levels or degrees of mastery here, and one can speak of "less" and "more" sophisticated comparative practices. Most profoundly, that "less" and that "more" refer to the level or degree of reflexivity, that is, to the degree to which one can step out of one's own mental and cultural conditioning, appreciate other expressions of our shared humanity, and become aware of how one is comparing these and why.

Related here is the fact that the level or sophistication of a comparative practice can also be judged by its *scale*, that is, by how many historical data, how much humanity one has put on the table of comparison. Generally speaking, the more material on the table, the more sophisticated the comparative practice. After all, it is one thing to develop a model of religion based on one's own Catholic Church and the Lutheran one across town. It is quite another to develop a model of religion that can make some sense out of hundreds of different religions spread across the globe over some thirty centuries.

How big is your table? How big is your humanity?

Comparative Practices Are Not Neutral

That "less" and that "more" of a comparative practice are also determined by the issues of accuracy and fairness. Skilled comparative practices will always strive to be *accurate* with respect to the historical and textual facts and *fair* in their insistence on applying the same critical standards to each religious system, preferably after having already applied them "at home," to the system the comparativists live in. This, as we have noted, is the "golden rule" of comparison.

But, please note, neither this accuracy nor this golden rule mean that comparative practices are value-free. Comparative practices are *never* value-free. Indeed, depending on their focus and methods, specific comparative practices can carry any number of real-world implications: religious, philosophical, political, social, emotional, moral, sexual, and so on. We saw this already with the comparativist miracle. Consider, as another example, what Rita Gross has to say about the inherent, inescapable critical edge of the comparative study of religion:

> The study of religion can never be value-free because the very existence of the discipline depends on this value: the development of a worldview that cherishes a neutral position vis-à-vis the various religions as well as an ability to see the internal coherence and logic that empowers each of them. This value is emphatically rejected by at least some segments of all major religions. … One *should* feel that sexist, racist, ethnocentric, and religious chauvinisms, if present, are being threatened by the academic study of religion.[4]

Rita Gross is right. As a simple exercise to demonstrate just how right she is, take the standard non-discrimination policies of almost any established research university or liberal arts college (maybe yours). Normally such policies explicitly forbid any discrimination based on gender, race, religion, or sexual orientation. But here is the catch: all major religious traditions routinely practice, indeed openly encourage, these very forms of discrimination, which they often consider to be the very epitome of piety and morality. What the academic institution sees as bigotry and prejudice born of an ignorance that should be directly addressed and openly challenged by an enlightened liberal education the major religions often see as a brave moral stand against a godless secular world—a stand that must be defended, sometimes at all costs.

Such differences, of course, only become more apparent, not less, when the academic project focuses in, on the religions themselves. Little wonder, then, that robust comparative practices applied to religion have not survived in any part of the world as a stable, broad, and public institution until very recently, and that in many parts of the world they are still actively suppressed, forbidden, or otherwise harassed and censored.

Defining the Humanities

The comparative practices that we will be engaging in here, however, are hardly suppressed in the social context for which they are intended: the college classroom. Quite the contrary, they lie at the very core of the modern study of religion, which is in turn a part of what we call the social sciences and the humanities. The social sciences traditionally encompass disciplines like sociology, psychology, anthropology (also sometimes located in the humanities), political science, and economics. The humanities traditionally encompass disciplines like history, philosophy, language, literature, and art.

Since the present textbook is oriented primarily toward the humanities although it will certainly engage the social, and even the natural, sciences, and

since almost no one outside a liberal arts college or university seems to have a clue as to what a phrase like "the humanities" means (I bet you don't), it is worth explaining the very special ways of knowing to which the term "humanities" points. The humanities are another way of defining our practice of reflexivity. The humanities are the red pill.

Here are four, increasingly technical, definitions of the **humanities** to discuss with your teacher:

1   Put most simply, the humanities are all those fields of study within a modern college or university that attempt to understand and analyze with the tools of critical reason whatever human beings do and make.
2   Put a bit more technically, the humanities are all those fields of study that attempt to understand and analyze the nature and construction of meaning, value, beauty, and narrative in the history of humanity as these have been crystallized in fields like philosophy, language, religion, literature, and art.
3   Put more technically still, the humanities are all those forms of modern thought that assert that reality is not just made up of matter, numbers, objects, and causality (which is what the natural sciences assert), but also of experiences, meanings, values, words, subjects, and stories.
4   Put most technically, the humanities are *the study of consciousness coded in culture.*

With respect to the fourth definition, it is important to clarify that scholars in the humanities do not study consciousness directly, nor do they generally claim to know what consciousness is. They study consciousness as it is reflected and refracted in cultural artifacts like texts, art objects, languages, ideas, rituals, and social institutions.

With respect to all four definitions, it is important to emphasize that the humanities as a whole assume *in principle* that all human beings share a common human nature and that their cultural productions can therefore be studied with similar methods and tools within a common field, be it history, anthropology, or the comparative study of religion. We may not ever be able to get to that shared human nature, and it is an especially fraught enterprise to try to describe whatever "it" is (for one is always in danger of confusing one's own very particular experience of human nature with an imagined "universal" one), but the disciplines, by their very existence, assume that there is such a shared human nature. As we saw with the time-traveling historians, they must assume this in order to do what it is they do.

This is an especially important point to make at the beginning of our journey together, since religious believers often operate on the opposite assumption: we find it in their acts, in their social institutions, and in their beliefs. That is, they assume that one is *first* and primarily a Christian, a Hindu, a Muslim, a Jew, or whatever, and only secondarily a human being. It is seldom (if ever) put this way, of course. The religious way of putting it is to claim that one cannot be "saved," be "twice born," be a "believer," be the "chosen," and so on unless one is part of a very particular community.

From the perspective of the humanities, this is the exact reverse of how things really are, although there *is* a profound truth hidden (and distorted) in these religious claims; for it is indeed the case that human beings need culture, language, and community to become fully human, and probably to become fully conscious. As Nietzsche had it: "Man is the animal whose nature has not yet been fixed."[5] Well, it is culture and community that "fix" that animal nature and turn it into something human—and always, please note, particular. An infant boy abandoned to wolves does not grow up speaking elegant British English, like Mowgli of the Disney film. He grows up dirty, mangy, and acting, howling, and eating like a wolf, if he is not eaten and grows up at all.

To sum up this second point, we might say that human beings do not need a *particular* culture or community to become fully human (which is what the religions commonly assert), but they do need *a* culture or community (which is what the humanities assert). This is another version of our earlier statement

that the power of belief, and not particular beliefs, is what comes to the fore in the fair comparison of miracles. The both–and again.

Defining Culture

So, if the humanities are the study of consciousness coded in culture, what is culture? When we say "**culture**" we generally refer to the entire network or web of institutions, laws, customs, symbols, technologies, and arts that constitute the life of a particular society and hence cultivate, control, and contain consciousness in very precise and specific ways. Turn on the television, go to a movie, attend a religious service, or read a newspaper. That is culture. Can you tell the difference between a wink and a blink? That is culture. So too is a handshake, an emotion of shame, a wedding, an insurance policy, a doctor's office, a pious bow, a tattoo on the shoulder, a piece of jewelry, a hairstyle, a pair of jeans, a veil, a dress, a piece of gum, or a party. Believe it or not, much of your own personal identity, including your most intimate thoughts and desires, is culture as well.

If we were fish, culture would be the watery environment that countless creatures before us helped create and in which we now swim, as if it were always there. If we were spiders, culture would be the web that we ourselves have spun (and that we'd imagine was always there, as if its particular pattern were somehow necessary and eternal). None of this is obvious, until, of course, the pond dries up, the fish is thrown up on the beach (or crawls out over millions of years), or the spider is trapped in a jar. Then it becomes patently obvious.

There are many more tricks here than the fish on the beach or the spider in the jar. After all, since this study of human consciousness coded in culture is practiced by human consciousness, we are caught in something of an infinite "loop." We are back to reflecting in front of the mirror again—this time a mind-bending double mirror. Maybe that is why no one seems to understand what the humanities are. They are not any "thing" at all. *They're us looking at us.*

And that is just a bit loopy.

Cultural Anthropology and Initiation Rites

We begin with such images and analogies because we think that they poignantly illustrate just what is at stake in the comparative study of religion and how it is that such a practice can well be understood as a kind of initiation.

A Beginning

An **initiation** (from the Latin *initium*, "beginning") is a comparative category that names any set of formalized activities and teachings through which a person's social or religious identity is transformed or redefined. There are innumerable types of initiation, but many can be understood as following a pattern that was first identified and developed in the field of **cultural anthropology**—a discipline dedicated to the study (*logos*) of human nature (*anthrōpos*) through the analysis of cultural expressions like symbols, myths, rites, kinship structures, and so on.

Shortly after the turn of the twentieth century, a Belgian anthropologist by the name of Arnold van Gennep noticed something particular about many of the initiation rituals of different cultures. They tended to follow a triple pattern. In van Gennep's language, these rituals moved from an initial state of "separation" from society through a "transitional period" and into a final state of "incorporation" back into the community. He also noticed something else about that transitional period: it functions as "a gap between the ordered worlds where almost anything could happen."[6]

Consider the case of John Fire Lame Deer recounted above. An elder of the community takes the boy up to a hilltop away from the community (the initial state of separation), where he is symbolically "buried" in a hole (the transitional period). During this "death" experience he sees visions of a race in the sky and of his dead-but-living grandfather and is empowered by the Great Spirit. This is not a metaphorical power. It is a living energy that he feels "flooding" through his body and soul just once, just then, during his initiation. He takes all of this back to the community. He is now a man and is accepted into the community with a new name (the final state of incorporation). This, of course, is very close to the triple structure of the ancient Greek practice of *theōria*, with which we began our journey together: separation from one's home-city, travel to a foreign city to witness a spectacle, and return home to report on what one has seen.

The In-between

Later in the twentieth century the British anthropologist Victor Turner picked up on van Gennep's tripartite structure. He extended the model into some influential reflections on what he called the "liminal" qualities of van Gennep's transition state. For Turner, the **liminal state** is a chaotic but creative condition, defined by paradox and ambiguity.[7]

The word itself comes from the Latin *limen*, which means "threshold." For Turner, the liminal is that middle space, that betwixt and between in an initiation ritual in which the earlier identity is symbolically dissolved or broken down so that it can be reconfigured into a new one. But that new self has not yet taken shape. The liminal stage is thus a place of intentional confusion and creative ambiguity. Common symbols are the womb, burial, darkness, water, death, bisexuality or transgenderism, and solar eclipse.

This textbook is designed to guide you through just such an intellectual initiation. We have chosen our comparative examples accordingly, that is, with Turner's paradoxical notion of liminality in mind. Please be aware of this. This textbook is designed to confuse and baffle, but also to enchant and bedazzle. Such is the nature of the liminal space. Like the ancient Greek traveling seer, we are after spectacles and oracles, not after the same old things we can see any day back home. The whole point is *to leave home*.

And then to come back and be re-incorporated into the human community—hopefully a bigger one.

Working Definitions and Their Histories

Before we can leave home, however, we need to understand the terms of our travel. It is these that we now turn to. There are seven such terms: religion, secularism, modernity, world religions, the sacred, experience, and magic.

Religion: Etymology and Politics

First, the really big one: religion. Because this seemingly innocent word is so commonly used, its philosophical and political implications are seldom recognized. Moreover, its historical background is almost never acknowledged, much less understood. We will try to do both here.

To begin, we might note that the term is often given one of two different etymologies: from the Latin *religare*, which means "to bind back, fasten tight, fetter," or, with a bit more imagination, from the Latin *relegere*, which means "to re-gather, re-collect" and "to go through/read again." Both etymologies— neither of which you should take too literally—have something to recommend to us. The first (which is, linguistically speaking, the more reliable etymology) speaks more to the social sciences, with their privileging of society and social bonding as the primary functions of religion. The second etymology (which is more of an invention nevertheless making a very serious point) speaks more to the humanities, with their privileging of the text as the primary locus of human meaning making.

In terms of the first etymology, we might say that religion is understood primarily through *what it does*: it unites a group of people by binding them together to a shared deity or sacred order. In terms of the second, we might say that religion is understood primarily through *what it means*, as a set of truths that are accessible only through a constant revisiting of the tradition in question.

It is important to note in this context that, historically speaking, the vast amount of religious activity has in fact been oral, not written. It is only very recently, in the past few thousand years, that human beings have developed written languages and begun to privilege them over orality and memory as means to preserve and pass on their cultural traditions. If, then, we are going to understand "religion" as a "re-reading," we would do well to keep in mind that most of this re-reading has in fact been a "retelling" and a "remembering."

So much for the etymologies of religion, imagined and otherwise. What of the term's political background? The first point to keep in mind here is that the very use of the word "religion" presupposes a certain political arrangement, more or less secular in orientation, and a subsequent psychological distance from the religions themselves. In the Christian West at least, the social and psychological effects of the Protestant Reformation cannot be overestimated: one can count among them the fact that religious piety was effectively removed from its traditional moorings and reattached to the individual and his or her relationship to God. Bible and belief—not symbol, sacrament, and tradition—became the primary markers of religious identity. The category of "religion," now understood, primarily, as a set of internal beliefs or intellectual propositions, was also shaped during the Enlightenment, under its rationalist, universalizing assumptions.

This category did not really come into common use, however, until two other major political transformations had taken shape: (1) Europe had its colonial encounters with other civilizations; and (2) the delinking of religion and the state was institutionalized, in different ways, throughout Europe and the USA. But—and this is really important— this was a Euro-American process, which was in constant conversation with a larger (in fact global) world. What we are really looking at is a global conversation that was at once democratizing, colonizing, and deeply conflicted. Only very gradually did it become more and more comparative and cosmopolitan. These processes, of course, are still all active today. We have hardly arrived at any definitive resolutions.

Secularism

The birth of religion in the modern world was also related to the birth of secularism. One implied, indeed demanded the other. To "have a religion," after all, implies that one might have some other religion, or no religion at all. Religion and secularism, then, are literally "terms" or end points along the same linguistic spectrum, like up/down, right/left, or yes/no.

Under **secularism** we generally refer to some version of being not religious. The English word comes from the Latin *saeculum*—"age, period, lifetime" and "generation, race" as in "this generation" and "this age." There are at least four things to keep in mind with respect to secularism: (1) there are multiple forms of secularism; (2) secularism does not necessarily mean anti-religion, indeed many forms of secularism end up making possible the *proliferation* of religions; (3) secularism is not some neutral state or a "natural" worldview but possesses its own, very specific histories and assumed values, which it does not generally question; and, finally, (4) explicit and open secularisms are exceptionally rare in human history (they are more or less restricted to the last few centuries).

Modernity

Hence the primary understanding of another key concept in our ensuing discussions: modernity. Modernity, as we have already noted, is generally defined as an historical era initiated gradually in the last two centuries through the development of institutionalized science and the industrial revolution, which resulted in a fundamental break with all that came before it. Modernity, then, implies newness, disruption, even a rejection of the past and its traditions. Unlike most religious ways of thinking, which look to a *past* revelatory event or a sealed scriptural text as representing the full truth, modernity looks to the *future*, for greater and greater displays of truth, promise, and human flourishing. Its fundamental value and hope can be summarized in one word:

progress. It is this sense of newness, of a radical break with the past, of a technologically driven world of infinite progress toward a promising future that defines the experience of modernity and, subsequently, most forms of secularism.

Secular Arrangements

The complex relationship between religion and secularism can easily be seen in the eighteenth-century American developments. Contrary to popular assumptions, the American separation of religion and state was not inspired by purely secular, much less anti-religious motivations. Quite the opposite, the American "separation of church and state" was an intensely moral project of deeply religious people who had been persecuted in their European homelands by forms of Christianity aligned closely with the state apparatus. These individuals understood, through real social suffering, loss of property, physical persecution, and religious exile, that, whenever religion aligns itself with the state, religious persecution directed at religious minorities is a real possibility. They wanted to assure that this would not happen again in their new homeland.

The new American separation of church and state and the specific form of secularism that it helped engender were not, then, designed to suppress religion, but to free it from the state and, most of all, from the influence and control of any present or future majority religion (and the once persecuted Christian communities were already attempting their own persecutions of other religions and peoples in the New World). The American Constitution's guarantee of "the freedom of religion" would thus come to mean not the freedom to practice only this or that particular faith (that is *precisely* what the framers feared), but the freedom to practice religion *in general*. And religion in general, of course, is not any particular religion at all. The "religion" of the "freedom of religion" is, in other words, a complex notion whose logic affirms religion in general by denying the exclusive claims of any and all religions in particular. Here, at least, freedom *for* religion is also freedom *from* religion.

Not every modern construction of "religion" and "secularism," of course, followed this American line.[8] Take the Indian and Chinese cases. Indian secularism, modeled on British secularism, resembles the American arrangement in that it helps produce a flourishing of different religious communities and forms. Indian authors today, then, write sometimes of the neutrality of the state with respect to religion as *dharma-nirapekshata*, literally "religion neutrality." Intense debate continues, however, about whether secularism is a truly adequate model for Indian culture and for its own specific histories and cultural resources (the same is true of the American scene—secular arrangements are always difficult for some types of believer).

The secular arrangement in China has played out very differently. For much of the twentieth century, because of its Marxist and Maoist roots, Chinese policy has been aggressively anti-religious. Secularism in China has thus involved open state persecution of religion, the destruction of temples, and the suppression of religious practices perceived to be a challenge to the communist authorities. This situation has loosened up considerably since the liberalization of China began around 1978, but the state suppression of specific religious practices continues, as can be seen in the violent suppression of the Falun Gong movement as late as 2000.

Muslim countries have had their own experimentation with secularism. In both Turkey and Iran, for example, there was a strong push toward secularism in the first half of the twentieth century, "progress" being the buzzword among both intellectuals and the ruling elite. Under the leadership of two powerful military commanders, Reza Shah in Iran and Ata Turk in Turkey, a militant anti-religious version of secularism was introduced into both cultures with the intent of reforming the social structure and of building a new public space. Religion, in all its manifestations, was to be limited to private spaces.

In Turkey, for example, the *madrasa* system (the institution of Islamic learning and teaching) was abolished, and the veil—*hijab*—for women was banned in public spaces. In Iran Reza Shah unsuccessfully made

similar attempts to put an end to the *madrasa* system and the hierarchy of Shiite clergy, but he was in the end forced to step back in the face of a better organized and financially independent religious opposition. Nevertheless, the government was thoroughly secularized.

It did not take long, however, for both projects to experience major setbacks. The sudden introduction of secularism as something forced upon the populace by the ruling elite from the top down naturally created a backlash. The Islamic Revolution of Iran, led by Ayatollah Khomeini in Iran in 1979, and the gradual resurgence of Islamic political parties like the Justice and Development Party in Turkey (JDP; in Turkish AKP, Adalet ve Kalkınma Partisi) and, more recently, the rise of the Muslim Brotherhood in Egypt are all examples of how the people in these countries have elected to increase, not decrease, the role of Islam in their own governance. Similarly, the striking resurgence of the veil as an expression of faith among young Muslim women across the Middle East in the first decade of the twenty-first century is a clear reaction to anti-religious versions of secularism implicitly or explicitly advocated by the previous secular governments.[9]

This is not at all to say that Muslim communities are naturally opposed to the idea of secularism in some form. Quite the contrary, there is a lively debate about the issues of democracy, governance, secularism, and human rights in virtually all Muslim majority countries today. In effect, "religion" and "secularism" are still being negotiated, still being constructed around the world.

World Religions

As already noted, the European colonial encounters with non-Christian religions during the eighteenth and nineteenth centuries also had a profound effect on the modern concept of religion. Most of the intellectual action here was in Europe. The eventual result was the birth of the new category of **world religion** among European intellectuals. The Dutch scholar Cornelis Tiele (1830–1902) was probably the first to bring a version of the expression "world religion" into broad use in the 1870s, in Dutch (*Wereldgodsdiensten*)—although there were precedents as early as 1827, in German (*Weltreligionen*). Significantly, Tiele taught in a state university, not in a religious one. As Tiele and others used the expression at this time, it meant something like "universal religion," as opposed to "national religion."[10]

The Problem and Promise of "World Religions"

Some scholars have argued that the categories of religion and world religion are inextricably bound to colonial history, European universalism, and false assumptions about the simple "essence" of complex cultures. Accordingly they should be abandoned. There is much to ponder in these criticisms. After all, it is indeed true that using a category like "Hinduism," "Islam," or "Christianity" implies that all Hindus, Muslims, or Christians believe and do the same things. This is, quite simply, nonsense.

The critique is then extended and radicalized. More troublingly, it is pointed out that such simplistic labels lay the groundwork for social conflict and, in extreme cases, for actual violence by encouraging individuals and communities to imagine themselves first and foremost through religious identities. Put too simply but not inaccurately, it is difficult to imagine, much less carry out, Christian–Muslim violence if there is no such eternal thing as a Christian or a Muslim. Or, to put the matter in a more sophisticated way, religious violence is unlikely if these Christian and Muslim identities are constructed as secondary features of a deeper and shared humanity, which is consciously cultivated as primary. "Christian" and "Muslim" have to be invented and socially constructed before there can be any such conflict. And scholars of "religion" or "world religions" who keep reinventing and constructing these essences are part of this problem, not its solution.

There is, then, much to be suspicious of in the categories of religion and world religions and in the various -isms that follow in their historical wake. But such criticisms tend to miss other, more positive and creative implications of the same categories, which work very much against colonialisms, ethnocentrisms, and violences of all kinds.

Take "religion" again. As the above discussion makes clear, it is most definitely not an innocent or neutral word. If you use the r-word, you are *already* doing comparison, and you are *already* thinking critically about religious behaviors and beliefs. You have already, in some sense, distanced yourselves from religion, since religion is now likened to an object that one can have or not have. It is *not* you. The distancing or critical effect of the category, moreover, often leads to a more or less inclusive worldview, since the category of "religion" assumes *both* sameness (for all are "religions") *and* difference (for each is a "different" religion). To speak of "religion," then, is a very modern and democratizing move, but—please remember—it also, necessarily, relativizes the absolute truth claims of each and every religion, including one's own. It cuts both ways, as we say. Another version of the both–and.

So, too, with the logic of the expression "world religions." It demands a recognition that we all exist and live in a single "world," even if we inhabit and practice different "religions" (sameness and difference again). But the category does much more work than this. As Peter van der Veer has pointed out, the category of "world religions" is not some simple western invention or one-way colonial imposition, as is often implied by the critics of the term. Rather, it is a positive construct of a shared modernity. This modernity, moreover, was created by imperial encounters and global interactions that emerged from the projects and intentions of countless actors, including Indian, Middle Eastern, and Chinese elites. In effect, "world religions" is a shared cosmopolitan creation. Moreover, and more helpfully still, the category of a "world religion," much like that of "spirituality" as an alternative to institutional religion, is a "moral category that transcends actually existing churches and religious groups," and hence it "implies a pacification of religious conflict."[11]

We need not be blind, then, to the positive effects of "religion" and "world religion" in order to recognize their potentially negative, even dangerous uses. A badly used idea is not the same thing as a bad idea.

Religion: Definitions

So much for the etymology, historical background, political origins, and some of the problems and promises of the word "religion." But what, exactly, *is* it? Hundreds, probably thousands of definitions have been offered in the last century and a half. Here are some of the most historically influential definitions for you to ponder and discuss with your teacher. We list them in the historical order in which they appeared.

> it seems best ... simply to claim, as a minimum definition of religion, the belief in Spiritual Beings.
>
> Edward B. Tylor, *Primitive Culture* (1871, vol. 1: 383)

> [Religion is] the feelings, acts, and experiences of individual men in their solitude, so far as they apprehend themselves to stand in relation to whatever they may consider divine.
>
> William James, *The Varieties of Religious Experience* (1902, 34)

> A religion is a unified system of beliefs and practices relative to sacred things, that is to say, things set apart and forbidden—beliefs and practices which unite into one single moral community called a church, all who adhere to them.
>
> Émile Durkheim, *The Elementary Forms of the Religious Life* (1912, 62)

> A *religion* is: (1) a system of symbols which acts to (2) establish powerful, pervasive and long-lasting moods and motivations in men by (3) formulating conceptions of a general order of existence and (4) clothing these conceptions with such an aura of factuality that (5) the moods and motivations seem uniquely realistic.
>
> Clifford Geertz, "Religion as a Cultural System" (1965, 90)

> Religion is the quest, within the bounds of the human, historical condition, for the power to manipulate and negotiate one's "situation" so as to have "space" in which to meaningfully dwell. It is the power to relate one's domain to the plurality of environment and social spheres in such a way as to guarantee the conviction that one's existence "matters." Religion is a distinctive mode of human creativity, a creativity which both discovers limits and creates limits for humane existence. What we study when we study religion is the variety of attempts to map, construct and inhabit such positions of power through the use of myths, rituals and experiences of transformation.
>
> Jonathan Z. Smith, *Map Is Not Territory* (1978, 291)

The following definition—a recent one, described by its author as "a legitimate form of science fiction"[12]—resonates strongly with the one that I will be working with in the present textbook:

> religion is a complex of practices that are based on the premise of the existence of superhuman powers, whether personal or impersonal, that are generally invisible.
>
> Martin Riesebrodt, *The Promise of Salvation* (2009, 74–75)

These practices are religious for Riesebrodt precisely to the extent that they enable human beings to "make contact" with a source of superhuman power. This contact is "religion's promise," which "remains astonishingly constant in different historical periods and cultures." This global constant is actually a triple promise: "to ward off misfortune, to help cope with crises, and to provide salvation."[13]

Much, of course, depends upon whether we consider those superhuman powers to be real and whether we think the religions can actually deliver on their promises of salvation. My own understanding of religion, which privileges individual contact with these superhuman powers, suggests that they are quite real and that the religions really do deliver, in the simple sense that people commonly experience such powers and attain such states. Accordingly, we will be paying special attention to what Riesebrodt describes as one form of religious contact: "activating superhuman potential that slumbers within a person."[14] In the spirit of Riesebrodt's description of religion as a "legitimate form of science fiction," we will even be looking at how science fiction can become a legitimate form of religion.

Individuals, then, are not always deluded or lying when they report such extraordinary powers and special states. They happen. What they *mean*, how we might interpret or explain them, and how they might be related to one another are all very different matters (and the matters of this textbook). For the sake of this textbook's initiation, I will define **religion** thus:

> any set of established stories, ritual performances, mind disciplines, bodily practices, and social institutions that have been built up over time around extreme encounters with some anomalous presence, energy, hidden order, or power that is experienced as radically Other or More.

Typically, this Other or More breaks into the ordinary everyday world and reveals itself, often to a single person, in overwhelming ways. Religion is *not* that original anomalous experience, revelation, or salvation event. Religion is the total psychological and social response to that breaking-in. Religion is the taking of that More and transforming it into narratives, performances, social structures, material objects, architecture, music, song, dance, and mental practices that are certainly less than that original More but can publicly point to, remember, re-enact, and above all make contact with it—all toward both the immediate practical needs of human life (protection, healing, and flourishing) and the ultimate or final salvation, enlightenment, or liberation of the human community.

It is worth emphasizing what is perhaps not immediately obvious in this working definition, namely that it refuses to equate the religious with the moral or the ethical. The religious and the ethical are certainly related, but they are not the same thing. Robert A. Orsi

has put this most powerfully, observing that the study of religion is not a moralizing discipline, but it is a moral practice, and this precisely to the extent that it refuses to idealize religion as somehow always good or beneficent. In his words, the study of religion "exists in the suspension of the ethical." As such,

> it steadfastly refuses either to deny or to redeem the other. It is a moral discipline in its commitment to examining the variety of human experience, and to making contact across boundaries—cultural, psychological, spiritual, existential. It is a moral discipline in its cultivation of a disciplined attentiveness to the many different ways men, women, and children have lived with the gods and to the things, terrible and good, violent and peaceful, they have done with the gods to themselves and to others.[15]

The Sacred

This is an especially important point to emphasize, since many people today insist on thinking of "the holy" primarily in moral terms. Accordingly, "holiness" becomes more or less equivalent to "being really, really good." This, it must be repeated, is a very serious mistake. If you are going to understand religion in any adequate fashion, you must abandon this naïve notion. You must also understand what scholars of religion mean by "the sacred."

The **sacred**, most simply put, is *that which is set apart from the ordinary or profane*. Much of this can already be detected in the etymology of the term "sacred," which can be traced back to the Latin words *sacer*, *sacrum*, and *sanctus*. All three belong to the vocabulary of ancient Roman religion. For the Romans, a *sacrum* (a "consecrated thing": this is a noun derived from the adjective *sacer*, meaning "dedicated, consecrated") was anything that belonged to the gods and could be encountered in the interior space of a temple, including that space or the temple itself—because that thing had been "consecrated" (*sancire*) and hence was *sanctus*. Moreover, what was "in front of," that is, "out of" (*pro-*) the "temple" (*fanum*) was *profanus* ("**profane**, unholy, common"):

this description was given to anything outside the *sacrum* or sacred interior space of the temple. The sacred is organized around a most basic binary, then: that of the inside/outside.

Something or someone set apart is, by definition, excluded from the community. The concept of the sacred, then, easily slides into the notion of the taboo, and even into those of the sinister or the damned. The category of the sacred, in other words, possesses a certain double character or moral ambiguity. The gods are sacred, but so are the demons. Moreover, the holy can liberate you from oppression, but it can also destroy you. The sacred is set apart, then, in order for us not only to honor and worship it, but also to contain it and to protect the community from its awesome superhuman power.

The sacred has had a long history in the study of religion, but nowhere was it more central than in *The Idea of the Holy* (1917)—a great work of the German historian of religions Rudolf Otto. Otto famously defined the sacred, or alternatively "the holy," in terms of a handy Latin sound bite. The holy or sacred, he wrote, is the human experience of a *mysterium tremendum et fascinans*: what I would gloss as a mystical presence at once terrifying (*tremendum*) and alluring (*fascinans*).

The sacred as a modern category has its uses and abuses. One of the category's main advantages is that its precise use in the comparative study of religion warns us away from simplistic moral readings of religion. Otto's sacred or holy, after all, is *not* the good, and it may or may not lead to what we consider to be moral behavior: some of history's most uplifting and positive moments were inspired by sacred texts and ideals, but so were some of history's most destructive and deadly. As with Riesebrodt's definition of religion above, the sacred is finally about *power* and *promise*.

The category's main disadvantage is the way it can too easily suggest that there is a single essence or thing "out there," called the sacred, that interacts with human beings in every clime and time. It is much more accurate to think of the sacred as an always local relationship or historical process. In actual fact,

almost *anything*—from a rock, a tree, an animal, or a place to a person, a temple, a totem, even a run-over beer can[16]—can become sacred within a particular social and historical context. So, clearly, the sacred is not some stable "thing" or essence.

The sacred, in other words, can be thought of as a bit like modern electricity. It needs two poles to work at all. Moreover, it can be harnessed and used toward the human good, for sure. But it can also electrocute anyone who gets too close or is not properly insulated from its force. It is a bit stretched, but one can also invoke here the analogy with a nuclear reactor. A traditional temple can be thought of as a nuclear reactor of sorts—that is, as a place that contains, produces, and protects the community from a most awesome power, *which it needs*. One approaches the temple with great care. In many religious systems, moreover, the average person can never enter the innermost recesses of a temple. That is too holy, too powerful, too dangerous. Only religious specialists, people set apart (just like nuclear technicians are), can enter there.

Two very different cultural examples might be useful at this point. Let us take an ancient Hebrew example and a modern American one, the latter from the history of the study of religion itself.

1   *The Ark of the Covenant*   The ancient biblical example involves the "ark of the covenant," which appears to have been a richly ornamented box that was believed to house, really enthrone, the God of Israel, who sat between the two cherubim on top of the box (the cherubim were a particularly high class of "angels" that vaguely looked like the Egyptian sphinx, half-human and half-animal). In this particular scene, King David and his priests are transporting the ark. Note what happens when a man named Uzzah innocently, and no doubt with perfectly good intentions, tries to prevent the ark from falling when the oxen carrying it stumble:

> David again gathered all the chosen men of Israel, thirty thousand. David and all the people with him set out and went from Baale-judah, to bring up from there the ark

of God, which is called by the name of the LORD of hosts who is enthroned on the cherubim. They carried the ark of God on a new cart, and brought it out of the house of Abinadab, which was on the hill. Uzzah and Ahio, the sons of Abinadab, were driving the new cart with the ark of God; and Ahio went in front of the ark. David and all the house of Israel were dancing before the Lord with all their might, with songs and lyres and harps and tambourines and castanets and cymbals. When they came to the threshing floor of Nacon, Uzzah reached out his hand to the ark of God and took hold of it, for the oxen shook it. The anger of the LORD was kindled against Uzzah; and God struck him there because he reached out his hand to the ark; and he died there beside the ark of God. (2 Samuel 6.1–7)

Such passages could be multiplied a hundredfold in multiple cultural contexts, with much the same result: the sacred has little, if anything, to do with internal intentions or "moral" concerns and everything to do with power. The sacred no more cares about a person's internal state than an electrical wall socket cares whether a saint or a sinner sticks a knife into it: either way, the person gets zapped.

2   *"Terrifying beyond Belief"*   For a modern example, consider the scholar of comparative religion Huston Smith and his description of his first experience with mescaline. On New Year's Day of 1961, Huston Smith ingested two capsules of mescaline in the home of Harvard psychologist Timothy Leary, after Aldous Huxley, then teaching at the MIT, had given Smith Leary's phone number. Here is what happened, in Smith's own words:

> The world into which I was ushered was strange, weird, uncanny, significant, and terrifying beyond belief. … It was as if the layers of the mind, most of whose contents our conscious mind screens out to smelt the remainder down into a single band we can cope with, were now revealed in their completeness—spread out as if by spectroscope into about five distinguishable layers. … As in Plato's myth of the cave, what I was now seeing struck me with the force of the sun, in comparison with which everyday experience reveals

only flickering shadows in a dim cavern. … It should not be assumed from what I have written that the experience was pleasurable. The accurate words are significance and terror.

Smith goes on to quote Rudolf Otto on the idea of the holy or sacred as "a distinctive blend of fear and fascination." He warns Leary that "there *is* such a thing as people being frightened to death." And he describes experiencing space in not three or four dimensions, "but more like twelve." It was a terrifying, beautiful experience of the sacred that changed the young intellectual forever.[17]

Huston Smith had taken the red pill. Two of them, actually.

Experience

Behind all of this discussion of religion, world religions, and the sacred is another modern category that you probably did not notice because you were simply assuming it as an unproblematic given: "experience." The term itself is Latin-based (*experiri*, "to try, submit to, learn, prove" and *experientia*, "trial, proof, knowledge") and related to the words "expert" (Latin *expers*) and "experiment" (Latin *experimentum*). In Renaissance Latin, for example, the word *experientia* can still mean "test," that is, the "practical reality" given to us by sense perception.[18]

Very generally speaking, the concept of **experience** now refers to a subjectively felt and directly perceived or cognized event that is self-evident to the person knowing it. Interestingly, in modern English we speak of a person "having an experience" (much as we refer to "having a religion"), which suggests that the experience is something other than the subject having it. In other words, the category carries connotations of both psychological immediacy *and* psychological distance.

As it is commonly applied in the study of religion, the category of experience goes back to a German professor, biblical critic, and philosopher named Friedrich Schleiermacher, who published a most influential book entitled *On Religion: Speeches to the*

Cultured Despisers (1799; the final text appeared in 1831). What Schleiermacher attempted to do in this book was rescue religion from its Enlightenment rationalist critics—the "cultural despisers" of his subtitle—by abandoning literal belief, even the immortality of the soul, in favor of an emphasis on what he called "intuition," "feeling," "pure contemplation," and the "direct experience of the infinite." In short, Schleiermacher moved from the question of whether this or that belief was true to the psychological fact that religious experiences happen. Beliefs, of course, come from the outside, whereas experiences, or so it was assumed, arise from the inside. Once this move was made, the cultured despisers could have their way with individual beliefs, which at this point were becoming increasingly unbelievable anyway, and Schleiermacher and his readers could still hold on to their faith in the presence and power of "the infinite." Belief was out. Experience was in.

This was an especially potent move, particularly for the future comparative study of religion (which did not exist yet), since one could now effectively separate the allegedly direct and immediate experience of religion from its social surround; that is, one could distinguish between a particular religious experience and the public institutional, doctrinal, and ritual forms in which it was embedded. Once such a "cut" or distinction was made, it was only a matter of time before intellectuals began using it to compare "religious experiences" across cultures and climes.

It is important to realize that this was not just a potent move. It was also one that had consistently been rejected as heretical before the modern period. Protestant leaders and writers in the seventeenth century, for example, had held up the pure doctrine and the revealed teachings of the Bible as the only legitimate means to preserve Christianity from what they called "Enthusiasm," a term of derision and condemnation for them. Enthusiasm (literally "state of being *entheos*," in other words "having a god within") referred to the phenomenon of ecstatic visionaries and prophets who were treating their own religious experiences as personal revelations, as a kind of direct and immediate conduit to God.

Protestant critics considered this reliance on Enthusiasm and the teachings that arose from such extreme states to be of pagan origin and hence untrustworthy. So, when a writer penned the Latin phrase "*Plato mysticus*" in 1699, he was not complimenting the philosopher; he was condemning him. He was calling him a "poisonous" infection on the body of Christianity.[19] Moreover, states of enthusiasm were also something that these same writers associated with the emotional states and swoonings of women, which made it all even worse. The basic problem with "Enthusiasm" in the seventeenth century, then, was that it could not be controlled by proper belief, revealed scripture, and (male) religious authority.

Schleiermacher's turn to "experience" was later picked up and developed in new directions in the late nineteenth and early twentieth centuries by a young discipline: the psychology of religion. Foremost among its new voices was William James, whom we have already met. James honed in on religious experience, and especially mystical experience, in his classic *The Varieties of Religious Experience*. He was clear about the fact that he considered religious experience to be primary and less prone to external manipulation or to later interpretation by church, tradition, and religious institution, all of which he considered secondary. In this he was being a good Protestant. Hence it is no accident that Catholic sources get very little attention or appreciation in *The Varieties*.[20] The later, secondary interpretations or institutional framings of direct religious experience James called over-beliefs—a word that, in its structure, looks remarkably like an English paraphrase of an earlier Latin-based word: "super-stition." For James, over-beliefs were not to be trusted on their own terms, nor were they necessary if you wanted to understand what was happening psychologically.

Not everyone has been convinced that experience can be so easily separated from public institution, tradition, and culture. Criticisms of the category of experience have been advanced, and with great sophistication. In 1978, for example, Steven T. Katz edited a multi-contributor volume entitled *Mysticism ical Analysis*, which set the tone for the ﹍ ﹍ decades through a robust criticism of this exclusive focus on experience. Katz and his co-writers argued that something like mystical experience is seldom, if ever, direct and immediate; that every form of human experience, and especially religious experience, is in fact *already* informed and shaped by culture, tradition, language, ritual, doctrine, and so on. Experience is neither "pure" nor "direct"—nor, they seemed to suggest, can it ever be so. Rather, experience is always constructed and mediated. Such events may or may not point toward or emerge from some larger reality, but scholars, as scholars, cannot know this and are much better off sticking to what they do know and can in fact analyze in great detail: the historically constructed nature of religious experience as the latter is expressed in texts.

Katz and his colleagues derived their criticisms largely from western philosophical sources. But a similar critique of experience has emerged from Asian ones. Robert Sharf, a contemporary scholar of Buddhism, has been particularly influential and helpful here. In a key essay he has demonstrated that, historically speaking, many of the Hindu and Buddhist traditions that are commonly called upon to prop up this approach through experience have not, in actual fact, been particularly interested in personal or subjective "experiences" as such.[21] The primacy and privileging of inner experience, he argued, is a modern phenomenon that finds little support in the premodern Hindu and Buddhist traditions. One can find such convictions, of course, in key modern Asian figures (like the Hindu philosopher and Indian statesman Sarvepalli Radhakrishnan, or the Japanese Zen writer D. T. Suzuki), but these individuals were working in a modern context that was deeply informed by western ways of knowing and speaking.

If, on the other hand, we look closely at Buddhist premodern traditions, we find that these texts and traditions regard what we would call "experience" as products of various mental and physical states, none of which is particularly helpful on the path toward liberation, enlightenment, or *nirvana*. Indeed, from many classical Buddhist perspectives, to focus on one's personal experiences is precisely the wrong thing to do, since it locks the practitioner into a constructed and illusory state of body and mind. Enlightenment or *nirvana* has nothing to do with anything constructed or "caused." Nor is it considered to be a subjective state. Quite the contrary, it is considered to be a direct perception of the nature of reality and, as such, beyond all notions of "person" or "subject." So the whole focus on inner experience is unhelpful here, and probably a very serious distraction.

Similar arguments can be advanced for the Hindu philosophical traditions, which also tend to understand mental states as unreliable—if not fundamentally illusory—material states. Many of these same traditions are extremely critical of any exclusive reliance on personal experience, preferring instead to discipline and contain it with the help of the authority of caste and, above all, the scriptural authority of the Veda.

The same deep reservations can be found again in the history of Islam, particularly around discussions of the role of visionary and ecstatic experience within Sufism. The learned elite, as opposed to what is known as popular Sufism, has generally been very suspicious of any exclusive reliance on personal visionary experiences on the *tariqah* ("spiritual path"). Such experiences, it argues, ought to be contained and regulated by the ultimate authority of the *pir* or "spiritual master," which is in turn informed by a sound understanding of the Quran and of the larger Islamic canon. Indeed, it could well be argued that the institutionalization of Sufism during the middle Islamic period (1100–1500) was a centuries-long effort, largely successful, to contain the unpredictable and threatening nature of personal religious experiences.

Sharf has been read as wanting to deny that premodern or non-western peoples had experiences at all. He is not arguing this. He is arguing that the contemplative traditions of Asia, and particularly the Buddhist ones, have developed very sophisticated reasons to be suspicious of "experience," including religious experiences, and it is therefore a mistake for modern scholars of religion to focus on the latter as much as they have done, as if such phenomena were some kind of simple, universal, or reliable guide to understanding the religious traditions the way they have understood themselves throughout history.

Magic

Secularism was not the only modern category to be born alongside that of religion. Magic was another. By "magic" we do not mean stage magic—that is, tricks of illusion or sleight-of-hand performed on the stage for the entertainment of a paying crowd (although some very interesting comparisons and historical connections between stage magic, religious ritual, and psychical phenomena could be made at this point). We mean something else. We mean something that goes to the very heart of the day-to-day practice of countless religions, whether they think of it as "magic" or not.

A few simple examples might help. We have already noted that, in the infancy story of the Gospel of Matthew (2.1–12), the first figures outside of Jesus' immediate family to recognize him as somehow special were the magi or astrologer-magicians from the East. What we have not said is that much of Jesus' later healing ministry strongly resembles the magical acts of shamans and wonder-workers from around the world: using his own spittle to cure blindness in two cases (Mark 8.22–26; John 9); healing and forgiving through spoken incantations or declarations; causing a fig tree to wither and die by simply cursing it (Mark 11.12–21); even manifesting what looks like a clairvoyant ability: when Nathaniel asks Jesus how he knew him, Jesus replies: "I saw you under the fig tree before Philip called you" (John 1.48).

Later Christianity built on these magical origins. When I was growing up in the American Midwest,

for example, I would often see, in cars, statues or medals of Saint Christopher placed on the dashboard or on the mirror, to help protect the car and passengers from harm. When I was living in Calcutta, I saw statues of the goddess Kali or of the elephant-headed god Ganesh on the dashboards of cabs, often with fresh flowers and burning incense around them. They reminded me of the Saint Christopher medals. The cab was now a rolling temple.

The Catholic practices have been quite controversial, particularly in some Protestant and Evangelical circles. For example, "hocus pocus," the popular expression of magicianship, was associated early on with Protestant bashings of the Roman Catholic Church, a tradition whose central rituals or sacraments the Protestant writers condemned as inherently magical, and therefore as "pagan." The expression "hocus pocus" is thought to be a corruption of the Latin sentence uttered at the heart of the Catholic Eucharist, which in turn is believed to have been spoken by Jesus himself, probably in Aramaic or Hebrew, over the unleavened bread during his "last supper." In Latin it reads: *Hoc est enim corpus meus.* "This is truly my body."

Asia is filled with similar reports and beliefs. It is common among Buddhists in Thailand, for example, to wear amulets attached to necklaces around their neck. These are decorated with images of highly revered figures, such as the Buddha or a revered monk, and they are believed to be repositories of auspicious powers that protect the wearer against evil or disease. In villages across India, yogis are believed to develop special techniques and powers (known as *siddhis*) as a result of their advanced yoga practices. Such techniques and powers include the ability to enter other bodies, read minds, and levitate.

Very similar practices can be found throughout the Islamic world. Among Shia Muslims, for example, there is a widespread practice called *istikharah* ("asking for the best choice"). People who are not sure about the consequences of a specific course of action they are considering might go to a religious specialist believed to have a special skill in consulting the Quran. They will ask this holy man to consult the Quran in order to determine whether or not they should take the course of action they are contemplating. The holy man might recite some prayers for a moment and then open at random the Quran. He would then interpret the verses and relate them to the situation of the person in front of him without knowing what that situation is; and he would give advice accordingly.

We might also list here the widespread Muslim use of the magical powers of different kinds of prayers and stones; or the belief that a particular verse in the Quran (68: 51–52) is deemed to be quite effective in dispelling the effects of the "evil eye" (this is a conviction, shared by many cultures, that the stare or look of a person can do harm to another). In some Muslim countries you will find this specific verse everywhere: at the entrance of homes and shops and, of course, on the dashboard of cars and of large transport trucks—especially there. We are back to the functions of Saint Christopher, Kali, and Ganesh, only now in a Muslim context that forbids such images, so it uses holy words to do the same work.

And, of course, countless human beings in countless religious contexts perform a public or a private ritual that we call "prayer." Such practices involve an intention, declared or not; they are designed to produce some effect in the external world—a healing, a rich harvest, guidance on a life decision, success on an exam, a safe birth or trip, and so on. To the theistic insider prayer does not generally appear as magic, because the believer works on the assumption that the true agent is an external deity. The magical practitioner's assumption, on the other hand, is that agency lies in the human practitioner or in the ritual act itself. There are, however, numerous "mixed" cases in which the agency is understood to be shared by the ritual magician with some kind of subtle being (an angel, a demon, a god, a spirit, and so on). In any event, it remains true that, very generally speaking, petitionary prayer is acceptable and unproblematic in theistic religions (since prayer involves submission to a deity), whereas the practice of magic is condemned as an inappropriate act of human pride (since such practices imply that human beings are themselves sacred or powerful).

But how should we define magic? Like with most other comparative categories, there are multiple problems here. Historically or etymologically, the word relates to the ancient Greek nouns *magos* ("magician," plural *magoi*) and *mageia* ("magic," the ritual culture or "religion" of these magicians). *Magoi* often referred to Persian (and more especially Zoroastrian) astrologers and dream-interpreters. How it is understood today in the English language, however, has little to do with Persian astrology and everything to do with Christian polemics against these sorts of practices.

These processes around magic were evident throughout the history of Christianity. If early Christian writers used the characterization "magic" to distinguish themselves from the pagans, later on the early Protestants used it to distance themselves from the Catholics. These writers were particularly anxious to separate their "true religion" (correct belief) from the "false religion" of Roman Catholicism (inappropriate ritual magic). Magic here equated bad religion.

These judgments were further developed in 1918, when, in a famous lecture given in Munich and entitled "Science as a Vocation," a German sociologist by the name of Max Weber announced that the modern world and its science depended on a gradual but inevitable process of "disenchantment" (*Entzauberung*). All legitimate knowledge, for Weber, required this exorcism of "sorcery" (*Zauber*)—which he explicitly related, with some venom, to what he called the "cult of experience" (note, again, the rejection of "experience," which is denied the status of a legitimate mode of knowledge). The universe could no longer contain "mysterious and incalculable powers." It was all about reason, measurement, and math now.

It would be a most dubious comparative practice to take this early modern Protestant understanding of false "magic" and true "religion" together with Weber's attempted exorcism of the sorcerers, and

Figure 3.2   *Zal Consults the Magi* (sixteenth century), attributed to Sultan Muhammad. Metropolitan Museum of Art, New York. Gift of Arthur A. Houghton Jr., 1970, Acc.n.1970.301.8. Image © 2013 The Metropolitan Museum of Art/Art Resource/Scala, Florence.

then to apply them to every other cultural context, as if this somehow explained anything other than those very particular Protestant and modernist convictions. Given, then, that we are speaking and thinking in English and that a fair comparison can harbor no judgment on the religious legitimacy of these near universal practices, how might we reframe "magic" for our own comparative purposes here?

Let us define "**magic**" as any ritual act, private or public, that works through an assumed correspondence between an internal or subjective state—a state of mind—and an external or objective event in the physical world, often with the intention of influencing or controlling the latter. The key word here is *correspondence*. Magical rituals and acts do not work through causation or mechanics. They work through hidden intentions and secret, unseen correspondences. Most simply, magical rituals set up "likes" or metaphorical relations between internal factors (intentions) and external results. Any ritual, event, or human experience that implies such a correspondence between inner and outer, between mind and matter, between the subjective and objective dimensions of human experience is "magic" in this understanding.

So then: the two things that we, today, call "religion" and "magic" are not so easy to separate, and we really cannot study the one without the other: these are "terms" along a shared spectrum again. It is also worth emphasizing that it is often difficult, if not actually impossible, to separate between "magic" and "science."[22] The origins of institutionalized modern science are usually located somewhere around the founding of the Royal Society in London in 1645. That society in turn appears to have emerged from an "Invisible College" of intellectuals well aware of the radical nature of what they were proposing (hence their "invisibility"). It is commonly pointed out that most of the members of the Royal Society were Protestants, Puritans to be precise, and that the principles of science that were institutionally embraced then resonated deeply with Protestant theology, which insisted on a transcendent God distinct from the material universe. This God had established regular natural laws, which were being increasingly seen as mechanistic and mathematical in nature.

The situation is, however, more complicated than this picture suggests. The historian Francis Yates famously argued for the thesis that the earliest strains of technological thinking did not appear with the Puritans and Protestants of the seventeenth century, but with the Renaissance philosophers, occultists, and magicians of the sixteenth, who had advanced the shocking idea that it was "not contrary to the will of God that man, the great miracle, should exert his powers" and so manipulate the material universe. In this model at least, "it is magic as an aid to gnosis which begins to turn the will in the new direction"— a new will that will eventually produce applied science.[23] We can hear echoes of this same fusion of occult magic and modern science in a novel like Mary Shelley's *Frankenstein* (1818), where the scientist is also an occult magician and "the will" to new knowledge operates via a kind of primitive biomedical technology that goes horribly wrong.

We must be very careful not to see here a simple progression from magic to religion to science, as so many thinkers in the nineteenth century did. A figure like Isaac Newton, for example, not only gave us a model of gravity and the foundations of modern calculus. He also believed in biblical prophecy, wrote about Atlantis, and practiced **alchemy**, a kind of magical chemistry that sought to transform matter into gold and, in some cases, the human being into an immortal one. After reading Newton's work on alchemy and other occult subjects, the British economist John Maynard Keynes wrote: "Newton was not the first of the age of reason, he was the last of the magicians."[24]

Well, no. Newton was by no means the last of the scientific magicians or magical scientists. The Invisible College lives on. We will encounter some of these scientists as we proceed.

At other moments in the history of science, there *was* a clear attempt to break with religious belief and, above all, with religious authority. The nine English gentlemen and scientists who met at Victorian dinner parties to talk about how to do battle with the clerics and fully integrate the new sciences into English government, society, and industry took for themselves a name that resonated with that of the earlier Invisible College (and with the names of later American superhero comic books): they called themselves "the X-Club." One of their own, T. H. Huxley, invented a new word to capture their own relationship to religion: **agnosticism**. Under this label Huxley meant to signal the position that we simply cannot know, *in principle*, about transcendent matters, and therefore scientific and religious things (and, most of all, scientific and religious *authorities*) should be kept apart. Way apart. He also meant, in between his other words, that religious matters are irrelevant to an understanding of the world, and that all reliable knowledge would come from empirical observation and measurement. Which is to say: from science.

The Uncertainty Principle: The Insider–Outsider Problem (and Promise)

It is often pointed out, correctly, that religious beliefs appear bizarre or absurd to those who do not inhabit that particular religious world. As the Romanian historian of religions Ioan Couliano used to quip, all religious beliefs are unbelievable, in the obvious and most simple sense that anyone outside a given religious tradition does not, and for the most part cannot, believe it. It is not that these non-believers are bad people. It is simply that they cannot in honesty bring themselves to believe an alien religious worldview, much less live in it. They live "outside" that worldview, not "inside" it.

An analogy might help us here. There is a special rule in quantum physics, called the uncertainty principle, which states that one cannot know the precise position of an electron at the same time as one knows its precise momentum. The more one knows about the position, the less one knows about the momentum; and the more one knows about the momentum, the less one knows about the position. Moreover, in order to determine either the location or the momentum, the physicist has to do something to the system that is being studied. She has to use laboratory instruments, for example, to shoot another electron into the invisible system in order to get it to react and so reveal its structure to the researcher. This strange, always "uncertain" feature of measuring electrons is not thought to be the result of inadequate measuring devices. Uncertainty is thought to be somehow fundamental—that is, built into the very structure of reality, at least as this reality presents itself to a human observer. The perspective an observer chooses by virtue of her measuring devices actually changes how matter behaves and how it can be measured in the laboratory.

I do not wish to make any identity claim here—I am drawing an analogy, not an equation—and I certainly do not want to present myself as understanding quantum physics (I do not). But I do think it is fair to say that something like the uncertainty principle is at work in the professional study of religion through what we call the **insider–outsider problem**. By "insider" we mean someone who has been raised in a particular religious tradition or has converted to it and accepts its basic belief system and values. By "outsider" we mean someone who has not been raised in a particular religious tradition and has not converted to it either.

This will take a little setup to explain, in three moves.

Move One. We know that certain insights into religious systems are generally not available to the believers themselves—so much are their thought processes determined by religious ideas and practices whose very purpose is, at least in part, to conceal all sorts of things (often these are the very things that scholars like to study) in order to justify their own "obvious" truths. As the great muckraking American journalist Upton Sinclair put it (in a different context): "It's difficult to get a man to understand something when his job depends on not understanding it." It is even harder when the man thinks that the eternal salvation of his soul depends on not understanding it.

Within any particular tradition, then, there is always an elaborate system of subtle and not so subtle practices and values that largely determine what ideas seem plausible, or even thinkable or imaginable. In other words, **plausibility**—the perceived likelihood of an idea being right or wrong—is relative and largely determined by social context, not by the intrinsic value of the idea itself. What is patently obvious to one community (say, a group of evolutionary biologists or psychoanalysts) is patently false to another (say, a fundamentalist Christian, Jewish, Hindu, or Muslim community). Put a bit differently, an idea can be utterly rejected by almost everyone in a community *and be correct.* An idea can also, of course, be accepted by almost everyone in a community *and be wrong.* This is why it is crucial to privilege the perspective of outsiders in order to assess, understand, and interpret a religious worldview, a worldview that would otherwise prevent this very project from happening on its own terms and conditions.

Move Two. Conversely, we also know that certain insights into religious systems are generally not available to outsiders who have not fully internalized the languages and ritual forms of the religious complex being studied. Life is short, our cultural and linguistic experiences are always severely limited, and hence it is impossible to know a religious system the way someone who was raised in it can. Any adequate comparative study of religion, then, must also rely heavily on the gifts, perspectives, and experiences of insiders.

Move Three. We are left, then, in something of a dilemma. The outsider knows what the insider denies (or cannot imagine), and the insider knows what the outsider denies (or cannot imagine). Critical insights into and experiential confirmation of a religious tradition are generally not available to a single individual. Both *are* possible, but not at the same time. What to do?

Different scholars take different positions here. Russell McCutcheon, for example, has famously argued that scholars should be "critics, not caretakers" in a 2001 collection of essays by the same name: for McCutcheon, only the outsider position is legitimate in the study of religion.[25] Other scholars disagree. They have taken different positions, arguing for various models that incorporate the insider perspectives within the outsider perspectives, or vice versa.

One of the most eloquent and influential voices here has been that of my own mentor, Wendy Doniger. Significantly, Doniger's primary medium of reflecting on religion has been that of the myth or story, which, of course, a reader has to "enter" in order to understand (the inside), even if the same reader can then "step out of the story" and critically reflect back on it afterwards (the outside). Because of this basic literary structure and the incredibly sophisticated materials with which Doniger works (ancient Sanskrit mythical and philosophical literature), Doniger's books are filled with radically reflexive images and paradoxical thought experiments. By "radically reflexive" we mean any image, idea, or practice that turns the view of an individual "back on itself," as in a mirror, in order to question that view's most basic assumptions about the world.

We encounter, for example, nested stories—that is, stories within stories; lovers sharing each other's dreams (which, by the way, really happens, even to famous skeptics);[26] people realizing that the world itself is a dream or an illusion in which they are embedded; and the prominence of double identities, such as gods pretending to be mortals or mortals realizing that they are gods (a comparative pattern that becomes "the Human as Two" in my own work, including here, in Chapters 9 and 12). There is also Doniger's comparative intuition of what she calls "the implied spider," that is, a posited shared humanity that spins the very different webs of the world's mythologies and religions but that we can never really know directly.[27] Finally, there is her most recent alternative history of Hinduism, which powerfully demonstrates that there are always many types of "insiders" who contribute to a tradition like Hinduism (in this case, insiders like untouchables, women, other Indian religions, and animals), and that every religious tradition takes on different meanings when viewed from the perspectives of these "inside outsiders" or "outside insiders," as we might recognize them.[28] Perhaps, though, the image that captures best these mind-bending forms of reflexivity is one that appears very early in her writing: that of the Möbius strip, a strip of paper whose inside becomes an outside and whose outside becomes an inside (see Figure 3.3).[29]

The position of the present textbook is much closer to the both–and position of Doniger than to the either–or position of McCutcheon. We suggest that both insider and outsider perspectives are appropriate for the field as a whole, as long as the student allows his or her conclusions to be challenged, criticized, and developed by the other perspective. The key—and we cannot emphasize this enough—is the ability or capacity *to move back and forth between insider and outsider perspectives*. Basically, the secret is to become that Möbius strip.

To privilege the outsiders is to lose touch with religious experience itself. To privilege the insiders is to guarantee the blunting of the scholar's critical edge. The goal here, then, is not to privilege the perspective of the outsiders at all costs, much less to privilege the

Figure 3.3 Mobiüs Strip. Computer artwork, Laguna Design/Science Photo Library. Corbis.

perspective of the insiders, but to turn the inside out and the outside in, toward a more and more radical analysis. The goal is to share one another's dreams, to step out of the story and realize that they are *all* dreams, and then to ask—perhaps the biggest question of all—just who is doing all of this dreaming. Who, or what, *is* the implied spider?

Perhaps we should have written this textbook on one long Möbius strip.

If push comes to shove, however—and, alas, it sometimes does—the outsider perspectives must be privileged over the insider ones as long as we are claiming to study religion instead of professing or practicing it. Otherwise the field as a field of critical study simply cannot exist on its own. The only position that is not, in principle, allowed in the professional study of religion is the position that one should not and cannot critically analyze a religion.

Whether one takes oneself to be an insider or an outsider, or—much more likely—a bit of both, we must also always realize that studying a religion, at least a living one, will likely challenge and change the religion in very small or in very big ways. Again, neutrality and objectivity are not options here. Like in the example of the physicist with her electrons, to study a system is to change it and, more often than is commonly recognized, to be changed by it in turn.

Religious Questions as Ultimate Concerns

It is not simply the case that we need to "come to terms" with comparison via the literal terms of the professional study of religion, as we have just done above. It is also the case that we need to "come to terms" with comparison in an existential, moral, cultural, religious, and emotional sense. Accordingly, it is time now to "get personal" and try to define your own worldview before we enter the comparative acts of Part II. This can best be done by attempting to answer a set of classical religious questions.

By "religious," in this particular context, we do not mean pious or faithful. Nor are we referring to any particular belief, or to the felt need to go to a particular building on a special day to perform a set of rituals. Nor are we referring to the sense or requirement of belonging to a particular community, ethnicity, or social group. By a **religious question** we mean *one that pertains to the ultimate meaning and purpose of human life*. We mean what the Protestant theologian Paul Tillich meant when he described the dynamics of faith as "reason grown courageous" about matters of "ultimate concern." To ask *how* human life is biologically put together is a scientific question. To ask what human life *means* or *why* we are here is a religious question. These are special sorts of questions, in the sense that they appear to be very nearly universal (they have been asked in some form by nearly all the cultures for which we have an adequate record)—and this despite the fact (or because of the fact?) that they cannot be answered with the usual tools of human reason and pragmatic technology. Measurement and meaning, after all, are two very different ways of knowing.

Tillich's questions of ultimate concern are hardly new. Over seventeen hundred years ago now, a Church Father named Tertullian noted down, with some contempt, the kinds of questions that "heretics" of his time were asking out aloud. He seemed annoyed. These audacious questioners were in fact gnostic Christians, followers of a visionary named

Valentinus, whose place in the early Christian community was so celebrated that he almost became one of the first popes. According to Tertullian, here are the questions that Valentinus and his followers were asking (and, even worse, answering) in the second century CE:

Who are we?
Where have we come from? Or, if you prefer, where were we before we were born?
What is this world in which we find ourselves?
How did we end up here, and why?
Where will we ultimately go after we die?[30]

The Tough Questions

1   So how would you answer the same five questions? Note that the purpose of this exercise is not to arrive at *the* "correct" answers. We certainly do not know the correct answers. What we do know is that it is very important for you to go through the exercise of trying to answer these questions—not so that you can tell yourself or your teacher what the truth of things is (trust us: you can't), but so that you may become more aware of your own answers to these perennial questions. Basically, we want you to become more aware of the water you are swimming in and the web you are crawling around on and, most of all, to know that it is water and that it is web.

2   Why do you think Tertullian associated these five questions with fellow Christians whom he deemed heretical—that is, what was so wrong with asking these questions?

Notes

1   I am indebted for this key metaphor to Wouter Hanegraaff's *Esotericism and the Academy: Rejected Knowledge in Western Culture* (Cambridge: Cambridge University Press, 2012).

2   Randall Styles, *Making Magic: Religion, Science, and Magic in the Modern World* (New York: Oxford University Press, 2004), 3.

3   All the quotations to follow in this section are from Gary L. Comstock, *Religious Autobiographies* (Belmont, CA: Wadsworth Publishing Company, 1995), 51–54.

4   Rita Gross, *Feminism and Religion: An Introduction* (Boston: Beacon Press, 1996), 13.

5   Friedrich Nietzsche, *Beyond Good and Evil: Prelude to a Philosophy of the Future*, translated by R. J. Hollingdale with an Introduction by Michael Tanner (London: Penguin, 1990), 88.

6   Arnold van Gennep, *The Rites of Passage*, trans. Monika B. Vizedom and Gabrielle L. Caffee (Chicago, IL: University of Chicago Press, 1961), 12.

7   Victor Turner, *The Ritual Process: Structure and Anti-Structure* (Chicago, IL: University of Chicago Press, 1969).

8   I am relying here on Peter van der Veer, *The Modern Spirit of Asia: The Spiritual and the Secular in China and India* (Princeton, NJ: Princeton University Press, 2014).

9   See Leila Ahmad, *A Quiet Revolution: The Veil's Resurgence, from the Middle East to America* (New Haven, CT: Yale University Press, 2012).

10   See Tomoko Masuzawa, *The Invention of World Religions: Or, How European Universalism Was Preserved in the Language of Pluralism* (Chicago, IL: University of Chicago Press, 2005).

11   Van der Veer, *The Modern Spirit of Asia*, 30.

12   Martin Riesebrodt, *The Promise of Salvation: A Theory of Religion*, trans. Steven Rendall (Chicago, IL: University of Chicago Press, 2010), 18.

13   Riesebrodt, *The Promise of Salvation*, 18. The definition and discussion occur at pp. 74–75.

14   Riesebrodt, *The Promise of Salvation*, 75.

15   Robert A. Orsi, *Between Heaven and Earth: The Religious Worlds People Make and the Scholars Who Study Them* (Princeton, NJ: Princeton University Press, 2005), 202–203.

16 I am thinking of the science-fiction writer Philip K. Dick, who once intuited the real presence of a divine cosmic force, which he called Valis, in an encounter with a crushed beer can.

17 Huston Smith, *Cleansing the Doors of Perception: The Religious Significance of Entheogenic Plants and Chemicals* (New York: Jeremy P. Tarcher/Putnam, 2000), 10–13.

18 Christopher I. Lehrich, *The Language of Demons and Angels: Cornelius Agrippa's Occult Philosophy* (Leiden: Brill, 2003), 87–89.

19 Hanegraaff, *Esotericism and the Academy*, 115.

20 I am indebted to this last point to Robert H. Abzug, editor of the abridged *The Varieties of Religious Experience (The Bedford Series in History and Culture)* (New York: St. Martin's, 2012).

21 Robert H. Sharf, "Experience." In *Critical Terms for Religious Studies*, edited by Mark C. Taylor (Chicago, IL: University of Chicago Press, 1998), pp. 94–116.

22 See Stanley Jeyaraja Tambiah, *Magic, Science, Religion, and the Scope of Rationality* (Cambridge: Cambridge University Press, 1990).

23 Francis Yates, *Giordano Bruno and the Hermetic Tradition* (London: Routledge & Kegan Paul, 1964), 156.

24 J. M. Keynes, "Newton: The Man." In *Proceedings of the Royal Society: Newton Tercentenary Celebrations, 15–19 July 1946* (Cambridge: Cambridge University Press, 1947). Quoted from Wikipedia's entry on "Isaac Newton's occult studies" (accessed March 4, 2012).

25 Russell McCutcheon, *Critics Not Caretakers: Redescribing the Public Study of Religion* (Albany: State University of New York Press, 2001).

26 Lynn Margulis and Dorion Sagan, *Dazzle Gradually: Reflections on the Nature of Nature* (River Junction, VT: Chelsea Green Publishing, 2007), 102.

27 Wendy Doniger, *The Implied Spider: Politics and Theology in Myth* (New York: Columbia University Press, 1998).

28 Wendy Doniger, *The Hindus: An Alternative History* (New York: Penguin, 2009).

29 Wendy Doniger O'Flaherty, *Dreams, Illusion, and Other Realities* (Chicago, IL: University of Chicago Press, 1986).

30 I am indebted to Wouter J. Hanegraaff for pointing these questions out to me and for putting them in this form. See his *Western Esotericism: A Guide for the Perplexed* (London: Bloomsbury, 2013), 72.

Leaving (2001), by Lynn Randolph, 16″ × 20″.

PART II

Comparative Acts

In Part II we leave our initial self-definitions, iden-tities, and identities, and locations behind and travel in our minds back through human history and around the world, on a journey through space and time. In the process, we will engage in a series of "comparative acts." These will be practiced on six comparativist foundations, which are as follows:

- the functions of myth and ritual (Chapter 4);
- the natural world (Chapter 5);
- the human sexual body (Chapter 6);
- religious prodigies, specialists, and their social institutions (Chapter 7);

- the paradoxical images, symbols, and powers of the religious imagination (Chapter 8);
- the final questions of the soul, salvation, and the end of the world (Chapter 9).

Such a list of comparative bases is by no means exhaustive. Not even close. These are illustrative case studies, that is, they are chosen to illustrate the how-to, not to narrate the general history of religions or the full sweep of comparative practice. There could just as easily be sixteen such chapters. Or sixty.

Comparing Religions: Coming to Terms, First Edition. Jeffrey J. Kripal, Ata Anzali, Andrea R. Jain, and Erin Prophet.
© 2014 Jeffrey J. Kripal. Published 2014 by John Wiley & Sons, Ltd.

Time's Journey (1987), by Lynn Randolph, 58″ × 46″.

4

The Creative Functions of Myth and Ritual
Performing the World

Man is a creature who makes pictures of himself and then comes to resemble the picture.
Iris Murdoch, "Metaphysics and Ethics" (in *Iris Murdoch and the Search for Human Goodness*, edited by Maria Antonaccio and William Schweiker)

Myths think themselves in man.
Claude Lévi-Strauss, *The Raw and the Cooked*

Chapter Outline

Comparing Religions: Coming to Terms, First Edition. Jeffrey J. Kripal, Ata Anzali, Andrea R. Jain, and Erin Prophet.
© 2014 Jeffrey J. Kripal. Published 2014 by John Wiley & Sons, Ltd.

Do you believe in Wednesday? I mean, do you *really* think that there is a space of time called "Wednesday" in the world that, say, a golden retriever would recognize as out there somewhere? For that matter, do you really believe that time is divided into neat seven-day and twelve-month cycles, and that it is the year "2014" or "2015," or whatever year in the western calendar we happen to be in when you are reading this?

Certainly, there is such a thing as a solar day. It is created by the earth's spin, which spins, by the way, in every culture. In the modern West, we have chosen to divide this spin into 24 "hours," which we then divide further into 60 "minutes," and so on. There is also, most definitely a (roughly) 28-day lunar cycle, and we know that the earth orbits the sun once about every 365 days. But we also now know that the length of our days and years is simply a function relative to the size of our planet and its orbital distance from the sun. If we were living, say, on Mars or Venus, our days and years would be of different lengths. As for the week thing or the month thing on planet Earth, they never really quite work, do they? The months, after all, have different numbers of days, which make them fit the solar year (did you ever memorize those?), and we have to add an extra day to our calendar every four years (the "leap year"), to prevent the whole system from eventually sliding into nonsense.

To take another, rather glaring example, we do not have the slightest idea on what day Jesus was born. December 25, or thereabouts, was chosen to replace the Roman winter equinox celebration, and even the different Christian traditions themselves do not agree on which day to celebrate Christmas. Moreover, no matter what the day actually was, there is good evidence to suggest, that the birth occurred sometime around the year 4 BCE.

That is just a little bit embarrassing.

Clearly, we are making this whole calendar time thing up. Which suggests another, less playful, more troubling question: What else are we making up?

The question is a bit unfair, as it suggests that making up something like Wednesday or the year 2015 is somehow a bad thing. It is clearly not a bad thing, for human beings need order and structure. Human beings cannot endure **chaos** for long—that is, complete disorder and non-meaning. And so they are always and everywhere constructing a **cosmos**— that is, an ordered system of meaning, structure, and purpose. Let us call any such symbolic system or structured cosmos a world, with the understanding that we are referring to a cultural system and not to an ecosystem.

The *content* of these individual worlds, of course, is very different in each case, but the *process* of creating a world is a universal human attribute: difference in content and sameness in function again. These shared functions of world building constitute our first and most basic foundation for doing comparison across cultures and times.

Without a doubt, two of the most ancient ways in which human beings create and maintain a world over time is through the linked processes of myth and ritual. Because of this, myth and ritual happen to be two of the most useful comparative categories that we possess. They also happen to be two of the most controversial. As with so much else in the modern study of religion, these difficulties revolve largely around those two tricky, mind-bending subjects we encountered in our previous chapter: the paradoxical, mirror-like nature of reflexivity and the promising problem of the insider–outsider flip.

Myth: Telling the Story Telling Us

Culturally and psychologically speaking, the world is made of stories and people acting them out. There are so many stories in the world. Each culture is a big story, each person a little story. Consider this. When you think of "you," what is this "you" about which you think? Most likely, you think of a few memories (selected out from potential millions), which you then string together to construct a very particular narrative, with a beginning (which you can't really remember), a middle (only tiny parts of which you can remember), and a present (which is gone as soon as you think about it), pushing out into the future (at which you can only guess). This is what a social self is—an extremely sketchy story that we put together from a few paltry pieces and tell ourselves constantly, as if to reassure ourselves that we exist at all. As for other social selves, well, we are all imagining one another within the larger stories we call cultures and religions, none of which come together in any neat way. This, then, is how comparison really works in a day-to-day fashion—as a self-story embedded in a cultural story, interacting, not so well, with countless other self- and cultural stories.

It's a real mess.

Muthos and *logos*

There is a long history of thinking about such stories. The baseline of this history, from the Renaissance to the present day, has been Greek mythology. Because of the ancient Greeks, we call these stories "myths." The word "myth" comes from a Greek word meaning "story" (*muthos*, plural *muthoi*), which was often contrasted, in ancient Greek thought, to "reason, argument, discourse" (*logos*, plural *logoi*). By the late fifth century BCE, the word was being used to describe invented or fictional stories or "tall tales." Plato, for example, used the term to refer to something opposed to the truth.

There are complexities here, though, and much depends upon which century of Greek culture we are talking about. For one thing, *both muthos* and *logos* also meant, at the most basic level, "word," which implies that they were thought of as related to language. More complexly still, Greek thinkers often used myths to express and explore some of their most profound ideas or reasons: in short, we might say that they used *muthos* to illustrate *logos*. We saw this with Plato's Cave. Plato could not have conveyed the same subtleties without his striking image of prisoners chained to the cave floor, where a sole escapee sees the light and returns, to face the total disbelief of his fellow prisoners. But, just as clearly, Plato was not asking his readers to accept that there is such a cave and set of prisoners somewhere. Plato was no literalist. He did not believe his myth, as we say; but at the same time he clearly thought that it was in some way true, or better—that it expressed some profound truth that could not be communicated in any other way. The myth pointed to the truth, but it was not itself the truth. Certainly by the first and second centuries BCE there were numerous Greek thinkers, particularly among the Stoics, whom we encountered earlier (Stoicism was one of the five major philosophical schools or "sects" of Hellenistic antiquity and a dominant cultural influence under the Roman Empire), who were engaging both myth and poetry as sources of philosophical wisdom in much the same way. Here was what Peter T. Struck calls "the birth of the symbol" and the beginnings of "mythic truth."[1] We will return to this moment in Chapter 8.

Finally, to paint an even more complex picture, the Greeks (particularly, again, the Stoics) also used *logos* in frankly mystical ways. A perfect example of the latter phenomenon is the ancient use of *logos* as the ordering principle of the universe, in both ancient Greek and early Christian thought. So, for example, Christ is called "divine Logos" or "Word" at the beginning of the Gospel of John: "In the beginning was the Word." *Logos* here does not refer to some form of rationalism or linear logic, but to a kind of cosmic Mind, universal intelligence, or super-language out of which all that is emerges and takes shape. *Logos* is not human reason here. It is "with God." It *is* God.

The ancient Greek writers, then, did not always see *muthos* and *logos* as opposed modes of human cognition; sometimes they saw them as complementary. Both terms, moreover, could be used to point to ultimate or cosmic truths. This duplication did not quite stick, though. The Romans translated the Greek noun *muthos* with the Latin noun *fabula*, which was in wide use in the West until the eighteenth century through its descendants in modern languages, all denoting fabricated or made-up tales.

Myth and History

Very roughly, this is how the word "myth" has come down to us—through the Greeks, the Romans, and their countless heirs in western intellectual life—as something negative. Mythical ways of thinking have been generally construed as simplistic, childish, or confused, as a mode of thought that eventually needs to be abandoned for the clean lines and straight thinking of pure reason, logic—and now, of course, modern science.

Much of this rejection of myth has orbited around the modern category of history, in the simple sense of what really happened in the past and can be reconstructed (always partially and selectively, of course) through archival, textual, or archaeological means. The uncomfortable truth is that mythical narratives have often been understood by their tellers and listeners as historical in a similar sense— that is, as what really happened in the past. This is a very hard pill to swallow, particularly since we know that every new generation "remembers" this sup-posed history in ways specific to its own particular needs and desires. There is myth, and there is history, and these are very different ways of remem-bering the past.

The Study of Myth

The modern comparative category of myth does not directly translate into "fiction" or "made-up tale," but rather suggests a symbolic story pointing to some deeper truth (be it cultural, psychological, historical, or philosophical). Very generally speaking, a **myth** is understood to be a sacred story that founds and grounds a particular world. Although such an under-standing possesses ancient roots, as Struck has clearly shown, it is primarily a modern project. Fritz Graf gives us a precise date for the appearance of "myth" in this new positive sense: 1764, by the German scholar Gottlieb Christian Heyne, who turned it into a Latin word: *mythus*.[2] So began the modern study of myths.

This new, essentially comparativist field of study goes under the rubric of "mythology." **Mythology** is, quite literally, the systematization or rational study (*logos*) of sacred stories (*muthoi*). This is a most interesting project, as it contains both *muthos* and *logos*. At least as a word, it seeks to combine the two different ways of knowing that human beings have expressed for millennia.

So which is it? Is a myth a made-up falsehood, or is it a symbolic expression of the profoundest of truths? Is it a piece of fiction to move beyond, or a piece of revelation to embrace and think with? Some, maybe many, would encourage us to choose sides here. We would encourage a different approach. We would encourage you to embrace the comparative category of myth as doubly powerful, *precisely* because it can mean both falsehood and truth *at the same time*. We encourage you to move back and forth again.

We offer this suggestion, however, with an impor-tant and (we hope) by now familiar caveat. We enter here, again, the paradox of reflexivity and the flips of the insider–outsider dynamic. From the inside, a major myth expresses how the world works and what a people's place in this world should be. From the outside, the myth is clearly a constructed, relative story that cannot possibly speak for anyone placed outside its particular cultural frame. The compara-tivist always finally privileges the latter perspective (there is the proviso or caveat), but also seeks, as best she or he can, to enter imaginatively the former and thereby to understand the religious world from within, as an insider might. The comparativist, in other words, honors both the inside and the outside of myth, but never mistakes the comparative study of myth for belief in a particular myth.

So where exactly are *you*? There is an easy test to determine whether you are inside or outside a myth. If you are outside, it is "just a myth." It is a piece of religious fiction or history, usually from another culture, but nothing more. If you are inside, it is "the way things really are." It is not a myth at all. It is not only true. It is as true as truth gets, and it is probably sacred to you—beyond questioning, incomparable. If you are truly outside a myth, on the other hand, you can study its history and how it was put together, how it relates to other aspects of the culture, and so on. If you are truly inside a myth, you can probably do none of these things, and you may even think that such critical study is inappropriate, perhaps blasphemous. It is too close to you. It *is* you. You are a fish still in the water, a spider still on the web.

So do you have a culture? Or does the culture have you? Do you have a religion? Or does the religion have you? Are you inside or outside your myths? How you answer these questions will largely determine how you compare myths and religions. Or don't.

Caught in a Story

One very useful analogy to think with here is the common literary trope of being caught inside a story. A character might realize that he or she is a character in, say, a novel that someone else is writing, as we see, for example, in the film *Stranger than Fiction* (2006). In this film the main protagonist, a man named Harold Crick, hears voices in his head. He thinks he is going crazy, until he seeks counsel with a literature professor named Jules Hilbert. Professor Hilbert suspects the voices that Crick is hearing are actually part of a novel that someone else is writing. He suggests to Crick that it would serve him well to find out what

the genre of the novel is, as his fate might hang on whether it is a tragedy or comedy.

Sometimes these patterns are more extreme in the sense that they appear to enter real life, as we see, for example, in the case of the science fiction writer Philip K. Dick. Dick repeatedly claimed to have met a woman in real life whom he had written into one of his sci-fi novels months before. It is a very odd experience, he confessed, to meet a person whom you thought you had made up. Dick's own firm conviction that we are living in a kind of virtual fiction and that, some day, we may be able to rewrite ourselves was captured beautifully in the film *The Adjustment Bureau* (2011), which was based on his short-story "Adjustment Team."

The film orbits around a mysterious "adjustment team" that controls people's lives according to "the plan," in order to protect them from their own free will, which, we are told, humanity had horribly abused in the slaughters of the twentieth century's two world wars. The protagonist, David Norris, works throughout the film to thwart the plan and to win back a woman named Elise Sellas, with whom he had fallen in love at the very beginning of the story. Eventually he succeeds, and the adjustment team and its chairman are duly impressed. At the very end of the film we watch David and Elise walk away and hear, in the voice of Harry Mitchell, one of the adjustment team, these closing words:

> Most people live life on the path we set for them, too afraid to explore any other. But once in a while people like you come along who knock down all the obstacles we put in your way. People who realize free will is a gift that you'll never know how to use until you fight for it. I think that's the chairman's real plan. That maybe one day we won't write the plan; you will.

That is pure Philip K. Dick. It is also a very good illustration of how the study of one's own cultural and religious myths might lead to a kind of self-awakening outside these plots and plans.

As these films suggest, living in a particular cultural story and *as* a particular mini-story (called the self) and then trying to study them all comparatively, as one whole, can lead to a dizzying sense of the fictional nature of social reality. It can also lead to a profound appreciation for our own, truly immense personal and collective creative powers. Science fiction is fact: we all really are caught in stories called "cultures" and "religions." The stories make all sorts of things possible that would not otherwise be possible. They also provide us with meaning, order, and a basic plotline for our lives. They can be quite wonderful. The problem, of course, is that their plotlines and plans can also lead, inexorably, to drama, conflict, and horrible violence, particularly when they come into conflict with competing plots and plans.

Our problem is Harold Crick's problem and David Norris's problem. Is the novel we are living in a comedy or tragedy? Or, more likely, is it a bit of both? And do we even like "the plan" into which we have been plotted? Comedy or tragedy, most of us consider these stories to be real, even though in actual fact they have been written through collective generational processes that we barely understand, which in turn witness to countless streams of influence, heated debate, and, of course, billions and billions of words stretched out over hundreds and even thousands of years. We are swimming in a boundless sea of words and stories.

Ritual: Acting Out the Story Acting Us

If a myth is a sacred story that founds and grounds a particular world, then **ritual** is the re-enactment of the myth that makes that world come into being. This is accomplished through scripted and repeated actions ("ritual"), usually performed in a culturally prescribed space and time and often by a religious specialist, who performs the myth through this ritual. If myth is the story of religion, ritual is its theatre, and both are aimed at a particular goal, be it an immediate practical one or a future state of salvation.[3] To employ a traditional category, to the extent that myth and ritual are about performing the world, causing some

very specific world to be, the processes of myth and ritual bear a very close resemblance to the practice of magic. Indeed, magical practices can be seen as rather obvious and acute forms of ritual and myth in action.

Or, if we prefer a more modern way of speaking, we might say that both myth and ritual are crucial components of "programming" a people into a particular religious world toward a particular task or goal. It is not enough to talk and tell stories. One has to *act out* those stories, over and over and over (and over) again—through communal performances, costumes, masks, chant and song, music, procession, artistic and architectural representation, the use of incense and special smells, and so on. Only through such sensuous, emotive, and physical means will the myths sink in and come to form the assumptions, values, and moods of a person's community life, often completely below conscious awareness and hence beyond any reasonable challenge.

Obviously, too, there can be no theatre, no effective ritual action without a good story. So ritual needs myth, just as myth needs ritual. We might say that *myth and ritual constitute a single performance aimed at the creative construction of a world to live in and experience as stable, secure, and real.* Scholars have debated endlessly which came first: the myth or the ritual. Once again, we can seldom, if ever, get back far enough in time to answer this "genetic question"— that is, the question of origins.[4] One thing is very clear, however: myths and rituals often become deeply intertwined and come to explain and reinforce each other.

The Study of Ritual

We have already seen that the comparative study of myth is only a little over two hundred years old. The comparative study of ritual is younger still. As Jan Bremmer has pointed out, the category of ritual as repeated symbolic behavior is a little over a century old. It was not until the 1890s that the term "ritual" began to be used in this broad comparativist manner.

Before that, it would have been associated with specific rituals, like the Roman Catholic mass or the ancient Indian sacrifices of the Rig Veda.[5] When it comes to theorizing about ritual in the twentieth century, probably no set of cultures has been more generative than African indigenous cultures. If Greek culture was the long background to the development of comparative mythology, African indigenous cultures were the most fruitful generators of theories about ritual—including Victor Turner's reflections on the liminal stage of initiation rituals, around which we have formed the present textbook.

It should be immediately added that there are at least two senses of ritual: a weak and a strong sense. The weak sense of ritual encompasses virtually all of human social behavior, taken as a coded and scripted set of actions that serve particular social and psychological functions. Here something like a baseball game is clearly a ritual: a set of coded behaviors of colorfully and bizarrely costumed men, with city totems no less, following very precise and very repetitive rules, in a marked-off space and time. So too is a handshake, a college graduation, a laboratory experiment, a commuting journey to work, a dance club, the naming of a child, or, well, just about anything else you can imagine doing in a public space. Perhaps only basic bodily functions, like breathing or farting, could be understood as lying entirely outside the realm of ritual, but even these are often disciplined by social norms and provided with specific cultural meanings. Believe it or not, both also enter the realm of myth.

The strong sense of ritual requires something else: an invocation of superhuman powers and a fundamental orientation toward an order of reality and an eventual state of salvation that transcends the social world and its material and pragmatic needs. We are employing the term *ritual* primarily, but by no means exclusively, in this second strong sense.

Like myth, ritual does not have a good name in the modern West, but for different historical reasons. In the case of ritual, it is mostly because of the Protestant Reformation, which repudiated and condemned Roman Catholic ritual in the sixteenth century as something dead, superstitious, repetitive, meaningless, pagan, decadently ornate, and so on. Today, then, conditioned as one is—like much of western culture—by these Protestant values, one often assumes that ritual is unimportant or irrelevant. In fact ritual lies at the center and core of any living religion, even if this religion claims to repudiate ritual. No religion can live without ritual of some kind—and this applies to all the Protestant traditions.

Nor, for that matter, can any secular society. Consider again the example of the modern seven-day week. It is not the case that we naturally experience the world in seven-day cycles and then ritualize that natural experience. Not at all. It is rather that the ritual of the seven-day cycle actually *produces* our experience of the flow of time and the different emotional and cultural nuances of the work week. Hence "Monday" feels very differently from "Friday," which we experience differently again from "Sunday," and so on. The ritual precedes the experience, shapes it, creates it, determines it.

Myth–Ritual Complexes in Three Monotheisms

Some concrete examples would be helpful at this point. For the sake of illustration, let us take the three western monotheisms and isolate three major myth–ritual complexes.

1   *Judaism*   There are many sacred stories within Judaism, of course, but a case could be made that the story of the Exodus is primary. The exodus is the story, related in the biblical book of the same name, of how the ancient Hebrews, under the leadership of the prophet Moses, were liberated from the slavery imposed on them by the Egyptians. Here we have the famous stories of the calling of Moses, the ten plagues, the parting of the Red Sea, and so on. These are great stories, for sure, but they probably would not have survived down into the present, not at least in any

living form, had they not been codified in ritual very early on and re-enacted each spring through the elaborate set of rituals that constitute the Jewish celebration of Passover. At the center of the Passover rituals is the *seder* meal, during which Jewish families and communities remember, through a series of scripted questions, answers, prayers, and pious acts, their ancient ancestors' dramatic escape from Egypt. Myth and ritual mirror each other almost perfectly here, and each reinforces the other in order to form a special community and a sense of solidarity over the generations.

2   *Christianity*   So too with Christianity. Here the central story is that of the death and resurrection of Jesus. Historically speaking, the Jewish preacher named Jesus was executed by the Roman state within the Jewish Passover cycle, probably on the Friday immediately after the *seder* meal, which, if we are to believe the scriptural accounts, Jesus consciously and creatively re-deployed as a ritual means to encourage his disciples to "remember" him. The early followers of Jesus, who, like him, were Jews and therefore very familiar with the Passover meal and its meanings, did just this; but they now attached new meanings to the ancient Jewish ritual (this, by the way, is a very common strategy of new religions—they adopt the inherited myths and rituals of their culture, but change their meaning). As numerous "gentiles" were converted to the new religious movement, this process was accelerated and eventually the Jewish Passover meal was transformed into the Christian Eucharist, which retold and re-enacted not the exodus from Egypt per se, but the death and resurrection of Jesus of Nazareth, now considered to be the Christ or Messiah. In the language of the tradition, the "old covenant" of the Torah and the giving of the Law have been replaced by the "new covenant" of the Gospel and the resurrection of the Christ.

3   *Islam*   Islam displays a special brilliance in the employment of ritual and myth. Getting a billion people to bow down five times a day facing a small

city in Saudi Arabia is an extraordinary ritual accomplishment, which unites peoples across radically different cultures and backgrounds. Not surprisingly, the ritual is a re-enactment of a powerful and defining myth: that of the *miraj* ("heavenly ascent") of the Prophet Muhammad. Like all other sacred stories, that of Muhammad's ascent through the seven heavens to the divine throne is found in a variety of versions, from the earliest sources of the hadith literature (a genre of Islamic literature dedicated to the sayings and deeds of the Prophet) to the oral local traditions preserved and passed down mainly by Sufis or Muslim mystics throughout the centuries. The basic structure of the myth, however, is relatively stable.

Muhammad is taken to Jerusalem by a magical beast, usually depicted as a winged horse named Buraq. From Jerusalem's Dome of the Rock, the Prophet ascends on Buraq through the seven heavens and finally comes before the divine presence. There he is commanded to enjoin his community to perform the prescribed ritual prayer fifty times each day. Descending through the heavens, however, Muhammad comes to the sixth heaven and meets Moses who, upon learning about the fifty prayers, warns the Prophet, on the basis of his own experience with the Israelites, that this is too much of a burden. Moses persuades Muhammad to go back and negotiate a lighter deal. So Muhammad returns and successfully gets the number reduced to forty-five. Moses is not impressed. The story continues with Muhammad going back and forth between God's throne and the sixth heaven, until the number of prayers drops down to just five. For Moses this is still too much, but Muhammad is too embarrassed to go back yet again, and so that is where it ends (see Figure 4.1).

From a historical perspective, the myth is fascinating, as it suggests that early Muslim identity was formed through a significant conversation with Judaism, here symbolized by the continual back-and-forth between Muhammad and Moses, the founding figure of the Jewish tradition. It is also significant that the heavenly ascent begins from

Figure 4.1 *The Prophet Muhammad's Ascent to Heaven* (1584), unknown artist. Folio from a manuscript of the Khamsa (Iskandarnama) by Nizami. Ink opaque watercolor and gold on paper, 39.5 × 26.2 cm (15 9/16″ × 10 5/16″). Harvard Art Museums/Arthur M. Sackler Museum. The Norma Jean Calderwood Collection of Islamic Art. 2001.50.33. Photo: Imaging Department © President and Fellows of Harvard College.

Jerusalem, which at that point in time had been understood for well over a thousand years in the Jewish tradition to be the earthly equivalent of God's throne in heaven. And indeed, in point of geographical direction, the Muslim prayers were originally set toward Jerusalem, not toward Mecca. The direction only shifted to Mecca later, in the aftermath of Muhammad's disillusionment with the Jewish tribes of Medina on account of their refusal to accept his new revelation. So not only does the central Muslim ritual of praying five times a day re-enact the myth of the *miraj*; it also encodes Islam's early indebtedness to Judaism (the centrality of Jerusalem) and subsequent break with it (the shift to Mecca). The myth, in short, likely encodes actual historical events.

Ritual Intention?

Whether or not a particular ritual complex is meaningful to an individual will depend largely on whether or not that individual accepts the basic story and is willing to perform it. There is an important qualification to make here, though; for ritual can do its work with or without the presence of personal belief. That is, getting a community together in order to perform a series of scripted ritual acts around a central sacred story can build and sustain a world with or without the belief of this or that community member. Complete consensus is simply not necessary (not to mention impossible), and private opinions are, in some real sense, irrelevant. What counts is the shared public religious act, repeated over and over again. What counts is the ritual.

Patterns in Myth

There are some well-established comparative patterns when it comes to the subjects of myth and ritual. With respect to the subject of myth, the patterns are nearly inexhaustible. In a related subject, that of comparative folklore, for example, in one classic index of folklore themes—Stith Thompson's six-volume *Motif-Index of Folklore Literature*—we find an elaborate mapping of over 2,400 plots! Obviously this kind of detail lies well outside our purposes. For the sake of discussion, then, let us isolate—this now sounds ridiculously simplistic—just three types of myth found throughout the world: (1) creation myths; (2) hero or quest myths; and (3) trickster myths. We will examine a fourth in our comparative

practice: founding myths, which are very much related to hero or quest myths.

Creation Myths

Arguably the most important myths in any religious system are its **creation myths**, that is, its sacred stories about how the world and/or human beings came to be. Creation myths are especially important, because they tend to express not only how the world came to be, but also what the proper place of human beings is in a world that came to be like this. Put technically, creation myths are not just descriptive; they are also prescriptive. They do not just explain how the world *is*. They imply or declare how the world *should be*. This is why creation myths, far from being some kind of objective or scientific snapshot at the beginning of time, display a very strong tendency to "slip in" all sorts of cultural values and activities that are specific to the particular culture telling this particular story (see Figure 4.2).

So, for example, in the first creation myth of ancient Israel as recorded in the first lines of Genesis, God creates the world in six days and rests on the seventh in order to model the seven-day cycle of the ancient Israelites and, perhaps most of all, the Sabbath (literally, rest or cessation), which the temple priests controlled and defined as holy. God honors the priests and the priests honor God, and so everyone else should honor both God and the priests. Or, no doubt more closely to the self-representation of the ancient priests, the priests honor the Sabbath and render it holy because it was on this day that God rested after creating the cosmos. In any case, the priestly ritual cycle mirrors and follows the creation myth, just as the myth undergirds and justifies the priestly ritual cycle. Each supports and justifies the other.

So too with the famous creation myth or "Hymn of Man" (*purusha-sukta*) in the Rig Veda (1200–900 BCE), the ancient scriptural text of what would later become Hinduism. Here a cosmic giant, called simply "the Man" (*purusha*), is described as both

Figure 4.2   A re-enactment of the Dogon people's creation story, Mali. © Amar Grover/Getty Images.

being the entire material cosmos and extending beyond it. In short, a cosmotheism. Hence the physical universe is the Man's body, and yet he is also immortal and more. Indeed, he is mostly more. We might say that the Man is both "immanent" in (and as) the physical universe and "transcendent" to it by being above or beyond it. Hence the opening verses, which can be read as pointing either to a Being that inhabits all limbed creatures or to a stunning many-headed, many-eyed, many-limbed superhuman, who will (much later) become the many-limbed deities of classical Hinduism:

> The Man has a thousand heads, a thousand eyes, a thousand feet. He pervaded the earth on all sides and extended beyond it as far as ten fingers. It is the Man who is all this, whatever has been and whatever is to be. He is the ruler of immortality, when he grows beyond everything through food. Such is his greatness, and the Man is yet more than this. All creatures are a

quarter of him; three quarters are what is immortal in heaven.

The gods then create the physical universe and the social world, both together, by sacrificing and dismembering this cosmic Man:

> When they divided the Man, into how many parts did they apportion him? What do they call his mouth, his two arms and thighs and feet? His mouth became the Brahmin [the priest]; his arms were made into the Warrior, his thighs the People, and from his feet the Servants were born. The moon was born from his mind; from his eye the sun was born. [The gods] Indra and Agni came from his mouth, and from his vital breath the Wind was born. From his navel the middle realm of space arose; from his head the sky evolved. From his two feet came the earth, and the quarters of the sky from his ear. Thus they set the worlds in order.[6]

What we have here, then, is a vision of human nature that is both cosmic, indeed divine, and linked to, indeed identified with, a very specific and very local social system, in this case an early form of the caste system and its four major divisions. Thus the Man's feet become the servant class; his thighs the merchant class ("the People" of the hymn); his arms the warrior class; and his head the priestly class. Like the seven-day priestly cycle of the Jewish creation myth, this early Indian creation myth both expresses and justifies a particular social system. It is not difficult to guess who probably wrote, preserved, and passed on this myth as sacred, and why: the people "at the top"—that is, once again, the priests.

If we look at different cultures, we find, of course, different concerns and social structures. Indigenous or tribal cultures, for example, know nothing of and care nothing for a seven-day priestly cycle or a four-fold caste system. Why should they? Their communities are often much smaller and do not require such elaborate classificatory schemes and social divisions. We find instead myths that reflect *their* experience of the world and of community life. We find stories about the lunar and the solar cycle, about people growing out of the earth like maize, and about a sky-father and an earth-mother.

The symbolic codes range widely in creation myths, but sexual intercourse (with a frequent reference to incest, since the original god was alone and had to create his partner from himself) and maternal birth, eggs, and plant growth are all especially popular modes. We also often notice that the creator god tends to be a **sky god**, that is, a male deity who lives "up above," in the heavens. This is what helped form the various theologies of **transcendence**—that is, those models that place divinity outside or beyond the world, as opposed to theologies of **immanence**, which place divinity in the world, or even identify it with the world.

Hero or Quest Myths

Is it significant that one of the oldest pieces of world literature, perhaps *the* oldest, is a hero myth? Already in the Sumerian *Epic of Gilgamesh* (very roughly, 2100–1000 BCE), we see what will become the classic plotline of **hero or quest myths**: departure from home, adventure in a foreign land or separate world, temptation, battle with a monster or adversary, discovery of some new revelation or secret knowledge, and return home in order to establish some new tradition or cultural innovation. In Gilgamesh's case, the hero fails to acquire the revelation sought after—the secret of immortality; but he returns nonetheless to rule over his people, a wiser man.

As a side note, comparison has played a key role in the modern deciphering and discussion of the *Epic of Gilgamesh*. The results have been provocative, to say the least. Here, after all, we encounter some clear parallels with both the (likely later) Adam and Eve story, complete with a snake as antagonist, and the biblical flood story. The parallels between the Mesopotamian epic and the biblical flood narrative (Genesis 6–8) are particularly striking: the Hebrew story follows the earlier Mesopotamian epic point by point, complete with a Noah character (named Utnapishtim), a released dove, and so on.

Although hero myths had been well studied and mapped out by figures like the Austrian psychoanalyst Otto Rank and the Russian folklorist Vladimir Propp in the early part of the twentieth century, this particular mythical pattern is most often associated with the popular work of the American writer Joseph Campbell. Popular assumptions aside, Campbell's approach to comparative mythology traveled straight through the body. Most fundamentally, he saw mythology as an expression of human biology.[7] More particularly, in his thinking, the mythology of the hero's journey follows the developmental paths of male sexuality. It's a male myth. Mythological language was, for Campbell, the male body talking. And one way the male body talks is through stories about a hero's journey, or quest tales. Here is how Campbell himself described the pattern: "*A hero ventures forth from the world of common day into a region of supernatural wonder: fabulous forces are there encountered and a decisive victory is won: the hero comes back from his mysterious adventure with the power to bestow boons on his fellow man.*"[8]

One of the most interesting aspects of Campbell's writing on the hero's journey is how it came to inform contemporary popular culture. Campbell's books and charismatic speaking style were deeply influential on cultural phenomena ranging from the human potential movement and a popular New Age aphorism ("Follow your bliss") to George Lucas's *Star Wars* movies and the general culture of Hollywood screenwriters. Lucas in particular modeled many of his plot narratives on the comparativist's ideas. He called Campbell "my Yoda."

Trickster Myths

My father used to tell me when I was a boy (he was a car mechanic at that time) that anything put together can also be taken apart, and the more parts something has, the more likely it will fall apart. He was thinking of things like car engines, transistor radios, and ten-speed bicycles, with that crazy chain traveling back and forth over all those exposed gears. The same is true of cultural systems and religious worlds.

Human beings everywhere are smart, and they often intuit this truth. They often understand that their worlds are composed of many parts and have lots of gears and that all this can be manipulated: the subsystems can be set against one another and the whole thing can be taken apart, either temporarily or permanently. We saw this already with Victor Turner's notion of the liminal stage of an initiation ritual, where the taking apart is performed through a ritual oriented toward the creation of a new social identity. We will see another form of this "taking apart" below, in Chapter 6, when we arrive at the explosive subject of transgression and sexuality. But there are still other religious ways to take apart a world. It can also be done through myth.

Such myths, in effect, see through the arbitrariness and relativity of the culture's claims to represent the way things really are. Accordingly, they encourage their listeners to understand themselves as cultural actors and to realize, well, *that they are acting* (or being acted upon), and that so is everyone else. It should not surprise us, then, that many mythical systems feature a set of stories or a set of characters that scholars have come to call "the trickster." The **trickster** is a mythical

Figure 4.3   Staff used by Yoruba peoples (Oyo subgroup), Nigeria, for the Worship of Esu/Elegba, *Ogo Elegba*, before 1930s (?). Wood, leather, cowrie shells, brass, bone, iron; H 19 1/4 in. (50.7 cm); Raymond and Laura Wielgus Collection; Indiana University Art Museum, 87.42.2. Photographed by Michael Cavanaugh and Kevin Montague.

character, variously named and imagined, of course, who through different comedic, ridiculous, violent, deceitful, and offensive behaviors upsets the established order and mocks the sacred and the right in order to renew, reform, and loosen up the system … or just to have fun. In a classic study of the trickster in West Africa, Robert D. Pelton has described this figure as "the transforming power of the imagination as it pokes at, plays with, delights in, and shatters what seems to be until it becomes what is."[9] (See Figure 4.3.)

These are poetic terms to be sure, but they point to a most basic universal human ability: the ability to step out of one's own cultural system, play with its codes and terms, and reassemble them in upside-down, contrary, and even ridiculous ways in order to demonstrate their arbitrariness and assert one's own final freedom from them. Put more simply, the trickster is a mythical embodiment of that human ability to laugh at, and thus to transcend, one's own most cherished beliefs and assumptions. Humor is holy here.

And the dirtier the humor, the better. "Legba everywhere dances in the manner of a man copulating," as the West African Fon say. Time itself sometimes falls before such a transcendent humor: "Eshu threw a stone yesterday; he killed a bird today," goes the Yoruba proverb.[10] In the North American Winnebago version, Wakdjunkaga, in the words of Lawrence Sullivan, "scatters all living creatures across the face of the earth with an enormous fart, which leaves them laughing, yelling, and barking." Sullivan goes on: "bodily functions and features are extreme: voracious appetite, insatiable lust, stupendous excretions, cosmic flatulence. … His head may be fastened to his bottom, or his penis to his back. … He craves modes of being other than his own: animal, plant, and so on." Both Pelton and Sullivan see *irony*, that is, a kind of intended and instructional duplicity, as one of the key messages of the trickster figure. Indeed the trickster myths are so deeply ironic that it is often impossible to say whether their protagonist is simply stupid or is pretending to be stupid for the sake of a deeper wisdom, beyond the illusions of the senses and the absurdities of religious certainty.[11]

More recently, Harold Scheub has made a case for considering both the trickster myth and the hero myth as related types. Both figures are about transition, about change, about movement from one state to another. In short, they are both about the liminal: "In the trickster and hero, all is change, transformation."[12] The emphases are different, of course. If the expertise of the trickster lies in taking things apart, in creating chaos, the hero is called upon to engage with this chaos and destruction directly, to refocus the creative energies through a particular vision and so to help put things back together again, hopefully in a new and more functional form: "The hero is a product of the old society, but he is making the movement to the new. … The hero is to be defined as the precursor and the carrier of social change."[13]

This is often true in secular contexts as well. And so, in modern American superhero mythologies, for example, we see these figures appearing a few years before the USA enters World War II (Superman initiates the genre in June of 1938) and then exploding in patriotic characters like Superman (again) and Captain America. The latter is actually punching Adolf Hitler on the cover of his first appearance in March 1941, just a few months before the USA entered the European theatre (which happened after the Japanese bombing of Pearl Harbor). When the world war ends, the superhero genre dips and declines, until it is revived again in another major American transitional moment—the 1960s counterculture. The trickster and the hero, then, help communities deal with historical and cultural transitions. They help people change by modeling the destruction and re-creation that are central to human life and human history.

Trickster myths are extremely common in human cultures. Scheub lists 191 different trickster figures, and his is a partial list. The trickster is often played by an animal, the hare or rabbit, jackal, hyena, coyote, monkey, spider, and fox appearing the most often.

Although trickster myths may seem relatively foreign to most western readers, western cultures do possess two fairly central secular institutions that serve a trickster-like function: the professional comedian and the political cartoonist. Comedians and cartoonists, after all, can say and do things that, say, a politician, an administrator, or a business leader could never say or do. Basically, western cultures have decided to carve out a space in their public discourse where their most central institutions and their most powerful figures can be exposed to some harsh criticism. By making fun of their own institutions, policies, and leaders, modern comedians and cartoonists serve a crucial function: they get their listeners to step out of their assumptions for a moment in order to look at their worldviews in a more honest and objective light. They are tricksters.

Patterns in Ritual

As in myth, in ritual too patterns are especially complex. We encounter, for example, **liturgical rituals** (designed to worship or honor a particular deity or founder), magical rituals (designed to manipulate the workings of the natural world, usually for some desired human good), **funerary rituals** (around death, burial, cremation, or some other method of handling the corpse), invocation or intercessory rituals (like prayer), healing rituals, exorcism rituals, seasonal rituals (like the New Year), **libation rituals** (in which some valuable liquid is poured over an image or before an altar), **pilgrimage rituals** (trips or travels to a place held to be sacred), and so on. Here, for the sake of brevity, we briefly treat just four: life-cycle rituals; civil religion rituals; rituals of sacrifice; and divination rituals.

Life-Cycle Rituals

We have already encountered one classical ritual pattern in our discussion of initiation rituals or rites of passage in Chapter 3. The vision quest of the boy about to become John Fire Lame Deer, the medicine man, is an excellent example.

These initiation rituals are usually treated under the more general rubric of **life-cycle rituals**, that is, rituals that tend to occur within different religious systems during marked biological events: pregnancy and birth, circumcision (in the Jewish and Muslim traditions), the naming of a child (as in the Hindu *namakarana* or "naming" ceremony), food production activities upon which a community depends (like a major hunt, or planting and harvesting during the agricultural seasons), times of calamity or danger (war, natural disaster, the depth of winter, draught), puberty or adolescence (as in the bar mitzvah and bat mitzvah celebrations of Judaism), marriage, and, of course, death.

Life-cycle rituals perform many functions, but two stand out as primary. First, they often both mark and effect some major change in the social status of the person undergoing the ritual. So, for example, a girl is no longer a girl when she has her first menstrual period. Through ritual means, themselves responding to dramatic biological changes, she is now recognized by the community as a woman. Similarly, the status and privileges of a young man and woman who have just gone through a marriage ritual alter their social identities dramatically. They are now expected to behave differently, take on further responsibilities, and bear children.

The second function of at least some life-cycle rituals involves the restoration of order and meaning after these have been disrupted or temporarily suspended. Death rituals are an obvious example here. A death always disrupts a community. The suddenness, brutality, and pure goriness of death often punch huge holes in a people's sense of security and safety. Hence a whole spectrum of rituals can follow: wakes, funerals, and memorials; bathing, burying, or burning the body in carefully controlled and scripted ways; and speeches, sermons, conversation, meals, and memory sharing. Clearly, funerary rituals are for the living, not for the dead.

Civil Religion Rituals

It is a well known feature of many ancient religions that the pre-eminent religious specialist was often the king. The sacred king stood in for and represented the community before the gods or God. He might possess secret ritual knowledge or secret texts that only he could read. When he died, he was often immortalized as a god. The gods, moreover, were often imagined and worshipped as a kind of royal court, with a king. Laws were believed to be given by the gods. The political structure of the heavens thus mirrored the political structure of the community: as

Figure 4.4   Fireworks on the Birds Nest National Stadium, opening ceremony, 2008 Olympic Games, Beijing, China. © Christian Kober/Robert Harding World Imagery/Corbis.

on earth, so in heaven. There simply was no clear division between the religious and the political. They were two divisions or expressions of the same political cosmos.

Our modern world, of course, has more or less gotten rid of its kings. Monarchy does not sit well with modern notions of democracy, liberty, and individual freedoms. So our political leaders are no longer generally sacred kings, and we have separated out "religion" from the "state"—again, more or less. But this does not mean that modern political life and institutions are devoid of sacral themes. Quite the contrary. The sacred king lives on—dethroned perhaps, but still there—in what scholars have come to call "civil religion" (see Figure 4.4).

Rituals do not simply construct religious identity and restore order to a community of faith. They also construct cultural identities and restore order to the life of a nation, city, or village. Accordingly, there are numerous civil or secular rituals that remain secular enough but also have vague religious or transcendent undertones. These are often studied under the rubric of civil religion, which was first introduced by the American sociologist of religion Robert N. Bellah in 1961. Scholars who use this expression generally mean to refer to the way in which modern secular or civil authorities employ traditionally religious means—like myth, ritual, and symbol—to create order, provide a sense of stability, and leave the impression that this is "the way things really are." One can read all these religious means as rituals in the weak sense, to the extent that they often lack a clear transcendent reference; but one can also often read them as rituals in the strong sense, since **civil religion rituals** often imply a connection, or even an identity, between the political order and the sacred order.

These civil ritual mechanisms are so powerful in the case of the modern nation-state that large segments of any given population feel what amounts to a kind of piety or devotion to entirely secular symbols, like a flag, a national story, a military battle, a founding figure, a memorial, or an imaginary line in the ground or in the middle of a flowing river—a line called a "national border." Indeed many nation-states go further and explicitly link these secular symbols to religious symbols, as if to suggest that the sacred order of reality has chosen or deigned to privilege *this* particular political arrangement or polity: one nation "under God," as the American Pledge of Allegiance has had it since 1954 (yes, it is that recent). Similar, if not identical statements can be found, of course, in countless other countries and their civil religious practices.

"Get down on your knees." Quick. What does that expression call up for you? What is the first thing that comes to your mind? You may have thought: "This is a call to prayer. He is asking for an act of piety." You may have just as well thought: "This is a threat. He is demanding an act of submission." You would be correct with either response. Both, after all, find deep support in the history of religious and political symbolism, and this for one simple reason: religion and monarchy have shared a similar set of myths and rituals for millennia.

Judaism, for example, is filled with references to God as "Lord" and "King." Biblical angels, far from being the cute effeminate figures of the child's bedroom, were understood to be warriors and army scouts of an invading or ruling king. Christians, moreover, may not realize it, but when they fold their hands and get down on their knees to pray, they are re-enacting ancient submission rituals to powerful kings and monarchs, who wielded tremendous (and, to our modern democratic sensibilities, entirely excessive) power over their political subjects. Although such acts possess clear precedents in both the Torah and the New Testament (since Israel was itself a monarchy at one time), this was not always the common posture of Christian prayer. The earliest textual, archaeological, and artistic evidence often represents Christians standing in prayer, with the elbows bent, the hands outstretched to the side, and the palms

up. This is sometimes called the *orans* ("praying") position.

Bodily acts of political and religious submission are not, of course, restricted to Judaism and Christianity. Many of the theistic traditions of Hinduism approach their chosen deities or their human spiritual teachers (gurus) as divine royalty, with all the recognizable hierarchies and postures of submission. Similarly, the different traditions of Buddhism often feature, as one of their central ritual prescriptions, the performance of bodily prostrations of various types and numbers. In some forms of Tibetan Buddhism, this is taken to great extremes: so for example in some forms of Buddhist Tantra, the aspiring practitioner is required to do up to one hundred thousand such prostrations.

In an entirely different religious context, the central act of Muslim piety is the full-body bow during daily prayer, and "Islam" is literally derived from the Arabic word for "submission."

Related to the latter point is a very old dispute between the Shi'i perspective and the majority Sunni view regarding the proper bodily gesture in prayers. The debate beautifully demonstrates this conflation of politics and piety. The Shiites oppose the practice of crossing the hands when standing for prayers, which is observed by most Sunni communities, on the grounds that one of the early caliphs introduced this innovation from a Persian political practice. The story goes like this. After the conquest of Persia by the Arab army, some Persian captives were brought to the second caliph. The captives stood in front of him crossing their hands. When he asked why they did this, they replied that it was customary for Persians to express their reverence for their kings with such a gesture. The caliph was very impressed and thought it would be a good idea to do the same while standing in front of God in prayer. We, of course, do not know whether this actually happened. That is hardly the point. The story clearly reflects the fact that some aspects of the mainstream Sunni practice of prayer were perceived, from outside that practice, to be a fusion of political submission and religious piety.

We could go through the other religions and find very similar conflations of piety and politics. What we would find in case after case is that the central religious rituals of prayer and worship are often modeled, quite directly, on a particular example of political authority: the absolute power of a king.

Which is all to say that constructing a world through myth and ritual inevitably involves real-world political processes, and that religious structures often mirror political structures and vice versa. As on the topic of civil religion, here too more difficult questions are lurking or are implied—like why modern peoples who are allegedly committed to the political arrangement of democracy continue to embody religious behaviors clearly modeled on the outdated and broadly rejected structures of monarchy. There is a Tough Question, if ever there was one.

Rituals of Sacrifice

The English word sacrifice derives from the Latin word family *sacrificium/sacrificari/sacrificare*, which in turn fuses a locution that meant "to make holy, to sanctify" (*sacrum facere*). That which is sacrificed is made holy or sacred. And the means of making something holy usually involves some act of either actual or symbolic violence. This is why by rituals of **sacrifice** scholars often mean **blood sacrifice**, that is, rituals in which some animal (or human being) is killed in a religious context, for a particular, sacred purpose, on the understanding that the "life" of the sacrificed being resides in the blood.

Human sacrifice is relatively rare in the historical record, but there are hints of it, for example in the biblical world (so the famous story of God commanding Abraham to sacrifice his son Isaac and then telling him to stop, which many scholars read as a sign of the Hebrews moving away from a practice common at the time), or in Hindu mythology and iconography (where, for example, decapitated heads are fairly common). It was certainly practiced in the history of Mesoamerican religions, as a culture like that of the Aztecs illustrates.

There are certainly other types of sacrifice—grain and vegetable sacrifices, fluid or libation sacrifices, and so on; but many scholars believe that these vegetable and fluid sacrifices are later "substitutes" for what was originally a blood sacrifice. It is, without doubt, the blood sacrifice that has received most attention in the scholarly literature, both because of this "substitution theory" and because its near universality poses some stark, obvious, and morally difficult questions: Why do people kill for religious purposes? Why do we find deadly violence at the very heart of so many religious systems? And, more speculatively now, is this ancient and widely distributed practice of blood sacrifice somehow connected to the fact that religion and violence are linked in our own modern world?

For now it is enough simply to note that many answers have been given to these honest questions, and that each answer functions as a beginning point for a different theory of sacrifice. Here we note only two such theories, which we might call the gift and scapegoat models.

1   *The Gift or Exchange Model*   Probably the most accepted model of sacrifice has been the **gift model of sacrifice** (or the exchange model). It was most famously advanced in the early twentieth century by the French sociologist Marcel Mauss in a book entitled, appropriately enough, *The Gift* (1923). Mauss noted that sacrifice often functions as a "gift" to the deity or the ancestors, a gift that, like all human gifts, sets up a reciprocal relationship, and hence a future response from the one so gifted. This gift model is sometimes captured in the Latin phrase *do ut des*, which translates as "I give so that you might give."

This is an especially powerful model of ritual sacrifice, with wide application and sometimes surprising implications. We might note here, for example, that, although all three major monotheistic religions—Judaism, Christianity, and Islam—hold up the willingness to sacrifice a human being as the model of faith (in the case of Judaism, Abraham's willingness to sacrifice Isaac; in the case of Islam,

Abraham's willingness to sacrifice Ishmael), only one major world religion carries out an actual human sacrifice as a reciprocal gift: Christianity.

Finally, before we leave the theme of the sacrifice as gift, we might note that, behind the motif of the gift, there often lies the deeper and more basic motif of *feeding*. One is not just giving to the god or to the dead, after all. One is feeding them. Often, but by no means always, the means of getting food through to the gods or ancestors is fire: one burns it.

2   *The Scapegoat Model*   Related to the gift model is the **scapegoat model of sacrifice**. This is an extremely old human practice. We have textual evidence for it that goes back as far as the thirteenth century BCE, in a Hittite text in which a man named Ashella describes how some army commanders deal with a disease spreading in their midst: they choose some rams, which are decorated and then tied to the main tents, with this prayer: "Whatever deity is prowling about, whatever deity has caused this pestilence, now I have tied up these rams for you, be appeased!" In the morning, Ashella drives the rams out into the desert, along with some beer, bread, and milk. Another, similar ritual involves rams, upon which the officers of the army place their hands, beer, and bread again, and a finely dressed woman, this time placed in front of the king's tent. Ashella goes on:

> And the officers point at the rams and the king points at the decorated woman, and the rams and the woman carry the loaves and the beer through the army and they chase them out to the plain. And they go running on to the enemy's frontier without coming to any place of ours …"[14]

The logic behind these ancient rituals is a very simple one, and it can be paraphrased like this: "Oh god, instead of eating us, please eat these rams and this food, or this woman." Note, though, that the practice does not necessarily or literally lead to the death of either the rams or the woman. It is in fact not at all clear whether they die in the desert or are killed by the enemy (and all that beer and bread would come in very handy). Certainly the rams, the food, and the woman are meant as substitutes for the community, but the community cannot bring itself to kill them outright, so it sends them out of sight, presumably to die or be killed. They thus become, as we say, "scapegoats." Or scape-rams and a scape-woman in this case.

The English word "scapegoat" almost certainly comes from the biblical version of this ancient Near Eastern practice, which preceded the Bible by many centuries. In Leviticus 16 we encounter the description of a major annual ritual called "the Day of Atonement." Here we see the high priest of the Israelites, a man named Aaron, selecting two goats and, by means of a lottery, assigning them to the Israelite god Yahweh and to a figure named Azazel—perhaps another deity, perhaps a demon. Aaron then puts his hands on the goat and transfers the impurity or pollution of the Israelites onto it. The goat is then driven out into the desert, again presumably to die. Jan Bremmer performs for us a model comparison of Hittite and Israelite practices. Notice how he expertly balances sameness and difference:

> It is not difficult to see the parallels between the Hittite and Israelite rituals. Yet at the same time, we also notice that the Israelites appropriated the ritual into their own sacrificial, theological, and calendric systems. The ritual is now supervised by the high priest, not the king; the object to be removed no longer is pestilence or another illness, but the sins of the people; the victim is only an animal, since the Israelites did not sacrifice adult humans; the mention of YHWH [Yahweh] *and* Azazel seems to point to the earlier polytheism of the Israelites; and, last but not least, the occasion is not an incidental event, such as a pestilence, but the ritual instead is attached to a fixed point in the religious year.[15]

Similar scapegoat rituals were performed in ancient Athens as well, where two male scapegoats were led out of the city, one to purify the men, one to purify the women. These were often selected from the low classes or from the large slave population.

Divination Rituals

The Greek historian Herodotus tells the story of Croesus, the king of Lydia. Croesus was trying to decide whether to invade the Persian Empire, one of the superpowers of the time. He decides to test the major **oracles** (we would now say "psychics") of the Mediterranean world to get help with this important military decision. More specifically, he sends out envoys and instructs them to ask the oracles of the different lands what he would be doing one hundred days out from the day he sent the envoys.

And it turns out that, on the one-hundredth day, the king of Lydia does the most unpredictable and specific thing that one can imagine: he boils tortoise and rabbit meat together, in a bronze cauldron with a bronze lid no less. Only two of the oracles could describe in sufficient detail what he was doing. One was the famous oracle of the god Apollo at Delphi. There a celibate woman, the Pythia, sat on a three-legged stool wearing a crown of laurels (Apollo's symbol) and uttered Apollo's answers at the request of inquirers who came to the sacred site. Croesus sent gifts to the two oracles that passed his test, but he put his real money on the prestigious Delphic oracle. Apollo subsequently informed him through the oracle that, if he did attack, "a great empire will fall." And so Croesus, very pleased by this information, mounted an expedition and invaded Persia.

But Croesus had not learnt the lesson of the trickster, including the tricks of oracles and psychics. Apollo's "prediction," after all, was a sure bet: if Croesus attacked, one empire would win and one would lose, hence, whatever the outcome, "a great empire will fall." The "great empire" of Apollo's prediction turned out to be Croesus' own Lydian empire, not that of the Persians. Croesus attacked and lost. He soon found himself standing before the king of Persia, on a pyre about to be lit. Croesus, alas, had "interpreted religion" wrongly, and he was now about to pay for this mistake with his life.

But this was not the end of the story. As the flames licked around his royal captive, Cyrus engaged Croesus in a debate on the meaning of happiness, of all things. The Persian king was so impressed with what he heard that he ordered the flames to be quenched. But it was too late. The flames were too strong. As the story goes, it took a prayer to Apollo to finally quench the raging fires with a downpour of rain. Cyrus and Croesus became close friends, and Croesus, now as Cyrus' advisor, helped extend the Persian Empire into much of the Mediterranean world. Ironically, none of this would have happened had not Croesus misinterpreted the original oracle. Sometimes mistakes, too, are providential.

There are many lessons to learn from this story: from the central importance of oracles and clairvoyants for military strategy in human history, through the inherent ambiguity of psychical phenomena and the prominence of "religious comparison shopping" in human history (which was as evident in the ancient world as it is our own), to the possibility of empirically "testing" oracular abilities and to the central role of empire in spreading a cosmopolitan spirit.[16] But only one feature of the story will capture our attention here: the nature, uses, and interpretation of divination.

Divination is a comparativist category that tries to capture both spontaneous, visionary, and dream-like phenomena and established ritual practices that attempt to intuit, predict, or fathom the future, usually to some practical end or decision. Such practices are distributed across the globe and throughout history and are known in countless forms.

Sometimes distinctions are drawn here between different types of divination. Very generally speaking, **prophecy** involves altered states of consciousness and is concerned with predicting or projecting future events: "prophecy," "prophet" and related words derive from the ancient Greek noun *prophētēs*, which meant "advocate," one who speaks (*phanai*) for (*pro-*) another, usually for a god—although, as we shall see, prophets often function as critics of political figures and their policies. Oracles are particular kinds of prophetic utterances, usually spoken through an established medium at the request of an inquirer. Finally, **omens** are signs detected spontaneously in nature or in a formal ritual context that signal something usually negative about to happen, if the appropriate actions are not taken. As the latter example makes clear, in ancient religious cultures fate and the future are seldom considered ironclad. They can be intuited or seen. They can be avoided. Hence the central importance and proliferation of divination rituals.

Like most other comparative categories, that of divination has had a difficult history, mostly because of Christian convictions and missionary concerns that equated it with sorcery, demons, and black magic. Christianity's demonic reading of divination goes back at least as far as Augustine of Hippo who, ironically, used a bit of divination himself—namely the interpretation of random children's voices, a traditional means of divination—in his famous conversion to Christianity. "Take up and read!" he heard some children playing in a garden say. And so he did: he read a Pauline letter and was converted on the spot.

The Christians hardly invented the demonic interpretation of divination, though. Further back still, this historical resistance to divination can be located in the Torah's various condemnations of Canaanite divination practices, even though the Torah, like the New Testament, is itself filled with divination practices: for example Joseph wins renown for his ability to interpret dreams, and then there is the entire Israelite institution of prophecy. Divination has hardly fared any better among secular interpreters, who have tended to dismiss it outright, as a reprehensible form of irrationalism, superstition, and wishful thinking. Colonial arrogance, western ethnocentrism, and scientific rationalism have also played central roles here.

Not so in Asia and in many of its religions. Consider the *Yijing* (a title sometimes transcribed into English as *I Ching* and translated as *The Classic of Changes*). The *Yijing* is one of the Five Classics (*Wujing*)—foundational texts of Chinese civilization attributed to the philosopher-sage Confucius (551–479 BCE). Indeed the *Changes* is considered to be the first and the greatest of these Five Classics. Much of what we know about the text and its earliest ritual uses can be traced back to the Han dynasty (206 BCE–220 CE), when it was declared a Confucian classic and one if its editions won imperial approval in 136 BCE.

The key point for us here, however, is that the *Yijing* is a divinatory text. Indeed, it is easily the most famous divinatory text in the world. As Richard Smith, the text's biographer, has observed, "for the past two thousand years or so, among all the works in world literature only the Bible has been more widely read and more extensively commented upon than the *Changes*."[17] The bare-bones core of the *Changes* is sixty-four six-line figures or hexagrams. The most common techniques for selecting a hexagram to read and interpret involved throwing coins or using milfoil (yarrow) stalks to build a particular hexagram with its six full or broken lines.

One engages with these hexagrams and the *Changes* through a ritual practice and, often, through a ritual specialist who provides commentary and interpretation, making it all "come alive" and speak in each new context and to each new concern. Historically, those concerns may have revolved around the choice of an appropriate marriage partner, a family crisis, the proper time to plant a field or to begin a new business venture, the hiring or firing of employees, or the likelihood of success on a government civil exam or on a military campaign.

Traditional Chinese commentators on the *Changes* clearly understood the interactive nature of the text and its ritual enactment. The Song scholar Shen Gua, for example, explained why the same divination technique could result in such different readings. "The ability to respond spiritually and make the truth manifest depends on the person," he wrote. Inanimate objects, like the ritual sticks, are necessary, because the human mind, though spiritually inclined, "is unavoidably burdened." "In order to gain access to it," one must "use as a substitute some thing that does not have a mind. The result of divination can only be explained by what makes one's own spiritual response possible."[18] Put in modern terms, we might translate Shen by suggesting that the person must be tricked into accessing his or her own precognitive intuitions, which are otherwise covered over or unavailable to the hardened social ego.

Dismissals aside, then, divination is widely practiced and celebrated around the world. Indeed it is so

Figure 4.5   *Ancient Rome: The Oracle of the Sacred Chickens,* colored engraving by Heinrich Leutemann (1824–1905). © Stefano Bianchetti/Corbis.

common that scholars have invented an entire glossary of new terms to get a handle on it. Here is a sampling:

belomancy	divination by pulling an arrow out of a quiver
dream incubation	sleeping in the temple of a god or in a special place for a special dream
hepatoscopy	divination by reading the liver of a sacrificed animal, often a sheep
lecanomancy	divination by staring, trance-like, into a vessel of oil and water
lychnonomancy	divination by staring, trance-like, into a burning lamp
necromancy	divination through the spirits of the dead or by enlivening a corpse
ornithomantics	divination by interpreting the flight or behavior of birds
pyromancy	divination by heating bones or shells to observe their cracks
scrying	divination by staring at water, a mirror, a glass, or a crystal ball

We could easily extend the list of neologisms, since, from a comparative perspective, it is obvious that *it does not matter what natural phenomena or artificial ritual techniques are engaged.* A flight of birds, the way a tortoise shell or deer bone cracks in the fire, the shape of tea leaves at the bottom of a pot, the examination of the details and direction of lightning bolts, the movement of a snake, the shape and colors of cowrie shells, the lines of a palm, the pecking of chickens, the fall of a handful of sticks, the sudden appearance of a fox in the forest, the random fall of palm nuts, the pattern in which an animal's entrails fall (spilled in a sacrifice for the god of the oracle), the shape of oil dropped in water or of flour on the floor, conversation overheard or utterances of children, the rising of smoke from a censor, a strange object, star, or lightform in the sky (this was called a *prodigium* in ancient Rome, which had its own "augural college" to look into such matters for the benefit of the state), the utterances of a man or woman in a trance state, the birth defects of a malformed infant, earthquakes, the contents of a dream, the sound of wind blowing through a sacred oak tree grove, the behavior of sacred crocodiles, the throwing of lots or dice—*all* of these can, and have, been read as signs of nature or of the gods guiding a human being or a community toward some particular action or potential future.

As such a list makes obvious, the human phenomenon of divination does not lie in a particular animal, natural phenomenon, or special ritual (as if the livers of sheep were somehow more precognitive than pecking chickens). Rather it lies in the relationship *between* a human diviner or seer and this animal, phenomenon, or artifice, usually the rules being set by a mythical tradition (dedicated to a particular god) or a ritual context (a chosen oracle or special temple). We might say, then, that random or anomalous events, however remarkable or interesting they might be in themselves, are not meaningful signs until they are engaged in as such by human beings and interpreted. We might finally say that *divination is interpretation* (see Figure 4.5).

Comparative Practice: The Awakened One and the Great Hero in Ancient India

Toward the end of each of these six middle chapters, we will model the practice and art of comparison by performing a series of comparative acts. These will

all be organized around a simple three-term formula: we will locate a comparative base or foundation (which we will call "our C") and then relate back to this comparative base at least two historical examples (which we will call "our A" and "our B"). For more on this formula and how to use it, please see "A, B, C: Six Guidelines for Comparing Religions Responsibly" on the accompanying website. Our first comparative practice will engage the subject of founding myths (our C), in this case those surrounding the founders of the Buddhist and Jain traditions of South Asia: Gautama Buddha (our A) and Vardhamana Mahavira (our B).[19]

Founding Myths and Hagiographies

A **founding myth** is, quite simply, a myth about the founder of a religion. Such sacred stories are often encoded in the religious titles that are given to these individuals, either during their life or after their death. Hence Jesus is often referred to simply as "the Christ" and Muhammad as "the Prophet." The man who would become "the Buddha" was named Siddhartha Gautama at birth, but his later disciples called him Buddha, "the awakened one," since the experience of enlightenment is often compared to the sudden experience of waking up from a bad dream. Likewise, a man named Vardhamana became "Mahavira," literally "the great hero," in the eyes of his disciples and for the subsequent Jain tradition, since he had striven so mightily to conquer and subdue his body and, indeed, all of material reality. We could almost stop here, as even these two seemingly simple titles capture so much about the two traditions—what they value, how they understand the state of salvation, and what they consider the ideal human being to be like. Waking up from a dream and battling all of material reality, after all, are two very different propositions.

Although scholars generally accept the historical existence of these two figures, they have struggled to locate the exact dates of their births and deaths. They generally agree, however, that both individuals probably lived some time during a period from the sixth to the fifth century BCE in India. This was an especially transformative period in the region, during which a culture of world-rejecting renouncers was emerging. These renouncers rejected society with its familial and material attachments and its duties and norms and strove for a more ultimate truth and for an end to the continuous cycle of rebirth (*samsara*), the underlying nature of which they identified as suffering, impermanence, and ignorance.

Many, if not most, of the details of the lives of Buddha and Mahavira are clearly legendary. Adopting the Roman Catholic language of medieval writings about saints, scholars sometimes refer to such stories not as founding myths but as hagiographies, literally "writings about saints." A **hagiography** is not an historical biography. It is not based on archival research, crosschecking, and historical records in the same way in which, say, a modern biography of a political leader is.[20] A hagiography may indeed represent a community's memory or experience of a historical founder or saint, or it may even reflect and express aspects of that person's lived religious experiences and teachings, but it has inevitably been written, preserved, and passed down in such a way so as to undergird and preserve the self-understandings of the tradition. In short, hagiographies do not so much reflect the actual lives of their historical subjects as they reflect the memories and interests of those who preserve and transmit the stories. Hagiographies are fundamentally about *memory* and *story*, not about historical accuracy. Put differently, hagiographies, particularly when they are about the founder of a religion, perform mythical functions. They are founding myths.

To Set Apart

Founding myths, above all, work to set apart their subjects from the ordinary lot of humanity. They thus often include stories of special births, which function to mark the founder or saint as someone different and destined for great things. Hence one story of the Buddha's birth describes how, upon existing his mother's womb, he immediately took seven steps and then announced that this was his final birth, in which he would save the world. Similarly, according to a version of Mahavira's birth narrative, Mahavira was first conceived in the womb of a brahman or Hindu priest but was then transferred to the womb of a member of the warrior caste.

Another function of founding myths is to separate or set apart the believing community from other communities in order to explain—in these two cases, for example, what makes a Buddhist a Buddhist or a Jain a Jain and not a member of ancient Hindu society. Mahavira's birth narrative does this quite explicitly. In addition to setting him apart from ordinary beings, the narrative was probably meant to relativize priestly power through its implicit, if somewhat ambiguous, claim that the brahman caste was not at the top of the religious hierarchy. Hence the special infant was born in a priest caste womb, but he was then literally moved to another, from which he was actually born. A profound connection is set up between the two wombs and therefore between the two castes; and yet they are also clearly distinguished, as the birth takes place in a non-priestly caste.

Both the Buddha and Mahavira were born within the ancient Hindu fold, but they introduced teachings that clearly opposed its established system of caste and ritual sacrifice. Both underwent dramatic crises whereby they renounced society and set out on quests to realize a truth that was not available in the context of their social world. Toward this end, they each put themselves through a set of trials that involved extreme fasting in both cases, before finally realizing or winning a new revelation, which they then successfully disseminated to others, thanks to their special personalities and their display of extraordinary magical powers (and here we recognize the clear outline of the quest or hero myth). Throughout South Asian history down to this very day, such special powers—like the ability to remember one's previous lives, or to project or manifest apparitions or visionary displays that others can see—have been believed to develop in those who achieve advanced states of knowledge, or who have engaged in extreme meditative practice or radical rejections of basic bodily desires, particularly sexual ones.

The phenomenon of people denying basic bodily needs and desires, such as food and sex, is found throughout the world's religious traditions in countless forms. Scholars of religion call this comparative phenomenon **asceticism**—a formation based on the ancient Greek noun *askēsis* ("discipline," "exercise"), which referred to the ways in which, for example, ancient Greek athletes trained their bodies for contest and public display (hence later Christian saints and ascetics were called "athletes for Christ"). In South Asia, similar "strivings" (*sadhana*), which include extreme forms of mental concentration, are believed to contain, preserve, build up, and redirect psychosexual energies, framed as "seed" (*retas*) or "heat" (*tapas*), until they morph and manifest as various paranormal powers.[21] There is, in short, a basic hydraulic metaphor at work here: if normal bodily energies are not "wasted" by being expelled or sent "out," they can be contained and redirected "in" and "up" until they manifest their true supernormal potentials. Hence the Hindu ascetic is sometimes called *urdhva-retas*, literally "he whose semen is turned up or reversed." More on these hydraulic metaphors below, in Chapter 6.

Comparative Enlightenment

Ultimately, though, for both the Buddhist and the Jain traditions, the goal is not superpowers but release from *samsara*—that round of birth, death, and rebirth in which we are all caught, as on a wheel. This is the state of salvation around which the two religions orbit and to which their various practices point.

Here is one classic description of the Buddha's enlightenment experience, from a text entitled *The Life of the Buddha*. At this point in the story, Siddhartha is incredibly weak, from excessive fasting and other ascetic practices. Exhausted and emaciated, he is about to despair, when a young woman named Nandabala appears. She is carrying some milk rice. Nandabala

bowed her head before [him] and made him take the milk rice. By eating that ... he became, with his six senses content, able to attain the Awakening. His body along with his fame having reached complete amplitude, the sage in his single person bore the stability and charm of the ocean and the moon ... from a reaper he then obtained some grass, repaired to the foot of that great pure tree, and sat down with the vow to become awakened. Then he took up the posture with folded legs ...[22]

After achieving full control over all the techniques of trance, he recalled ... the series of his former births ... After recalling births and deaths in all the various rebirth states, that man, full of compassion, then felt compassion toward all beings ... he became convinced that samsara had no substance.[23]

And here is an account of Mahavira's enlightenment, from a text called *The Limbs of the Teaching*:

Then [Mahavira] formed the following resolution: I shall for twelve years neglect my body and abandon the care of it; I shall with equanimity bear, undergo, and suffer all calamities arising from divine powers, men or animals... The Venerable Ascetic Mahavira passed twelve years in this way of life; during the thirteenth year ... in the field of the householder Samaga, in a north-eastern direction from an old temple, not far from a Sal tree, in a squatting position with joined heels exposing himself to the heat of the sun, with the knees high and the head low, in deep meditation, in the midst of abstract meditation, he reached Nirvana, the complete and full, the unobstructed, unimpeded, infinite and supreme, best knowledge and intuition ... he was a Kevalin, omniscient and comprehending all objects, he knew all conditions of the world.[24]

As can be seen from these two accounts, both Buddhists and Jains agree that, once one achieves enlightenment, one attains omniscience or "all-encompassing knowledge," a preliminary stage along the path to the ultimate goal. The two traditions even use a common word for the ultimate achievement: *nirvana*, literally a "blowing out" or "cessation." From there, however, they diverge significantly. For instance, whereas the Buddha prescribed what is called in the Buddhist tradition "the Middle Way"—a monastic lifestyle between the extremes of radical asceticism and worldly indulgence—Mahavira argued that radical asceticism is indeed necessary for advancement along the path toward enlightenment. Hence the Buddha achieves enlightenment under the shade of a tree, on some soft patch of grass, after taking nourishment from a young woman, whereas Mahavira achieves enlightenment while baking in the sun in the middle of a field, after thirteen years.

These two distinct paths, it turns out, have everything to do with the two traditions' conceptions of soul. Jains are dualists. They believe that the *jiva*—"soul"—is real, unchanging, and eternally distinct from the material world. The final goal of Jain practice, then, consists in the realization of this soul as an entity completely separated or isolated from all physical reality. It follows that the body, which is a part of the material world, keeps the soul entrapped in the cycle of rebirth as long as one is subject to desires stirred by the senses. It logically follows, then, that one must conquer the body and gain control over the senses through rigorous ascetic practices in order to attain enlightenment. This is called *kaivalya* ("isolation"), and the person who achieves it is called a Kevalin, literally "he who has achieved isolation." Upon the now enlightened person's death, the luminous soul, often imagined as a perfect ball of conscious light, will float up to the top of the universe, attain *moksha* ("release") from the cycle of rebirth, and enter a state of pure and absolute consciousness, forever perfectly isolated from the phenomena of suffering, darkness, and death in the material world below.

Buddhists are not dualists, nor are they striving for an isolated soul. Quite the contrary: in Buddhism there is "nothing substantial in existence," that is, nothing that is permanent or lasting. There is no unchanging, eternal soul. Indeed, from the Buddhist perspective, it is *precisely* the idea of an eternal soul or of a permanent and stable self that causes human beings to suffer. Hence much of Buddhist meditation is aimed at helping the person realize that there is no soul, no self, and hence—and this is the key—literally no one to suffer. Accordingly, upon successfully traversing the Middle Way and achieving indifference

toward all desires, the Buddhist adept experiences enlightenment, which includes the realization that what people mean by self or soul is really only an ever changing stream or flow of experience, made up of different, separable qualities or strands. The enlightened person attains *nirvana*—in other words is "blown out"—either during life or at death. All remnants of the self or the ego are dissolved into an all-encompassing state of peace and bliss that is beyond all suffering and all limitation. If the enlightened Jain soul is a perfect, all-knowing sphere of conscious light at the top of the universe, here, in the Buddhist *nirvana*, the soul is forever dissolved into an all-encompassing state of emptiness, compassion, wisdom, and peace.

The two founding myths play out these core differences. In the Buddhist myth, we see the Buddha just after his rejection of radical asceticism and his adoption of the Middle Way. He accepts an offering of food, sits underneath a tree, and vows that he will not move from that place until he becomes free of ignorance. In artistic renditions of these events, we see that his body is draped in simple robes and he sits comfortably, with his legs crossed in his lap, in the classic lotus posture of Indian yoga. As the story continues, we hear of a malicious being named Mara attempting to distract the Buddha from his meditation by producing illusory images of horrible demons designed to elicit fear and of beautiful dancing women designed to elicit lust. But the Buddha remained calm and did not stir from his meditation. At last he achieved enlightenment and awoke to the liberating knowledge that there is nothing, absolutely nothing that is permanent in the world, and hence that there is nothing and no one left to suffer.

Mahavira's biographers tell a very different story. Here we encounter "the great hero" in the midst of one of his prolonged fasts, having gone without food or water for two and a half days. The ascetic is crouched down in the rigorous squatting meditative posture. Completely naked and exposed to the scorching heat of the sun in the middle of a field "not far from" a tree, he enters into a deep meditation until he achieves enlightenment, awakening to the knowledge that the eternal soul is real and is radically distinct from the body and the rest of the material world.

In Conversation

These stories are found in separate textual traditions, but they appear to be in conversation with one another. Besides the fact that both stories are about the attainment of enlightenment, they also both feature the presence of a tree. We might speculate that the tree in the Buddhist story signifies the balance and wisdom of the Middle Way. Hence the Buddha chooses to sit comfortably under the protective branches of a tree rather than expose himself to the natural elements. In the Jain story, on the other hand, the tree appears to signify the radical asceticism characteristic of the Jain religious path. Mahavira, after all, *could have* sat underneath a tree, like the Buddha, but he refused to do so, because that would have meant that he had succumbed to normal bodily desires. He was better than that. This lesson of extreme Jain asceticism is equally evident in the other features of the founding myth, such as the oft-mentioned details that Mahavira was naked, that he had been fasting without water, and that he was crouched in the painful squatting posture.

These differences are reflected in the religious art of the respective religions. The most famous Jain statues, for example, are immense—over fifty feet tall in some cases. The Jain heroes are portrayed here in the meditative posture of either standing upright or being seated and completely naked. The two features associated with these postures—the incredible height and the full nudity—emphasize the heroes' utter transcendence from and indifference to the material and social world. In one such figure displayed here (Figure 4.6), a Jain figure named Bahubali stands isolated in the wild, completely motionless. He has been standing there for so long that ants have built mounds around his ankles and vines have grown up around his legs. Nothing stirs his meditation. He has achieved perfect enlightenment.

The traditional images of the Buddha and his Middle Way are quite different. The Buddha is

Figure 4.6   A fifty-five-foot tall icon of the Jain *kevalin*, Gomateshwara Bahubali, Shravanabelagola, Karnataka, India. Every twelve years, Jains consecrate the image with various libations in a ritual called the Mahamasthak Abhisheka. Here, devotees pour turmeric water over the image. Photographed by Andrea R. Jain (2006).

almost always seated. This is itself a "middle" position, we might observe—neither standing over and above the world nor engaging in any worldly activity. If the Buddha is sometimes represented as standing, he adopts that position in order to teach or to bless, not to stand utterly aloof in isolation. His face, like that of the Jain heroes, is in absolute peace and absorbed with this state, but he has achieved this complete and total release from suffering by taking a very different path and through a very different conception of soul (see Figure 4.7).

As we can see well in these Buddhist and Jain founding myths, comparison is not just a modern scholarly practice, indulged in for the sake of understanding religious traditions today. It is also

Figure 4.7   Buddha, thirteenth century, Bangkok, Thailand. Jim Thompson House. Image by © Luca Tettoni/Corbis.

characteristic of the religious traditions themselves, however ancient they might be. These two religious communities clearly recognized each other as competitors and developed their founding myths to acknowledge the differences between them and to claim superiority over each other. We might say, then, that founding myths function to identify not just what a particular community believes, but also what it does *not* believe and, by implication, how it understands itself to be different from other religious communities. Founding myths do not just create sameness within a community; they also create difference between communities.

Beginning a Toolkit

We have already discussed, in Chapter 3, how religion looks very different depending on which material one chooses to "put on the table" and, just as importantly,

to "take off the table." We have also discussed how something like a miraculous healing can mean one thing in a particular historical context and quite another when placed on the table of comparison. Behind this table metaphor is another: the worktable.

There is a long tradition in the comparative study of religion of using the metaphors of the "workshop" and its attending "tools." Indeed the father of the field, Max Müller, published his collected essays in five volumes, under the title *Chips from a German Workshop*. These metaphors are still very much with us today. Wendy Doniger has written of the "toolbox" of comparison, and, as we shall see in Chapter 12, Ioan Couliano wrote of a "historian's kit for the fourth dimension," by which he meant using Einstein's space–time model to re-imagine the nature of time, and hence the writing of history. Similarly, today, a scholar like Ann Taves employs the language of "building blocks" and "kit" in order to communicate what she is doing, through her own approach, to the "special things" of religion and how they are built up, over time, through a finite set of cognitive and social processes.

Although each of these authors has meant something different with these worktable metaphors, they all share at least two basic ideas: (1) that the study of religion works through a finite set of models and cognitive skills, or "tools," which can be identified and learned; and (2) that not every model or skill is appropriate for every situation the student of religion encounters. Different tools are needed for different jobs.

In this same workshop spirit, as we move through these middle chapters, we will be collecting tools for your own toolkit and teaching you how to use them. We have already begun this process in Chapter 3, of course, with our discussions of the key skill sets of both–and thinking, reflexivity, and the ability to move back and forth between the perspectives of the insider and the outsider. We have also introduced a number of comparative categories or "tools": initiation, religion, world religion, the sacred, experience, and magic. Indeed all of our glossary terms are, in some sense, tools for you to pick up and use. But there are also the "big ideas" of each chapter, which you might think of as major skill sets or instruction manuals on how to use these word tools. A tool, after all, is never sufficient unto itself. It must be learned, and only a few people will master it. The same tool in different hands can create *very* different things, depending on the user's skill level and on the materials to which it is applied.

If our glossary terms are our tools, then the primary skill sets collected in the present chapter might be summarized this way:

1   *How to Think about Myth*   One initial way to compare religions is by looking for their central stories, narratives, or "myths" and asking how these narratives shape the respective moods, beliefs, customs, and behaviors of their communities. We have seen that creation myths, hero or quest myths, trickster myths, and founding myths are especially common.

2   *How to Think about Ritual*   One can then also look for the "rituals" that re-enact these grounding narratives as a kind of repeated performance, which makes the sacred narratives come alive and remain relevant for their respective actors and future generations, and enables individuals to come in contact with the superhuman powers of the mythical world. We have seen that central myth–ritual complexes that perform the central truths of a particular religion, along with the pragmatic rituals of the life cycle, civil religion, sacrifice, and divination, are especially common.

3   *The Insider–Outsider Möbius*   Such a comparative practice, of course, is descriptive of an outsider's perspective. There are no myths inside a religious worldview, but every religious narrative is a myth to someone standing completely outside of it. One must always be aware of and sensitive to this insider–outsider "flip," that is, to whether one is "inside" or "outside" a particular myth–ritual complex. We have encouraged you to appreciate and imagine both positions when comparing religions. We illustrated the profundity of comparing myths and rituals with our discussion of the oft-reported experience of being inside a novel or being a character in a movie. To the extent that we inhabit a language and a culture, we are all living inside a story and acting it out, be this religious or secular in nature. The central question then becomes: Are we aware of this?

4   *Function over Content*   Finally, we have observed that the comparative tools of "myth" and "ritual" point toward a globally distributed need to create narratives, to create rituals to celebrate those narratives, and to come in contact with the sacred source of the world. There is difference, for sure (the relative content of the myths and rituals). But there is also real sameness (the fact that every community recites and performs its own myths and rituals, toward both practical ends and states of salvation). The key of the skill set here is to locate sameness in the function and not in the content.

The Tough Questions

1   The question of myth is an especially poignant one in the modern world, where countless stories (or myths) are in constant contact and potential conflict. Was there some point in your life when the story into which you were born (as family, culture, religion) began to break down, began not to work any longer? What resources did you find to put a self-story back together again, either as a new version of the inherited story or as an entirely new one?

2   Does your community have trickster myths? Can you laugh at your own beliefs, whatever they are? If so, why? If not, why not? Should we "make fun" of religion?

3   Here is a scene from my own youth with my own remembered reflections. Comment on

this passage with the help of what you have learned about civil religion rituals. Can you think of any similar scenes from your own life?

When I was a teenager, I played (American) football at a public, that is, secular high school. Before each game, the team would gather in a circle and recite the Lord's Prayer. It was not entirely clear why we did this. It may have been a prayer for protection (as American football is quite dangerous, and young men were always getting seriously hurt). It may have also been a prayer to win, to defeat the other team. Whatever it was for, it certainly worked, in the simple sense that it focused our attention, ritually united the team (in that circle), and raised our adrenaline levels (the implied danger part). Precisely because the ritual was never explained

or rationally justified, its meanings remained ambiguous, and I am certain that both the protection and the winning intention occurred to virtually everyone in the ritual circle.

The first intention struck my young mind as reasonable enough. We were, after all, a bit scared, and we had some reason to be. But the second? Was the God who created the entire universe, all those billions and billions of galaxies and countless species on this single grand planet, rooting on the side of eleven spindly teenage boys trying to get an inflated pigskin over a chalk line on a grassy field, as eleven other spindly teenage boys from a nearby town tried to stop them through minor, scripted acts of violence? The Lord of the universe had chosen sides in a Friday night football game?

Notes

1 Peter T. Struck, *Birth of the Symbol: Ancient Readers at the Limits of Their Texts* (Princeton, NJ: Princeton University Press, 2004), 150.

2 Fritz Graf, "Myth." In *Religions of the Ancient World: A Guide*, edited by Sarah Iles Johnston (Cambridge, MA: Harvard University Press, 2004), 45.

3 This theory goes back to Jane Harrison, who in 1912 suggested that myth "is the plot of the *dromenon*," this being the Greek term designating what is acted out in the ritual; see Jan Bremmer, "Ritual." In *Religions of the Ancient World: A Guide*, edited by Sarah Iles Johnston (Cambridge, MA: Harvard University Press, 2004), 42.

4 Graf, "Myth," 52.

5 Bremmer, "Ritual," 32.

6 For the whole hymn, see Wendy O'Flaherty, trans., *The Rig Veda* (New York: Penguin, 1981), 30–31.

7 Joseph Campbell, *The Hero's Journey: Joseph Campbell on His Life and Work*, edited by Phil Cousineau (Novatao, CA: New World Library, 2003), 138.

8 Campbell, *The Hero's Journey*, 28.

9 Robert D. Pelton, *The Trickster in West Africa: A Study of Mythic Irony and Sacred Delight* (Berkeley: University of California Press, 1980).

10 Pelton, *The Trickster in West Africa*, 71, 113.

11 Lawrence E. Sullivan, "Trickster: An Overview." In *The Encyclopedia of Religion*, edited by Lindsay Jones (2nd edn., New York: Macmillan, 1987), 9351.

12 Harold Scheub, *Trickster and Hero: Two Characters in the Oral and Written Traditions of the World* (Madison: The University of Wisconsin Press, 2012), 6.

13 Scheub, *Trickster and Hero*, 196–197.

14 All the quotations in this section come from Bremmer, "Ritual," 33–34.

15 Bremmer, "Ritual," 35.

16 For the point about "religious comparison shopping," see Sarah Iles Johnston, ed., *Religions of the Ancient World: A Guide* (Cambridge, MA: Harvard University Press, 2004), ix, xiv.

17 Richard J. Smith, *Fathoming the Cosmos and Ordering the World: The Yijing* (I Ching, *or* Classic of Changes)

and Its Evolution in China (Charlottesville: University of Virginia Press, 2008), xiii. See also *The "I Ching": A Biography* (Princeton, NJ: Princeton University Press, 2012).

18 All these quotations are from Smith, *Fathoming the Cosmos*, 144.

19 Although the scholarly consensus is that Mahavira first systematized the ideology that became the basis for the Jain tradition and that he is in effect the tradition's historical founder, Jain doctrine considers him to be not the founder, but the most recent of twenty-four *jinas* ("conquerors"), all of whom together, as a lineage, created the present tradition.

20 This is not to say that modern historians are not themselves formed by particular assumptions, values, and worldviews. They are; but these are very different from those of the traditional hagiographer. We will question some of these modern historical assumptions in Chapter 8, around the subjects of magic and miracle.

21 See, for example, Knut Jacobsen, *Yoga Powers: Extraordinary Capacities Attained Through Meditation and Concentration* (Leiden: Brill, 2011).

22 Ashvaghosha, *Life of the Buddha*, trans. Patrick Olivelle, in the Clay Sanskrit Library series (New York: New York University Press, 2009), 12.111–120.

23 Ashvaghosha, *Life of the Buddha*, 14.2–6.

24 Hermann Georg Jacobi, trans., *Acaranga,* in *Jaina Sutras*, Parts I–II (Charleston, SC: Forgotten Books, 2008), 2.15.25–26.

Big Bend Lightning (1985), by Lynn Randolph, 36″ × 36″.

5

Religion, Nature, and Science
The Super Natural

Hydrogen is a light, odorless gas that, given enough time, turns into people.

Anonymous

I think the plants love us. I have no idea why. We certainly have done nothing—at least recently—to deserve it. I think that they want us to be human beings again.

Stephan V. Beyer, *Singing to the Plants*

Comparing Religions: Coming to Terms, First Edition. Jeffrey J. Kripal, Ata Anzali, Andrea R. Jain, and Erin Prophet.
© 2014 Jeffrey J. Kripal. Published 2014 by John Wiley & Sons, Ltd.

"We are star people!" That's what my college astronomy professor said when he walked into class one day. He happened to be a Christian monk, but he also possessed a PhD in chemistry, and he was speaking that day as a professional scientist who knew all about the basic building blocks or elements of the natural world and how they come together to form bigger and more complex molecules, which then form into various sorts of chemicals, solids, fluids, gases, and eventually living, carbon-based bipeds like you and me.

He was being quite literal with the shocking "star people" line. It turns out that large dying stars, with their unimaginable heat and pressures, are the only places in the universe where the heavier elements that are required for organic life can form. It also turns out that the universe is about fourteen billion years old, that it probably emerged from a mind-boggling burst of energy, space, and time called "the Big Bang" (easily history's greatest understatement), and that it now consists, depending on whose calculations you accept, of something between one hundred billion and two hundred billion galaxies. A single one of these galaxies, say ours, contains somewhere between two hundred billion and four hundred billion stars. You do the math. More crazily still, many theoretical physicists champion something called string theory, in which all of matter is composed of tiny, invisible "strings" vibrating at unbelievable speeds in multiple dimensions (ten, in one widespread model); and we are now more or less certain that most of our universe is composed of "dark matter," whose nature and purpose we do not understand. Moreover, what we call "the universe" may be just one of multiple universes that branched off that original—well, *whatever*

it was. We may, in other words, be actually living not in a universe but in a multiverse.

Evolutionary biologist J. B. S. Haldane's famous and oft-quoted quip is getting truer and truer with each passing decade: "My own suspicion is that the universe is not only queerer than we suppose, but queerer than we *can* suppose."[1]

In the billions of years it takes the sun stars of our local universe, particularly the larger ones, to burn out and collapse, heavier and heavier elements are fused together in the ungodly hot interior cores of these dying stars. The dying stars then eventually explode (as our own sun will, one day) and, like some giant orgasms, they cast the elemental seeds of life into the black womb of space. There, through the forces of gravity, they might eventually collect together again, in a much cooler environment, and form the new worlds that we call "planets" and, eventually, that most mysterious of all cosmic expressions: life. Put simply but majestically, we carry around in our bodies, through and *as* those bodies, the cosmic stuff of exploded stars. We are indeed, every one of us, star people. That is the truth. That is who we really are.

We are also all Africans. Every human being on this planet can trace his or her genetic lineage back to groups of *Homo sapiens* that decided to leave Africa for some reason; and this happened at different times, somewhere between forty thousand and one hundred and twenty-five thousand years ago (the numbers are shifting with new data and new research). The Africans, of course, did not just appear there. They had been evolving from earlier hominid and primate species that lived on the African continent for millions of years. From Africa, our ancient ancestors migrated into what is now the Middle East, into the Mediterranean basin, and into modern-day Europe and Russia; they went over to South Asia, East Asia, and Australia (about forty thousand years ago), over what was probably a frozen Bering Strait into North America during the last ice age (about fifteen to twenty thousand years ago), then down into what is now Latin America. It was a vast journey that began in Africa and ended at the tip of South America, probably no more than ten thousand years ago. Even later dates are commonly given for our arrival in the Polynesian islands, perhaps as late as three thousand and five hundred years ago, when, likely with the help of the stars as a kind of celestial map, we spread out over vast stretches of ocean and colonized the islands of the Pacific.

These long years saw many travels, settlings, disasters, starvations, battles, and civilizations, countless mythological systems, rituals, deities, and moral codes, and numerous subtle mutations and minor ethnic distinctions (skin color, eye shape, body size, and so on)—as we collected into locally settled groups, had sex among ourselves, created little gene pools, and tried to survive and flourish in this and that ecosystem—in the mountains, by the sea, on the islands, on the plains, in the freezing cold, in the searing heat. We also had sex with other species of hominids—with the Neanderthals in Europe, for example, probably somewhere between forty-seven and sixty-five thousand years ago; and with the Denosivans of Melanesia and Southeast Asia. All of this is encoded, woven tight within the trillions of cells that make up each one of us. All of this is "written" (to be more precise) in those molecules—the sex texts—that we so boringly call "DNA" (deoxyribonucleic acid). We are hybrids, all of us.

We certainly succeeded in our travels. We colonized the entire planet. Nowadays, of course, it does not take us thousands of years to get from Africa to the tip of South America or the Polynesian islands. If we can book the right flights, it takes us a day or so; and, if we happen to be lucky enough to be floating in a space station, it takes a few minutes at a cruising speed of 17,500 miles or 28,000 kilometers per hour. But we remain—to this day, in our genetic heritage, in the deepest hidden codes of our bodies—Africans all. This is the truth. This is what we really are.

Religion and Contemporary Science

These two stories are modern creation myths. The first is a **cosmogony**, a myth about how the universe came to be. The second is an **anthropogony**, a myth about how human beings came to be. Unlike many—maybe all—religious creation myths, these particular stories reflect actual cosmic, planetary, biological, and historical events as best we are able to trace them through the mathematical equations and empirical findings of modern science—especially astrophysics, evolutionary cell biology, and genetic anthropology.

Already in 1978, in his *On Human Nature*, the biologist and ant specialist E. O. Wilson used the phrase "epic of evolution" or "evolutionary epic," calling it "the best myth we will ever have."[2] Other scientists have reacted differently. The British astrophysicist Fred Hoyle, who actually coined the name "Big Bang," later famously rejected the thesis behind the name, partly because it sounded way too much like a creation myth and appeared to imply … well, a creator. That, it seems, was just too much.

Although we will immediately qualify the issue, there is no point in dodging it. We are in a rather embarrassing situation here. Such scientific stories and accomplishments, after all, seldom sit comfortably with traditional religious accounts of how things came to be. Indeed, generally speaking, the scientific plots flatly contradict the religious plots. This is a common pattern, which has led to a thesis technically called the **Draper–White thesis**, after its two nineteenth-century proponents: Andrew Dickson White and John William Draper. Simply put, the Draper–White thesis argues that, although religious thinkers and authorities have long tried to block or prevent the progress of science in the interest of belief and tradition (the Roman Catholic suppression of Galileo is the iconic example here), religious belief will eventually lose out to the relentless march of science and its empirically based models.

But, if we have a "conflict model" about science and religion in the Draper–White thesis, we also have a "harmony model" in the **Merton thesis**, named after the sociologist Robert Merton, who argued in

1938 that it was English Protestantism, and in particular the Puritans, that catalyzed the scientific revolution—as we have already noted in Chapter 3. Sometimes religion attempts to block science. At other times it inspires and produces it.

Neither thesis should be taken as absolute. The historical truth is that the relationship between science and religion is an extremely diversified and complicated affair, and that it shifts from period to period and from culture to culture, even from person to person. Take my opening "star people" story. This story moved me deeply when I first heard it from the monk who was my professor. Why else would I still remember it, thirty years later? I was no less moved when I learned, years afterwards, that my believing professor almost certainly borrowed the line from one of the twentieth century's most famous atheists, the inimitable Carl Sagan, who uttered it with a not so different sense of awe. Does that fact make the slightest difference? Does it make the truth of our stellar nature any less awe-inspiring?

The complex relationship between science and religion, of course, extends far beyond this single personal example. On a much larger scale, we might observe that technological inventions are often inspired or made necessary by religious sensibilities. We find obvious examples of this in the calendrical and astrological systems of ancient stone temples, or in the scientific and mathematical achievements of medieval Islam. It very much appears that religion came first in instances of this type, and that the technology followed, to aid religious practice.

Wherever one lands on the assumed incompatibilities between science and religion, one thing seems clear enough: the findings of modern science provide us with a most powerful foundation from which to do responsible comparison. The findings of science, after all, are only scientific to the extent that they apply everywhere, and not just in this or that culture—that is, to the extent that they are universally true. Science has no problem with sameness. It assumes it, indeed it proves it. Minor variations, mutations, and adaptations there always

are, but in the end no fundamental difference is allowed here. It is sameness all the way down to the molecules and subatomic particles of our cosmic star bodies. We are all the others. We are the same star stuff.

The Paradox of the Super Natural

And so we arrive at our second major base or C for comparing religious systems across space and time: the natural world. Like myth and ritual, the natural world is a very good foundation from which to launch a comparative practice with respect to religion, and this for one very simple reason: all religions arise from and participate in the same natural world. The same sun, moon, and stars, the same atmosphere and ecosystem, the same water, wind, and weather.

The Ecologies of Religion

Almost. Note that, even here, we must qualify this "sameness" with a series of important "differences." Alaskan Inuit peoples, after all, do not live in the same natural world as the indigenous tribes of the Amazon, much less the same world as a modern-day Parisian, New Yorker, or citizen of Kolkata, Tokyo, or Mexico City does. None of these communities eats the same mammals and fish, nor do they experience the same weather. They do not even see the same stars or experience the sun in the same ways. So too with every other "same," from the weather to the wind and water—it is all "different" as we move from one local ecosystem to another. Such observations and their analysis are part of what we call the **ecology of religion**, that is, the study of religions as experiences and expressions of their natural environments.

The Human Keyboard

It is not all difference, of course. All human beings, from Alaska and the Amazon to Africa and Australia, from Hawaii to Hong Kong, share the same basic physiology (a bilateral, more or less symmetrical form with two ears, two eyes, two arms, and two legs), the same neurological system, the same set of sensory capacities, and so on. They all must also meet the same biological needs of protection, nourishment, and reproduction. Perhaps most importantly of all, any sexually healthy man and woman anywhere can mate and produce a child, who, as an infant, can learn to speak the sounds, words, and grammar of *any* language and culture on the planet. Potentially, any of us is all of us.

There are metaphors to balance and qualify such a universalism. As has often been noted, the human being may be thought of as a fantastically sophisticated musical instrument with an immense keyboard. Like with the sounds of a particular language, however, only some of these potential keys will be activated and "played" within any single culture; but they are all there at birth in every healthy infant. As the infant learns a particular language, all of the other connections necessary for all of the other languages "collapse" and "shut down." Culture literally, neurologically, changes the brain.

So, even with respect to the natural world, we are all the same, and we are all different. We might say that nature and biology are what unite us, and that culture and religion are what separate us. Body, not belief, is that through which we can see most clearly that we are, in actual genetic and biological fact, one. We will zoom in on that body in the next chapter. For now, let us zoom out, into the shared natural world from which this human body has evolved and of which it is an expression.

The Hierophany

What do we find if we compare religions through their understandings of nature, that is, through their sacred ecologies? As with the patterning of myth and ritual, the complexities and variants are endless here. As a way of illustrating this, consider Mircea Eliade's *Patterns in Comparative Religion* (1958). In this classic work, Eliade examined what he called the **hierophany**—literally, a "manifestation" or "appearing" (-*phany*, from *phainein*, "bring to light, reveal, cause to appear") of

"the sacred" (*to hieron*)—mostly through human interaction with the natural world. Eliade's notion of a hierophany is extremely useful but also controversial. It is also based on a subtle and frankly paradoxical idea, which is often misunderstood. So let us try to explain it.

For Eliade, human beings are constantly encountering the sacred, but only and always *through* something else, for example a rock, a tree, an animal, a body of water, a sacred symbol, a myth. Literally anything can become a means for the manifestation or "shining through" of the sacred. Put differently, there is no such thing as a pure experience of the sacred, nor is the experience "out there," as a stable object or thing. Experiences of the sacred rather are always relational, embodied, local, and historical events, even if, at the same time, they also point beyond these local, historical contexts to something Other or More, which we, as historical human beings, can never really get at in and as itself.

There are many ways to think about this both–and. Particularly helpful is the work of Bryan Rennie, who has written about the sacred in Eliade's thought as a special dimension or mode of consciousness that is activated through these kinds of relational experiences with the natural world.[3] The point is this: a hierophany is not a matter of either–or, as if the sacred were either some sort of direct and unmediated revelation of ultimate reality, or just an object mistaken for a deity, like a rock or a tree—an "idol," as we say. Rather, the experience of the sacred is more often a both–and, the sacred appearing *through* or *by means of* the human encounter with some natural object or event. In a single phrase, the hierophany is quite simply a "shining through." In another, we might think of it as the "super natural," that is, as the natural world manifesting the sacred.

Eliade himself was quite clear about this. Evoking everything—from the worship of the sacred in stones and trees (God as pipul tree in Hinduism or as burning bush in Judaism, for example) to the Hindu theology of the *avatara* (God's "descent" as a human being) and the Christian doctrine of the incarnation—Eliade considered this paradox or "coexistence of contradictory essences" (sacred/profane, spirit/

matter, temporal/non-temporal, divine/human) to be "*the* cardinal problem of every religion."[4] The liminal again.

The Thunder God

However central to the general history of religions this both–and nature of the sacred might be, we recognize that it is likely also confusing. Let us, then, look at a single concrete example. It came to me, unbidden, from an undergraduate student. At the time of the letter I'm about to present, this particular young man was studying comparative religion, and so he was well equipped to think about his experience in reflexive ways. Note in particular how his language does not appeal to but clearly performs the both–and structure of Eliade's hierophany.

We break in, mid-way into this young man's letter (an unpublished manuscript):

> The ground on my farm had been parched by an almost year-long drought. I was about 10 years old … I was an acre or so from my house down a cow-trail. I took off my shirt and let it hang and flap like a flag of surrender on the barbed-wire fence, and the cool wind pricked my skin. It was, as I recognize now, an almost sexual experience with the wind, certainly a sensual one. It felt completely intimate, and reached into my shorts and under my arms.
>
> Then came the thunderclouds. The sun was behind them, so by the time they were really blackened by the anxious rain, the sky had turned that electric blue-grey that Texas is famous for. And it was everywhere, that color. And the clouds—I could see the tops falling towards me and then falling under the bottom, like a giant vaporous wheel in the sky. As they rolled and tumbled towards me, I was overcome with—with what? A sense of beauty, perhaps? But it was much more than that. It was a sense of meaning, that somehow my life was intimately tied up with the atmosphere and the land. … I began to weep, sob actually, and fell to my knees grabbing my face and whimpering, "Oh God, thank you, thank you, thank you for this, thank you." It didn't stop. I slammed my hands on the ground and that's when I heard the first thunder. The thunder

didn't come from the lightning—it came from inside me. I literally created the thunder by hitting the ground.

> More was to follow. Every time the thunder rolled, I felt it coming from my body, and I knew the thunder was going to happen a split second before it sounded its rumble. I began to direct the movements of the clouds, moving my hands in a beckoning gesture as the cumuli stumbled forward. Every time I pointed at the cloud, a lightning bolt struck. I know how utterly insane this sounds, but, for a moment, I was the thunder-god. I was controlling that cloud. It was an extension of myself, like a third hand, or another way of sensing. I knew the shape of every lightning-bolt before it struck, and [I] didn't only know the sound and timing of the thunder, but [I] made the sound and timing of the thunder. I was directing it like an orchestra.
>
> Then, as the cloud became too close and too tremendous to even imagine let alone see, I felt something weird happening. The ground on which my knees rested was as parched as one could possibly imagine. It was cracked and hard and dusty. But suddenly I felt the sinews in my leg muscles unbind and reach through the skin of my knees. … My sinews became woody and fibrous and gnarly, in other words, became roots. I felt my roots sink deep into the ground, the dry, dry ground, even felt them go down below the topsoil to the layer of caleche, which tasted (to my roots) like white chocolate. I tell you, I know what it feels like to be a thirsty tree. Presently, I felt water rush up through my roots and feed my veins. I could feel the water travel through my circulatory system, feel its coolness in my arteries, and even felt when it reached my heart. The water flowed and flowed until I felt that my blood had been utterly replaced with the water from the ground. I had gone from hot and red and sweaty to cool and refreshed and dry … Then it began to rain.

Note that this experience cannot possibly be described as a simple subjective state, as if it were nothing more than an experience of awe or beauty before a Texas storm. But also note that the event ceases to be an experience of the sacred if we remove the subjective element. Without this very particular young man's presence on that plain at that time, the storm would have simply been another storm, as it no doubt was for the rest of his family. In short, *both* the subjective state *and* the objective storm were necessary to transform this natural event into a super natural one.

The young man then offered his own thoughts on the experience:

> My understanding of this experience was immensely life affirming. … I felt awe at the power channeled through my own consciousness. The paradox is this: I realized that I was (merely) a vessel for something much grander than me. But the "something much grander than me" depended on me just as I was humbled by it. "It" depends on my selfhood to exist, therefore it was self-affirming. I don't know how to make sense of this, frankly.

Does it matter that this same young man and I, together in a classroom, later heard a very similar story about an elderly Native American who could manifest thunder by shaking his sacred gourd, and this from a Houston lawyer who spent three decades defending the Native American church and its members' sacramental consumption of peyote?

Food and Purity Codes: "You Are What You Eat"

Nature, of course, is not just a matter of what appears above, in a storm. It is also about what appears below, in and on the ground. All human societies are embedded in this "on the ground" natural world. And yet all human societies have worked very hard to separate themselves from the same natural world. The primary mechanism of this attempted separation from nature may surprise you. That primary mechanism is food.

The Raw and the Cooked

This primordial division between nature and culture has been famously framed in anthropology through the symbolism of "the raw" and "the cooked." Wild nature eats its food raw. Socialized humanity eats its food cooked. The passage from nature to culture is through fire and, more particularly, through the cooking of meat. Very roughly, paleo-anthropologists currently think that deliberate butchery began around two and a half million years ago, and that the ancestors of humans began controlling fire somewhere around one million and eight hundred thousand years ago. So we've been moving (and cooking) from nature to culture for a very long time.

Cooked food, however, does not simply signal the passage from nature to culture. It also functions as a boundary marker between this community and that community. Hence the elaborate control systems put in place around the eating of food. It is certainly no mystery why this is the case. Food, after all, is the most common and easiest way to "get inside" someone.

Everyone has to eat every day, and many times a day, so, if a religious or social system can manage to attach a whole set of meanings and values to what one puts in one's mouth, then that system will have numerous opportunities each day to strengthen itself, to remind social actors of itself to the point where the worldview becomes obvious and natural (even though it is neither obvious nor natural to any outsider). Food helps make a world. Food is belonging. Food is boundary. Food is story. Food is performance. Food is self.

Fake Reasons

Religious dietary rules seem arbitrary to many people. That's because they are. Even if reasons are sometimes given for eating this or not eating that that seem rational (for example, that pork gave ancient peoples trichinosis, or that vegetarian food is healthier, or that purity codes are really about hygiene), it is a serious mistake to see such so-called "reasons" as explaining much of anything.

The truth is that such rationalizations may paint a veneer of modern reasonableness here and there, and they may even work in a few isolated cases—as in the explanation of why a culture like Indian Hinduism prohibits the eating of cows: because it makes little sense to eat something that might function as your dairy, your source of energy (the dung), *and* your transportation truck. Still, rational explanations of this sort (which are seldom the explanations given by the cultures whose rules they seek to account for, anyway) do not even come close to encompassing the full range and specificity of dietary rules, let alone their social power. Nor can they explain why the exact same food (say, pork) is considered impure and highly polluting in one culture (say, an orthodox Jewish or Islamic one) and healthy and beneficial in another (say, a traditional Chinese one).

Function versus Content

From a comparativist perspective, the truth is that it does not matter what the dietary rules are, *as long as there are dietary rules*. Put a bit differently, what the dietary codes are about is not the *content* of the codes themselves, but their *functions*. And these functions boil down to two: (1) the formation of an individual religious identity and of a set of emotions (purity, pollution, shame, guilt, disgust, and so on) through a necessarily repeated daily act; and (2) the subsequent segregation or separation of a community around these identities, biological acts, and emotions. In short, eating regulations not only help shape and maintain a very particular religious identity; they also form and police a very particular community. They help make a world.

Purity Code Systems

It is not simply food that provides boundaries and meaning, though. Dietary regulations are part of a larger system of rules or purity codes. One might think of **purity codes** as rules, moods, and assumptions that structure a particular community around a basic **binary** or set of opposites—in this case, the binary of purity and pollution—toward the construction and performance of a religious world.

By assigning the categories of "purity" and "pollution" to daily acts, foods, places, and persons, a society defines not only what a people can eat, but also what it can touch, with whom the individuals belonging to it can mingle or eat, whom they can marry, how ill, wounded, or dead bodies are to be handled, what constitutes a "polluting" sore or disease in that community, what kind of sexual act is proper, and so on. Purity codes are one way in which religious communities structure daily life and maintain both psychological and social boundaries.

Not all religious systems emphasize or employ purity codes to the same extent, of course. But those that do often display common features that are worthy of comment. There are four such features: (1) the structural relationship between purity codes and hierarchical models of society; (2) the use of **contagion** or touch as the primary means of transmitting pollution; (3) the symbolism of the body-as-container, implicit in most purity systems; (3) the very different ways purity codes are perceived by insiders and outsiders; and (4) the tendency of purity code systems to produce or encourage their own transgressions or intentional violations—in essence, their own subversions or "countercultures." We will deal with the first three here and turn to the fourth in our next chapter.

Hierarchy   The word **hierarchy** comes from ancient Greek, where the equivalent compound means to "rule" (*archein*) over "the holy rites" (*ta hiera*, from *hieros*); thus a *hierarchēs* was a "high priest," the one who conducted the performance of sacred rituals. Literally, then, the word refers to societies that base their social structures on what those societies claim to be a divine order. The word means both more and less than this, however, as it is used more technically to describe any social structure (religious or secular) that includes "lower" classes of people and social functions and subordinates them to "higher" classes of people and social functions within a greater social whole or meta-system. Hierarchical social structures are the opposite of egalitarian social structures: in terms of our present inquiry, we might say that the former privilege difference, whereas the latter—and egalitarian models in general—privilege sameness.

In some sense, of course, all large societies are hierarchical, as all of them produce social structures that distribute wealth, power, and authority unequally. Smaller tribal or, we assume, earlier hunting and gathering societies were/are generally rather egalitarian, since social stratification appears to be a function of size: the larger the group, the more hierarchy one tends to see. However, there is good evidence that, historically, hierarchical modes of social organization run deep and in fact predate the evolution of hunting hominids and humans—primates, for example, organize their communities around a hierarchy, even as they also display clear modes of egalitarian behavior. Anyone who has owned more than one dog knows that the same is true about our canine friends.

What sets apart traditional religious hierarchies from modern secular ones is that they accomplish social stratification and hierarchical ordering through the categories of purity and pollution. Perhaps the clearest and most instructive case of such a religious organizing principle is the Indian caste system.

The English word "caste" is not of Indian origin; it comes, through Portuguese (*casta*, "race"), from Latin, where it meant "pure" (*castus*). Although an ancient four-group model functions as the social ideal in India (what is called "the four *varnas*"), in practice there are innumerable castes or hereditary classes. These are called *jati* ("birth"), since one is born into one's caste and cannot choose it. A series of purity codes regulate the boundaries between the castes. Male members of each caste, ideally anyway, share the same occupational role and social duties. Moreover, there are rules regarding what anthropologists call endogamy and commensality. Both are widely distributed practices around the globe. **Endogamy**, literally "marriage within," refers to the requirement to marry within one's own close group or subgroup (or very near it in the hierarchy). **Commensality**, literally "eating together," refers to the requirement to share food only with those within one's social group or

subgroup. What we see here, again, are sex and food being used as mechanisms to regulate and control social and psychological boundaries.

Social status in traditional Indian society is determined not simply by wealth, but also by caste and purity (one can thus be very pure and very poor, or very rich and very polluted). The castes are ranked in a hierarchy based on a polarity between purity (which is at the top) and pollution (at the bottom). The more pure one's caste, the higher it is in the system—and the more vegetarian the food regulations tend to be; the more impure or polluted one's caste, the lower it ranks in the system—and the more loose and broad the food restrictions become. In order to regulate the pure or impure substances that may be exchanged in occupational, marriage, and eating contexts, the caste system relies on purity codes and on social markers such as surnames.

In the classic study of the Hindu caste system, Louis Dumont's *Homo Hierarchicus* (1966), Dumont argued that, in order to understand caste hierarchy, one must evaluate it as a whole, including the rules that regulate the arrangements of and the boundaries between its parts. Such an evaluation reveals how the religious dichotomy between purity and pollution functions to reinforce social hierarchy. Put most simply, Dumont argued that castes cannot be understood in isolation, because the purity of one depends on the impurity of another, and vice versa.

Consider the following simple illustration. Castes belonging to the brahman or priestly social group are at the top of the hierarchy. Members of these castes are associated with the cow, an animal that is venerated for its ability to purify (hence to kill a cow is traditionally considered tantamount to killing a member of the brahman caste). On the contrary, the members of the "untouchable" castes are people at the bottom of the hierarchy or, from another point of view, people outside the sacred social order altogether, since the untouchables are held to be excluded from the traditional fourfold caste system. These are people responsible for performing the most impure tasks and for having the most polluting occupations, like cleaning sewers or dealing with the carcasses of dead cows, which are believed to be extremely polluting. Considered in isolation from each other, the respective roles and duties of brahmans and untouchables appear arbitrary. When we consider them as two parts of a whole social system, however, it becomes clear that the polluted status of the untouchable depends on how his duties are contrasted with those of the pure brahman, and vice versa for the status of the brahman.[5] In essence, the brahman and the untouchable are two sides of the same social coin.

Purity codes are hardly unique to South Asian Hinduism. Very similar notions can be found throughout the world in many forms of Judaism and Islam to this day. Traditional forms of Judaism, for example, follow **kosher laws** (rules around eating properly prepared or ritually pure foods), which stem from ancient ritual and sacrificial notions of purity around the Jerusalem Temple, its animal and grain sacrifices, and its Levite or priestly culture.

As in the Hindu case, these purity codes extended into every aspect and nuance of ancient Jewish (and modern Jewish Orthodox) life—including, if we are to believe the biblical texts, how women experienced (or at least were expected to experience) their polluted status after childbirth. In the biblical book of Leviticus, for example, if a woman gives birth to a daughter, she is rendered "unclean" for twice as long as after she gives birth to a son (Lev 12.4–5). In short, purity codes did not just construct hierarchical societies. They also constructed hierarchical models of gender.

Contagion   Traditional notions of pollution and purity should not be confused with modern notions of moral agency, although it is true that they overlap significantly, causing endless confusions in the modern mind. Pollution is usually passed on not through any kind of intention or act of the will (as modern people tend to think of moral acts), but through contagion or touch. Pollution is contracted automatically, the moment one touches an "impure" object, food, or person. From a comparative perspective, of course, this "pollution" is not any kind of epidemiological or chemical reality "out there." We are not talking about germs. Rather, pollution is a ritual notion that performs or creates that which it claims to describe, rather like magical speech.

If purity codes are about social hierarchy, fixed social and gender roles, and automatic contagion, it follows that they will come into serious conflict with modern notions of morality, which generally assume the opposite values of egalitarianism, individual agency, and moral intention. The situation is exacerbated further here, because religious systems commonly conflate ritual states of purity and impurity with moral states of being good and being bad. The result of anachronistically combining ancient hierarchical social values based on purity codes and modern egalitarian social values based on moral agency is confusion and conflict. This is essentially what happens, for example, within modern debates about homosexuality. Ancient religious texts based on hierarchy and purity codes are invoked to condemn acts that are a matter of individual agency and human rights in the modern egalitarian context. The two models cannot be reconciled, and so the result is confusion and controversy.

The Body as Container   As the British anthropologist Mary Douglas famously argued in her classic study *Purity and Danger* (1966), purity codes imply a symbolic understanding of the human body as *a container*. Cultures then project this body-as-container outward and imagine the community as a kind of "social body" or communal container. Purity codes function to preserve the integrity of this container-body, whether it is operating at an individual or at a political level. At the individual level, what "gets in" is food and sexual fluids, and therefore these are fraught with anxiety and control. At the political level, what "gets in" is not food and sex, but immigrant communities, invading armies, and "foreign" ideas and values. Accordingly, political borders are, like the borders of the body and of the social self, fraught with anxiety and elaborate ritual defenses.

On the Importance of "Dirt"

Douglas's larger point here is the same one that we articulated with respect to the Hindu caste system, namely that, to understand purity codes, one must locate them in a larger whole or system. Douglas points to the influence of Gestalt psychology (the noun *Gestalt* means "shape, form" in German, and Gestalt psychology studies the ways in which human perception "constructs" or "creates"—*gestalten*—meaningful wholes out of the bits and pieces of the senses), which in turn led to an approach called **structuralism**. The latter is an approach that, in anthropology, privileges the entire system of a society over its individual pieces and parts, much as we saw in Dumont's analysis of Indian caste. Douglas's analogies and summary are well worth quoting:

> In the 1930s car designers found that they could eliminate the steel frame if they treated the whole car as a single unit. The stresses and strains formerly carried by the frame are now able to be carried by the body of the car itself. At about the same time Evans-Pritchard [a British anthropologist working in Africa among the Nuer] found that he could make a political analysis of a system in which there were no central organs of government and in which the weight of authority and the strains of political functioning were dispersed through the whole structure of the body politic. ... It follows that anyone approaching rituals of pollution nowadays would seek to treat a people's ideas of purity as part of a larger whole.[6]

As a side note, this "view from the whole" explains well why religious leaders and believers are often so concerned about what seems to be, to outsiders anyway, extremely minor ritual or doctrinal matters. The leaders and the believers are correct to be concerned, it turns out, as all of these seemingly minor details are in fact working as a whole, to provide integrity and strength to the car frame, as it were. Once the individual features are moved or eliminated, it is only a matter of time before the "car frame" of the religious system is compromised.

Humorously, there was one more inspiration for Douglas's famous approach to the subject of purity and pollution: her husband. He, it turns out, was much more concerned about cleanliness in their home than she was. This conjugal difference forced her to ask the simple question: Why is "dirt" good in the garden but bad in the house? It is the same dirt, after all. So why does it take on entirely different meanings in these two different contexts? Dirt, she concluded, is not the same thing as soil. *Dirt is symbolic disorder.* "Dirt offends against order. Eliminating it is not a negative movement, but a positive effort to organize the environment. ... In chasing dirt, in papering, decorating, tidying we are not governed by anxiety to escape disease, but are positively re-ordering our environment, making it conform to an idea."[7] Dirt, then, is about ambiguities and anomalies within a system of meaning; it is a symbol for something that does not fit in or should not be "in the house." She was beginning to understand her husband.

And Leviticus. According to Douglas, a text like Leviticus understands holiness to be more or less equivalent to wholeness, that is, to a consistent system. Purity codes are all about creating a "unity in experience."[8] "Where there is dirt," she famously observed, "there is system."[9] Accordingly, purity and pollution in ancient Judaism make sense only if they are understood as parts of a system held together by this sense of wholeness or unity of experience. They served the same function that cleaning up one's own home does in a more secular frame: they kept the dirt out and the order in.

To create a whole or to secure a sense of unity of experience, a system must, however, exclude most of the rest of the world of experience, which is inherently untidy, if not actually and flatly chaotic with respect to whatever order a culture creates. A house can only become a house if you build four walls that separate the inside from the outside and hence keep out all that "dirt." Hence the importance of what Douglas calls "rituals of separation."[10]

As we saw above, Hindu castes are separated from each other by rules pertaining to occupation, marriage, and diet. Similarly, in Leviticus, the Israelites are separated from other communities by the fact that they distinguish between foods and sexual acts that are pure or "holy" and foods and sexual acts that are polluted or "abominable." We will get to the sexual acts in the next chapter. As for the foods, animals that chew their cud and possess cloven hooves, or fish that possess fins and scales are considered "pure," whereas animals that do not chew their cud or do not possess cloven hooves, or sea creatures that do not possess fins or scales are considered "polluted" or "abominable." So cows and fish can be eaten, but pigs and shellfish cannot. By following these purity laws, the Israelites maintained a holy community that was separated from the rest of mankind. They sought the blessings of their god, which they believed could only be obtained if the community was holy, that is, if it demarcated holy foods and acts from abominable foods and acts and kept itself apart from the surrounding cultures and communities. Holiness meant *being set apart*, and it demanded excluding the other as foreign, polluted, and abominable.

New Directions: Space Exploration, Dark Green Religion, and Popular Culture

It is sometimes assumed that religious encounters with the natural world are a thing of the past. As we saw in the thunder god story, this is not true. Modern peoples, like ancient or contemporary indigenous ones, still encounter the sacred in and through the natural world. Three interrelated phenomena seem worth mentioning in this context: (1) the profound role that space exploration has had on the religious imagination; (2) the influence of the ecological crisis and of environmental concerns on the development of new religious sensibilities; and (3) the manner in which the biological sciences are being integrated into popular culture and non-traditional forms of religious expression, particularly through the framework of evolution. Let us look at each of these phenomena in turn.

A New Heaven

A **cosmology** is a model of the universe. If a cosmogony is an origin myth about how everything came to be, a cosmology is an account of the already existing (or created) cosmos and of how it all works. In countless traditional cosmologies, the gods dwell in the sky. They descend from and return to "the heavens," an English expression that still carries this double sense of "the sky" and "the place of the divine." Hence the first line of that most common prayer: "Our father, who art in heaven …" The reason why angels and other mythical beings are given wings is to fly up to the heavens; and people often look up when they are praying because they would like to do the same (or they hope their prayers might). This general inclination to locate deity in the sky or "up" is also why many of the traditional terms for "god" stem from a common ancient Indo-European root that meant "to shine"—which is what the celestial bodies do. This root has produced, for instance, the Sanskrit *deva*, the ancient Greek Zeus, and the Latin *deus* (which in turn is the ancestor of Spanish *dios*, French *dieu*, Italian *dio*, Romanian *zeu*, and so on—words inherited from Latin in all romance languages—and also of loanwords like the English *deity*). They all refer to a god who lives in or is associated with the sky, with "up."

But now we might reasonably ask: Which "up"? We know, after all, that our home planet is orbiting around an average star, which is orbiting in a gigantic whirlpool of a galaxy, probably around some spinning super-massive black hole. We also know that there is no such thing as "up." Up is entirely relative to one's place on this spinning globe, or relative to one's position in this seemingly infinite space.

What now? What does "heaven" mean, what *can* it mean, to modern, scientifically savvy human beings? How should we imagine the moon mythically, now that we have actually walked, even hit a golf ball, on its dry, powdery surface? What happened to us, religiously, when human beings traveled to outer space and knew, beyond a shadow of a doubt, that there is no heaven "up" there? Put most bluntly, what did NASA do to the religious imagination?

Figure 5.1   The ancient Hebrew conception of the universe (2010), by Michael Paukner.

There is a negative answer here, and a positive one. First the negative answer.

The negative answer boils down to the conclusion that, eventually, space exploration will almost certainly render irrelevant or meaningless any traditional religious symbolism that relies on the metaphorical equation of verticality with transcendence. As we will have occasion to see later, this does not mean that transcendence will become obsolete; but it does mean that human beings will eventually stop associating transcendence with "up." This obsolescence of an earlier religious symbolism, we must immediately add, is nothing new, as "the heavens" have changed considerably over the millennia. Ours is hardly the first era to abandon a cosmology or a particular view of the sky.

Let us start with the ancient Hebrews (see Figure 5.1). The ancient Hebrew cosmology, which is also the oldest biblical cosmology, imagined the universe as a remarkably cozy place, with the earth at the center of things and the sky as a kind of dome or ceiling upon which the sun, moon, and stars

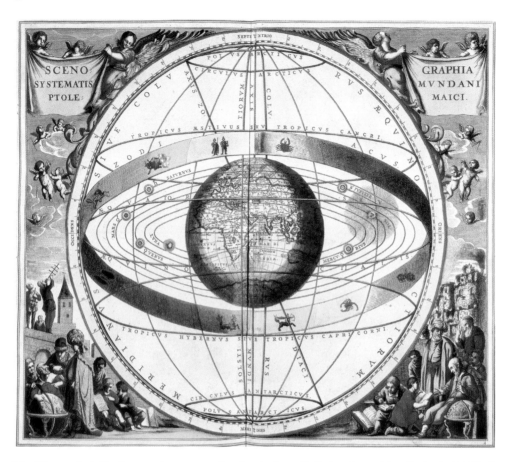

Figure 5.2   The ancient Greek cosmology, engraving by Andreas Cellarius from *Atlas Coelestis* (1661). Barcelona, Biblioteca de Catalunya (National Library of Catalonia). Photo © Mary Evans/M. C. Esteban/Iberfoto.

moved and out of which things like rain poured down. This would not last. As we move through the ancient Hebrew texts into the Greek and Roman worlds of the New Testament, early Christianity, and Jewish rabbis, things shift considerably and various ancient Middle Eastern astrological conceptions enter the picture. We eventually get a model of multiple spheres moving in harmonious sequence within one another, with the earth at the center of it all. This is sometimes called the Ptolemaic or geocentric model (see Figure 5.2).

Eventually there were thought to be seven heavens or spheres, through which a particularly gifted or graced soul could move as it ascended in an ecstatic trance, getting closer and closer to God, who was imagined as dwelling outside or above all of these spheres, or in the seventh of them. Some communities imagined an eighth still, while still others worked with three. It was to some version of this spherical model that a Jewish rabbi named Saul or Paul was referring when he spoke of being taken up "into the third heaven." The same conception would later become common in Islam, particularly around the Prophet's famous *miraj* ("night journey"), which we have already noted in our previous chapter. So this was a geocentric model of the physical universe that was assumed by all three of the West's monotheistic traditions in the first millennium of the Common Era.

And it was wrong. Clearly none of this can work anymore. We are on different ground now, or, perhaps better, under a different sky. There are no embedded spheres, no third, fourth, or fifth heaven, and there really is no middle to the universe. Clearly, moreover, the ancients believed that their journeys "through the heavens" went through the actual physical structure of the universe. They were not metaphorical journeys, they were being quite literal. But can we believe this? How can we continue to speak of the "heavens above" or of sky-dwelling deities, let alone of something as specific as the "third heaven"? What can this mean for modern religious individuals and communities?

This is where the positive answer comes in. For modern religious individuals and communities, this means exactly what new discoveries have always meant for the religious imagination: it is time to change. The religious imagination worked one way in ancient hunting and gathering societies (around the sacred power of animals, totems, and the hunt). It worked very differently when agriculture was invented (with the mysterious "death" and "rebirth" of seeds). It worked very differently again when iron could be mined and shaped and the horse and the chariot came on the scene (with winged horses and chariots now appearing in myths and mystical visions; see Figure 5.3). And it works entirely differently again in the modern world after electricity, nuclear power, television, and space travel.

We are no longer living in the Stone Age, the Bronze Age, or the Iron Age. We are living in the atomic age, the cement age, the silicon age, and the genomic age. And the ages are coming *fast*. Accordingly, modern people who experience themselves as leaving their bodies during a near-death experience (NDE) or out-of-body experience (OBE) seldom travel through spheres or ride horses and chariots. They travel, as we shall see soon enough, through "dimensions," they speak of "parallel universes," and they step out of "space–time."

Figure 5.3 Chariot of Elijah, from the Verdun Altar by Nicolas of Verdun (c. twelfth century). © Alfredo Dagli Orti/ The Art Archive/Corbis.

NASA and the Cold War space race between the United States, Europe, and the former Soviet Union inspired an entirely new set of mythologies and mysticisms, and on all sides. A long and careful look, for example, at something like the history of science fiction literature (a genre that came into clear focus just before and during the Cold War) can quickly reveal any number of camouflaged religious themes and sensibilities. The gods still descend from the sky. They are just in spaceships now. It is not, then, that modern science has made the religious imagination irrelevant. It is rather that modern science has helped to inspire different forms of the super natural (see Figure 5.4).

Here is a lunar story for you. Edgar Mitchell walked on the moon on February 5, 1971. On his trip

Figure 5.4   A field of galaxies through the Hubble Space Telescope. One of the most distant regions of the universe ever imaged, near the limit of the visible universe. © Corbis.

back home in the Kittyhawk command module, he became absorbed in a weightless contemplative mood before the beauty of planet Earth, that blue jewel of a planet suspended in black space. In this altered state, Mitchell had an overwhelming mystical experience of the universal connectedness of all things within an intelligent, evolving, self-aware universe. This was not an abstract idea or a vague feeling. It was a direct knowing of the mind and intelligence of the evolving cosmos itself.

It changed his life. This "grand epiphany," as he described it, led him the following year to found the Institute of Noetic Sciences in order to pursue the study of psychical phenomena and what he would eventually call the "dyadic" relationship between the material and the mystical worlds. He would later refer to his experience in outer space as his "samadhi," a Sanskrit term meaning yogic "union." He had, in effect, become one with an evolving universe that he knew to be conscious, intelligent, and alive.

Such a both–and vision of the material and the mystical is the key to assuring the survival of the species for the NASA astronaut. After rejecting the usually misplaced trust in artificial intelligence (as if mind were nothing but properly arranged matter), the astronaut proposes a new kind of mysticism, one that seeks to make more and more conscious the evolutionary intelligence that he himself had known in outer space and was now studying in paranormal prodigies:

> I find it more promising were we to allow the natural process of evolution to continue, aided and augmented by an informed, kindly, and intentional science that fully understands the processes of consciousness. … A dyadic model [which posits the fundamental unity of mind and matter] predicts that evolution is ongoing but coming under conscious control. To suggest that evolution is coming under conscious control also implies that it has been under subconscious or unconscious control … The individual who exhibits startling conscious control with mind-over-matter processes represents only the tip of an iceberg in an aware and intentional sea. The untapped potential that lies just under the surface is almost incomprehensible at our current stage of evolution.[11]

Obviously the sky is still sacred for many modern, very modern, people. It is simply sacred in different ways.

Deep Ecology

The other realm in which a new super natural has emerged is a wide spectrum of new religious movements; hence broad-based movements like neopaganism (a modern self-conscious renewal of various nature-based pagan and polytheistic religions of the past, often around the practice of ceremonial or ritual magic). Or that whole host of ecologically inspired religions that Bron Taylor has recently brought under the umbrella of "dark green religion." With this phrase Taylor means to name "religion that considers nature to be sacred, imbued with intrinsic value, and worthy of reverent care."[12] More specifically, dark green religion is "based on a felt kinship with the rest of life, often derived from a Darwinian understanding that all forms of life have evolved from a common ancestor and are therefore related." This kinship is "accompanied by feelings of humility and a corresponding

critique of human moral superiority" and emphasizes notions of interdependence and interconnectedness, that is, a "kinship ethics," particularly as these notions are established by the sciences of ecology and physics.[13]

Also of importance here is **deep ecology**. Deep ecology is a diverse philosophical, political, and spiritual movement that seeks to awaken both cultures and individuals to the biological truth of our existence, to the fact that we exist only because of the larger ecobody of which we are a most rare and astonishing expression. The historical roots of deep ecology lie in a fusion of the natural sciences, various forms of western philosophy and literature (European romanticism and the American writers Ralph Waldo Emerson, Henry David Thoreau, and John Muir, in particular), and Hindu spirituality. The expression itself can be traced back to the Norwegian intellectual and activist Arne Naess, who was both a trained philosopher and a student of Mahatma Gandhi.

Historian of religions David Haberman frames the principles and spirit of deep ecology through a simple set of questions: What is your body? Where did it come from? We actually have an answer to these questions. We know now that *every* molecule, *every* atom of our individual body comes from the larger ecobody out of which we evolved and upon which we depend for our daily sustenance and survival: the earth and its organisms. The water from the nearby lake or river is the water you drink, which becomes most of your body (about 75 percent of it). If the lake or river is polluted, so are you. The air in the sky is the air that becomes your breath, enters the intimacy of your lungs, and oxygenates your blood. If that air is polluted by the coal plant upwind or by the millions of cars driving around your city, so are you. Similarly, the food that you constantly eat and excrete is part of a larger ecosystem. If the food contains pesticides and preservatives, so do you. Finally, the oxygen upon which life itself depends is produced through the elaborate chemical processes of photosynthesis in the trillions of leaves of the trees and plants that surround us. If those trees and plants are cut down or are compromised in any serious way, you are in big trouble. You breathe *with* the trees. You depend on them.

Like any worldview, the deep ecology vision implies a set of values and practices. But there is a difference here. We are not, after all, addressing a set of moral values that came from the sky, were written on stone tablets, or were proclaimed by a prophet or saint. We are talking about a set of moral values that sit seamlessly with a set of scientific facts (which nevertheless are not sufficient to produce those moral values). Put a bit differently, this moral dimension does not work like a command or duty from the outside, as if you had to do this or not do that because some external authority or political party decided so. As this moral dimension is conceived by a figure like Naess, there is no such "external" authority within deep ecology. Environmentalism is not an imposed duty. It is rather understood as *self-defense*. To defend the health and welfare of the natural world is to defend the health and welfare of one's own body.

The signature moment for all this arrived well before any of these modern movements, in the heart of Victorian England. Taylor sums up the watershed moment and the manner in which it has split the religious responses into two basic camps—a traditional camp of denial or grafting, and a new camp of dark green religion:

> In 1859, Charles Darwin published *On the Origin of Species*, shattering traditional explanations of the fecundity and diversity of the biosphere. Religion would never be the same. Where this cognitive shift has been most deeply made, traditional religions with their beliefs in nonmaterial divine beings are in decline. Where traditional religions have not declined significantly, and to the extent their practitioners encounter societies that have adopted an evolutionary worldview, such conventional religions find themselves on the defensive. Yet the desire for a spiritually meaningful understanding of the cosmos, and the human place in it, has not withered away. Some

find ways to graft evolutionary understandings onto long-standing religious traditions. Yet increasingly, new perceptions, both explicitly and implicitly religious, have filled the cultural niches where traditional religious beliefs have come to be seen as less plausible.[14]

Taylor argues that these new forms of eco-religion are far more common and important than we normally recognize. Neopaganism and deep ecology are two of them. But so also is that ultra-modern, all-embracing realm of modern "spirituality," which more often than not is intertwined with both environmentalist concern and a willingness to rethink divinity from the ground up, as it were. This is not generally the case with traditional historical religions, however, particularly those that emphasize "transcending this world or obtaining divine rescue from it."[15]

Quite the contrary, the traditional monotheistic religions have historically been quite hostile to nature religion, which they have long associated with paganism, polytheism, and idolatry, that is, with their exact imagined opposites. Early nineteenth-century scholars of religion implicitly followed in the well-worn paths of these same theological convictions with their category of "animism." The latter they defined as the false attribution of mind or soul (Latin *anima*) to inanimate objects. They understood this as a form of intellectual error and associated it with "savage" or "primitive" religions, as well as with the origin point of religious consciousness itself. In short, for the early study of religion, nature religion = animism = bad thinking.

More recent analyses of the relationship between religion and nature have reversed this early assessment. The most famous of these reversals was by an American historian named Lynn White, Jr., who, in a 1967 article in the widely read and respected journal *Science*, argued that Christian monotheism was at the root of our modern ecological crisis. Christianity, he argued, promoted a dualistic approach to nature (with nature "out there"); fostered the exploitation of nature as object, property, and resource; and encouraged a callous attitude toward non-human creatures through its **anthropocentrism**, that is, through an exclusive focus on human beings as of sole intrinsic value and integrity. White held up Asian religions, indigenous religions, and both paganism and animism as counterexamples to this kind of western Christian arrogance and exploitation. Perhaps most interestingly of all, he also insisted that we cannot solve our present problems unless we address their religious roots: "More science and more technology are not going to get us out of the present ecologic crisis until we find a new religion, or rethink our old one."[16]

White's thesis is among the most often discussed in the literature on religion and nature. The thesis is widely shared for its precision and insight, but also widely criticized for its historical and comparative simplicities. Scholars have pointed out, for example, that it is simply not the case that non-theistic or non-Christian religions are always paragons of environmental concern. The Chinese geographer Yi-Fu Tuan has pointed to massive deforestation in traditional China, and a number of scholars of Hinduism have examined the massive pollution of sacred rivers in India.[17] The list of such examples could go on for a long time.

Nor should we idealize the eco-religions that privilege the environment as an ultimate good. Taylor has been especially careful to point out the potentially destructive or violent dimensions of eco-religions. For the most part, such dimensions derive from these religions' holistic ethics, which can sometimes occlude or even deny the importance and value of individual rights. Hence Taylor's description "*dark green religion.*" The "darkness" is meant to signal both a profound engagement with the natural world *and* these potentially destructive dimensions. Such a model is an excellent example of comparison done well—sympathetically toward every religious system encountered, but idealizing none and always applying the same principles to all.

Evolution and Popular Culture

Evolution is a fact that no educated person can deny. Its precise mechanisms or dynamics will continue to be debated by scientists and philosophers of science, but the facts are clear, well established, and beyond doubt: all life, including human life, has evolved from simpler life forms. What these biological and historical facts all *mean* is quite another matter, and this question science is ill equipped to handle. It does not, after all, appear to be a scientific question. It is certainly a religious question, though. To put the question most clearly: We know the *what*, but what about the *so what*? What about the *why*?

Among those who accept the *what* of evolution, this is precisely where the debate splits into two further camps: those who read evolution, with Darwin, as random and fundamentally meaningless, that is, as *going nowhere*; and those who read evolution against Darwin, as fundamentally meaningful, animistic, and ensouled, that is, as *going somewhere*.

Contrary to popular assumptions, there are sophisticated reasons for speculating about some sort of conscious dimension to the evolutionary process, if, certainly, not in the ways in which biblical literalists and the creationist movement have generally done. We are not talking about an ancient Israelite creation myth or yet another sky god here. We are talking about the mind-blowing complexity and microchemistry of the cell and its DNA "digital codes," which look very much as if they were written, or of the incredibly precise ways in which the four fundamental forces of matter (gravitational, electromagnetic, weak nuclear, and strong nuclear) are calibrated "just right" for the evolution of life.

There are multiple voices here. Some are simply open or deeply skeptical of the present orthodoxies. The philosopher Thomas Nagel, for example, has recently expressed very serious doubts about the materialist Darwinian picture, mostly on the grounds that it simply does not, and cannot, in principle, explain *us*—that is, conscious beings.[18] Other voices, like the primatologist Jane Goodall, have openly abandoned scientific orthodoxy altogether and effectively embraced a positive form of dark green religion. Once, she writes, we can "reestablish our connection with the natural world and with the Spiritual Power that is around us … then we can move … into the final stage of human evolution, spiritual evolution."[19]

The vast majority of evolutionary biologists, the first camp, clearly reject these speculations on the basis of Darwinian orthodoxy, which insists that evolution is random and pointless. The modern religious imagination that we are examining here has sided with Goodall and the second camp. Although its framing and nuances are very modern, this second camp sits comfortably with the cosmotheisms and evolutionary monotheisms of the ancient world that we examined briefly in Chapter 1. We first saw an explicit modern form of the ideology of this second camp in the New Testament biblical scholar David Friedrich Strauss and his bold assertion, already in 1872, that ours might yet be a "religion of cosmic evolution." These beliefs have only intensified since Strauss was kicked out of his professorial post. They are certainly no longer matters of religious speculation. They are now experienced in and *as* ecstatic states, as we saw with Apollo astronaut Edgar Mitchell. Whether particular scientists like the fact or not, scientific narratives like evolution are becoming enchanted. They are spawning new religious worlds and making new religious experiences possible.

Consider these two examples.

1   *The Dolphin DVD*   Jenny Wade's *Transcendent Sex* is a book about spontaneous mystical experiences reported during or around sexual activity. One such case involves a most extraordinary telepathic exchange with a super-intelligent animal (interspecies communication, particularly with elephants, dolphins, cats, and dogs, is a commonly reported phenomenon).[20]

"Max" is a former secret agent and now inventor who once found himself in a tank, swimming with two dolphins at a research facility. The female, a dolphin named Rosie, boldly engaged him in very physical ways that he experienced as sexual, as a kind of foreplay, as the male dolphin, Joe, swam neurotically at the bottom of the tank. Rosie exhausted Max, who real-

ized quickly that he was *way* out of his element, both literally and metaphorically. He climbed up out of the pool to rest. Here is how Max describes what happened next:

> Rosie pops her head up out of the water three feet from me. Her head's bobbing, and she's looking at me, and *it happened.*
>
> If they were making a movie of it, you'd see this stupid red beam coming out of her forehead, and it went *bam!* Right there to the pineal gland [he points to the center of his forehead].
>
> It was like *wow!* Suddenly this whole quick-time movie that was stored somewhere in me or in her began, like a DVD of all the evolution of this planet, the unfoldment of all life: all the structures, the elements of it, the species, the birth and death of species, the whole thing.
>
> I saw it as if on fast-forward, in full-color, in more than three dimensions in high resolution. It was like taking a film that would run six billion years and speeding it up to run in fifteen seconds so that you got the patterns, the codes … and when it stopped, she went under.

Max adds that this was all sixteen years before the Internet, "*years* before humans started languaging things like that in the culture." In other words, Max is looking back and using his training in computer science to make sense of his sexual–spiritual encounter with a cosmic dolphin. He calls Rosie's blast a "virtual-transmission implant." "It was *off the charts* in terms of communication. And it was stored in this species. That's how they communicate."[21] We are back to nature as super nature.

2   *The Infant God*   Does it matter that a scene almost identical with Max's telepathic transmission was featured in the comedy *Paul* (2011), an American–British film about a sarcastic alien (voiced by Seth Rogen) and two British comic book geeks on a UFO pilgrimage in the US? Or that Edgar Mitchell's claim that there are select individuals gifted by evolution with paranormal powers is the signature idea behind

the mythology of the X-Men? Or that Max actually invokes the "bad sci-fi movie" comparison?

These "loop" effects between the paranormal and popular culture are even more obvious in our second example, the work of Grant Morrison, a Scottish punk rocker and bad boy turned mega-popular comic writer, whose mind-bending writing has influenced such blockbuster films as *X2–X-Men United*. Morrison, it turns out, is a real-world X-Man, as his work is suffused with a dramatic contact experience he underwent in Kathmandu, Nepal, in 1994. It is also suffused with the central notion of *being written*. Recall that this is how we defined the condition of being inside a myth.

And what a myth Morrison found himself in! As he tells the story in his memoir, *Supergods*, he had gone to Nepal on a kind of personal pilgrimage. Morrison's own mystical encounter occurs in a Kathmandu hotel room, just after he had visited a Tantric Buddhist temple. As Morrison chills on the roof of the Vajra Hotel, he sees the temple come alive and begin to rear up, like one of those living sports cars in the *Transformers* movies. He retreats to his room, only to find chrome-like "presences" emerging from the walls and the furniture. Their liquid mercurial forms stretch even the writer's way with words: they were "rippling, dribbling blobs of pure holographic meta-material angels or extraterrestrials."[22]

Whatever they were, they communicated with Morrison, transported him to what looked like a distant planet, and then showed him the secret of the universe, which involved a kind of hyper-dimensionality, that is, the understanding that we live in a universe not restricted to the three-dimensional geometry we can sense and think about. In his own italicized terms, "I was *turned around*." As he put it, "my being was rotated through a plane I could not now point to" into an azure hyper-field laced with shimmering, lattice-like information grids.[23]

Morrison had been "twisted off the surface of the universe into the fifth dimension," into a new kind of eternity. The revelations followed fast and furious. One involved his realization that all of life

on this floating planet is a "single weird anemone-like mega-Hydra with its single-celled immortal root in the Precambrian tides and its billions of sensory branches, from ferns to people," stretching into the present and the future. It was as if he had been shown "an infant god, attached to a placental support system called Earth."[24]

Such language echoes the **Gaia theory** of the British environmental scientist James Lovelock. The Gaia theory, named after the Greek goddess of the Earth, postulates that the earth is a single organism that regulates itself for the maintenance and evolution of life. Lovelock intended "Gaia" as a metaphor, not as the invocation of a literal deity. But Morrison appears to be saying something more. Much more.

Like many visionaries (and hero myths) before him, Morrison understood that he had to return from these heights, in his case so that he could help "midwife" the infant earth-god. And so he came back—back into the flesh body. But back with a superpower. For a time at least, he could sense things, from a coffee cup to a coffee barista, in five dimensions: "I could see the shapes of things and of people as the flat plane surfaces of far more complex and elaborate processes occurring in a higher dimensional location." A human being now looked like a billion-limbed Hindu god, extending through time as it wormed back from the present moment and evolved forward into the future. "Everything was immortal and holy not as a result of some hidden supernatural essence but as a consequence of its material nature in time."[25] The super natural again.

Much like Mitchell, Morrison speculates that consciousness is the sought-after unified field that ties everything together. He also recognizes that things like telepathy and reincarnation would not be much of a mystery within this eco-mystical vision, as they would be easily possible if everything everywhere were one giant meta-organism stretched through eons of time. For what, in such a super reality, is *not* already in communication, already connected, already one body, already always one?

Comparative Practice: The Human Plant

Is it significant that Grant Morrison was smoking a little marijuana on the roof of that hotel in Kathmandu before the Buddhist temple morphed into a Transformer and chrome beings emerged from the walls? Does that relieve us of the responsibility of taking his experience seriously? Can life-changing religious experiences catalyzed by a plant really be understood through the long names, English letters, and Arabic numerals of a chemical formula? How about delta-9-tetrahydrocannabinol, or $C_{21}H_{30}O_2$? Is it *really* that easy?

In his historical study of drugs in American religious history, Robert Fuller put the matter most pointedly, and most correctly:

> [The subject of drugs and religion] is one of the most fascinating in all of religious history. It is also one of the most controversial. The fact that even a tiny amount of LSD [lysergic acid diethylamide] or mescaline can trigger mystical rapture raises challenging questions. What, after all, is an "authentic" religious experience? Is it possible that religious experiences are nothing more than aberrations in our brain chemistry? Or is it possible that the Kingdom of God is truly within us, but awaiting release through whatever means we can discover?[26]

Historically speaking, mind-altering or "psychoactive" plants or fungi (our C for the sake of this comparative practice) and religion go together very well, indeed.[27] We have spent some time in this chapter looking at the human relationship with nature through food and its cultural coding. But not everything that human beings put in their mouths is for nourishment or, for that matter, for the sake of stable social structures. Human beings also consume things to make contact with superhuman powers and presences, in effect, to *transcend* their social circumstances. There is a spectrum here, of course. Muslim Sufis have employed coffee (and much stronger plants in other contexts) to fuel their chanting and meditative practices. Many Native American cultures have smoked tobacco plants for centuries in their religious rituals. Some have also used peyote, a powerful psychoactive cactus. The famous

soma of the ancient Hindu Vedas, which helped inspire the ancient sage-seers to hear the sacred revelations, may have been derived from a psychoactive plant or fungus (or from the memory of one), and many Hindu holy men smoke marijuana to this day (so Morrison would have had company in the Kathmandu valley).

Nor are these practices a thing of some distant past, from which we can now protect ourselves. Psychoactive plants, fungi, and chemicals have also played important roles, if behind the scenes, in the recent history of modern psychology, medicine, science, technology, and, yes, the comparative study of religion. Particularly important here is what the research psychologist James Fadiman calls "cognitive enhancement." William James, for example, famously reported that one of the key inspirations for his model of mind in his comparative classic *The Varieties of Religious Experience* was an altered state of consciousness that he knew on nitrous oxide (we will return to his description in Chapter 12). Kary Mullis, who won the Nobel Prize in chemistry in 1993 for inventing the polymerase chain reaction (which made possible the human genome project), was on LSD intermittently as he developed his groundbreaking biotechnical innovation (we will meet Mullis again as well). And Steve Jobs, the visionary founder of Apple, described LSD as "one of the two or three most important things" that he had experienced.[28]

The point of these brief religious and intellectual examples is not to encourage the use of illegal substances, some of which have also had devastating social effects and ruined many a life. The point rather is to underline the profound relationship that has always existed between human beings and special plants and fungi (and, much more recently, man-made molecules related to the plant molecules). Indeed, I can think of few instances in the general history of religions in which the relationship between "nature" and "religion" is more obvious, more dramatic, and more revelatory than here. If we are going to understand the relationship between nature and religion, we had better try to understand this.

Toward this end of understanding the plants–fungi–humans religious nexus (which corresponds to

C in our online Appendix), let us look at two historical examples: the ritual ingestion of a sacred tea made from a vine and a bush within the traditional shamanisms of the Amazonian basin of Latin America (what we have defined as "our A"); and the discovery, naming, theorization, and cultural explosion of "psychedelics" among mid-twentieth century European and American elites and the counterculture of the 1960s and early 1970s ("our B" in the scheme of our guideline). It should be observed immediately that it is difficult, if not actually impossible, to separate A and B in any artificial way here. As we shall soon see, there have been countless historical interchanges between "North" and "South" America around these sacred plants and fungi. Accordingly, we would do well to see the Americas, particularly in their warm equatorial zones, as a single eco-zone producing a stunning array of vegetal revelations and religious traditions. If the truth be told, plants and people alike have never

really been very good at recognizing lines drawn on a map. And they often travel together.

Shamanism

Before we can engage in this comparison, however, we must introduce another comparative term. The word **shaman** is one of those major comparative categories that scholars worry about and argue over, but use anyway. It is taken from Siberian culture. More specifically, it is a Tungus word that means something like "sorcerer." "Medicine man" has been another common translation, particularly in the study of Native American religions (see Figure 5.5).

As with the comparative category of the sacred, there is an important moral ambiguity embedded in the term "shaman." Idealizing assumptions aside, while shamans do generally act as healers, mediums, and psychic hunting and military scouts for their own

Figure 5.5 Young shaman dancing during initiation. Inchon City, South Korea (2008). Photographed by Stefano De Luigi/ VII/Corbis.

communities, they can—and they do—sometimes act as sorcerers or black magicians toward their enemies.

Anthropologists and scholars of religion have long used "shaman" as a generic term designating a religious specialist within indigenous religions around the world who might serve any number of different functions. These shamanic patterns might include:

- an initial "calling" or "initiatory illness" in youth, often connected to a special dream or vision, that effectively separates the young shaman from an ordinary life;
- claims of bodily transformation, altered states of energy or "shamanic heat," and magical powers;
- an ability to alter consciousness or to enter dissociative trance states—through singing, drumming, dancing, and/or the ingestion of sacred plants, for example—in order to travel in spirit to the world of the dead or to the intermediate world to recover lost souls, guide departed ones, or do battle with threatening spirits, intermediate beings, or other shamans;
- a special relationship with a "power animal" or totem;
- an ability to heal the sick and suffering in the community;
- the role of keeper of the community's mythical lore and symbolic knowledge;
- the role of master of the ritual skills of divination and symbolic art;
- an anomalous, sacred, or "queer" sexuality (more on this in Chapter 6).

The above list is taken largely from Mircea Eliade's *Shamanism: Archaic Techniques of Ecstasy* (1964). This book has played a tremendously influential role not only in the scholarship that followed it, but also in the countercultural development of what we now call neo-shamanism, that is, the practice of a generically named "shamanism" by individuals living in urban secular societies who were not raised in indigenous societies. There are real insights in Eliade's classic study (like the repeated suggestion that virtually all of the later history of mystical and visionary experience can be found in the "archaic" practices and experiences of traditional shamans). But there are also real problems. One is that Eliade never lived or worked with shamans. Two others concern the fact that he dismissed the importance of psychoactive plants and spirit possession. He considered practices involving both plants and possession, which are extremely common in the history of shamanism, to represent "degenerate" forms of true shamanism, and he insisted on associating the latter only with ascension or spiritual flight, that is, with going "up."

Traditional Shamanism in the Amazonian Basin

Scholars who have lived and worked with traditional shamans often strongly reject these last two claims, and with good reason. The traditional shamanisms of the Amazonian basin (our A) is a case in point. Among the plant practices found here are ones that involve ayahuasca ("the vine of souls"), the name that the Quechuan peoples of the Upper Amazon and Peru have given to the vine component of a powerful sacred tea brewed by skilled shamans.

There is a real botanical mystery here, which boils down to the chemical fact that the active property of the leaves of the Amazonian bush that is used in the shamanic rituals is dimethyltryptamine, or, more mercifully, DMT. Here is the catch: DMT is not psychoactive if ingested alone, since an enzyme in the human digestive system called monoamine oxidase immediately recognizes and changes it. Put in less technical terms, our bodies easily recognize the chemistry of DMT and neutralize its effects. Our bodies have clearly known and done this for eons. The shamans of the Amazonian basin have somehow figured a way to get around the neutralizing process. They interlay psychoactive leaves of the bush and crushed stalky fibers from the ayahuasca vine in a pot of water and then boil it for hours. Because the ayahuasca vine contains a chemical that suppresses the enzyme in our stomach that would otherwise neutralize the DMT in the bush leaves, the result is a potent tea whose DMT remains active for the human being who drinks it.

Often enough, its effect is vomiting, in many cases followed by astonishing, hyper-real visions involving plant and jaguar spirits, orbs of light, and discarnate entities or disembodied beings. Interestingly, one of the most common modern descriptions of the ayahuasca experience, by both natives of the basin and foreign pilgrims, is that it is like "watching a movie," but a movie that one is *inside*. Many others have used sci-fi terms to liken the effects of ayahuasca to entering a parallel universe, an alternative dimension, or a hyper-space—which they describe as inhabited by real aliens, often of an insectoid nature. Anthropologist Stephan Beyer puts it this way: "What is most striking about ayahuasca visions is the sense of personal *presence*—first, that one is interacting with *persons* and second, that the persons are external, solid, three-dimensional, *real*."[29]

This is weird enough. But it is even weirder from a purely botanical perspective. Anthropologist Jeremy Narby presses the point we briefly made above:

> So here are people without electron microscopes who choose, among some 80,000 Amazonian plant species, the leaves of a bush containing a hallucinogenic brain hormone, which they combine with a vine containing substances that inactivate an enzyme of the digestive tract, which would otherwise block the hallucinogenic effect. And they do this to modify their consciousness. It is as if they knew about the molecular properties of plants *and* the art of combining them …[30]

But how did they come to know such things? If one asks them, the answer is swift and simple: the plants told them. And they are completely serious. Over and over, the reports come back: the plant speaks; the plant is conscious; the plant is a person; the plant is intelligent. Indeed, the plant is super-intelligent. And really, really *old*.

The religious and artistic dimensions of ayahuasca, both in the traditional indigenous contexts and in a series of modern transnational religious movements (particularly the Santo Daime and União do Vegetal traditions), have become the focus of much scholarship in the last few decades. This is really where most of the discussion of sacred plants and religion is

taking place now. There and in the American court system, around the key constitutional question of religious freedom and of whether religious people should be allowed to use prohibited or criminalized plants to make contact with superhuman powers and presences in their sacred rituals.

Two volumes of recent scholarship stand out in this quickly growing body of literature: one by an Israeli psychologist: Benny Shanon's *The Antipodes of Mind* (2009); and one by an American anthropologist: Stephan V. Beyer's *Singing to the Plants* (2009). Each of these tomes is massive, and each is deeply personal. Words like "insider" and "outsider" cease to have much meaning here, as both authors depend heavily on their own ingestion of the sacred tea and the luminous worlds of spirit-knowledge into which they were initiated. Because of space limitations, we will have to restrict ourselves to the hopelessly inadequate strategy of focusing on each man's personal experiences of these worlds, which they themselves privilege by describing them in the first pages of their respective books.

Shanon's quest began in the summer of 1983 in Ecuador, where he had a long conversation with an Indian woman guide whose psychological sophistication stunned him. Eight years later he was back in Latin America, this time in Brazil, for a scientific conference, after which he traveled, on the advice of a friend, to a "strange mystical group" in another part of the country. There he had his first encounter with "the Daime" (the local name there for ayahuasca). A dilapidated room became brilliant and beautiful. He saw giant butterfly-birds and a beautiful arabesque from which emerged reptiles, and he seemed to know what total strangers were feeling, who they were. This is an oft-reported phenomenon in the literature. Indeed it is so common that, when the first alkaloid was isolated from the vine, it was given the name "telepathine," that is, telepathic element or substance.

Shanon's second encounter took place during a formal *feitio* or ritual preparation of the brew in the middle of the night. He drank. "All of a sudden, the forest was aflame." He saw human history unfold before him. He also saw a kind of Eden, that is, the super natural world suffused now with the myths of his own Jewish heritage: "At one point I gazed at the forest, which was now washed by the fresh morning light. It seemed that this was the first day of creation."

Then what he calls "philosophical thoughts" came to him. They sound like the thoughts of the astronaut Edgar Mitchell and of the comic-book writer Grant Morrison, whom we met above:

> In particular, it occurred to me that process theories, such as psychoanalysis or Darwinian evolutionary theory, miss the point. The essences of persons and of species are not determined by the processes that these theories specify. The essences at hand are determined on another level. The processes only define the realization of these essences in the physical world and in time.

In short, we are not these species or these psyches. We are beamed and bent into here from elsewhere.

As Shanon advanced further and further into this research, the questions became more and more of a quest. He realized that "what I was actually entering was a school." The end result? "For years I have characterized myself as a 'devout atheist.' When I left South America I was no longer one."[31]

Stephan Beyer—a man with two doctorates (in psychology and in religious studies); a wilderness guide; and the author of a classic study of Tibetan Buddhism—brings numerous tools and gifts to the study of ayahuasca. His book dwells at length on his training under two mestizo healers of the Upper Amazon. It traces the mythologies and folk traditions around sacred stones, spirit possession, sex, harming and healing magical practices, and plant medicine, and it ends with discussions of present-day ayahuasca tourism and legal issues surrounding the use of psychoactive plants in the Americas. Like Shanon, Beyer begins his book with a deeply personal vision:

> Here is a story. I am drinking ayahuasca. Suddenly I find myself standing in the entry hallway of a large house in the suburbs, facing the front door. ... Standing at the door is a dark woman, perhaps in her forties, her raven hair piled on her head, thin and elegant, beautiful, dressed in a red shift with a black diamond pattern. She silently holds out her right hand to me. On her hand is a white cylinder, about three inches long, part of the stem of a plant, which she is offering me.
>
> I was concerned about this vision, because the red and black dress might indicate that the dark woman was a *bruja*, a sorceress. But don Roberto, my maestero ayahuasquero, and dona María, my plant teacher, both immediately and unhesitatingly identified her as *maricahua*, whom they also call *toé negro*, the black datura. They told me that this plant is ingested by splitting the stem and eating a piece of the white inner pith, about three inches long. The lady in my vision was handing me just such a piece of the plant, a part of herself.
>
> Ayahuasca teaches many things—what is wrong or broken in a life, what medicine to take for healing. It teaches us to *see through* the everyday, to see that the world is meaningful and magical; it opens the door to wonder and surprise. I need to open my front door, look out onto a bland suburban street, and see standing there the Dark Lady, the black datura—thin and dark, raven hair piled on her head, elegant and beautiful, silently holding out to me a stem of maricahua—and follow her into her dark and luminous world.[32]

Such a decision would not be a simple thing, and it would involve far more than a single experience, however remarkable. At one point, it would even result in him realizing that he had become a sorcerer, with actual and potentially destructive powers.[33] If Shanon used the metaphor of *the school* to describe what he would enter, Beyer invoked the traditional religious language of *the path*.

The New Shamans: Sacred Plants and Modern Elites

Now, our B. Narby, Shanon, and Beyer are all, of course, trained intellectuals writing for modern English readers. As this simple fact attests, the vine of souls has also played a real role in the northern hemisphere, and particularly in North America.

In the last half-century, the sacred vine has interacted again and again with poets and writers, scientists, anthropologists, scholars of religion, artists, and seekers of every sort in order to produce a stunning array of visionary material. Here we might just briefly mention the Beat writers William Burroughs and Allen Ginsberg, whose joint 1963 *The Yagé Letters* is usually pointed to as the definitive beginning of this hyper-interchange between North and South; the Harvard botanist Richard Evans Schultes, who called the Amazonian species "plants of the Gods"; and the remarkable American brothers Terence and Dennis McKenna.[34] We might also point to James Cameron's blockbuster movie *Avatar* (2009), which was widely seen by those in the know as gesturing toward the visionary worlds of ayahuasca, particularly in the dreamhunt scene—which was deleted from the released film but preserved on the extended DVD.[35] If Shanon had concluded from his own ayahuasca experiences that we are beamed in from elsewhere, Cameron's *Avatar* put this visionary experience to dramatic cinematic use, and this under the blue banner of a classical Hindu expression: the *avatara*—the "descent" of God.

Perhaps no one in this American history, however, has written and spoken more eloquently about ayahuasca than the late Terence McKenna (1946–2000)—a modern shaman and bard, if ever there was one. When Beyer summarizes the classic ayahuasca encounters with intermediate beings under the rubric of "elves and spirits," he is invoking McKenna. In a stunning series of comparative fusions that mixed everything, from Latin American mythology and modern chemistry to science fiction, flying saucers, and *The Wizard of Oz*, McKenna famously described these interdimensional beings as "self-transforming machine elves," "tryptamime Munchkins," and "hyperdimensional machine-elf entities." Beyer cannot help but quote McKenna on what is perhaps the most distinctive feature of the ayahuasca experience: the utter and absolute realness of this other inhabited dimension: "you are conveyed into worlds that are appallingly different from ordinary reality. Their vividness cannot be stressed enough. They are more real than real … and

Figure 5.6 Poster for Dennis McKenna's lecture at Rice University (2013), by Dean Mackey, Rice University Public Affairs. Dean Mackey

you realize that you are not looking in on the Other; the Other is looking in on you."[36]

The mirror again: this time as an interdimensional portal. Or door.

Figure 5.7   *St. Albert and the LSD Revelation Revolution* (2006), by Alex Grey. Oil on wood panel, 24″ × 36″.

Assumptions aside, the most immediate origins of the modern use of psychoactive plants and of the comparativist practices they have inspired (we might call these "psychedelic comparativism") were not among the youth culture and hippies of the mid and late 1960s. We can trace this sacred plant use as far back as we wish really; but the psychedelic era itself is most often thought to have started on a Friday, April 16, 1943, in a pharmaceutical lab in Switzerland. This was the Sandoz lab, where the chemist Albert Hofman first synthesized LSD-25 on a day that the later psychedelic subculture calls, playfully but seriously, "Better Friday" (by analogy with Good Friday, the day that memorializes the crucifixion of Jesus in the Christian calendar; see Figure 5.7).

The story then continues into the 1950s, with an American banker and his Russian wife—R. Gordon Wasson and Valentina Pavlovna—studying mushrooms around the world in consultation with professional scholars, for example the classicists

Robert Graves and Albert Ruck and the Sanskritist Wendy Doniger O'Flaherty. Graves would later write an ecstatic essay on his own experiences with psilocybin mushrooms in Mexico, suggesting that these experiences had something profound to do with ancient Greek mythology: another psychedelic comparativism.[37] For his part, Ruck would speculate that the ancient Greeks had used a drink derived from ergot (a kind of fungus, mold, or tiny mushroom) in their famous Eleusinian Mysteries—the same mysteries with which we began our own journey.[38] The story then moves on again, to a renowned novelist (Aldous Huxley), to two Harvard psychologists (Timothy Leary and Richard Alpert) one of whom became a Hindu guru (Alpert as Ram Dass), and to a famous, best-selling scholar of comparative religion whom we have already met (Huston Smith).

In short, the later American and European counterculture's engagement with sacred plants did not begin in the margins of society but among cultural elites, scientists, and academics, most of whom were associated with research universities. As for the term "psychedelic"—literally "mind manifesting" or "-illuminating," but also "-revealing" (*dēloun*)—it was coined not in a hippie love-in or by a rock band, but in a private correspondence between a famous writer and a doctor: Aldous Huxley and the British psychiatrist Humphrey Osmond.[39] We will return to this story in Chapter 12.

Comparative Reflections

What we have with these psychedelic comparisons, of course, is another comparative practice, through the super natural world. We might make three brief observations here.

1   *The Power of a Name*   First, we might observe that these two examples teach us an important comparative lesson: naming things is never innocent. The shamanic cultures of Latin America align their own use of sacred plants with expressions like "the vine of souls" and, in other contexts, with the Christian Eucharist. They see their ingestion of the ayahuasca

tea or consumption of psilocybin mushrooms as a sacrament—that is, as the ingestion and consumption of a ritual substance through which they can make contact with superhuman powers and presences. *And they do.*

What, then, happens to our comparative understanding of such religious events when we reframe these natural plants and fungi as "drugs," as in "drug store" or the "drug wars"? Is "hallucinogen," which means "generator of hallucinations," any better? "Psychedelic" is certainly historically and philosophically appropriate enough. As we have just seen, it means "mind-manifesting." But the word is now so loaded down with moralisms and extreme reactions to the counterculture that its usefulness is limited at best, and always controversial.

In 1979 a collective of botanists and scholars of religion (including Ruck, Schultes, and Wasson) got together in order to create and then propose a new word: **entheogen**. The word means something like "having the property to engender the divine within/ to generate one's own god/divinity." This is provocative enough, and it certainly answers the earlier prejudices, but the word has yet to catch on in the broader culture.

Our point here is not to pick a correct term. The point is simply to underscore the fact that it very much matters what we call things. Categories count. Words matter. Here, once again, we have to "come to terms" with a religious subject—and to *better* terms.

2   *The Chemical Technologies of Mysticism*   Perhaps we should not be relying so much on words. Perhaps we should be turning more to the sciences of botany, psychopharmacology, and neurochemistry. As we now know from these disciplines, the altering of human consciousness in every clime and time is neither accidental nor historically relative, since these psychoactive super-molecules are built in such a way that they can "plug into" chemical receptors in the human brain, which appear to be ready-made *just for this*. There is really no getting around the fact: we are made this way. This is how we co-evolved with the plant world. There is even some evidence, if still speculative, that our brains themselves may produce "endogenous" or internally generated psychedelic substances (including DMT), which in sufficient quantity could initiate visionary dreams, psychosis, and near-death experiences, particularly around trauma and physical death.[40] We might be our own best psychedelics or mind-illuminators.

Clearly, with the known chemistry of these natural psychoactive plants, and now with the production of new psychoactive substances (LSD, for example), what we have is yet another instance of a new technology and of a new body of scientific knowledge throwing light on, or even actually producing, new (and very old) types of mystical and visionary experience. Hence the potential power of the psychedelic comparativist practices. We saw this phenomenon above, in the case of modern cosmology producing new conceptions of "heaven"; in the case of the disciplines of ecology and physics helping to produce new dark green religions; and in the case of evolutionary biology helping to produce new evolutionary mysticisms.

3   *The Human Plant*   Finally, we might comment on the profoundly *relational* nature of all of this. When the great Spanish surrealist artist Salvador Dali was asked about whether he "took drugs" to paint his fantastic scenes, he quipped back: "I do not *take* drugs. I *am* drugs."[41] He was perfectly correct. We all are drugs. Every second, our neurological systems work through countless chemical reactions, whose speed and complexity can only boggle the conscious self. The religious use of sacred plants is an expression of this same universal human chemistry. As in Eliade's hierophany, however, there is no pure subject *or* simple object here. The spiritual inrush is not exactly "out there" (as it requires a human subject), but neither is it purely "in here" (as it requires a plant or chemical). The trip is not "in" the plant. It is really a "we"—the human world and the plant world, working together—that reveals, that manifests the sacred. Put a bit differently, if a sacred plant is psychedelic, it is only psychedelic *because we are.*

The Toolkit

The present chapter has been interested in developing five basic skill sets, again with the tools of the glossary terms. Like at the end of Chapter 4, here too we have given each one of these a short name. Here they are:

1   *The Ecology of Religion*   The natural world constitutes one of our strongest and most obvious foundations for comparing religions across temporal and spatial boundaries, just as we do with myth and ritual. Because different human communities live in different ecosystems, however, we also find a great deal of variance or "difference" across the religions here.

2   *Science and Religion*   We need to acknowledge the fact that many traditional cosmologies are simply untenable now, in the light of modern science, particularly those that involve a conception of "up" as some sort of heaven or as the realm of the gods, or those that deny the facts of evolution.

3   *The Super Natural*   But we also need to beware of projecting the western categories of the "natural" and the "supernatural" onto religious worldviews in which such divisions are simply not operable. We have suggested instead that you employ the category of the "super natural." With this simple little space between two letters, we can now begin to recognize that the religious experience of the natural world is seldom a form of "idolatry," as if it were a simple matter of worshipping stones and trees. Rather, it is more often the case that the sacred is manifesting itself *through* the natural world and its various objects, including—yes—stones, trees, and sacred plants.

4   *Purity as System*   Some of the most basic ways in which human beings have related to (and separated themselves from) the natural world are through the technology of agriculture and the production and cooking of food, along with the subsequent marking of particular foods as "pure" and "impure." The *content* of specific dietary systems, much like the content of myths and rituals, is culturally relative; but their *function*—to mark identity, to construct a world, and to separate a community—is remarkably consistent across climes and times. Similar markings of "pure" and "impure" are applied to particular bodily fluids, sexual acts, and specific communities toward the same ends, as we shall soon see in our next chapter.

5   *Science to Religion*   Finally, we noted that it is not the case that science and religion are always opposed. Indeed modern science is now helping to inspire new ways of being religious, which is what the reigning models of the natural world have always done. Science is also triggering new kinds of religious experiences, especially around space exploration, environmental science, evolutionary biology, and neurochemistry. The super natural does not disappear with the rise of science. It morphs into new forms.

•••

We began this chapter with a funny epigraph that captures the history of everything: "Hydrogen is a light, odorless gas which, given enough time, turns into people."[42] I suppose we could have just shut the book and stopped there. After all, as it stands, that one sentence of the history of the cosmos is true enough. It leaves a few things unanswered, though. Like where the hydrogen came from, and what exactly a person is. As we move from prehistory into history and watch the human experience of the sacred go more and more out of nature and into the book, we will see that these are the kinds of questions that come to the fore. The sacred in the storm, in the mushroom, in the oracle, in the prophet, and in the sheep's liver will become myth, scripture, commentary, and eventually philosophy.

As we shall see soon enough, all that speaking (and now writing and reading) hydrogen had more than a few answers to those perennial questions about itself, about where it all came from and why.

1 Are there any sacred animals in your world-view, that is, are there in your world any animals "set apart," which cannot be eaten because they are sacred or polluting? If your answer to this question is some version of "No," then ask yourself this: could you eat your pet, or, if you do not have a pet, the pet of a friend?

2 Would it change your relationship to the natural world if you firmly believed that that world was your larger body? Or God's body?

3 How is a religious experience, say, in a car accident or on a deathbed any different from a religious experience on a sacred mushroom? Are not fantastic levels of chemicals operating within the body in both circumstances? So why should we consider one authentically religious and the other not? Or are simply the chemicals speaking in both? If your answer is the last one, what does *that* mean?

Notes

1 J. B. S. Haldane, *Possible Worlds and Other Papers* (London: Chatto and Windus, 1927), 286.

2 Quoted in Bron Taylor, *Dark Green Religion: Nature Spirituality and the Planetary Future* (Berkeley: University of California Press, 2010), 32.

3 Bryan S. Rennie, *Reconstructing Eliade: Making Sense of Religion* (Albany: State University of New York Press, 1996), especially chapters 2–3.

4 Rennie, *Reconstructing Eliade*, 29.

5 Louis Dumont, *Homo Hierarchicus: The Caste System and Its Implications*, trans. Mark Sainsbury, Louis Dumont, and Basia Gulati (Chicago, IL: University of Chicago Press, 1980), 150–151.

6 Mary Douglas, *Purity and Danger: An Analysis of the Concepts of Pollution and Taboo* (London: Ark Paperbacks, 1988), viii.

7 Douglas, *Purity and Danger*, 2.

8 Douglas, *Purity and Danger*, 2.

9 Douglas, *Purity and Danger*, 35.

10 Douglas, *Purity and Danger*, 51.

11 Edgar Mitchell and Dwight Williams, *The Way of the Explorer: An Apollo Astronaut's Journey through the Material and Mystical Worlds* (New York: G. P. Putnam, 1996), 186–187.

12 Taylor, *Dark Green Religion*, ix.

13 Taylor, *Dark Green Religion*, 13.

14 Taylor, *Dark Green Religion*, x.

15 Taylor, *Dark Green Religion*, 3.

16 Quoted in Taylor, *Dark Green Religion*, 10–11.

17 See Taylor, *Dark Green Religion*, 12.

18 Thomas Nagel, *Mind and Cosmos: Why Materialist Neo-Darwinian Conception of Nature Is Almost Certainly False* (New York: Oxford University Press, 2012).

19 Quoted in Taylor, *Dark Green Religion*, 29.

20 For examples, often of scientists reporting these experiences, see Taylor, *Dark Green Religion*, 18–19, 23–24, 28.

21 Jenny Wade, *Transcendent Sex: When Lovemaking Opens the Veil* (New York: Pocket Books, 2004), 67–68.

22 Grant Morrison, *Supergods: What Masked Vigilantes, Miraculous Mutants, and a Sun God from Smallville Can Teach Us about Being Human* (New York: Spiegel and Grau, 2011), 279.

23 Morrison, *Supergods*, 280–281.

24 Morrison, *Supergods*, 290–291.

25 Morrison, *Supergods*, 292–293.

26 Robert C. Fuller, *Stairways to Heaven: Drugs in American Religious History* (Boulder, CO: Westview Press, 2000), vii.

27 Technically speaking, we are also talking about fungi here (mushrooms, for example); but, for the sake of simplicity, I will usually only reference "plants."

28 For the problem-solving uses of LSD in the lives of Jobs and Mullis, see Tim Doody, "The Heretic." In *The Morning News*, July 26, 2012. Francis Crick is often cited in this context, but his story remains speculative and likely apocryphal.

29 Stephan V. Beyer, *Singing to the Plants: A Guide to Mestizo Shamanism in the Upper Amazon* (Albuquerque: University of New Mexico Press, 2010), 238.

30   Jeremy Narby, *The Cosmic Serpent: DNA and the Origins of Knowledge* (New York: Jeremy P. Tarcher, 1998), 11.

31   I am relying here on the Prologue to Benny Shanon's *The Antipodes of the Mind: Charting the Phenomenology of the Ayahuasca Experience* (New York: Oxford University Press, 2002), 1–9.

32   Beyer, *Singing to the Plants*, xiii.

33   See Steve Beyer, "How I Became a Sorcerer," at http://www.singingtotheplants.com/2008/04/how-became-sorcerer/ (accessed August 2, 2013).

34   Dennis McKenna, *The Brotherhood of the Screaming Abyss: My Life with Terence McKenna* (St. Cloud, MN: North Star Press of St. Cloud, 2012).

35   Martin W. Ball, "Why Psychedelics Make Avatar More Sophisticated," at http://www.realitysandwich.com/psychedelics_make_avatar (accessed August 2, 2013)

36   Quoted in Beyer, *Singing to the Plants*, 239.

37   Robert Graves, *The Greek Myths* (New York: Penguin Books, 2012), xvi–xvii.

38   R. Gordon Wasson, Albert Hofmann, and Carl A. P. Ruck, *The Road to Eleusis: Unveiling the Secret of the Mysteries* (Los Angeles, CA: William Dailey Rare Books, 1998; first edition 1978).

39   See Don Lattin, *The Harvard Psychedelic Club: How Timothy Leary, Ram Dass, Huston Smith, and Andrew Weil Killed the Fifties and Ushered in a New Age for America* (New York: HarperOne, 2010).

40   Rick Strassman, *DMT: The Spirit Molecule* (Rochester, VT: Park Street Press, 2001).

41   My thanks to Dennis McKenna for this factoid.

42   Quoted in David Christian, *Maps of Time: An Introduction to Big History* (Berkeley: University of California Press, 2004), 27.

Sacred Wedding in the Night (2002), by Lynn Randolph, 36″ × 28″.

6

Sex and the Bodies of Religion
Seed and Soil

*Sexuality is a tangible yet invisible reality embedded in the dynamics of the cosmos. …
As an elemental cosmic force, sex is a reality that demands the attention of individuals
and communities. To ignore sex or repress it is to be excessively vulnerable to the
inevitable surprises this force will visit on the rigid or unsuspecting. Such visitations can
transform or undermine one's world. The discourse one has at hand shapes one's response
to these visitations.*

Dale Launderville, *Celibacy in the Ancient World*

Comparing Religions: Coming to Terms, First Edition. Jeffrey J. Kripal, Ata Anzali, Andrea R. Jain, and Erin Prophet.
© 2014 Jeffrey J. Kripal. Published 2014 by John Wiley & Sons, Ltd.

If I had to name two things that most define the day-to-day structure and dynamics of a religious world, I would not pick myth and ritual. I would pick food and sex. What one eats and with whom one has sex, after all, are matters of extreme importance for many religious communities. To make these matters more important still, food and sex are often combined, since both involve substances and fluids going "in" and "out of" the body. You do not have to think for long to come up with examples and colloquial expressions that combine these two basic human activities.

However humorous or vulgar, this deep symbolic linkage between food and sex is historically grounded. And I do mean *grounded*, since agricultural practices, which produce food, have been compared countless times to sexual acts, and vice versa. In contemporary American English, for example, we have all those sexual euphemisms drawn from the biblical world: "seed," "plowing," "forbidden fruit," "barren" women, and so on. We might summarize this sexual–agricultural symbolism as the ancient and widely distributed symbolism of "seed and soil," which imagines the planting of the male seed in the female soil.

It is here, on the subject of sex and religion, that many will experience a kind of "Aha!" moment. And nothing will be the same again. Having said that (and probably *because* of that), no other comparative base is more fraught with anxiety and potential controversy. We are on dangerous ground here. Before you proceed,

then, it is important that you *choose* to proceed; that you assent, morally and intellectually, to what follows. If you thought it felt slightly dangerous to approach religions as comparable performances of myths and rituals, or as a super natural world revealed through a thunderstorm or through the ingestion of sacred plants, you may want to think twice (and then thrice) about going any further. You may want to sit down.

But then you're probably sitting down already.

In the Beginning …

It is really quite remarkable. It could well be said that western monotheism begins (in the first few chapters of the first book of the Bible) with the subject of sex and religion.

The Serpent's Gift

It is a talking snake that gets the ball rolling. After the two creation myths of Genesis 1 and 2, patched together as they are, the action begins in Chapter 3:

> Now the serpent was more crafty than any other wild animal that the LORD God had made. He said to the woman, "Did God say, 'You shall not eat from any tree in the garden'?" The woman said to the serpent, "We may eat of the fruit of the trees in the garden; but God said, 'You shall not eat of the fruit of the tree that

is in the middle of the garden, nor shall you touch it, or you shall die.' " But the serpent said to the woman, "You will not die; for God knows that when you eat of it your eyes will be opened, and you will be like God, knowing good and evil." So when the woman saw that the tree was good for food, and that it was a delight to the eyes, and that the tree was to be desired to make one wise, she took of its fruit and ate; and she also gave some to her husband, who was with her, and he ate. Then the eyes of both were opened, and they knew that they were naked; and they sewed fig leaves together and made loincloths for themselves. (Genesis 3.1–7)

Put away all your assumptions concerning what you think you know about this myth: that the serpent is Satan, that the couple ate an apple, and that the story is about "original sin" or "the Fall." None of those things is in the story. Look again. What do we really see here? We see a story about a desire for knowledge and a subsequent sexual emotion, namely Adam and Eve's shameful sense of being naked after accepting the serpent's gift of the knowledge of good and evil. The story moves directly from the eating of the fruit to the shame of the couple's exposed genitals. Moreover, in the first line of Chapter 4, which follows immediately, we read of Adam "knowing" his wife Eve, who then gives birth to Cain. Some modern translations, like the New International Version, just ignore the verb "to know" and give us "Adam made love to his wife Eve" (Genesis 4.1). "To know" was a Hebrew euphemism for "to have sex with." Hence the "knowledge" of the tree that the young couple ate.

Modern readers, socialized by two millennia of euphemistic readings, normally miss the obvious; but ancient and medieval authors were generally not so naïve. The second-century Church Father Clement of Alexandria, for example, wrote about a community of early Christians who drew exactly these connections between the forbidden "knowledge" of the Garden and "sexual intercourse." And so they did the logical thing: they rejected sexual intercourse as forbidden.[1] Similarly, the medieval Jewish mystic Abraham Abulafia unabashedly identified the

Figure 6.1   *Adam and Eve Banished from Paradise* (1610), from *Hadiqat al-Suada* (*Garden of the Blessed*), Baghdad (vellum), Islamic school (seventeenth century). Topkapi Palace Museum, Istanbul, Turkey/The Bridgeman Art Library.

knowledge of the forbidden tree with sex: "Intercourse is called the Tree of Knowledge of good and evil and is a matter of disgust and one ought to be ashamed at the time of the act."[2]

In these traditional readings, the fruit of the tree of knowledge of good and evil that God forbade the first couple to eat was what we today call "sex." Why else would they become aware of their genitals immediately after taking a bite out of a piece of fruit? In truth, even today we know this. Hence the contemporary English expression that he or she is "forbidden fruit," or the grinning comment that so-and-so "knew" him or her "in the biblical sense." We know, in other words, that eating and knowing can and do function as symbolic codes for sexual acts.

The Androgynous God

The sexual complexities of the Bible hardly end here, though. Or begin here. In the first creation myth of Genesis, at 1.1–2.4, we are told that God created human beings "in his own image." Translators have a devil of a time with this passage. Here is a literal translation, this time from the Revised Standard Version:

> So God created mankind in his own image, in the image of God he created him; male and female he created them. (Genesis 1.27)

To an ancient Hebrew reader, the phrase "in his own image" would have referred to a physical likeness. So, for example, a little later, at Genesis 5.1–3, Adam begets Seth "in his own likeness, after his image," that is, Seth looks physically like his father. But what does God look like? Stunningly, what the Hebrew myth suggests is that God's body is "male and female," or what we would today call a **male androgyne**, that is, a being who is both male and female but whose maleness is nevertheless privileged (as is usually the case with androgynous figures in the history of religions). The human being is created in God's image, male and female, because God is male and female, or so it appears. Early Jewish rabbinic authorities certainly understood as much. Some of them suggested that Adam, made in this same "image of God," was in fact an androgyne before woman, contained within him, was removed from his body: she was split off Adam to form the first couple.

The Wife of God

God, it seems, was once a couple, too. We know from other ancient Hebrew texts that the Hebrew God-king once had a spouse, or a wife, who, in these non-biblical texts, is called the Queen of Heaven. Even from evidence in the Bible itself, we know that the ancient Israelites were commonly setting up wooden images or poles called "asherahs," named after Asherah, the goddess worshipped by the Canaanites. Hence the inscriptions, which date back as far as 800 BCE, containing blessings "by Yahweh and his Asherah." April DeConick draws the following conclusion: "These inscriptions show that in the old Israelite religion, the great Near Eastern goddess Asherah was associated with Yahweh. They appear to have been a very popular divine couple worshiped for centuries prior to the religious changes introduced by King Josiah in 622 BCE."[3]

Josiah and his prophet Jeremiah were the ones who began the purge of Asherah, a process that extended over the next few centuries, as the priestly writers blamed the Israelite worship of Asherah for the political and military disasters that befell them. As in the Garden, so here: the strategy was simple—blame the woman. The prophet Ezekiel went further than blaming the woman. He used images of spousal abuse and rape to assault Israel, now imagined as the wife of God, for its "idolatry," which he sexualized as conjugal unfaithfulness (Ezekiel 16.8–42). The Queen of Heaven, the lover and spouse of Yahweh, would now leave the historical stage to come back only in secret and visit places like the Jewish mystical tradition, to which we too will return.

Owning Up to What Is at Stake

We began the present chapter with this early Hebrew myth about a sexual transgression in a garden and an androgynous God/dess not in order to suggest that the Jewish and Christian traditions are somehow more problematic than other religions. Indeed these particular readings, *all of which were developed by Jewish and Christian intellectuals*, could easily be used to argue the exact opposite, namely that the most gender-redemptive re-readings of religion have emerged from the Jewish and the Christian traditions. No, we begin here to acknowledge the complexity and potential danger of what *we* are doing in this chapter.

A myth like that of Adam and Eve, after all, forces us to take seriously the highly conflicted emotional field in which this discussion seems always to take place, namely that defined by the human desire to know the truth about sexuality and religion (hence the serpent and the couple) and by the human desire to *not* know the same truth (hence the prohibition and punishment). Precisely because the realm of sexuality structures so much of the religious institution, practice, and experience, any extended attempt to study the sexual dimensions of religion will likely reveal (and implicitly challenge) some of the deepest roots of piety, sanctity, and religion itself. Put mythically again, we should not expect the gods of the religions to be terribly happy about this sort of inquiry.

Let me put the matter another way. When I was a boy, the common adult wisdom was that there were three subjects that one should avoid in polite conversation: sex, religion, and politics. The reason is obvious enough: these are the three subjects that divide communities and individuals most. We know why this is so. It is through these same three functions that communities and individuals define themselves as bodies/borders/containers. So, by addressing directly and honestly any of these functions, what one is doing is either defending one's own boundaries/borders/containers or calling into question someone else's. In any case, this is exactly how religion commonly functions both on a psychological and on a social level—through boundaries, borders, and belonging, all of which are arbitrary and historically constructed. There is thus *no way* to understand religion without thinking and talking incessantly about sex, religion, and politics, and at the same time no less. Which is all to say that there is no way not to be "impolite."

But at least we can be precise, responsible, and fair in our impoliteness. We certainly have enough new words. We have "come to terms." Indeed, one could argue that no topic has garnered more attention in the humanities over the last one hundred years or so than sex. As the French philosopher Michel Foucault liked to point out, we really, really like to talk about it; in some ways, modern thought has been defined by this constant talking about sex. One of the results is that the language we use has grown increasingly sophisticated and precise.

To talk about sex today, then, requires that we use our words carefully. In particular, we must practice at least five new ways of talking and thinking about

human sexuality: those defined by the comparative categories of gender, sexuality, sexual orientation, sexual transgression, and sexual trauma.

The Social Body: Sexuality, Gender, and Sexual Orientation

The category of **sexuality** refers to a biologically driven instinct that, although genetically determined to varying degrees, is nevertheless open to the profound cultural conditioning and influences of the social environment in which it comes to maturation. Whereas the biological and cognitive sciences have generally focused on the "biologically driven instinct" part, the humanities and social sciences have turned to that "nevertheless open to" part. We do not speak and write of sexuality, then, but of *sexualities*. These comparative practices were developed most fully in the last one hundred years (not accidentally, the same time period that saw the development of the study of religion) from a variety of systems of thought, particularly psychoanalysis, feminism, and French philosophy, or what I like to call "the Three Fs": Freud, Feminism, and Foucault.

Much of this discussion has been dominated by the category of gender. Gender is not the same thing as sexuality. We might define **gender** as a culturally variable model of masculinity or femininity, that is, as the meanings, values, moods, and practices normally associated with being a man or a woman in a particular social system. To put it a bit differently, a person's gender is not something that he or she is born with, fully formed. Rather a person's gender is something that he or she acquires over time through elaborate interactions between biology and culture, between genetics and custom, between nature and nurture, between sexual desire and social repression, and so on. It is not entirely set, but neither is it simply relative. Another both–and.

If feminism and the category of gender taught us to adopt a wide range of perspectives on religious phenomena that had been otherwise erased or hidden from view by the standard male gaze and its tendency not to question (or even see) how women might be perceiving and experiencing a religious system, that of sexual orientation honed this sense of perspective even further, by warning us away from what looks now like extremely naïve heterosexual assumptions about religion. By **sexual orientation** we mean the general (but not necessarily exclusive) direction of sexual desire in a particular individual, that is, whether an individual is sexually attracted to males, females, or both. It is very important here to distinguish between sexual *orientation* and sexual *acts*. The former does not require the latter. We will signal this distinction in our language. Hence we might write of "homoerotic" images, institutions, or desires, which implies the presence of sexual desire between men or between women that need not involve any literal or genital sexual act at all.

With such distinctions in place, what we did not see, what was always there "right before our eyes," suddenly becomes obvious.

Celibacy

And then we see. Consider, for example, all those religious practices of **celibacy** (a religious state defined by a commitment not to engage in any sexual activity for the sake of some religious end). Celibacy is, again, a form of asceticism, which is the name scholars give to a wide range of practices that discipline the body and mind, often altering their function in dramatic ways toward some religious end.

We should not imagine asceticism in only negative terms. In historical fact, these practices have been pursued toward truly fantastic ends, often involving the accrual of magical powers or access to some transcendent deity or hidden super-reality. The athletic metaphor is more than apt here. The Olympic swimmer, for example, does not get up at 4:00 a.m. every morning, count every calorie, and endure intense suffering (training) every day for years on end simply to "give up" something. That would be ridiculous. She does all of this to win a gold medal, to achieve some measure of fame, and to set herself

apart from everyone else. "No guts, no glory," as we say in colloquial English. That is ascetic logic through and through.

We see the ascetic practice of celibacy in many of the major world religions, in Buddhist, Hindu, Jain, and Christian **monasticism**, that is, in the practice of living celibately in same-sex communities ("monasticism" comes, through the Latin *monasticus*, from the ancient Greek *monos*, "single," "alone," which is at the origin of *monachos*, "unique," *monazein*, "to live alone," and the whole family of derivatives later on related to "monastery," "monk," and the solitary life). The claimed powers, the social and psychological complexity, and the fascinations of celibate discipline cannot be overestimated. Hence we see celibacy being practiced in religions that otherwise do not encourage celibacy, or even actively discourage it. Islam, for example, like Judaism, does not generally encourage celibacy as an ideal, but we nevertheless see it practiced in some Sufi groups.

The practices around celibacy have had real social consequences as well. Foremost among these is the production of new familial–spiritual relationships not determined by biology, whence all the familial language of religion: "father," "mother," "brotherhood," "sisterhood," and so on. We might also note here other possible consequences, such as increased physical mobility, economic discipline, advanced learning, and martial training. Not being married makes possible other modes of life.

Before the modern study of sexuality and religion, most interpreters were assuming that such practices are ascetic in both principle and psychology and require the effective suppression of sexual desire and affection. In other words, most assumed that these religious celibates really were "giving up" something that they deeply desired. We now understand that it is often more complicated than this. It all depends on how we imagine that the person is doing that "giving up."

Consider this. For a heterosexual male, celibacy most certainly would be a "sacrifice," as we say (in another religious register), since it is likely that such a man truly desires a female sexual partner, a wife, and generally feels at home in the heterosexual structures of society and in its central institution, the family. But how do such a celibate vow and the abandonment of "this world" (read: the heterosexual family) appear when we imagine them being enacted by a homosexually inclined man, or by almost any type of woman within a traditional society? They could well appear as *freedom*, as an abandonment of heterosexual structures that never fit the homosexual desires of the male in the first place or, in the case of the woman, violate her wishes—and in many cases her physical safety and wellbeing (she, of course, may also desire other women).

In both these cases, then, the individuals concerned would have "given up" something they did not in fact want for a life of love and companionship in a close-knit, usually same-sex community (a monastery, a brotherhood, or a convent, for example). Hence what appears to be an ascetic denial of basic sensual and emotional needs turns out, on closer inspection—that is, with the new categories of sexual orientation and feminine empowerment—to be an affirmation of a very different sexual orientation or gender position within a society that allowed no other meaningful or attractive outlets.

Queer Criticism

This approach is sometimes called **queer criticism**. Here "queer" is not a derogatory term. It is not a name calling. It is a technical term used by scholars, many of whom self-identify as queer intellectuals, to refer to any kind of sexual lifestyle, orientation, institution, text, or symbolic system that is fluid, ambiguous, and constantly morphing with respect to the direction of desire and/or the gender identity of the figures involved. It turns out that such comparative patterns are extremely common in the general history of religions. Religion is a very queer thing.

Related here is the concept of the **third gender**, an umbrella phrase for all those mixed genders, alternative sexualities, bisexualities, or transsexualities that do not follow the traditional binary logic of male/female or heterosexual/homosexual but break

out into other queer modes of sexual being and religious experience. Here we might think of the transgendered person whose body is male but thinks of "herself" as female, or whose body is female but thinks of "himself" as male. This shows up in the religious literature, for example, through patterns like the motif of cross-dressing (quite common in religions) and that of children remembering past lives in which they were someone else, of the opposite gender.

A commonly held notion in queer scholarship today is that societies before the nineteenth-century West, while holding socially constructed sexual and gender norms, had little or no model of homosexuality per se and, instead, had more fluid and less categorical conceptualizations of sexual orientation. Put a bit differently, premodern cultures tended to think of human sexuality in terms of specific sexual *acts*, whereas modern westernized cultures tend to think of it in terms of sexual *orientations*. This is generally true.

But this is not always true. Consider the case of Jainism, one of the most ancient religions of India. Jain monastic literature from the second to the eighteenth century CE provides us with recurrent discussions of gender and sexual orientation, including a systematic explanation of heterosexuality and homosexuality in the premodern world. The Jain term for sexual orientation or the direction of sexual desire was *veda*. Jains believed that there were three kinds of *veda*: *striveda* (the sexual feelings usually found in women directed toward men), *pumveda* (the sexual feelings usually found in men directed toward women), and *napumsakaveda* (the sexual feelings usually found in a hermaphrodite, which might be directed to either men or women, or to both). However—and this is key—regardless of the body's biology, all humans were believed to be capable of having any *veda*. For example, a person could be anatomically male and simultaneously be psychologically female, that is, a biological male could be sexually attracted to male bodies: he would thus possess a *striveda*. In our contemporary English-language terms, he would be a male homosexual.[4] It is very difficult to not see an ancient model of sexual orientation, and a very sophisticated one, in the Jain discussions of the three kinds of *veda*.

Such queer "clicks" of the lens can change pretty much everything with respect to the study of religion. These new clicks have found their greatest sophistication and most dramatic effects in biblical studies, where we now have dozens of elaborate studies of the queer nature of major biblical figures—from ancient Hebrew figures like King David and Jonathan, through Jesus and the apostle Paul, to God himself, who, after all, is imagined as "marrying" an Israel represented by men. But similar gender-bending patterns can be found in other religious systems. The Hindu deity Ardhanareshvara—"the Lord who is half woman" of the Hindu pantheon—is a particularly striking example: here we encounter a God/dess whose body is both male (on the right) and female (on the left), that is, another male androgyne (since the masculine is privileged as "Lord").

The bottom line of all of this? Spirit and sex are two sides of the same human coin. Indeed we should probably be speaking of sexual–spiritual orientations, and not simply of sexual orientations.

Feminist Criticism

Another key comparative category with respect to the subject of gender is that of patriarchy. The term has been developed mostly in feminist criticism, that is, in reading cultural documents and practices from the perspective of the women involved. **Patriarchy**—literally the "rule" (*archē*) of the "father" (*patēr*), whence *patriarchēs* in Hellenistic Greek and *patriarchia* in Byzantine Greek—is a modern critical term that refers to the observation that traditional cultural systems are heavily weighted toward male interests, values, authority, power, privilege, and perspectives. To take the simplest of examples, despite key queer passages like Genesis 1.27, "God" is assumed to be male in most western religions, whether this is stated or not. And, as the radical feminist theologian Mary Daly famously observed, "[i]f God is male, then the male is God."[5]

Because of these patriarchal patterns, women in the world's religions have been subjected to a most depressing list of sufferings, double standards, prohibitions, and outright violence. They have been forbidden to study their own scriptures and therefore have been deprived of any real religious authority; they have been married around puberty to much older men and forbidden to remarry if their husbands died; they have been blamed, imprisoned, even killed by their families for being victims of rape; they have been denied the right to divorce their husbands, no matter how abusive these were; they have endured physical mutilation, such as "female circumcision" or genital mutilation (particularly in Africa) and foot-binding, which is really a kind of foot-breaking (in China); they have been deprived of sufficient nutrition, of healthcare, and of birth control options; and they have been aborted in extraordinary numbers, far, far out of proportion by comparison with males (in India and China).

As the Indian Hindu case is explained by Anantand Rambachan, the dowry system (which makes having daughters extremely expensive, since the family of the woman must essentially pay the family of the man as part of the marriage arrangement) not only leads to thousands of "dowry deaths" each year (the murder of a young wife by her in-laws, often through fire, in a kitchen "accident," after the dowry is collected), but also contributes to some incredible female abortion rates. In one study done in Maharashtra, India, for example, out of 8,000 abortions performed, 7,999 were of female fetuses. The one exception was a Jewish mother who wanted a daughter.[6]

Moral Judgment

As the content of the above paragraphs makes clear, the category of patriarchy, really the whole field of the study of gender and religion, raises the obvious issue of moral judgment. This is a very complicated point, as most comparative work on culture and religion has operated with the assumed value of **moral relativism**: the position that it is in principle impossible to judge fairly between different cultural value systems, each of which is internally consistent and self-justifying. It is very difficult, after all, to judge another culture without implicitly or explicitly privileging one's own culture over the one being judged. How does one know that one is not simply thinking and judging out of one's own cultural biases and assumptions?

Still, judgments will be made, and many have equally worried out loud that models that rely only on cultural relativism prevent us from dealing with our own honest questions and moral crises. Many, for example, have noted that sexuality and gender are implicated in an astonishing range of contemporary global crises. Here they point to the debates surrounding abortion and reproductive rights, homosexuality, gay marriage, clerical sexual scandal, and the ordination of women in the American Christian churches; honor killings in some Islamic societies; religious resistances to the education of women around the globe; religious rejections of effective birth control that exacerbate population problems and encourage the spread of sexually transmitted diseases (including and especially AIDS in Africa); and, perhaps most dramatically, the "disappearance" (or cultural killing) of one hundred and sixty million women, mostly in China and South Asia, which was famously brought to our attention by the Indian economist and Nobel laureate Amatrya Sen. Such crises are, for these thinkers, fundamentally unanswerable within any framework that divides the single species into separate solipsistic cultures, each with its own infallible moral, religious, and sexual norms. From this perspective at least, cultural relativism (which we might frame as the affirmation of pure difference and the denial of sameness) is not just bad history; it is also bad ethics.

Many scientists would add: it is also bad biology. Evolutionary psychologists and sociobiologists—that is, scientists who study human behaviors and social practices as evolutionary adaptations and biological expressions—have been particularly vocal in their rejection of constructivist models of sexuality and gender, which they believe are flatly contradicted by the biological evidence.

The Paternity–Patriarchy Principle

The truth is that humanists and historians, who tend to emphasize the relative or socially constructed nature of gender and sexuality (that is, difference), and biologists, who tend to emphasize the universality of sexual biology (that is, sameness), are both correct. Nature *and* nurture, genetics *and* society appear to work together. With respect to the comparative study of religion, then, we suggest a double model that can be applied to a broad array of religious systems. This double model involves two extremely stable comparative patterns: a biological fact (paternity) and its anxieties, and a common social structure (patriarchy) and its religious results.

With respect to the first pattern, we might simply observe that, to a very large degree, religious purity codes about proper sexual behavior can be explained by one simple biological fact: until very recently, a man could never really be certain if a child was his. As the old Latin proverb went: *pater semper incertus est.* "The father is always uncertain." A more modern, south Chicago version, is perhaps a bit more memorable: "Mama's baby, Papa's maybe." With respect to this social pattern, we might simply observe that in most (patriarchal) societies wealth, inheritance, and the family's name are passed through the male line, that is, through the son, and not through the daughter.

If we put these two observations together (anxieties around biological paternity and the social fact of passing the family name through the male line), we get a very stable and very helpful (if troubling) method for comparing sex, gender, and religion across traditional cultures. Let us call it the **paternity–patriarchy principle**.

This is why religions generally prefer sons over daughters—to ensure the correct flow of inheritance and the accumulation of wealth in the father's line. *This* is why religions so often insist on female but seldom male virginity—to ensure that the child born to a woman is really the husband's. *This* is why religions often want to control the location and physical movement of women—to prevent their sexual access to other men. *This* is why religions so often encourage the marriage of young women or girls shortly after, or even before, puberty—to ensure that they have not yet been impregnated. *This* is why religions often condemn any kind of sexual behavior that either cannot produce a proper son or confuses the proper lines of inheritance—adultery, incest, homosexuality, bestiality, and so on. And *this* is why religions cultivate elaborate emotional fields of shame, "dirtiness" (read: impurity), and guilt around any acts or feelings that work against either these rules—to control from within the sexual behavior of individuals. Everything here is designed to produce sons that can inherit the patriarch's wealth and authority and hence to carry on the father's social name. Women are crucial, of course, but primarily as containers for these sons. As the feminist critics have so powerfully put it, women are basically wombs in most traditional systems. They are sexual possessions, "fields" to plow and harvest, certainly not agents or authorities in their own right.

Circumcision

There are a number of stunning illustrations of this paternity–patriarchy logic, but perhaps nowhere is the logic more obvious and more historically influential than, once again, in the first book of the Bible. Consider the mark of the covenant that God made with Abram in Genesis 17, whereby God changed the patriarch's name to Abraham and promised him that he would become the "father of many nations." This covenant is, in many ways, the beginning of all three monotheistic religions. And what is the sign of this patriarchal contract? It is **circumcision**—the "cutting around" of the tip of the foreskin.

Circumcision was widely practiced in the ancient Near East (by Egyptians and by Canaanites, for example) and was seen as a kind of "pruning" (another agricultural metaphor), that is, as a means of increasing male fertility. Similar agricultural motifs are implicit in the biblical story of Abraham. The penis, of course, is the male organ of procreation, and hence the instrument through which Abraham would "be fruitful"

and bear sons—countless descendants—and would become the father of many nations, encompassing three world religions. From that point on, every male in Abraham's family was supposed to be circumcised as a sign of belonging to this sacred covenant. The connections between paternity, patriarchy, and religion do not get much more obvious than that.

The patriarchal practice of circumcision is continued to this day in most Jewish and Muslim traditions, as well as in many Christian communities, if only for medical or cultural reasons in the latter. Interestingly, the early Christian communities, which were largely Jewish, would eventually break with Judaism; they did this for many reasons, one of the major ones being the dispute over whether the gentile followers of Paul (whom the apostle called the "foreskinned") had to be circumcised. Paul's position, rooted in the Jewish Torah, was quite complex, if not actually confusing, and would lead to much debate and division. It took one contemporary biblical scholar, for example, twenty-eight carefully reasoned pages to summarize the religious complexities around penises and foreskins in the Hebrew Bible, the New Testament, and the later history of Christianity.[7]

Very briefly, it appears that the apostle Paul taught that Jews should continue to be circumcised, since they were God's chosen people and circumcision was the sign of the covenant that God had made with them, but that the gentile followers of Jesus should not be circumcised, since they were not true Jews but now shared in the covenant by adoption. Eventually Paul's careful division was dropped and a more simple anti-circumcision position won out, as early Christianity moved out of its original Jewish matrix and took on a whole range of anti-Jewish polemics and attitudes. In this the Christian churches reflected the social mores of the Greek and Roman societies of late antiquity out of which they emerged, which considered Jewish circumcision to be a superstitious barbarism, a kind of genital mutilation.

Christianity, in other words, broke with Judaism on the penis and, more specifically, on the ritual removal of the foreskin. We can well guess that there were other reasons as well, less symbolic and more practical, like how to recruit adult males to the new religion if the first requirement was an extremely painful procedure on their most sensitive organ. Not exactly your best recruiting tool.

Ritual Nudity

Christianity was by no means the only major tradition that split on a sexual controversy (in this case, whether to cut the penis ritually). For a most remarkable analogue in Asia, consider the early split in Jainism. By the fifth century CE, the two largest Jain communities, the Shvetambaras ("the white-clad ones") and the Digambaras ("the sky-clad ones"), had split over disagreements concerning an ascetic sexual practice: monastic nudity. In fact the communities are literally *named* after the side they took in this dispute—whether or not their male monastics wear "white" robes or remain permanently nude, clad only by the "sky."

Again, to recap, Jains are dualists. They believe that the *jiva* ("soul") is real, unchanging, and eternally distinct from the material world, and that the body keeps it entrapped in the cycle of rebirth. It follows, then, that one must conquer the body and gain control over the senses through rigorous ascetic practices in order to attain *kaivalya*—"isolation." If one is successful in such practices, one becomes enlightened; upon such a person's death the luminous soul, often imagined as a perfect ball of self-conscious light, will float up to the top of the universe, attain *moksha*—"release" from the cycle of rebirth— and enter a state of pure absolute consciousness, being forever isolated from the material world below.

Ritual nudity was one central expression of this quest for total transcendence, since nudity is a powerful social marker of rejecting society. The question underlying the early debates was (and remains) whether or not it is appropriate for monks to wear robes. The sky-clad Digambaras argue that the robes infringe upon the spiritual path by perpetuating

attachment to social conventions, whereas the white-clad Shvetambaras argue that robes facilitate greater concentration on the spiritual path by preventing the distractions that nudity would cause. Such debates saturate Jain monastic literature.

There were also prolonged debates, in male literature, over the question whether women can achieve liberation. This particular feud includes expressions of revulsion from *both* communities discussed above toward the female body and its sexual organs, which are believed to be the centers of massive levels of "pollution." The focus of much of this anxiety is menstruation—a source of impurity in many traditional religious systems. The Digambaras argued that female anatomy is largely to blame for women's incapacity to achieve spiritual liberation, as it makes them impure by nature. On the contrary, Shvetambaras argued that, despite their anatomical impurity, women are still capable of spiritual liberation. Both groups, were, however, in full agreement that women cannot be permanently nude. Both held the unquestioned social assumption that the presence of nude women would destabilize society. Shvetambaras took it one step further, arguing that the reality of women's spiritual abilities, combined with the fact that they shouldn't be permanently nude, justify the male practice of wearing robes.

Padmanabh S. Jaini has convincingly argued that the question of women's spiritual abilities became central to the Jain schism, not because male monastics were overwhelmingly concerned with the question of female liberation—both Shvetambara and Digambara monastic literature express a strong vein of misogyny— but because of the need to justify each community's own definition of being a Jain monastic, which contained a provision on nudity. To this day, in a way that is very similar to how the presence or absence of circumcision defines religious identity in some monotheisms, the presence or absence of robes signals religious identity for Jain monks. Nudity is *precisely* what makes a sky-clad male—and not a white-clad male (or the other way round)—a monk.

Sex and Transgression

Recall our discussion of purity code systems in the previous chapter. What we did not tell you there is that cultures and individuals do not simply create structures of meaning and order through purity codes. They also take them apart by intentionally violating these same codes. We call this process of consciously violating a purity system toward some positive religious end **transgression**. The logic of transgression is a clear function of the "inside" and "outside" of any religious system. Consider a simple thought experiment like the following one.

Purity systems around the body-as-container are often extremely powerful because, once internalized through child-rearing practices, custom, and socialization, these codes are experienced as part of the self, that is, as *one's own* feelings, fears, attitudes, moods, convictions, emotions, and so on. The orthodox Jew or Muslim avoids pork or the orthodox upper-caste Hindu cannot eat beef not because he or she feels pressured by some external arbitrary authority, *but because this is precisely how he or she feels*. The common assumption from the insider's perspective, of course, is that he or she feels this way because this is the way things really are.

But the insider is wrong about that, as can be easily seen by simply lining up the dietary practices of different cultures and time periods. The comparative method, in short, effortlessly reveals the arbitrary nature of dietary rules. What is a horrific impurity or a devastating pollution in one cultural arena is an expensive delicacy in another. The simple truth is that human beings, as a species now, will eat practically anything that provides nourishment (and a large number of things that do not). From a comparative perspective, it is clear that dietary codes are historically constructed and culturally relative.

I, for example, feel nothing but pleasure and nourishment when I eat pork or beef, because I was not raised as a Jewish, Muslim, or Hindu. Quite the contrary, I was raised by a Roman Catholic family that included many cattle ranchers and beef farmers.

My sensibilities, of course, are also historically constructed and relative. Obviously the religious emotions of disgust, purity, and pollution around food practices are not natural. They do not correspond to, or reflect, the way things "really" are. They have to be taught and internalized. They have to be constructed and then constantly repeated and policed. They are products of culture, not of nature.

One of the most interesting aspects of purity systems is that they do not always work, not even with insiders. There are always individuals, even in traditional purity systems, who are not successfully conditioned, or who see through the arbitrary system and consciously seek to challenge, reform, or even overturn it, either in public or—much more commonly—in secret. One of the most widespread ways to do this is through sexual practices. This makes good sense: if, as we have already argued, a social world is structured largely around gender and sexual norms, then it follows naturally that one of the most effective ways of challenging the social order is to transgress the gender and sexual norms that undergird and support it.

Consider, for example, the figure of the "hero" (*vira*) of the Hindu Tantric traditions. He consumes impure substances and engages in forbidden acts, often of a sexual nature, in a bold attempt to break the bonds of society, to transcend the wheel of birth and death, and to become "divine" (*divya*). Similar undertakings can easily be found in the history of Buddhism, where practices like drinking from a human skull (used as a bowl) or meditating on a rotting corpse, either metaphorically or literally, in order to realize the impermanence of all things, are well established.

Similar creative–transgressive acts can be found throughout the history of Islam. We have already noted the Prophet's iconic smashing of the idols that were placed inside the Kaba. The old pantheon and the social order that supported it had to be destroyed for the new monotheistic social order to take effect: here, in other words, a form of religious transgression (the literal destruction of other people's deities) was the logical expression of the new faith. A very different sort of Islamic transgression occurred in the summer of 1848, when Qurrat al-'Ayn, the most prominent female follower of the Bab (the nineteenth-century founder of the Baha'i faith), astonished a council of men who had gathered to discuss the future of their nascent movement in the aftermath of their prophet's imprisonment. Qurrat al-'Ayn appeared in front of them unveiled (to be precise, without covering her face with the *burqa*) in order to announce that the followers of the Bab are no longer bound by the Islamic dispensation and its laws.

Individuals, it turns out, often suffer grievously for such simple symbolic gestures: George Fox (1624–1691), for example, the English founder of the Quakers, was beaten up and imprisoned many times for things like refusing to tip his hat to his social superiors (since, for him, all human beings were equal). It was not the tipped hat, of course. It was all about defending and preserving what the tipped hat ritually re-enacted: social hierarchy.

Probably the most well known case of religious transgression, however, is that new religious movement that emerged in ancient Judaism around the figure of Jesus of Nazareth. A second word of warning. We are about to engage here in an analysis that some may find shocking. I am treating this particular case for two reasons. First, I do so because the scholarship is especially sophisticated and developed; indeed, more sexual and gender analyses have been performed on the New Testament and early Christianity than on any other religious complex. *Way* more. Second, I do so because of the golden rule of comparison, which states that one should apply to one's own cultural tradition the same methods of analysis that one applies to the traditions of others. Very similar gender and sexual analyses, of course, could easily be done on any number of Muslim, Hindu, Buddhist, or indigenous figures, and indeed have been done. *No* religion is exempt from comparative practices around gender and sexuality. *No one* gets a free pass here. That's the flipside of the golden rule.

The Transgressions of Jesus

Jesus was a transgressive figure. It is very difficult to read the gospels, as a whole anyway, and not to come away with a distinct impression that this man tried his best to scandalize the pious and that one common target was the purity codes of Leviticus, as these were interpreted by the conservative religious authorities of his culture. He was certainly schooled in these purity codes and generally honored them. Indeed, as we shall see, he often radicalized and *extended* them. But his understanding of these purity codes was hardly in line with that of the religious authorities of his place and time. "Truly I tell you, the tax collectors and the prostitutes are going into the kingdom of God ahead of you," he declared to them (Matthew 21.31). It is not what goes in the mouth that makes one impure, he insisted, but only what comes out of it (Matthew 15.16–19). In short, it is not this or that food that renders one impure. It is intention. Put differently, literal purity codes are not the point. This was truly radical stuff in the hierarchical, purity-based culture of his place and time, where you were what you ate (pure or polluted), *regardless* of your intentions.

Like in the Hebrew Bible, the sexual shockers begin with the very first chapter of the very first book of the New Testament. It is listed in that first chapter of the Gospel of Matthew (1.1–11) that Jesus' reputed lineage contains three women, each of whom were famous for committing bold sexual acts: Tamar, who disguised herself as a prostitute to sleep with her father-in law, Judah (Genesis 38); Ruth, a Moabite who sexually seduced Boaz at the encouragement of her Israelite mother-in-law, Naomi (Ruth); and Rahab, a Canaanite prostitute who protected some Israelite spies (who appear to have abandoned their spying for other pursuits with Rahab) before the Israelite army slew every single person in the city, sparing only Rahab's family (Joshua 2). The sexual controversies continue right along with the story of Jesus' conception. His adopted father, Joseph, naturally assumed that the child was illegitimate (a form of radical pollution, technically worthy of the death penalty). Because of a dream, Joseph married the pregnant woman, who was probably still a young teenager, in order to protect her from the law (Matthew 1.18–20).

And that's just the beginning. As an adult, Jesus was a figure whose first miracle reported in the Gospel of John consisted in turning large vats of water into delicious wine for an already drinking wedding party (John 2). He was someone commonly described by his contemporaries as "a glutton and a drunkard, a friend of tax collectors and sinners!" (Luke 7.34); someone who openly violated the Sabbath, one of the strongest markers of conservative Jewish identity (Mark 6.1–11); someone who socialized and ate with sinners and sex workers (Matthew 5.30; Mark 2.16); someone who taught that there is no marriage in the afterlife (Mark 12.25; Matthew 12.30; Luke 20.35); someone who declared that a man cannot be his disciple unless he "hate father and mother, wife and children, brothers and sisters, yes, and even life itself" (Luke 14.26); someone who made his chosen messenger, to her own people, a Samaritan woman with five husbands and living extra-maritally with a sixth man (John 4); someone who does not appear to have been married but did have a male "beloved disciple" (a well-known biblical fact that some scholars have suggested, had it referred to a woman, might lead some to assume an erotic relationship).[8] someone who insisted that his disciples eat his flesh and drink his blood, a fantastically polluting act that his contemporaries immediately recognized as outrageous, gross, and deliberately offensive. Even many of his own disciples abandoned him at this point (John 6.51–66). Hence the conclusion of Theodore Jennings, Jr., that Jesus' attitude to the conventional rules of piety and purity was "one of insistent, persistent subversion. From the very beginning, Jesus's intention seems to be to drive the representatives of conventional piety crazy."[9]

Castrated for the Kingdom

Perhaps nowhere is this more obvious than in the famous passage in which Jesus holds up, as ideal disciples, those "who have made themselves eunuchs for the sake of the kingdom of heaven" (Matthew 19.11–12). A eunuch is a castrated man, that is, a male whose testicles have been surgically removed. This passage is worth dwelling on for a moment, since few people, as Jesus himself observed in the same passage, are able to receive it. "Let anyone accept this who can."

Not many can.

The textual and the social contexts are crucial here. First, as we have it in the passage itself, this appears to be an esoteric or secret teaching, for it is offered to Jesus' disciples alone, and the passage goes out of its way to acknowledge that few will be able to accept it. Second, it is important to understand that eunuchs were, in the words of Jennifer Wright Knust, "much reviled and yet well-known figures in antiquity, represented as not-men who were either overtly sexed or not sexed at all." Besides, castration was illegal under Roman law. Becoming a eunuch, then, meant a clear loss of social status: "Eunuchs were presumed to be either foreigners or slaves, castrated by their masters." Knust's conclusion seems more than justified: "Whatever Jesus intended, the saying in Matthew was clearly intended to shock the reader."[10]

Shock, indeed. Should we ignore the obvious here, namely that castration metaphorically feminizes the male, and hence makes him a potential object of male desire? Moreover, should we overlook the historical fact that the bishops of the early fourth century explicitly forbade priests to become eunuchs?[11] Clearly, at least some Christians were castrating themselves. Even if we interpret the eunuch passage at Matthew 19.11–12 metaphorically and argue that Jesus was calling on his closest disciples not to be married, which is exactly how it has traditionally been read, we are still left with the difficult image of a Jesus who was using a violent sexual image to encourage his closest disciples not to enter the heterosexual institution of the family.

Obviously none of this is meant to suggest that Jesus can be read as a kind of modern liberal or social prophet of sexual freedom. He cannot be. The truth is that Jesus actually *extended* the Jewish prohibition against something like adultery, making it encompass the lustful gazes of men and the private fantasies of masturbation. Hence Jesus encourages cutting off the right hand or plucking out the right eye that "causes you to sin"—almost certainly cultural allusions to manual masturbation and to the lustful look (Matthew 27.30). It is not, then, that Jesus transgressed every purity code all the time, or that he rejected purity codes in principle. Not at all. But the transgression of purity codes is only powerful if there *are* purity codes to transgress. It is more the case, then, that Jesus appears to have aimed his transgressions precisely and intentionally, and to both deadly and fantastic effects. The eventual result was his own arrest and state execution and, in the few next centuries, the eventual development of the largest religion on the planet today.

The Gender Wars of Early Christianity

The truth is that what we, today, consider to be Christian attitudes toward sexuality is the product not of anything Jesus said or did, but of what amounted to a series of "cultural wars" that took place in the centuries that followed his grisly execution. Much of this process—I mean the formation of attitudes to sexuality—was catalyzed by the rabbi Paul, who was not married and encouraged his followers to become permanent "virgins" like him. Marriage, Paul taught, was acceptable, but as a kind of compromise, certainly not as an ideal. Why? Because the world, as it was, was ending and there would soon no longer be any need or purpose for sex or procreation. There may have been other psychosexual reasons. Paul writes, for example, that "a thorn was given me in the flesh, a messenger of Satan to torment me" (2 Corinthians 12.7), a possible reference to sexual temptation or desire. Moreover, there is something very queer about Paul's desire to marry *everyone*, man and woman alike, to a single god-man: "for I promised you in marriage to one husband, to present you as a chaste virgin to Christ" (2 Corinthians 11.2). The sexual complexities of such a passage boggle the mind, at least any mind thinking in "straight" heterosexual terms.

The sexual understandings and practices of the early Christians became more and more diverse as the centuries proceeded. They ranged from complete rejection of sexuality and marriage (always after the celibate models of Jesus and Paul) to a call for the traditional domestic roles of respectable Roman society (a veiled subservient woman who obeys her husband and does not speak or lead in public); then to a secret sacrament

called the "bridal chamber" or the "mystery of intercourse," which appears to have employed prayerful contemplation, during sexual intercourse, in order for the married couple to participate in the union of the male–female Godhead and to produce pious children; and finally to a reported masturbatory ritual that involved the manual collection of semen and menstrual blood for consumption, as the "body" and "blood" of Christ, in a ritual context, for the purpose of "collecting the souls" (believed to be in the semen) and of "saving" them from dispersal in the material world.[12] We have to be careful to distinguish what the early Christians actually did from what they said they did (or claimed that their enemies in the Christian or pagan folds did), but the bottom line is clear enough: the positions Christians took on matters of gender and sexuality were diverse and, above all, contested.

These cultural wars—which, like most cultural wars, were male wars—were fought over two types of female body: (1) the veiled female body; and (2) the body of Mary Magdalene. It was the letters of Paul that sealed the former, as Paul argued that women must remain quiet and veiled "because of the angels" (1 Corinthians 1.10). This is probably a reference to the ancient belief that angels desired to have sex with human women (see Genesis 6). Unveiled women were considered promiscuous in Roman society; and, yes, angels were believed to have sex with humans. Paul also insisted that women show subservience to the natural authority of their husbands; for, just as Christ is the head of every man, "the husband is the head of his wife" (for the full argument, see 1 Corinthians 11.2–16 and 14.34–35). It was in this way, DeConick explains, that "Paul effectively threatens the women of Corinth into submission by suggesting that they have left themselves open to angelic invasion and rape by male demons." Moreover, he "orders the women of Corinth to put their veils back on their heads because their veils represent the authority of their husbands."[13]

As for the body of Mary Magdalene, her identity ranged in early Christianity from first witness of the resurrection, and hence first apostle, to a formerly demon-possessed woman, to the consort or wife of

Jesus, and to a repentant whore and model ascetic. It was the last trope that finally won out. But this process took *centuries*. Indeed it was not really sealed until the end of the sixth century, in a historically influential sermon by Pope Gregory the Great, which fused a number of diverse gospel passages into the single story that would become standard. We even have a precise date for this sermon: September 14, 591.

The two female icons of Roman Catholic Christianity—the Virgin Mary and Mary Magdalene—were now set. One was a contradiction: a lifelong virgin who was also a mother. The other was a repentant whore.

Super Sexualities

A biological sexuality, a socialized gender, a sexual–spiritual orientation, and the spiritual potentials of sexual transgression: these four have dominated much of the comparative study of religion and sexuality, and rightly so. But what has been left out, or not put on the table? One glaring omission is the historical fact that human beings have consistently reported moments in which the body functions as a window or star-gate into other dimensions of reality. Indeed in religions we encounter paradoxical descriptions—such as a "spiritual body," a "subtle body," a "rainbow body," an "energetic body," a "diamond body," a "glorified body," a "resurrected body," and so on. In art, moreover, the body literally *glows* (see Figure 6.2 and Figure 6.3).

Consider the liberated sages of Jainism, who are understood to be perfect spheres of conscious light at the very top of the universe, but here on earth are represented by giant bodies, in the likeness of their historical human incarnations. These bodies tower over their devoted crowds, utterly naked, immobile in perfect isolation and freedom from this world and its social mores. Perhaps, then, it is no accident that the Jain tradition calls its most recent historical founder Mahavira, "great hero" (*maha-vira*) or, with the slightest twist, "super hero."

Many religious traditions, then, have understood, and no doubt experienced, the human body in truly

Figure 6.2 Rainbow body (c. 2007), Tibetan ritual painting or thangka. Private collection of Timothy Morton. Photographed by Jenna L. Kripal (2013).

fantastic ways that overflow and transcend our present biomedical models, which assume, of course, that all the action stops at the skin.

We might recall the Adam and Eve myth again. The serpent's gift, after all, promised not only moral knowledge. It also promised **divinization**, that is, it promised to turn the young couple into gods. And indeed, once the two eat of the fruit, the god observes (in that confusing plural again) that the man and the woman have become "like one of us." Moreover, we learn that, if the two were to go on and eat from the second tree of life, they would be further divinized; they would become immortal. They would become gods.

Figure 6.3 *The Resurrection of Christ* (c. 1512–1516), from the Isenheim Altarpiece, right wing (c. 1512–16), oil on panel by Matthias Grünewald (Mathis Nithart Gothart) (c. 1480–1528). Musée d'Unterlinden, Colmar, France/The Bridgeman Art Library.

The snake was right. The truth is that human beings sometimes experience themselves as divine and, believe it or not, sometimes experience this human divinity in sexual activity. Let us give this comparative pattern a name. Let us call these experiences **super sexualities**. Consider, for example, the aforementioned work of Jenny Wade, whose *Transcendent Sex* chronicles, classifies, and compares the experiences of ninety-one individuals who knew mind-blowing forms of transcendence, empowerment, and illumination during sexual activity, many without any preparation or expectation at all. Wade's researches began when she herself—raised as "a good girl" in the Baptist, Methodist, and now Episcopalian denominations—spontaneously saw what looked like a past-life memory (of ancient Crete) during sexual activity and later had an episode in which "the whole world disappeared in a wash of white light that became clear, and then nothingness, nonduality, the Void." She expresses amusement over the fact that, although she was Christian herself, her life-changing mystical experience was clearly a Buddhist one.[14] The nonlocal self again.

She then proceeds to chronicle a series of sexual–spiritual events that include things like:

- streams of liquid light shooting out of the top of the head or skull;
- extreme body heat being spontaneously generated (a phenomenon, she points out, that is known as *tummo* in Tibetan Buddhism);
- sexual activity invoking or attracting "beings from other realms";
- visions of shamanic shape-shifting into animals like bears and wolves;
- the development of paranormal abilities, particularly telepathy or mind-reading;
- past-life memories or visions, often compared to "watching a movie";
- the stopping of time and a sense of eternity;
- the experience of every cell in the body vibrating at an extremely high frequency, which in turn leads to an out-of-body experience and a sense of being both in and outside the body.

The Erotic

There is really no way of understanding such moments in their full force with our modern, strictly biological notions of "sex." We need another category, one that can at least remain open to the most fantastic potentials of human sexuality and embodiment. I have proposed such a category. I call it the **erotic**. By the erotic I do not mean simply "sexuality." By the erotic, I mean to point to a sexual experience that also functions—we really do not know how—as an opening to altered states of consciousness and energy.

I am hardly being original here. I am doing little more than attempting to give a modern voice to some very ancient convictions. Plato, for example, wrote eloquently of *erōs* (the Greek term for sexual desire) as the very secret of the philosophical life in the *Symposium*. As that famous text explains, the philosopher is the one who knows how to take these sexual energies, not to spend them on lower things, and to redirect them toward the divine world. Plato, like many Greek philosophers, was discussing here a very particular kind of erotic desire: homoerotic desire. In later readings of the dialogue, this was the "heavenly" love that aimed at artistic achievement, the education of young men, culture, and the eternal truth (also related here was the public nudity of the male Greek athletes)—and not the base or "vulgar" love that aimed at procreation, women, and children. In the Renaissance, Plato's homoerotic concept of *erōs* would be framed as "Platonic love" by none other than Marsilio Ficino (whom we met in Chapter 2), who was a Roman Catholic priest deeply infatuated with another man, Giovanni Cavalcanti.[15]

We find other fusions of the mystical and the sexual throughout the general history of religions. We have already met briefly an early gnostic Christian community that employed the marriage bed as a sexual sacrament that could unite the genders of the Godhead and produce pious children. Something similar can be found in the history of Jewish mysticism, the Kabbalah, where the female aspect of God is known as the *Shekhinah*. Some Jewish mystics have made love to their wives on the Sabbath to arouse the Shekhinah and to reunite her with the male Godhead and so "repair" (*tikkun*) the world. In such cases, then—both Christian and Jewish—sex was not just sex; it was redemptive. Sex was salvation.

Similar super sexualities can also easily be found in the different Tantric traditions of Hinduism and Buddhism, where they positively abound. Consider the Tibetan traditions, where something called *bodhichitta* ("the thought [*chitta*] of enlightenment [*bodhi*]") is used in a conscious double way. This key term can be used *either* as an expression of the compassionate intention that all beings attain enlightenment *or* as a secret code for semen and menstrual blood—or, if you prefer, for sexual energy. Geoffrey Samuel explains the paradox and the profundity:

> Thus *bodhicitta* is not just a generalised desire to relieve the sufferings of sentient beings, it also has a direct and explicit link to the sexual drive and to male and female sexual secretions. The central issue here is about controlling and directing these flows so that they assist in the attainment of Buddhahood. The sexual practices are not necessarily physically performed, but they are intrinsic to the structure and imagery. Thus, while this is not stated directly, it is easy to read the practice as a directing and channeling of sexual energy and desire into the compassionate and altruistic central motivation of Buddhism.[16]

It is not for nothing, then, that the Sinhalese anthropologist Gananath Obeyesekere called the "transcendental eroticism" of Tibetan Buddhism "one of the most radical forms of sublimation on record." Here, after all, we have a system that imagines and portrays a practice "in which one has sexual intercourse with a select consort whereby orgasmic bliss is transformed into the bliss that promotes one's salvation quest."[17] It was this same worldview, at once spiritual and sexual, that produced all those images of Buddhas copulating with their consorts right in the middle of the image. Such transcendent sex, whether ritually enacted or meditatively imagined, is not a marginal feature of Tibetan Buddhism. It sits, quite literally, right at the center (see Figure 6.4).

Or consider the *ch'i*—the "life energy" of traditional Chinese cosmology. If there ever was a broad cultural system organized around a super sexuality, it is the ancient *yin–yang* system, known to us from

Figure 6.4 Vajrasattva (c. 2007), Tibetan ritual painting or thangka. Private collection of Timothy Morton. Photographed by Jenna L. Kripal (2013).

ancient Chinese civilization (it came to the fore under the Han dynasty, which reigned from 206 BCE to 220 CE). This cosmology teaches that all reality is composed of complementary pairs or "opposites" that work at all levels, be they in the natural world or in human experience and social life. The *yin–yang* model was the ultimate means of ordering the world and of comparing its patterns. *Yang* was considered male or active; *yin* was considered female or passive. *Yang* was heaven, sun, day, life, hard, waxing, above, hot, dry, fire, older, father, giving, and so on. *Yin* was earth, moon, night, death, soft, waning, below, cold, moist, water, younger, child, receiving, and so on. The key here is not to choose one over the other but to keep these two cosmic poles in balance and, moreover, to see them as two poles of some underlying fundamental mystery, a "supreme ultimate" or *Taiji* (often imaged as a simple circle), an undifferentiated unity, or a cosmic way—in short, the Dao (see Figure 6.5).

In human experience, the most fundamental way of combining apparent "opposites" into a greater whole is, of course, sexual intercourse between a man and a woman. After quoting a Daoist text on how "[t]he sexual union of man and woman is the *tao* of *yin* and *yang*," the scholar of Chinese Daoism Douglas Wile can observe that "[s]ex is *yin* and *yang* in action; *yin* and *yang* are sex writ large." Indeed, as Wile goes on, "one senses that much of Chinese metaphysics itself was actually inspired by the mundane physics of sex."[18] It was through sexual yoga practices, sometimes with a partner, sometimes "solo," that some Daoist masters and texts claimed to be able to preserve, master, and re-route the sexual energies and fluids toward the creation of a very special and subtle super body. They employed this "alchemy" to create a super body that they experienced as immortal and divine. Through a sexual yoga they became gods.

The Sexual Ignorance of the Religions

We have already discussed above how a huge swath of religious practices around sexuality are products of a dual logic involving paternity and patriarchy. What we did not discuss were the mythical dimensions of these sexual structures. There are two comparative patterns to identify here, which in turn lead to what I will call the sexual ignorance of the religions.

The first comparative pattern involves the identifications between male/spirit and female/nature. It can be mapped as follows:

male : female :: spirit : nature

That is, male is to female as spirit is to nature. It is astonishing how common cultures liken the male or

Figure 6.5   Sages with Yin Yang symbol, Kang Hsi period (1661–1722). Painted ceramic, Chinese School. Private collection, Ancient Art and Architecture Collection Ltd., The Bridgeman Art Library.

masculinity to spirit, soul, seed, and culture and the female or femininity to body, sexuality, soil, nature, and death. This, of course, implies that the divine order, too, is male and "up," whereas the natural order is female and "down"—and, well, you can see where that is all going. Anthropologist and gender theorist Sherry Ortner has critically engaged this comparative pattern in an influential essay entitled "Is Female to Male as Nature Is to Culture?"[19] If we stick to traditional cultures, the answer to the question in her title is generally "Yes."

The way this worked in the ancient Mediterranean world was through a simple and devastating understanding of gender that in turn informed, shaped, and determined most of western religious history up to the present day. The female body was considered a deviant or incomplete body. It did not, after all, possess a penis. In the words of April DeConick, the

female body was considered "as a body deficient, as an imperfect male, even as subhuman."[20]

The second comparative pattern may lie behind the first. Let us call it the **agricultural pattern**. Traditional cultures generally understood human sexuality in relation to agricultural practices, which, of course, involved planting seeds in the soil. The planting of the seed was understood as the male act and the soil or earth was understood to be female. This understanding in turn was connected to the common claim that women are the sexual property of men, just as the fields are. Hence all of those economies in which men exchange women as objects or possessions through practices like prostitution, negotiated marriages, and dowries.

Once these two broad metaphorical systems are in place, much of the traditional religious systems develop around them. Here is the problem, though. We now know that most of the bodily metaphors that structure and give meaning to traditional religious worlds are grossly biased in favor of the male body and, in many cases, are flat-out wrong in their biological implications. The history of this religious symbolism is based on what we now know is a form of sexual ignorance. That is a very strong claim, so allow me to explain.

Premodern peoples noticed that, when they planted, say, a seed of maize or wheat into fertile ground, a stalk of maize or wheat would come up. A seed of maize would never produce a stalk of wheat, nor would a seed of wheat ever produce a stalk of maize. The conclusion was clear and unambiguous: the "substance" or "essence" of a plant resides in the seed, not in the soil, although both are crucial for its development. They then carried over this agricultural model to the realm of human sexuality and compared male semen to "seed" and the female womb to "soil." They concluded, of course, that the "substance" or "essence" of the person so planted was in the male seed and not in the female soil. The essential soul or true spirit was male; the outer body or mortal frame of the person female.

This is perfect logic.

But it is perfect logic based on an agricultural metaphor, not on our real biology. We now know that this is wrong. The "substance" or "essence" of a human embryo, fetus, and child most definitely does *not* lie solely in the male seed. It lies in the male seed and in the female ovum, *equally*. Each sexual partner contributes exactly half of the genetic material. Moreover, it is the woman's body and time, not those of the male, that carries, gives birth to, and then generally nurtures and raises the human being. If anything, it is the female that is primary in the creation of a human being, not the male.

There is a second irony here, this time around what the male genetic material does in fact determine. Traditional practices around the world witness men taking concubines and multiple wives until one of these women can produce a male heir, as if it were the woman's fault that no son was born (again: blame the woman). We now know that this is doubly wrong, since the man can be infertile too; and it is the man, not the woman, who determines the gender of the child by contributing an X or a Y chromosome to the

Figure 6.6   Reading DNA strands with ultraviolet light. © Karen Kasmauski/Corbis.

woman's stable X chromosome (hence an XX is female and an XY is male).

There is, then, a massive mismatch between premodern agricultural understandings of human sexuality, a basic ignorance that almost all ancient religions share, and our modern biological knowledge of the mathematically even (23/23) genetic contribution of male and female chromosomal material via the event of ovum fertilization and subsequent cell division (see Figure 6.6). The result? We now know that we cannot turn uncritically to ancient religious texts to resolve our own moral questions about gender and sexuality, since the ancient religions advanced models of human sexuality that are grossly inequitable and biologically false.

Comparative Practice: The Two Ann(e)s

Finally, there is another comparative category that we have not yet treated. It is the most difficult of all (if that is possible), so we have kept it here until the end. We now approach the topic of **sexual trauma**, that is, the psychological condition of being prone to dissociative states of consciousness that "split" a person's sense of self because of earlier sexual violence or abuse, often of an extreme or extended fashion.

Sacred Trauma

The general idea is that human beings learn to dissociate in traumatic contexts—be they emotional, physical, or sexual—as a mode of survival. In effect, a person learns to separate his or her sense of self from the context and person being abused—which, of course, is also he or she. Hence the dissociative "split" state.

One of the difficulties of interpretation here involves the fact that human beings can also dissociate in non-traumatic contexts. The ability to enter trance states, for example, appears to come from a universal human potential, some individuals being more adept at it than others. Dissociation, then, like any other skill, is distributed unevenly throughout the population, and it is often actualized in particular life contexts or accidents.

A related difficulty involves the fact that dissociative states can be profoundly negative or profoundly positive. This fact is in turn relevant to understanding that broad range of ecstatic experiences, trance states, possession states, and dissociative forms of consciousness in the general history of religions, since these altered states often display two seemingly contradictory features: (1) they are often described as profoundly meaningful, even as ecstatic and transcendent events; and (2) they can sometimes be traced back to earlier life crises and can be read as traumatically catalyzed.

Please note the adjective "catalyzed" here. Note that I did not write "caused." My terms are carefully chosen, as I think it must remain an open question whether the initial trauma produces these states, or rather it somehow breaks down the normal workings of the psyche, to "let in" other states of consciousness or mind that are normally suppressed.

This is a very difficult point, which introduces a key nuance to which we will return in later chapters, so let me explain the situation through a simple analogy. People often report profound religious experiences during or after horrible car accidents. They experience themselves leaving the body, floating above the scene, seeing a light, and knowing degrees of peace and religious insight that completely change their lives, almost always for the better. Now no one would call an automobile accident a moral event, and no one would suggest that we deliberately drive our cars into oak trees so that we might have an out-of-body experience. Still, it is extremely doubtful whether these people would have had such experiences had they not been in those accidents. The physical trauma appears to be a necessary condition for the religious event, but it is not at all clear that it caused the personal revelation.

Something similar may well be true of other forms of trauma, including sexual trauma, and the positive religious experiences that sometimes appear to follow, often years later. We might thus speak here of sacred trauma, that is, of extremely positive religious events characterized by dissociative or "split" states of consciousness, which themselves encode histories of extreme forms of human suffering. In effect, something really bad catalyzes/causes something really good.

As a way of illustrating this comparative pattern further, we end this chapter with a study of sacred trauma (our C) in two historical female bodies: Mother Ann Lee, the foundress of the Shakers (our A), and Anne Heche, the contemporary Hollywood actress (our B). Mother Ann experienced a divine split self she called "Ann the Word." Anne Heche experienced a divine split self she called "Celestia."

Mother Ann

Mother Ann Lee (1736–1784) was the charismatic founder of the American Shaker community. This tradition emerged from a small English group of

Quakers, technically known as the Wardley Society (from its two founders, John and Jane Wardley) but popularly known as the "Shaking Quakers" (from the way they shook or quaked in their devotional rituals). Shaking and quaking mean the same thing: the redundant expression was originally intended as a jab or slur. Hence what we have here is another religious community named by outsiders.[21]

Much as we did in the opening pages of this chapter, Mother Ann quite literally identified the sin of Adam and Eve with sexual intercourse. She did this not because of modern scholarship (which did not exist), but because of an "open vision" she had around 1770 of the original couple engaging in the shameful sexual act. In other words, what Christians call the Fall (that is, Adam and Eve's violation of God's commandment not to eat of the fruit) was not simply about sex for Mother Ann. It *was* sex.[22]

Lee herself took this traditional sexualization of sin to an unusually dramatic conclusion, insisting on complete celibacy for her community in order to restore the original bliss of Eden. The logic was simple: if sin is sex, then salvation is no sex. It was an all or nothing proposition, a zero-sum game, for Mother Ann. This is why Mother Ann was understood to be a kind of counter-Eve. She was here to reverse what Eve had wrought through her lustful wiles.

Practically speaking, this meant strict gender segregation in the Shaker communities; shockingly intolerant prohibitions against married couples engaging in intercourse or bearing children; the breaking up of nuclear family attachments (children were raised communally); an obsessive concern with the control of sexuality and its many symbolic manifestations, including things like long hair;[23] and the famous marathon "shaking" and dancing sessions, which were used to express devotion, cement community, and probably spiritualize sexual desire. What we have here, in light of our previous discussions, is yet another example of erotic transformation: stop up sexual energies here, and they express themselves over there, in symbolic form—in this case through the devotional spasms of "quaking" and "shaking."

Mother Ann worked with a bisexual or queer theology based on an already familiar passage, Genesis 1.26–27 ("Let us make man in our image …"). Accordingly, God was believed to be both male and female, both an "Eternal Father" and an "Eternal Mother." If God is both male and female, it stood to reason that Christians could now expect a female incarnation of God. After all, they had already had a male incarnation of God in Jesus. Accordingly, just as Jesus had been the male manifestation of the Christ-spirit in the First Coming, Mother Ann was believed to be the female manifestation of the Christ-spirit in the Second Coming.

It is unclear and a matter of historical debate if Mother Ann herself claimed exactly this. When addressed, she would say, slightly more simply, "I am Ann the Word." But this is very close, since "the Word" is a traditional description of Christ from the beginning of the Gospel of John. Regardless, her followers, and particularly those who later systematized the community's teachings, certainly believed that she was the second incarnation of God or the spirit of Christ. In the words of the community, "Christ did verily make his second appearance in *Ann Lee*."[24]

Such understandings of sex, gender, and God had profound effects on Shaker life. For one thing, it undermined the usual structures of patriarchy, with men "on top" of women in every way. Not these men. Not these women. The segregated men and women may have performed traditionally gendered work roles, but they also enacted a leadership and authority system that was dramatically egalitarian by the standards of the time. Men and women were certainly recognized as different, but also as equals. As in early Christianity, celibacy, and particularly female celibacy, had radical countercultural consequences in the Shaker community. And almost all of them worked to the advantage of the women, who were now free to pursue many cultural and religious ends that were both unthinkable and practically impossible in the hierarchical subordination and with the procreative burdens of the traditional American household. Shaker women had it well.

Not that there was no hierarchy. There was. Ann once commented that "a body without a head is a monster."²⁵ *Someone* has to be on top. God may have been a kind of androgyne for the Shakers, then, but he remained a male androgyne: the maleness of God was ultimately privileged over the femaleness of God, even when both aspects were present and acknowledged.

But there was a dark side here, too. By all accounts, Mother Ann was absolutely terrified of sexual intercourse. As well she should have been. According to tradition, the poor woman had lost *all four* of her babies in infancy. Little wonder that she so feared sexual intercourse. She did more than fear, though. She prayed that no man "might suffer in hell on my own account" (by "stirring up the affections").²⁶ And she resolutely refused to continue conjugal relations with her husband, a long-suffering man named Abraham Standerin. His response? After bearing innumerable persecutions in the community, untold emotional turmoil with his wife, and a dangerous trip across the Atlantic, Abraham brought a prostitute to the house and told Ann to sleep with him or he would choose the prostitute.

He left with the prostitute, never to be seen again in the Shaker community.

Not that Mother Ann was any less harsh on other couples. Ann the Word saw, in her own phobic ways, that the bearing of children, or what she called "the filthy works of the flesh," was a terrible financial and emotional burden on women.²⁷ She wanted them to stop. Immediately. Hence her vision in Niskeyuna, New York, not long after the community (of just nine) landed in America to escape the barrage of physical abuse and criminal charges of blasphemy that they had faced in England. Niskeyuna was a plot of land in the wilderness up the Hudson Valley, where the community first settled. Ann saw a black cloud on the horizon, "as black as a thundercloud; and it is occasioned by men's sleeping with their wives." She then explained what would happen to these filthy spouses in the afterlife: "their torment appears like melted lead, poured through them in the same parts where they have taken their carnal pleasure."²⁸

Oooph.

And there was more. As her biographer observes, her nine-year spiritual crisis was a long struggle that, given what she says about the dates and the years, must have begun "at about the date of her wedding."²⁹

This sexual–spiritual crisis culminated in the revelation that she was Ann the Word and that the sin of Adam and Eve was sex. The revelation occurred some time around 1770, while Ann was released from internment in the Lunatick Ward of the Manchester Infirmary (or just around that time). The poor woman was not sleeping at night (she would hold her eyelids open with her hands), and she had become a walking skeleton, with what she describes as "down" for skin (a phenomenon known in cases of modern anorexia as well).

What role, if any, we might well ask, did Ann's traumatic experiences of sexuality and birth play in her sexual theology and in her subsequent deification as the Second Coming or as daughter of God? And can we locate the source of the trauma even earlier, in her childhood perhaps? As historians point out, children could have easily have heard their parents or older siblings having sex, as "rooms" were often little more than simple partitions.³⁰ The results were not often positive. "It is remarkable that, in early youth, she had a great abhorrence of the fleshly cohabitation of the sexes," a very early Shaker document tells us. "[A]nd so great was her sense of its impurity, that she often admonished her mother against it; which coming to her father's ears, he threatened and actually attempted to whip her; upon which she threw herself in to her mother's arms and clung round her to escape his strokes."³¹

The historian attuned to psychological matters is allowed to be suspicious about such scenes, particularly when we read that, even later in life, "sometimes, for whole nights together, her cries screeches and groans were such as to fill every soul around her with fear and trembling," and that "[b]y such deep mortification and sufferings her flesh wasted away till she became like a mere skeleton."³² The poor woman was really suffering. And, apparently, anorexic.³³ "Traumatized" seems far too tame a word to describe what had happened to Ann before she "split" and evolved into Ann the Word.

Anne Celestia

Such questions are complicated further when we place them, in an act of strong comparison, alongside another, more modern "Ann"—an Anne. In her courageous autobiography *Call Me Crazy*, Anne Heche graphically chronicles a childhood of repeated sexual abuse at the hands of her father, whose homosexual activities outside the home resulted in him contracting AIDS and dying on March 4, 1983, when Heche was only thirteen (he was one of the first reported cases of the disease). Not that his illness stopped his abusive behavior: he had stripped in front of her, crawled into bed, and asked her to join him as a sick and dying man.[34] Heche's brother Nathan drove off the road exactly three months after his father died and perished in the ensuing car crash.

While Anne's father was still alive, a family culture of total denial, a squeaky clean façade, and an Evangelical Christian piety in the home worked together to translate everything into obfuscating patriarchal terms that both vaguely legitimated and successfully camouflaged the father's abusive activities. These included whipping his children with a belt on their naked buttocks until the flesh broke and bled. In the patriarchal biblical logic, remember, fathers literally own their wives and children as possessions, and this can lead to real emotional, physical, and sexual abuse.[35] It certainly did in Heche's case.

The details here are absolutely horrific. According to her own accounts, Heche was orally raped via forced fellatio before she could speak, that is, when she was an infant.[36] A sister, named Cynthia, had died as a baby under unexplained circumstances. Anne had the obvious symptoms of herpes by the age of eight.[37]

The suffering, of course, extended well beyond the physical. The lack of cultural and psychological resources to give Heche's experience an adequate voice outside her family's religious register led to extreme forms of suffering and self-loathing (since she could not psychologically separate herself from the beliefs and behaviors of her family). The little fish could not think her way out of the water that surrounded her, despite the fact that this same water was polluted and was drowning her. As a young woman, Heche would thus feel profound shame and guilt around her sexuality ("A child of abuse thinks that sex is wrong").[38] She would also become sexually promiscuous, often with much older men, that is, with father figures.

Eventually, however, now as a young woman living and working in New York City as an actress on a soap opera, Heche sought help at the advice of a close friend. She practiced a most modern and most radical form of reflexivity: psychotherapy. Through this ritual practice, she learned to release and recognize her emotions and the past traumas. She would see two therapists (one male, one female), who helped her to release what she calls "pockets" of memory and emotion through gentle touch and the famous "talking cure" that lies at the basis of all forms of psychoanalysis. She would also engage with her past through LSD therapy, that is, through the investigation of the unconscious mind through this chemical catalyst and the visions it induced within a safe therapeutic environment. Heche is quick to point out that this form of therapy was illegal and deeply, deeply traumatic (it involved visions of things like "becoming shit" and being raped by her father), but that it was also ultimately healing and helpful.

Three years after these therapy sessions, Heche had a conversation with her mother on the phone, during which she confronted the older woman about what had happened to her as a baby and young girl. A little less than three weeks after this phone call, it happened. God spoke to the actress audibly. What did he say? He informed her in front of Ray's Manhattan pizza parlor that she was the daughter of God, just as Jesus had been the son of God. The impact of the voice was so strong that it threw her down, until she was straddling the curb. Here is what I take to be Heche's reconstruction of that conversation:

"Hello? Hello?" You might call out while checking for broken bones. "God, What the fuck was that?"
And like nothing you've ever imagined, God answers back. "Yes, Anne?"
"What?"
"You asked, 'What the fuck?'"
"God? Is that you?"
"Yes, it is true."
You search the sky for loudspeakers and see none. "Jesus, I must be crazy."
"No, but you *are* Jesus."

Now you get even more concerned about your mental
health than the moment before. "Oh, God!"

"That's right. Jesus, God, Anne. That's what you are,
Anne. Jesus. God."

There was more than a little critical perspective on
religion in these heavenly exchanges. And more than
a little of the trickster. Humor shines through the
traumatic opening that was this conversation:

"But what about Jesus? I thought he was coming back."

"It wouldn't be very fair to have me be a male both
times on earth, would it?"

"Why not? Isn't that what the Bible says?"

"The Bible was written by men."

"So it's prejudiced?"

"Very."

"I've always wondered about that."

"I know."

"But I didn't come from a virgin."

"Neither did he."

I always knew the Bible was full of it. "That's really
gonna piss some people off."

"People believe what they want to believe," God said.

"You can say that again," I said.

"People believe what they want to believe," God said
again.

"Thanks, God."

"You're welcome."[39]

And then things got weirder. For twelve days, Anne
Heche was ushered into another dimension of experience (she calls it "the fourth dimension") in which
she manifested striking clairvoyant, precognitive,
and paranormal capacities (although she uses none
of these familiar adjectives). She was guided by a
voice to walk—actually float, as she felt and experienced it—into a previously unknown leather shop to
buy two leather books for the new Bible she was
about to author. The clerk didn't even know he had
any leather books, but he then remembered and
found both of them under the counter for her. She
was guided down the street again to a record store,
where she now walked through a CD section and,
with her eyes closed and her fingers touching the
plastic covers, picked up a small pile of CDS, all
twelve of which, it turned out later, had religious
themes or images on them.

And that was just the opening act. She would soon
channel symbols and a language that she did not know
("I let the energy guide me") and wrote out, automatically and not knowing what or how, lines from a new
piece of scripture, none of which she understood in the
least but whose basic message was this: "*God is love.
The world is love. There is no pain unless we agree to
pain. War is an ugly battle of ego. Ego must die. We are
all God.*"[40] She healed the swelling and pain of a badly
sprained ankle of one of her friends named Light. She
found herself on the floor of a director friend's
apartment, reliving his birth as a breech baby with the
umbilical cord wrapped around his neck (two correct
facts he had never told her). She even woke up toward
the end of twelve days to discover that she had the stigmata on her feet, that is, the wounds of Christ. "I didn't
even believe in stigmata. I thought it was a Catholic
thing."[41] Finally, she went into a trance state and began
to sing something that sounded like opera. Heche's
response? "I'm singing fucking opera for God's sake,
and I have holes in my feet that I didn't put there. I'm
sick. Either I'm sick or I'm God, and I think I'd rather
be sick. I hate fucking opera."

Her friend Anna tried to record Anne's operatic
singing: "the tape recorder didn't record. It spun.
The record light was blinking, but it did not record."[42]
A comparative side note: the literature on UFO
sightings is rife with similarly timed technological
failures.

Which brings us to how this all ended. It came to a
head in the year 2000, in the desert, just outside of
Fresno, California, where the famous actress wandered, half-dressed, in the heat and sun, looking for
the spaceship that was going to take her home, to
heaven. Luckily she wandered into the home of a
gentle family, who gave her water, shower, fresh
clothes, and shelter until the police arrived. The
police were gentle and kind, and so was a nurse at the
hospital who taught Heche through an innocent
conversation to be at home here, on the earth. Her
best friend Kathy arrived and took her home.

As she looks back in the book, Heche does not claim to understand all of this, but she does have a theory. She believes that her telephone conversation with her mother was too painful to deal with. Deprived of human love and understanding, "I believe that my mind created a false reality that directly connected me with God." She no longer needed love. She *was* love. She *was* God. Having said that, she was also not in control. Anne Heche went off line, and a second self named Celestia came on line (Heche's middle birth name is Celeste). Celestia was the reincarnation of God, the Second Coming who had returned to teach the world that "each and every person on this planet was God." Heche later describes these twelve days as "the scariest, most invigorating, most insane-making period of my life. It is a time that affected my whole being for the next four years, until I could get a handle on what it was about and let it go."[43]

That certainly explains the religious content and shape of the events, of the psychological splitting, and of the message, even of the symbolic stigmata, the glossolalia (speaking in another language or tongue is a common phenomena in American Evangelical communities), and the sensation of floating, all of which could have easily been conjured by her mind from her childhood religious education and social surround. Indeed she says as much. But what about the clairvoyance with the two leather books and CDs, the birth reading, and the ankle healing, not to mention the stigmata and the opera scene? The honest reader is left with few simple options here.

Comparative Reflections

The act of comparing these two Ann(e)s, of getting them, in effect, to speak to each other in our own minds pulls all sorts of vague details from the background and brings them into the foreground, where we can ask some of the most difficult questions. We must be humble here, and we must recognize that our questions are speculative; but the patterns remain striking, indeed eerily similar: both women, after all, experienced serious and repeated sexual trauma, and both came to see themselves as a kind of female Christ figure. What

we might not have noticed in Mother Ann's case, though a biographer like Richard Francis mentions it several times, is that her contemporaries and converts would swear that she could read their minds and hearts. It is tempting to chalk this off to pious exaggeration. Until, that is, we encounter a Hollywood actress knowing where to buy two hidden leather books and psychically reading a director while curled up on his floor, as if she were a baby being delivered—as if she were *him*.

The differences between these two most extraordinary stories—and this is really key—finally lies well outside the religious register. They lie in the social contexts and final acts of the women's specific interpretations. The bottom line is that Mother Ann lived a hundred years before Freud and Anne Heche lived a hundred years after him. And that made all the difference.

Mother Ann may or may not have realized the connection between her early sexual life and her later religious experiences, but she found adequate meaning living entirely within a newly minted religious language that her community supported, celebrated, and ritualized. Francis sums up this reading:

> Ann Lee sublimated her terrible experience of motherhood into images of spiritual birth, and pictured herself, redeemed, as a new-born baby. By doing this she had transcended her trauma in two ways simultaneously: switching the terms of her experience from negative to positive by replacing tragic physical births with a glorious spiritual one; and consigning her previous miseries to a past that was as irrelevant as it was irretrievable. But much the same occurred with her sexual experience. She jettisoned physical love for the spiritual variety, but still saw herself in a male–female relationship [with Christ as her "lover"].[44]

It was in this way, Francis suggests, that the woman who lost all of her children in infancy thus became a mother of thousands.[45]

In another context—this time a young man who had the audacity to warm his back, as opposed to his front, against a fire (Mother Ann insisted that the former "enrages lust")—she declared that "God will break in pieces the man and maid. If you want to marry, you may marry the Lord Jesus Christ."[46] Since Mother Ann, like the apostle Paul, meant this to be applicable to both "man and maid," the historian sensitive to queer readings speaks up about right here. He or she speaks up a bit louder when one reads, on the very next page of Francis's biography, that, when a seventeen-year-old woman named Hannah Cogswell converted to the Shakers, she shared a room, and often the same bed, with Mother Ann for four and a half months.[47]

Heche lacked such a community, not to mention such converts. But she had something Mother Ann did not: modern psychotherapy. Through this set of ritual practices and this form of radical reflexivity, Heche learned to translate the religious phenomena into psychological categories and in this way she moved beyond them, in an act of healing and in a defiant act of public speaking and self-affirmation: her published autobiography. In short, whereas Mother Ann accepted her experience of divinity, rejected her sexuality, and created a new religion to be healed, Anne Heche rejected her experience of divinity, accepted her sexuality, and left religion in order to be healed.

"A child of abuse thinks that sex is wrong." Mother Ann accepted the equation of sex and sin. Heche finally refused it. With the historical tools and forms of reflexivity that are the comparative study of religion, we can well understand and sympathize with both these brave women.

The Toolkit

When I was being formally examined by my PhD mentors in the late 1980s, Wendy Doniger asked me what tool I choose to privilege in my methodological toolbox. I grinned and answered: "a very big Freudian screwdriver." The joke got the laughs, and it was certainly true enough, but it was more than a joke. It was an accurate reflection of the already noted historical fact that there are few subjects in the study of religion that have achieved as much sophistication as that evolutionary impulse, reproductive instinct, erotic inspiration, cultural shaper, ecstatic trigger, emotional anxiety,

and pure physical lust that we so casually capture under the hopelessly inadequate description "sexuality."

In the present chapter we have tried to say more around six basic ideas or skill sets. They might be summarized like this:

1   *Comparative Bodies*   As an evolved expression of the natural world, the human body is an especially reliable base from which to do effective comparison across cultural and temporal boundaries, since all human beings possess a shared anatomy, physiology, neurology, and biology. We are all members of the same family, all temporary waves on the surface of the same swirling gene pool. Biologically speaking, cultural differences are surface things. Deep down, in the tens of trillions of cells of each of our human forms, we *are*, each, all the others.

2   *The Male Gaze*   Having said that, it also remains true that culture plays an especially powerful, really definitive role in how we understand ourselves and our day-to-day experiences of these universal bodies. "Gender"—the standard cultural models of what a "man" or "woman" should be—is especially amenable to these social conditionings, and hence it is highly variable from culture to culture. Gender, moreover, is a key driver of most religious experience and expression, if in a profoundly uneven way. Traditional religious systems are inevitably defined from and for the male perspective, that is, from the "male gaze." When trying to understand any religion, then, one should also ask: "But what does, what could, what should this mean for a female member of the community?" Since the traditional answers to what religion means are male answers, the answers one gets to this question will seldom, if ever, be traditional. So be ready.

3   *Spiritual Orientation*   The same is true about the skill set of recognizing the liniments and signs of sexual orientation. Very common religious institutions (like celibacy or same-sex communities) take on entirely different meanings once we ask the simple question: "But what does, what could, what should this practice, institution, ritual, or experience mean if

we do not assume a heterosexual orientation in its subject or participants?"

4 *Super Sexualities*   We should also recognize that the history of religions witnesses numerous examples of how human sexuality can manifest dimensions and powers that *far* overflow any and all secular or biomedical understandings of the human body. Sex can, and does, morph into spirit. We saw this in the Tantric traditions of Hinduism, Buddhism, and Daoism, but also in ancient Christian gnosticism, in Jewish mysticism, and in the spontaneous modern American cases studied by Jenny Wade.

5 *Traditional Sexual Ignorance*   We must eventually come to terms with the fact that most traditional religious understandings of human sexuality are built upon the agricultural metaphors of "seed and soil,"

which we now know to be fundamentally false and grossly uneven with respect to the genders.

6 *Sacred Trauma as Breakthrough*   Finally, we must also ask how sexual trauma might be acting as a psychological catalyst for some of the extreme states that we see in specific founders and visionaries. We must be compassionate and careful here. In terms of the care, we should ask such a question in a way that does not presume a straight causal mechanism. Sometimes a "break" might also be an "opening." We saw this pattern most dramatically in our comparative discussions of the two brave Ann(e)s.

What such new skill sets and tools will build in our communities has yet to take shape. What will *you* build? And, just importantly, what will you have to take apart first?

The Tough Questions

1 In contemporary American culture, a bride generally wears white instead of, say, black or red, and a pornographic magazine is called a "dirty magazine," despite the fact that it is in chemical fact glossy and perfectly clean. Comment on both with what you now know about purity codes.

2 Read Amartya Sen's famous *New York Review of Books* essay "100 Million Women Are Missing" (December 20, 1990). Do some cultures eliminate millions of women through neglect and the inequitable distribution of nutrition and healthcare? Comment.

3 There are certainly plenty of "fathers" and "sons" in religious mythologies. Why are there so few "daughters"?

4 Comment on the historical background of a father "giving away" his daughter at a Christian wedding ceremony.

5 What would happen to the religions if they abandoned their biologically false agricultural models of human sexuality and adopted the biologically correct genetic models? Would this produce a new **gender equity**, that is, the ethical principle that the genders (all of them) should be treated equally?

Notes

1 April D. DeConick, *Holy Misogyny: Why the Sex and Gender Conflicts in the Early Church Still Matter* (New York: Continuum, 2011), 85.

2 Quoted in David Biale, *Eros and the Jews: From Biblical Israel to Contemporary America* (Berkeley: University of California Press, 1997), 109.

3   DeConick, *Holy Misogyny*, 10.

4   See Padmanabh S. Jaini, *Gender and Salvation: Jaina Debates on the Spiritual Liberation of Women* (Berkeley: University of California Press, 1991).

5   Mary Daly, *Beyond God the Father: Toward a Philosophy of Women's Liberation* (Boston, MA: Beacon Press, 1993), 19.

6   Anantand Rambachan, "A Hindu Perspective." In *What Men Owe to Women: Men's Voices from World Religions*, edited by John C. Raines and Daniel C. Maguire (Albany: State University of New York Press, 2001), 23.

7   Jennifer Wright Knust, *Unprotected Texts: The Bible's Surprising Contractions about Sex and Desire* (New York: HarperOne, 2011), 191–218.

8   Dale B. Martin, *Sex and the Single Savior: Gender and Sexuality in Biblical Interpretation* (Louisville, KY: Westminster John Knox Press, 2006), 100.

9   Theodore Jennings, Jr., *The Man Jesus Loved: Homoerotic Narratives from the New Testament* (Cleveland, OH: Pilgrim's Press, 2009), 68.

10   Knust, *Unprotected Texts*, 68. Jesus' teachings on divorce are also relevant here, since the eunuch passage appears in response to a question about divorce.

11   Knust, *Unprotected Texts*, 68.

12   See DeConick, *Holy Misogyny*, 106–110, 139.

13   DeConick, *Holy Misogyny*, 59.

14   Jenny Wade, *Transcendent Sex: When Lovemaking Opens the Veil* (New York: Pocket Books, 2004), 8.

15   Wouter J. Hanegraaff, "Under the Mantle of Love: The Mystical Eroticisms of Marsilio Ficino and Giordano Bruno." In *Hidden Intercourse: Eros and Sexuality in the History of Western Esotericism*, edited by Wouter J. Hanegraaff and Jeffrey J. Kripal (Leiden: Brill, 2008). For my own thoughts on this homoerotic comparative pattern, see pp. xviii–xix.

16   Geoffrey Samuel, "Panentheism and the Longevity Practices of Tibetan Buddhism." In *God's Body: Panentheism in the World Religions*, edited by Loriliai Biernacki (New York: Oxford University Press, forthcoming).

17   Gananath Obeyesekere, *The Awakened Ones: Phenomenology of Visionary Experience* (New York: Columbia University Press, 2012), xiii.

18   Douglas Wile, *Art of the Bedchamber: The Chinese Sexual Yoga Classics Including Women's Solo Meditation Texts* (Albany: State University of New York Press, 1992), 11.

19   Sherry B. Ortner, *Making Gender: The Politics and Erotics of Culture* (Boston, MA: Beacon Press, 1996).

20   DeConick, *Holy Misogyny*, xii.

21   Lawrence Foster, *Sex and Religion: The Shakers, Oneida Community, and Mormons* (Bloomington: Indiana University Press, 1981), 27.

22   Foster, *Sex and Religion*, 46.

23   Richard Francis, *Ann the Word: The Story of Ann Lee, Female Messiah, Mother of the Shakers, the Woman Clothed with the Sun* (London: Fourth Estate, 2000), 137.

24   Francis, *Ann the Word*, 48.

25   Quoted in Francis, *Ann the Word*, 135–136.

26   Francis, *Ann the Word*, 41.

27   Francis, *Ann the Word*, 10.

28   Quoted in Francis, *Ann the Word*, 90.

29   Francis, *Ann the Word*, 30.

30   Francis, *Ann the Word*, 7.

31   *Testimonies of the Life, Character, Revelations and Doctrines of Our Ever Blessed Mother Ann Lee, and the Elders with Her; Through Whom the World of Eternal Life Was Opened in This Day of Christ's Second Appearing* (Hancock: J. Tallcott & J. Deming, Junes, 1816), 3. This document quickly became controversial and was withdrawn and restricted to senior officials. Hence it became known as the "Secret Book of the Elders" (Francis, *Ann the Word*, 332).

32   *Testimonies*, 5.

33   Francis, *Ann the Word*, 41 suggests the same.

34   Anne Heche, *Call Me Crazy* (New York: Scribner, 2001), 98.

35   For the masking of sexual abuse in the language of piety, see Donald Capps, *The Child's Song: The Religious Abuse of Children* (Louisville, KY: Westminster John Knox Press, 1995).

36   Heche, *Call Me Crazy*, 32–33.

37   Heche, *Call Me Crazy*, 54.

38   Heche, *Call Me Crazy*, 100.

39   Heche, *Call Me Crazy*, 188–189.

40   Heche, *Call Me Crazy*, 195. Heche points out that "[n]one of these concepts were foreign to me. I had heard them in churches and on radios."

41   Heche, *Call Me Crazy*, 201.

42   Heche, *Call Me Crazy*, 202.

43   Heche, *Call Me Crazy*, 191.

44   Francis, *Ann the Word*, 93.

45   Francis, *Ann the Word*, 322.

46   Quoted in Francis, *Ann the Word*, 153.

47   Francis, *Ann the Word*, 154.

Ecstatic Man (1988), by Lynn Randolph, 58″ × 46″.

7

Charisma and the Social Dimensions of Religion

Transmitting the Power

It is society that thinks in me.

Karl Marx, as quoted by Louis Dumont, *Homo Hierarchicus*

[O]nly in the perfect uncontamination and solitariness of individuality may the spirituality of religion come forth at all.

Walt Whitman, *Democratic Vistas*

We know that God is experienced in the brain as a social relationship. (Put someone in the scanner and ask them about God, and the same region of the brain lights up as when you ask them about a friend.)

T.M. Luhrmann, *When God Talks Back*

Chapter Outline

Comparing Religions: Coming to Terms, First Edition. Jeffrey J. Kripal, Ata Anzali, Andrea R. Jain, and Erin Prophet.
© 2014 Jeffrey J. Kripal. Published 2014 by John Wiley & Sons, Ltd.

Franklin Jones was born in the Borough of Queens, New York City, in 1939. He grew up on Long Island. He completed a BA at Columbia University, studied English at Stanford University, and moved to Greenwich Village, where he came into contact with his first spiritual teacher, a man named Albert Rudolph. "Rudi," as he was called, made a living as an oriental art dealer in New York City. He himself had been taught by an Indian spiritual teacher named Swami Muktananda, whom Franklin would soon take as his own guru too.

In the fall of 1970, while sitting in a Hindu temple in Hollywood, California, Franklin awakened fully into "the Bright," his expression for complete and total enlightenment. Through this experience and countless others that followed, Franklin came to understand what he claimed was the ultimate nature of Consciousness (he capitalized terms that express the divine). He would go on to describe this Consciousness, in decades of teaching and in dozens of books, as both Transcendent and Radiant, as the Source-Condition of everything that is, as the uncaused immortal Self, as a Conscious Light utterly beyond the limited perspective of any ego, any religion, or any culture. Out of this same Conscious Light, he taught, all of physical reality, the entire material universe, arises as an unnecessary, playful appearance.

Put in more traditional language, Franklin Jones came to realize that everything is God, and that God is still more—infinitely more—than this everything. In short, is was not a God "out there" or somewhere "up." This is not another sky god, not a God separate from the material world. This is the Real God, he taught, the Divine Person who *is* Reality itself, who is everything that exists, and infinitely More. You might recognize such a teaching as a most dramatic instance of panentheism or cosmotheism, which we first encountered in Chapter 1.

Franklin Jones did not use this kind of abstract language, though. After all, there was nothing abstract about what he now knew. He had come to know "the Bright," which was also, somehow, himself. Later on he would sum up all of this in just three brief sentences:

There is no ultimate "difference" between you and the Divine.
There is <u>only</u> the Divine.
Everything that exists is a "modification" of the One Divine Reality.[1]

This is who we are, he taught. This is what everything is. We just don't know it. We are asleep.

Franklin decided to wake some of us up. And so he began teaching around a small bookstore that he started in Los Angeles, together with some friends, in the early 1970s. To say that he was an effective teacher would be a gross understatement. Weird and wonderful things happened in his presence. Disciples routinely reported feeling an immense "Presence" or "Force" in the room, which they would feel as if it were descending on them, pushing on them, changing them. The guru would later speak of this phenomenon as "the Thumbs" and describe, in elaborate detail, how these energies enter "from above," move down the front of the body and then up the backside until the Spirit manifests as a perfect sphere of Conscious Light.

The disciples themselves routinely reported how their bodies would spontaneously erupt, quite out of their own control, into specific patterned movements (this, by the way, is a well-known phenomenon, from Indian yoga to American tent revival meetings during the Great Awakenings of the eighteenth and nineteenth centuries). They would laugh uncontrollably. Or weep in joy. They would feel waves of bliss and utter love. When the guru touched them, they would feel bolts of electric energy pass from his body into theirs. They would scream in delight. Here is how James Steinberg, a long-time devotee who was there in 1974, described to me what it was like to encounter Bubba Free John (the guru's name at that time):

> Bubba would look into my eyes and transmit spiritual energies that would fill me instantly, invading the entire front of my body and then traveling up my spine, and filling my brain with powerful and radiant energy and light. It was as tangible as if someone had thrown a bucket [of water] on me. I saw Him wave his hand, and clouds would rush across the sky and thunder would sound. I saw and felt thin streams of rain even inside the rooms, full of light and mild moisture, felt to be grace rain and a blessing itself, falling on all of us. There was an endless stream of phenomenal manifestations of all types, inside my body, but also in the environment itself.[2]

Franklin Jones changed his name many times between the early 1970s and the day he died, on November 27,

2008, in the Hermitage Ashram that he had established in Fiji. First it was Bubba Free John, then Da Free John. Many other names followed over the years. By the time he died, as Adi Da, he had long claimed, and his community had long experienced, that he was in fact an Avatar: the Divine Person or Source-Condition, who had taken on a human form to teach humanity the ultimate lesson—the lesson of Real God, of Reality Itself.

What are we to make of such claims, and of all those capital letters? Many, no doubt, are comfortable with virtually identical teachings, as long as they are located squarely in the past and fit comfortably into their own social worlds and religious beliefs. When reading the texts of Adi Da, it is difficult, for example, not to be reminded of the language of the Christian Gospel of John, with its opening declaration of the Word or Christ, through whom all things were created and came to be; or of the Hindu Bhagavad Gita, with its stunning, terrifying cosmic vision of Lord Krishna as all there is.

But in the counterculture of California and of the Fijian islands? Surely, this cannot be. Obviously Mr. Jones was making all this up, and his young disciples were just imaging these bolts of palpable energy, both in their bodies and in the sky.

Charisma and Community

But were they? In actual fact, although what happened to Franklin Jones and his youthful community in the early 1970s was fantastic and extraordinary by any measure, these events fit seamlessly into a long history of similar awakenings, transmissions, and altered states of consciousness and energy. These are the historical facts of the history of religions. We need to recognize them and deal with them, not to normalize, ignore, or deny them.

The guru and his community certainly did the former, not the latter. This period in the life of the community is called the "Garbage and the Goddess" period. The guru was clear that such miraculous phenomena were temporary and could not produce any state of enlightenment (since enlightenment is not

Figure 7.1   Shakti-Pat ("Descent of the Power") from Franklin Jones (Adi Da), Mountain of Attention Sanctuary (1974). Middletown, California. Image ©1974, 2013 ASA. All rights reserved.

any "thing" that can be caused or mechanically produced). One must "throw them away," like a greasy bag of garbage, he would say. Hence the line that was attached to the photograph in Figure 7.1 when it was used as a movie poster for the community's first film, "A Difficult Man" (1974). The caption read: "I could press the mystical life force into your brains for eternity, and it would still not produce Enlightenment."

So what would? The poster's point is a dramatic version of one of the most basic questions that the student of religion can ask: What is the essence of religion? What makes it work so dramatically sometimes, and not at all at other times? Does the core of religion lie in some historical event of revelation, some prophetic or visionary experience that occurred to a particular person at a particular place and time, usually a long, long time ago? Or does the core of religion lie outside any such individual subjective event, however profound, in the more stable and accessible roles and rites of special institutions and special people—"special" precisely to the extent that they invoke some revelation of the sacred as the source and foundation of their authority? Put most simply, "where" is it? Is the core of religion "inside" or

"outside"? Is it in the guru or in the community? Is it a matter of the soul or a matter of society?

Clearly, if you pick either alternative as your position, there would be truth in both. The special institutions of religion, after all, always hark back to the special experiences of individuals, just as the special experiences of individuals are usually catalyzed and shaped by these special institutions. If, then, we imagine psyche and society, the private and the public as two end points or "terms" on a single line, we need to bend back that line and close it upon itself. We need to turn that line into a circle or loop.

Nowhere is this more obvious than in the literature on **charisma**. The German social theorist Max Weber (1864–1920), who did more than anyone to turn this word into a searching lens for the study of religion, defined charisma as "a certain quality of an individual's personality by virtue of which he is set apart from ordinary men and treated as endowed with supernatural, superhuman, or at least specifically exceptional powers or qualities."[3] Charisma, we might say, is the "electricity" felt in the presence of a person set apart as special or holy. Charisma is what the disciples of Franklin Jones felt in his presence. Charisma is what many a Catholic felt in the presence of the late Mother Teresa. Charisma is what Mahatma Gandhi and Martin Luther King, Jr., had. If we wish to expand the category into a more secular realm, it is also what Marilyn Monroe, Elvis Presley, and Michael Jackson manifested on screen and stage. It is probably no accident that we call such people "stars" (in the ancient world, the stars were often considered to be divinities); or that the English word "fan" comes from the Latin *fanaticus*, which applied to the enthusiast or true believer attached to the "temple" (*fanum*) of his god.[4]

Weber himself wrote about charisma in both sacred and secular contexts. And indeed, it is not entirely clear how sacred and secular charisma are really different. With either form, we are already back to our opening question about the inside and outside of religious experience. What, after all, makes charisma? How is it generated? The believer thinks that the energy is produced by the charismatic person— saint, guru, godman, or prophetic reformer. The sociologist, on the other hand, argues that the felt energy is produced by the total social field in which the charismatic person is acting and in which he or she is recognized, indeed constructed, as a special, holy, or "set apart" person. There is no rock star without fans, the sociologist might point out, nor can there be rock-star fans without a rock star, and they *all* need the public ritual performance on the stage.

Still, not just anyone can be a rock star; and there was only one Marilyn Monroe. Individual traits *do* appear to matter, and matter a great deal—talent, beauty, body, and that most mysterious thing of all, "personality."

The Radioactive and the Electric Arc Models

To appeal to an energy metaphor, we might say that, for the religious believer, the charisma is experienced as emanating directly from the special person, as if that person were somehow radioactive. Hence all those halos, rainbow bodies, and glowing superhumans of religious art around the world. For the sociologist, on the other hand, this experience of charisma is fundamentally a social experience and, as such, it is a care-fully crafted performance, constructed by very specific social dynamics—including those countless artistic representations of halos and glowing superhumans.

If we combine these two perspectives, we could think about charisma as an electric arc or magnetic field generated by two poles: the charismatic or "magnetic" personality and the social field in which he or she is revered as special. As in phenomena of electricity or magnetism, remove either of these poles and the "spark," "arc," or "attraction"—the charismatic effect—goes away. It is no more.

Here is a little thought experiment to help you with this idea. A Hollywood starlet or the pope may indeed manifest charisma on the silver screen of the movie theater or within the ritual theater of an elaborate ritual service at the papal altar of St. Peter's Basilica in Rome. These are indeed very impressive displays of charisma and power. But is the starlet still the starlet and the pope still the pope, say, when she or he is snoring in bed, really loudly? Or suffering from severe diarrhea? The sociologist has a point.

As my combination of the two models suggests, I am not entirely persuaded by the sociologist's point. I have had too many experiences of interacting with religious communities (including that of Franklin Jones or Adi Da), and I have heard too many stories from too many people who have written me out of the blue. They write long intimate letters about getting "zapped" by a light or beam, after which they feel the deepest interiors of their bodies "vibrating" at unbelievable speeds, more or less exactly as if they had been, well, *magnetized*. Sometimes these extraordinary energies spike during sexual arousal. At other times they spike during meteorological phenomena, as we saw in Chapter 5 with the thunder god story, or during hurricanes, as was once explained to me by a professional therapist in my hometown of Houston. Other individuals have reported that their spouses and children, and even sometimes their pets, sense or see the glow. Afterwards many of these people describe being endowed with special powers (spiritual intuitions, precognition, telepathy, healing gifts, and so on), which then often fade away after a time.

Moreover, I myself have had very palpable experiences with two different female healers: one worked on my injured knee and on a torn meniscus—and as a result the orthopedic specialist was quite surprised when he could not find (in the office) the same level of injury that had shown up on the MRI (magnetic resonance imaging) a few weeks earlier; the other worked on an old back injury at the base of my spine. In both cases I could feel, *very* clearly, a kind of subtle energy or magnetic field working. In the former case, it felt like a gentle heat wrapping around my knee. In the latter, it felt like a "ball" of subtle plasma, or like magnetism (which was not subtle at all), pushing into the base of my spine and into those displaced muscles. Neither healer touched me.

The causal chains at work in such events are not at all clear, but these events are not simply imagined. They cannot be dismissed as purely subjective affairs or wishful thinking. Neither can they be understood as products of strictly social processes, although, of course, they are clearly social events as well. Indeed I suspect that they depend heavily on emotional–relational states like trust, acceptance, and belief. In my own case, I doubt very much that anything would have happened had I approached either gifted woman with the suspicion and doubt of the (almost always male) professional debunker. Still, these events are not just social. There is a More at work here.

For these reasons, I tend to think that many of these individuals really are different, really have been zapped, really do have special powers, whether or not there is a community to recognize this or not. I also suspect—and this is a much more subtle point—that the community or social field is often the "trick" that allows the "truth" to manifest. For some reason, we normally block ourselves from experiencing such things. We thus need to be tricked—via a ritual, a community, or a charismatic person—into accessing our own supernature. More on that later, at the end of our next chapter.

Where I am in total agreement with the sociologists is in their observation that the social field is essential if these sorts of anomalous experiences are to "get traction" in the culture and to survive beyond the individual who first knew them so dramatically and intimately. Perhaps the community is needed to manifest fully what is already latent in the psyche of the charismatic person. I do not really know, nor do I claim to understand these things. I just know that they happen.

Max Weber on Charisma and Social Change

Weber had an answer to what charisma is about. He thought that charisma is the engine of social change and creativity, particularly as these changes are catalyzed by individuals who have broken out of the conditionings of their own societies. It is not all about society, then, for Weber. Charisma is also about individuals. It is about freedom. It is about experimentation.

And offense. Weber observed that charisma often erupts at especially dramatic historical moments, moments of radical change and profound social suffering. He also observed that charisma, by its very nature, is often destructive of the status quo. Its apparent purpose, though, is not to destroy simply for the sake of destruction. Charisma is transgression. Charisma destroys the old in order to create the new. It is, after all, impossible to create something new without destroying something old. As Charles Fort, American humorist and collector of all things anomalous, put it: "I do not know how to find out anything new without being offensive."[5] The believer always forgets: his or her religion usually began as an offense to the previous social and religious order. Fort was right. So was Weber.

Sometimes these charismatic experiments work and produce massive social movements and radical social change, as the tiny community of the early Jewish followers of Jesus did, or the first followers of the Buddha, or the family and first followers of the Prophet Muhammad. Each of these little communities went on to become worldwide movements that dramatically reshaped the social, cultural, and political future of the globe. Sometimes, however, and really most times, these charismatic experiments last but a single generation (or a few more), and then they die out. The world has not seen five or six religions. It has seen tens of thousands. And it will see other tens of thousands.

It was for this reason that S.N. Eisenstadt summed up Weber's position on charisma through an evolutionary analogy:

> The development of such "charismatic" personalities or groups constitutes perhaps the closest social analogy to "mutation," and the degree of their ability to forge out a viable symbolic and institutional order may be an important factor in the process of survival, or selection of different societies or cultural creations. This analysis brings out again the fact that a crucial aspect of the charismatic personality or group is not only the possession of some extraordinary, exhilarating qualities, but also the ability, through these qualities, to reorder and reorganize both the symbolic and [the] cognitive order.[6]

To invoke a different set of metaphors, we might say that the charismatic personality or group is "playing with the codes" of the culture in question, effectively "reprogramming" the software of the society so that the society can better respond to new challenges.[7] The society, of course, does not always see it this way. What the charismatic personality or group sees as a necessary rewriting or reprogramming of the worldview, the religious and social authorities in power may well see as a kind of "virus" that has invaded the stability and proper order of things. One sees a new world on the horizon, whereas the other sees hacking or, in a more traditional vein, a disease.

The Institutionalization of Charisma: Passing on the Charge

Sometimes what the powers see as an invading virus gets into the social body anyway, helps take down the old constitution, and mutates the society from within, now very slowly, now very quickly. To capture something of this process, Weber wrote about what he called the **institutionalization of charisma**. This is a key phrase that captures an important moment in

the development of a **tradition**—which is a "passing on" or a "handing over" (from the Latin abstract noun *traditio*, derivative of *tradere*, "to transmit"). Weber recognized that, when prophets, saints, and reformers die, they leave their communities in a difficult position, which boils down to the question of how to continue to transmit the electric charge of the charismatic leader's original energy. With the death of the charismatic founder, one of the poles of the electric arc is gone. And, when one pole goes, the flashing arc flashes no more.

There are many strategies that can be employed at this point. Here we might list six: (1) the interpreted dream or vision; (2) the institutional role or office; (3) the scriptural text; (4) the institution of religious law; (5) sacred architecture and art; and (6) the relic.

The Dream or Vision

One of the most common means of passing on charisma from one generation to another is the dream or vision, often interpreted by the elders of the community and recognized as special, as holy, as a kind of "calling." Sometimes, but not always, this vision or dream occurs in the context of a serious illness or life crisis.

The problem with dreams and visions is that anyone can claim them, and in the end it is quite impossible to control them. If charisma is passed on through dreams and visions alone, then who is to say *whose* dreams and visions get to count? This problem is somewhat mollified in indigenous cultures through the presence of elders and of the still living shaman—these often act to interpret and authorize the dream or vision of the new shaman; but it remains nevertheless a very real problem.

The Office

The charisma of the founder can also be passed on formally to a successor—a follower or family member—before the founder's death. Weber called this comparative pattern the "charisma of the office" or, in the case of the family member, the "charisma of kinship" or "hereditary charisma." Christianity employed a version of the charisma of the office in its notion of apostolic succession, that is, the notion that there is an unbroken change of transmission, leading from the present back to Jesus and the disciples. Here the charisma is formalized—"institutionalized," as Weber put it—until it resides not in a person but in an office or role. In Weber's technical terms, the inspired "prophet" has become the socially recognized "priest."

This is an important distinction in Weber's writings. Although these terms are clearly derived from the Jewish and Christian traditions, they are nevertheless worth explaining, as they carry more than a little comparative utility. For Weber, the **prophet** is the religious individual par excellence, the man endowed with special superhuman gifts who speaks for God. The charismatic authority of the prophet is generated by the prophetic gift itself. It speaks for itself, as it were, even as it claims to speak for another, that is, for the god. The **priest**, on the other hand, is a priest not by virtue of any prophetic or charismatic gift, but to the extent that he faithfully fulfills a formal role or a recognized office within the special institution of the religious tradition. The priest does not necessarily manifest any personal charisma himself. Rather he channels and mediates the charisma of the tradition through ritual and role.

The Scriptural Text and Commentary

The charisma of the original revelation event can also be de-coupled from the founder or from any office and located in that which was revealed through the founder or prophet. In this model, the religious power of the revelation is crystallized and contained in a stable reproducible text—that is, in a sacred scripture. Think the Veda of Hinduism, the Torah of Judaism, the Bible of Christianity, the Quran of Islam, the Guru Granth Sahib of Sikhism, and so on.

It is seldom this simple, though, as most religions end up employing multiple strategies in order to transmit charisma from one generation to the next. To take one instructive example, Buddhists throughout the world speak of three "jewels" or three "refuges": the Buddha, the *dharma* ("teaching"), and the *sangha*

("monastic community"). Which is to say that they understand the charismatic succession of Buddhism to pass through the founder, his teaching, and his community *all at once*.

In a very different mode, Judaism originally functioned through elaborate priestly lineages, sacrificial rituals, and multiple temples until these were all more or less consolidated into a single central temple in Jerusalem. This temple was then destroyed twice: once in 587 BCE, by the Babylonians, and again in 70 CE, by the Romans; after this it was never rebuilt. After the first destruction, the tradition rebuilt the temple (hence this period of Jewish history is often called "Second Temple Judaism") and put together the texts that would eventually become the Torah, no doubt to preserve its traditions and teachings. After the second destruction of the temple in 70 CE, the tradition, now deprived of any possibility of offering grain and animal sacrifices in the temple, increasingly focused on scholarly commentary on the Torah, which was practiced by a class of scribes called rabbis, and to this end it developed a series of local communities around meeting places that came to be called synagogues. The text, read and interpreted by specialists in the context created by these communities, became a privileged way to transmit charisma (see Figure 7.2).

The case of Islam is similarly complex. On the central problem of prophetic transmission, early Islam split, deeply and so far permanently, into two basic traditions: Sunni and Shia Islam. Here Weber's central question about the institutionalization of charisma came to define the entire Islamic tradition.

Whereas for the majority of Muhammad's followers—who were later called Sunni—it became customary to think of the prophetic charisma as distinct from that of the revelatory message, a minority among his followers—who became known later as Shia— were strongly opposed to this separation between prophetic personality and divine revelation. For the Shias, it was inconceivable to understand fully the text of the Quran, which they called the "silent" Quran, without having access to a divinely inspired person who embodied the totality of the revealed message.

Figure 7.2   Rabbi and Torah. Szeged, Hungary. ©Nathan Benn/Ottochrome/Corbis.

This was the Imam—the leader. He was the "talking" Quran in whose heart the true meaning of the Quran was inscribed by God. He was considered to be, and exclusively so, not only the inheritor of the prophetic knowledge through a sacred blood line, but also the rightful successor of Muhammad in all social and political matters. He was, in short, the Imam—the leader—in all matters of life.

Quite in contrast, the Sunnis believed that Muhammad's personal charisma and authority were transferred to the immediate community of his followers or "companions," and from there to the whole community of Muslims—the *umma*. That, indeed, is what the title "Sunni" conveys. As an abbreviation, it stands for the people of the *sunna* (the "prophetic tradition") and the *jama'a* (the "community"). It is this community of Muhammad's companions, Sunni Islam professes, that gained the right to choose one of its members as the rightful leader. These chosen leaders were later called by Sunnis the "rightly guided caliphs," that is, the "rightly guided successors." From the Shia point of view, however, these successors—

with the exception of the fourth, who happened to be the first Shia Imam—were nothing but misguided usurpers of the rights of the family of the Prophet.

Islam, in short, split on the question of prophetic or charismatic transmission: the Shiites emphasized the charismatic authority of the living and infallible Imam and the Sunnis emphasized the institutionalized charisma of the community and its religious and political leaders. In effect, whereas in the Shia model charisma was "concentrated" in a single individual, in the Sunni model charisma was "spread out" and distributed through the community and its leaders.

Religious Law

One of the most effective and far-reaching techniques to institutionalize charisma is the practice of religious law, which is in turn related to the whole realm of religious ethics or morality.

The first five books of the Bible, for example, consist largely of stories about the original "contract" or covenant Abraham and his descendents made with God; its detailed laws were later given to the prophet Moses. Much of the history of Judaism consists of rabbinic or scholarly commentary on these laws and on how to interpret and follow them in each successive generation.

Christianity is a complicated case, since, as we have already noted, a good deal of early Christianity was inspired precisely by the rejection of the Jewish laws and by an attempt to move beyond the categories of purity and pollution upon which many of these laws were based. Indeed "the law" took on a primarily negative connotation among early Christian communities, where it was opposed to "the spirit." This is one reason why the Jesus movement eventually became a gentile or non-Jewish religion.

But, as Christianity became one of the central institutions of European society, particularly after the Emperor Constantine abandoned Rome and headed for the East to found Constantinople in the fourth century, the church took over the legal terms and practices of the Roman Empire. This legalization of the church was manifest everywhere. For example, the very word for a church authorized by the papal power, *basilica*, is simply the Latin or Roman term for a court of law. In ancient Rome a *basilica* was the place where one went to hear court cases. A basilica in Roman Catholicism is where one goes to connect to the charismatic power and authority of the pope. The church also developed an entire branch of "canon law." Canon law concerns itself with all legal matters pertaining to the church. There are also canon lawyers trained to determine everything, from the rules of marriage and priesthood to who becomes an official saint, as we will see in a moment.

Islam is much closer to Judaism here; for, outside the Quran itself, Sharia—"Law"—is easily the most important and influential feature of Islamic society, wherever we look. Like Judaism, Islam is a legal tradition as much as a religious one, or rather it is a way of being religious that orders itself through legal reasoning. Like all other aspects of human life and culture, though, Muslim understandings of Sharia have gone through some dramatic changes since the dawn of Islam. The earlier revelations of Muhammad in Mecca, mostly of an apocalyptic nature (that is, dealing with the end of the world as we know it), bothered little, if at all, with legal matters. It was only

after Muhammad's migration to Medina and the establishment of the first Islamic community and polity that matters of law appear to have come to the fore. Naturally, in the absence of any solid and coherent Quranic direction, the tapestry of local costumes and codes were consulted. In an intimate conversation with local Bedouin and Jewish codes of conduct, legal judgments were issued by the Prophet—and later by his companions—to provide the precedence upon which, well after the death of the Prophet, distinct schools of law were established.

Eventually, in a long and contested process that took more than two centuries, thousands of prophetic traditions were remembered and debated. To deal with this enormous body of literature, a class of religious specialists, later called the *fuqaha*, emerged throughout the heartlands of the Islamic world. Just as the practice of authoring gospels spread in the early Christian world, so here: many of these specialists compiled their own versions of what they considered to be the legally binding collection of prophetic traditions. Eventually, however, only a handful came to be recognized as "authentic" enough to become sources of legal reasoning. Accordingly, four official schools of law were established as orthodox. Although each of these schools has gone through many changes, the fact remains that, for the majority of Muslims, these four are still the only officially acceptable schools of Islamic law.

The case is somewhat different in the Shia world. Shia Muslims consolidated their own canonical works and developed their own understanding of Sharia, slightly after their Sunni counterparts. Their version, however, was built not only upon the prophetic traditions, but also, and more importantly, on the traditions of their infallible Imams.

Asian religions have their own legal traditions too, of course. Hinduism, for example, has its central category of *dharma* (a word that can be translated as "duty" or "established order" or, with a bit of stretching, "religion")[8] and its *dharma* literature, which is essentially legal literature: a series of code books on purity, pollution, caste, marriage practices, the stages of life, and proper behavior in this or that social context. The Buddhist traditions also possess an immense and immensely complicated legal literature, but it mostly involves the rules and regulations of the monastic life. Confucianism is perhaps the legal Asian religion par excellence, since it sees what we might recognize as law—here framed as social custom, ritual, familial relations, and emotional comportment—as the key to the proper and fullest human life.

Sacred Art and Architecture

It is an often forgotten fact that the vast majority of people in human history were illiterate. They could not read their own sacred scriptures. The situation was often more dramatic still, for in many traditional religious systems people (especially women) were *not allowed* to read the sacred scriptures. Religious institutions, then, had to turn to other means to instruct and edify their members. One of the most common means of doing this has been what we call **material religion**—all those physical objects or "things," from miniature statues and posters to holy cards and amulets, that enable people to imagine their religious worlds into being on a daily basis. Often the objects of material religion are things of pop culture—cheap, colorful, kitschy, and trinket-like. Not always, though. Cultures sometimes invest incredible amounts of time and wealth into material religion. The results are sacred architecture and sacred art.

An especially instructive example here is St. Peter's Basilica in Rome, which functions both as the pope's primary church (though it is not technically his official "seat") and as the sacred center of Roman Catholicism. The structure was designed by some of the greatest artists of the Italian Renaissance—men like Raphael, Peruzzi, Michelangelo, and Bernini—and built over an already existing one, in the sixteenth and seventeenth centuries, largely from huge blocks of white stone taken from Rome's ancient Colosseum, in a deeply symbolic pillaging.

As one approaches the immense structure, one is met by two huge colonnades reaching out from the church, like giant arms, to surround an equally immense courtyard, called St. Peter's Square. The basilica is the largest church in the world. And it wants you to know this. Embedded into the floor of the center line of the church are little stars that mark the depth or length of the other church contenders, like

St. Paul's Cathedral in London. They would all fit easily inside St. Peter's. The ceilings and vault of the church extend hundreds of feet into the sky. One might feel very small in such a sacred space. One might also feel awe and be moved by the grandeur of it all. Both effects were clearly intended by the architects.

The art plays a key role here. It is inspiring. It is gorgeous. And it is famous. Michelangelo's *Pietà*, for example, resides now in St. Peter's, and probably the most revered painting in the western world, the same artist's *The Last Judgment* (1536–1541), is just next door, in the Sistine Chapel. The chapel is where the cardinals gather to elect the next pope. It would be difficult to imagine a much more significant sacred space for the institutionalization of charisma in Roman Catholicism.

It would also be difficult to imagine a more erotic one. The painting has been controversial from the very beginning. Cardinal Biagio da Cesena, the papal master of ceremonies, famously criticized the painting as disgraceful and shameful, as something that belonged in a tavern or a public bath. Michelangelo was furious. He painted the prudish cardinal into his hell scene, gave him donkey ears, and wrapped a huge snake around his body. He also made sure the cardinal would not need to complain about his own genitals being exposed. Michelangelo covered the cardinal's genitals completely: with a huge snake biting them, one would imagine, clean off. As the story goes, the cardinal complained to the pope about this serpentine penectomy in hell. The pope is said to have responded that he did not have any jurisdiction in hell, and so there was nothing he could do to change the painting.

Surely some of these men had a sense of humor. If nothing else, the story does.

Still, the censoring cardinal eventually won. After Michelangelo's death, when the Council of Trent condemned nudity in religious paintings, artists were commissioned to paint pants over all those exposed genitals. Most of these now robed genitals were penises, but even the women Michelangelo painted are all basically muscle-bound men with odd breasts. In short, Michelangelo was a "queer" painter, whatever his own sexual orientation was.

This case carries a very important, really crucial, lesson about religious art and the institutionalization of charisma. That lesson is this. Religious imagery is seldom simple, and it often works at multiple levels. Religious art can question, make fun of, and subvert religious authority as easily as it can justify and support that authority; and often, moreover, it can do both at the same time. We might say that religious art can institutionalize charisma by glorifying a religious leader, but it can also bite him in the balls. If you don't believe me, just go to Rome and see for yourself. Or just take a virtual tour of the painting here: http://www.vatican.va/various/cappelle/sistina_vr/index.html

The Relic

St. Peter's Basilica is not just filled with astonishing art and grand architectural design. It is also filled with dead people. Dead popes, mostly. Over one hundred corpses are interned in the church, most in the grotto below the main floor. But a few are in the church above, including one (Pope John XXIII) displayed in a glass altar structure that encourages the veneration of his body. The logic at work here should be very familiar to you by now. By virtue of the holy body, the place in turn becomes holy, special, set apart, as if the sacred power contained in the body of the saint functions as a kind of electricity or contagion, as if it can be transmitted through simple presence or touch. Following the terminology of medieval Catholicism, we can well call these preserved or interned charismatic bodies **relics** (see Figure 7.3).

It would be difficult to over-emphasize how important these relics were to the religious life of medieval Christian Europe. Indeed, the culture practiced a veritable trade in the body parts of saints: saints' bodies were often dismembered and cut up so that they could be distributed to multiple locales and employed there as pilgrimage attractions. They were also traded, stolen, copied, and used in military operations.[9] On a humorous note, one of my graduate teachers used to joke that, if one could collect all the relics of the true cross of Jesus spread across medieval Europe, one would have enough wood for the true ark of Noah.

Figure 7.3 *The Relics of Saint Genevieve Carried through the Streets of Paris* (c. 1890). ©Stefano Bianchetti/Corbis.

To take a most famous example, a single set of relics functioned, and still functions, as the sacred center of Roman Catholicism. The central claim of St. Peter's Basilica in Rome is that the main papal altar (on which only the pope can celebrate the eucharist or mass) is built on the grave of St. Peter himself: *his* bones, buried directly below the altar, are believed to transmit something special, that is, some charisma, right up into the altar and, through that central altar, into the physical church and, through this physical church, into the entire global community of believing Catholics. That is what makes St. Peter's Basilica so special, so holy, for Catholicism: its claims a *physical* link to St. Peter himself, the man to whom Jesus gave "the keys of the kingdom" (hence the central icon or coat of arms of the papacy features a set of keys).

One could hardly ask for a more clear instance of what Weber called the institutionalization of charisma. After all, those holy bones beneath the papal altar and those symbolic keys of the kingdom embedded into the floor (and inscribed, in huge Latin, across the top of the interior of the church) function in exactly these ways: they claim the religious authority or charisma of St. Peter—and, by extension, of Christ—as their own. And the tradition does not simply claim this. It builds an immense, fantastically impressive structure to mythologize and ritualize this claim, this charisma. It is in this way that the Roman Catholic tradition quite literally performs, and in this way creates, a religious world.

The veneration of relics is by no means restricted to Catholicism. The sacred teeth of the Buddha, for example, have attracted immense religious, political, and military attention in India, Sri Lanka, China, Taiwan, and Japan. Moreover, visiting the tombs of saints is an especially common practice in some Muslim communities. One is also reminded here of the Kaba, the sacred black stone of Mecca. It is not exactly a relic, for it is no one's body part, but it functions in ways similar to the bones of St. Peter: it orients faithful Muslims from around the world toward a single charismatic pole or center. Some believe that the sacred black stone may have literally fallen out of the sky, as a meteorite. Maybe it did.

Patterns of Special Institutions

There are many types of special people. There are also many types of special institutions that attempt to preserve, ritualize, and pass on the charisma of these religious prodigies. Sociologists of religion have spent over a century honing their ways of thinking about the special institutions we call religious institutions. One of the most influential models was first advanced by a German Protestant historian by the name of Ernst Troeltsch (1865–1923). Troeltsch laid down this model in his *The Social Teachings of the Christian Church* (1912), one of the undisputed early classics of the sociology of religion.

This is an immense, two-volume work that spans the first eighteen centuries of Christian history. What it is most known for in the field today, however, is the tripartite model that Troeltsch laid out in the last few pages of the work, to make sense of the mind-boggling diversity of Christian history that he had just described in the previous thousand pages—a kind of final theoretical revelation on the mountain of historical facts, if you will.

Here he suggested three ideal types. An **ideal type** is an abstract description of some social pattern that exists nowhere in the real world in this pure form, but that can nevertheless be used as an interpretive tool to think about history in rigorous and insightful ways. We all, of course, use ideal types every day. "Democracy" is an ideal type, as is "college," "corporation," "capitalism," "religion," or "circle" and "square," for that matter (there are no perfect circles or squares in the real world). We *have* to generalize. We *must* create abstractions. Otherwise we would be frozen by the complexity of the world.

Troeltsch thought that Christian history could be better understood if we distinguish three ideal types of religious organization: the church, the sect, and mysticism. He thought, moreover, that each of these social organizations was related to a "real religious fundamental idea" that "lay in the unconscious."[10] Put differently, he thought that these three types of social organization functioned as definitive influences on

Christian belief and community, secretly shaping, and limiting, what it is possible to believe in, and what can exist, within each kind of fellowship. As Karl Marx had it in our opening paragraph, we do not think. Rather we are being thought. "It is society that thinks in me." Troeltsch would add: "It is also society that believes in me."

This is an incredibly important point. For Troeltsch, what a particular religious community or individual believes is generally not the result of some simple conscious choice. That is a naïve position. Rather, *religious belief issues from, and is largely determined by, the social structure of the religious community itself.* We might also say that *the social form determines the belief system, and not the other way around.*

The implications are immense, as this thesis suggests at least two further key ideas. First, it suggests that, if you are imagining that people have generally chosen their beliefs via some universal value or mechanism called religious freedom, you are quite mistaken. As we will see in Chapter 10, religious choice and religious freedom are very recent, very modern ideas and are themselves products of the social structures of liberal democracy and modern pluralistic societies. Second, the thesis suggests that real religious change does not, and cannot, arise from arguing about conscious beliefs or from debating dogmas. These, after all, are surface things. They are not what is really driving the show. Real religious change can only come about through social and institutional change. This is what is really driving the show.

I do not mean to offer such a thesis as a foregone conclusion. One could easily advance some serious challenges to it. For example, it is also obviously true that individuals *do* break with their social systems, *do* have thoughts they are not supposed to have, *do* convert to religions in which they were not raised, *do* reject, entirely and utterly, the religious beliefs in which they were raised, and so on. If this were not all true, no real social change would ever occur, and the general history of religions would look entirely differently.

So, again, there were three ideal types through which Troeltsch thought about religious belief and social structure: church, sect, and mysticism. Troeltsch's

successors in the sociology of religion have since taken up these types and developed and qualified them in numerous ways. Some explanation is in order with each.

The Church

The first ideal type is the **church**, by which Troeltsch and his successors mean something very precise and not at all what you probably have in mind. They mean a religious organization that is closely aligned with the political polity of the land and its elites; that has toned down its otherworldly orientation and recognized the wisdom of a certain practical compromise with the social world; that is privileged economically and socially by virtue of this religious–political alignment; and that instills in its subjects, through public ritual and doctrine, a comprehensive and singular worldview, in which people participate more or less automatically. One is born into such a church; one does not choose to belong to it. Defined this way, a church is like the water the fish swim in and the web the spider crawls on without questioning it.

Such a church structure, moreover, accomplishes the work of salvation "objectively," that is, through public ritual and religious authority. Personal experience and subjective states of piety are secondary, if they are relevant at all. What counts is the overarching public presence of the church, its authority, and its ritual accomplishment of salvation. What counts is the people's occasional presence at these rituals and their implicit submission to the church's authority and saving work, done on their behalf. What counts is the water and the web, not the individual fishes or spiders.

Because the church understands its message as universal and absolute, and because it is aligned with the political powers of the day, it shows little interest in what we would today call religious tolerance, much less in religious pluralism or religious freedom. None of these values makes sense to the church type. The truth, after all, is the truth, and no compromises can be made with other competing claims. The water and the web are the whole world. Period.

Such a church exists nowhere in the modern West today. It cannot exist because the essential religious pluralism of modern society has eroded the unified social structure upon which it depended for its existence. But this particular social structure once existed in medieval Europe. Indeed what Troeltsch really has in mind with his notion of the church type is medieval European Roman Catholicism.

Sociologist of religion Steve Bruce captures well how such a church type worked. Let us put the date somewhere in the fourteenth century. Here is what we would have seen:

> A small number of highly trained officials, acting on behalf of the state and the people, glorified God. They did so with a liturgy and with music that was far too complex for the active participation of lay people. Religion was done, not in the local language, but in Latin, which united religious professionals across Christendom but separated them from the laity [the common people] ... There were no hymns and only sometimes a sermon. Until the late fourteenth century, later in many places, there were no seats in the part of the church used by the audience; they either stood or knelt in an unheated building. Ordinary people were expected to behave morally, to attend church on the great feast days, and to finance the professionals who did the serious religious work on behalf of the community and the nation.[11]

One cautionary word before we move on. Obviously "church" is a Christian word. Troeltsch, after all, was writing about the history of Christianity. The social structure that this word named for him, however, is hardly restricted to the history of Christianity. Some historical forms of Islam, for example, work more or less in the same way: that is, through a fusion of religious and political authority, an alignment with social elites, and an overarching ritual and legal system with an absolute claim on the truth, with little real sympathy for other forms of religion. If you prefer another word, go ahead and use it, although we cannot see what that word would be at this particular historical moment.

The Sect

Troeltsch's second ideal type, that of the sect, is first and foremost a voluntary organization. One *does* choose to belong, but what one is choosing here is still well within the worldview of the larger religious society or church. One is not choosing to be, say, a Buddhist in fourteenth-century France. One is choosing to be a different sort of Christian, usually because of some powerful personal religious experience or conviction. Troeltsch wrote of this personal experience as "the new birth," but we might offer a more contemporary example: the Christian Evangelical expression "born again."

The **sect**, then, represents a group of people, usually from the lower economic and uneducated classes, who have become disillusioned with the public church for its formality and have broken away, to form a smaller community in order to intensify the religious life of individuals around some traditional doctrinal point or ritual practice. To the extent that the sect is a breakaway tradition, the sect is always related to the church type, if only through disillusion, protest, or dissent. It does not wish to be at peace with the state or the church. It knows that its message is only for the chosen few. In a similar spirit, members of a sect, unlike those of the church, accept the principle of religious tolerance, but only to a very limited degree. They expect those in power to extend toleration to groups like them, but they themselves are generally not tolerant of other religious beliefs and practices.

Historically speaking, sometimes the church reincorporated these breakaway sects, as the Roman Catholic Church did with its religious orders throughout its history (Benedictines, Franciscans, Dominicans, Jesuits, and so on). Sometimes these sects, however, could not be reincorporated back into the church, either because they were too radical or because their teachings and practices were too "deviant" (another sociological term, meaning something like "too different to be incorporated into the broader social order"). These deviant sects thus became "heresies" and were often persecuted.

The early Protestant movements of the sixteenth century were sects in Troeltsch's sense. They, of course, eventually came to align themselves with the apparatus of the state and the power of elites as well. They thus approached the ideal type of the church, even if they could never quite reach it, except perhaps in a few restricted local cases—like John Calvin's Geneva, which for a time operated essentially as an all-encompassing Protestant city-state.

Local exceptions like Geneva aside, well over a century of spasmodic religious violence between Catholics and Protestants in Europe, in the sixteenth and seventeenth centuries, resulted eventually in the practical compromise of the modern notion of "religious tolerance." This history of European religious violence, combined with immigration patterns in the United States and Europe, which involved innumerable religious communities (many of them fleeing religious intolerance and violence in their homelands), further eroded any hope for (or trust in) an all-encompassing church structure. The eventual result was a social situation in which the church ideal became an impossibility, and in many cases—like in the founding of the United States of America—an undesired and illegal social danger.

The Denomination

One result of this history was the development of what we now call denominations. Bruce defines it as "mutually tolerant respectable religious bodies which certainly sought to bring in as many people as possible, often had a professional clergy, and typically imposed few substantial demands on their members—and yet were clearly no 'churches' in the classic sense."[12] A **denomination** is basically a modern sect that no longer takes a hostile or contentious position vis-à-vis the world and other religious communities, but instead has become respectable and gone mainstream in a modern pluralistic society.

Mysticism

Finally, Troeltsch advanced a third form of social organization, which he chose to name mysticism. We have focused above, at various points, on the mystical

element of religion as a form of experience. Here we will focus on the sociological structures of mysticism, that is, on the effects that mystical experiences tend to have on social institutions.

Troeltsch had a very specific understanding of mysticism. For him, the mystical type of Christianity is one that turns Christian doctrine and ritual into *interior* realities. As such, **mysticism** tends to be highly individualistic, which is to say that it puts a very high premium on some direct and personal encounter with God. The "objective" work of salvation of the public church is not enough for the mystic; nor are the usually literal and uneducated understandings of faith advanced by the sect. The mystic wants to *know* salvation personally, directly, and dramatically. But he or she has also come to the conclusion that the doctrines and rituals of the church are symbolic, that is, they point to actual states of the soul and not necessarily to anything literal or historical.

A single example might help here. Consider the fourteenth-century Christian mystic and professor Meister Eckhart: "Master Eckhart." Eckhart preached of an inner light that makes men divine and of a power beyond space and time that he called the eternal Now. "This light," he wrote, "is so potent that it is not merely in itself free of time and space, but … this light takes away time and space."[13] In other words, this light grants a type of consciousness that has nothing to do with spatial or temporal boundaries. To employ our modern scientific register, it is outside space–time. To employ the traditional religious terms, it is infinite (beyond space) and immortal (beyond time). "Anyone powerfully seized by this light," the professor preached, "would be as far superior to another man as a living man is compared to one painted on a wall."[14] The painted man lives in only two dimensions, we would say today. He is "flat." The superior man now lives in three, or four, or more. He is hyper-dimensional, we would say.

Meister Eckhart re-read numerous traditional Christian doctrines peeled off the wall of space–time. Instead of focusing on the incarnation of God in the historical birth of Jesus of Nazareth, for example, he wrote of "the birth of the Word in the soul"—that is, of the divinization of human nature in the innermost core, root, or ground of the human being. This particular teaching appears to stem back to his own queer mystical experience. Here is how he describes becoming a woman and becoming pregnant with God: "It seemed to a man as in a dream—it was a waking dream—that he became pregnant with Nothing, like a woman with child. And in the Nothing God was born: He was the fruit of Nothing."[15] Hence the "birth of the Word" was no longer a single historical event that happened once, a long, long time ago. In Eckhart's teaching, it became an eternal process that is happening right now in the soul, outside of time and space. He thus begged his listeners to "take leave of God for God," that is, to abandon their simplistic and naïve notions of God as an objective person "out there," so that they might experience true divinity in and as their own souls.[16] In short, he re-read scripture and Christian doctrine in light of his own inner experiences.

Troeltsch understood such examples in ways that were in conversation with his own place and time. Hence he associated mysticism with "the religious life of the cultured classes"—that is, with people like him.[17] Mysticism, for Troeltsch, was the religious form of intellectual elites and of the educated. It sees the language of the Bible or of Christian belief as of "merely relative significance." The truth is expressed through such forms, but these forms are not the truth, nor can they ever be.

Troeltsch further argued that from mysticism alone "are toleration and freedom of conscience" possible, since only through a mystical type of religion can different types of religious practice be seen as justified and appropriate approximations of a universally shared truth. "Mysticism," then, was no fuzzy or easy term for Troeltsch. It was radically critical of religious tradition, and it was an inherently paradoxical and reflexive comparative practice. Hence Troeltsch ends his massive study with a paraphrase of Jesus in the Gospel of Luke: "The truth is—and this is the conclusion of the whole matter—the Kingdom of God is within us."[18]

Which is all to say: not in any institution or religion.

Having said all of that, Troeltsch did not idealize mysticism. He in fact saw this type as possessing a real structural weakness. That weakness boiled down to the observation that—let me put it bluntly—mystics are often just awful at organizing themselves. Their independence of spirit and their conviction that religious truths are symbolic of interior realities can prevent them from organizing into tight, well-formed, authoritarian communities. And so we arrive at the most basic and most important modern dilemma that Troeltsch's model implies, when it does not actually shout it. That dilemma can be framed in this way: *whereas the most "true" form of religion (the mysticism type) is generally the one that is most poorly organized and cannot, in principle, be organized on a large scale at all, the most effective and most highly organized form of religious organization (the church type) is usually the one that leads to religious intolerance and violence and is now impossible in the modern world.* Or, as Adam Gopnik put it referring to the early gnostic Christianities, whose texts we only know because they buried them on a desert cliff: "The truth is that punitive, hysterical religions thrive, while soft, mystical ones must hide their scriptures somewhere in the hot sand."[19] The result? *No one* is happy with the state of religion.

Probably the best contemporary example of what Troeltsch called "mysticism" is the very modern sensibility of being "spiritual but not religious." The profoundly unorganized group of people who correspond to this description—which at the moment represents the fastest growing demographic in American religion, particularly in the youth culture—is in fact expressing a belief system and a social form that mirrors closely what Troeltsch meant by mysticism. Troeltsch in fact wrote about "spiritual religion," which he associated, among other things, with "the universal movement of religious consciousness in general," with the inclinations of the modern world, and, perhaps most importantly, with a general inability to connect to the churches, and therefore to the masses.[20] He would have likely recognized the spiritual but not religious crowd as advancing *the* modern expression of religion, which he would have understood as mystical in structure and intent.

The Miracle and the Saint: Signs of the (Im)possible

Both the electric arc of charisma and community and the formation of special religious institutions are helpful in understanding two central religious subjects that we have briefly invoked above but have never really defined or explored: the miracle and the saint.

Miracles, not unlike divination rituals, have posed very special problems to the study of religion from its earliest beginnings in nineteenth-century Europe, mostly because they appear to violate the laws of nature, which, since the rise of science (in that same nineteenth century), have been increasingly seen as unbreachable. Although this is seldom recognized, the situation is more complicated today, and for two reasons.

First, the situation is more complicated because the scholarship on miracles and anomalous phenomena has advanced to a point where many now find it unreasonable, if not actually perverse, to continue denying that such things happen. Many anthropologists, who routinely witness such wonders in the field, seem especially open-minded about the subject. And even those scholars who do not recognize that such things happen all the time, or who wish to remain silent or agnostic on the matter, often appear to be much more willing to take a careful and balanced look at the subject. It is a new day with respect to the study of the miraculous.

There is another reason why miracles are getting a second look, however, and that reason is, oddly enough, science. The bottom line here is that science itself has now developed all sorts of utterly bizarre theories and models, which appear to be necessary if you want to describe and explain the nature and structure of the physical universe. These include ideas like quantum nonlocality and "teleporting" quantum particles (in which quantum particles communicate instantly beyond space and time); a growing suspicion that consciousness somehow participates in, or even determines, how matter behaves; talk of

dark energy, which we are now told comprises most of the universe; black holes; and multiverses that overlap or move through one another like immense cosmic ghosts. Such scientific models make *any* of the miracles of the general history of religions look downright simple, unimaginative, and banal. With weird science like this, who needs miracles?

My point here is not to pretend that I understand any of these scientific models in their mathematical precision. I do not. My point is that it was the simple nineteenth-century materialism that rendered any sympathetic discussion of the miracle impossible, and that we now know that this kind of surface materialism is a fundamentally inadequate model with which to understand even physical reality.

There were other reasons why the miracle was rejected in the nineteenth century, including the advances of textual criticism and the growing awareness that the biblical stories could no longer be responsibly read as eyewitness accounts of real historical events. For all of these reasons, and more, the miracle story, and particularly the New Testament miracle story, came to function as a kind of litmus test for separating the study of religion from religion itself, the true scholar from the pretender. The believer continued to see miracle stories as accurate descriptions of real historical events. The scholar, however, became a scholar precisely to the extent that he read them as textual fabrications, or at least exaggerations, designed to illustrate a religious teaching or, more darkly, to prop up the religious claims of the religion and its authorities.

Comparative Miracles

If we put this stark either–or (miracles are either literally true or ideological fictions) aside for a moment and open out our perspective from a single religion to many religions, we can make a number of useful observations about the miracle in the general history of religions. David Weddle has recently given us an exceptionally calm and balanced comparative study of miracles. He opens his book by defining the miracle this way: "A **miracle** is an event of transcendent power that arouses wonder and carries religious significance for those who witness it or hear or read about it."[21] He also notes, correctly, that the miracle is first and foremost a narrative or story. "The story of miracles," he writes, "begins with the miracle of story: the power of narrative to draw readers into alternative views of reality."[22] In this narrative function, the miracle shares very much in the power of myth.

So *miracles are stories*. That is the first key.

The second key is that *miracles are signs*.

That is to say, miracles carry meaning. They signal some important truth of the religion in question. Let me illustrate this second key point with a bit of humor. A religious miracle is not simply an anomalous event, a bizarre happening that violates the ordinary workings of the world. If tomorrow a huge baked potato materialized in the sky over the northeastern seaboard of the United States and appeared to drop immense ghost-like blobs of sour cream, tree-like chives, and boulder-sized bacon bits into the ocean, would that be miraculous? No. That would be ridiculous. If, however, a crowd of faithful claimed to see an apparition of the Virgin Mary hovering over a church in Madrid on Christmas Day holding a glowing baby, would that be a miracle? Yep. That would be miraculous.

What is the difference? The difference is that, whereas the floating baked potato fits into no established cultural or religious narrative and so means nothing, the apparition of the Virgin Mary with child fits into a well-established cultural and religious narrative presently active in Spain and so would immediately be interpreted as meaningful, as a "sign."

Put more precisely, a miracle is not just an anomalous event, but *an interpreted and meaningful anomalous event* that is "set within a tradition's broader system of beliefs and understood as signifying something about transcendent reality."[23] We might say, then, that, technically speaking, there can be no private miracles. To mean something, a sign must be communicated to a community within a particular religious framework. In this, the miracle is very much like charisma as understood by the sociologists. Indeed, we might well define the miracle as a charis-matic event that needs a social field to happen at all. We are back to the electric arc of charisma and community.

This, by the way, also explains a most curious feature of the comparative study of miracles, namely the fact that religious communities do not generally recognize the miracles of other, competing religious communities. How could they? This would be an implicit recognition that truth also lies there.

The third key is that the *miracles involve transcendence*. Miracles, in Weddle's apt phrase, are "signs of transcendence."[24] If we prefer a modern, non-religious language, we might say that miracles always happen at a particular time and place, but they appear to issue from a dimension beyond space–time. That is, they signal the presence of another order of reality, a hidden dimension that is speaking to a human community in the only way it apparently can "speak"—through symbols, myths, and signs.

Weddle looks at five traditions to illustrate his point about the miracle as a sign of transcendence: Hinduism, Judaism, Buddhism, Christianity, and Islam. He demonstrates that these major religions all have miracle stories, and in abundance, but that these stories mean different things to each tradition. In short, he is an excellent comparativist, balancing sameness and difference. More specifically, Weddle draws a distinction between the vastly different *contents* of the miracle stories and the very similar *functions* they serve in each of the world religions (this move should strike you as a familiar one by now). He isolates four such common functions or comparative patterns with respect to miracles. Miracles in the world religions, he concludes, do four things: (1) they support the hope that humans are not completely bound by material forces that otherwise appear to fix human fate; (2) they confirm the conviction that there is a world or dimension beyond this one that occasionally shows itself to the human community by manipulating physical reality; (3) they illustrate the teachings or doctrines of the religious tradition in question; and (4) they express a particular community's hope for justice and political freedom from unjust rulers, despots, and social suffering.

Miraculous People

Very much related to the subject of miracle is the subject of the saint. The English word "saint" derives from the Latin word *sanctus*, "holy." Like the Siberian term "shaman," the Roman Catholic term "saint" has come to function as a comparative category in the study of religion. In this comparativist usage, a **saint** is a person considered to be especially holy by a particular religious community. But we have to be careful here, for by "especially holy" we do not mean "really, really nice." We mean "really, really *powerful*." We mean someone who embodies in a most dramatic fashion the core values and beliefs of the tradition and can transmit these truths, like a contagion or electric charge, to those who come in contact with him or her. We mean charisma.

Different religions understand, recognize, and establish their saints in different ways. Many traditions, for example, establish saints more or less by popular acclaim, that is, by the local people building shrines over graves, preserving folklore about their deeds and intercessory powers, and mass-producing images of their likenesses in various media. Many forms of Hinduism, Sufism, and Buddhism work like this.

Other religions insist on tighter control. The case of Roman Catholicism is especially instructive here again, and for at least four reasons. First, this is the tradition that produced the comparative category of the saint. Second, the Catholic tradition has recognized that its own faithful often do some dubious things when it comes to assessing a person's sanctity—like when the monks of the monastery of Lisieux, France, insisted on honoring their departed steward as a saint (this was in 1181). The problem was that he "had in fact been killed in a drunken brawl."[25] Third, the Catholic tradition has amassed large archives of historical material on the subject, rich in first-person descriptions from sworn witnesses, recordings of examinations and cross-examinations, even physical, chemical, and medical analyses. And, fourth, the same tradition has developed sophisticated rational principles of doubt and legal procedures of analysis to assess these materials through a patient and exhaustive process.

These legal procedures are formally handled by a special office in the Vatican called the Congregation of Rites. The procedures involve years (indeed often decades, and sometimes centuries) of preparation and extensive court hearings, all designed to examine the evidence, pore through the historical materials, advance arguments and counterarguments, and come to a final decision. To ensure a correct outcome, a special canon lawyer is assigned; his job is to try to frustrate, challenge, and, if possible, disprove the case. This is the famous Promotor Fidei (literally "promoter of the faith"), better known today as "the devil's advocate." As a friend of mine puts it, Catholicism is the only tradition to put its saints on trial. And that is not a metaphor.

The process of determining whether someone can be declared a saint consists of two stages: beatification and canonization. The first stage results in the title of "Blessed," the second in the title of "Saint." The first thing to prove in this legal process is that the candidate exhibited what the tradition calls "heroic virtue" in life, that is, lived out the highest moral principles of the faith. Related to this first and primary criterion is the demand that nothing in the saint's teachings be in conflict with the orthodox teachings of the church. If such heroic virtue is not found, the case ends, no matter how many strange powers the individual manifested. If such heroic virtue and orthodox faith are demonstrated, the process proceeds.

Now the case involves establishing whether or not genuine miracles occurred after the person's death. The church is careful to attribute such miracles to God, but it also understands them as connected to the intercession of the saint-to-be. Two such miracles are needed for beatification; four are needed for canonization. Popular acclaim or hearsay is never sufficient. All miracle stories have to be proven in a court of law. In general, the tradition has been extremely suspicious of claims to the miraculous. It sets the bar high. Historians, medical experts, and scientists are routinely employed to comb through the evidence and determine whether the miracle in question is empirically miraculous, that is, inexplicable in medical or natural terms.

The key point to remember here is that a Catholic saint, like the miracles attributed to her, is finally a sign witnessing to the moral and doctrinal truths of the tradition. One could manifest all sorts of miracles—cure the sick, know the future, raise storms, even raise the dead—and none of this would matter in the least, if one taught, say, that there is no Trinity, or that the Virgin Mary was no virgin. What matters is the truth of the tradition, not the presence of the seeming miraculous, which is often no such thing at all.

Comparative Practice: The Flying Saint and the Levitating Medium

The subjects of charisma, saint, and miracle all come together when we compare the same anomalous phenomenon in two very different contexts. Take the extreme case of levitation, as extensively reported around Saint Joseph of Copertino (1603–1663) and the Scottish medium Daniel Dunglas Home (1833–1886).

Joseph was the "flying saint" who became the patron of pilots, astronauts, and air travelers (an airplane appears on the back of medals worn in his honor to this day), as well as—it is difficult not to smile at this point—the patron of poor students and test-takers, who need their grades "raised." He himself was an abysmal student. Home (pronounced "Hoom") was a Scottish super-medium with an American accent (he had lived in the States as a boy), red hair, and freckles, who became the star of nineteenth-century European occult culture. If we set these two men side by side, we have a fruitful opportunity for comparison, as we are comparing a "same," that is, levitation (our C), via two significant "differences," that is, a traditional saint within an intensely Catholic Italian society (our A) and a modern medium within a Protestant and quickly secularizing society (our B).

There is a most interesting feature of this very particular kind of comparison, which sets it apart from most others. Our "same" here, after all, is more empirical than most, since, with levitation, we have a phenomenon that is not simply internal to a reporting subject or that is functioning on the plane of myth, belief, or doctrine. Rather we have an alleged

physical phenomenon that was reported by numerous external and corroborating witnesses.

No one can see the religious experience of another. No one can see a myth or a doctrine. No one can see Freud's notion of sublimation or one of Weber's ideal types. But, presumably, anyone can see a man floating three feet off the ground. There are difficulties here, of course, around the reliability of witnesses, the adequacy of the lighting, and the possibility of fraud. But the simple fact remains that a flying saint or a floating medium is something very different from a belief or an ecstatic vision.

Joseph's most recent English biographer is the American philosopher Michael Grosso, on whose work with an Italian colleague and translator, Cynthia Clough, I am relying here.[26] Grosso is sympathetic to the possibility, indeed likelihood, of Joseph's levitations, mostly because he sees no plausible way around the historical facts—which, as we shall see, are as embarrassingly numerous and well attested as they are extreme. On the other hand, Home's most recent biographer, Peter Lamont, is deeply skeptical of the phenomenon of levitation, even as he clearly adores his historical subject and writes about him with much humor and verve. Lamont sees Home both as a charlatan whose tricks were never discovered and as a trickster figure who played a creative role in the drama of Victorian culture. Given these features, the two biographies of Joseph and Daniel grant a most instructive comparison of levitation.

Joseph

Let us look at Joseph first. Known to his contemporaries as Padre Giuseppe, Joseph is easily the most well documented case of human levitation on record. It was a difficult life, to say the least. Joseph was born in utter destitution to a reportedly cruel and abusive mother, in a stable no less; his father was in hiding from pistol-toting debt collectors, who had just impounded their home. Four of his five siblings died in childhood. And he came close. As an adolescent, Joseph was bed-ridden for five full years: he had on his back a stinking tumor the size of a melon, which was eventually cut off and cauterized by a hermit. When he finally crawled out of bed, he had underdeveloped motor skills and highly developed dissociative skills. They called him *Boccaperta* ("gaping mouth") for his habit of staring into empty space with his mouth wide open.

As an adult, Joseph would manifest what Grosso calls "near frightening psychophysical powers." These included the traditional ability to "read hearts," which meant in this case Joseph's ability to see people's sins in the form of muck or dirt on their faces and then to hector them into guilt and repentance. The poor people were terrified of what Grosso calls "the super bully and nosey telepath." He would learn to tone it down.

Joseph's religious career spanned some thirty-five years, during which thousands of individuals witnessed him, usually in broad daylight, do things like float to the top of churches and fly into trees. These were his *voli* ("flights"). One time "he flew up into an olive tree and, like a rash kitten on its first climb, could not get down again; his companion [a Benedictine monk], after a quarter of an hour or so, had to go and fetch a ladder."[27] These *voli* were more or less constant throughout his adult life, and they did not decline with age, as psychical abilities often do. Indeed, Joseph's last levitations took place on his deathbed and were reported by his surgeon, who noted that Joseph floated and felt no pain as his right leg was being cauterized.

Everyone, from peasants to kings, came to see Joseph. Among royalty was the king of Poland and the Protestant duke of Brunswick, who converted from Lutheranism to Catholicism after witnessing Joseph's flight (a conversion confirmed by the duke's employee, the philosopher and mathematician Gottfried Wilhelm Leibniz). We have private diaries witnessing to Joseph's abilities. We have Inquisition reports (Joseph was called up twice). And we have extensive written depositions made under oath (called *processi*) from the legal proceedings that eventually declared him officially to be a saint. These legal documents contain some 150 eyewitness reports, including from scholars, from two cardinals, from Pope Urban VIII, from kings, and from princesses. As if this were not enough, the devil's advocate of the church's legal process to canonize Joseph was none

other than Prosper Lambertini, admired friend of Voltaire, who, as Pope Benedict XIV, finally beatified Joseph in 1753 and sent him on his way to full sainthood in 1767.

All of this adds up to this fact: if we are going to explain Joseph away, we have a whole lot of explaining to do. Whatever they were, Joseph's ecstatic flights were not staged, and he was routinely both horrified and embarrassed by them. As was the church, whose authorities continued to move Joseph from place to place his entire life, lest the crowds grew too great. Grosso writes of a succession of popes putting Joseph under what was essentially house arrest. His physical charisma had to be contained, disciplined, made obedient, and then whisked away.

Grosso notes the symbolic nature of Joseph's flights, as if the levitations were waking dreams materializing their primary spiritual and emotional meanings as "ecstasy," "spiritual flight," and, of course, "up." The ecstasies were usually preceded by a scream and involved physiological signs of death such as rigidity, the eyeballs being turned up, an insensitivity to pain or touch, and a warping of space that violated what we think of as gravity. Weirdest of all (as if "weird" continues to have any meaning at all here), his robes often appeared frozen while he was in flight, as if he had become a living statue. Grosso puts it this way: "It is as though Joseph were being composed, modeled and framed as a living work of Baroque art … something is propelling Joseph to mount a display of himself, as if he were a living transcendent art-object: out of time and space, a vision to be admired and venerated."[28]

There was also something vaguely erotic about some of these screaming ecstasies—"erotic" in the sense in which we have already defined that adjective: at once spiritual and sexual, if not necessarily genital. Two scenes, one involving a divine and beloved male body, the other a human and despised female body, bring this feature out. Consider the first scene:

> In the company of two priests from Copertino, [Joseph] asked them: "Brothers, if it were to happen that you found Christ crucified on these crosses and each one of

us were able to touch and kiss him, on what part of the body would you have kissed him? You, for example, Donato Antonio?" And Donato Antonio replied that he would have kissed him on the soles of his feet. "And you, Father Candeloro?" Padre Giuseppe asked the old priest. Brother Candeloro said, "I would kiss him on his most holy rib-cage, from which the seven sacraments originated." Then Padre Giuseppe began to respond, as the two brothers say in the *processi*: "I … I … and I" swelling up more and more as though he could not say another word, but instead let out a great scream and all of a sudden flew from the brothers all the way to the cross, embraced it, and landed on his knees supported by the cross-beam about three metres from the ground.[29]

Now consider the second scene, this one involving Joseph basically bouncing around the interior of a church, partly, it appears, as a means of avoiding having to speak to a sexually active woman:

[In 1646] the Admiral of Castile came to Assisi from Rome with his wife and children, attracted by Giuseppe's fame, and met with the Padre in his cell. Afterward, the Admiral told his wife that he had seen and spoken with another St. Francis. The wife, also wanting to talk to Giuseppe, asked the Custodian if she could speak in private with the holy one. The Custodian, anticipating the repugnance of Padre Giuseppe in having to deal with this woman, asked him to go into the church to meet with her and her companions for the sake of obedience. Padre Giuseppe smiled and said that he would obey but did not know if he would be able to speak to them. In fact, he foresaw that he would not be able to speak because the greater force of the Immaculate Mother of God would transport him elsewhere. After leaving his cell, he entered the Church through a small door in front of the altar on which a statue of the image of the Immaculate Conception had been erected. The moment he entered, he looked at the statue, screamed, and flew a distance of twelve steps *above the heads of the Admiral and the women*, to embrace the feet of the statue of the Queen of Heaven. Then, after remaining in that pose of adoration for some time, he gave another scream and, still flying through the air, returned near the little door where he bowed in reverence to the Mother of God and kissed the floor, his

head inclined so that his hood fell over his face. He then walked away back to his cell, leaving everyone dazed if not traumatized. The wife of the Admiral fainted and the Admiral had to revive her, splashing water in her face and holding smelling salts to her nose; the Admiral himself raised his eyebrows and, opening his arms, stupefied, did not faint, but became weak-kneed and flustered.[30]

Grosso notes that the statue Joseph embraced was well off the ground (five to six feet), so Joseph was hovering in mid-air as he embraced the Virgin to escape the wife. Joseph does not just levitate. He flies like a Catholic Superman (see Figure 7.4).

Figure 7.4   Joseph of Copertino levitates in the presence of Pope Urban VIII. Mary Evans Picture Library.

Figure 7.5 Daniel Dunglas Home levitates in the presence of an astonished crowd (1871). Lithograph from Louis Figuier, *Les Mystères de la science* (vol. 2, Paris, 1887). Microfilm courtesy Cornell University Library. Scan courtesy Rice University.

Daniel

"In the history of the paranormal," Lamont writes, "no one was greater than Daniel Dunglas Home." Home was, in Lamont's apt phrase, the "first psychic," since the term "psychic" was first used publicly around 1871 by the chemist Sir William Crookes. After discovering the element thalium, Crookes was experimenting with Home's abilities, which he traced back to a still unknown "Psychic Force." The term "psychic," in other words, was invented by a scientist to describe Daniel. For Lamont, Daniel is not just the first psychic, though. He is "the most interesting person who ever lived," and this despite the fact that you have probably never heard of him.[31]

It is easy to sympathize with Lamont's hyperbole. Daniel appeared to be able to foresee the future, produce ghostly hands that ended at the wrist (and shook living ones), elongate his body (about eleven inches, according to one witness), psychically move furniture (in one documented case, a table with five men standing on it),[32] play musical instruments from a distance, shake walls, handle hot coals without getting burnt, and, most famously of all, float horizontally out a window and levitate up to ceilings, where he liked to scratch a mark as a sign that he had really been up there. Such feats consistently polarized Victorian and European culture all the way up to the era's most famous scientists, writers, and political leaders. Perhaps most astonishing of all is the fact that no one ever caught Daniel cheating (see Figure 7.5).

Lamont summarizes this most remarkable of careers this way:

> In Britain, he would be attacked by Dickens and defended by Thackeray; Faraday would refuse to meet him while Darwin would be eager to test him. In Europe, he would be a guest of the Pope but later be expelled from Rome on the charge of sorcery, he would be detested by Tolstoy yet become a confidante of the Tsar.[33]

And—get ready for a long list—this is before we even get to:

- Napolean Bonaparte and Empress Eugenie, who hosted and admired him;
- or Mark Twain, parts of whose *A Tramp Abroad* Daniel translated into Russian (Twain joked that he couldn't find a single error in Daniel's translation);
- or Robert Chambers, who foreshadowed Darwin's theory of natural selection in his *Vestiges of the Natural History of Creation* (1844), wrote an introduction to Daniel's first autobiography, and tried to reconcile evolution with psychical phenomena;
- or the poet Robert Browning, who carried a real hatred for Daniel and wrote an angry poem about him entitled "Mr. Sludge, 'The Medium'";

- or the sexual innuendos and scandalous rumors that consistently circled around his "effeminate" nature, "unnatural practices," and intimacies with men;
- or the two apparent attempts on his life by would-be assassins;
- or his conversion to Catholicism;
- or—one of my personal favorites—the female spirit who entered a marble-topped bedside table to chase her famous musician nephew around an apartment and throw herself around his neck, at which point he fainted.

The last event allegedly happened one night after Daniel had communed with the spirits on his way to Russia (to marry a Russian princess, of course).

Then there was the time when the anthropologist E. B. Tylor, who pioneered the anthropological study of religion, asked the question: "Is Mr D. D. Home a were-wolf?" Tylor was probably making fun of Alfred Russel Wallace—the co-originator of the evolutionary theory, with Darwin—who had taken exception to Tylor's suggestion that folklore was simple superstition and ignorance. The pioneering biologist believed, like many after him, that folklore and legend are rooted in actual psychical phenomena, and not simple superstition and bad logic, as Tylor had famously argued.[34]

Well, *whatever* he was, Daniel makes the rest of us look downright boring.

The first levitation that Lamont reports occurred in August 1852, in South Manchester, Connecticut, while Daniel was still living in the US: during a séance, he was lifted about a foot off the floor, and witnesses were holding his feet: "Again and again he was taken from the floor, and the third time he was carried to the lofty ceiling of the apartment."[35] Years later, the British *Cornhill Magazine*, a prestigious publication edited by Thackeray, published an anonymous piece called "Stranger than Fiction," which described another scene in which, in semi-darkness, Daniel lifted himself off the floor and headed for the ceiling again: "We watched in profound stillness, and saw his figure pass from one side of the window to the other, feet foremost, lying horizontally in the air."[36]

By far, though, the most famous of Daniel's levitations occurred on Sunday, December 13, 1868 before three men, one of whom, Lord Lindsay, would later become president of the Royal Astronomical Society and a fellow of the Royal Society (a very prestigious scientific institution). The accounts of two of the men, Lord Lindsay and Lord Adare, differ in details but agree that Daniel appeared to have floated out of one window, head first, stiff, and more or less horizontal, and then climbed in another, and all of this "85 feet from the ground." Lamont ably documents the discrepancies in the two accounts and the strange fate of the little book that recorded it. Lord Adare and his father co-wrote and privately printed about sixty copies of *Experiences in Spiritualism with Mr D. D. Home* (1869). Most of the copies were then almost immediately destroyed by the father, whose Catholic faith, Lamont reasonably suggests, likely gave him second (and third and fourth) thoughts. The result? "Daniel might have floated out of a third floor window but, to his frustration, hardly anybody knew this."[37]

They would find out anyway, through an eighteen-month inquiry into psychical phenomena and a whole host of scientists and highborn Brits who came to defend the reality of such events, including Daniel's third-story levitation and double-window adventure. Not surprisingly, the event remains mired in controversy and completely unresolved to this day.

Welcome to the study of religion.

Comparative Reflections

Well, what to do with the flying saint and the floating medium? The first thing we can observe is that everything depends upon our comparative ground or foundation, that is, on the nature of the world that *we* are assuming. We have seen this principle working throughout our comparative acts in these chapters. This feature is even more acute here. If we happen to inhabit a scientific materialism, all of this can only be pious wish and conscious fraud. Gravity is gravity, and people don't float and fly. End of story. If we happen to inhabit a traditional Catholic world-view, St. Joseph is one more proof that the Catholic faith is true. But Daniel? Well, he can only be a fake. Or a sorcerer. Or a werewolf. And, even if he really did float, what exactly did this miracle signal or sign? The existence of spirits and an afterlife, perhaps. But whose? The historical truth is that Daniel never really found a theology that could handle his powers or a religious community that could accept him. Indeed, even after his conversion to Catholicism, he was kicked out of the city of Rome.

So much for being a saint.

Daniel fared little better with the Protestant Victorians back in England. Lamont nails the comparative crisis that ensued there: "So how could a Christian believe in the miracles of Jesus, yet reject the miracles of Daniel Home?" One answer came easily enough to the Victorians: the miracles of the Bible proved the Bible and the truth of the Christian tradition. Daniel's miracles proved nothing, as they were not in the Bible and sat in no ancient tradition. This allowed the Protestant Victorians "to accept the word of Matthew, Mark, Luke and John, while dismissing the word of Daniel as blasphemous."[38]

One wonders what the Victorian Protestants would have thought of Joseph, the flying Catholic saint. Probably not much. One also wonders what they would have thought of Grosso's simple observation that there are between *two and three hundred* cases of levitation in the annals of Catholic hagiography alone, including in the Spanish autobiography of Saint Teresa of Avila, who describes in some detail how her mystical raptures sometimes resulted in literal levitation and how she once stretched out on the floor and asked her fellow nuns to hold her down, lest her levitations cause a scene on a feast day (when some noble ladies were present). One can only wonder what the visiting ladies thought of a group of nuns pinning one of their own to the floor.[39] Nor have such things ceased in the modern period. Grosso notes that a priest from southern California, Fr. Aloysius

Ellacuria, was witnessed levitating at mass in Paris as late as 1975.

Perhaps the non-Catholic can dismiss all of this. It is not so easy for the professional comparativist, who privileges neither the Roman Catholic nor the Victorian Protestant, nor any other religious world for that matter. The comparativist knows, after all, that, while the historical evidence around figures like Joseph and Daniel may be well nigh unique, floating and flying people can be found everywhere in world mythology, shamanism, and folklore. Such genres no doubt exaggerate and certainly cannot be read uncritically, but, once we have met a historical and obsessively documented figure like Joseph or Daniel, we cannot help but wonder whether historical realities may not lie behind the most fantastic folklore traditions as well.

The Toolkit

This chapter has been about the social manifestations of religion, that is, about how individual religious experiences or anomalous events are crystallized into a stable, public form that can then be passed on from generation to generation. Since "electricity," "conductivity," "transmission," and "charge" have been the primary working metaphors, these tools clearly go in the toolbox drawer marked "electrical work" or "electrician." There are at least five ways to work with this electricity:

1 *Charisma and the Body Electric* Founders, prophets, saints, and spiritual teachers often manifest "charisma." Charisma is best thought of as a kind of palpable social energy that arcs between a leader and a community. We also suggested an alternative "radioactive" model of charisma, which suggests that these energies may not always be completely dependent on a social community. They might also be physiological or metaphysical.

2 *Passing On the Charge* What most certainly does rely on a social community is the "transmission"

or passing on of this charisma to new generations: "tradition." We saw how this transmission was done through dream and vision, office or role, scripture and commentary, religious law, art and architecture, and the relic or sacred body part.

3 *The Social Body Electric* Religious institutions attempt the same electric transmission, but they do so in different ways, depending on their historical context and on their relationship to whatever religious worldview is socially dominant. We looked at three types of religious institutions: the church (an all-encompassing institution that is more or less identical to the social order and is socially dominant), the sect (an intense group of people that breaks away from the church on a particular doctrinal point or ritual matter), and mysticism (a highly individualistic approach to religion that relies on personal experience and is very difficult to organize). We noted that the church type is now impossible in modern pluralistic societies.

4 *The Miracle as Sign* A "miracle," we noted, is not simply an anomalous, unexplained, or weird event. A miracle is a "sign" of the transcendent breaking into history in order to give witness to the truth of a religious tradition. A miracle, moreover, gives witness through narrative or story. In this it shares in the function of myth. All established religions, we observed, possess such miracle stories.

5 *The Social Production of Sanctity* Very much related to the comparative pattern of the miracle is the comparative pattern of the saint. A saint is not a really nice person. A saint is an exemplar of a religious community who manifests the truths of the tradition in an especially powerful, dramatic, or heroic manner. A saint is a "miraculous person," which is to say a person functioning as a miracle of the tradition. We looked at the legal processes of Roman Catholicism around the canonization of saints to demonstrate the miracle as sign and the saint as traditional exemplar. We also compared the levitations of St. Joseph of Copertino and Daniel Dunglas Home in order to show how and why the social context of the former made him a saint and the social context of the latter made him an assumed charlatan. Social context is not everything, but it's most things when it comes to social memory, institution, and tradition, that is, when it comes to the sociology of religion.

The Tough Questions

1 Do you believe in relics? If your answer is no and you possess, say, the stage cape of Elvis Presley or the diamond glove of Michael Jackson, can I have it? Why do we value these material objects, which are worthless as simple objects?

2 What do you make of our statement above that, whereas the most "true" form of religion (the mysticism type) is generally the one that is most poorly organized—and cannot, in principle, be organized on a large scale at all— the most effective and most highly organized form of religious organization (the church type) is often the one that leads to religious intolerance and violence and is now impossible in the modern world?

3 If you are a religious person and are committed to a single tradition, what do you do with the fact that miracles are reported and revered in all religions, and that each miraculous complex witnesses to the truth of a different and quite contradictory set of doctrines? How do you practice fair comparison here?

Notes

1   These three passages, widely cited throughout the tradition's literature, are most easily accessed here: http://www.adidam.org/newsletter/issue1/ (last accessed on August 24, 2013).

2   James Steinberg, personal communication, February 20, 2013, responding to this chapter.

3   Quoted in S. N. Eisenstadt, ed., *Max Weber on Charisma and Institution Building* (Chicago, IL: University of Chicago Press, 1968), xviii.

4   For more on the religious dimensions of modern fandom, see Victoria Nelson, *Gothicka* (Cambridge, MA: Harvard University Press, 2012).

5   Charles Fort, *Lo!* In *The Book of the Damned: The Collected Works of Charles Fort*, Introduction by Jim Steinmeyer (New York: Jeremy P. Tarcher/Penguin, 2008), 547. *Lo!* was first published in 1931.

6   Nelson, *Gothicka*, xl.

7   I am indebted here to Jess Hollenback's analysis of mystics as agents of quick cultural change, in his magisterial *Mysticism: Experience, Response, and Empowerment* (University Park: University of Pennsylvania Press, 1996).

8   The Buddhist and Hindu uses of *dharma* are very different. In Hindu contexts, this word generally means duty or appropriate role, whereas in Buddhist contexts it generally means teaching and sometimes, in philosophical texts, "essence."

9   See especially Charles Freeman, *Holy Bones, Holy Dust: How Relics Shaped the History of Medieval Europe* (New Haven, CT: Yale University Press, 2011).

10 Ernst Troeltsch, *The Social Teachings of the Christian Churches*, vol. 2, translated by Olive Wyon (New York: Macmillan, 1931), 996.

11 Steve Bruce, *Religion in the Modern World: From Cathedrals to Cults* (Oxford: Oxford University Press, 1996), 2.

12 Bruce, *Religion in the Modern World*, 75.

13 Maurice O'Connell Walshe, trans. and ed., *The Complete Mystical Works of Meister Eckhart* (New York: Crossroad Publishing Company, 2009), 145.

14 O'Connell Walshe, *Complete Mystical Works of Meister Eckhart*, Sermon 24.

15 O'Connell Walshe, *Complete Mystical Works of Meister Eckhart*, Sermon 19.

16 O'Connell Walshe, *Complete Mystical Works of Meister Eckhart*, 296.

17 Troeltsch, *The Social Teachings*, 994.

18 Troeltsch, *The Social Teachings*, 1013.

19 Adam Gopnik, "The Big Reveal." *The New Yorker*, March 5, 2012: a review of Elaine Pagels, *Revelations: Visions, Prophecy, and Politics in the Book of Revelation* (Viking, 2012).

20 Troeltsch, *The Social Teachings*, 996–997.

21 David L. Weddle, *Miracles: Wonder and Meaning in World Religions* (New York: New York University Press, 2010), 4.

22 Weddle, *Miracles*, xi.

23 Weddle, *Miracles*, xiii.

24 Weddle, *Miracles*, 214.

25 Renée Haynes, *Philosopher King: The Humanist Pope Benedict XIV* (London: Weidenfeld and Nicolson, 1970), 83.

26 Michael Grosso with Cynthia Clough (trans.), *Wings of Ecstasy: Mind and Body in the Life of Joseph of Copertino* (unpublished manuscript).

27 Haynes, *Philosopher King*, 35.

28 Michael Grosso, *The Strange Case of St. Joseph of Copertino: Ecstasy and the Mind–Body Problem* (New York: Oxford University Press, forthcoming).

29 Grosso, *The Strange Case of Joseph of Copertino*.

30 Vita, ch. 11. In Grosso, *The Strange Case of Joseph of Copertino*.

31 Peter Lamont, *The First Psychic: The Peculiar Mystery of a Notorious Victorian Wizard* (London: Abacus, 2005), ix–xiii.

32 Lamont, *The First Psychic*, 30–31.

33 Lamont, *The First Psychic*, 3.

34 For the last, see Lamont, *The First Psychic*, 101.

35 Lamont, *The First Psychic*, 33.

36 Lamont, *The First Psychic*, 109–110.

37 Lamont, *The First Psychic*, 188. See pp. 185–196, and 265, where Lamont suggests that the three men were somehow hypnotized. This is one of those cases where the debunking "answer" is as fantastic as the reported event.

38 Lamont, *The First Psychic*, 225–226.

39 See Teresa of Avila, *The Book of Her Life*, translated with notes by Kieran Kavanaugh and Otilio Rodriguez, Introduction by Jodi Bilinkoff (Indianapolis, IN: Hackett Publishing, 2008), 121–124, chapter 20, paragraphs 4–9.

Nocturnal Clouds (2005), by Lynn Randolph, 41″×36″.

8

The Religious Imagination and Its Paranormal Powers

Angels, Aliens, and Anomalies

Should he admit the probability of even one of these stories? How important would such an avowal be, and what astonishing implications could one foresee, if even only one such occurrence could be supposed to be proven?

Immanuel Kant, *Dreams of a Spirit Seer*

Reflexivity begets paradox: it blurs the distinction between subject and object. Psychic phenomena do also.

George P. Hansen, *The Paranormal and the Trickster*

We are part of a symbiotic relationship with something which disguises itself as an extraterrestrial invasion so as not to alarm us.

Terence McKenna, quoted in Mac Tonnies, *The Cryptoterrestrials*

Comparing Religions: Coming to Terms, First Edition. Jeffrey J. Kripal, Ata Anzali, Andrea R. Jain, and Erin Prophet.
© 2014 Jeffrey J. Kripal. Published 2014 by John Wiley & Sons, Ltd.

Consider the following three encounters with a light-form. All three are of European origin, and all three are from the 1980s.

Someone reported over the air: "Here it comes. Here it comes. Here it comes." Over the far end of the field, from the direction of the North Sea I noticed a small red light. The light came closer each second. At first I thought it was an aircraft, but it came at us too fast and silently … The red light cleared the pines bordering the field and quickly made a downward arc until it was directly over the illuminated fog. Only about 20 feet above the ground, the object was not stationary and roughly the size of a basketball … As my mind tried to register what I was looking at the ball of light exploded in a blinding flash. Shards of light and particles fell into the woods. I couldn't move; I tried to cover my eyes, but was too late.

About 50 neighbours went along … All at once seven or eight of us began shouting, "Look at that light." It came from the sky, as if the sky had opened up about ten metres, and it came towards us. It stopped over the hole in the ground (he pointed to where the people had been digging up the earth) … the light seemed to stream from it. It was as if a balloon of light had burst and there were thousands of tiny stars everywhere. We were just bathed in light … We were all crying. As long as I live I shall never forget that night.

[My mother] had told me that she had sensed that she had company in the house. The final "out of the ordinary" thing happened just four days before she died [from a long terminal illness] on 8th July '85 on a Sunday evening … When I arrived her words to me were that she had had a "strange visitation." I asked what happened, and she told me that firstly her TV screen had gone all ZIG-ZAGY and then black, then through her sitting room window had come a broad band of silver light. Mum demonstrated the bridth by holding her hands about 1 foot apart. This band of light passed through the room and out through the kitchen which leads from her sitting room. After it had passed through the room the TV came back to normal. My mother's little Border Collie also sat up and saw it.[1]

These three accounts are taken from Mark Fox's comparative study of spiritual encounters with light-forms, a study that tracks some 400 unpublished accounts from a large database of similar stories begun by the British zoologist Sir Alister Hardy. Hardy was convinced that such events signaled something important about the species and its evolutionary adaptation to a deeper dimension of reality. Through his own comparative practice, Fox demonstrates that these encounters display common cross-cultural patterns and can be shown to possess a "common core." This core reveals a broad band of light phenomena that are "typically manifested at times of crisis," are "overwhelmingly benign and loving," and often result "in 'turning-points' towards new spiritual and creative directions in the lives of those who experience them."[2]

Lightforms are a global constant in the history of religions. They are seen in ancient texts like *The Revelation of the Magi*. They are common in Roman Catholic Marian apparitions. They are omnipresent in contemporary American UFO accounts, being often framed now in a cold war mythology of invading extraterrestrials. They are routinely encountered, even by professional anthropologists, in Africa and Latin America, where they are given numerous and conflicting interpretations, from the flight of witches and the magical battles of shamans through ghost riders and treasure lights to UFOs again.[3]

If there is a shared light here, however, it is a shared light that is refracted through various historical prisms and psychological filters, which end up producing a veritable rainbow of different meanings and interpretations: sameness (the light) and difference (the historical and psychological prisms) once again. Take the three stories with which we began. The first is a scene from a famous series of UFO sightings, near the US military base in Rendlesham Forest, England. The second is an apparition of the Virgin Mary in the town of Medjugorje in former Yugoslavia, from the years before religious and ethnic tensions

there exploded into horrific civil war. I removed just two brief phrases from this second account, to hide, temporarily, its religious context: "and we all began praying"; and "a wooden cross"—which is what was in the hole. The third account appears to be a premonition of the visionary's own impending death.

Significantly, it appears that none of these light-forms offered up its own clear and unambiguous interpretation, although each was certainly given, almost immediately, a whole set of plausible meanings by those who witnessed it, largely no doubt because of the context in which it occurred (a military base, a religiously soaked scene, and a dying woman). Accordingly, these interpretations ranged from the eerily extraterrestrial, through the deeply pious, to … to what? Spiritual comfort in the face of death? If so, this was a spiritual comfort that, oddly, could interact with both a television set and a dog. So: a UFO, the mother of Jesus, and an electromagnetic spirit visible to a Border Collie.

Again, sometimes comparison just gets you into trouble.

System and Anomaly: Paranthropology

In this chapter we turn to the central subject of *the image* in the study of religion, which in turn will require us to come to terms with the imagination, the symbol, and the vision. What we will see over and over again is the basic paradox of something imagined communicating through symbol and myth something sensed or cognized as hyper-real, that is, something *not* imaginary. Sometimes the mediated reality will be of an explicitly religious nature (a discarnate being or a special state of the soul, for example). At other times this reality will be some historical event in the physical world (like a funeral or car accident, for example). In both types of case, however, we will see that the imagination manifests a basically paradoxical structure—and for one simple reason: as an organ of cognition, it stands *in between* that which it mediates and a human mind to whom this is shown. The paradox boils down to this: the

Figure 8.1   Exterior of Wat Rong Khun Temple, Chung Rai, Thailand, showing hell with hungry ghosts. Photographed by Mister Jo.

vision, symbol, or image *is and is not* that which it communicates or translates.

There are profound social and psychological dimensions to be dealt with here. In terms of the social aspects, Mary Douglas's work on purity is particularly helpful again. Douglas observed that societies based on strong purity codes do not deal well with the "dirt" of anomalies. An **anomaly** (from the Greek *anōmalos*, "uneven, irregular": *homalos*, a derivative of *homos*, "same," "regular," with the privative prefix *an-*) is any figure, event, or thing that does not fit into an explanatory system. Birth defects or the birth of twins are such anomalies in some cultural systems, as are strange lights in the sky or solar eclipses in others. The "hells" of the religions are extreme examples of the same: these are the places where a cultural system puts those acts, beliefs, and identities that violate its own structure and order, *that cannot be fit in.*

They are finally made to fit in precisely by being excluded from the system (see Figure 8.1).

Whatever the anomalies happen to be, social systems often have a very difficult time tolerating them, since the anomalies openly challenge the completeness, indeed the "realness" of the world in question. So, when something appears that does not fit into this world, the exception or anomaly must be punished or expelled, or at least brushed aside, derided, or ignored. But—and here is the catch that comparison clearly and definitively reveals—no social or religious system is complete, and none can speak for everything that happens in the world. Exceptions and anomalies always exist. Dirt happens.

So too with our own modern scientific worlds. Lightforms appear to military personnel, pious Catholics, dying women, anthropologists, and college students, and we have *no idea* what these things are or, for that matter, if all of these things are in the end very different. Nor do we know how to represent such events in any shared, acceptable language. We cannot even agree that they happen, even though, oddly enough, they do all the time.

Dirt and Parapsychology

If we have not come to terms with these anomalies, at least we have resources in the study of religion to make good sense of our failure. Recall that the sacred is traditionally defined as the Other, that which does not and *cannot* be fit into the profane world. We might suspect, then, that an anomalous event might well function as much more than the odd or the dirty. It might also manifest the sacred. And indeed this is what Douglas shows. Her examples are mostly drawn from ancient Israelite religion, classical Hinduism, and tribal religions from around the world. But there are other, closer contemporary examples of this systemic dirt or impurity.

Consider the modern category of the paranormal, or **psi** as it is technically called, after the first Greek letter in the word *psuchē* ("soul"). Psi is the central concern of **parapsychology**. Parapsychology is that branch of modern psychology that studies mental–material phenomena that appear to issue from "beyond" (*para*) the normal range of the human mind, as the latter is commonly understood in academic psychology. Its usage arose among British, French, and German scientists in the late nineteenth and early twentieth centuries, but its most famous professionalization occurred in the US in the early 1930s, around the Duke University lab of the botanist J. B. Rhine. Rhine, working closely with his wife Louise, used controlled laboratory experiments and statistical analyses to study, isolate, and measure psychical phenomena. It was Rhine who brought the popular expression "extra-sensory perception" (ESP) into broad public use.

The Psychical

There were earlier words. The words *psychic* and *psychical*, for example, came into use in the early 1870s through the writings of a prominent British

chemist named Sir William Crookes, who was studying what he came to describe as the "Psychic Force" of the super-medium whom we have met above: Daniel Dunglas Home. By **psychical** the early English researchers meant to refer to an as yet unexplainable force, which clearly pertained to the human psyche but could also, somehow, affect physical objects or sense events distant in space and/or time. They coded this double form of consciousness in a new phrase, somewhere between "psychical" and "physical." They dubbed it a "psychical Force."

The Paranormal

The word *paranormal* came a little later. It appears to have been first coined around the turn of the twentieth century by French scientists who studied **poltergeist** or "angry ghost" phenomena. They chose the word *paranormal* ("beyond the normal") as a naturalizing replacement for the word *supernatural*. In short, "paranormal" was originally a skeptical term, designed to call into question the assumed religious nature of a phenomenon. The French scientists did not believe, after all, in angry ghosts.

But they did believe in angry human beings with some most unusual unconscious powers. By postulating the **paranormal**, these scientists meant to refer to the human organism's apparent ability to "exteriorize" energies, usually of an extreme emotional or sexual nature, into the external environment. It was as if such individuals could manipulate material objects and physical events around them in order to express or symbolize their psychic condition. The classic cases involved, say, a person's anger making things around "explode," or a medium's excited trance state moving furniture, blowing curtains, and pushing people around with phantom hands, or, in even weirder instances, physical objects "disappearing" from one place in a home and "appearing" in another, in the manner of a teleportation scene in a science fiction movie.[4] Researchers came to realize that these events were generally not ghostly phenomena. They were symbolic phenomena. Moreover, the true nature of things appeared to be the precise reverse of what the religious language suggested. At stake was not an "angry ghost" but the "ghost of anger."

It is worth noting here that, once again, we have a comparative category descended from a more or less Protestant context. The paranormal was a modern reframing of a much older Catholic term, the *preter-natural*, which literally meant the same thing ("what is beyond the natural") and was used in a different skeptical mode, namely as a means of acknowledging strange, bizarre, or magical events without neces-sarily attributing these effects to God. Demons, after all, could also produce preternatural phenomena, or so the earlier Catholic skeptics had argued. The Protestant paranormal was a more secular version of the earlier Catholic preternatural. But the demons would return, nonetheless. Just wait.

Parapsychology as Anti-structure

Such ideas did not last long in the official culture. Although they were once common among intellec-tuals and scientists in and around places like Cambridge, Harvard, and Duke, these forms of research would become increasingly marginalized as the decades ticked by. And so today the paranormal is lazily associated with tabloid journalism, cranks, fraud (of which there is aplenty), and horror movies. In effect, the paranormal has become a taboo—even in the study of religion, where one would think it would be a central concern. Much like the subject of magic (of which it is a clear modern variant), the paranormal has been taken off the table of comparison and serious inquiry.

Can we make some further sense of this situation? Consider the work of the parapsychologist, stage magician, and professional skeptic George P. Hansen. In *The Trickster and the Paranormal* (2001), Hansen draws on cultural anthropology and literary criticism to shed light on paranormal events, which he sees as a form of communication appearing in the gaps and fractures of the modern scientific worldview. For Hansen, the paranormal is about *destructuring* or *anti-structure*. It is about destructuring, change, transition, disorder, marginality, ambiguity, paradox,

and the blurring of boundaries. The paranormal thus tends to spike in moments of profound social change (like the American counterculture) or of personal crisis (like a near-death experience, or the death of a loved one).

Hansen's work is especially helpful when it comes to understanding why such subjects are so difficult to study in an institutional setting like a university. Why, asks Hansen, is it that the only US government agencies that consistently invested in psychical research during the Cold War were the military and intelligence branches, that is, those dedicated to the use of control and deception? Why can the word "magic" refer to both a religious event and a trick on a stage? Why have numerous movies about UFOs and extraterrestrials grossed hundreds of millions of dollars, whereas the largest group of researchers dedicated to the study of UFOs (the Mutual UFO Network or MUFON) was still housed in the home of its founder three decades later?[5] And why has para-psychology never really found a stable home in the universities?

According to Hansen, it is certainly not because of a lack of good evidence. Evidence there is, in abun-dance, for anyone who takes the time to actually read the vast historical and scientific literature. Hansen does not see a conspiracy in this lack of institutional-ization. He thinks that psychical phenomena have not become the object of institutional study because they, by their very nature, resist any and all insti-tutionalization. The paranormal is marginalized because it *is* the marginal. It cannot be rationalized, that is, be made to fit into a system, because its whole point is *not* to fit into the system. The paranormal is an anomaly that points *beyond* the system. And so "the critics are partly right: psi *is* irrational, but it is also real."[6]

The Sixth Super Sense

What is our comparative base here? If the five senses act as the primary medium between our internal mental states and the external physical world, what acts as the medium for communications from outside such a system? What, if you will, constitutes the sixth sense?

One possible answer is a deceptively simple one: the imagination. I write "deceptively," because the imagination is no longer generally seen as a potential organ of cognition. It has become simply a spinner of "imaginary" things—fluff, fantasy, schlock. But is that really the whole truth? Is it possible that the imagination sometimes takes on other powers and mediates other dimensions of the real to us? Is it possible that not everything imagined is imaginary?

The Empowered Imagination

There are resources in the comparative study of religion for entertaining exactly this possibility. One of them is the **empowered religious imagination**. By such an expression I do not mean to refer to "imaginary" things, to the common experience of fantasy or day-dream or ordinary dream, although all of those psychological processes are certainly related and draw on the same human capacities to think through image and story. Rather, when I say "empowered imagination" I mean to evoke those very special moments when the imagination is "electrified," "zapped," or "magnetized"—and it just *knows*. What is known or "seen" in such special states remains "imagined," for sure, but it is now experienced as somehow more real and more true. The empowered religious imagination is no longer simply constructing and projecting; it is now also mediating and translating and, in some quite extraordinary cases, even apparently materializing its fantastic content. In a phrase, *something is coming through*. And this something is both real (hence the "something is coming" part) and imagined (hence the "through" part).

I am drawing here on the work of Jess Hollenback.[7] For Hollenback, psychological and ritual techniques that make consciousness focus and lead it into deeper and deeper states of concentration somehow catalyze remarkable transformations. These focusing techniques can be private, as in many forms of Hindu and Buddhist meditation practice, or communal, as in the "gifts of the Holy Spirit" of Pentecostal meetings, or in the extraordinary energy or "num" phenomena of the dance rituals of the Kalahari Kung people of southern Africa. In whatever context they are known, such altered states of mind and energy can lead to the manifestation of genuine paranormal powers like precognition, telepathy, clairvoyance, and out-of-body flights, to healing events, and even to apparent mind-over-matter effects and moments of materialization.

Since this last claim will return later in the present chapter, with both a monstrous fury and a spinning weirddom, we would do well to define it now. Hollenback writes of the phenomenon of **materialization**, by which he means the human imagination's apparent capacity to inform, influence, or even "project" (like a film projector) material or quasi-material events. As hard as it is to believe this, historical data suggest strongly that the human imagination can affect biological bodies and the physical environment in extraordinary ways, even create quasi-material shapes and apparitional bodies.

We can see this materializing capacity of the empowered imagination at work, from the ancient resurrection appearances recorded in the Gospels (the resurrected body of Jesus as described there could be touched, but it could also walk through walls) to modern-day encounters with dead loved ones, which are recorded in extraordinary detail in the parapsychological literature. Contrary to assumptions, these last cases are often reported as *physical* encounters in broad daylight (we will treat one in some detail in our last chapter). We can also come across striking cases of materialization in the anthropological literature. Hollenback, for example, finds his own ideas confirmed in the work of Paul Stoller and Edith Turner, both of whom worked in Africa and both of whom have reported dramatic paranormal encounters with materializing effects. Stoller fled the country after experiencing a sorcery attack in eastern Niger after apprenticing with a local sorcerer.[8] Turner witnessed an *ihamba*—an ectoplasmic spirit-substance—emerge from a body during a healing ritual in Zambia.⁹ In both of these cases the symbol had become concrete or quasi-concrete. It had materialized.

The Symbol

All of this, in turn, involves what is traditionally called the symbol. Scholars of religion who employ this term (and not all do) generally do so with something very specific in mind. Since for scholars who work with this category so much of religion is "symbolic," a great deal hinges precisely on how we understand the word. It is well worth dwelling for a moment, then, on its technical meanings and deep history.

First, it is important to understand what a symbol is *not*. A symbol is not a representation that mimics or reproduces what it signifies, in an objective or naturalist mode. That is, it does not work like a realist painting of a natural landscape, or like the photograph of a family—that is, through a one-to-one correspondence between the sign and that which it signifies. Nor does a symbol function as an artificial social convention that signifies through some arbitrary social agreement: for example, it does not work like an octagonal red metal sign whose eight sides and bright redness carry no natural connections to the message "Stop!"

So what is it? Most simply, we might say that a **symbol** is a very special type of sign, "with a life of its own." More technically, we might say that a symbol is a sign that appears spontaneously in the psyche of an inspired poet, prophet, dreamer, or visionary and is understood—and here is the really important part—*to somehow share in the essence or nature of that which it signifies* (since it is believed to have emerged from, or to have been revealed by, that which it points toward). Once such psychic events are expressed in language and elaborated in art, doctrine, myth, or ritual, they, of course, no longer need to be spontaneously produced. They are now part of the cultural currency. They have gone public. Accordingly, they can now take on different meanings, even entirely new or opposite meanings, as future generations

encounter, appropriate, and trade them within a shared social environment. A private symbolic event has become a public image, which in turn informs future private symbolic events, and so on, in a never-ending circle of inside and outside, of psyche and culture.

The key point to remember here is that symbols are not treated as arbitrary conventions or as strict products of any conscious manipulation or technical skill. Rather they are treated as mini-revelations, mini-miracles, or, as the great Neoplatonist Olympiodorus (495–570 CE) put it so well, as "little myths."¹⁰

Implicit in such an understanding of the symbolic is the existence of at least two orders of reality that need to be crossed for a message to be received by the individual or human community. The symbolic event is just such a mediation or translation "across the threshold." Note that—and here is the twisty part with which we began—a symbol *is and is not* that which it signifies. It would thus be a serious mistake to take the symbol literally, but it would also be a serious mistake to take it as pure fancy, as imaginary.

Consider a stained glass window in a church, with sunlight shining through it. There are pictures in the window telling a particular story (a myth). The light itself is not constructed or created by the church community and its historical tradition, but the window and its art most certainly are. The light is real, and it utterly transcends the little earthly community, but it can only be processed and engaged in by the community after it has been shaped and "colored" by the medium of the window. Something is really shining through, but both the "really shining" and the "through" are part of the process. Without the sun, there would be no window, but no one can live on the sun. Distance and mediation are crucial, but so is the light. So too with the image as symbol.

Another provocative analogy might help at this point. Consider the number. Science and mathematics operate through a rule-bound or logical manipulation of these entirely abstract signs. Are numbers social conventions or symbols? The squiggly lines that we identify with the decimal system inherited from Arabic science is conventional and historically constructed enough. These are clearly social conventions or signs. But what about the numbers themselves?

One could well argue that numbers are "eternal" and "transcendent," in the sense that they operate the same way in any historical period and exist in a "space" that is entirely unaffected by historical events. Moreover, conventional science assumes that numbers are not arbitrary signs; that they somehow participate in that which they signify; indeed, that they express and make understandable the hidden structures of the cosmos, which would otherwise not be available to us. Through them, we, like legendary wizards, can envision and even manipulate what we cannot see. Numbers render the invisible visible. They are symbolic realities. Little wonder, then, that, when it comes to figures like Pythagoras (of the famous theorem), and even Plato, the early western history of the number is deeply intertwined with esoteric communities, initiations, and religious notions of transcendence, reincarnation, paradox, and secrecy.

And the "symbol." The classicist Peter T. Struck has recently given us a profound history of the term and its three-millennia run in western history. That history, it turns out, has everything to do with the ancient poets and myth-makers (called *theologoi*, "theologians" or people who speak or create discourses about the gods). These myth-makers worked with the same mundane words as everyone else, of course; but they managed to use them in a way that enabled some of their readers to "hear in their words the faint but distinct promise of some truer resonance, or a subtle and profound knowledge that arrives in a concealed form and is waiting for a skilled reader to liberate it from its code." The hope was, and remains, "that we might find in poetry some palpable trace, at last, of the transcendent."[11]

The ancient Greeks came to mark these special places in these special texts with a number of words, the most important of which was *sumbola* ("symbols"). In Struck's elegant expression, such symbols marked "the limits of their texts," the places where the oracle, the poem, the myth, or the riddle carried their readers and listeners over into another realm of truth. As it turns out, those textual limits often had to do with the most scandalous and perverse scenes of Greek and Roman mythology, as when Ouranos/Caelus ("Heaven") is castrated, or Kronos/Saturn ("Time") eats his own children. Impossible scenes were also favorites, as when Athena, the goddess of wisdom, is born out of Zeus's head (Freud had it just right: it's always about sex and the kids).

The etymological background is fascinating here. The word itself literally refers to two things "put" or rather "thrown" (*ballein*) "together" (*sun: sumballein*). Originally it had nothing to do with literary or religious mysteries. Rather it designated an "agreement," the token that authenticates a "contract."[12] Thus the earliest meanings on record involved Greek "businessmen," who would break a pottery shard into two separate pieces, would each keep one, and would use the jagged pieces (which, of course, fitted each other perfectly and had no other match) as proof of the identity of the business partners in a later transaction (for example, the delivery of goods at a port, which was accompanied by one of the two shards). A "symbol" here was literally a whole that had been split off into two and later recombined to form the whole again.

In a fascinating display of these earliest "symbolic" meanings, Plato uses the same term in the *Symposium*, in a famous myth about the origin of gender distinctions and sexual desire that is put there in the mouth of the comic playwright Aristophanes. Each of us, says Aristophanes, is a "symbol" of the original human being. That original human being was round, two beings joined as one at the back before Zeus cleaved it into two. Those of us who were originally of two male or two female beings naturally desire a person of the same gender in order to be whole again. Those of us who were originally of the "hermaphrodite sex" naturally desire a person of the opposite sex in order to be whole again. "So each one of us," says Aristophanes, "forever searches for his/her own *sumbolon*."[13] The "symbol" here is all about spiritual wholeness. And sex.

The symbol was not just the two shards of a piece of broken pottery or a split human sexuality, however. It was also a chance "meeting" on the road that was experienced as an omen or sign, that is, as a form of spontaneous divination. Struck calls these divinatory incidences "meaningful coincidences."[14] Here the symbol's power lies in its ability to connect, or to make *co-incide*, two seemingly separate realms: those of matter and mind as objective event and subjective state.

Struck demonstrates that, although these symbolic notions were deeply embedded in Greek culture, they were rejected by a number of important figures, including the fourth-century BCE philosopher Aristotle, whose influence on later western thought can hardly be overestimated. Thereafter there were two basic ways of reading poetry and mythology in the ancient world: the mode associated with Aristotle, which saw the poet or myth-maker as a skilled rhetorician following a unique set of rules—a mode that Struck calls "analytical"; and the "mode of criticism that sees the text primarily as a repository of hidden wisdom and envisions its task as the extraction of these meanings," which Struck calls "interpretive" or "hermeneutical."[15]

This last term is the adjectival form of **hermeneutics**, which is probably our best name for this second mode or method of reading religious texts and of understanding the religious imagination and its symbols. Hermeneutics can be glossed simply as "interpretation," but its Greek ancestor, the verb *hermeneuein* ("to interpret," "to translate"), was actually related to the name of Hermes, the Greek god of language, communication, liminal spaces, trickery, and secret wisdom.

The first, "analytic" way of reading is after clarity, clean rational lines, mechanisms, rules, style, and social effects. It is after *how* meaning is mechanically produced, not after *what* that meaning is. It basically trusts everyday human language, which it sees as sense-based, descriptive, and representative, that is, as possessing a more or less one-to-one correspondence with reality. It mistrusts the symbol and prefers instead to speak of **metaphor**, which it sees as a conscious artifice that joins two things for

the sake of clear and unambiguous communication. Struck sums up this first way of reading in the trope of *the label*.

The second, "hermeneutical" way of reading, on the other hand, is after allusion, density of meaning, illumination, secrets, and salvation. It is much more suspicious of language's everyday ability to represent the way things really are. It sees language as a kind of mystery rite or magical invocation. The work of symbolic language here is not about re-presenting or passively receiving an external world through the supposedly reliable senses, like a modern camera. Rather, poetic language is understood to be autonomous and capable of creating a world of its own. Struck sums up this second way of reading in the trope of *the talisman*.

Reading labels requires training, but its results are finally public and reproducible ones—anyone with the proper training can and will arrive at more or less the same descriptions or labels. Reading talismans, on the other hand, requires initiation, creates a separation between the enlightened and the unenlightened, and is neither public nor reliably replicable. Quite the contrary; as Struck demonstrates at great length, the text-as-talisman relies most fundamentally on the trope of *the secret*. In Struck's phrase, such a way of reading "draws more from Delphi than from the agora," that is, it emerges more from the divinatory practices at the temple at Delphi, where Greeks went to receive enigmatic oracles from the psychics of their time, than it does from the public market in Athens, where goods were exchanged in a shared economy and the philosophers debated the rules of reason.[16]

As the latter reference to the oracle of Delphi suggests, "the literary symbol, then, emerged under the influence of both the symbol as omen and the symbol as the secret piece of wisdom possessed by members of esoteric sects. It grew, in other words, out of coincidence and secrecy."[17] And its purpose? "The symbol makes the impossible happen; it becomes the node on which the transcendent can meet the mundane."[18]

This "history of the image" as constructed public metaphor or enigmatic secret symbol is by no means a tangential exercise, since the contemporary study of religion remains deeply split on the nature of the image and, by extension, on the nature and scope of the imagination. As in the ancient world, there are two basic camps, which we might capture in Struck's terms, as the label and the talisman.

The "label camp" rejects the notion of the paradoxical symbol outright and opts for the artificial metaphor of Aristotle and his many rationalist successors. Here all poetry and all religious expression should be approached as a kind of artful ruse, a product of skill aimed at a particular social function or rhetorical effect. Metaphor is fine. Symbol is definitely not. Cognitive scientific approaches to the study of religion, to which we will return soon enough, are probably the best examples of this standard rationalist approach to the image.

The "talisman camp" employs the analytical or rational mode, but it also insists on employing the esoteric, symbolic, and interpretive modes when appropriate (for example, when deciphering mystical or visionary literature). Accordingly, these interpreters continue to see the image, at least potentially, as an expression of some hidden wisdom or secret truth, whose meaning is available only to the illuminated initiate or, short of that, to the gifted reader. The history of religions school, often associated with the figures of Mircea Eliade (whom we have already met) and Henri Corbin (whom we will meet soon), is probably the best example of this hermeneutical approach to the nature of the image and the scope of the imagination.

What is most striking about the present split in the field is the same thing that was striking about the ancient split: whereas analytic readers reject outright the symbolic approaches to the image, symbolic readers understand the analytic approaches and do not hesitate to employ them. I will return to this lack of reciprocity in our last chapter, where I will attempt to resolve it, not unlike the ancient Greek businessmen who would join the two pieces of jagged pottery to re-create the whole and thereby to seal a profitable business transaction. Then you can decide for yourself whether you "buy" my offer.

The Imaginal: Not Everything Imagined Is Imaginary

Let us consider two concrete examples of how the empowered imagination might know things that were not first registered in the five senses, and how it speaks through symbolic events. Because both are modern western examples, neither is technically religious, although both involve two classic religious topics: death and dream.

The Mental Telegraphy of Mark Twain

Consider, first, the American writer Samuel Langehorne Clemens, better known to the world as Mark Twain. Twain, dressed in his famous white "dontcaredam suit," was famous for mocking every orthodoxy and convention—including, as it turns out, the conventions of space and time. "History," Clemens is said to have written, "may not repeat itself, but it rhymes." Life, in other words, is not simply linear, temporal, and causal. It is also organized around meaning, metaphor, and poetry.

And dream. Sam and his brother Henry were working on the riverboat *Pennsylvania* in June of 1858. While they were lying in port in St. Louis, Twain had a most remarkable dream:

> In the morning, when I awoke I had been dreaming, and the dream was so vivid, so like reality, that it deceived me, and I thought it *was* real. In the dream I had seen Henry a corpse. He lay in a metallic burial case. He was dressed in a suit of my clothing, and on his breast lay a great bouquet of flowers, mainly white roses, with a red rose in the centre.

Twain got dressed and prepared to go view the casket. He was walking to the house where the casket lay, before he realized "that there was nothing real about this—it was only a dream."

Alas, it was not. A few weeks later, Henry was badly burned in a boiler explosion and then accidentally killed when some young doctors gave him a huge overdose of opium for the pain. Normally the dead were buried in a simple pine coffin, but some women had raised sixty dollars to put Henry in a special metal one. Twain explains what happened next:

> When I came back and entered the dead-room Henry lay in that open case, and he was dressed in a suit of my clothing. He had borrowed it without my knowledge during our last sojourn in St. Louis; and I recognized instantly that my dream of several weeks before was here exactly reproduced, so far as these details went—and I think I missed one detail; but that one was immediately supplied, for just then an elderly lady entered the place with a large bouquet consisting mainly of white roses, and in the center of it was a red rose, and she laid it on his breast.[19]

Who would not be permanently marked, at once inspired and haunted, by such a series of events? Who among us, if this were *our* dream and *our* brother, could honestly dismiss it as a series of simple coincidences? Twain certainly could not. He was obsessed with such moments in his life, of which there were all too many. He even made up a new expression to capture the sense and feel of them: "mental telegraphy."[20]

The technological metaphor points to Twain's conviction that such events were often connected to the acts of reading and writing—a key point to which we will return. Indeed, Twain suspected that whatever processes this mental telegraphy named had some deep relationship to the sources of his literary powers. For Twain, *the paranormal is about reading and writing.* Hence Twain's fascination with something he called "crossed correspondence," that is, the phenomenon of writing spontaneously to an old friend or acquaintance, only to have, out of the blue, a letter from that very person "cross" one's own letter in the mail. Clemens came to believe that human intentions could somehow reach out and influence the minds of distant subjects. It is worth describing a single instance of this, as it illustrates powerfully just how paranormal events often work—not like a proof or a debunking, but like a piece of true fiction.

Twain told a most dramatic case of such crossed correspondence in his first *Harper's* essay. On a particular 2nd of March, he explains how a "red-hot new idea" for a book about the Nevada silver mines

came blazing into his mind. He wrote down the book's details, order, and sequence in the form of a letter to a colleague who he thought was best poised to write this book, a certain Mr. Wright. But he never mailed that letter. However, when he received a letter in the mail from Mr. Wright just a week later, on the 9th of March, after years of silence between the two friends, he knew already the date of the letter's signature (the 2nd of March) and what it contained (the outline of the book on the Nevada silver mines that had come to him, as if out of nowhere). But Twain did not stop here with this internal conviction. As a little experiment, before he opened the envelope, he described in detail the content of the letter to a cousin who happened to be present. He was correct on every count. "I could not doubt," Twain wrote, "that Mr. Wright's mind and mine had been in close and crystal-clear communication with each other across three thousand miles of mountain and desert on the 2nd of March."[21]

Note here how what we would today call a paranormal event is communicated *through a story.* And a fictional one at that. The communication was very real for Twain. The story was "made up," and yet also somehow *given.* A fictional story truly given, we might say. Like a little private religion.

The Wife Who Knew

As another case of the same mixing of death and dream, consider the story of the contemporary American forensic pathologist Dr. Janis Amatuzio. Amatuzio works for hospitals as a specialist figuring out how and when someone died. One night she encountered a very troubled hospital chaplain in the course of her work. The chaplain asked to go back to her office, where he then asked her if she knew how they found the body of a young man recently killed in a car accident. She replied that her records showed that the Coon Rapids Police Department had recovered the body in a frozen creek bed at 4:45 a.m.

"No," the man replied, "Do you know how they *really* found him?" The chaplain then explained that he had spoken to the dead man's wife, who related how she had had a vivid dream that night of her husband standing next to her bed, apologizing and explaining that he had been in a car accident, and that his car was in a ditch where it could not be seen from the road. She awoke immediately, at 4:20 in the morning, and called the police to tell them, with absolute certainty, that her husband had been in a car accident not far from their home, and that his car was in a ravine that could not be seen from the road. They recovered the body twenty minutes later.[22]

The two death dreams, of the American writer and of the widowed wife, are very good examples of the empowered imagination. Both dreamers sensed or knew that that which was imagined was *not* imaginary, that "something was coming through." Somehow Twain's mind knew that his brother would be dead in a few days—he even knew *precisely* what kind of flower bouquet would sit on his brother's breathless chest. In an even more certain fashion, the wife's dreaming mind knew that her husband had just been killed and where his body lay. Words like "inside" and "outside" or "mind" and "matter" cease to have much meaning in these historical events. We are back to the loopy nature of the Möbius strip, only more loopy. Both dreamers knew something perfectly true about the world "out there," even though they were still "inside" their dreams. Space and time, moreover, were clearly transcended in these moments. The dreaming widow knew of an event that had just taken place elsewhere. The dreaming writer sensed an event that would not play out for weeks along the space–time continuum.

The Traumatic Technology of Telepathy

Twain would have known about another recently invented word: telepathy. The term was coined in 1882 by a Cambridge reader and teacher of Latin and Greek by the name of Frederic Myers (1843–1901), who intended to express through this new word the fact that most dramatic psychical communications occur between loved ones in extreme emotional states, often in dangerous or deadly contexts. Hence the new word "telepathy," from the two Greek words *tēle* ("at a distance") and *pathos* ("suffering, being passive, being affected," in turn a derivative of *paschein*, "to suffer/be acted upon"): "affection/thing suffered at a distance"/"being acted upon at a distance."

The new word was a precise one. This was not a matter of something as boring as card guessing in a laboratory. The events this new word referred to were anxious symbolic communications, often made through dream or waking vision, between family members at that most poignant of all human moments—death. Myers and his colleagues collected, classified, and compared thousands of death narratives before they could come up with a word like telepathy. Many of these stories were indistinguishable from those of Twain and Dr. Amatuzio. We are left with a humble conclusion: *strong emotion (pathos), particularly around trauma and death, is the most common catalyst of robust paranormal events.* Trauma, it seems, is what "electrifies," "zaps," or magnetizes," and hence empowers the imagination. Trauma is the technology of telepathy.

This, by the way, is what the debunkers misunderstand when they ask, with a sneer, why all psychics do not get rich on the stock market, or why robust psychical phenomena cannot be made to appear in the controlled laboratory. Putting aside for the moment the fact that psychics sometimes do get rich and that humble forms of psychical phenomena do in fact appear in laboratories all the time, the answer to why *robust* paranormal events do not generally appear in the lab is simple enough: there is no trauma or pathos there. No one is dying. No one is in danger. The professional debunker's insistence, then, that the paranormal play by his rules and appear for all to see, in a safe and sterile, controlled laboratory, is little more than a mark of his or her own serious ignorance of the nature of the phenomena. To play by these rules is like trying to study the stars at midday and then claiming that they don't exist because they do not appear under those particular conditions.

The Imaginal

Myers and his colleagues struggled to come to terms with how the human imagination might be able to know distant things, or even to know about historical events before they happen. Alas, the English language was a blunt instrument. At first they used the patently paradoxical expression "veridical hallucination." The expression was meant to capture the simple fact that in cases like those reported by Twain and Dr. Amatuzio the individuals know perfectly well that they are dreaming, but they also know that the dream is "veridical," that is, true.

But "veridical hallucination" was an awkwardly ugly phrase, and Myers was a poet. He had to come up with something better. As a poet, he naturally turned to the rich language around *the image* and the literary experience of inspiration. He noticed in particular that the telepathic subject often reported being energized by an "influx" of spiritual energy (early nineteenth-century reports also used the language of being "magnetized," and they meant this quite literally). Myers became convinced that these altered states of energy had something to do with the mind's new imaginative powers, and—in an especially bold move—that these powers were early examples of how the imagination would function some day, in the far future. Much like astronaut Edgar Mitchell and Sir Alister Hardy, Myers thought that abilities like telepathy are part of our evolutionary inheritance. Myers thought that, in capacities like telepathic communications and precognitive dreams, we, like a wormy caterpillar witnessing the graceful wings and bright colors of a floating butterfly nearby, are witnessing the early signs or buds of a still evolving future supernature—ours.

This is poetic language to be sure, but it also makes some sense. After all, something like precognition—even of a few seconds, and even if functioning unconsciously (which is exactly what the most recent laboratory evidence of Dean Radin and Daryl Bem suggests)[23]—would carry *immense* adaptive and survival benefits. In any case, it was within this evolutionary framework that Myers proposed a new term, to distinguish what comes through an empowered imagination from the purely imaginary. He called the former **imaginal**.

That was better. A Swiss psychiatrist by the name of Théodore Flournoy picked up on Myers's new term and used it in his study of a young Swiss medium by the name of Élise Müller, who claimed to be both the reincarnation of a Indian Hindu princess and a regular visitor to Mars. Whoa. Flournoy's book was entitled *From India to the Planet Mars* (1899). His lively, novelistic retellings of the medium's various personalities and channeled adventures (in India and Mars, no less) made it an instant hit. In the process, Flournoy also helped to revolutionize the study of mediumship and trance formations through a relatively new tool: hypnosis. This is quite significant, as the same technique would later play a major role in the production of the alien abduction literature in the 1960s, 1970s, and 1980s—"to the Planet Mars" again, as it were.

Flournoy was devastatingly skeptical and deeply sympathetic at the same time. Hence he could demonstrate how Müller's claims to speak a Martian language, to remember a past life in India, and to communicate with dead spirits were simply not true. They were creative imaginative products of the medium's present life memories, which she had forgotten and unconsciously wove back together in her various sittings with the hypnotist. Flournoy marveled at the astonishing creativity of this process: it was like being present for the inspiration and production of some serially published Jules Verne novel.

But the psychiatrist could also take very seriously the "**supernormal** appearances" of the medium's life. Under this description (which he also got from Myers), Flournoy summed up things like telepathy and telekinesis, which he concluded were likely real. His final conclusion? That the common assumption that one must choose between the "brutal alternatives" of spiritualism (the medium was really talking to the dead) and materialism (there is nothing to any of it and human life ends at the grave) "is surely puerile."[24] That is to say, childish and stupid.

Flournoy would have none of this immature either–or thinking. Nor would he jump to conclusions about what it all meant and where it was all going. He refused to take a position about whether these imaginal visions and supernormal abilities were "forerunners of a future evolution" (which is what Myers thought) or evolutionary survivals from some previous condition (which is what Freud would suggest), or "whether they are purely accidental" and hence meaningless.[25] He just did not know.

That was not the end of the story. Flournoy and Müller were taken up as patrons of the surrealist art movement (and, significantly, Müller later became a religious painter herself). Flournoy, moreover, became the older mentor of a young Swiss psychiatrist by the name of Carl Jung, whose writings would profoundly influence the study of religion in the twentieth century. Among Jung's colleagues was a French scholar named Henry Corbin, who used Jung's psychology and the category of the imaginal to write about Islamic Iranian mysticism. By the time we get to Corbin's usage, the imaginal has been stripped entirely of its evolutionary connotations and linked to an intricate theology of visionary experience and Sufi sayings like this comparativist gem from the mystic Junayd: "The color of the water is that of the vessel which contains it."[26] In Corbin's understanding, the imaginal, however, still carried fantastic paranormal powers and objective veridical content, as is evident in his treatment of clairvoyance, mind-reading, telepathy, even materialization and teleportation in the life and teachings of Ibn 'Arabi.[27]

It was from the books of Corbin that later writers picked up the term "imaginal" (usually unaware of the term's indebtedness to the earlier psychical research tradition). They found it useful in a very general sense, that is, as a both–and understanding of the image that could acknowledge *both* the imagined nature *and* the veridical content of some visionary experiences. Something is coming through. Not everything imagined is imaginary.

Like when a brother dreams of a red and white funeral bouquet, or a sleeping wife "sees" her dead husband apologizing to her and talking about his corpse in a ditch.

The Comparative Practices of Popular Culture

Not all comparative practices involving the empowered imagination are performed by academics, of course. Nor, moreover, does every instance of a symbolic event take place in a recognizable religious context. There are also the **comparative practices of popular culture**.

Such practices are usually ignored by scholars. This is unfortunate, as these practices often demonstrate real insight, and these writers do not hesitate to treat anomalous "impure" subjects that conservative academics refuse to touch. What such writers sometimes lack in intellectual rigor, discipline, and historical precision, they often make up in intellectual courage and moments of real genius. Two subjects have attracted many of these popular comparisons: monsters and UFOs.

Monster Studies

Monsters are good to think with. They are dramatic expressions of the liminal. They combine things that should not be combined. Hence the zombies or the "living dead," the werewolf, at once half-human and half-wolf, or the Frankenstein monster, at once scientific and super natural. They "throw together" (remember *sumballein*) things that should not be thrown together. They are also profoundly impure. Timothy Beal calls them "threatening figures of anomaly within the well-established and accepted order of things."

These modern monsters, of course, are very much related to the various demons, troublemakers, haunting ghosts, sprites, and *jinn* (a species of demon in Islam) of the traditional religions, as well as to the whole subject of exorcism, which we might reframe in the present context as the ritual expulsion of the anomalous, the monstrous, and the demonic toward a re-establishment of order. Alas, where there is order, there is disorder. Someone, or something, is always trying to mess things up (see Figure 8.2).

Related here again is the category of the uncanny. The uncanny is the English equivalent of the German word *unheimlich*, which means "un-homely" and was much discussed by Freud. The uncanny is precisely "the awareness that something that should be outside the house is in it."[28] Note how similar this definition is to Douglas's discussion of "dirt" and impurity, religious notions that she first came to understand, recall, through the metaphor of the house or home. The uncanny monster is "dirt" come alive, which has gotten into the house. It is the paranormal with wings and teeth in the bedroom.

Figure 8.2   *Exorcist and Clients* (c. 1900), attributed to Muhammad Ghaffari, Kamal al-Mulk or his circle. Tehran. Oil on canvas, 22 1/4″ × 29″, private collection.

As we saw with other forms of the paranormal as the impure, the monster can also function as a figure of revelation of the deeper order of things. Indeed monster, as a word at least, comes from the Latin *monstrum*, literally "that which is shown or revealed": *monstrare*, "to show, point to," derives from this noun. But *monstrum* itself derives in turn from *monere*, "to warn" or "to portend."; As Timothy Beal emphasizes, "[i]n this sense, a *monstrum* is a message that breaks into this world from the realm of the divine."[29] We might say, then, that the **monster** is a revelation of the sacred in its "left" or "negative" mode.

Scholars have struggled with monsters. There is now even a new field called, charmingly enough, "monster studies." There is also something called "monster theory," which is really a form of literary criticism, that is, a method to interpret or make sense of texts *about* monsters. Fair enough. But what are we to do with those cases, which are numerous and sometimes surprisingly well documented, when this in-betweenness, this "showing," takes on a definite

form and enters modern human experience as a … well, *as a monster*? What is there to do when, to invoke Hollenback here, the symbol frick'n materializes?

We have to go well outside the professional study of religion to find extensive studies of these real-life monsters. Emblematic here are the writings of John Alva Keel (1930–2009). By profession, John Keel was a writer and journalist. He is most famous for his writings about a particular American monster, the Mothman of Point Pleasant, West Virginia, to which we will return soon enough (or too soon, depending on your purity codes). But the Mothman was really part of a much larger cultural phenomenon, which Keel had been writing about for years before he ever struggled with the Mothman: the UFO phenomenon.

The UFO

In 1970, after extensive interviews with over two hundred "silent contactees" (his term for individuals who encounter a UFO but seek no publicity for it),

Keel's *UFOs: Operation Trojan Horse* appeared.[30] Keel offered here a model of the modern UFO phenomenon that places it squarely in the in-between. As he had it from his study of the silent contactees, UFOs are not "hard" stable objects, much less high-tech space ships. They are "soft" paraphysical manifestations, "transmogrifications of energy," as he put it, very much akin to the apparitions of traditional **demonology** and **angelology** (the study and classification of demons and angels, respectively). In short, UFOs are materializations of the cultural imagination, now dominated by sci-fi and Cold War terms.

The secret of the contactee experience, then, is not in the light shows in the sky, or in some secret government file or paranoid conspiracy theory. The secret of the contactee experience is in the *contactees themselves*. In this way Keel sought to remove the UFO phenomenon from the purview both of the air force (which had already decided that this phenomenon did not represent a real security threat, not at least one it could address) and of scientific skeptics (who insisted, and still insist, on dismissing it as completely unreal), and to place the problem squarely among professional intellectuals who actually know something about the history and analysis of unusual states of mind, mystical illumination, possession, and apparitions—that is, among scholars of comparative religion.[31]

The UFO is ours. Or at least it should be.

Like a good comparativist, Keel noted the phenomenon's "reflective" quality: its tendency to reflect back to the witnesses whatever cultural assumption or religious beliefs they bring to the events. The demons and angels of medieval Catholicism and the elves, fauns, and fairies of early modern European folklore thus became the sci-fi aliens, invading Martians, and beneficent Venusians of Cold War America.

Keel's insistence on the reflective quality of UFO encounters, of course, is yet another version of what we have called "the mirror." Looking into that mirror, Euro-Americans should not be tricked by what they often see: some Cold War anxiety or technological

fantasy. Very similar encounters can be found, after all, in modern Native American cultures, where they are generally (but not always) experienced, very positively and quite consciously, as matter-of-fact encounters with ancient ancestors, often called Star People, Observers, or Keepers, and function as the numinous sources of religious belief and community feeling.[32] There is little Cold War paranoia here.

Like Hollenback and Myers, Keel understood that these were imaginal forms, "veridical hallucinations" mediating something real. "The flying saucers," Keel insisted, "do not come from some Buck Rogers-type civilization on some distant planet. They are our next-door neighbors, part of another space–time continuum where life, matter, and energy are radically different from ours."[33] They come from the in-between. But this in-between is a tricky place, and Americans would do well, Keel thought, not to naïvely believe everything they were being shown through this new code of the monstrous. Beware, Keel tells his readers. The demons and deities of the ancient world are still with us, and they deal, as they have always dealt, in tricks, illusions, and distractions. If the motto of *The X-Files* television program in the 1990s was "I want to believe," Keel's advice in the 1970s was: "Don't."

It is important to understand that Keel's conclusions have been shared and advanced in different forms by others, including the French astronomer and computer scientist Jacques Vallee, whose ideas and personality became the basis for the character of Dr. Claude Lacombe in Steven Spielberg's *Close Encounters of the Third Kind*—one of countless cases where popular culture has fused with the paranormal. In books like *Passport to Magonia* (1969) and *The Invisible College* (1975), Vallee was one of the first writers to trace out in detail how the modern abduction phenomenon follows the contours of western occultism and European folklore around human encounters with small humanoids (the thesis of *Passport*) and the data of parapsychology (the thesis of *The Invisible College*).

Other writers, inspired by Keel and Vallee, have suggested similar comparisons. As a single example, consider the professional writer James Gallant and his powerful little essay "The Humiliating UFOs." In a most bold act of comparison, Gallant points out that the modern UFO phenomenon bears a very precise similarity with ancient religions like those of Sumeria or ancient Greece, which revolved around a pantheon of immortal superhumans who lived, normally undetected, among humankind, but who also occasionally disguised themselves as human beings in order to bestow culture and to guide human history. It was in this same Greek mythological context, of course, that we have already witnessed the "birth of the symbol."

Gallant hones in on the notion of intermediate worlds as the key to these ancient systems. Citing a scholar of ancient Mesopotamia, he writes: "Nothing in polytheism is more difficult for the modern Western mind to negotiate … than the idea of a 'plurality of spiritual dimensions.'"[34] The problem here is that all the rational models offered to explain these polytheistic experiences fail to take into account the very notion of plural worlds that polytheistic systems inevitably express and rely on. The rational models thus confuse their plural premodern worlds with our single modern world. In short, we cannot possibly understand an ancient polytheistic religion like that of the Sumerians or the Greeks without at least entertaining the possibility of other dimensions and of intermediate worlds.

Gallant then takes the next step: "Is it possible," he asks, "that our kinship with the cosmos can become explicit," like that of the ancient Sumerians and Greeks? The answer appears to be: "Yes." After all, "there is a phenomenon today sufficiently common and overwhelming in its uncanny immediacy as to suggest a parallel with earlier humanity's experiences of other planes of being: the UFO."[35]

Gallant finds this comparative link at once fascinating and humiliating, as the weird both–and nature of the UFO phenomenon completely frustrates any attempt to understand it, much less to "prove" it. The "objects" appear on radar and yet are never quite physical. Their presence can cause serious, even apparently deadly, illnesses. Or they can effect stunning

cures. And their wildest features—for example, the motifs of genetic manipulation and alien–human hybridity—recall "fairy changelings, amours between fairies and mortals, and the mixed parentage demigods of mythology." "It is as if," Gallant wryly notes, "abduction were the work of Kafka or the Marx Brothers, if not a Zen master." An alien abduction, Gallant concludes, "is a kind of humiliation that undermines the ego." And again: "The lesson of the UFO may be that those content with the little island of intelligibility on which the sciences have marooned us will be reminded forcibly of the sea of their unknowing."[36] Still, we also have to recognize that not every UFO sighting is so—well—religious. Sometimes the darn things are embarrassingly physical.[37] As has often been noted, deciding between a paranormal reading and a "nuts and bolts" spacecraft interpretation of the UFO phenomenon is often impossible, and that is probably the point. The both–and again, this time in the sky.

The Mothman

Keel's most famous case of how these ancient tricky gods and humiliating UFOs work among us today was the Mothman of Point Pleasant, West Virginia. In *UFOs* he had already noted that great winged beings, often headless, haunt the modern contactee experience, very much like medieval demons and angels, and he told tantalizing stories of his traumatic research experiences in West Virginia.[38] Five years later, in *The Mothman Prophecies*, he told his readers the full story.

For thirteen months in 1966 and 1967, a seven-foot, human-like, brown figure with huge bat-like wings, no visible head, and glowing red eyes on its upper chest terrorized the community of Point Pleasant. The residents at first called it a "bird-like creature," "Birdman," and "Bird-Monster," likened it to an immense man-bat, and then landed on the name "the Monster Moth Man" and eventually simply "Mothman," probably because "Batman" was all the rage on TV then, and this seemed like a real-world super-villain to the residents of Point Pleasant (and, besides, "Batman" was already taken) (see Figure 8.3).

Figure 8.3   The Mothman pursues a car, drawing by Gary Gibeaut. From Jeff Wamsley, *Mothman: Behind the Red Eyes* (2005).

But it wasn't a bird or a bat, much less a moth. According to different witnesses, the thing stood around 7 feet tall and boasted immense shoulders, that is, its physique reproduced the standard he-man frame of the superhero. Reports described clawed hands, a running speed of up to 100 miles per hour, a flight speed that allowed it to perform circles around a speeding vehicle, an unnerving scream that blew up a television set (remember the electromagnetic ghost of our opening story?), and a strange ability to control people like a magnet. Weirder still—if that means anything here—it seemed to provoke a kind of sacred sixth sense of intense fear in many, as if they could "feel" the thing before they saw it.[39] Most of all, though, people spoke, in awed terror, about its haunting, mesmerizing red *eyes*.

One odd detail may be relevant to our earlier comparative discussion around super sexualities: the

Mothman's first appearance, on Tuesday, November 15, 1966, was to four teenagers "parking" in a black '57 Chevy, almost as if the thing were attracted to the altered, ecstatic energies of human eros. It was certainly attracted to *something*. It chased the two young couples down Route 62 into the city limits of Point Pleasant.[40]

Okay, we are getting into trouble again.

Predictably, the debunkers wanted to claim that the Mothman was a balloon (the weather balloon functions similarly in the debunking literature on UFOs), a large sandhill crane, or a barn owl. The latter suggestion is an ironic one, since the owl holds a classic place in the alien abduction literature, where it is often read as a "screen memory" of the alien (a screen memory, a concept derived from Freudian theory, is a false memory of an event that hides the true event behind a symbolic screen or stand-in).

In an only slightly more rational, but much more understandable and traditional vein, a local Evangelical Christian witness put what he calls a "spiritual interpretation" on his experience and concluded that it was "the Devil."[41] The local residents, many of whom had actually seen this thing, were deeply offended by the crane and barn owl "explanations." The Evangelical interpretation, we might imagine, was harder to dismiss. And at least it was closer to what they had felt and seen.

Whatever the thing was, it played havoc with the local peace. The place went more or less wild for thirteen months. This havoc included a dramatic spike in UFO sightings (unfortunately for just about any model, UFOs and winged or hairy monsters often appear together). Indeed, the "window" area where UFOs were appearing on an almost nightly basis—an old ammunition dump ominously called the TNT area with God-only-knows-what buried below—became a veritable parking lot, as the roads filled up with hundreds of cars driving out to watch the strange lights in the sky, and men armed with shotguns went "monster hunting" in the night.

But close readers of Keel already knew how it would all end, since he had given away the final chapter in his earlier book *UFOs: Operation Trojan*

Horse. There he described how, around this same time, "more than once I woke up in the middle of the night to find myself unable to move, with a huge dark apparition standing over me."[42] He reported that in October 1967 he had had a "lengthy long-distance call from a being who was allegedly a UFO entity."[43] He told Keel two things: that many people would die in an Ohio River disaster, and that there would be a huge black-out when President Johnson turned on the Christmas lights in the White House. On November 3, Keel wrote his journalistic colleague Mrs. Mary Hyre in Point Pleasant about the possible river calamity.

When he returned to Point Pleasant for Thanksgiving, things got more ominous still. He learned that Mrs. Virginia Thomas, who was living in the very epicenter of the apparitions, was having horrible dreams. She was dreaming "of pleading faces and brightly wrapped Christmas packages floating on the dark water of the Ohio [River]."[44] Then, on December 11, Keel was awakened by another mysterious caller, who informed him of an upcoming plane crash in Tucson. The next day an air force jet careened into a Tucson shopping mall.

On December 15 President Johnson hosted the annual tree-lighting ceremony. Keel watched the event on his television in New York City, waiting for the worst. Nothing happened. The tree lit up, and the East Coast stayed lit up. Then, just thirty seconds after the twinkling Christmas tree, an announcer broke into the broadcast: "A bridge between Gallipolis, Ohio, and the West Virginia has just collapsed. It was heavily laden with rush-hour traffic. There are no further details as yet." "I was stunned," Keel writes. "There was only one bridge on that section of the river. The Silver Bridge between Point Pleasant, West Virginia, and Ohio. Christmas packages were floating in the dark waters of the Ohio."[45]

There were more than Christmas presents floating in those waters. There were people. Thirty-nine individuals died that evening, crushed and drowned in what was, by one account, the worst bridge disaster in American history.[46] Whatever it was, or was not, the

apparitions more or less ceased after the bridge collapse. Others would continue to encounter the being, but only sporadically now.

Miracles in the Making: The Fortean Lineage

It is easy to dismiss the exaggerated forms in which an author like John Keel chooses to express his ideas. There are no doubt more than a few stretched stories here, and I really have no idea how to disentangle everything. But that is probably the point: we can't. We can't because the cultural imagination is not something separate from real history; it *is* real history too. Keel at least was convinced that reality participates in fiction and fiction in reality. And he marveled many times at how some of the phenomena around Point Pleasant appeared to rely on his own presence, how the events "pulled him in" and made him a part of the plot. It was as if he and his colleagues were caught in a novel or movie, which he himself was writing.

They were, and he was.

One way we can make sense of such a comparative practice is to contextualize it within an older stream of thinking about religion. John Keel was a **Fortean**, that is, an author inspired by the original archival research and irreverent books of the American humorist turned obsessive collector of anomalies Charles Fort (1874–1932). Fort was a bit like Twain. Only more so—fascinated by telepathy, outrageously funny, incredibly insightful, and occasionally really, really wrong. His books are filled with both embarrassing missteps and stunning moments of originality. Fort is easily one of the most neglected, insightful, and just plain weird comparativists in recent memory.

It was Fort, for example, who did more than anyone to envision and bring into focus what we now call "the paranormal." His methods were decidedly bookish and nerdy. Fort sat in the New York Public Library every day for decades, reading pretty much every periodical in French and English back to 1800 (including all the journals of Myers and his colleagues).

The Damned

He was looking for what he provocatively called "the damned": events that happen everywhere all the time but are immediately ignored, dismissed, or ridiculed because they do not fit into the religion or science of the time. Fort's "the damned" was a version of Douglas's cultural "dirt." Two of the things he kept finding in the newspapers were reports of "super-constructions in the sky" (what would much later be called UFOs) and paranormal people, whose strange powers he called "wild talents."

The Super

In works like *The Book of the Damned* (1919) and *Wild Talents* (1932), Fort threw out an entire "super" vocabulary to capture the excitement and pure mischievousness of his "data of the damned." Here we encounter things like a super-bat, super-biology, super-chemistry, super-geography, super-imagination, super-magnets, super-mind, super-religion, super-scientific attempts, super-sociology, super-sight, super-vehicles, super-voyagers, super-whiskeys (with ultra-bibles, no less), and super-wolves.

Through such a vocabulary Fort sought to communicate an emerging worldview defined by what we would recognize today as the paranormal and the extraterrestrial. In other words, he meant more or less what superhero comics mean by the prefix "super." Except that he was claiming this was the stuff of our daily lives. He was claiming that the fiction is real or, better, that the real is itself a kind of fiction. We are written.

By what or whom, it is not at all clear.

Intermediatism

Particularly relevant for our own purposes is what Fort called his Intermediatism (you cannot get more "in between" than this). With this term Fort meant to refer to a philosophical position, his own, that involves the refusal of all easy, polarizing answers to the problem of the paranormal and the related insistence that, whatever such phenomena are (or are not), they cannot be mapped onto the cognitive grids of the pairs mental/material, real/unreal, subjective/objective, and so on. Most of all, Fort argued, things like UFOs and monsters cannot and should not be "believed," as the "Dominant of Religion" once had it, or "explained" or "proven," as the present "Dominant of Science" now wants to claim. They are much more fruitfully understood as "expressions" within a new "Dominant of Intermediatism" or, as Fort liked to call it in his more colorful phrase, the coming "Era of Witchcraft."

The Paranormal and the Miraculous

All of this invokes, again, the "miracle." Are paranormal events miracles? Probably not. They are better understood as "miracles in the making," that is, as private wonders that are in search of some larger mythical and ritual complex that they themselves are, of course, helping to create. Recall that a miracle, as we have defined the term, is a "sign" of some greater religious truth and of some stable tradition, usually with elaborate ritual and institutional resources. "Proving" that truth and tradition is the real point of a miracle. The miracle, then, always gestures toward some larger social institution, which we call a "religion." Intermediate beings like UFOs and the Mothman still lack such a social institution (although there *are* tiny UFO religions). But what we might call the cultural imagination is certainly hard at work creating one. Just go to the movies and see for yourself.

Fact and Fraud: On the Trick of the Truth

Finally, before we close this chapter and turn to our comparative practice and toolkit, it is well worth pointing out that not every intermediate state involves lightforms taking on the appearances of electromagnetic ghosts, the blessed Virgin Mary, or red-eyed, headless mothman monsters. Sometimes intermediate states happen in the most common of places.

The Placebo Effect

Like hospitals. Consider the **placebo effect**. *Placebo* ("I will please") is a Latin word—the future first person of *placere*, "to please"—and its use in this form is drawn from the Latin Bible. Medical researchers know that a placebo—a sugar pill, for example—will often work just as well as a real drug in a particular drug trial. They do not know how, but they know that it happens all the time. Recent research has suggested—in perfect line with the study of religion, I would add—that the self-healing may be effected by the cultural and ritual context (the hospital, the cultural authority of the doctor, and all those white coats) as much as by anything else.

Medical professionals know that sometimes there is also a **nocebo effect**. *Nocebo* is the Latin for "I will harm." This is the negative version of the placebo effect: if a patient believes that a substance or procedure will harm him or her, the substance or procedure in question often does just that. Anthropologists, by the way, have observed the same in other cultures: if an individual believes that he or she has been cursed, has been the victim of the evil eye, or has been assaulted by a dream demon, he or she may well get ill, even die. We thus often refer to "white magic" and "black magic." In modern medicine we refer to placebos and nocebos. These are different cultural and ritual contexts, to be sure, but they are clearly related.

Fraud as Mask and Trigger

The placebo and the nocebo raise the fascinating issue of deception and truth within religious rituals and institutions, particularly those involving magic or modern paranormal phenomena. There is no getting around it: a placebo is a fraud that works, a trick that manifests a truth.

I am always reminded at this point of the German mathematical genius Kurt Gödel, who left us a body of work that demonstrated that no mathematical model can ever be complete (rather like a culture or a religion, I might add). Gödel, like many intellectuals, was fascinated by the paranormal. He believed that his wife could predict numbers generated at random, and there is some evidence that he attended séances. Where he was most sophisticated on this particular subject, though, was on the subject of fraud: "The result and *the sense* of the fraud," he wrote, "is … not that it *simulates*, but that it *masks*, the genuine phenomena."[47] Fraud as a social phenomenon, in other words, is not about faking something that is not real. It is about faking something that *is* real so that we will think that it *isn't*. It is finally about confusion, misinformation, and distraction.

But sometimes, more weirdly still, fraud also *triggers* the real deal. Consider the laser physicist turned parapsychologist Russell Targ, who helped lead a psychical espionage program for the US government in the 1970s. I once heard Russell describe how he first became interested in psychical phenomena. As a teenager, he was an amateur stage magician and, more precisely, a mentalist. He faked psychical abilities on stage. One day, during a show, he realized that real telepathic information was coming through the stage trick. He realized, in short, that the fraud was manifesting a fact, the trick a truth.[48]

Whatever we choose to call such reported events, we might venture to speculate that the mind has an incredible influence over the body (and maybe even over its immediate physical environment), that it is able to heal (or hurt) the body in the most extraordinary ways, but that it sometimes needs to trick itself into using these unconscious powers via a sham, ruse, magical spell, sugar pill, white-coated modern priest, or dark candle-lit room. In short, we seem to have here a truth that will sometimes *only* manifest itself through, or with the help of, a trick.

Which, come to think about it, is not a bad definition of religion.

Comparative Practice: Supernatural Assault Traditions

Consider the following stories. Like our opening three lightform stories, all three happened in the 1980s, this time to three American males.

The Glowing Racoon

The first took place in a private cabin in northern California around Mendocino, about three and a half hours north of San Francisco:

> I was living in Berkeley at the time, and I'd drive up to my property on Friday nights. One night in 1985 I got there just around midnight. I had driven up alone, and I had passed the functional sobriety test—I had made it through the mountains.
>
> I turned on the kitchen lights, put my bags of groceries on the floor, and grabbed a heavy, black flashlight. I was headed down to the john, which was about fifty feet west of the cabin … I walked down the steps, turned right, and then at the far end of the path, under a fir tree, there was something glowing. I pointed my flashlight at it anyhow. It only made it whiter where the beam landed. It seemed to be a raccoon. I wasn't frightened. Later, I wondered if it could have been a hologram, projected from God knows where.
>
> The raccoon spoke. "Good evening, doctor," it said. I said something back, I don't remember what, probably, "Hello."
>
> The next thing I remember, it was early in the morning. I was walking along a road uphill from my house. What went through my head as I walked down toward my house was, "What the hell am I doing here?" I had no memory of the night before. I thought maybe I had passed out and spent the night outside. But nights are damp in the summer in Mendocino, and my clothes were dry, and they weren't dirty.

The next day he remembered the "the little bastard and his courteous greeting" with "his little shifty eyes." He searched for his flashlight (nothing), felt

terribly confused, took a nap, and then set out to fix a pipe on the property that fed a pond from a nearby spring. He was approaching the woods about two hundred yards from his cabin.

> Just inside the shade of the trees, I began to panic. I turned around and walked as rapidly as I could toward the daylight. I didn't run or look over my shoulder—I walked fast. I didn't want anything to know that I was panicking. When I got well out into the open, I turned and looked back into the woods. "What the hell am I doing?" I had no idea… Whatever happened to me last night must have happened there, in those woods. I remembered that the road I had been walking on that morning when I came to my senses came toward my house from that direction. I got the hell home and didn't go back. I didn't tell anybody about it.[49]

The Visitors

The next story comes from the same year. This time we have an exact date: December 26, 1985, that is, the night after Christmas. It took place at a forest cabin too, but this time on the other side of the country, in the Hudson Valley, north of New York City. As the subject recalled the scenes later, under hypnosis, with a professional psychiatrist, he remembered how, in the middle of the night, he woke up suddenly to "a peculiar whooshing, swirling noise" in the living room, as if a large number of people were moving around the room. Then "the visitors," as he calls them, appeared. They were three and a half feet tall, with two dark holes for eyes, and "a black down-turning line of a mouth that later became an O."[50] They carried him out of his bedroom, naked and paralyzed. One of the creatures, who he sensed was a woman, asked him what they could do to help him stop screaming. Her voice had "a subtly electronic tone to it, the accents flat and startlingly Midwestern."[51] All in all, the subject saw four different types of visitors that night, but the most memorable was the female, about five-foot tall, slender, "with extremely prominent and mesmerizing black slanted eyes." Most of all, he remembered *those eyes*.[52] The traumatic experience was dominated by a kind of raw sexuality, which he recalled under hypnosis as violent and abusive.

Immediately after the event, however, he knew none of this, not at least in any conscious way. He was angry when he woke up the next morning, feeling a profound unease and remembering a barn owl staring at him through his window. He knew he had seen no barn owl, and he had read his Freud, so he suspected that this was a kind of "screen memory"—that is, as I already explained in this chapter, a literally false but meaningfully true memory, which encodes a real memory behind its symbolic face. Abductees, he notes, often remember animals in strange places when they attempt to recall the traumatic event, particularly big-eyed or "masked" ones (like owls and raccoons).

The initial abduction set off a long series of visitor experiences, spanning many years, and a whole spectrum of bizarre mind-over-matter effects, palpable plasmic energies, out-of-body experiences, and stunning visions, some of which were extremely positive (and erotic). Like this one, which involved getting radiated by a brilliant sphere floating outside his New York cabin:

> This light had rays that I could feel penetrating my skin with gentle prinpricks. And, as it entered me, there also entered in me the sense and presence of another person, and of an explosively childlike joy, and of a peace that is the peace that is outside of time altogether. I had something close to a seizure, a paroxysm as my body responded with fearsome, tingling pleasure to the most intimate touch I have ever felt, and I knew then utter compassion and an ancient love.[53]

Eventually he began to wonder whether the alien experience is "what the force of evolution looks like when it acts on conscious creatures."[54] In our own terms now, we might add: "that is, when this evolutionary force is 'pictured' by a temporarily empowered imagination." He is a professional writer of fiction, many of whose books are based largely on his own real experiences; hence this particular subject is incredibly sophisticated when it comes to

understanding the role, scope, and paranormal powers of the imagination. His is a comparative practice of the most radical and reflexive kind. I once heard him reflect, for example, on how he is perfectly aware that his own experiences were shaped and colored by the "bad science fiction movies" that he had seen as a kid, but that this hardly means that what was coming through those encounters can be explained by those bad B-movies. The filter is not the filtered. What we need to do now, he went on to muse, is make better science fiction movies, so that future encounter experiences will be more productive and creative and less terrifying and traumatic. A mind-bending example, if ever there was one, of reflexivity and of the fusion of fiction and fact.

The Energy

The last story took place in 1989 on the other side of the world, in northeastern India. The subject describes both the ritual context and the mythical shape of the experience:

> For days, I had been participating in the annual Bengali celebration of the goddess Kali in the streets and temples of Calcutta (now Kolkata). One morning I woke up asleep, that is, I woke up, but my body did not. I couldn't move. I was paralyzed, like a corpse, more or less exactly like the Hindu god Shiva as he is traditionally portrayed in Tantric art, lying prostrate beneath Kali's feet. Then those "feet" touched me. An incredibly subtle, immensely pleasurable, and terrifyingly powerful energy entered me, possessed me, completely overwhelmed me. My vibrating body felt as if I had stuck a fork in a wall socket (all sexual innuendos intended … and wall sockets in India, by the way, put out far more voltage than American ones). Perhaps more significantly, my brain felt as if it had suddenly hooked up to some sort of occult Internet and that billions of bits of information were being downloaded into its neural net. Or better, it felt as if my entire being was being reprogrammed or rewired.
>
> A door in the Night, a portal had opened.
>
> And this was all before I felt my soul or subtle body (for it still had a shape) being pulled out of my physical body by some sort of invisible Super Magnet.

"Electromagnetic" would work extremely well as a descriptor, as long as one understands that this Energy was both obviously conscious and super-intelligent.

And somehow completely Other or, well, *alien*. In terms of the alien abduction literature … abductees commonly speak of the "cellular change" they have undergone. Before they are beamed through a wall or ceiling, Star-Trek style, it is "as if an intense energy is separating every cell, or even every molecule, of their bodies." After such experiences, moreover, they "feel that powerful residual energies are left in their bodies, as if stored in the cells themselves."[55]

That is *exactly* how it felt, and still feels in my memory. It is almost as if some kind of direct, right-brained, mind-to-mind transmission took place, as if those residual plasmic energies were encoded with ideas or structures that could not be "languaged" but could be stored and later intuited and consciously shaped in the mirror of other resonant or echoing authors until they could appear, now through the prism of the left-brain's words, as my books.[56]

I chose these three stories carefully, to shake the reader from any notion that imaginal encounters with intermediate realms happen only to the pre-modern, the pious, or the uneducated. The first story is from Kary Mullis, the biochemist whom we met briefly in Chapter 5. Mullis won the Nobel Prize in 1993 for inventing the polymerase chain reaction or PCR process, which in turn made possible the human genome project. The story is taken from his autobiography, *Dancing Naked in the Mind Field*. The second story is from horror writer Whitley Strieber's *Communion*, probably the twentieth century's most influential and most nuanced autobiographical account of an abduction experience. The third story is my own, taken from the introduction to my book on the paranormal roots of American popular culture, *Mutants and Mystics*.

The plot thickens further when we learn that something very similar happened to Mullis's daughter on the same family property, and that both recognized their own cabin experiences in Strieber's, when they independently picked up a copy of *Communion*—

which appeared in the winter of 1987, a few years after their own encounters. They were not alone. After *Communion* hit the best-selling charts, it set off an avalanche of corresponding stories. Over the next few years, Strieber would receive a *quarter million* letters from individuals all over the world who recognized either the iconic "Grey" on the cover (painted, like a police sketch, by Ted Seth Jacobs after Strieber's instructions) or traces of their own spiritually traumatic experiences in his. Many of these comparing readers believed that they had been abducted by aliens.

Mullis is more careful: "I had one of those experiences myself. To say it was aliens is to assume a lot. But to say it was weird is to understate it. It was extraordinarily weird." What he insists on is that it really happened. He recognizes, of course, that he cannot do science with such a single anomalous experience, "but I don't deny what happened … it happened."[57]

The plot thickens again when we learn that only the right brain appears to be able to read the emotional nuances of the upper part of the face—the eyes—whereas the left brain focuses on the lower part—the mouth.[58] The classic alien head that we see in Strieber's visionary experience and on the cover of his famous book—with huge, almond, meaning-filled eyes and a kind of abstract or cartoon mouth, only a line or circle standing in for it—looks very much like an exaggerated version of what the right brain would put together if it were to imagine and process an anomalous encounter.

Strieber is equally sophisticated about the identity of the beings he prefers to call simply "the visitors." He took a battery of psychological, neurological, and physiological tests after his abduction event and bravely explored, through the comparative study of religion, the blatant sexual dimensions of his experiences: "It is terrifying, of course. But reflect also that mankind has had a sexual relationship with the fairies, the sylphs, the incubi, the succubi, and the denizens of the night from the very beginning of time."[59] He would eventually come to a paradoxical position, which should strike the reader as familiar by now. He came to the conclusion that the question "must be left open," that there is something about the modern abduction experience that frustrates any attempt to lock it down into a single explanation or model. As he explained to the Harvard psychiatrist and alien abduction researcher John Mack:

> If you start saying, "Well, they are aliens and they're from this planet," you're lost … I've often been in positions where the question has been impossible to live with. You can't not answer it, and you can't answer it either. And there you have it. You sit in a situation where you can't bear to be—and you grow.[60]

In the in-between.

Comparative Reflections

What do we notice when we put these three cases side by side? Three things all three cases share are a common gender (male), a shared cultural context (the US), and a single decade (the 1980s). But we can certainly say more. There is a female presence here as well in two of the cases. Moreover, although we are given no details, both Mullis and his daughter saw a clear and obvious connection between their experiences and that of Strieber. In essence, they were comparing out of the eerie depths of their own anomalous experiences.

There are other linking patterns. Is it significant, for example, that two of the three cases summarized here (that of Strieber and of myself) involved some kind of physical paralysis? It is perfectly possible that the third (that of Mullis) did as well, but we do not know, and probably we cannot know.

We all "paralyze" when we go to sleep. Otherwise we would hit our partner during a bad dream, or worse. But sometimes this natural sleep system misfires. There is a particular psychophysical condition called "sleep paralysis" (SP), in which the mind comes online and wakes up (or seems to wake up), while the body remains frozen, paralyzed by the chemicals it has released into the bloodstream during deep sleep. We know quite a bit about this condition,

including the fact that it is often accompanied by extremely realistic visions and terrifying nightmare scenarios.

David Hufford has spent much of his professional life studying—both in the humanities, as a folklorist, and in the neural and behavioral sciences, as a medical researcher—what he calls "supernatural assault traditions" around the world, particularly as they are connected to sleep paralysis. His *The Terror That Comes in the Night* (1982) has become the classic study of this global pattern. Let us begin, then, by suggesting that our C, which links these three cases, is the category of supernatural assault, that is, the experience of being attacked, overwhelmed, or invaded by an intermediate being, often via paralysis in bed. John Keel's description of waking up in the night and being "unable to move, with a huge dark apparition standing over me" around the time he was investigating the Mothman is a classic example. These are usually highly charged negative events, but they can also "flip over" into ecstatic and visionary events of extreme power and beauty. Which is all to say that these are modern manifestations of the sacred.

Hufford began his work on the phenomenon in Newfoundland, an island just off the east coast of Canada, where he worked and taught between 1971 and 1974. There he encountered multiple stories about what the locals call "the Old Hag." They spoke of being "Hag Rogue," probably a corruption of "hag rode" or "hag rid." To be hagged or "hagrid" is to be ridden by a supernatural being (the English "haggard" may be related as well). As a comparative side note, we might note that possession phenomena often use the same basic metaphor to explain what being possessed feels like: the human being is the "horse" or "vehicle" of the intervening spirit or deity. After leaving Newfoundland, Hufford went on to explore the Old Hag pattern throughout the United States, with further research and extensive interviews in Pennsylvania, Nebraska, California, and Kentucky. What he found was a variable pattern, but also a remarkably stable one. When asked, about 15–25 per cent of North American subjects report such an experience, whether they have access to a folk tradition involving something like the Old Hag or not.

These supernatural assaults are often once in a lifetime affairs. But not always. They are also sometimes clearly sexual in nature. Significantly, it turns out that, as with the Mothman and Strieber's female visitor, the being's eyes are the feature most mentioned. Occasionally the event reaches extremely strange proportions: reports of rocking or moving beds, accompanying psychical phenomena, communications with the dead, and tingling, vibration- or electrocution-like sensations, often located in the spine.

Through his ethnographic research, Hufford came to reject what he calls the "cultural source hypothesis," that is, the notion that such experiences can be explained away as products of cultural beliefs and local folklore: he rejected the model of pure difference. He found rather that the assaults are not associated with ethnicity, religious background, or any other ethnographic variable. The reports have every appearance of being based on actual empirical experiences, which, of course, are imagined and processed through whatever local mythical grids happen to be present. Finally, then, Hufford opts for what he calls the "experiential source hypothesis." The experiential source hypothesis suggests that these events are neither "fictitious products of tradition" nor "imaginary subjective experiences shaped (or occasionally even caused) by tradition."[61] Rather, the phenomenon "appears to have worldwide distribution and has been a part of the empirical foundation for a great variety of supernatural traditions."[62] What we have here, of course, is a model comparative practice—a balancing of sameness and difference.

This does not necessarily mean, Hufford is careful to point out, that the experience is somehow objectively true, only that people are being perfectly rational and empirical when they report these experiences, and that these same events cannot be explained away in a facile manner, by appeal to local folklore traditions or to the sleep paralysis factor, which functions in many of them. Sleep paralysis, after all, may be a common physiological condition of the event, but not a direct cause. We already encountered this kind of both–and reasoning in our discussion of sacred trauma in Chapter 6.

The implications of the supernatural assault literature for the comparative study of religion are obvious. Hufford, for example, notes that Old Hag attacks are easily and readily applied to witchcraft beliefs and can be detected in the historical records of the Salem witchcraft trials. The comparisons with the medieval *incubus* and *succubus* (male and female demons who were believed to have sex with human beings in their sleep) are also obvious enough, although Hufford points out that the Old Hag experiences are not always sexual, whereas the *incubus/succubus* experiences were, by definition, sexual. The relevance of Hufford's work for the very modern alien abduction phenomenon is also apparent, and indeed Hufford wrote a paper on the subject for a conference at the Massachusetts Institute of Technology on the topic (see Figure 8.4).[63]

Finally, it can hardly be an accident that a large percentage of abductions happen in bed and involve some form of paralysis. This is why John Keel called their protagonists "Bedroom Invaders." The problem is that such events do not always happen in bed. Many of the most famous cases have occurred while the subjects were driving on lonely dark highways—as we see, for example, in the famous Barney and Betty Hill case, which initiated the alien abduction literature in 1965. Others are encounters in broad daylight or at dusk. Others still display objective electromagnetic effects, particularly involving cars, tractors, and (as we saw both in our opening vision of the dying woman and in the Mothman case) television sets. As with all comparative patterns related to religious experience, we have to be careful about easy solutions. We have to learn to keep the question open. We have to learn to dwell in the surreal landscapes of the empowered religious imagination and come to terms with what we see there.

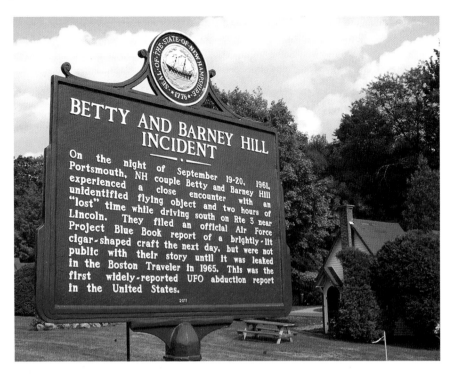

Figure 8.4   State historical marker of the first widely publicized abduction case in the USA: the Betty and Barney Hill Incident. Photographed by Kathleen Marden.

Adding to Our Toolkit

The primary point of this chapter has been to help you develop both–and thinking, particularly with respect to religious images, symbols, and visions. We have focused on those events that call into question the assumption that human beings can be thought of as stable, contained subjects, isolated in bony, box-like skulls that interact with a world "out there" through the relatively trustworthy and more or less exhaustive medium of the senses.

In this commonsense view of things, something is either "in here" (and hence "subjective") or "out there" (and hence "objective"). Something is either "mental" or "material." Moreover, the subjective or mental dimension is assumed to be largely unreal or unimportant. The objective or material dimension is what is real. This is how the world usually works for us. But, unfortunately (or fortunately), this is not

how it always works, as we have seen. This in turn led us to the following ideas:

1   *The Rational Offense of the In-between*   Paranormal and psychical phenomena are the "dirt" or "impurity" of the present orthodox worldview of scientific materialism. These events "offend" the way things really are (or are supposed to be), and so they are commonly met with excessive or hysterical forms of rejection, shaming, and humiliation.

2   *The Imaginal*   Because such paranormal events are commonly mediated by the imagination, it does not follow that they are all "imaginary" or unreal. As we saw with the Twain and Dr. Amatuzio cases, the dreaming imagination can pick up and communicate *empirically correct information* about the external world miles away and, more weirdly still, days ahead. We have labeled these moments "imaginal."

3 *The Symbol* Other forms of the imaginal are symbolic. A symbol is not the same thing as a sign. From the ancient Greeks on, a symbol has been experienced as a talisman or portal, a medium of some profound and often paradoxical truth. A symbol is, quite literally, a form of co-incidence, here of two different dimensions of reality or mind. A sign, on the other hand, is an arbitrary social convention. Although these two categories clearly overlap and often inform one another, distinguishing between them can bring much clarity in the handling of extreme religious events.

4 *The Pathos of the Paranormal* Profound emotional bonds, trauma, danger, illness, and death are especially important in the triggering of paranormal, imaginal, and visionary events. Hence the nineteenth-century category of *telepathy* or "pathos at a distance." It is this traumatic technology key that debunkers of paranormal phenomena commonly miss.

5 *The Trick of the Truth* Finally, we noted that the relationship between trick and truth, fact and fraud, is not as simple as is often assumed. We saw this in the role that the imagination can play in mediating empirical events and in the biomedical fraud of the placebo. We also suggested that something similar is at work in the "tricks" of myth, ritual, and magic, and indeed in religion itself.

The Tough Questions

1 Read the *New York Times* piece on Daryl J. Bem's scientific research on precognition: Benedict Carey, "Top Journal Plans to Publish a Paper on ESP, and Psychologists Sense Outrage," January 6, 2011, page 1. The outrage came soon enough. Using Hansen's model of the paranormal as anti-structure, comment on the excessive nature of this outrage. For more background, see Dean Radin, *Entangled Minds: Extrasensory Experiences in a Quantum World* (New York: Paraview, 2006).

2 What would happen to our religions if we understood religious doctrines as mediating "symbols" rather than as literal "dogmas," that is, if we came to terms with the role of the imagination in religion? What if we took to heart the Muslim mystic Junayd: "The color of the water is that of the vessel which contains it"?

3 If one accepts the veridical contents of some imagined dreams or visions, where exactly does one stop? That is, if one accepts the empirical accuracy of the imagined dreams of Mark Twain and of Dr. Amatuzio's female subject, what do we do with the imagined dreams and symbolic visions of the abductees and the supernatural assault folklore? Where is your line? Should we draw a distinction between the imaginal as an empirical cognition of something happening in the physical world and the imaginal as a symbolic vision mediating some other spiritual world?

Notes

1 Mark Fox, *Spiritual Encounters with Unusual Light Phenomena: Lightforms* (Cardiff: University of Wales Press, 2008), 59–60, 158.

2 Fox, *Spiritual Encounters*, back cover summary.

3 Diego Escolar, "Boundaries of Anthropology: Empirics and Ontological Relativism in a Field Experience with Anomalous Luminous Entities in Argentina." *Anthropology and Humanism* 37.1 (2012), 27–44.

4 For a most remarkable case reported in detail by a professor of experimental physics, see John Hasted, *The Metal-Benders* (London: Routledge & Kegan Paul, 1981), chapters 18–20.

5   George P. Hansen, *The Trickster and the Paranormal* (n.p.: XLibris, 2001), 20.

6   Hansen, *The Trickster*, 22, 24, 32.

7   Jess Byron Hollenback, *Mysticism: Experience, Response, and Empowerment, Response* (University Park, PA: The Pennsylvania State University Press, 1996).

8   Paul Stoller and Cheryl Olkes, *In Sorcery's Shadow: A Memoir of Apprenticeship among the Songhay of Niger* (Chicago, IL: University of Chicago Press, 1989).

9   Edith Turner, "The Reality of Spirits: A Tabooed or Permitted Field of Study?" *Anthropology of Consciousness* 4.1 (1993), 9–12.

10 Peter N. Struck, *Birth of the Symbol: Ancient Readers at the Limits of Their Texts* (Princeton, NJ: Princeton University Press, 2004), 193.

11 Struck, *Birth of the Symbol*, 1, 20.

12 Struck, *Birth of the Symbol*, 90–96.

13 Plato, *Symposion*, 192d5; for commentary see Struck, *Birth of the Symbol*, 79.

14 Struck, *Birth of the Symbol*, 171. With this expression Struck is silently invoking C. G. Jung, who used the same two words to gloss his notion of "synchronicity" (which we treat below, in Chapter 12).

15 Struck, *Birth of the Symbol*, 3.

16 Struck, *Birth of the Symbol*, 75.

17 Struck, *Birth of the Symbol*, 179.

18 Struck, *Birth of the Symbol*, 213.

19 *Autobiography of Mark Twain*, vol. 1, edited by Harriet Elinor Smith (Berkeley: University of California Press, 2010), 274–276.

20 See "Mental Telegraphy" (1891) and "Mental Telegraphy Again" (1895) in Mark Twain, *Tales of Wonder*, edited by David Ketterer (Lincoln: University of Nebraska Press, 2003), 96–111.

21 Twain, *Tales of Wonder*, 99–100.

22 Janis Amatuzio, MD, *Beyond Knowing: Mysteries and Messages of Death and Life from a Forensic Pathologist* (Novato, CA: New World Library, 2006), 84–85.

23 See Tough Question 1 at the end of this chapter.

24 Théodore Flournoy, *From India to the Planet Mars: A Case of Multiple Personality with Imaginary Languages*, with a new Introduction by Sonu Shamdasani (Princeton, NJ: Princeton University Press, 1994), 250.

25 Flournoy, *From India to the Planet Mars*, 224.

26 Henry Corbin, *Creative Imagination in the Sufism of Ibn 'Arabi* (Princeton, NJ: Princeton University Press, 1969), 266.

27 Corbin, *Creative Imagination*, 42, 47–48, 68, 222–224. The Sufi lore around teleportation (not named as such, of course) occurs at 237–238.

28 Timothy K. Beal, *Religion and Its Monsters* (New York: Routledge, 2001), 4–5.

29 Beal, *Religion and Its Monsters*, 7.

30 John A. Keel, *UFOs: Operation Trojan Horse* (New York: G. P. Putnam's Sons, 1970), 212.

31 Keel, *UFOs*, 217, 270–272, 304.

32 Ardy Sixkiller Clarke, *Encounters with Star People: Untold Stories of American Indians* (San Antonio, TX: Anomalist Books, 2012).

33 Keel, *UFOs*, 291.

34 James Gallant, "The Humiliating UFOs." *Raritan* 30.4 (2011), 74. My thanks to Victoria Nelson for this reference.

35 Gallant, "The Humiliating UFOs," 76.

36 Gallant, "The Humiliating UFOs," 88–89.

37 The best book on these cases is Leslie Kean's *UFOs: Generals, Pilots, and Government Officials Go on the Record* (New York: Harmony Books, 2010).

38 Keel, *UFOs*, 255.

39 Jeff Wamsley, *Mothman: Behind the Red Eyes* (Point Pleasant, VA: Mothman Press, 2005), 22, 38, 50, 72, 74.

40 Wamsley, *Mothman*, 44.

41 Wamsley, *Mothman*, 132.

42 Keel, *UFOs*, 274–275.

43 Keel, *UFOs*, 276.

44 Keel, *UFOs*, 277.

45 Keel, *UFOs*, 277–278.

46 Wamsley, *Mothman*, 276–278.

47 Quoted in Hansen, *The Trickster*, 277; see also 289–291.

48 Russell Targ, *Do You See What I See? Memoirs of a Blind Biker* (Charlottesville, VA: Hampton Roads, 2008), 34.

49 Kary Mullis, *Dancing Naked in the Mind Field* (New York: Pantheon Books, 1998), 131–133. This chapter is entitled (ironically?) "No Aliens Allowed."

50 Whitley Strieber, *Communion: A True Story* (New York: Harper, 2008), 11–12.

51 Strieber, *Communion*, 19.

52 Strieber, *Communion*, 75.

53 Strieber, *Communion*, xxii.

54 Whitley Strieber, Foreword to Jacques Vallee, *Dimensions: A Casebook of Alien Contact* (London: Souvenir Press, 1988), vii.

55 John E. Mack, "How the Alien Abduction Phenomenon Challenges the Boundaries of Our Reality," in *UFOs and Abductions: Challenging the Borders of Knowledge*, edited by David M. Jacobs (Lawrence, KS: University Press of Kansas, 2000), 254.

56 Jeffrey J. Kripal, *Mutants and Mystics: Science Fiction, Superhero Comics, and the Paranormal* (Chicago, IL: University of Chicago Press, 2011), 5–8.

57 Mullis, *Dancing Naked*, 130, 136.

58 Iain McGilchrist, *The Master and His Emissary: The Divided Brain and the Making of the Western World* (New Haven, CT: Yale University Press, 2009), 59.

59 Strieber, *Communion*, 247–248.

60 John E. Mack, *Passport to the Cosmos: Human Transformation and Alien Encounters* (Largo, FL: Kunati, 2008), 3. Whitley Strieber develops the same paradoxical point in *Solving the Communion Enigma: What Is to Come* (New York: Jeremy P. Tarcher/ Penguin, 2011), for which I wrote the Foreword: "Reading as Mutation."

61 David J. Hufford, *The Terror That Comes in the Night: An Experience-Centered Study of Supernatural Assault Traditions* (Philadelphia: University of Pennsylvania Press, 1982), 14.

62 Hufford, *The Terror That Comes in the Night*, 55.

63 David J. Hufford, "Awakening Paralyzed in the Presence of a Strange 'Visitor.'" In *Alien Discussions: Proceedings of the Abduction Study Conference held at MIT, Cambridge, MA*, edited by Andrea Pritchard, David E. Pritchard, John E. Mack, Pam Kasey, and Claudia Yapp (Cambridge, MA: North Cambridge Press, 1992), 351.

Lamentation (2001), by Lynn Randolph, 29″ × 30″.

9

The Final Questions of Soul, Salvation, and the End of All Things

The Human as Two

I am He whom I love,
and He whom I love is I.
We are two spirits
dwelling in one body.

Muslim mystic al-Hallaj (858–922)

Imagine a book which speaks of nothing but events which lie outside the possibility
of general or even rare experiences—the first language for a new range of experiences.
In this case, nothing will be heard!

Friedrich Nietzsche, *Ecce Homo*

Comparing Religions: Coming to Terms, First Edition. Jeffrey J. Kripal, Ata Anzali, Andrea R. Jain, and Erin Prophet.
© 2014 Jeffrey J. Kripal. Published 2014 by John Wiley & Sons, Ltd.

Two Scenes

How does one study something that one has never known? How does one speak of the soul, much less study it, in an officially scientific culture that denies the very existence of the soul? How does one take seriously a witness that, in Nietzsche's words, "speaks of nothing but events which lie outside the possibility of general or even rare experiences"?

Two scenes.

The British Architect

In 1962 a British writer named Douglas Harding wrote a lovely little book entitled *On Having No Head*. In its pages he treats the day "when I found I had no head." "This," he goes on, "is not a literary gambit, a witticism designed to arouse interest at any cost. I mean it in all seriousness: *I have no head*."[1] How did he come to this odd conclusion? Harding was trekking in the Himalayas when he suddenly discovered that he was not at all who he thought he was, that he was not a body or a brain. Here is how he later explained it:

Somehow or other I had vaguely thought of myself as inhabiting this house which is my body, and looking out through its two round windows at the world. Now I find it isn't like that at all… Victim of a prolonged fit of madness, of a lifelong hallucination (and by "hallucination" I mean what my dictionary says: *apparent perception of an object not actually present*), I had invariably seen myself as pretty much like other men, and certainly never as a decapitated but still living biped. I had been blind to the one thing that is always present, and without which I am blind indeed—to this marvelous substitute-for-a-head, this unbounded clarity, this luminous and absolutely pure void, which nevertheless is—rather than contains—all things.[2]

Now staring into a mirror (there it is again), he puzzles at the sheer lunacy of confusing consciousness with the brain, the ego, or the body:

In my saner moments I see the man over there [in the mirror] … as the opposite in every way of my real Self here. I have never been anything but this ageless, adamantine, measureless, lucid, and altogether immaculate Void: it is unthinkable that I could ever have confused that staring wraith over there with what I plainly perceive myself to be here and now and forever![3]

This realization was certainly dramatic, but it was not entirely surprising. Harding had long been a free spirit and an open mind. At the age of twenty-one he was excommunicated from his ultra-conservative church, the Exclusive Plymouth Brethren, in which everything, from newspapers to laughter, was forbidden. He had confronted the elders of the community with a ten-page list of objections. Estranged from his family for the rest of his life (for being "in league with the Devil"), Harding trained as an architect—hence the importance of direct observation, perspective, and precision in his writings—and pursued a philosophical vocation before his headlessness in the mountains set him off on a more direct spiritual search. He eventually discovered the "original face" of Zen Buddhism (the nature of mind before one's individual existence) and the immortal *atman* or "Self" of Hinduism as the most adequate approximation to what he knew. But he joined neither tradition. Instead he became something of an independent spiritual teacher. As his obituary had it, he had begun "with the attitude of a scientist and ended with the insights of a mystic."[4]

A humorous side story. In 1986 another British gentleman, named Vic Burnside, took a copy of Harding's *On Having No Head* with him on a Tibetan Buddhist meditation retreat at Conishead Priory in Cumbria, England. He had himself photographed with the book in his pocket. The photo clearly shows an image of Mr. Burnside with—gulp—no head. It seems that the camera at least took Mr. Harding quite literally, as cameras are wont to do, and then winked with a shutter click (see Figure 9.1).

The Teenage Hippie

In 1975 a nineteen-year-old American named Bill Barnard was living in Gainesville, Florida. He considered himself spiritual and hence signed up for a workshop on awakening one's "latent spiritual energy" with a visiting Hindu guru named Swami Muktananda, whom we have already met briefly above, in our discussion of Franklin Jones. Bill scraped together the thirty dollars and arrived at a suburban house at 8 sharp in the morning, ready to go.

Figure 9.1   Vic Burnside appears without a head in the second photograph (taken just after the first) while he was on retreat with a copy of D. H. Harding's *On Having No Head* in his pocket. Fortean Picture Library.

The house had been refitted for the event: no furniture, incense wafting, Indian chants playing on a stereo system. The workshop began with some talks about what would happen over the course of the day and how one might focus on a mantra, a single-syllable sound that is meant to be repeated over and over again in order to make one concentrate on one's meditation. Then the guru came into the room, dressed in a silk tailor-made orange dress shirt, a lungi, a knit skull cap, and orange socks (orange is the color monks wear in many forms of Hinduism). The overall effect on the young man was mesmerizing and bears all the characteristics that we have learned to recognize as features of charisma. Bill was "transfixed." "Time itself seemed to shift" and the whole room "was surrounded and interpenetrated by this shimmering globe of energy."[5]

Then the moment arrived for the *shakti-pat*, that is, the "descent of power," which was the specialty of this particular holy man, bestowed either with the gentle swipe of some peacock feathers or by the touch of a hand on the head (or in a dream, as in my own case, recounted in our previous chapter). "As I chanted," Bill writes,

I listened as this man began to pad around the room in his orange socks, going up and down the rows of people, thumping them with his peacock feathers … I could hear the rustle of his robes, I could smell the thick, exotic scent of the Indian perfume that he wore, then at last, the peacock feathers thwacked me over the head.

The results were certainly dramatic enough:

My consciousness dramatically shifted inside of me after those feathery whacks. The shift wasn't subtle at all. Instantly, I felt my awareness being powerfully pulled inside … It was as if I had split into two parts: one part was watching this mantra arise within me, while the other part of me *was* the mantra … Then, something shifted again. All at once, I was no longer split into two, I was no longer looking for the source of the mantra; instead, I felt myself to *be* the source of the mantra. It's here that I begin to sympathize with many mystics' frustration with the ineffability of mystical experiences [that is, with the impossibility of putting it into human grammar and words]. I can say that the experience had something to do with complete and utter freedom … It's also not completely false to say that it felt like an awakening, like an ecstatic recognition that I was this dynamic, expansive, swirling mass of joyous consciousness, that I always had been that and that I always would be … In fact, at one point during this experience, I remember laughing, realizing on some level of my being that my previous identification with my body and my ego was a cosmic joke, knowing that I never was just an ego and I never would be just an ego, recognizing in the core of my being that, contrary to what I'd always believed, I never had suffered and I never would.

The nineteen-year-old could not have possibly described the experience in these words. Indeed, he jokes about how the young hippie would have vocalized the experience then: "Wow, you know, man, it was like, you know, really incredible." But the experience was so life-altering that Bill eventually joined Swami Muktananda's community in India for a number of years and then completed a PhD in the social scientific study of religion. Armed with the very categories and ideas you have been learning here, he can now articulate the experience. He now teaches at Southern Methodist University in Dallas, Texas.

If we compare the accounts of Harding and Barnard in these two sections, we are struck by any number of similarities. Foremost among these are a certain "splitting" or separation between the common sense of self—what Harding calls the man in the mirror, or simply "the head," and Barnard calls the "limited, suffering, ignorant ego with a body." We also notice in both men an expansive humor, a transcendental mocking of the previous ways of seeing the human being. Harding calls this previous ignorance a "lifelong hallucination," Barnard a "cosmic joke." We also notice that both men ultimately connected their experiences—but only later—with Asian religious traditions: in Harding's case, it was Zen Buddhism and Advaita Vedanta; in Barnard's case, it was a form of Hindu idealism (everything is "mind") known to scholars as Kashmir Shaivism.

Of particular interest to the student of religion is the fact that neither man trained for or expected his particular realization. Both certainly had contexts (Harding was an architect and an independent philosopher, Barnard a spiritual hippie), but in other respects both experiences came unbidden and certainly overflowed any expectations on the part of the subject.

What would happen if we practiced comparison in a way that left the door open to the "rare experiences" of which Nietzsche spoke in our epigraph, experiences that took a British engineer to Japan and an American hippie to India? What if we did not assume the absolute reality of the local self but left a door open to other forms of mind and subjectivity, to the nonlocal self? Remember Plotinus hitching a ride to India with the Roman army?

The Nature of Embodied Consciousness

If I had to say what I thought the general history of religions is in the end *really* about, I would not say that it is about the nature of God or the sacred, about a particular story and its repeated performance, about nature, about the sexual body, about charisma and its special social institutions, or about the paradoxical paranormal powers of the religious imagination. I would say that it is about the nature of the human being and, finally, about the nature of embodied consciousness. I would say that it is about the ancient human experience of being not one, but two. I would say, in four simple words, that the general history of religions is about *the human as two*. I would also say that, once we make this "split" in our thinking about human identity, much that is mysterious or nonsensical about religion immediately becomes obvious and eminently sensible.

The specific identity of the first member of this "human as two" is more or less consistent, if also always different: it is the body-ego, the local, historical social self, the day-to-day awareness of "fill in the blank with your name." This first half of who we are is the sole object of most of our standard methods of studying religion today, from historical criticism through sociology to cognitive science. It's all we know. And maybe all we can know with our academic methods.

The specific identity of the second member of this "human as two" is not at all clear. Sometimes it is experienced outside the embodied self, as an external deity or presence. This is what we generally get in the western theistic religions. Sometimes it is experienced inside the embodied human being, as a kind of deeper or cosmic inner Self, or as an empty and blissful void. This is what we generally get in the Asian

religions. Sometimes, moreover, it is a little of both, as we get in our opening epigraph from the great Muslim mystic al-Hallaj (who, by the way, lived between the West and Asia and was crucified, and then cut into pieces, for proclaiming this kind of relationship to God). We do not quite know how to "study" this other half, since it is not an object at all. It cannot really be described, and it certainly cannot be measured or manipulated.

I am not alone in my conclusions. The early scholar of religion Ludwig Feuerbach (1804–1872) (pronounced "*foyer*-Bach"), already back in his *Lectures on the Philosophy of Religion* (1851), wrote more or less the same thing with respect to what he called "the true seat and source of religion":

> The ultimate secret of religion is the *relationship* between the *conscious* and *unconscious*, the *voluntary* and *involuntary in one and the same individual* … Man with his ego or consciousness stands at the brink of a bottomless abyss; that abyss is his own unconscious being, which seems alien to him and inspires him with a feeling which expresses itself in words of wonderment such as: What am I? Where have I come from? To what end? And this feeling that I am nothing without a *not*-I which is at the same time my *own* being, is the religious feeling. But what part of me is I and what part is not-I?[6]

This sounds a lot like Sigmund Freud, who would not come on the scene with his influential language of "the unconscious" for another half-century.

We do not need to frame the "human as two" in religious, or even in philosophical terms. We can say the same in modern neuroscience. David Eagleman, for example, has compared our day-to-day consciousness, our ego (that is, what I have called the first half of the "human as two"), as a tiny CEO or king sitting on top of a vast corporation or kingdom, imagining that he is "doing all of this," when in fact he is simply directing the actions of countless other agencies and invisible workers.

The analogy of a business or kingdom is, in the end, inadequate. Our twoness in neuroscience is much more outrageous than that. And so Eagleman points out that the human brain, *your* brain, contains hundreds of billions of neurons and glia, which are

> connected to one another in a network of such stagger-ing complexity that it bankrupts human language and necessitates new strains of mathematics. A typical neuron makes about ten thousand connections to neighboring neurons. Given that there are billions of neurons, this means there are as many connections in a single cubic centimeter of brain tissue as there are stars in the Milky Way galaxy.[7]

Put differently, there are more connections between your ears than there are on the entire global internet. And you—and this is the punch line—you are aware of *none* of this. There is a good reason, then, why religious prodigies have consistently reported that human beings contain a universe within them: we do.

We will return to some of these ideas in our final two chapters. For now, we return to the questions that Harding and Barnard asked as young men: Who are we? What are we? A state of pure consciousness surrounding and interpenetrating a headless walking monkey biped, as Mr. Harding had it? A created soul destined for damnation or eternal life depending on what beliefs one holds and what church one attends, as Mr. Harding's family had it? An immortal, joyous Self temporarily playing the part of an ignorant ego in a suffering body for a time, as Prof. Barnard puts it? A surface ego sitting on top of an indescribable, virtually infinite inner cosmos, as Prof. Eagleman has it? Or, or … *what*?

Patterns of the Soul and Salvation in the History of Religions

What we are really addressing here is the nature of the soul in the history of religions, which is inevi-tably tied to what Martin Riesbrodt has called the "promise of salvation" in each religion. For the sake of conversation, we might define a particular reli-gion's promise of salvation as its soteriology (from the ancient Greek *sōzein*, "to save," and *sōtēria*,

"safety, preservation," later "salvation"), and the **soul** as that animating identity or core of the human being that is generally believed to be separable from the body and, in consequence, is the primary con-cern and object of this promise of salvation. In essence, if salvation is the end point or goal of a reli-gious path, the soul is what walks it and is finally saved. This really will not do, however, as there is a vast multitude of doctrines, models of salvation, and practices or paths concerning the soul that make these definitions look ridiculously simple. Consider these three perennial questions.

First, is the soul created or uncreated? Various the-istic religious systems in Judaism, Christianity, Islam, and Hinduism see the soul as created by a deity. Others see the soul as uncreated or as itself infinite, immortal, and "divine." We often find both models within a single religious tradition, moreover. Hinduism is a particu-larly obvious case here.

Second, does the soul live once or many times? The monotheistic religions generally see this soul as possessing a single life on earth, then being judged at death by a creator-deity and being sent to some eternal state of reward or punishment—the "heavens" and "hells" of the monotheistic imagination. But not always. Sikhism, for example, accepts the doctrine of reincarnation, and it is a rigorously monotheistic religion. Other religions, particularly those that emerged in Asia, see the soul as reincarnating count-less times through the life cycle (including through many heavens and hells) before it is sufficiently mature and capable of some final state of salvation, which is often assumed to be a release from this round of births and deaths. Other systems still, like many forms of Buddhism, deny the final existence of a soul altogether, even as they also recognize that something *like* a soul is necessary to make sense of the (very Buddhist) doctrines of *karma* and reincarnation.

Third, what of the soul's relationship with the body and the material world? This is an especially compli-cated matter. Some religious systems operate with a very clear and very distinct dualism here, the soul and the body being conceived as entirely different substances, as in Jainism and many forms of Indian yoga. Others operate with various notions of a "subtle body," an intermediary or liminal body participating in both the material and the spiritual world.[8] Such notions can be found in various forms of Daoism, Hinduism, and Buddhism, late antique Neoplatonism (a form of Greek philosophical religion), Sufism, Spiritualism, and modern ritual magic. Of particular note here is the spherical body of light and "spirit vehicle" (*ochēma pneuma*) of the Neoplatonists (and of some modern UFO encounters). Ioan Couliano wonderfully described the notion captured by this ancient Greek phrase as a spiritual "space shuttle" that descends from the Milky Way and the planets down into the human form before it ascends back up again in ecstasy, mystical union, and death. Still other religions operate with the hope of a future spiritualized, glorified, or resurrection body (Judaism, Christianity, and Islam).

These spirit–matter relations are complicated by two further issues. The first is the question whether divinity can manifest itself in human flesh. Christianity depends on the belief that it can, and that it did manifest itself in a single human being named Jesus, who was worshipped as resurrected and divine, as Lord, after his death. The Hindu doctrine of the *avatara* ("descent") of God into a human being depends on the belief that this kind of event can happen as well, and many times—perhaps countless times. The same belief, however, is rejected in Judaism and is considered a serious heresy in Islam, where it is known as *hulul* (usually translated as "incarnation"; the Arabic root is h-l-l, which means "taking up residence" or "descending upon," and this is the infinitive form). But, significantly, we do find the idea within mystical movements in both the Jewish and Islamic traditions. The second issue is the practice—found in many traditions, from ancient Egypt and Greece to contemporary Hinduism and Roman Catholicism—of "charging" or "animating" statues with the presence of a deity, saint, spiritual presence, or soul. Roman Catholicism is a trickier case here, since, even though it is forbidden to worship a statue or to consider it divine, statues of the representations of the Virgin and of the saints are commonly believed to "bleed" or "weep"—which of course implies that they are animated or "ensouled."[9]

Whether they affirm or deny it, whether they see it as operating in a single life or in countless lives, and however they understand its relationship to matter, each of these religious systems engage what Ioan Couliano has simply described as the **separable soul**. They must, as this is clearly one of the most basic, long-lasting, and ancient religious ideas on the planet. The phenomenon of the separable soul is clearly behind most indigenous shamanic practices, for example—the shaman being now understood to be *the* expert in separation. The idea was probably already popular in the Paleolithic period. As best we can tell, even the Neanderthals worked with some concept of soul and life after death, which they appear to have understood as both a journey and a state of sleep. Hence Neanderthal burial sites contain food and tools (that is, supplies for a journey), and the bodies are carefully laid to rest in sleeplike positions. The symbolism of death as sleep is one of those forms of religious expression that have remained unambiguously consistent over the millennia. To this day, for example, metaphors based on this "Neanderthal" symbolism (or a very similar one) are commonly employed in English: "May she rest in peace," "He was laid to rest."

Symbols of the Soul

Earlier, when we tried to define the humanities, we came to the view that they consist in the study of consciousness coded in culture. Something similar happens when we pursue the soul in the general history of religions: what we find there is not the soul itself, but refractions and reflections of people's experience of soul, now coded in myth, ritual, doctrine, art, dance, song, and symbol. The countless doctrines and practices around the separable soul likely emerged over millennia of extreme anomalous events like those experienced by Harding and Barnard, as these were then variously narrated, ritualized, artistically rendered, socially disciplined, suppressed, and encouraged by religious authorities and institutions within different historical contexts. There is hardly a "beginning" here, and there is certainly no end in sight. Once again, however, there are patterns.

1 *The Double Soul* One of the most consistent of these patterns is established by the notion that the human being possesses not one, but two animating forces. In the ancient and in the medieval Christian world, for example, the concept of "soul" (*psuchē* in Greek, *anima* in Latin) tended to refer to the life principle or living energy of a sentient creature, whereas "spirit" (*pneuma* in Greek, *spiritus* in Latin, both of which refer primarily to air, wind, and breath) tended to refer to that transcendent aspect or dimension of a human being that was believed to survive the ravages of physical death. Other cultures have arrived at similar dichotomies. The ancient Egyptians, for example, conceived of the *akh*—the human soul—as consisting of numerous parts (often listed as five), two of which were the animating principle or life-force (*ka*) and the individual personality (*ba*). Many of the peoples of Oceania draw a distinction between a "free" soul that departs the body during dream and trance and a "body" soul that carries the basic functions of biological life. A very similar pattern is evident on the island of Sumatra, where a general opposition is drawn between a "life soul" that bestows vitality on the body and a "death soul" that is released at death.[10]

Ancient Daoism also proposed a composite or "two-soul model" of the human being. Here the person was said to possess both a *hun*—a "heavenly soul," which was associated with *yang* and the subtle or ethereal aspects of the self—and a *po*—a "corporeal soul," which was associated with *yin* and the "flesh and bone" aspects of the human being. At death, these two animating forces were thought to separate. The heavenly soul would ascend and, for a time (for seven generations, according to one standard account), would become an ancestor; the corporeal soul would return to the earth while the body decomposed. Both animating principles are ephemeral, however, and eventually they both dissipate into the cosmos.[11]

2 *Radiance and Light* Another widely attested pattern in the general history of religions is the soul's or the spirit's association with light. From the "mind of clear light" in Tibetan Buddhism to the loving lightforms of contemporary near-death experiences, this theme is remarkably stable across space and time, even though its local meanings are endlessly various. Scholar of Buddhism Matthew Kapstein, in the introduction of a volume on the same theme in the world's religions, invokes a famous Christian poet to make the same comparative point: "The traditions themselves, in their interplay of convergence and difference, seem to confirm the vision of the whole and its many modes revealed in the *Paradiso* of [the medieval Italian poet] Dante Alighieri"—which goes like this:

> The Primal Light the whole irradiates,
> And is received therein as many ways
> As there are splendors wherewithal it mates.[12]

3 *Subtle Energy or Force* Very much related to the theme of divine radiance or light is the motif of the soul as energy or force. We have already looked at a number of examples of erotic transformation, all of which assume a type of spiritual energy or eroticism that can be spent, directed, preserved, increased, and transfigured. We might mention in this context late antique Greek Neoplatonism, which often saw the soul as a kind of conscious ball of light or "spirit vehicle" that needed to be formed and stabilized through prayer and ritual; or modern New Age revelations that describe the soul as a malleable and morphing "energy" or "vibration."

4 *The Heart and the Head* Behind this particular pattern lies another: the question of the "where" of soul or spirit. Are such conscious energies localized in the region of the heart, as we have it in so many religious systems? Or in the brain, as we tend to assume today, in the age of neuroscience—a location that we also find well represented in the general history of religions? Or just above the brain, as we have it in many traditional Indian yogic models? Or is the

"seat of the soul," as Descartes would have it, in an embarrassingly precise answer: in the pineal gland at the core of the brain? Or is the question of "where" itself misplaced (forgive the pun)—a naïve attempt to lock something down that is in fact nowhere? As the alien intelligences tried to explain in Grant Morrison's comic-book series *The Invisibles* (itself based on Morrison's own hyper-dimensional awakening in Nepal): "The soul is not in the body. The body is inside the soul. Do you understand? Look. We are you. Try to remember."[13]

But "where" does this remembering take place? In the brain? What, then, is there to do with all of those documented cases of organ transplants that transmitted vivid and detailed memories, and even radically different personalities, from the previous owner to the new one, to the great consternation of the medical establishment? And so a white racist befriends black people and begins listening to classical music after receiving a heart from a black man killed on his way to a violin lesson. Or a small child picks out the father of his donor in a crowd, runs up to him, and cries, "Daddy!" That sort of thing. Such medical facts are rich in religious implications. The scholar of medieval Christianity Barbara Newman has compared these modern medical cases to the medieval devotional theme of "exchanging hearts," a Christian understanding that locates the soul not in the head, but in the heart.[14]

5 *Soul-Breath* Another extremely common pattern is that the human spirit is connected to the breath. The English word *spirit*, for example, is derived from the Latin verb *spirare*, meaning "to breathe"—as is, by the way, the whole symbolic conception of "inspiration," which literally means "in-breath." So too with the ancient Hebrew *ruah*, the Sanskrit *atman*, the Greek *pneuma*, and the Arabic and Quranic *ruh*: all of these words refer to the act of breathing and are related to the soul one way or another.

The same symbolic complex is also assumed in all sorts of contemporary western customs, from the practice of saying "God bless you" when someone sneezes (the person's spirit-breath, after all, was just violently expelled, and so he or she is vulnerable to other spirits now, until the breath-soul can be recovered) to the American teenage custom of holding one's breath as one drives by cemeteries (where there is no breath). It is not difficult to see why this same physiological–symbolic complex is so common in world mythology. Ancient peoples, after all, repeatedly noticed a simple universal biological fact: when human beings die, they stop breathing. They drew the following conclusion: breath = life = spirit.

6 *Shade, Shadow, and Image* There are other symbolic complexes, of course, like that of the soul as shade, shadow, mirror reflection, or body image. We might invoke here the western horror trope of the vampire—a creature that is technically dead, casts no shadow, and does not appear in mirrors. The soul is often believed to possess a body, as we have already noted, which is seen in apparitions and dreams.

7 *The Soul as Female* Another common pattern is that the soul is female. We find this gender complex particularly in religious traditions that imagine God as male and the human being or the human community as his wife, bride, or lover. So in much of medieval Christianity, for example, the soul is female, even in grammatical gender (*anima*), and every soul, including every soul in a male body, is a woman in a relationship with God. Something very similar can be found in the Jewish tradition, where both the people of Israel and individual holy men have been imagined as God's bride since the prophetic period. The doctrine of the soul as a woman is especially strong in mystical forms of Islam, as Annemarie Schimmel has pointed out in a book entitled, appropriately enough, *My Soul Is a Woman*.[15] It can also be found in many forms of devotional Hinduism, particularly those traditions in which God is worshipped as Krishna and the human soul is understood to be his female lover.

8 *The Transhuman Soul* One common assumption of the nineteenth-century scholarship on religion

was that ideas of God evolved from ideas of soul, and that the earliest model of deity or soul was provided by **animism**. The name of this concept derives from the Latin word for soul (*anima*) and refers to the belief that all things, from people and animals to trees and rocks, contain souls or spiritual intelligences—that everything is in effect alive or animated. Another term for this worldview, this time from the Greek, is **panpsychism**, which literally means "soul (*psuchē*) [in] everything (*to pan*)." The Greek derivative is preferred these days to the Latin one, perhaps because it has been taken up by philosophers and does not seem to carry the negative baggage of animism, which was often used as a stand-in (or sweeping common denominator) for the beliefs of the "primitive" or the "savage" in the colonial era.

Whichever word one uses, the message is that *the soul is not simply human*. Animals often have souls and indeed function as "spirit helpers" or "power animals" of shamans, hunters, warriors, witches—and today pet owners. Similarly, plants are often said to have souls, particularly those that are ingested for their abilities to transport their human hosts into other dimensions, as we saw in Chapter 5. Even what we in the West normally think of as completely "dead" matter—rocks, mountains, waters—has been, and still is, experienced as fiercely alive by countless peoples. Sacred trees, for example, are treated as conscious agents in many forms of Hinduism to this day, as David Haberman has recently shown in great detail.[16] And this is before we even get to the subject of reincarnation, which assumes in most of its forms that the soul can take on different kinds of bodies, including non-human ones.

We might sum up all of this, then, by saying that the soul in the general history of religions is **transhuman**—that is, it extends "beyond" (Latin *trans*) the human species. This category goes back to the medieval Christian poet Dante, whom we met briefly above. When Dante wrote *Transhumanar significar per verba/Non si possia* ("It would not be possible to render in words the act of going beyond the human") in his *Divina Commedia* (Paradiso, Canto 1, lines 70–71), he probably implied that having a vision of the divine results in just such a process of "transhumanization" or "going beyond the human."

Soul Practices

The separable soul is not simply believed in as an abstract idea or doctrine. It is also practiced and, perhaps, even "made."

Prayer

One of the most common soul practices is prayer. One tends to find prayers in theistic traditions in which there is a clear notion of a separate and personal deity. In non-theistic traditions, like Buddhism, Jainism, or many forms of Hindu yoga, we are more likely to find another type of practice, **meditation**, which is not necessarily directed at any external deity (although it can be).

There are numerous forms of prayer. Among these are **petitionary prayer** (request for something to happen), **liturgical prayer** (communal praise or formal worship of a deity), and **contemplative prayer** (communing, often without words or images, with a deity or some ultimate state). A rich spectrum of phenomena are known to occur during prayer or around states of prayer. They usually involve one of two sensory systems: sight or hearing. The most common of these phenomena are visionary events or "seeing things" (which makes good sense, given the human brain's immense investment in sight). Less common are pleasant or "heavenly" smells, internal sensations of heat or "fire," and various paranormal phenomena (like the stigmata or poltergeist manifestations). Still others consist in what is traditionally known as **auditions**, that is, hearing a spirit or deity speak to one—in short, "hearing things."

The anthropologist T. M. Luhrmann has recently studied these audible events "when God talks back" among American Evangelical communities. She approaches belief and the practice of prayer as a learned technique of *paying attention*. As she puts it:

"the way you learn to pay attention determines your experience of God." Her project thus becomes a means of explaining how ordinary Americans come to believe what the skeptic considers to be absurd, namely that God cares about them, even speaks to them directly and personally. How? Luhrmann's triple thesis is that

> people learn specific ways of attending to their minds and their emotions to find evidence of God, and that both what they attend to and how they attend changes their experience of their minds, and that as a result, they begin to experience a real, external, interacting living presence. In effect, people train the mind in such a way that they experience part of their mind as the presence of God.[17]

In my own terms: "the human as two."

Part of this prayer practice involves hearing voices—really and truly. Such voices, it turns out, are much more common than is usually realized, and, contrary to popular assumptions, they seldom are symptoms of mental illness. Quite the contrary: unlike schizophrenic voices, which tend to be deeply threatening and demeaning, these religious auditions are often comforting and ultimately profoundly positive in their effects (although they are often very disconcerting at first). Such audible voices, Luhrmann reminds us, have also been known to inspire extremely successful professional careers (as in the case of the psychiatrist Oliver Sacks, who traces the beginnings of his own writing career to just such an event) and acts of great historical courage (as in the case of Martin Luther King, Jr.). Luhrmann is clear: "These practices work. They change people."[18]

None of this, of course, solves the problem of how we should interpret such voices. One could certainly read auditions theologically, that is, as a dialogue with God or some other external divine presence, which is how the Evangelical Christians read them (along with figures as diverse as Socrates, Muhammad, Joan of Arc, and William Blake). Or one can read prayer practices and auditions psychologically, that is, as a particularly common means of realizing

other forms of mind, which is how an author like Oliver Sacks would likely read them. In short, the phenomenon is one thing, the interpretation another. The important point is this: such voices *are* heard; they are real experiences; and they need to be taken seriously by the student of religion. We need to come to terms with people really and truly "hearing things."

Ancestor Worship or Veneration

As the early anthropologists suggested, there are some good ethnographic reasons for speculating—and this can only remain speculation—that the idea of deity emerged gradually from the idea of soul. One of these reasons is that **ancestor worship or veneration** is extremely common throughout human cultures, particularly in African and Chinese religions. People worship or venerate their dead, sometimes to appease them, sometimes to remain in contact with them, mostly, no doubt, simply because they miss them and this is the custom. In any case, the whole concept of community or family clearly extends beyond a single generation in these cultures.

Whether one "worships" or "venerates" the ancestors is, in the end, in the eye of the beholder and a particular worldview. Take Roman Catholicism, for example. The tradition has its own version of sacred ancestors, a "community of saints" that extends through every generation back to the original apostles or disciples of Jesus. Moreover, it remembers this community of saints at every mass and actively encourages the faithful to "venerate" them along with the Virgin Mary. The oft-repeated logic of this veneration and prayer is simple enough: Mary and the community of saints are now closer to God, and therefore they can pray for the living in an especially effective way. If the living can pray for one, why not also the dead—and even more the dead? The church forbids the faithful, however, from "worshipping" Mary and the saints. Such worship is proper only when directed to one of the persons of the Trinity. Distinctions aside, however, if one actually observes much of the Catholic piety directed toward the saints, and particularly toward the Virgin Mary, it is often not at all clear that this is not in actual practice "worship." The Protestant reformers certainly thought it was. They thought it was idolatry, and so they demoted Mary, broke the statues of the saints, and removed them from the churches.

I mention this bit of western history not in order to take sides, but simply to underline the fluidity and ambiguity of the categories of worship and veneration as these are commonly used in western scholarship on religion and—just as importantly—to call attention to some of the theological or religious assumptions behind yet another comparative category: ancestor worship/veneration. The two descriptions clearly go back to these Catholic–Protestant debates and do not reflect the anxieties of other cultures and religions, which commonly worship their ancestors much as they worship their deities. In short, they don't have a problem with this; the western Christian does.

The Medium

If ancestors are spirits that demand or deserve worship, sacrifice, and regular offerings, they are in effect active members of the community. Not surprisingly, they often make their presence felt, and in some fairly dramatic ways. In particular, they speak through individuals whom we generally call mediums: these are so named because such a person is functioning as the go-between or "**medium**" for this kind of spirit communication.

Spirit Possession

Spirits can possess individuals and speak through them in positive or negative ways. We call this pattern **spirit possession**, which is generally understood to be a particular cultural shaping of what looks like a nearly universal human capacity: trance. If **trance** is the ability to focus and to direct one's awareness in ways that block out most sensory input and in this way allow other forms of consciousness to manifest themselves, spirit possession is a particular shaping

and interpretation of the altered states of consciousness that manifest themselves in trance. Whatever it is, spirit possession is as common as water in the general history of religions. Ancestors do it. Deities do it. Intermediate beings do it. Even living religious prodigies—shamans, witches, wizards, and yogis—do it.

Spirit possession is clearly a soul practice, but it is also a social practice. Much of the scholarship around spirit possession has pointed out that not just anyone becomes possessed and not every community values possession. In general, communities that are being suppressed by imperial or colonial forces are especially porous to "possession," and individuals on the lower or lowest ends of the social spectrum—particularly the abused, women, and the socially marginalized (often the same people)—are the most usual objects of spirit possession. These patterns, for example, are quite obvious in nineteenth-century American spiritualism, where mediums tended to be women (that is, individuals without a voice or authority in the churches) and where female mediums were advancing the most progressive social agendas of their time (or ours, for that matter) around topics like gender, sexuality, and the comparison of religions.

Channeling

We might mention here the modern phenomenon of **channeling**, through which a particular person communicates or "channels" a new text or scripture that functions to guide a community of readers in its spiritual development. The word is modern, but the phenomenon is not. The romantic poet William Blake, for example, claimed that he received inspired lines of poetry from immediate dictation—twelve, or twenty, or thirty lines at a time. He simply wrote down what he heard. Similar ideas are encoded in the very ancient Hindu notion of sacred scripture as *shruti*: revealed truths that were "heard" by the ancient sages from a divine, non-human source.

As a recent example, consider the New Age classic *A Course in Miracles* (1975). The *Course* was channeled from 1965 to 1972 through a reluctant New York Jewish atheistic psychologist by the name of Helen Shucman, who was encouraged by another psychologist, her colleague Bill Thetford, to accept and transcribe the material. Both Shucman and Thetford were professors of medical psychology at Columbia University's College of Physicians and Surgeons. The text was then edited by a third psychologist, Kenneth Wapnick. The *Course* itself—the product of, please note, three PhDs—is a creative combination of numerous streams of influence, including Christian mysticism, psychoanalysis, and Neoplatonism. The channeled text's origins can be traced back to Shucman being overwhelmed by a series of highly symbolic dreams and finally submitting to a kind of inner-directed source that she came to call "the Voice." (When she did not give expression to "the Voice," she would get sick or could not sleep.) One of the most interesting aspects of this particular instance was Shucman's own personal reaction to the revelations. As she once put it to a friend: "I know the Course is true, Bill, but I don't believe it."[19] Bill felt something similar: "I always thought that a Higher Authority must have goofed in selecting Helen and me for this assignment."[20] And yet Helen was very proud of what had come through her; and Bill, who was originally agnostic about the material, did come to believe in the *Course*. Both forms of ambivalence and belief are perfect examples of what we have called "the human as two." A person can doubt and believe at the same time, not because she or he is confused or inconsistent, but because she or he is two.

Channeling phenomena continue into the present, as can be seen in a figure like the American channeler Paul Selig, whose work has been featured on television, in film, and in two contemporary pieces of channeled literature, both witnessed by literary critic Victoria Nelson: *I Am the Word* (2010) and *The Book of Love and Creation* (2012). I have personally witnessed Selig work on a number of occasions and have also helped film him for a feature documentary. He "tunes into" the living, not the dead. He demonstrates both **clairvoyance** (the ability to see things at

a distance) and **clairaudience** (the ability to hear voices speaking to a particular issue at hand), as well as a most remarkable ability to take on the physical characteristics of the person he is "reading"—for example, the unique facial expressions of one of my family members or, in the case of one of *The UneXplained* television episodes, the jerky muscular movements of a child with cerebral palsy, neither of whom he knew or had seen before the reading.[21] It is easy to dismiss such things when you have not personally witnessed them. It is not so easy once you have.

Comparative Corpses

Finally—perhaps most importantly, and certainly most commonly—there are funerary practices, that is, cultural rituals designed to deal with the dead body and to process the inevitable traumas in the community that a death effects.

Probably the most spectacular examples here come from ancient Egypt, which invested unimaginable resources into building the pyramids: these were understood to be immense machines, staircases, or eternal abodes for securing the immortality of the pharaoh and his family. The sheer size and the small number of these architectural feats speak volumes about the earliest Egyptian attitudes toward the afterlife: it was for royalty—and for royalty alone. It was also "up." Hence one of the most common images of immortality was the transformation into a bird or bird soul, for example a falcon, an ibis, a heron, or a vulture. Gradually, as the Old Kingdom gave way to the Middle Kingdom, these beliefs "democratized" until the nobles first, then even the common people could enjoy some kind of postmortem existence.

The answers were very different in Asia. In Indian religious complexes like Hinduism, Buddhism, and Jainism, for example, where bodies are understood to be temporary forms that a reincarnating soul (or, in Buddhism, a pseudo-soul) puts on and takes off as it would a set of clothes, cremating corpses has been a common and sensible means of handling dead bodies for millennia. The clothes, after all, are no longer needed. There are obvious practical benefits here as well, like the effective prevention of the spread of disease and the preservation of land for other uses.

Cremation, on the other hand, has been quite controversial in the Christian West, largely due to the doctrine of the resurrection and the consequent belief that the body itself will share in the world to come. The body has generally been buried in Christian communities, since it is believed that this same body will some day rise in a glorified form. The Jewish and Islamic views are similar. There is a widespread consensus that resurrection is about the soul and the body in equal measure, that the dead will rise from their graves, and that their bodies will be reconstructed by the power of God. Cremation is explicitly forbidden in both religious systems.

The comparative point is a simple one: how a community handles its dead is a reflection of what it thinks about the soul, the body, salvation, and the afterlife. Different beliefs lead to different funerary practices.

Traumatic Technologies of the Soul

There are also "technologies of the soul," as we might call them: by this we mean both practiced techniques and spontaneous, uncontrollable life experiences as a result of which the innermost subject of the person is "split off" from the social ego and felt, on its own plane, as something self-existent and hyper-real.

As it turns out, in many of the most dramatic cases the soul is realized through intense human suffering, crisis, danger, illness, excruciating pain, disaster, or near-death. Such a pattern goes back to the very beginning: religion itself has been laced with the themes of death, sacrifice, and rebirth from as far back as we can see. In the twentieth century, particularly after the post-traumatic sufferings witnessed by medical professionals in the two world wars, we became more and more aware of the effects that intense suffering has on the human psyche and of the

manner in which the latter tends to "split" or dissociate in order to survive otherwise unendurable circumstances.

It was not long before similar models were being used to understand intense religious states. Already back in *The Perennial Philosophy* (1945), Aldous Huxley had employed a telling chemical metaphor that we might recognize as an early traumatic model for accessing the soul:

> Nothing in our everyday experience gives us any reason for supposing that water is made up of hydrogen and oxygen; and yet when we subject water to certain rather drastic treatments, the nature of its constituent elements becomes manifest. Similarly, nothing in our everyday experience gives us much reason for supposing that the mind of the average sensual man has, as one of its constituents, something resembling, or identical with, the Reality substantial to the manifold world; and yet, when that mind is subjected to drastic treatments, the divine element, of which it is in part at least composed, becomes manifest ...[22]

We could make the point even more contemporary. Nothing in our everyday experience gives us any reason to suppose that matter is not material, that it is made up of bizarre forms of energy that violate, very much like spirit, all of our normal notions of space, time, and causality. Yet, when we subject matter to certain drastic treatments, like the Hadron Collider near Geneva, Switzerland, we can see quite clearly that matter is not material at all. But—and this is the key—we can only get there through a great deal of physical violence, a violence so extreme and so precise that it cost billions of dollars and decades of preparation to inflict and then analyze it.

Is this part of the answer to our opening question about why most religious people do not and cannot experience those "events which lie outside the possibility of general or even rare experiences" of which Nietzsche wrote? We now have one possible answer to this original question: they have not been split into two.

Yet.

Doing Nothing

There is certainly nothing that the ego or social self, much less the laboratory scientist (who, after all, is just such a social ego), can do to cause the soul to appear, since, if we are to believe the traditions, it is *precisely* that social self—the ego—that is veiling the soul in the first place. The more the ego does, the stronger it gets, and so the less likely it is that soul will become manifest. We are in a kind of catch-22 here.

Ironically, then, one of the oldest techniques to make the soul manifest itself beyond the self is to do *nothing*. Jainism is probably the most instructive example here again. The tradition's all-out assault on *karma*—that is, on action of any sort, as a quasi-physical covering of pure spirit—works from exactly this kind of logic. And so does the classical definition of yoga in Patanjali's *Yoga-Sutras* (*Aphorisms on Yoga*). The first aphorism reads: "Yoga is the stopping of mental currents." In other words the practice of yoga is the practice of stopping all mental function, including, of course, the function of the ego.

One wonders if a similar psychological suppression is involved in the Protestant framing of the doctrine of grace, that is, in the notion that there is absolutely nothing the person (read: the ego) can do to be saved, because salvation is a gift and not something to be earned or won. Once again, nothing can be done to "earn" or "cause" the desired religious state.

Nothing.

Sacred Pain

People try anyway, and sometimes they succeed. One way they try is through self-inflicted pain and suffering. A sixteenth-century Christian saint by the name of Maria Maddalena wore a corset studded with nails, because she believed that the consequent pain would bring her closer to Christ. Hindu pilgrims walk barefoot, with cut and blistered feet, across rocky terrains in excruciatingly hot climates in order to instigate their loving union with the Lord. Some Native American communities participate in a ritual called the Sun Dance, in which men have their chests pierced with sticks or eagle claws that are fastened by a rope to a post from which they must break free by tearing their own flesh. A similar kind of "hook-swinging," often in a public procession, is practiced in Sri Lanka as a means to commune with a deity. The lives of shamans and famous saints are filled with severe "initiatory illnesses" and various forms of abuse, which often function as the origins of their calling and spiritual transformation. Modern alien abduction phenomena are often correlated with histories of earlier trauma, be these of a physical, emotional, or sexual nature. And on and on we could go, for a *very* long time.

The indubitable truth is that human beings have endured and/or sought out pain for the sake of higher religious aims for millennia. From the modern biomedical perspective, this is a bit odd, to say the least. For most modern people, pain lacks value. The biomedical tradition's definition of pain reflects this sentiment: pain is an unpleasant physiological sensation related to tissue damage. Pain is something to take away or remove. It is *bad*.

This is clearly not the whole story, though. For one thing, for most of human history, pain was unavoidable (imagine going, just a few years ago, to a "dentist" wielding a hammer, a pair of pliers, and a bottle of whiskey). Suffering had to be dealt with. It could not be medicated away. But there is more. Different authors, mostly from anthropology and the comparative study of religion, have demonstrated that pain is not only physiological. It is also a cognitive and social event: pain is shaped and conditioned by a person's social context, and it is often "put to work."

As a simple example, imagine two people without food and water from dawn to dusk. A prisoner who is punished in this way will likely experience this lack as a privation, as an undesired and undeserved torture. A pious Muslim, on the other hand, who is celebrating the sacred month of Ramadan and fasting for religious reasons, will likely experience the same lack in positive ways.

Many forms of sacred pain are much more extreme, of course. And these in particular can have radical effects on what Ariel Glucklich calls the "body-self template," that is, one's sense of being a physical self.[23] Pain can powerfully disrupt the homeostasis of the body-self and consequently transform consciousness. Pain, then, need not be a simple negation of the body-self but the means of producing a *different* one. Pain can become a technology of the soul. We can thus well understand why religious individuals might value and cultivate pain: they want *to be changed*.

The Traumatic Secret

Extreme states of the soul and salvation generally only appear in a human life once or twice, if they ever appear at all. This is a psychospiritual fact of immense significance for the study of religion and its various present debates. I call this fact the "traumatic secret."

I call it a "secret" for two reasons. I do so in order to draw attention, first, to the rarity or special nature of states of transcendence triggered by trauma, and, second, to the ways in which trauma can function as a kind of master-key to the general history of religions—a key that can serve as an answer to one common question: "Why do some individuals experience extreme religious states and consider them the summation and goal of all human life, while others are left utterly cold by such claims and never know such special events?" The answer is that the former have experienced sufficient trauma and the latter have not. Trauma is the key. Trauma is the secret. Trauma is the technology of soul. Even the resurrected body of Jesus, as described in the Gospel of John, displays the clear signs of trauma and traumatic memory: holes.

The traumatic secret, please note, does not simply explain the presence of faith and belief. It *also* explains the presence of indifference and disbelief. It does not just explain why so-and-so knew God after a severe illness or grasped the immortality of the soul in a car accident. It explains why so-and-so did not (and may be just fine with that, illnesses and car accidents being what they are). Moreover, and perhaps most helpfully of all, the traumatic secret humanizes the believer and the unbeliever alike. We can now

easily see that both types of responses are operating out of their own honesty and integrity.

A strong word of warning. We must not romanticize trauma. Trauma is awful. Trauma does *not* automatically produce a religious experience. Indeed it probably seldom does. Much more often trauma simply destroys, maims, and mangles us. Trauma, we might more safely speculate, is sometimes a *necessary* but never a *sufficient condition* for an experience of transcendence or salvation; in other words it does not automatically cause such an experience. Sometimes, for reasons we do not understand, trauma cracks an individual open and reveals what the psychotherapist Janet Elizabeth Colli has called "the dark face of heaven"—yet another version of the sacred as allure and terror. Colli arrived at such a conclusion through her suffering patients and through what she describes as their "true stories of transcendence through trauma."[24] The latter phrase could well function as a one-line description of the general history of religions.

Comparative Eschatologies

And, finally, we arrive at the end of all things. Most religions have some views about how it will all end. We call a religious model of the last things an **eschatology**, literally a "doctrine" (*logos*) about "last things" (*to eschaton, eschata*).

Recall that we began our comparative chapters with a discussion of myth, especially the creation type of myth. If creation myths or cosmogonies are about the beginning of the story, eschatologies are about its end. The end is not just an end, then. It is also the *culmination* or *purpose* of the entire religious narrative. It is where the story is headed, what it is all ultimately about. It is where the sacred breaks into cosmic history, definitively and dramatically, and changes everything. We might think of the end of all things, then, as a state salvation writ large, and often on a cosmic scale. There are many things that could be said about eschatologies, but just three will have to suffice.

The Line and the Circle

The first thing that can be said with some measure of certainty is that a religion's model of the end of the world (what we might call its cosmic eschatology) tends to look more than a little like its model of the end of a human being and of the state of salvation (what we might call its personal eschatology), and vice versa. We see this relationship between the end of the person and the end of the cosmos in an especially striking fashion if we take the world religions and separate them very roughly into two camps, as "western" and "Asian."

Much too simply (but quite instructively), the western monotheistic religions work with a one-shot, linear view of the cosmos and the human being. The human being is created by God, is born once, lives once, and dies once. Everything depends on that single life; everything is "judged" on that one-shot chance. So too with the universe. It was created by God at a single point in time. God now guides its history, and some day it will all come to an end. There is only one universe, one temporal stream, one end. We might think of this as the modal western "line model."

The modal Asian model works differently. The soul here has known countless births and deaths in innumerable bodies of all sorts, and it will know countless more births and bodies before it achieves salvation, enlightenment, or release from the cycle of births and deaths. The soul does not have only one chance in this cosmology; it has countless chances. Indeed, apparently, it has as many as it needs. So too with the universe. In a religion like Hinduism, the cosmos is not created once. It is created over and over again, in an endless cycle of creation, preservation, and destruction. The cyclical life of the cosmos, moreover, mirrors the cyclical life of the soul. We might think of all this as the Asian "circle model."

There are complexities here, of course. We do sometimes find cyclical models in the West. Reincarnation, for example, was a relatively common belief in ancient Greece, as it was in some forms of Jewish Kabbalah, which taught reincarnation (known as *gilgul*) at different points. It should also be noted that there are Asian religions, like many schools of Buddhism, that refuse to address questions like the origin or end of the universe altogether, mostly because they consider them to be unanswerable and a huge waste of precious time, which could be better spent on the removal of the self and of suffering.

Eschatological Violence

The second thing to note with respect to eschatologies is that they tend to come with a great deal of violence. Part of this is logical: as with transgression, in order to create something new, one must destroy the old. Part of it is psychological: eschatology is the traumatic secret writ large—a violent in-breaking of the transcendent into space and time through the cracks of suffering and disaster. Hence the word **apocalypse**, which refers to an "uncovering," that is, a final revealing of a secret, here of a cosmic nature. Finally, part of this violent logic is social and historical. Eschatologies often find their origins in persecuted or even paranoid communities, whose persecution leads to a narrative of revenge.

The case of the Christian apocalypse as it is laid out in the New Testament book of Revelation is particularly instructive here. The strong scholarly consensus is that this text was written during the Roman persecutions of the Christian communities in the last decade of the first century CE, as a means to give these suffering communities hope. Part of this hope involved imagining the Roman persecutors dying grisly deaths by sword and fire. Certainly much of the highly symbolic language of the text consists, in its origins at least, of coded expressions about Roman persecution and the Roman Emperors Nero and Domitian. The famous "666" is the name "Nero" with each letter given a numerical value according to Hebrew letter magic and added up; the seven-headed dragon is Rome with its famous seven hills; the exploding mountain is the volcanic Mount Vesuvius, which really did explode in 79 CE; and so on.

Another aspect of this hope giving involved, however, imagining that fellow Christians whose views and practices the author violently opposed perished alongside the despised Roman persecutors. In one recent scholarly reading of Revelation, these inimical Christians seem to be the ones who followed Paul and hence were not obeying the full Torah regulations; they were indeed bringing impure gentiles into the pure Jewish fold. In short, Revelation may have well been aimed precisely at the churches and teachings that would become "Christianity."[25] An ironic conclusion, to be sure.

Revelation was the very last book to be included in the New Testament canon, probably because it was so controversial. Not a few bishops in the second century wanted it condemned as blasphemous (they may well have known that it was aimed at them). Since its inclusion in the canon in the late fourth century (all the other books of the New Testament were more or less set two hundred years before this), this same book has taken on all sorts of other lives and helped end even more. The book, after all, advances a most violent logic, which involves the demonization of the outgroup or enemy, the sanctification of revenge as an act of God, and the conviction that history must end in spectacular violence.

The Christian apocalypse is hardly unique here. Many of the contemporary Islamist terrorist campaigns have been linked to similar apocalyptic visions of violence toward an outgroup, in this case the West, the infidel, the wrong kind of Muslim, and the nonbeliever. Suicide bombings, moreover, have been ritually constructed, and no doubt experienced, as pious acts of martyrdom. Historically speaking, the "**martyr**" is an ancient Christian concept that refers to an individual whose persecution or death gives "witness" to the truth of his or her faith. Another kind of violent religious end.

Comparative Practice: Re-Death, Near-Death, and After-Death Experiences

There is something very interesting about mythologies of the end, something that may well set them apart from other types of myth. As Gregory Shushan has suggested, mythologies surrounding death and the afterlife are unusually similar across cultural and temporal

boundaries in ways that other types of mythologies are not. This, he suggests, is because mythologies of the end are "correlates" (which is not to say literal descriptions) of actual human experiences of death, whereas mythologies of the beginning can only be speculative.[26] This makes some simple sense: everyone everywhere dies, but no human being was present at the Big Bang.

What is it like to die? One might imagine that such a question is impossible to answer, since no one returns from the dead. This is a very modern assumption, however, and one flatly denied by most of the religious traditions on the planet. Moreover, we now possess two immense bodies of modern literature that pose the same kind of challenge to this modern assumption, namely those organized around the **near-death experience (NDE)** and around **cases of the reincarnation type (CORT)**. The expression "near-death experience" was coined by Dr. Raymond Moody (who also had a PhD in philosophy) while he was still a medical student; it was intended to describe the reported experiences of individuals who entered the death process but were brought back, usually through advanced medical technologies. The second expression was coined by the late University of Virginia psychiatrist Dr. Ian Stevenson and applies to individuals, usually young children, who claim to remember previous lives, often in incredible detail, which can subsequently be confirmed or plausibly supported.

For our final comparative practice, we will treat a few examples of traditional religious literature around the death process as our A, the modern NDE and CORT literatures as our B, and that undeniable universal—the event of physical death—as our C.

The Traditional Literature

Mythologies around the world are filled with humans, heroes, and deities journeying to and returning from the land of the dead. Moreover, the Asian concept of reincarnation or rebirth—one of whose earliest appearances in Indian Sanskrit literature (as the compound *punar-mrityu*) really means "re-death" or "repeated death"—*requires* a return from the dead, if it is to make any sense at all. It is difficult, however, to on actual experiences, perhaps passed on orally and fashioned into folklore and eventually into religious doctrines (see Figure 9.2). Two examples are worth examining to demonstrate this possibility.

The Story of Er   The first example of a western piece of ancient literature that appears to reflect an actual near-death experience is Plato's retelling of the story of a warrior named Er in the tenth book of *The Republic*, a text written in the fourth century BCE, that is, twenty-four hundred years ago.

Er was a warrior apparently killed on the battle-field. As Plato's Socrates recounts the story, Er's body is dumped into a pile of rotting corpses ten days after the battle. Two days later, the bodies are about to be burnt on the pyre when Er revives and tells a remarkable story. His story is described as a journey—a kind of travel as transformation again. If this was a journey, though, it was one with a purpose: he was told to observe everything so that he could teach humanity about the afterlife.

And so Er explains how, in the company of very numerous souls, he encountered two passageways in the ground. He saw how just souls turned "right" and "upward" and unjust souls turned "left" and "down-ward." He was then shown the mechanisms that determine the soul's next birth into human or animal form. This amounted to a Greek version of *karma*, the soul's previous life determining the bodily form of its bearer's next life. After the souls have chosen their lots, they are led to the Plain of Oblivion and made to drink from the River of Forgetfulness. Er was not allowed to drink from these waters, no doubt so that he could remember. He was then somehow—he did not know how—returned to his body.

The first near-death experience recorded in west-ern literature, then, is a reincarnation story in which we encounter a number of standard themes. A judg-ment scene is said to follow death. Right/left and up/down are coded as good/bad. Other religious themes are not stated, but they are implicit. We might gather from the story, for example, that some animals have souls, and that the soul cannot be equated with the character of a particular lifecycle: after all, the soul

Figure 9.2   Apparent "Near-Death Tunnel": detail from *Ascent in the Empyrean* (fifteenth century), by Hieronymus Bosch. © Marco Secchi/Corbis.

glean individual experiences from these ancient liter-atures, since pre-modern peoples did not generally write about themselves. Regardless, it seems reason-able to speculate that some of these texts were based changes these surface identities with every new birth. Plato is not content with such implicit lessons, though. He wants to make it plain what the moral of the story is: that the soul is immortal, and that it should strive to live righteously and well, so that it may fare well on its long journey through life after life.

Er's story is usually framed in discussions of ancient philosophy as the "myth of Er," with the assumption that it is a fanciful tale without basis in actual history. That assumption is a questionable one, since we now possess very similar stories that can be traced back to historical individuals. The University of Texas M. D. Anderson Cancer Center critical care nurse Debbie James, for example, once related to a class of mine the story of a Vietnam veteran who was taken for dead on the battlefield, thrown in a pile of dead bodies on the rescue helicopter, and only much later, now back on base, "came back" from a near-death experience—in essence, a modern version of the "myth of Er."[27]

Recognizing the Mind of Clear Light   The Tibetan Book of the Dead (1927) was one of those popular texts that helped Buddhism establish itself in the West and eventually "win" the counterculture. It is a dramatic text filled with elaborate visions and striking claims about the ultimate nature of mind. On the surface at least, the book presents itself as a text to be read to a departed soul as it hovers around the corpse after death in what the Tibetans call the *bardo*, that is, the "intermediate realm" between one life and another. Essentially these are instructions to the discarnate soul about what it will see and how not to be fooled by these visions, be they blissful or terrifying (the double sacred again).

All of these visions, the text teaches, are projections or manifestations of a deeper and immeasurably more wondrous reality—the "mind of clear light." The secret is to not be tricked, *not* to believe what one sees, but rather to use the traumatic opportunity that is physical death to realize one's own Buddhahood. What decades of meditation or moral effort cannot do—take away the ego—death can do literally in a heartbeat. This is *the* moment, the great opportunity. If one takes it and realizes the mind of clear light, one is free, one is enlightened, one becomes a Buddha. If

one misses this opportunity and does not realize this truth, one will enter another "womb door" and will be born again into the cycle of births and deaths, according to one's *karma* and previous choices.

In a wonderful recent "biography" of the text, Donald Lopez begins by explaining that *The Tibetan Book of the Dead* "is not really Tibetan, it is not really a book, and it is not really about death."[28] What he means by this humorous one-liner is that this modern classic of spiritual literature is far more popular in the West than it ever has been in Tibet; that it was put together and edited from a series of original woodblocks that its American promoter and editor, a scholar named Evans Wentz, purchased in Darjeeling, north India, in 1919; and that, although parts of it were traditionally used for funerary purposes, much of it was originally intended for advanced Tantric initiates who used it to re-live the death process as a means of realizing the mind of clear light while still alive.

Lopez also points out that the text is part of a larger genre of literature in Tibet known as *terma* ("treasure texts"). Treasure texts are traditionally associated with a partly historical, largely mythical figure named Padmasambhava, a Tantric master who is believed to have helped bring Buddhism to Tibet in the eighth century. A treasure text is what Lopez calls a "time-release revelation," that is, a Buddhist scripture that was hidden by Padmasambhava for future discovery by his initiated disciples. Lopez lays out some of the textual and sexual complexities this way:

> Knowing that his teachings would be needed in the distant future, he [Padmasambhava] dictated books to his consort and scribe (the queen of Tibet) and buried them—sometimes in a cave, sometimes in a lake, sometimes in a pillar, sometimes in the heart of a disciple yet unborn—to await discovery when the time was ripe for their contents to be revealed to the world.
>
> The revealers of treasure are regarded as the reincarnations of Padmasambhava's own disciples, students to whom he had personally bestowed tantric initiation. In order to find the treasure, it was said to be necessary for the reincarnated student to manifest the mind of clear light … The mind of clear light manifests at death, but it also manifests during orgasm. The discovery of treasure

is therefore often preceded by the practice of sexual yoga with a consort.[29]

There are many features of *The Tibetan Book of the Dead* that capture the comparative reader's attention: from the intimate connection this literature makes between sexual ecstasy and textual inspiration; through the historical fact that the American spiritualist tradition that so deeply influenced Evans Wentz began in 1848 in Hydesville, New York, just ten miles or so from where a man named Joseph Smith had just dug up another kind of treasure text in a hillside, *The Book of Mormon*; to the uncanny fact that revealers of treasure texts in Tibet normally have "Ling" as part of their name, and Evans Wentz was born in 1878 as "Walter Yeeling Wentz."[30]

As Charles Fort used to say, that is just a bit too much.

But, for our own purposes here, the real take-away is the central psychological point that the text itself makes: that the visions of heavens and hells witnessed by the soul in the *bardo* should not be believed, should not be taken literally. Rather they should be "worked through" or "seen through," as we say in modern parlance, until one realizes them as projections of the projector—the mind of clear light.

The NDE Literature

Now our B: the modern NDE and CORT literatures. The beginning of the near-death literature can be dated to 1975, when Raymond Moody published his best-selling *Life after Life* and brought the expression "near-death experience" into broad public use. In a chapter entitled "Parallels," Moody not only discusses the story of Er, but also notes "a striking similarity between the account in this ancient manuscript and the events which have been related to me by twentieth-century Americans."[31] In short, the NDE literature begins on a strong comparative note.

This literature has grown increasingly rich and sophisticated over the years, as individuals have described thousands of near-death experiences. The power of these modern NDE accounts is quite impossible to appreciate without an example. Anita Moorjani's *Dying to Be Me* (2012) will serve us well here. The book

tells the story of Moorjani's upbringing in Hong Kong, advanced cancer, near-death, and what can only be called a miraculous healing through a transcendent loving presence and energy influx during a coma. The book is really about still more than this, though. It is very much a model example of comparison, as it functions as a robust critique of religious identity and conservative gender roles.

The book begins with a comparative crisis. Moorjani grew up in Hong Kong in an Indian home, where she was educated in a British Catholic school run by nuns. She grew up, that is, in three different religious cultures, among what she calls "distinct and often contradictory beliefs" that "shaped me and fostered the fears that turned out to manifest in disease."[32] These fearful shapings manifested themselves in three primary forms: as painful gender inequity in her home, where she felt inferior as a girl ("gender inequality is rife in my culture"); as dogmatic religious beliefs in the Catholic school, which would send her to hell for all eternity for not holding the right religious creed; and as racism in many of her blue-eyed blond classmates at a subsequent English school, who made fun of her darker skin.

Other cultural contradictions were also painfully apparent to her young mind, for example the different purity codes of Indian and Chinese culture. She noticed that foods held to be profoundly impure and polluting in her Indian culture (like pork and beef) were considered pure and healthy in Chinese culture. At one point in her story she relates how she effectively ended a prospective arranged marriage simply by innocently ordering a tuna sandwich at a restaurant. Food separates.

In the spring of 2002 Moorjani learned that she had Hodgkins lymphoma. Four years passed as the cancer spread until she could no longer hold her head up. Her body was now emaciated from months of not being able to absorb any food. On the morning of February 2, 2006, she could not even open her eyes. Her face and body were horribly swollen. Her husband took her to the doctor, who immediately had her rushed to the hospital. She was now in a coma.

Oddly, Moorjani felt fantastic. She could not understand why her family was so upset. For one thing, new kinds of extraordinary abilities kicked in.

I wasn't using my five biological senses, yet I was keenly taking everything in, much more so than if I'd been using my physical organs. It was though another, completely different type of perception kicked in, and more than just *perceive*, I seemed to also encompass everything that was happening, as though I was slowly merging with it all.[33]

A kind of telepathic link was set up between Moorjani and those rushing and worrying around her in the hospital. She now knew what they were thinking and feeling, even if they were not in the room.

She also felt no attachment to her body. "It didn't feel as though it were mine. It looked far too small and insignificant to have housed what I was experiencing. I felt free, liberated, and magnificent." *Magnificent.* That is the word she comes back to again and again. Part of this magnificence was the fact that space and time ceased to have much meaning. She became aware "that I was able to be anywhere at any time … It was as though I were no longer restricted by the confines of space and time." She expanded further and further, becoming everyone and everything, until her emotional attachments dropped away and she felt what she describes as "superb and glorious unconditional love" surrounding her. In a single word (one deeply embedded in her own Indian culture), she had "awakened."[34]

Not only did she realize the human is two. She also realized that *time is two.* In that other realm, Moorjani describes how she felt "all moments at once." She felt everything that involved her in the past, present, and future as one moment, as spread out as a single space–time sheet, as it were. Time does not move, she now realized. *We* move through time. She also sensed the presence of multiple lives, but a past life did not feel like it was actually in the past. It was all happening in the present, in the eternal now.

This experience caused her to reflect philosophically on the nature of time and how it appears to be created by our brains and senses. "It's as though our earthly minds convert what happens around us into a sequence; but in actuality, when we're not expressing through our bodies, everything occurs simultaneously, whether past, present, or future." Our senses,

she speculates, focus on a single point in time and space, but this is not how reality actually *is*. Time does not move, unless we are using "the filter of our physical bodies and minds."[35]

Through this experience of time as two, Moorjani concluded that the reincarnation model she had grown up with was not finally supported by her NDE. It was not completely wrong, but it was not completely correct either. She concluded that there really is no sequential or linear soul reincarnating through life after life. Rather "the concept of reincarnation is really just an interpretation, a way for our intellect to make sense of all existence happening at once." When someone "remembers" a past life, then, she is not really remembering a past life but a parallel or simultaneous one, since "all time exists at once."[36]

Then she realized something even more fantastic, namely that "God isn't a *being*, but a *state of being … and I was now that state of being!*" This was a most extreme realization of the human as two:

In that state of clarity, I also realized that I'm not who I'd always thought I was: *Here I am without my body, race, culture, religion, or beliefs … yet I continue to exist! Then what am I? Who am I? I certainly don't feel reduced or smaller in any way. On the contrary, I haven't ever been this huge, this powerful, or this all-encompassing.*

And then she uses a most traditional word: "I felt eternal, as if I'd always existed and always would without beginning or end."[37] In our own language, the *eschaton* had really and truly arrived. History, as a linear series of events, was effectively relativized or "ended."

Such an ending, of course, had profound consequences on how Moorjani subsequently understood culture and religion. She now saw them as the comparativist sees them: as a relative and anxiously policed set of codes and beliefs. But she saw something else: she saw them as a relative set of codes and beliefs, whose conflicting messages and gross gender inequities had literally made her sick. All of those hells and judgments, she recognized now are simply projections of our own fears and our own very human sense of revenge.[38] Her

NDE, on the other hand, was "a state of pure awareness, which is a state of complete suspension of all previously held doctrine and dogma." It was in turn this suspension that allowed her physical body "to 'reset' itself."[39]

Ironically, it was an *absence* of belief that was required for her healing.

Now that she knew who she really was, an "infinite self" or a "universal energy," she could return to her body and heal it, in days. Her emaciated body, the lemon-size tumors, the huge skin lesions, so serious that reconstructive surgery had been planned—all of this began to heal immediately, and at a fantastic rate. She went home five weeks after entering the hospital. The doctors were stunned.

The CORT Literature

There is another type of modern literature around death that is equally rich for the serious comparativist, although it is not cited as much as the NDE literature: the CORT literature. CORTs, "cases of the reincarnation type," display the phenomenon of children remembering previous lives, often regardless of the cultural context. The nonlocal self again.

These cases were originally collected by Ian Stevenson. Over the course of his professional career, Stevenson churned out hundreds of elaborate case studies of past life memories, particularly in Hindu and Buddhist South and East Asia (India, Sri Lanka, Thailand, and Burma), Shiite Lebanon and Turkey, West Africa, and Northwest America. As of 1997, Stevenson had collected 2,600 reported cases of past life memories and had published 65 detailed reports on individual cases, including a massive and eerily suggestive study of 225 cases of what he calls "the biology of reincarnation," that is, the phenomenon of birth marks or birth defects as physical "marks" from a previous life's violent ending by knife, rope, or bullet wound.[40] This particular comparative study runs to over 2,300 pages.

Through his entire database (still being coded, organized, and analyzed by his colleagues), Stevenson isolated what he calls "four universal features" found in every cultural complex that he studied, including in Europe. These are:

> an early age (usually between 2 and 4 years) of a subject's first speaking about a previous life; a slightly older age (usually between 5 and 7 years) when the subject stopped speaking spontaneously about a previous life; a high incidence of violent death in the previous life; and frequent mention of the mode of death in the child's statements.[41]

Interestingly, the gender of the previous life also tends to be male, probably because males are much more likely to die violently than females in most cultures.

It is worth noting that the CORT literature has been taken very seriously by professional skeptics, such as Carl Sagan and Sam Harris, and has been positively reviewed in such weighty venues as the *Journal of the American Medical Association* and the *Journal of Nervous and Mental Disease.*

Comparative Reflections

There are many things to say here from both a historical and a comparative perspective.

The first thing to note is the central role that modern technology is playing in the production of NDE experiences. It is now possible, after all, to "bring back" individuals from much more advanced stages of dying. At no point in human history could so many individuals have gone so far into the death process and return. This is no doubt one reason why we have seen an explosion of near-death visionary accounts in the modern period—we now *can*. What we are witnessing is a kind of technologically aided vision quest.

The second thing to note is that the near-death phenomenon has long been linked to Asia and reincarnation. From the very first story in western literature (the story of Er) to the close linkage today between the NDE and CORT research communities, this is an especially telling pattern. Put differently, the near-death experience has always been a comparative category.

The third thing to note is that NDE events display near-universal features (like supernatural environs, deceased humans, or beings of light), but also real cultural differences. Western NDE events, for example, often (but not always) assume a one-life model, whereas an NDE like that of Moorjani engages directly and critically a reincarnation model. Of particular note is the apparent pattern in which the famous "life review" or "panoramic memory" is not generally present in NDE events within hunter–gatherer or tribal societies (the data here are drawn from Guam, Native America, Aboriginal Australia, Africa, and Maori New Zealand), although it is present in accounts from the USA, Europe, India, China, Thailand, and Tibet. This makes some sense if we posit, with a number of philosophers and anthropologists, that the "self" or "individual" as a stable biographical entity with a particular life story is a relatively recent phenomenon in the history of human civilization and is by no means a cultural universal.[42]

Fourth, it is important to note that, like all religious experiences, near-death experiences are seldom "innocent" or neutral with respect to their religious implications. Quite the contrary: they are commonly put to work within various cultural and religious projects. Sometimes these projects are Mormon in accent, as in Betty J. Eadie's *Embraced by the Light* (1992). Sometimes they are Christian and Evangelical in tone, as in the affirmation of the reality of hell in Maurice Rawlings' *To Hell and Back* (1993). Mostly, though, they have been broadly inclusive in both tone and project. At least here, the judging God and the certainties of dogmatic religion have been effectively replaced by the formless loving Light of the modern NDE.

Given this general project, it should not surprise us that the presence and the percentage of "negative" or "hellish" NDEs have been a particular bone of contention. Researchers have long insisted that negative NDEs are quite rare (Moody, for example, includes none in his original book), while more recently others have observed that negative NDEs are more common than is usually recognized, although these phenomena can be interpreted in various ways (for example, as incomplete NDE events, as symbolic expressions of the death of the ego, and as expressions of the paradoxical structure of ultimate reality as positive *and* negative—the sacred

again).[43] There is also the real question of whether we have so few negative NDE reports because people are simply too afraid or too embarrassed to report them.

The religious implications of NDE reports are clear in the life and work of Moody. As he himself has explained in his recent autobiography, early on Moody resisted the conflation of the near-death experience with any particular religious doctrine, and this despite the fact that one of his initial mentors, who had had an NDE of his own (a psychiatrist by the name of George Ritchie), encouraged him to dedicate his book to Jesus Christ. Moody refused to do that.[44] He had taken what was in effect a strong comparative stance, not a specific doctrinal one.

Such a stance was not always well received. Christian fundamentalist readers in particular would write Moody hostile letters. He had shown, after all, that people of all faiths—or, even more shockingly, of no faith at all—have profoundly positive religious encounters within near-death experiences. Belief is often simply irrelevant to what happens. This was a clear affront to fundamentalist readers, who insisted that only Christians like themselves could see God after death, and that what these other people were encountering had to be "Satan himself." Moody's NDE was thus the "work of the devil."[45] The comparative method, which lies at the basis of Moody's approach, can be extremely threatening to particular religious worldviews.

Not every Christian comparative practice, of course, has been so unfair and judging. John Price, an episcopalian priest, has recently offered a much more balanced and much more positive assessment of the near-death experience from a hospital chaplain's perspective.[46]

The Toolkit

At the end (and "end" in more ways than one), here are some final skill sets and tools for you to collect and put in your toolkit:

1   *The Human as Two*   If the witness of the history of religions means anything, there is more than

one "you" in you. We have named this intuition, experience, or full-blown realization "the human as two." We have also identified this pattern as the separable soul.

2   *Spiritual Multiplicity and Morphing*   It is really not this simple, of course. Perhaps we could more accurately say that the self is seldom considered to be singular within the general history of religions. There are not just two of you. There might be many of you *and* one of you. Or none of you, as we see in most forms of Buddhism. Still, all major religious systems have had to deal, positively or negatively, with the religious concept of the separable soul.

3   *Refractions and Reflections of Conscious Light*   We can never get to the soul as an object of direct replicable knowledge. It is, after all, not an object. What we can do is see "soul" indirectly refracted and reflected, like light, through the medium of culture and language. Among these refractions and reflections, we have noted the globally reported experiences of light and energy and the local but still common symbolisms of breath, shadow, reflection, and image. We have also looked at whether the experience of soul is said to be located in the heart or the head, at whether it is transhuman, and at the fact that it is usually gendered female, particularly in male monotheisms.

4   *The Traumatic Secret*   We also looked at different soul practices (prayer, ancestor worship, mediumship, possession, and channeling), most of which assume the human as two and/or involve some ritual technology to suppress, silence, distract, or temporarily take offline the surface self. We also noted that sometimes illness, accident, or near-death can do the same, and much more definitively. We noted that this "splitting" of the self into two appears to be the secret generator of many beliefs about "the soul," and that the presence or absence of this splitting in an individual helps us to understand and appreciate *both* sincere belief *and* sincere skepticism around the subject of soul.

5   *The Line and the Circle*   Just as the soul can live once or many times, so too can the universe, in different mythological systems. We looked at these two basic types of eschatologies or "myths of the end" and named them "the line and the circle." We noted the central role that violence plays in these narratives, both as imagined and as acted out.

Finally, a closing note. The nineteenth-century British anthropologist Edward Burnett Tylor famously argued that the origin of the belief in the soul stems from the apparitions of dead family members and ancestors in the dreams of the living. Along similar lines, it has been theorized countless times that religion is, at base, a human response to death. What is usually meant by this statement is that religion is a salve or an emotional mechanism designed to deal with the inevitability and brutality of death. This is no doubt true. But it leaves unanswered questions: Is religion *just* a salve? Is it *just* an emotional mechanism, an efficient denial? Were these dreams of the dead just dreams? Tylor clearly thought so. He considered the dreams of the departed souls to be illusions, and the subsequent beliefs in the soul, which these dreams generated, to be mistakes of the primitive mind, which we would do well now to leave behind.

If, however, one pays heed to some of the accounts we have compared in the last two chapters, one can begin to see a different kind of answer emerging, one that embraces the importance of death and dream apparitions in the formation of religious beliefs around the soul and immortality but sees these formations as based on real historical events. Put bluntly, doctrines of the soul and salvation may be so widespread and so consistent across human cultures because they reflect something fundamentally accurate about human nature. What would Edward Tylor say, for example, to Mark Twain? Or to Dr. Amatuzio?

What do *you* think?

And, perhaps most importantly of all, which "you" is doing this thinking?

1   Is the death experience of a Hindu fundamentally different from that of a Jew, Christian, or Muslim? If you identify with one of the latter labels, how do you know that you will not be reincarnated? If you were born in Thailand, you would most likely be a Buddhist now, with convictions and beliefs as sincere and strong as the ones you presently hold. If you were born in the American Midwest, you would most likely be a Christian now, with convictions and beliefs as sincere and strong as those of the Thai Buddhist. How do you explain that?

2   Does your body "have a soul"? Or does your soul "have a body"? What's inside what? Or do you think of yourself as only a material body that somehow produces the illusion of spirit or soul? What difference do your answers to these questions make?

3   One of the key problems in addressing a possible environmental crisis is that many individuals and communities, particularly those in privileged parts of the world, imagine themselves to be *outside* the effects of such events. To invoke a distinction, the looming possibility of an environmental crisis is understood to be a "disaster," not a "catastrophe." A *disaster* is an event that one observes from the outside, as in "on the news." A *catastrophe* is an event one finds oneself and one's community in, as in "Oh my God, there goes my house!" Religious eschatologies, it must be noted, are likely major contributors to this common conviction, often unconscious, of being outside the problem and finally immune to its effects, since their narratives usually remove or "save" their communities from the final disaster. How, then, might specific religious beliefs about the soul and "the end" encourage such a lack of concern and hence impede effective responses to something like global climate change?

Notes

1   D. E. Harding, "On Having No Head." In *The Mind's I: Fantasies and Reflections on Self and Soul*, edited by Douglas R. Hofstadter and Daniel C. Dennett (New York: Basic Books, 1981), 23.

2   Harding, "On Having No Head," 24, 25.

3   Harding, "On Having No Head," 28–29. Hence the symbolic importance of decapitation and severed heads in the art and meditation practices of Indian and Tibetan Buddhism and Hindu Tantra. Harding was hiking in the Himalayas, where these traditions are especially prominent.

4   Obituary, *The Independent*, February 15, 2007.

5   Personal communication made in writing to me. This is the source for all subsequent quotations from Bill Barnard in this section.

6   Ludwig Feuerbach, *Lectures on the Essence of Religion*, trans. by Ralph Manheim (New York: Harper & Row, 1967), 310–311.

7   David Eagleman, *Incognito: The Secret Lives of the Brain* (New York: Pantheon, 2011), 1, 19, 1–2.

8   For a wonderful collection of essays on the same topic, see Geoffrey Samuel and Jay Johnston, eds., *Religion and the Subtle Body in Asia and the West: Between mind and body* (New York: Routledge, 2013).

9   See especially Lisa Schwebel, *Apparitions, Healings, and Weeping Madonnas: Christianity and the Paranormal* (New York: Paulist Press, 2004), who treats such Catholic events through the surprisingly well-documented phenomena of psychokinesis or mind over matter.

10   I. P. Couliano, *Out of This World: Otherworldly Journeys from Gilgamesh to Albert Einstein* (New York: Shambalah, 1991), 34, 37, 74.

11   Louis Komjathy, *The Daoist Tradition: An Introduction* (London: Bloomsbury Academy, 2013), 125–126.

12 Dante, *Divina Commedia*, Paradiso, Canto 29, lines 136–138; quoted in Matthew T. Kapstein, ed., *The Presence of Light: Divine Radiance and Religious Experience* (Chicago, IL: University of Chicago Press, 2004).

13 Grant Morrison, Jill Thompson, Chris Weston, John Ridgway, Steve Parkhouse, and Paul Johnson, *The Invisibles*, vol. 2: *Apocalipstick* (New York: Vertigo, DC Comics, 2001), 195. A Möbius strip appears on the same page, visually "flipping" our notions of "inside" and "outside."

14 Barbara Newman, "Exchanging Hearts: A Medievalist Looks at Transplant Surgery." *Spiritus* 12 (2012), 1–20.

15 Annemarie Schimmel, *My Soul Is a Woman: The Feminine in Islam* (New York: Continuum, 2003).

16 David L. Haberman, *People Trees: Worship of Trees in North India* (New York: Oxford University Press, 2013).

17 T. M. Luhrmann, *When God Talks Back: Understanding the American Evangelical Relationship with God* (New York: Alfred A. Knopf, 2012), xxi.

18 Luhrmann, *When God Talks Back*, xxii.

19 Robert Skutch, *Journey without Distance: The Story behind a Course in Miracles* (Berkeley, CA: Celestial Arts, 1984), iv.

20 Neal Vahle, *A Course in Miracles: The Lives of Helen Schucman and William Thetford* (San Francisco, CA: Open View Press, 2009), 3.

21 See "Trapped in His Body," A&E Biography Channel's *The UneXplained*, August 2012.

22 Aldous Huxley, *The Perennial Philosophy* (Cleveland, OH: The World Publishing Company, 1962), v–vi.

23 Ariel Glucklich, *Sacred Pain: Hurting the Body for the Sake of the Soul* (New York: Oxford University Press, 2001).

24 Janet Elizabeth Colli, *The Dark Face of Heaven: True Stories of Transcendence through Trauma* (2013).

25 See Elaine Pagels, *Revelations: Vision, Prophecy, and Politics in the Book of Revelation* (New York: Viking, 2012).

26 Gregory Shushan, *Conceptions of the Afterlife in Early Civilizations: Universalism, Constructivism and Near-Death Experiences* (London: Continuum, 2009).

27 Debbie James, "The Human as Two Lecture Series: The Near-Death Experience." Lecture delivered at the Houston Jung Center, October 24, 2012.

28 Donald S. Lopez, Jr., *The Tibetan Book of the Dead: A Biography* (Princeton, NJ: Princeton University Press, 2011), 11.

29 Lopez, *The Tibetan Book of the Dead*, 2, 59.

30 Lopez, *The Tibetan Book of the Dead*, 119.

31 Raymond A. Moody, Jr., *Life after Life: The Investigation of a Phenomenon—Survival of Bodily Death* (New York: HarperCollins, 2001), 114.

32 Anita Moorjani, *Dying to Be Me: My Journey from Cancer, to Near Death, to True Healing* (Carlsbad, CA: Hay House, 2012), xiv.

33 Moorjani, *Dying to Be Me*, 60.

34 Moorjani, *Dying to Be Me*, 64–65.

35 Moorjani, *Dying to Be Me*, 142.

36 Moorjani, *Dying to Be Me*, 142–143.

37 Moorjani, *Dying to Be Me*, 68–69.

38 Moorjani, *Dying to Be Me*, 144.

39 Moorjani, *Dying to Be Me*, 137.

40 Ian Stevenson, *Reincarnation and Biology: A Contribution to the Etiology of Birthmarks and Birth Defects* (Westport, CT: Praeger Publishers, 1997).

41 Ian Stevenson, *European Cases of the Reincarnation Type* (Jefferson, NC: McFarland & Company, 2003), 250.

42 See Allan Kellehear, "Census of Non-Western Near-Death Experiences to 2005: Observations and Critical Reflections." In *The Handbook of Near-Death Experiences: Thirty Years of Investigation*, edited by Janice Miner Holden, Bruce Greyson, and Debbie James (Santa Barbara, CA: ABC CLIO, 2009), 135–158.

43 Nancy Evans Bush, "Distressing Western Near-Death Experiences." In *The Handbook of Near-Death Experiences: Thirty Years of Investigation*, edited by Janice Miner Holden, Bruce Greyson, and Debbie James (Santa Barbara, CA: ABC CLIO, 2009), 63–86.

44 Raymond Moody with Paul Perry, *Paranormal: My Life in Pursuit of the Afterlife* (New York: HarperOne, 2012), 95.

45 Moody with Perry, *Paranormal*, 107.

46 John Price, *Revealing Heaven: The Christian Case for Near-Death Experiences* (New York: HarperOne, 2013).

Listen to the Amniotic Cosmos—Once Upon a Time again (1991), diptych, right panel, by Lynn Randolph, 36″ × 28″.

PART III

Putting It All Together Again

It is time to come back. It is time to leave our liminal wanderings and wonderings in foreign lands and try to refashion our worldviews in the light of the spectacles we have seen and oracles we have heard. It is time to do theory, to put things back together again.

Perhaps you feel like nothing of real significance has changed for you after all these historical and comparative exercises. That would be a legitimate conclusion. Or perhaps you feel more like Humpty Dumpty. Perhaps you feel like things *cannot* be put back together again. That too would be a kind of conclusion.

Regardless, the purpose of this third and final stage of our textbook initiation is to help you put things back together again. More particularly, these final three chapters are about helping you come to clarity in answering the single, all-encompassing question that has glowed between the lines of this textbook, namely, the question of religious pluralism, or why there are hundreds, really thousands of religious answers to life's questions and not just one or two. We have thus moved from the "What?" questions …

- What is the history of comparison?
- What do Muslims or Buddhists believe?

- What is a myth or a ritual?
- What do the religions teach about the afterlife?

… to the "So what?" questions:

- So what does this mean for me and my community?
- How should comparison change, or not change, the ways in which I think about Muslims or Buddhists, or about other people's myths and rituals?
- Or about my own myths and rituals?
- Do I really have myths and rituals??

As thinking human beings have struggled with these questions over the last few centuries, three broad types of response have emerged. Taking up the (most likely fanciful) etymology of religion as *relegere* that we discussed in Chapter 3, that is, as a "re-reading" of scripture and tradition, we will call these three broad responses faithful re-readings, rational re-readings, and reflexive re-readings.

We are not exactly being original here. In his *On the Nature of the Gods*, the great first-century BCE Roman philosopher-statesman Cicero staged a three-way debate between three individuals. One of these was a Stoic philosopher named Balbus whom Cicero has argue, in the words of the classicist Peter T. Struck, that "a truly religious person 'retraces' or 'rereads' [*relegere*] *everything* that has to do with the gods and makes what sense he or she can from it." For Balbus, these pious re-readings have everything to do with *reading*. Struck explains for us that Balbus stresses

> the literate nature of true piety, characterizing the study of the gods with terms that self-consciously repeat forms of the verb "to read." True religion is selective [*e-ligere*], diligent [*di-ligere*], and demands understanding [*intel-legere*]. He contrasts this sincere devotion with the superstitious person, who takes up the whole day pleading through prayer and sacrifice for a particular outcome.[1]

What we intend in this last section of the textbook is a re-reading along the lines that Balbus imagined, although, as we shall see soon enough, many of these re-readings will hardly be pious ones.

Note

1   Peter T. Struck, *Birth of the Symbol: Ancient Readers at the Limits of Their Texts* (Princeton, NJ: Princeton University Press, 2004), 117.

La mestiza cosmica (1992), by Lynn Randolph, 40″ × 24″.

10

Faithful Re-readings

Exclusivism, Inclusivism, Pluralism, and Justice

[T]he King cares little that in allowing everyone to follow [his or her own] religion he was in reality violating all.

A Catholic priest on the religious tolerance of the
Indian Mughal Emperor Akbar

If there were only one religion in England, there would be danger of tyranny; if there were two, they would cut each other's throats; but there are thirty, and they live happily together in peace.

Voltaire, "On the Church of England" (Letter 5 in *Letters Concerning the English Nation*)

Chapter Outline

Comparing Religions: Coming to Terms, First Edition. Jeffrey J. Kripal, Ata Anzali, Andrea R. Jain, and Erin Prophet.
© 2014 Jeffrey J. Kripal. Published 2014 by John Wiley & Sons, Ltd.

On February 20, 1974, the doorbell rang at the California apartment of the American science fiction writer Philip K. Dick. The author was feeling a bit woozy from some sodium pentathol that he had been given at the dentist's office for an oral surgery earlier that day. A young woman was at the door. She was delivering a packet of painkillers. Dick was struck by her long brown hair, her eyes, and her beauty. He was also attracted to her gold necklace, which featured the fish sign used by the early Christians as a symbol for Christ. "Attracted" may be exactly the right word. Dick's wife at the time, Tessa Dick, has suggested that he was gazing at the necklace as a stratagem for staring down the young woman's blouse, which sported a "plunging neckline."[1]

Breasts or not, this golden symbol that gleamed in the sun triggered something in the author. For the next two months, Dick would find himself passing through a most remarkable series of events, including the appearance of various memories of past lives that caused him *to remember*. Remember what? "Your celestial origins," Dick explains, "this has to do with the DNA because the memory is located in the DNA (phylogenetic memory) … You remember your real *nature*. Which is to say, origins (from the stars) … You are here in this world in a thrown condition, but you are not *of* this world." More specifically, on that winter day Dick remembered who he really was: a secret Christian living in fear of the Romans in the first century—a space–time dimension, he speculated, that was somehow layered over his own space–time dimension, as if they somehow existed all at once, like grooves on a vinyl record, as he once put it (we are reminded of Anita Moorjani's descriptions of her near-death experience outside of linear time). Such impossible thoughts were fired into his brain by what he calls "a transcendentally rational mind." He could not help but be reminded of the ancient Christian mystical doctrine of the Logos, the divine Word or cosmic reason, through which all things came to be and which is one with God, which *is* God. This transcendentally rational mind did more than fire things at him, though. It killed and resurrected him so that he could now also know what he really was: "an immortal being."[2]

Dick would go on to write three novels—his last three—about the events of those months before he died eight years later, in 1982. He would also type and scrawl some 8,000 pages of private journal entries now known as *The Exegesis*, in a vain attempt to recover the meanings of those events through analysis and acts of interpretation. Eventually Dick began to claim that he had been "resynthesized" or "reprogrammed" by a pink beam emanating from a vast

Figure 10.1 *A Philip K. Dick Moment* (2012), by Robert Jiménez. At zerostreet.com.

super-consciousness that he called VALIS, an acronym for "vast active living intelligence system."

He made the name up, but he did not make up Valis. Nor did he make up the pink light. Both were autobiographical facts of immense power and immeasurable, really infinite significance. Indeed Valis was so meaningful that Dick could interpret its appearance in his life in a hundred different ways; but every interpretation, every attempt to frame or capture it always found its opposite, or, more weirdly, ended up in another paradox, which looped back on itself within a kind of infinite reflexivity, as in a double mirror. Somehow Valis remained beyond any single name, interpretation, or reading. It could not be "languaged." It could not be reasoned.

Not that it didn't "speak." This, after all, was a light that beamed into Dick the information-laden energies of entire books. Valis, he came to understand, was

what his life was all about. It was what he had been writing "toward" in all those earlier sci-fi pulps; because he now realized that those were so many pointers toward *this*. The Robert Jiménez painting reproduced in Figure 10.1 captures beautifully this notion of Dick's pink revelation from above and the effect it had on his writing, on his words. The fish sign that triggered it all hangs on his hairy chest. His late friend, Bishop James Pike, who helped him to learn about ancient Christian gnosticism and who (Dick suspected) possessed him via the Valis event, hides mysteriously behind the writer's collar.

None of this, of course, "makes sense": it is not rational in the simple, secular sense of that word. Which is just to say that whatever Dick experienced cannot be slotted into the working of the world as we normally experience it through our five senses, our logic, and our normal notion or feeling of what is real. And yet it happened. It was real to Dick; indeed Valis was the most real and the most important event of his entire life.

If Dick had been living in a previous era, he would have certainly framed Valis in traditional religious terms—as an angel or a demon, as a god or a goddess, or, more likely, as God—instead of using his own colorful sci-fi expressions to do it. He would not have written three science-fiction novels to explain it, either. He would have channeled another religious scripture or would have written a commentary on the New Testament, the Torah, or the Upanishads. Actually the latter is more or less what he ended up doing in his private journals: he related his experience of Valis endlessly to the world religions he knew, and especially to the mystical traditions of ancient Greece, Christianity, Judaism, Hinduism, Buddhism, and Daoism.

In the end he settled for a position that recognized that the sacred manifests itself in all the religions and yet overflows each of them; that transcendent truths are scattered throughout space and time in the different religious systems of the planet; that these glowing shards can be located, identified, picked up, and put together into a new revelation by someone imaginally empowered (like him); that belief can never exhaust revelation; and that revelation falls fundamentally outside and beyond the rules and boundaries of human reason. Religious revelation, Dick realized, is its own thing, even if it can only "speak" to us in our own thing, that is, in the structures and symbols of cognition and culture.

The Task of Theology: Relating Reason and Revelation

Throughout this textbook we have been emphasizing that the sameness of the religions resides primarily in their *functions*, not in their content, teachings, or final states of salvation, which are all very different. We can now name these re-readings of religion as instances of **functionalism**. In the last three chapters we will return to the functionalist models, but we will also turn to those different revelations and to those final states of salvation *as ultimate truth claims*. We might call these comparisons focused on the truth claims of the religions **substantive comparative practices**. Such practices are not strictly concerned with the similar functions of religion. They are concerned mostly with the different truth claims of various religions and with how to relate these claims to one another within some larger or global understanding or theory of religion.

We begin with a sci-fi writer for three reasons. First, Dick's Valis reminds us that revelation honors and recognizes no distinction between "elite" and "popular" culture. Revelation can take on almost any cultural frame, including the pop-cultural frame of a cheap paperback. Second, we begin with Dick because his brave but finally futile attempt to understand Valis illustrates in glowing colors just how deep and vast the abyss can be between the experienced realities of religious revelation and the logical structures of reason. It is this fundamental *gap* between revelation and reason—mediated, in part, through the symbols and narratives of the religious imagination—that we will repeatedly stress here. Third, we begin with Dick's Valis because this case powerfully

demonstrates that religious revelation and different states of salvation continue into the present. Such events are *by no means* things of the past.

Ongoing Revelation

We have come across this truth before, of course. Here we might recall *The Revelation of the Magi*, which featured the star-being who proclaims that he is "a ray of light whose light has shone … in the entire world and in every land by unspeakable mysteries."[3] We met this idea again in Ralph Waldo Emerson, who got kicked out of Harvard for suggesting, among other scandalous things, that Christians should stop idolizing the Bible since revelation was an ongoing phenomenon; and again in the poet Walt Whitman, who suggested that all the bibles are shed out of us, like leaves off a tree.

It is worth observing that this "revelation of ongoing revelation" is often extremely problematic for the more conservative forms of religious systems, many of which are heavily invested in the position that revelation does *not* continue into the present. This is why new revelations, like Mormonism or the Baha'i faith, were vehemently denied by their surrounding cultures. When these two movements—Mormonism and the Baha'i faith—emerged in the nineteenth century, both were violently resisted by American Protestant Christians and Iranian Shia Muslims, respectively. The logic of this resistance is not difficult to fathom: if the new revelation is valid, then the older revelation is incomplete and imperfect, something to leave behind.

The Baha'i Religion The case of the Baha'i religion is especially instructive in this regard. In 1844, a young Shia merchant from Shiraz, Persia named Sayyid Ali Muhammad, after going through a number of profound religious experiences, announced that the end of the age was near and declared himself to be the "gate" (*bab*) to the hidden Imam. The latter is the messianic leader who Shia Muslims believe has been in occultation for some twelve hundred years; they await his return at the end of time. Moved by this new revelation, the Bab, along with a number of his close confidants, began missionary activities across the Middle East. But this kind of activity stirred up much tension within the Muslim communities. The Bab was summoned and questioned a number of times and eventually imprisoned in 1847, after he refused to denounce his beliefs and declarations about being the Gate of the hidden Imam.

Then, early in 1848, he went further still and announced that he was not the Gate, but the awaited hidden Imam himself. He then declared the abrogation or end of Islamic law and announced his desire to replace it by a new social order, which he delineated in a book. His disciples followed and began to announce the end of the Islamic era and the inauguration of this new dispensation. This was a radical claim, but it was hardly a new move. In fact it was quite traditional. Recall that this is more or less what the early Christians proclaimed in relation to the Torah or "Old Testament" and what the early Muslims proclaimed in relation to the Torah and the Gospel.

The response from the orthodox was swift and severe. The Bab was executed in July 1850. A period of heavy persecutions and religious violence followed. After more than a decade of exile, soul searching, and disarray in the nascent community, it was a close disciple, Mirza Husain-Ali Nuri, better known as Baha'ullah ("God's glory"), who announced himself to be the promised prophet of the new era. A great number of writings from Baha'ullah followed in which he referred to his followers as the "people of Baha." It was during the last decades of his life (he died in 1892), which he spent in exile in the Ottoman prison city of Akka (in present-day Israel), that Baha'ullah laid the theological foundation for what was later called "the Baha'i religion" or the religion of the followers of Baha'ullah.

The notion of ongoing or progressive revelation often leads to a broadly tolerant understanding of other people's religions. Accordingly, the writings of Baha'ullah and other Baha'i leaders are emphatic about the unity of all religions (including the Asian ones) and their prophets (including figures like Krishna and the Buddha). From a Baha'i perspective,

all religions, in spite of their historical specificities, originate in the same divine source and carry a similar message to humanity. The Baha'i faith is believed by its followers to be privileged today not because it is absolutely true and the other religions are false, but because of this very notion of progressive revelation. In other words, in the lineage of prophetic cycles that includes figures like Adam, Moses, Zoroaster, the Buddha, Christ, and Muhammad (Platonic orientalism and the ancient wisdom narrative again), Baha'ullah has brought a religion that belongs to the present prophetic cycle by being the most recent "manifestation of God." Not that this particular manifestation is final, either: even the Baha'i faith itself is subjected to the principle of ongoing revelation. Revelation is never over. God speaks only with commas, never with full stops. There will thus come a time when a new prophet will arise, to usher in a new cycle and to renew the divine message according to the always changing needs of the human race and its increasingly connected "global village."[4]

Mormonism   Similar notions of ongoing revelation can be found in Mormonism. This new revelation was born in the USA, in upstate New York. in the early decades of the nineteenth century, around a man named Joseph Smith. Smith claimed to have discovered, at the direction of a white-robed angel named Moroni, a collection of golden plates buried in a hill near his farm outside of Palmyra, New York. These golden plates recorded the prehistory of the Americas and its peoples, especially two groups called the Nephites and the Lamanites; the latter group, Smith revealed, became the Native Americans of known history.

These ancient civilizations, the revelation went on, were connected to the ancient Israelites of the Bible through the family of Lehi, which left the ancient Near East and traveled to North America in the middle of the first millennium BCE. Through such narrative means, Joseph Smith's golden plates drew a direct connection between ancient Israel and the ancient Americas. They proclaimed in effect that a new revelation had been made and—just as importantly—that *there was more to come*, since Smith was instructed not to translate all of the plates: some of them were ordained for the future.

Smith claimed that his original discovery of the *Plates of Mormon* (named after a fourth-century prophet and scribe who compiled the plates) took place on September 21, 1823. In the following years he proceeded to translate a portion of the plates, which became the *Book of Mormon*. The text was published in 1830.

Smith's career as a prophet began, however, before all this, with what the Mormon tradition calls "the First Vision" and what we might now recognize as a comparativist crisis. As a young man, he was severely bothered by all the competing denominations and sects of the early United States. According to the traditional account, he wanted to know which one was the correct one. God the Father and his son Jesus Christ appeared to Joseph and gave him a very clear answer: none of them. He was to wait for the true faith, which would soon come.

It did.

Such claims were immediately countered by accusations of intentional fraud that came from many people close to Smith and his family. It was not just the message of the plates, but their very existence that many doubted; and the skeptics included people like Smith's own father-in-law, Isaac Hale. When the content of the revelations began to spread, these doubts and accusations escalated into threats of violence and active persecution from angry mobs. The publisher of the first edition of the *Book of Mormon*, for example, was legitimately concerned for his personal safety and for the security of his print shop. Smith and his brother Hyrum were eventually murdered by an angry mob while they were in jail. A large portion of the early community responded to these events by traveling to Utah for self-protection and safe haven.

The comparative point to make with respect to these two religions is this: new revelations announcing new eras are, in principle, poised against previous revelations and established social orders. The fact of ongoing revelation, then, is not just a challenge to reason. It is also a challenge *to religion*.

Revelation and Reason Defined

We have been employing two terms that deserve clear definitions. By **revelation** we mean a set of particular claims about transcendent realities or ultimate matters. These matters are not available to the five senses and it is not possible to work them out by rational means, but they are revealed to an individual or to a community, usually in a most dramatic way: through a vision; through the hearing, channeling, or inspired writing of a revelatory text; or through a visionary journey, an internal auditory event, or a miraculous event or sign of some sort. These revelations or "promises of salvation" are eventually written down or remembered in some relatively stable form (through a lineage of shamans, a sacred priesthood, or a scriptural canon), and then passed on from generation to generation in a variety of oral, ritual, institutional, textual, artistic, and oral forms.

By **reason** we mean a way of knowing that is guided by the senses; limited to information derived from them; and determined by some standardized form of logic and by the basic structures of human cognition (inductive and deductive inference, the law of the excluded middle, coherence, and so on). In a modern college or university "reason" is celebrated as a form of knowledge that is shared, debated, and honed through free and open conversation and not bound or controlled by any external authority, be it political or religious: essentially, Enlightenment reason.

Commentarial Traditions

For the sake of discussion, we might understand revelation as *something given* and reason as *something done*. We have to be careful here, though, since established religions never function simply as "givens." To begin with, this "given" is always given within a particular cultural context and together with its codes, which are themselves products of human agency and community labor—in a specific language, in an image become symbol, in a narrative vision or dream, and so on. Moreover, after the revelation is given, it is inevitably taken up and actively shaped—through further acts of interpretation, artistic and ritual performance, and so on—into something usable and understandable. Particularly important here is the **commentarial tradition**—that is, a specific body of literature and interpretive techniques that in effect "extends" and adapts the original revelation or scriptural text to new generations, through interpretation and application to the problems and questions of later historical periods.

This is especially evident in a tradition like Judaism, where the process of *midrash*—scriptural interpretation—is itself seen as an ongoing revelation and the ancient collections of *midrash*, called Talmud, are treated as authoritative. Indeed there are stories in the Jewish tradition about God attempting to intervene or to interrupt a group of rabbis debating the interpretation of a particular Torah passage. He is told to stay out. There is humor here, but there are also at least two profound points being made: *interpretation is itself a form of revelation;* and *human agency is an integral part of this process.*

Theology Defined

As we noted in Chapter 1, the systematization of a revelation is called "theology," a word of Greek origin that can be analyzed into the compounds *theos* ("god"/"divine") and *logos* ("word, reasoning, discourse, science"). Most simply put, theology is the attempt to relate reason to revelation and revelation to reason. Put a little more complexly, theology is the attempt to understand, organize, and institutionalize revelation through reason. Theology, then, is not at all the same thing as belief, although every theology begins with beliefs and every belief is a kind of implicit or beginning theology.

We might define **belief** as intellectual assent, either implicit or explicit, to the truth of some proposition or statement of faith. One believes that there is a God. Or one believes that one's ancestors can interact with the living community. Or one believes that the shaman can extract a disease, like an object, from a sick woman's body. Or one believes that eating pork is polluting (or that it is good for you). And so on.

Theology, on the other hand, is the process of picking up the various beliefs and practices of a community, which are seldom consciously systematized, and of attempting to organize them into a coherent system, which can be rationally discussed, debated, and defended before other competing systems of belief (or unbelief).

Historically, the practice of theology in the Jewish, Christian, and Muslim worlds has been closely connected—conceptually and institutionally—to the development and practice of philosophy. It is not for nothing that the earliest European universities developed directly out of monasteries, that medieval academics were almost all monks and clerics, and that to this day professors wear long flowing robes at graduation ceremonies, robes that are modeled on medieval monastic ones—another clear sign that the humanities and the liberal arts possess deep mystical roots.

Having said this, it is also true that there has been a great deal of angst expressed around the application of human reason to divine revelation. Not every era and tradition has been receptive to this project. Already the Church Father Tertullian (160–225), for example, famously asked: "What indeed has Athens to do with Jerusalem, the Academy with the church, heretics with Christians?"[5] His own answer? In so many words: "Nothing." Echoing Tertullian, early Protestant writers spoke of the "scandalous mixing" of philosophy and the Bible; one even named the comparative method itself as the real danger. More precisely, this Protestant author wrote of the *indignam comparationis arenam* (the "unworthy arena of comparison").[6] Comparison here was precisely what got one into trouble, what was incompatible with Christianity's exclusive truth claims.

Apologetics and Polemics

Theology, most broadly conceived, attempts to handle two sorts of problems that any religious system generates. The first sort is the sort encountered by the revealed tradition outside the tradition itself. For example, how might the Jewish, Christian, and Muslim creation stories in Genesis and the Quran be reconciled (or not reconciled) with the findings of modern evolutionary biology? Or how can the teaching of the Buddha that there is no self or soul be understood in relation to the common Hindu understanding that there is an immortal self beyond the social self? These are the sorts of question that theologians ask and try to answer.[7] Recall that, as we explained in Chapter 1, theological work aimed primarily at explaining, justifying, or defending, to outsiders, one's own received revelation is called apologetics. Theological work aimed at critically engaging the revelatory claims of other communities, usually in order to relativize them, is called polemics.

The second sort of problem that theologies address is one that arises from contradictions within the revealed tradition itself. In some sense, these problems are more serious than the ones of the first type, since they suggest that the system itself is incomplete, self-contradictory, or maybe just plainly mistaken.

Theology, as one very influential definition, or rather description, by Saint Anselm of Canterbury (1033–1109) had it, is "faith seeking understanding" (*fides quaerens intellectum*). We might expand on Anselm's definition here in light of our above discussion and define theology, for our own comparative purposes, as belief in a revelation seeking some reasonable framework that can "make sense" of the original revelation for the believing community in a particular place and time. This last clause, "in a particular place and time," is key. It explains why a community's theology in one century is not the same as in another century.

Comparative Theology

When a believer takes religious diversity seriously, looking at it as a potential source of new religious insight and not as a simple threat to his or her own beliefs, we might begin to speak of **comparative theology**. Comparative theology, in the words of Francis X. Clooney, involves "acts of faith seeking understanding which are rooted in a particular faith tradition but which, from that foundation, venture into learning from one or more other faith traditions." These acts of "deep learning across religious borders" involve both intuitive and rational forms of knowledge. Comparison here

> is a reflective and contemplative endeavor by which we see the other in light of our own, and our own in light of the other. It ordinarily starts with the intuition of an intriguing resemblance that prompts us to place two realities … near one another, so that they may be seen over and again, side by side.[8]

For Clooney, comparative theology is a type of religious reading that involves detailed study of specific religious texts. When done responsibly and deeply, it "intensifies rather than dilutes religious commitment and devotion."[9]

Clooney's comparativism is an explicitly and committed religious practice. It is a faithful re-reading that emerges from the conviction that the basic problem (and promise) of religious **pluralism** is *the* most basic challenge to any revealed tradition, and that religious diversity represents, to the believer, a much more serious and consequential crisis than, say, atheism might be. Why? Because the atheist positions "solves" the problem of religious pluralism by ignoring or by denying the phenomenon in question—that is, the very ancient and very modern human experience of revelation. A discipline like the comparative theology conceived by Clooney, on the other hand, acknowledges the reality of multiple revelations, affirms the necessity of commitment to a particular revelation or tradition, *and* is honest about the fact that the different revelations and traditions disagree with one another, sometimes profoundly, on important issues.

Religious Tolerance and Religious Freedom

There are two modern values that you have, no doubt, swimming around in your head about now.[10] The first is religious tolerance. The second is religious freedom.

We might define **religious tolerance** as the civic virtue or political policy that does not attempt to suppress or eliminate religious worldviews competing with, contradicting, or even denying one's own worldview. Robert Erlewine offers the following definition: tolerance is

> a principle which claims that more good arises on a societal or even a moral level in not acting rather than acting on one's moral disapproval regarding the actions, beliefs, and practices of the Other, so long as the Other does not directly obstruct the well-being of oneself or other Others.[11]

Note that such tolerance in no way implies moral acceptance or intellectual agreement and in fact is practiced mostly *by not acting on one's beliefs*. Religious tolerance is more of a social truce or agreement to differ: a pragmatic decision to "coexist," as we say today.

We might define **religious freedom** as the related civic legal structure that protects the civil rights of a society's citizens to practice their religions in peace, as long as these practices do not unduly impact in negative ways the religious lives and civil freedoms of other communities and individuals. Religious freedom is, in effect, the legal expression of the moral value of religious tolerance.

Both religious tolerance and religious freedom are central to most modern liberal societies; but it should also be recognized that both come at real religious costs and produce blindspots that are seldom addressed. Moreover, the religious costs of the two civic virtues are very much related to those of comparison, which, when done sufficiently well, is not at all blind to such costs. We have been owning up to these religious costs, coming to terms with them, all along, and via multiple channels: through our constant emphasis on the radicalism of the comparative method itself; through our repeated observations on the censorship, harassment, and persecution that have defined the history of comparison both in the ancient and in the modern period; and, of course, through the initiation structure of the textbook itself, which implies "Look out!"— when it does not actually shout it.

All along, we have tried to warn you.

What's the big deal? What is so costly about religious tolerance, religious freedom, and, of all things, about a "merely academic" enterprise like the comparative study of religion? Let us consider a typical American example. Throughout recent American history, numerous court cases have involved things like the attempt to institute prayer in public schools, or to erect nativity scenes or the Ten Commandments in or around a courthouse. When such acts are later declared illegal (since they clearly violate the separation of church and state), conservative Christian voices reply that their religious freedoms are being "violated." But this is simply incorrect, since such individuals are perfectly free to practice their faith in their own communities and religious institutions. There they can pray and set up all the nativity scenes and Ten Commandments they want. What they are *not* free to do is to impose those practices and that faith on the rest of the public; but this is exactly what they are doing with, say, the Ten Commandments in the courthouse.

In these contemporary cases people are really arguing not for religious freedom but for **religious primacy**: they are claiming that their religious views should be the ones defining the public space and conversation. The conservative Christian response would be very different if the local Hindu community wanted to set up a statue of the goddess Durga on the courthouse lawn, or if the local Muslim community wanted to impose Muslim prayers in the public schools. Neither of these acts would be possible in the American context.

Having said all this, there is real insight in the offended conservative Christian voices. They are accurately perceiving that there *are* real costs to religious freedom and religious tolerance. One of these costs is that no particular religious community gets to impose its will and its ways on the others. Such a legal practice is also a comparative practice.

Particularity and Universality

Very much related to this discussion are features that scholars sometimes call the **particularity** and **universality** of the world religions. What is meant here is that religious revelations and the respective states of salvation are almost always experienced as *particular* revelations that claim to be of *universal* significance to the community to which they are addressed and, often through that community, to the whole of humankind. The case is somewhat different in indigenous religions, which emphasize particularity and locality and do not usually make universal claims for the whole of humankind.

As we have it in a sacred story like that of Exodus, the God of Israel did not appear on Mount Sinai to Moses with an option to believe this or that, to do maybe this, maybe that, or with an encouragement to coexist in peace with Egyptian polytheism. This was an awesome, terrifying, literally burning event that demanded of Moses, and then of the Hebrew people, a stark set of choices and acts, literally carved into stone, as the story has it. Nor did this same God later call on his people to live as good citizens in Canaan within a civil pluralistic society, to respect, as it were, the religious freedom of others. Within the text of the Torah at least, he demanded that they conquer Canaan as their own and destroy anyone who stood in the way—and especially all those competing "idols" and Canaanite temples.

The Asian revelations are different, but not that different. The Buddha, for example, did not preach to north Indians that only they did not have a self or soul; that only they suffered by virtue of believing that they were a self or soul; and that only they could reach *nirvana*—the end of all suffering and self. No, as we have it in the early Buddhist texts, he preached that *everyone* and *everything* lacks a self or stable substance, and that *everyone* suffers. Moreover, the later history of Buddhism, which spread from north India throughout South and East Asia and eventually to Europe and the Americas, only makes sense if that salvation message was understood in the way it was originally intended: *as a universal fact, capable of being practiced and realized by anyone anywhere.*

Religions' revelations and states of salvation are not, then, experienced under an option to believe or not to believe them. They intervene with overwhelming power and force into the lives of individuals and communities and make ultimate, universal,

absolute truth claims. The problem, of course, is that there have been not just one or two, or maybe even three such revelations and salvations, but hundreds, if not actually thousands. This most fundamental challenge posed by multiple but exclusive and absolute revelations and states of salvation is what the civic virtues of religious tolerance and religious freedom fail to address—what they sidestep or, most likely, politely ignore.

This same challenge is what faithful re-readings take up with courage and rigor. As already noted, a **faithful re-reading** is an interpretation of religion that attempts to engage religious pluralism from within a particular religious stance or faith position. It is a *religious* response to religious pluralism. If we desire that a litmus test distinguish a faithful re-reading from a rationalist or reflexive one, we could employ such a test in the form of a question. Let us call this question "the faith test." It goes like this: "Does this particular type of re-reading religion privilege a particular faith tradition or an articulated faith stance?" If the answer is yes, we have a faithful re-reading. If the answer is no, we do not.

Please note two things here. First, note the "or" of the litmus question. A faithful re-reading does not require that a recognizable, common, or traditional faith tradition be present. A non-traditional faith stance will suffice as well, as long as it is an articulated and conscious one. Second, the litmus question does *not* preclude other forms of inquiry, not even strong rationalist or reductive forms. Faithful re-readings, remember, are as concerned with the principles of reason as they are with the revelations of religion. What makes a faithful re-reading "faithful" is the presence of an articulated faith stance, not the absence of reason.

There are three basic types of faithful re-readings that have been endlessly discussed over the last few decades. They are as follows:

- **exclusivism**: the rejection of other religious worldviews on the basis of the categories of one's own religious worldview;
- **inclusivism**: the acceptance of other religious worldviews on the basis of the categories of one's own religious worldview;

- **pluralism**: the potential acceptance of all religious worldviews as cultural approximations of the sacred, which is understood to overflow or transcend them all.

We suspect that, if you remember nothing else about this textbook in twenty years, it will be these three terms (okay, and the aliens). There is a good reason for this. These three categories are extremely useful in describing the positions individuals and communities take vis-à-vis other competing worldviews, whether they happen to be yours or not. They work really well. To continue our toolkit metaphor, these are three major skill sets without which you will have a very difficult time "comparing religions."

Let us now look at some examples of each in order to get a better handle on these first three re-readings of religion.

Excluding the Other Religious Worldview from One's Own

One of the most common responses to religious pluralism, especially in the western monotheistic religions, is exclusivism. The logic of this re-reading is simple: there is only one God or way of being religious: ours. Therefore anyone who worships a different god, no god, or even our God, but in the wrong way is to be rejected, "damned"—to use one especially common (and cruel) religious code (see Figure 10.2).

Figure 10.2 Compulsory colonial conversion. ©Bettmann/Corbis.

We saw these forms of exclusivism early on in our very first chapter, with our first look at forms of comparison in the scriptures and in the histories of Judaism, Christianity, and Islam. But there are also numerous contemporary expressions of the same logic. To take two fairly typical Protestant examples, the great German theologian Karl Barth, who was probably the most influential theological voice of the twentieth century in Protestant circles, wrote:

> the Christian religion is true, because it has pleased God, who alone can be the judge in this matter, to affirm it to be the true religion … it alone has the commission and the authority to be a missionary religion, i.e., to confront the world of religions as the one true religion, with absolute self-confidence to invite and challenge it to abandon its ways and to start on the Christian way.

Similarly, in 1960 the Congress on World Mission explained that, "in the years since the war, more than one billion souls have passed into eternity and more than half of these went to the torment of hell fire without even hearing of Jesus Christ, who He was, or why He died on the cross of Calvary."[12] And we need not pick on what the theologian John Hick calls the "sublime bigotry" of Barth and the Protestant missionaries. Similar quotations from other world religions could be listed for a very long time. Consider the radical Islamist whom I once heard on the radio talking about non-Muslims: "They are infidels. What do I care of them? They will all burn in hell." The logic in each of these statements is very clear: to conserve a religious worldview one must reject and condemn every other. Again, we are in a zero-sum game: "If we are right, they must be wrong." End of story.

It would be easy to reject such a position outright. But it would be a serious mistake to see such forms of exclusivism as things of the past or as products of nothing more than simple religious intolerance. In actual fact, these worldviews are both powerful and popular and seem to be grounded in some very basic human needs.

Strengths and Weaknesses of Exclusivism

For example, such types of belief and identity carry very strong psychological and social benefits, to the extent that they construct a very clear **ingroup**, to which the believer belongs and in which she feels at home, and a very clear **outgroup**, against which the believer identifies herself and her community and which she considers other, foreign, dangerous, impure, and so on. From the same functional point of view, it can be seen that such forms of exclusivism also grant very dramatic forms of certainty. There is little ambiguity here, and much conviction about how the world works, what history means, who God is, and what the purpose of human life is. A profound sense of belonging, community, meaning, and certainty are hardly minor accomplishments, and it is in fact quite easy to see why exclusivistic worldviews are so common and so popular.

The problem is that, whereas such a community of individuals may benefit from these forms of certainty and from those thick, high walls of exclusion—benefit, namely, via things like full parking lots, swelling rolls of membership, extensive financial support, large voting blocs, and psychological security—these very same certainties, when put next to other certainties, which are mutually contradictory, can easily result in social tension, even conflict and violence. It is really a simple matter of scale. It is one thing to be a Christian, a Muslim, a Jewish, or a Hindu exclusivist in one's own community, among people who look like you and believe more or less the same things about the world as you do; it is quite another when the globe becomes a village and all these mutually excluding worldviews are forced to share the same social or political space and the same natural resources, not to mention the same schools, hospital wards, and places of business.

The Bridge–Bonding Dilemma

Put a bit differently, a religious strategy like exclusivism can result in real benefits at a personal or individual community level but can be highly dysfunctional and even dangerous at a larger social, national, or international level. Sociologists refer to this scaling problem as the **bridge–bonding dilemma**. The larger society requires "bridge capital," that is, social forms that link and connect people together into a large social unit, like a city, state, or nation, whereas the ingroup requires bonding capital, that is, social forms that bond only certain people together in tight-knit communities. The dilemma arises from the simple fact that the one often comes at the expense of the other.[13] These problems, of course, have been vastly exacerbated in our modern world, where the ingroups or local communities of a nation-state are (a) much more numerous because of immigration patterns and (b) much more aware of one another because of technology, transportation, and the global media.

There is also the intellectual problem of the ingroup's "certainty." As any good education can show, many of the things that exclusivistic forms of religion claim as certain about the world and history are in actual fact not at all certain. Indeed many of them are patently false. This is why strongly exclusivistic forms of religion in a culture like the USA are generally correlated with lower levels of education (although there are some *very* sophisticated and *very* educated forms of exclusivism). Generally speaking, in the United States, the more education an individual has, the less likely he or she is to hold a strongly exclusivistic religious worldview.

Including the Other Religious Worldview within One's Own

Numerous contemporary religious communities have seen these same basic problems and have answered the challenge of religious pluralism with a different kind of faith response: with inclusivism. Inclusivistic re-readings insist on the uniqueness and absolute claims of their own revelation, while also acknowledging that other communities have experienced their own unique revelations, which they honor but subordinate to the absolute claims of their own.

Sometimes these re-readings represent real breaks with, or even reversals of, the tradition. One of the most instructive examples of such a change is that of Roman Catholicism and Vatican II. Vatican II was a series of official meetings of church leaders and scholars that took place in Rome from 1962 to 1965 and resulted in a set of documents that represented some new, more open, and more humble orientations to the modern world, biblical scholarship, science, and religious pluralism—among other things (see Figure 10.3).

Before Vatican II, that is, for most of Catholic history, the consensus was clear that salvation resided in the Catholic Church alone. To quote the well-worn Latin sound bite (dating back to the Church Father Irenaeus in the second century CE), *nulla salus extra ecclesiam*: "there is no salvation outside the church." In short, exclusivism. This position held firm until the twentieth century, when the cosmopolitan realities of the modern world, the findings of science, the developments of biblical scholarship, and the sophistication of anthropology and of the comparative study of religion began to render many of the church's "certain" claims both emotionally unbelievable and intellectually untenable. The result was a phenomenon that amounted to a Catholic "conversion" from exclusivism to inclusivism, perhaps best articulated in the Vatican II document *Nostra aetate* (*In Our Age*).

This "Declaration on the Church's Relationship to Non-Christian Religions" stated the church's admiration for Hinduism, where "men contemplate the divine mystery and express it through an inexhaustible abundance of myths and through searching philosophical inquiry," where they "seek freedom from the anguish of our human condition either through ascetical practices or profound meditation or a flight to God with love and trust." Similarly, Buddhism is praised there as teaching "a way by which men, in a devout and confident spirit, may be able either to acquire the state of perfect liberation, or attain, by their own efforts or through higher help, supreme illumination." The same document states that the church "regards with esteem" Muslims and acknowledges its profound debt and ties to "Abraham's

Figure 10.3   Second Vatican Council. Photographed by Hank Walker © Time & Life Pictures/Getty Images.

stock," that is, to the Jewish people. "The Church reproves, as foreign to the mind of Christ, any discrimination against men or harassment of them because of their race, color, condition of life, or religion." The key inclusivistic move, however, occurs at the heart of the document:

> The Catholic Church rejects nothing that is true and holy in these religions. She regards with sincere reverence those ways of conduct and of life, those precepts and teachings which, though differing in many aspects from the ones she holds and sets forth, nonetheless often reflect a ray of that Truth which enlightens all men. Indeed, she proclaims, and ever must proclaim

Christ "the way, the truth, and the life" (John 14: 6), in whom men may find the fullness of religious life, in whom God has reconciled all things to Himself.[14]

In short, the other religions contain or reflect "a ray" of truth, but not the full truth, which can only be found in Christ and the Roman Catholic Church. To employ the language of one of the Council's most distinguished theologians, Karl Rahner, non-Christian peoples can be thought of as "anonymous Christians" who can be saved in their own cultural and religious traditions by the grace of Christ working secretly or anonymously through these very traditions. To translate this back into our own comparative terms, the other religious worldviews are accepted, but only on the conditions and categories of one's own religious worldview—in this case, those of the Roman Catholic Church.

Things, of course, are not always this dramatic or official. Sometimes inclusivistic re-readings are more playful. There is a funny scene in one of the episodes of a well-used comparative religion film series produced by the BBC, *The Long Search* (1977). The editorial consultant of the series was the influential Scottish scholar of comparative religion Ninian Smart (1927–2001). This particular episode happens to be on Theravada Buddhism. Narrator and guide Ronald Eyre, who became famous (at least among professors of comparative religion) for his wit and bad polyester suits, is at a Buddhist festival in Sri Lanka. If I remember it correctly (it's been a while), he is speaking to some women there, who are standing around him and smiling. They are having a conversation, which is half-serious, half-teasing. Eyre asks the women what they think of him and his Christian faith. He is a very nice man, they say it in so many words, but he must have done something bad in his former life. Otherwise he would not have been born in a country like England (this is the point where they begin to giggle more). If, they assure him with their smiles, he can live a better life in this present life, perhaps he will have the good fortune of being born again in a better culture and religion, that is to say, in a Buddhist one.

The Buddhist women, in other words, do exactly what the Vatican document did. They accept the other person or worldview, but only on the terms and conditions of their own worldview, in this case, Theravada Buddhism. Whereas the Catholic document has the Buddhist secretly saved by the grace of Christ, the Buddhist women have the English Christian reincarnating and progressing, gradually, toward Buddhism and its ultimate truths. Same move, different worldview.

Inclusivism and Canon Formation

There are other forms or comparative practices of inclusivism. Foremost among them in the world religions is **canon formation**, that is, the manner in which a later tradition defines the boundaries and scope of its sacred scriptures. Particularly common here is the

strategy of defining one's own scriptural texts so as to "include" or "supersede" those of previous religions.

We have already noted this strategy in Chapter 1. In the seventh and eighth centuries, for example, the new religion of Islam relegated the much older Jewish and Christian scriptural canons to lower rungs of revealed truth: the Quran was now the full and complete word of God, which had been revealed to correct the errors of the Jewish Torah and Christian Gospels. Muhammad was declared to be the "seal of the prophets": the final and perfect spokesman for God, after whom no further revelation was possible (the "seal" here refers to the unbroken wax seal on ancient business contracts or letters that guaranteed that no one had tampered with the contents, that the letter or contract was, if you will, "genuine"). In short, Islam thus "included" the earlier histories and incomplete truths of Judaism and Christianity into the full and complete truth of Islam. It did not entirely reject or exclude the revelations of the Torah and of the Gospels—of what it calls the "people of the Book." Quite the contrary. But it did not fully accept them either. It included them within its own system.

Christianity, of course, had done the same thing to Judaism five centuries earlier with its notions of an "Old" and "New" Testament, as both religions emerged and argued over who would take up the mantle of the true Israel. And the followers of Baha, or the early Baha'i movement, would adopt the same superseding strategy via-à-vis Islam in the nineteenth century. Similar inclusivistic moves, different worldviews.

Hindu Tolerance and Hierarchy

What we now call Hinduism has used similar strategies, if on very different religious stories and scriptures. Hinduism is often described as "tolerant." This is true enough, but it is also partly false and sometimes deadly wrong, as we see, for example, in recent Hindu communalist riots and organized acts of violence and destruction aimed at Muslims in modern India. It is in fact much more accurate to say that traditional Hinduism works on the basis of an ancient hierarchical principle of inclusivism. This more ancient social and religious system is called Brahmanism. Its fundamental principle is hierarchy: non-brahmanical sects and groups are not excluded; they are included, but—and here is the crux—always at a lower level of this same social and religious hierarchy, where the brahmans or priests are at the all-inclusive top.

The Hindu tradition, for example, declared the Buddha to be an *avatara* ("incarnation") of its own god Vishnu, stating quite explicitly that he had descended to earth in order to spread the heresy of Buddhism in order to lead astray the anti-gods. Similarly, when the Christian missionaries arrived in India in the nineteenth century preaching the incarnation of God in the person of Jesus Christ, they were often dismayed to encounter a Hindu attitude that amounted to saying: "Well, of course, he can be one of the avatars too, just like Rama and Krishna." Not exactly what the missionaries had in mind, but extremely effective. The other foreign incarnation was not excluded, but included within the broader and more universal embrace of "Hinduism." In this way the Christian challenge was to a certain extent contained and neutralized.

Strengths and Weaknesses of Inclusivism

As with exclusivism, there are real strengths and weaknesses here. On the strength side, inclusivism allows a tradition to acknowledge what is already obvious to many of its adherents, namely the integrity, honesty, and humanity of religious people with different beliefs and practices. Perhaps most of all, though, inclusivism avoids, or at least seems to avoid, the obvious intolerances and potential violences of exclusivism. It thus represents a strong compromise position that manages to do two different things at once: (1) to acknowledge the other religions as legitimate; *and* (2) to insist on the fuller and more complete truths of one's own religion. Essentially, inclusivism wants it both ways. It wants to hold on to one's own religious certainty without erasing or eliminating the other competing truth claims.

As with exclusivism, there are not just promises here. There are also problems. Most obvious are those embarrassing scriptural passages present in any

ancient tradition that simply cannot be slotted into generous inclusivistic readings (that demanding God on Mount Sinai, or that universal teaching of the Buddha again). Exclusivistic individuals are always pointing these out. They are certainly there. There are many passages in almost any ancient scriptural canon that cannot be read—at least on their own, in isolation from the rest of the tradition and texts—in inclusivistic ways. Like the Torah passages on slaughtering whole villages, or the Gospel of John passage on the Jews as children of the Devil, or the Quran passages portraying the Jews as irreconcilable enemies of Muslims alongside the idolators, some scriptural passages are simply unredeemable from an inclusivist position, let alone a pluralist one.

Encountering the Sacred within and beyond All Religious Worldviews

The faith response that has embraced the methods and findings of the comparative study of religion the most enthusiastically is pluralism. Indeed, in many ways, modern pluralism can be seen as a direct historical outgrowth and religious expression of the comparative study of religion. It is, however, also the most rare, the least traditional, and consequently the most difficult for many religious people to understand and appreciate, much less to accept and put into practice. It is what we had in mind when we added "faith stance" (as opposed to "faith tradition") to our earlier faith question litmus test.

If we take a culture like the USA, for example, pluralism is, numerically speaking, a most uncommon position among the established religious institutions. Indeed the traditions that have clearly and unambiguously adopted pluralism, like the Unitarian Universalists or some branches of Reformed Judaism and Quakerism, are among the smallest religious communities in the USA. If, however, we refocus our lens and look at what we might call non-institutional religion—for example, the "I am spiritual, but not religious" crowd—then pluralism as a theological position can be recognized as one of the most popular and common of American religious responses to religious pluralism as a social fact. There is also a clear age or generational pattern at work here. At the time of writing this particular faith response is easily the most common religious position among people younger than 30 in the USA.

Assumptions aside, pluralism is not a strictly modern phenomenon. In the sixteenth century the Mughal Emperor Akbar created a small college of comparative religion at his north Indian court and, taking this comparative spirit one step further, established in 1582 a new universal religion later called "the divine faith" (*Din-i-Ilahi*). Emperor Akbar thus acted on his pluralism. Indeed he legislated according to it. He repealed both the hated Pilgrim's Tax, which his predecessors had imposed on Hindus visiting their own shrines, and the traditional *jizya*—the religious tax for non-Muslims. Within this same pluralist vision, Akbar also commissioned translations of classical Hindu scriptural texts and invited Muslim, Hindu, Zoroastrian, Jain, and Parsi scholars, even Catholic priests from Goa, to argue their points together in his presence. The Sikh community flourished under Akbar's reign.

As a modern intellectual practice, pluralism can best be seen in comparative theologians who have embraced and developed these faithful re-readings over the last few decades: figures like John Hick, Raimundo Pannikar, and Paul F. Knitter. Hick's *God Has Many Names* (1980) can be treated as an early and paradigmatic example of how the method approaches the problem and promise of religious pluralism.

In this text, Hick wrote of a "Copernican revolution" in Christian theology. Copernicus, recall, famously argued that, contrary to what the church and common sense had it, the sun, planets, and stars do not revolve around the earth. Rather the earth and the planets revolve around the sun. The truth is *the opposite* of what was universally assumed. Copernicus (who was also a priest) was correct, and the Christian tradition was wrong on this point. Period.

So too with respect to God and the world religions in Hick's modern allegory. The "sun" is God, and the "planets" are the world religions, each of which imagines (falsely) that the cosmos revolves around its own worldview. Modern social experience and the advances of knowledge have made it intellectually impossible to believe any longer that the history of humanity's religious experience orbits around the center of the Christian religion or any other religion. Religious people need to rethink their "Ptolemaic" ways, that is, their insistence that the universe orbits around them. All sorts of clever strategies (like inclusivism, Hick points out) can be used, of course, to explain away the historical and anthropological facts and to make one hold on to one's sense of religious primacy; but, much like the early attempts to explain away Copernicus, none of these is really convincing and now they are all looking, to the outsider anyway, as "slightly ridiculous or slightly dishonest."[15]

Hick at first called this new pluralistic conception of the divine "the Eternal One." He preferred this expression, since it can be read *either* in personal theistic ways *or* in non-personal mystical ways. Hence it can apply to western monotheisms as well as to traditions like Hinduism, Greek mysticism, and Daoism (although, we must observe, it does not really work for a tradition like Buddhism). Here is Hick in 1980 on his title phrase "God has many names" (which, you might recall, had already been invoked millennia ago by India's ancient Rig Veda):

> When I say in a summarizing slogan that God has many names, I mean that the Eternal One is perceived within different human cultures under different forms, both personal and non-personal, and that from these different perceptions arise the religious ways of life which we call the great world faiths.[16]

No doubt thinking of Buddhism, often the glaring exception to world religion patterns, he would later move away from "the Eternal One" and switch to a more inclusive referent: "the Real."

Pluralism Is a Truth Claim

Sometimes pluralism is read as a kind of happy, fuzzy "anything goes" response, in effect a kind of intellectual laziness or irresponsible denial of real difference and real-world complexity. One can certainly find examples of such moments, but this is hardly a necessary feature of the pluralist logic, which is also radically *exclusivistic*. Pluralism insists on affirming *and* negating religious forms at the same time. The Jesuit missionary in India with whom we began this chapter was correct: to affirm all religions, as the Mughal Emperor Akbar was doing, is also to deny the claims of each and every one of them.

We are *all* exclusivists, in the simplest sense that any clear position we take must, by necessity, exclude and deny those positions that are logically contrary to it. Perhaps that is why we are so seldom clear.

The pluralist, then, like the exclusivist and the inclusivist, is making an absolute claim, which denies and excludes other faith claims. But this absolute claim is not rooted in, limited to, or exhausted by any single historical religious tradition. *That* is the truth claim.

Strengths and Weaknesses of Pluralism

Again, there are both real advantages here and real problems, just as we saw in the case of exclusivism and inclusivism. The advantages come down to the simple observation that pluralism is easily the faith response that is the most adequate to the history of religions as we know it today. Put simply, it is very difficult for many people to learn something of the full scope of human religious belief and practice and then to imagine that God just happened to speak the full or only truth to one's own very particular culture or ethnicity. That strikes many as suspicious and, well, more than a bit self-serving. It certainly suggests a rather flippant, ethnocentric, even cruel God, who plays favorites and who leaves most of humanity in darkness or only partial light. Pluralism will have none of this.

The problems or dilemmas arise from this same universalism. It is clear, for example, that all sorts of human knowledge are by no means evenly distributed between cultures and times. It is difficult to see why this unevenness would not extend to religious, moral, and philosophical subjects as well. A related issue here

is that we also know that moral positions that become widely admired often begin in marginal or persecuted individuals and communities that claim religious inspiration for their very particular positions. We see exactly this in historical instances—from the radical gender equity of spiritualists in nineteenth-century America, through the non-violent campaigns of Mahatma Gandhi in British India in the twentieth, to the **civil rights movement** of Martin Luther King, Jr. These were all religiously inspired movements, and they argued for or accomplished dramatic moral ends, none of which would have been possible without these same very particular and very specific religious inspirations and motivations.

The pluralist's egalitarianism also produces a most acute pragmatic problem: if God speaks more or less equally to all human communities, then why belong to this particular community instead of that one? Indeed, why belong to any religious community at all? The walls of the ingroup are so thin and so low here that it is not even clear that there are walls to be had. Consequently, the parking lots of pluralist religious communities tend to be very small and their membership lists very short. The more pluralist a religious tradition becomes, the smaller it becomes. To return to the bridge–bonding dilemma model, we might say that the pluralist community has put all of its eggs in the "bridge" basket, and so its ability to "bond" is seriously compromised. The exclusivist or fundamentalist community does the opposite: it puts all its eggs in the "bond" basket, and so its ability to "bridge" is seriously compromised.

Other dilemmas are logical and moral ones. Can the pluralist, for example, really accept the exclusivist and his or her own religious claims as a legitimate expression of the sacred? Can a pluralist tolerate intolerance? Can the pluralist take a firm moral position on religious practices that violate his or her own religious humanism, say, on female circumcision or female genital mutilation (FGM), so prominent in northeastern Africa, on the Hindu caste system, on Christian fundamentalist hate-mongering around the issue of homosexuality, or on the Muslim Pakistani practice of imprisoning or killing daughters who are raped? Clearly, some kind of distinction must be made between the revelatory core of a tradition and its cultural and social expressions. But can such a distinction *really* be made? These are some of the problems that any pluralist must face.

Comparison Is Justice: Liberation, Black, Feminist, and Queer Theologies

Exclusivism, inclusivism, and pluralism, then. Here are three ways to put your world back together again after it has been taken apart in the bright light that is religious pluralism. Here are three ways to be religious among the countless religions.

But the social fact of religious pluralism is not the only problem that confronts the believer in the modern world. There are other major concerns that call for new ways of thinking. There are thus other specifically religious ways of re-reading religion. Foremost among these is a whole set of faithful re-readings that do not compare religions primarily on the basis of their approach to other religions, but on the basis of how they lead (or do not lead) to social practices, personal attitudes, and stable political, economic, and legal institutions that are just and fair. The fundamental concern with these faithful re-readings is not the type of God or ultimate reality one assumes, but how this model of divinity or reality leads to real and lasting social justice and human flourishing.

For own comparative purposes here, we might define **social justice** as *the moral insistence on being treated the same*. We might even say that justice is itself a kind of universal comparative practice, that *sameness is justice*, as long as we understand that this sameness does not mean that everyone must be the same (the same religion, the same race, the same gender, the same sexual orientation, and so on), but that everyone should be treated the same by a society's public, educational, legal, and political institutions, regardless of one's religious, ethnic, gender, and sexual differences. In short, sameness is justice only

to the extent that it can also acknowledge and accept real and lasting difference.

Put differently, *comparison is justice*.

Different forms of modern theology have arisen in the last century or so that operate on this same fundamental comparativist logic according to which justice is the balancing of sameness and difference. As we shall see, all of these ways of doing theology are linked, both conceptually and historically, since it is extremely difficult to argue effectively for the equality of one group or class of people while demeaning or rejecting another (although, ironically, this is often precisely the case in particular communities to this day). So, for example, many minorities will argue strenuously for religious equality in contemporary democratic societies, even as they deny full equality to women in their own communities and belief systems; or many churches in the USA or Africa will witness powerfully to, say, racial equality, even as they seek to deny basic civil rights to gay and lesbian peoples; and so on.

It is precisely these sorts of inconsistent discriminations that this particular group of faithful re-readings of religion have sought to address. Together, they have produced massive literatures and an immense sweep of powerful social movements that have, together, helped reshape modern society in fundamental ways. We will concern ourselves here with just four major chords in this long moral symphony: liberation theology, black theology, feminist theology, and queer theology.[17] Each of these theological traditions rose to prominence in the Americas within the last sixty years (more or less in the order in which we have just listed them), but each one also possesses deep roots that stretch back into global history. As we shall see, three nineteenth-century movements in the USA were particularly influential: the social gospel movement, the abolition movement, and the early women's movement.

Liberation Theology

Most simply put, **liberation theology** is a way of thinking and speaking of God that understands God as identifying with the poor, the marginalized, and the oppressed. It arose in the 1950s and 1960s among Latin American intellectuals who were increasingly concerned about how the Roman Catholic Church was aligning itself with the rich and powerful and how this religious–political alignment was helping to produce all sorts of authoritarian and oppressive political regimes. Gustavo Gutiérrez, a Roman Catholic priest from Peru, is usually identified as one of the movement's key figures. It was he who coined the expression "liberation theology" in 1971, in his book *A Theology of Liberation* (originally published in Spanish). Other key figures include the Jesuit priest Jon Sobrino from El Salvador and the Brazilian and former Franciscan priest Leonardo Boff, both of whom have come into conflict with the Vatican for their writings.

If one reads the Bible from the perspective of the oppressed and the poor, these intellectuals argued, it is obvious that the biblical God sides in this life and world with the poor, not with the rich; with the oppressed, not with those in power. The Jewish salvation narrative orbits precisely around an enslaved people (the Hebrews of Exodus) being liberated from an oppressive political regime in Egypt (hence the importance of this biblical story for the black slaves in the American South of the eighteenth and nineteenth centuries). The same applies to the biblical prophets: they witnessed to a God who was angered by the injustices and gross inequalities of Israelite society and by the corruptions of political power, which were so often evident in Israel's institution of monarchy. The God of the prophets is a God who demands justice and fairness. Here salvation is not some post-mortem place of rest and reward. Indeed, shockingly, the Hebrew Bible knows virtually nothing of an afterlife until very late, in just a few pages—those of Daniel, for example. In the older prophetic books, salvation is all about political liberation and social justice. It is about the here and now. It is about justice.

So too with the New Testament, the gospels, and the moral message of Jesus. That Galilean firebrand, the Latin American theologians pointed out, did not preach: "Blessed are the rich, for they have worked hard for their wealth and deserve it." He preached: "Blessed are the poor, for theirs is the kingdom of heaven" (Luke 6.20). And, lest you jump to conclusions here, the "kingdom of heaven" did not mean the heaven of modern piety. It was an alternative expression for the "kingdom of God" in the gospels (since pious Jews would avoid using the word "God" in their speech and writing). Numerous gospel passages describe such a kingdom as a mystery or state of salvation available in the here and now.

Moreover, this same historical Jesus did not die quietly in his sleep or of old age, feted by politicians and churchmen and made wealthy by an adoring flock. He died a gruesome, horrible death as a tortured political prisoner, as a hated and rejected criminal. In effect, he was brutally killed by a deadly cocktail of religion and politics. And why not? He had given powerful witness to the gross injustices that these two institutions had imposed on the poor through their purity codes, their sacred hierarchies, and their colonizing ambitions and imperialistic violences.

As the Latin American intellectuals developed these kinds of faithful re-readings, their theology began to form around a few core interpretive principles. One of these was what Gutiérrez popularized through the phrase "the **preferential option for the poor**." He meant by this expression that the Bible should be read, and so Christian life should be lived, in ways that, like God, identified with the poor and the downtrodden. But the liberation theologians went further. Because they were schooled in sociological theory, and particularly in Marxist theory, they realized that the injustices of society are *structural* and not simply personal: they realized that people suffer and are oppressed not primarily because of their individual choices or intentions (this is what those who want to conserve the inequalities of a society always argue—they effectively blame the victims), but because the social, political, and religious *institutions* they live in are set up in a way that makes it impossible for people to be treated equally and justly. It is not that the poor and the marginalized are playing the game badly; it is that the rules of the game are set up in a way that makes it impossible for them to win—or even to get in the game, for that matter.

The corollary of this basic sociological insight followed closely: if things were going to change, they would have to change at a social and institutional level, and not just at a personal level. No "change of heart" by this or that individual would do. Salvation could no longer be simply a personal matter, about "saving one's soul." It would now have to be also a social matter, about transforming society into the kingdom of God. The game itself has to change.

These were not entirely new ideas. Earlier versions of these same faithful re-readings had been advanced in the nineteenth and early twentieth centuries in the USA, within something called the **social gospel movement**, perhaps best embodied by a Baptist minister named Walter Rauschenbusch in his classic works *Christianity and the Social Crisis* (1907) and *A Theology for the Social Gospel* (1917). What Rauschenbusch was so concerned about in his own day was the gross wealth of the business magnates—or "robber barons," as they were called (since they "robbed" the wealth of society and hoarded it for themselves)—and the way these wealthy businessmen were using poor people to work in their factories and on their railroads. Child labor was a particularly obvious and noxious social problem here, as were the grueling hours of the working poor, who were basically little more than legal slaves.

Black Theology

The basic insights of the social gospel movement and later Latin American liberation theologies were persuasive. Accordingly, they helped inspire other types of theology, whose primary concerns were liberation from economic oppression and social injustice. Arguably the earliest of these developments in North America was **black theology**: a way of doing theology that thinks and speaks of God from the perspective of the historical experience of African Americans, who, like the Hebrews, were once chattel slaves and continue to suffer all sorts of prejudices and injustices because of their skin color and assumed racial characteristics.[18]

Black theology was by no means simply a response to Latin American liberation theology, however. It emerged organically from the North Atlantic slave trade (the first African slaves arrived in Virginia in 1619) and from the long African American experience of forced servitude and violent oppression over two and a half centuries. Particularly important here were the horrific public lynchings that lasted well into the twentieth century (dummies of President Barack Obama were lynched in a number of states as late as 2012, during the presidential election); the white Christian terrorism of the Ku Klux Klan; and the dramatic social transformations of the 1960s.

The northern black intellectual W. E. B. DuBois, who was a student of William James at Harvard, set the agenda early on for this form of thought in his *The Souls of Black Folk* (1903), namely around the various subtle and explicit ways in which American racism created a "double consciousness" in black people, denying them the public power to signify and thereby define their own souls; but he also established—and this is crucial—a perspective outside the social system that grants them particularly acute insights into how it works (and does not work for black people). He called the former—the denial to signify oneself—a "veil," and the latter—the ability to see through the social fiction—the gift of "second-sight":

> The Negro is sort of a seventh son, born with a veil, and gifted with second sight in this American world—a world which yields him no true self-consciousness, but only lets him see himself through the revelation of the other world. It is a peculiar sensation, this double consciousness, this sense of always looking at one's self through the eyes of others, of measuring one's soul by the tape of a world that looks on in amused contempt and pity. One ever feels this twoness—an American, a Negro; two souls, two thoughts, two unreconciled strivings; two warring ideals in one dark body, whose dogged strength alone keeps it from being torn asunder.[19]

There are other ways to be "split in two"—social and political ways. Trauma can be social.

Of particular interest here was the civil rights movement of the 1950s and 1960s. This was a widespread social movement in the USA that sought to overturn an array of "Jim Crow" and "Jane Crow" laws (which segregated and restricted black people from particular public places, like restaurants and transportation services), institutions, attitudes, and policies deeply embedded in American society. Two figures were of iconic importance here: Martin Luther King, Jr., and Malcolm X (born Malcolm Little). King, a Baptist minister with a PhD, was a powerful preacher and eloquent voice who took up non-violent means of protest as his primary method of social change. He believed in the full integration of blacks and whites within American society. King was partly inspired here by the Hindu political and religious leader Mahatma Gandhi, who was assassinated by a Hindu fundamentalist for his inclusive policies toward Muslims. Probably King's most famous speech is "I Have a Dream," which he gave in front of the Lincoln Memorial on the Washington Mall in the summer of 1963, a little over one hundred years after President Lincoln issued the Emancipation Proclamation, on January 1, 1863. King was assassinated in 1968 by the segregationist James Earl Ray (see Figure 10.4).

Malcolm X took a different approach. Originally he preached black supremacy, sought a policy of separation of blacks and whites, and joined the Nation of Islam. Later he took a pilgrimage to Mecca, converted to Sunni Islam, and renounced racism of any sort after he saw races of all kinds interacting as equals on the Hajj (the Muslim pilgrimage to Mecca). One consistent theme throughout his life, however, was his standing argument that African Americans cannot be liberated with their oppressors' religion, that is, through Christianity. Malcolm X was assassinated in 1965, at a public meeting, with twenty-one shots to his body, at close range. Three Nation of Islam members were convicted.

In its origins in the late 1960s, black theology was a synthesis of the legacies of Martin Luther King, Jr., and Malcom X. King's Christian gospel of love and non-violence is carried by the "theology" part; Malcolm X's

Figure 10.4 National Memorial to Dr. Martin Luther King, Jr. Washington, DC. © Stephen St. John/Getty Images.

message of black power and self-determination is carried by the "black" part.[20] James Cone was the principal architect of black theology. Cone's two first books, *Black Theology and Black Power* (1969) and *A Black Theology of Liberation* (1970), set the tone and context of much that would follow, including his central and controversial notion of God's ontological blackness.

The term "ontological" refers to the being, nature, or core reality of something. Cone was arguing that God's being is indistinguishable from the being of black people, and that this gives rise to God's action on behalf of black peoples.[21] Cone was not, of course, referring to God's skin color, but to God's identification with the oppressed, which in the USA means an identification with the plight and sufferings of African Americans or black people. In this view, anyone who works for justice and freedom is ontologically "black."

Black theology does not generally read the Bible literally, and for good reason. The Bible has been used to justify both American slavery and South African apartheid.[22] And this is because the Bible itself tolerates and even implicitly promotes the practice of slavery. Consider this passage, with the usual biblical notion that women in particular are male property (sex, marriage, and slavery are deeply intertwined in the religious imagination):

> When you buy a male Hebrew slave, he shall serve six years, but in the seventh he shall go out a free person, without debt. If he comes in single, he shall go out single; if he comes in married, then his wife shall go out with him. If his master gives him a wife and she bears him sons or daughters, the wife and her children shall be her master's and he shall go out alone. (Exodus 21.2–4)

Or this one from the same book and chapter:

> When a slaveowner strikes a male or female slave with a rod and the slave dies immediately, the owner shall be punished. But if the slave survives a day or two, there is no punishment; for the slave is the owner's property. (Exodus 21.20–21)

Numerous New Testament passages could also be cited here and discussed at great length (and to devastating effect to any literal reading of the Bible).[23] Here, after all, we find lines on how slaves should obey their masters "with respect and fear," as they would obey Christ (Ephesians 6.5); the apostle Paul returns a runaway slave to his master (Philemon); and a passage in 1 Peter actually encourages slaves to endure unjust beatings as part of their salvation (1 Peter 2.18–21). Also relevant here are the commonly cited passages on why wives should be subject to their husbands and why children should obey their parents (Colossians 3.18–4.1; Ephesians 5.21–6.9). Always left out of this discussion today is the fact that these same passages explicitly link a patriarch's authority in his household, over his wife and children,

to his authority over his household slaves. The patriarchal family and the institution of slavery are clearly understood to participate in the same divine order, the free man at the top of the hierarchy standing in for Christ as the ultimate "master" or "head."

Little wonder that many sincere Protestant Christians in the USA assumed that the Bible was on their side in the nineteenth-century debates around the abolition of slavery. Read literally, it was. Even the pope agreed with them. In 1866 Pope Pious IX signed a declaration that "[i]t is not contrary to the natural and divine law for a slave to be sold, bought, exchanged or given." Similar notions can again be found in the Quran and in the history of Islam, particularly around the legal status of female slaves. From the perspective of early experts on Islamic law, the slave concubine is considered to be the *milk* or "property" of her owner, who has a legal right to have sex with her as his sexual property, as did slave owners in general in the ancient Near East.[24]

The bottom line is this: the social worlds from which the three monotheistic scriptural canons emerged *assumed* the institution of slavery. They did not seriously question it. Hence the prominence of the practice of slavery in the histories of Christianity and Islam. Interestingly, Judaism is a relative exception here again. Whereas Christians and Muslims enslaved peoples in immense numbers for centuries, Jews engaged in the practice only sporadically, although examples can be found.

Such biblical texts and ugly religious histories have led black historians of religions and theologians like Charles Long and Anthony Pinn to question whether discussion and analysis of the black religious experience should be restricted to Christian sources (an echo of Malcolm X). They have also pointed out that the black religious experience in America is hardly restricted to the Christian churches. African Americans, after all, inhabit countless religious worlds, from Africa-inspired conjuring and magical traditions like Voodoo and Santería, through various Catholic, Muslim, and Jewish traditions, to humanism, Buddhism, and various esoteric traditions (think Masonic Lodges and UFO encounters, as we find, for example, in the Nation of Islam and in the leader Louis Farrakhan's Mother Wheel).[25] Scholars have also turned to African American slave narratives, to literary, material, and popular culture (black literature, quilting cultures, and rap music, for example), and to traditional black folklore for their source materials and to African religions and humanism for some of their new theoretical perspectives.

It is really quite impossible to overemphasize the importance of the African American experience for the modern study of religion, particularly in the latter's North American forms. We have dedicated an entire chapter in this textbook to gender, but we could have just as easily dedicated an entire chapter to race. Clearly race is just as foundational for the moral underpinnings and social expressions of the study of religion.

Feminist Theology

The subjects of race and gender are deeply intertwined, both historically and conceptually. For example, in the nineteenth-century **abolition movement**, it was the issue of black slavery that first inspired American Christian women activists to work for the abolition of slavery, which in turn made them realize something of the depths of their own subservient condition. These women attempted to take leading roles in the movement—at meetings, in churches, in the press, at the pulpit. Again and again, they were denied those leadership roles, those voices, and that pulpit. They were forced to the conclusion that it was more than a little ironic to work for the freedoms of black slaves when most of these same freedoms were explicitly denied to their gender, both in churches and in town squares.

They responded with what was, in essence, the first American "wave" of the women's movement, which focused on the issue of **suffrage** (the right to vote) and produced wonderfully colorful figures like Susan B. Anthony and Elizabeth Cady Stanton and classic texts like Stanton's *The Woman's Bible* (1895–1898)—an extraordinary commentary on many of the biblical books from the perspective of a female reader. All this was in effect one of the modern beginnings of what would become feminist philosophy and feminist theology in the 1960s through the 1980s—a period often referred to as the second wave of the women's movement.[26]

Feminist theology is a way of doing theology that thinks and speaks of God from the perspective of those who have traditionally been excluded from thinking and speaking of God in every world religion: women. Feminist theologians recognize that most traditional language about "God" is male language that privileges male psychology and authority, along with notions of transcendence and omnipotence and the imperial and colonial violences that lie behind those notions. Feminist theology generally rejects such models of divinity as dangerous and one-sided, preferring instead to emphasize the female qualities of relationship, connectedness, and nurturing. More specifically, feminist re-readings of religion work through a balancing of the principles of sameness and difference: sameness is viewed, again as justice, in the sense that women should be treated as equals at every level (legal, cultural, and personal), and difference is defined mostly through the principles of mutuality, connectedness, and relationship— with family, with social others, with the environment, and so on.

As feminist theology developed, it became more and more apparent that the women from whose perspective the theology was to be done were themselves very different. It became apparent that there is no such thing as just a "woman." There are white women, black women, Latina women, Asian women, straight women, lesbian women, married women, single women, middle-class women, poor women, mothers, wives, lovers, daughters, grandmothers, and so on. And each community, each perspective produces different social concerns, and hence different models of divinity and religious practice (see Figure 10.5).

Feminist theology thus began to branch out further, particularly after 1982, when the African American author Alice Walker published her pioneering book *In Search of Our Mother's Gardens*. With this book

Figure 10.5   Members of the Good Shepherd Anglican Church march for peace, Warri, Nigeria, 2004. © Ed Kashi/Corbis.

and this author, whose novel *The Color Purple* also functions as a key text within this tradition of re-reading, a new expression was born: womanist theology, which we might define as feminist theology done from the perspective of black women. These women pointed out that black theology was also a male theology, and that it more or less ignored the experiences and perspectives of a full half of black people—women. Such a logic was persuasive, and it was quickly extended into Latina feminist theology (which is sometimes called mujerista theology) and into Asian feminist theology (Asian women constitute a full quarter of the world's population).

The central lesson here is this: thinking about God and religion is never neutral, never objective—nor should it be. Theology, as James Cone pointed out, is always interested, always local, always done from a particular perspective for a particular community. The corollary of this obvious truth quickly follows, and it is a radically pluralistic one: no single model of God and religion should be imposed on anyone, since no single model of God and religion can possibly represent and

express the historical experiences of every community or body. Once again, religion is radically, fundamentally, irreducibly *plural*.

Queer Theology

The next major development in these comparative theologies of justice was **LGBT theology**. LGBT (lesbian, gay, bisexual, and transsexual) theology takes up the basic principles of earlier liberation theologies and employs them to reinterpret the biblical texts and to think and speak about God from the perspective of people with socially marginalized sexualities, be these lesbian, gay, bisexual, or transsexual.

In feminist theology one often has to speculate about the perspectives of the women involved in a particular scriptural text or teaching, since these texts and teachings—Jewish, Christian, Muslim, Hindu, Buddhist, Confucian, you name it—were almost always written by and for men. In male gay theology, however, the situation is often quite different, in the sense that the homoeroticism of a text or tradition is often explicit; it is an open secret, if you will. After all, many of their authors were men, and as men they had access to voices and modes of expression that their female counterparts did not. The result is that the male homoeroticism of a scriptural or ritual tradition is often quite easy to see. Scholarship on the Hebrew Bible, the New Testament, and Roman Catholicism are particularly rich and provocative here, mostly because these were the traditions of the scholars who developed these same gay or queer faithful re-readings.

One of the foundational texts of LGBT theology is Yale historian John Boswell's magisterial work *Christianity, Social Tolerance and Homosexuality* (1980), which demonstrated that, along its history, Christianity was not particularly concerned about "homosexuality" until the medieval period, somewhere around the twelfth century. Indeed many texts from the Bible and from Christian history—especially texts produced in the clerical and institutional ranks of the Roman Catholic Church—can easily be re-read as celebrating homoerotic love, Boswell pointed out. Hence his famous subtitle: *Gay People in Western Europe from the Beginning of the Christian Era to the Fourteenth Century.*

This subtitle became famous because it sat as a direct challenge to one of Boswell's own inspirations: the work of Michel Foucault and his three-volume *History of Sexuality*. Foucault had previously argued that categories like "homosexuality" and "gay"—and indeed the whole notion of a "sexual orientation"—were modern constructions of the nineteenth century (this, as we have seen, is a questionable assumption). For Foucault, human sexuality is always more fluid than such simplistic categories would suggest, and sexual practices and identities are products of constantly shifting and changing cultural norms and social "discipline." The latter is a very broad term that points to the ways our innermost desires and norms are shaped and controlled by all the surrounding social factors, from religious principles and moral norms through the official categories of professional psychiatry to civil and criminal law codes.

Beginning with her classic work *Gender Trouble* (1990), the feminist philosopher Judith Butler has

advanced this model yet further, through her fundamental notion of gender as a socially enacted performance and of desire as a function of social norms. To put it very simply (perhaps too simply), in this model one does not "have" a sexual orientation—one does not just "desire" anything; one *performs* a gender and a sexuality via stylized acts and scripts provided by the surrounding culture.

This last approach to human sexuality, which emphasizes fluidity and the social construction of all sexual desire and identity, is technically referred to as queer theory. Although the two share many intellectual influences and values, queer theory is in fact quite different from LGBT theology, since it is much more reticent about locating clear sexual identities in pre-modern history or in non-western cultures. This difference has major implications for the kinds of justice that each approach advances. Whereas LGBT theology claims justice for lesbian, gay, bisexual, and transgendered people throughout history and across cultures (since such people really existed), **queer theology** wants to critique the very notion of a sexual identity as a limiting and often dehumanizing, even sinful social construction—an *invention* used to discriminate against particular people and their always fluid desires.

Later on contemporary scholars like Robert Goss and Mark Jordan took up this line of thought, which is specific of queer theology. Goss, a public activist and a scholar, has written two provocative books that present Jesus as a radical social reformer who "acted up," that is, who sided with the poor and marginalized (and hence would definitely side with the sexually marginalized today) and was likely anything but "straight."[27] For his part, Jordan, a trained medievalist and theologian, has employed queer theory in elegant theological studies of the invention of "sodomy" in medieval theology (the term originally covered everything from anal sex to masturbation) and in the institutional paradoxes of contemporary Roman Catholicism, which is at once internally homoerotic and externally homophobic.[28]

Much of this work flows from the insight that sexual desire is never free from internal and external restraints—or, as Foucault put it, from "policing" and

Figure 10.6 Gay rights rally, Tyne and Wear, England, 2012. © Matt Dinnery/Demotix/Corbis.

"disciplining"—and that, moreover, sexual desire itself often requires these social repressions to work. Human beings often desire most precisely that which is forbidden: prohibition *increases* desire. Hence human sexuality is seldom simple or without conflict. Accordingly, a religious tradition can be deeply homophobic in its social teachings (the prohibition part) and deeply homoerotic in its inner institutional structures and spiritual life (the desire part). The two poles are by no means mutually exclusive. Indeed, they often work together as the very psychosexual "engine" of holiness itself (see Figure 10.6).

As Jordan demonstrates in *The Silence of Sodom*, for example, a tradition like Roman Catholicism may condemn the expression of homosexuality, but one result of this moral discipline (or prohibition) is that Catholic gay men, being deprived of a licit or acceptable outlet in society, find celibacy and priesthood (read: freedom from straight life) particularly attractive. Accordingly they come to dominate the demographics, and hence the institutional cultures, of those celibate (read: non-heterosexual) professions. In effect sexual repression leads to different kinds of erotic sublimations, and in this case it leads to spiritual lives that may not be overtly sexual at all but are expressed through all sorts of coded queer acts—from loving a perfect god-man to eating his body (never the body of a woman, please note) and to living in same-sex communities. This same queer re-reading also explains the Catholic prohibition against married men and women becoming priests: straight men or women would obviously weaken, if not eventually dissolve, the strong male homoerotic dynamic of clerical culture.

It bears repeating that similar observations could easily be made, and have been made, in other religious contexts, from Buddhist monasticism and Hindu sainthood to Native American shamanism and Islamic Sufism. What we have here is another clear gender and sexual pattern in the general history of religions.

We can also see reactions to these common gender and sexual patterns: we can see rabidly homophobic strains in numerous religions on any continent. The roles of some of the African states and Christian churches have been especially evident recently. Robert Mugabe, the president of Zimbabwe, blamed gays and lesbians for the problems of his country. In Cameroon gays and lesbians have been imprisoned for their sexual orientations. The former Anglican archbishop of Nigeria, the Most Reverend Peter Akinola, led his church in an attempt to break away from the Anglican community because an American church ordained an open homosexual, the Reverend Gene Robinson. There was even a draft bill in the Ugandan parliament that would have defined same-sex relations as a capital offense. It failed, but not before one of its opponents was murdered.[29]

The struggle goes on around the world.

Thinking Justice

All of these theologies of justice are related, and this for at least two reasons. First, they are related because these modes of re-reading religion are not disinterested, or simply descriptive. They are openly concerned re-readings, designed to change people's hearts and society's institutions. They are *religious* re-readings of religion.

Second, they are related because the logic of religious discrimination has worked in remarkably similar ways in different historical contexts. Hence they must be confronted and addressed in similar ways. We might summarize this process of religious discrimination, re-reading, and social liberation in four basic movements:

1   A cultural majority decides that a particular class of people, defined by some physical or cultural characteristic, is less than human ("damned," "infidels," "impure," "primitives," "low caste") and hence not deserving of the same rights, dignity, and opportunities that the cultural majority enjoys.

2   The same cultural majority uses its revealed texts and teachings to justify this oppression; and all traditional scriptures, produced as they were in ancient cultures that assumed things like slavery, the subordination of women, and the necessity of war, are rich in such prejudices.

3   The literal authority of these same scriptures or traditions breaks down in the light of modernity, historical criticism, and commentary, particularly as these re-readings are performed by members of the oppressed class.

4   Finally, the oppression and social injustice is removed or at least ameliorated, inevitably against the received readings of the religions and through a new modern (and often partly secular) logic of human freedom, dignity, and equality.

What is so interesting about this process from a historical perspective is how consistent it is and how short the historical memories of the discriminating religious communities are. Quoting the discriminatory passages from the Bible, for example, was *the*

defense of those who argued for the biblical roots of slavery; as it was for those who argued for the "proper place" of women in the home and away from the voting booth and the pulpit; as it was for people who argued for the persecution of Jews in Europe; as it was for those who insisted on the segregation of blacks and whites in the American South or, more recently, in South Africa; as it is now for those who argue against the integrity of gay, lesbian, and transgendered peoples. The actors and the proof texts change, but the project is basically the same: go back to a set of ancient social values "frozen" in a scriptural text and attempt to impose them on people today.

No major world religion is immune from this discriminatory logic and this difficult history. They have only used different scriptural texts to discriminate against different types of people. Specific religious communities, however, have engaged in discriminatory practices to different extents. As we have already noted, whereas the Torah, the New Testament, and the Quran all contain passages clearly supportive of slavery, only Christianity and Islam engaged in the massive enslavement of peoples over the centuries. Judaism did not. If we turned our focus on caste and social oppression in Asia, similar comparisons could be drawn between Hinduism (which assumes the institution of caste) and Buddhism (which generally rejects it). Hence the career of one of India's greatest modern social reformers, B. R. Ambedkar (1891–1956), whose movement involved the conversion of Indian Dalits to a socially progressive form of Theravada Buddhism.

Again, *no* religion or culture is immune from these sorts of comparisons from the perspective of justice defined as "being treated the same." Accordingly, when the editors of the second edition of *The Encyclopedia of Religion*, one of the standard and most distinguished reference books in the field, sought to update the first edition after the turn of the millennium, they asked their chosen contributors to emphasize three crucial categories: sex, class, and race. Through this move the editors made explicit and highlighted what had long been implicit in the scholarly tradition: the link between academic method and social justice, and the imperative that, when it comes to the study of religion, *nothing* should be removed from the public table of critical analysis. Nothing can be sacred here.

Nuances: Faith and Scholarship

Finally, it seems appropriate to add a note on the need for nuance in understanding and practicing faithful re-readings. One's stance on faith does not simply impose a position on religious pluralism or social justice. It also informs *how* one studies religion: the kinds of questions one asks, what one sees in another faith, what one misses, the kinds of moral positions that this study produces, and so on.

George Marsden, a historian of Evangelical Christianity, has noted that, whereas all sorts of other identities are valued and freely displayed in the academy (ethnic identities, racial identities, sexual identities, and so on), religious identities are generally discouraged, or even demeaned as illegitimate intellectual perspectives.[30] This is clearly a double standard. It is also clearly wrong, as religious subjectivities, just like other types of subjectivity, grant particular insights and nuances to scholarship, especially on humanist subjects like literature, philosophy, art, and, of course, religion. If handled in a nuanced, sophisticated, and self-critical way, a faith position need not produce scholarship of any lower quality. Indeed it might actually produce *better* scholarship. It certainly produces scholarship with different accents and nuances.

To take just one example, it has been observed that the history of comparative theology displays the prominence of Catholic theologians and intellectuals. In this reading, Catholicism encourages and nurtures a particular kind of comparative practice. Similar observations could also be made, of course, about black theology, feminist theology, and queer theology, which display, respectively, a prominence of black, female, and queer intellectuals.

So we do not want to leave you with the impression that religious perspectives simply lead to discrimination. This is not true. Religious belief can sharpen as well as distort. Religious conviction can produce better and worse re-readings of religion, depending upon how it is handled and, most of all, depending upon how reflexive it is.

The Tough Questions

1 How is the statement "A Buddhist is going to hell" or "Non-Muslims are infidels" any different from "Blacks are inferior"? Are not all three forms of bigotry and ignorance, the former couched in religious language, the latter in racist language? Why do we generally tolerate the former, but not the latter?

2 What is your community's position on mixed marriages, that is, marriages between two people of two different faith traditions? Where does religious community end and religious discrimination begin?

3 Watch Mende Nazar describe her experience of slavery and the Jewish, Christian, and Islamic scriptural passages that are used to justify it, at http://www.brandeis.edu/projects/fse/conferences/beyond-slavery/videos/mende-nazer. How can a scriptural text that is "revealed" justify a social practice that almost everyone today would consider morally abominable? And, if these scriptural passages on slavery can no longer be supported, why take other scriptural passages on other ancient social practices and convictions (like the "impure" status of homosexual acts) as relevant or authoritative?

4 Can a person who adopts a pluralistic position really be tolerant of all other worldviews? Can one tolerate intolerance?

Notes

1 Tessa Dick, *Philip K. Dick: Remembering Firebright* (CreateSpace, 2009), 75–79. The details of this story shift from one account to another, of which there are many (a not uncommon phenomenon with religious narratives). I am telling here the standard version, as it were. Tessa Dick has the young woman delivering the author's regular high blood pressure medicine on the third day after the oral surgery and states that the pink light was sunlight bouncing off a bumper sticker with a silver fish sign on their west window, not off the young woman's Christian necklace. Whatever happened, it changed the author in dramatic ways.

2 Lawrence Sutin, ed., *In Pursuit of Valis* (Nevada City, CA: Underwood Books, 1991), 102, xvii, 81.

3 Brent Landau, *Revelation of the Magi: The Lost Tale of the Wise Men's Journey to Bethlehem* (New York: HarperOne, 2010), 91.

4 For an excellent summary of Baha'i theology, see William Garlington, *The Baha'i Faith in America* (Westport, CT: Praeger, 2005).

5 Tertullian, *On the Prescription against Heretics*, Ch. 7.

6 Wouter J. Hanegraaff, *Esotericism and the Academy: Rejected Knowledge in Western Culture* (Cambridge: Cambridge University Press, 2012), 121, 108, 91.

7 This question is best framed as a question of Hindu theology or Buddhist philosophy, since, technically speaking, there is no such thing as Buddhist theology, there being no "God" there.

8 Francis X. Clooney, *Comparative Theology: Deep Learning across Religious Borders* (Oxford: Wiley-Blackwell, 2010), 10–11.

9 Clooney, *Comparative Theology*, 21.

10 See Robert Erlewine, "Monotheism, Tolerance, and Pluralism: The Current Impasse." Chapter 1 in his *Monotheism and Tolerance: Recovering a Religion of Reason* (Bloomington: Indiana University Press, 2010).

11 Erlewine, "Monotheism, Tolerance, and Pluralism," 7.

12 Both quotations are taken from John Hick, *God Has Many Names* (Philadelphia, PA: The Westminster Press, 1982), 30, 90.

13 Michael O. Emerson, *People of the Dream: Multiracial Congregations in the United States* (Princeton, NJ: Princeton University Press, 2008), 93.

14 This document can easily be found on the Vatican's website at http://mv.vatican.va/3_EN/pages/x-Schede/CSNs/CSNs_G_Giud.html (last accessed on August 23, 2013).

15 Hick, *God Has Many Names*, 68.

16 Hick, *God Has Many Names*, 59.

17 There are other important traditions not treated here, including Native American theologies of justice and emerging eco-theologies.

18 For a summary of black theology upon which I am relying here, see Anthony B. Pinn, "Black Theology." In *Liberation Theologies in the United States: An Introduction*, edited by Stacey M. Floyd-Thomas and Anthony B. Pinn (New York: New York University Press, 2010), 15–36.

19 W. E. B. DuBois, *The Souls of Black Folk* (New York: Cosimo, 2007), 2.

20 James S. Olson, *Equality Deferred: Race, Ethnicity, and Immigration in America Since 1945* (Belmont, CA: Wadsworth, 2003), 64–66; quoted in Pinn, "Black Theology," 20.

21 My thanks to my Rice colleague, Anthony Pinn, for help on this point, and so much more.

22 For the African case, see Elias Bongmba, "African Theology." In *The Wiley-Blackwell Companion to African Religions*, edited by Elias Kifon Bongmba (Oxford: Wiley-Blackwell, 2012), 241–254.

23 For two stunning studies, see Jennifer A. Glancy, *Slavery in Early Christianity* (Minneapolis, MN: Augsburg Fortress, 2006); and J. Albert Harrill, *Slaves in the New Testament: Literary, Social, and Moral Dimensions* (Minneapolis, MN: Augsburg Fortress, 2005).

24 We are relying in this paragraph on Bernadette J. Brooten's unpublished paper "Overcoming the Legacy of Slavery: A Challenge for Religion," delivered at Rice University, February 19, 2013, which is in turn based on Bernadette J. Brooten, ed., with Jacqueline L. Hazelton, *Beyond Slavery: Its Religious and Sexual Legacies* (New York: Palgrave Macmillan, 2010). For the issue of slave concubinage, see Kecia Ali, *Marriage and Slavery in Early Islam* (Cambridge, MA: Harvard University Press, 2010).

25 For a map of this diversity, see Anthony B. Pinn, *The African American Religious Experience in America* (Westport, CT: Greenwood Press, 2006).

26 There were, of course, other influences, particularly European literary and philosophical ones, from key texts like Virginia Woolf's "A Room of One's Own" (1929) and Simone Beauvoir's *The Second Sex* (1949).

27 Robert E. Goss, *Jesus Acted Up: A Gay and Lesbian Manifesto* (New York: HarperCollins, 1994) and *Queering Christ: Beyond Jesus Acted Up* (Cleveland, OH: Pilgrim Press, 2002).

28 See, for example, Mark Jordan, *The Invention of Sodomy* (Chicago, IL: University of Chicago Press,

1998) and *The Silence of Sodom: Homosexuality in Modern Catholicism* (Chicago, IL: University of Chicago Press, 2000).

29 Elias Kifon Bongmba, "Introduction." In *The Wiley-Blackwell Companion to African Religions*, edited by Elias Kifon Bongmba (Oxford: Wiley-Blackwell), 2012, 19.

30 George M. Marsden, *The Outrageous Idea of Christian Scholarship* (New York: Oxford University Press, 1998).

Annunciation of the Second Coming (1996), by Lynn Randolph, 58″ × 46″.

11

Rational Re-readings

Masters of Suspicion, Classical and Contemporary

If we take in hand any volume of divinity, or school metaphysics, for instance, let us ask: Does it contain any abstract reasoning concerning quantity or number? No. Does it contain any experimental reasoning concerning matter of fact and existence? No. Commit it then to the flames; for it can contain nothing but sophistry and illusion.
David Hume, *Inquiry Concerning Human Understanding* (1748)

Do we hear nothing as yet of the noise of the gravediggers who are burying God? Do we smell nothing as yet of the divine decomposition? Gods, too, decompose. God is dead. God remains dead. And we have killed him.
The Madman in Friedrich Nietzsche's *Thus Spoke Zarathustra* (1885)

Comparing Religions: Coming to Terms, First Edition. Jeffrey J. Kripal, Ata Anzali, Andrea R. Jain, and Erin Prophet.
© 2014 Jeffrey J. Kripal. Published 2014 by John Wiley & Sons, Ltd.

There are other ways of re-reading religious experience than those of faith. It is quite possible, after all, that there is another way of resolving the historical fact that there are countless religions and hundreds of revealed scriptures. That resolution goes something like this: it is not the case that one religion or revelation is true and the rest are false, or that one is more true than the rest, or that they are all partially true; rather, it is simply the case that they are *all* false.

When Religion Doesn't Work

There are many reasons for thinking as much. No doubt one of the biggest is something that Christian theology calls **theodicy**: literally the "justice of God," but here better rendered as the problem of suffering, injustice, and evil in the context of belief in a loving and all-powerful God. Consider the immeasurable sufferings of countless human beings ravaged by war, dislocation, hunger, natural disasters, and gross economic injustice. Or the unthinkable historical massacres, wars, and genocides of the twentieth century, the murderous campaigns of Hitler, Lenin, Stalin, Mao, and Pol Pot, which together slew us in

the *hundreds of millions*. Or the daily countless racial, gender, and sexual bigotries often carried on in the name of God or religion. Or those centuries-long historical sufferings of slavery and, today, human trafficking. Or all of those natural diseases too gruesome to describe, which invisibly feed on us every day before the worms do. And this is before we even get to the untold sufferings of animals, who show every sign of sharing sentience with us and whom we slaughter, often quite cruelly, by the millions *each day*, for our own pleasure and sustenance.

Clearly, if the religions are meant to "explain" all of this, they have failed, and spectacularly so.

There are other problems still. There are all those countless daily, quiet, and largely invisible failures of ritual, prayer, and religious hope. Religious systems routinely fail to do what they claim they can do. We might frame this last problem under the banner of "when religion doesn't work." This is a major theme, if often submerged, in the study of religion. At least part of the issue boils down to the double fact that (1) religious traditions are often based on singular revelations, anomalous events, or states of enlightenment that happened "in the beginning," or once, often to a single individual, within a very specific and probably unique state of consciousness, and that (2) these revelations, events, and states are not repeatable in any other human being in exactly the same way. The religious traditions will often claim that the original revelation, salvation event, or enlightened state is accessible if one does a, b, and c or believes x, y, and z. But the truth is that doing or believing anything seldom (ever?) results in exactly the same original event, and that for the most part these practices and beliefs result in little.

Or in nothing at all.

Religions are aware of this problem, of course, and so they have developed elaborate explanatory models for why this is the case. The models of *karma* and reincarnation in many of the Asian traditions, the presence of a trickster figure in so much indigenous folklore, and the doctrines of grace and God's inscrutable will (or that trickster, Satan) in the monotheisms: each can be re-read as a reflection not on some mysterious cosmic moral principle or human failure, but on *why that particular system usually does not work*. Phrases like "the achievement of *nirvana* or enlightenment is the fruit of many births and the burning of all karmic bonds," "if God wills it," or "by the grace of God" can all be translated in the same way: "This is why it didn't work for you." All too often, moreover, what they really mean is this: "It's your fault."

That is just a bit cruel.

The fact that the anomalous states of revelation, salvation, and enlightenment cannot be reliably reproduced has also had a significant impact on how the professional study of religion is practiced. This is one major reason why the field has focused generally on things that can be reproduced and observed, things like texts, rituals, the formation of social identities and institutions, artistic representations, material objects, buildings, doctrines and beliefs, and temporal linear histories, preferably with numbers attached to them. At least these things stay put. At least these things behave. The field is wise to focus on them. But it must also hold in balance the fact that all of these things and selves only make sense as "religious" to the extent that

they point back to and express states of extraordinary experience that are not things at all, to which we have no direct access, and that we certainly cannot reliably reproduce in a book, a classroom, a laboratory, a number, or anywhere else for that matter.

Finally, this common failure of the religions is also, no doubt, one reason why there are so many different religions and subsystems in the first place. The bottom line? People are different. And that is a fantastically gross understatement, as the variables here are basically infinite, as we now know from brain science and all those gazillion connections in our heads—which, of course, are *different* connections, a gazillion times over, in each and every head.

Perhaps the most common result, however, is that many people experience nothing special at all. Hence also the common phenomenon of unbelief, agnosticism, or simple religious indifference. These negative responses are not an indication of sinister, insincere, or bad people, as the religious systems too often want to claim. Usually they are rather perfectly honest and heartfelt responses to that difficult fact of the history of religions: religious practices and beliefs often accomplish nothing at all.

Zilch.

Nada.

Zip.

On the Heart of Reductionism: "There Is No Gap"

Not only are such questions honest. They often have also taken great moral courage to formulate and have come with heavy costs to the person asking them (asking them out loud, anyway). But questions are questions, and they do not go away just because people in power want to squash them. And the power of these particular questions is simply immense.

Take western culture. Once faith seeking understanding began to question its own foundations, it was only a matter of time before reason separated itself entirely from its religious engagement and sought its own integrity entirely outside the special institutions of revelation. Accordingly, the last two centuries have witnessed a whole series of radical thinkers whose thought defines, inspires, and guides the study of religion to this day. Among the greatest of these were three men whom the French philosopher Paul Ricoeur called our "masters of suspicion": Nietzsche, Marx, and Freud. These three men are so influential in western thought today that we do not need their first names.

As the poet W. H. Auden observed in 1939 in his eulogy for Freud, such a thinker leaves behind a legacy that does not so much contribute a piece or a part to a culture but comes to define an entire worldview. And so Auden wrote of the fallen psychologist, who changed so dramatically how we think of human sexuality, childhood, mothers, and fathers, and who brought expressions like "Freudian slip," "oedipal complex," and "phallic" into our everyday vocabulary (and humor):

> if often he was wrong and, at times, absurd,
> to us he is no more a person
> now but a whole climate of opinion
> under whom we conduct our different lives.[1]

In the present chapter we have chosen to concentrate on a duo of thinkers: Sigmund Freud and Émile Durkheim. We have chosen these two men because, together, they succinctly represent the psychological and sociological modes of rational re-readings that dominated the twentieth-century study of religion. We will also, toward the end of the chapter, treat some rational re-readings of religion that have arisen more recently around three further complexes: empire and colonialism, evolution and the brain, and religious violence.

But all five of these **rational re-readings** are expressions of the same basic conclusion, namely that *there is no gap* between revelation and reason. That is, the literal claims of revelation are finally false ones and must be rejected as illusory from the side of reason. This is why we are calling these re-readings

rational: not because the other re-readings are not rational (as we have just seen, faithful or theological re-readings are all about relating reason and revelation and are thus rational forms of thinking as well), but because the present ones recognize as valid *only* rational forms of thinking. In short, rational re-readings solve the disjunction or gap between revelation and reason by removing one side of the apparent disjunction: the side of revelation.

Reductionism Defined

These are much more than simply rejections of revelation, though. They are also thoughtful, often elegant explanations. They do not simply say "No" to religion. They explain exactly *how* religion is about something else, which is not religious at all. They "reduce" religious experiences, expressions, and institutions to more basic mechanisms. They identify deep underlying structures that give rise to religious phenomena but that are not themselves religious. Enter another skill set, which is vital for putting the plural pieces of religion back together again:

> **Reductionism:** the explanation of religious phenomena as the effects of some deeper, more basic non-religious causes, processes, or mechanisms.

The Intellectual and Moral Integrity of Reductionism

We will leave it at that for now. As we proceed through this chapter, what reductionism is and how it works will become more than apparent. Just now we want to issue a preliminary caution, which is really a kind of moral plea: please do not misread robust forms of reductionism as some kind of simple, uncaring, or angry rejection of religion. Sometimes reductionist thinkers are indeed "angry" (often for very good reasons). Sometimes they are superficial and simplistic (often for not very good reasons). And sometimes reductionism is employed as a blunt tool with which to ridicule religion. But, historically speaking now, this is not how reductionist re-readings arose, nor is it how they generally function in the professional study of religion today.

As we have already had many an occasion to note, the critical study of religion originally arose in the hearts and minds of well-meaning individuals who came, often at some risk to their professional lives (or just to their lives), to the painful conclusion that what they formally believed is simply not true. More precisely, they came to the conclusion that their former beliefs could no longer be reconciled with what they now knew to be true about history, the biblical texts, the natural world, and the advances of science. They did not "choose" these thoughts. Such thoughts were forced on them as inevitable conclusions of years, sometimes decades of intense research. In short, such conclusions were finally not acts of anger or apathy at all. They were acts of courage, profound concern, and moral outrage. There is much reason, it turns out, to be suspicious of religion.

Before we get into some of the specifics of our own two masters of suspicion, it will serve us well to discuss the two fields with which they are mostly identified: the psychology and sociology of religion. These are, if you will, two different drawers in your toolkit, which is perhaps getting rather full about now.

Religion and the Social Sciences

Some scholars are interested in the psychological dimensions of individual religious experience, while others choose to focus on the demographics and social structures of religion. The study of religion has branched out into different specialties roughly along these same lines. The internal or experiential dimensions are the primary concern of the **psychology of religion**. The external or institutional dimensions are the primary concern of the **sociology of religion**. We write "primary," because these two approaches are not truly separate. It is a matter of accent, as psychologists of religion are perfectly aware that religious

experience is deeply shaped by social institutions (hence all their intimate focus on the family unit), and the sociologists are hardly denying the importance of personal experience. Still, that accent, wherever it lands, makes a big difference to how one sees and understands "religion."

Strong and Moderate Forms of Reductive Inquiry

There is a further important distinction to draw here. There are strong and moderate forms of reductive inquiry. The **strong forms of reductive inquiry** reduce religious events and experience entirely to natural mechanisms and unequivocally deny the transcendent or ultimate truth claims of the religions as false. The **moderate forms of reductive inquiry** are not so sure. They either leave the door open to the possibility of some transcendent force or truth at work in religion or avoid the truth questions altogether and focus instead on the psychological or sociological functions of religion.

As with the faithful re-readings, there is a fairly easy litmus test to apply in order to distinguish between moderate and strong forms of reductive inquiry and then to distinguish between strong forms of reductionism and both faithful and reflexive re-readings. Let us call it "the 'nothing but' test." Again, this test can be applied in the form of a question: "Are religious experiences and institutions *nothing but* the transformations of perfectly natural states of emotion, cognition, and social process?" Strong forms of reductive inquiry can easily be identified by their clear answer to this question: "Yes." Faithful and reflexive re-readings answer the same question with a "No." Moderate forms of reductive inquiry answer it with a "Maybe," or, more commonly, they avoid the question altogether.

We will get to the strong forms of reductionism in due time. As an example of moderate forms of reductionism and of avoidance of the truth question, consider the way in which religion is normally handled in the media. The media are most interested in demographic patterns, in who believes what—and not for the sake of that "what," but for the sake of how effectively or broadly that "what" forms a particular voting bloc or social group. The journalist never asks: "Well, is it really true what so-and-so believes?" Rather the journalist asks: "How many such believers are there? And in what ways will their numbers affect the next election or the next social issue?" Truth is actually irrelevant here, since falsehood is never seriously entertained as an option and all we really have at the end of the day is a kind of counting. All that really matters is how people act in the public square on their beliefs, not whether those beliefs are profound or absurd.

Psychologists and sociologists of religion practicing strong forms of reductionism and some radical theologians stand for a very different set of concerns. They want to know what is true and what is false, and they are willing to consider that it may *all* be false. They want to know what the deeper mechanisms of religion are. They couldn't generally care less about how full the parking lots are, or what the impact of a particular belief on a religious institution or particular election might be. Indeed, they might even suspect that the fuller the parking lot or more successful the election campaign belief, the *less* likely a claim is to be true. They are after truth, not after votes. Perhaps most importantly of all, they come from a long line of thinkers who knew the truth but did not have the votes. They remember the towers, the fires, and the censors.

Sigmund Freud: Religion Is a Childish Illusion

Sigmund Freud is the most significant founder of what would later become the psychology of religion. There are certainly other major figures, including William James and C. G. Jung. But Freud's thought has had an especially formative influence on the field, particularly in the ways it has so fruitfully taught us that cultural and religious phenomena are deeply inscribed by psychological dynamics that can be traced back to childhood and, more particularly, to the manner in which fathers, mothers, and children interact within what Freud called the family romance—that complex of sexual and aggressive feelings between mother, child, and father that defines how a child develops and becomes a person.

It is good to admit up front and immediately that Freud's thought is very controversial to this day and that, whereas it is widely used and celebrated in the humanities—especially in the study of literature, film, popular culture, and religion—it is generally rejected in academic psychology as grossly dated, particularly in light of the advances of cognitive science and evolutionary psychology—which, rather ironically, have more than a little in common with Freud's strong biological reductionism, his insistence that most of human behavior is controlled "offline," and his infamous insistence on the centrality of sexuality (re-figured as reproduction or "**fitness**" in evolutionary psychology).

Freud himself had a quick and too easy answer for his critics. He psychoanalyzed them. He pointed out that their "resistance" was a **defense mechanism** encountered often in therapy, where it expressed the psyche's attempt to protect itself from difficult material that would expose its own illusions. We are here in the realm of Shakespeare's oft-quoted line from *Hamlet*: "The lady doth protest too much, methinks." In other words, people vehemently reject Freud's thoughts because, to take these ideas seriously, they would have to examine whole regions of their mental, emotional, social, and sexual lives that they would rather leave alone.

Freud's point about defense mechanisms may have been too easy, but it contains more than a grain of truth. Who would deny that human beings often reject plausible ideas for emotional rather than rational reasons? In other words, if Freud gets people worked up, this is itself likely significant: "a button has been pushed," as we say. It is also worth remembering that Freud's ideas have been the object of active censorship and moral condemnation among various types of offended communities—academic, political, and religious. Freud ended his life not in professional comfort, but in terrible physical pain (his death was an assisted suicide, a requested overdose while suffering the end stages of mouth cancer) and in the emotional turmoil of a political exile from Hitler's Germany. He had to flee his beloved Vienna for a distant London shortly after the Nazis temporarily kidnapped his daughter and staged public burnings of his books. To the latter he responded along these lines: "At least we have advanced a little. In a previous age, they would have burned me."

Alas, Freud was terribly wrong, for this, of course, is exactly what the Nazis would do—burn books *and* people, by the millions—including his own sister, it turned out. From the very beginning, Freud stood bravely against all of this. He knew what it meant to be despised, to be censored, and to be exiled from his home for both his ideas and his very person. Another version of the tower.

Censorship and the Unconscious

Nor was (or is) this only a political issue for fascists and hate-mongers. Freud was clear that *censorship is internal to the psyche itself and its conscious/unconscious structure.* What Freud had learned from his suffering patients is that the human psyche censors its own thoughts and wishes and so encodes them in more safe or distant forms within the narratives of dreams and the symptoms of mental illness. What Freud called the **unconscious** contains everything that the psyche has censored and pushed "under." The unconscious is that realm of the human mind of which the conscious individual is unaware but which nevertheless influences, if not determines, much of the individual's thinking, emotional life, and social behavior. If there were no internal censorship, there would likely be little or no unconscious, not at least in the Freudian sense of the term.

There is one corollary here that Freud did not pick up on, but that numerous later anthropologists and cross-cultural psychoanalytic thinkers did. It goes like this: if the unconscious is a product of what is censored, and if different cultures censor different things, then the unconscious will be different in different cultures. Freud was very much a universalist

when it came to such things. He did not generally recognize the profound influence of different cultural practices on the human psyche.

The most basic method of psychoanalysis, then, boils down to this one rule: Look for the defense mechanism, the resistance, the denial, the attempted censorship, *and go there.* That is where the truth lies. That is where the secret abides. And psychoanalysis is all about secrets: identifying them, decoding them, and finally speaking them in the open. Because the unspoken secret, as the repressed, is what makes individuals and whole societies sick, the revealing of the same secret is what heals and makes whole. At the end of the day, then, psychoanalysis is all about *speaking secrets in order to heal.*

Consider, as a most simple and mundane example, the whisper. Imagine having a long conversation with a friend about anything. At some point in the conversation, the friend bends closer, looks around, and begins to whisper something to you. What do you immediately assume? You assume that whatever this friend is about to say is far more important than anything that came before it and anything that will likely come after it. What you assume is exactly what Freud concluded with his patients—that the secret is the key.

This twin notion of secrecy and censorship goes to the very heart of what Freud was trying to show us. In his later writings he would extend this dethroning of the "I" and write of how our conscious sense of self, or what he called the **ego** (simply the Latin for "I"), is in fact a rather superficial social construction floating precariously between a sea of submerged, largely unconscious desires and aggressions (the **id**, the "it") and a threatening sky of moral judgments, themselves derived from social interactions with the parents and, later, with other social actors and institutions (the **superego**, the "over-I"). This was Freud's version of how we are a double product of both nature and nurture, biology (the id) and society (the superego).

Religion, for Freud, was an illusion. And not just any illusion, but a childish one at that. All human beings are born from a woman and most grow up in some sort of family arrangement in which they are radically dependent on parents for their sustenance and security. Most people never really grow up, however. People remain in need of the securities of infancy and childhood. They remain in need of a nurturing mother and a protecting father. And so they project these emotional needs, these infantile wishes, into the sky: "Our Father, who art in heaven …" God, for Freud, is essentially an illusion that people create in order to feel safe and secure. In reality, of course, there is no father in the sky, nor is there any real security. We all die. It all ends badly for each of us. Better to accept this than to live in the illusion that religion represents, Freud argued. Better to grow up.

The Oedipus Complex

At the heart of Freud's developed system is one of his most fruitful and most controversial ideas: that of the **Oedipus complex**. Freud himself clearly saw this as the master key to all sorts of cultural forms, especially art, literature, and religion. Put very simply, Freud argued that the child's early relationships with his parents (Freud focused on the son) set the psychic patterns that will be worked out—or not worked out—in later adult life. More specifically, Freud argued that a male child's first love object is his mother (and, more specifically, her breasts), and that the infant son experiences fear, aggression, and anger towards his father as he competes with him for possession of the mother-lover. Eventually, if all goes well, the young boy accepts defeat, surrenders the mother, and identifies with the victor, that is, with the father. In this way he learns to be a man like his father and will some day go in search of another woman, one who most likely reminds him of his first love, that is, of his mother. Freud named this drama the Oedipus complex, after King Oedipus in Sophocles' ancient Greek play *Oedipus Rex*. In this play, Oedipus falls in love with a woman who, unbeknownst to him, is in fact his mother and kills a man who, unbeknownst to him, is actually his father.

Freud argued that how a small child resolves these early family conflicts determines in large part his later emotional and sexual make-up, and that child-rearing practices determine a culture's mythology and religion. As we have already noted, Freud himself was a universalist here. He did not recognize just how different child-rearing practices and family structures are in different cultures. Later psychoanalytic thinkers would correct and develop Freud's thought here. They adjusted it to different cultures and in this way showed how different family structures produce different sorts of mythologies and religions. Of particular note here is South Asia, where gifted analysts and anthropologists like the Indian analyst and novelist Sudhir Kakar and the Sinhalese anthropologist Gananath Obeyesekere have been particularly eloquent and prolific in correcting Freud's thought and extending it into the study of various Hindu and Buddhist traditions.

The basic comparative conclusion goes something like this. If the father is supreme in the family household, he will also be supreme in the culture's mythology and public ritual. Similarly, if the mother or a small community of mothers raise the children in the relative absence of the father (who may, after all, be literally unknown in many traditional cultures), then the mother or these mother figures will dominate the mythology. Moreover, the degree to which the son is bonded to the mother (and this varies widely from culture to culture) will determine the emotional lengths to which the culture must go to separate him from this female world and to insert him into the world of men and fathers. The secret of religion and mythology, in other words, lies in that exceedingly strange and mysterious drama in which a man emerges from the vagina of a woman, shares intimate contact with her breasts and nurturing body for years, and then must be banished from this same physical and emotional union for the sake of becoming an individual and starting the whole drama all over again, as an adult, with another woman.

And you wonder why men are so confused?

Entire religions and cultures based on childhood and sex and childhood sexual impulses? Sounds outrageous, doesn't it? Think again. Think about how commonly religious people employ family terms to speak of their deepest beliefs about the divine. In religion after religion, the divine is a "father" or a "mother" (or both), or a "son" (but almost never a "daughter," for all the reasons we explored in Chapter 6). Similarly, religious titles of honor and respect are routinely taken directly from family life. From the Catholic practice of referring to priests as "father" to the Hindu practice of honoring religious leaders with the title of "Swami" ("lord" or "husband") and to the innumerable religious communities in which individuals address one another as "brother" or "sister," the practice is so common that we tend to forget the this-worldly origin of such titles and all they imply.

As for the "bizarre" idea of aggression between fathers and sons, all we have to do is open our comparative eyes to see that this is a salient feature of all three western monotheisms, in which the model and exemplary act of faith is the willingness of a father to kill his own son. In Judaism we have the story of Abraham and Isaac, in Islam the story of Abraham and Ishmael, and in Christianity we have a Father who wills an order of salvation that demands the gruesome murder of his own beloved Son.[2] This strong comparative pattern of son sacrifice made little rational sense before Freud and his oedipal theory. It makes sense after him.

Such oedipal patterns are not restricted to the West, as is often falsely claimed. They are evident, if not always so obvious, in Hindu India and Buddhist Asia as well. As a most striking example, consider the following Buddhist scripture, translated into the Chinese from the Sanskrit around 542 CE, in which the author advances a theory of gender and sexual orientation that is virtually identical to the Freudian one:

> Finally, as the time of his death approaches he sees a bright light, and being unaccustomed to it at the time of his death he is perplexed and confused. He sees all sorts of things such as are seen in dreams, because his mind is confused. He sees his (future) father and mother making love, and seeing them a thought crosses his mind, a perversity (*viparyasa*) arises in him. If he is going to be reborn as a man he sees himself making love with his mother and being hindered by his father; or if he is going to be reborn as a woman, he sees himself making love with his father and being hindered by his mother. It is at that moment that the Intermediate Existence is destroyed and life and consciousness arise and causality begins once more to work. It is like the imprint made by a die; the die is then destroyed but the pattern has been imprinted.[3]

Freud, of course, would locate these processes in infancy and childhood, whereas the Buddhist text locates them in the intermediate state between lives. But the classical oedipal structure of this process (the child loving one parent and feeling aggression toward the other) is nevertheless obvious. Note also that the soul's witnessing of the parents having sex (Freud called this the **primal scene**) is not some minor accident without consequence. On the contrary, its primordial "die" or "imprint" is permanent, even if its source is no longer obvious or conscious. Moreover, it is precisely this same witnessing and these same sexual and aggressive drives that set the wheels of causality and existence into motion again. They actually *create reality*. Basically the Buddhists out-Freud Freud here.

Libido, Repression, and Sublimation

Freud not only had an eye for the aggressive and sexual sides of life. He was also an admirer of art and literature, which he considered successful transformations of libidinal energies. Freud used the word **libido** to refer to energies in the body that are closely aligned with sexuality but can be employed for all sorts of nonsexual ends. What the reigning public morality cannot accept, the psyche of the artist, writer, or religious seer has to disguise somehow or, better, to transform into art, text, or vision. Thus Christ may be denied an erect and useable phallus in the Christian imagination, but when one of his female saints (Teresa of Avila) unites with him in a mystical marriage, she sees a gorgeous male angel

Figure 11.1 *Ecstasy of Saint Teresa of Avila*, by Gian Lorenzo Bernini (1647–1652). Church of Santa Maria della Vittoria, Rome. © Gianni Dagli Orti/Corbis.

with a flame-tipped arrow, which he thrusts again and again into the middle of her body as she moans in intense pain and ecstatic pleasure. This visionary sublimation worked: Bernini's marble version of this erotic vision now hangs suspended over the altar of a chapel in Rome (see Figure 11.1).

Freud called this process, from sex to spirit, "sublimation." The term was probably originally derived from alchemical literature, where the concept thus named was used to describe the mysterious transformation of base metals into gold. Modern chemistry redefined the same term to describe the chemical process by which a solid is translated directly into a gas, as when, for example, ice evaporates into the air without first becoming a liquid. In the same way we too, for Freud, have a process that goes from a solid (the sexual body) to a gas (the cultural) while skipping the liquid phase (sexual emission). Freud, in other words, used **sublimation** to describe how

libidinal energies are diverted from their original sexual aims and converted into cultural accomplishments, such as art or literature.[4]

If we were to update Freud's notion here, we might recall our discussions of super sexualities in Chapter 6 and say this. By "sex" we do not mean sex. We mean everything in a truly vast range—from the DNA sex texts wrapped tight around one another in the inner depths of the trillions of cells of our bodies to the lust and passions of sexual intercourse that these same DNA coils require for their transmission from one body to another; to the love a mother and infant or husband and wife feel for each other; to the compassion of the social worker, the minister, the rabbi, the mullah, and the priest; to the creative urges of the artist and writer who helps to draw the lineaments of human culture; to the spiritual flights of religious ecstasy and divine love. *All* of this is of and from the same energy. And all of it is erotic.

How exactly this occurs Freud did not claim to understand (nor do we). In the end, this sublimation or "making sublime" went unexplained. It is the point at which Freud's thought ends, and the master falls silent and simply admires.

Émile Durkheim: Religion Is Society Worshipping Itself

Sociology, like psychology, is an immensely diverse and complex form of thinking practiced by tens of thousands of professionals. But perhaps its most basic argument boils down to this: *a society is not made up of individuals; individuals are made up by society*. Put metaphorically, we might say that individuals are best thought of not as hard billiard balls bouncing around on a flat green, two-dimensional carpet, but as moving, morphing nodes in a constantly shifting, multidimensional web of meaning, social practice, economic exchange, relationship, and language. "You," as an ego, as a social self, do not "have" relationships and transactions. You *are* those relationships and transactions. It may be true that "you are what you eat," but it is also true that "you are who you know and love (and hate)."

Perhaps the easiest way to get a handle on this is to consider the role of language in forming a social identity. At the end of the day even one's name is a word, and all of our thoughts are basically silent sentences in our heads. So too with most all of our social interactions, business transactions, social identities, professional practices, and so on—they are *all* carried on in and through language (as is this textbook). But language is not a personal invention. It is a social process into which one is born—again, like a spider in a web. We cannot even have a conversation with ourselves in our own heads without this web. We rely on what is fundamentally a social practice of communication to create and maintain what we think of, probably incorrectly, as a stable personal identity.

The Totem

Religion is one major tool through which the social web forms, constitutes, and controls its individual nodes. In the sociological view, religion is a set of beliefs and practices that hold a society together around a common authority. We have already had occasion to "think with" this approach in our brief study of Max Weber and Ernst Troeltsch and their respective analyses of charisma and religious institutions. Another major thinker in this line of thought was the French sociologist Émile Durkheim.

Durkheim is a classic reductivist thinker who resolved the problem of religious plurality and the apparent absurdity of religious beliefs by tracing them all back to a single, deeper, and finally natural and rational source. Here is how he announces his project through the trope of "surface" and "depth":

> When only the letter of the formulae is considered, these religious beliefs and practices undoubtedly seem disconcerting at times, and one is tempted to attribute them to some sort of a deep-rooted error. But one must know how to go underneath the symbol to the reality which it represents and which gives it its meaning. The most barbarous and the most fantastic rites and the strangest myths translate some human need, some aspect of life, either individual or social. The reasons with which the faithful justify them may be, and generally are, erroneous; but the true reasons do not cease to exist, and it is the duty of science to discover them.[5]

What are these "true reasons" beneath the surface of erroneous beliefs, fantastic rites, and strange myths that science must discover?

Society.

Durkheim thought that this thesis about the social basis of religion could be most effectively demonstrated by going back to the most archaic and simplest of religious forms: the totem. This is what he did in his classic work, *The Elementary Forms of the Religious Life* (1915). A **totem** is an animal or object that is made to represent a particular group of people, for example a family, a tribe, or a clan. Totems are commonly found in indigenous religions around the world, in places like Australia, the Americas, Asia, and Africa. Totemism, Durkheim argued, is the most archaic and "elementary" religious phenomenon on the planet. Indeed it is so simple that it scarcely involves any notion of divinity at all.[6] Studying the totem, then, should logically lead to a general theory of religion, or so Durkheim assumed.

For Durkheim, when a community worships or honors a clan totem, what they are really worshipping and honoring is their own social structure. Religion, in other words, is not about private pious feelings, and it is much less about hopes for some individual or personal salvation. These are all erroneous surface notions or later developments. Deep down, religion is "an eminently collective thing."[7] Religious myths, symbols, and rites are, first and foremost, "collective representations that express collective realities."[8] When human beings bow down to a god, they are in effect bowing down and submitting to their own collective social systems. Hence two of Durkheim's memorable sound bites: "religion is society worshipping itself" and "God is society writ large."

Such "divine" collective representations, it should be noted, are always the product of immense stretches of time, numerous generations, and countless individuals, because a very special kind of wisdom or intelligence results when all these factors come together. Religion is not simply rational, then. It is also super-rational. "A special intellectual activity is therefore concentrated in them [the collective representations] which is infinitely richer and complexer than that of the individual." This is Durkheim's version of what I have called "the human as two," through which he explains the remarkable powers of any single human reason "to go beyond the limits of empirical knowledge":

> It does not owe this to any vague mysterious virtue but simply to the fact that according to the well-known formula, man is double. There are two beings in him: an individual being which has its foundation in the organism and the circle of whose activities is therefore strictly limited, and a social being which represents the highest reality in the intellectual and moral order that we know by observation—I mean society ... In so far as he belongs to society, the individual transcends himself, both when he thinks and when he acts.[9]

Basically, we are way smarter as a group than we are as individuals, and we worship that which is greater than us. But the sacred, the "other" of the human as two, is the social, not the soul.

The Sociology of Knowledge

In this same line of thought, intellectuals will sometimes speak and write of the social construction of knowledge. This in turn is the basic idea of the **sociology of knowledge**, a field that explores how "truth" is not discovered in some objective and clear way, say, like a mineral in the ground or a distant planet, but "constructed" through elaborate social processes and institutions—like churches, empires, laboratories, nation-states, and universities.

As in other forms of reductive inquiry, there are strong and moderate forms of this thesis. The strong forms assert that *all* forms of human knowledge (including science) are socially con-structed and can best be understood as pragmatic truths that are good at doing particular things for particular people, but by no means can any such truth be claimed as absolute or entirely objective. The moderate forms suggest that all human know-ing is indeed shaped, and even severely restrained, by social processes and contexts, but that human beings nevertheless can arrive at, or at least approximate, real truths, truths that are not entirely dependent on or relative to this or that social practice and institution.

Peter Berger and the Sacred Canopy of Religion

The sociological theories of Troeltsch, Weber, and Durkheim, like the psychological theories of Freud, James, and Jung, spawned a rich and diverse legacy. But perhaps no sociologist has had a deeper and more lasting influence on the contemporary study of religion than the American sociologist Peter Berger. Berger co-wrote, with Thomas Luckman, one of the classics in the sociology of knowledge: *The Social Construction of Reality* (1966). The following year he published *The Sacred Canopy* (1967), a potent and especially clear little book that has become a kind of classic of the modern study of religion.

Berger begins *The Sacred Canopy* with an oft-noted observation about the human species: in contrast to all other higher mammals, which are born with a more or less fully wired instinctual apparatus, humans are born "unfinished." They are born with an underspecialized instinctual apparatus, which is not hard-wired toward a species-specific environment. As a result, "man must make a world for himself." This world-building activity is not to be understood as a "biologically extraneous phenomenon, but the direct consequence of man's biological constitution."[10] If bees build hives and birds build nests, we build worlds. These constructed worlds we call "culture"— probably with insufficient awe.

But how exactly do we build worlds? Berger portrays a dialectical or two-way process, in which society is a product of individual human beings and individual human beings are products of society. In fact we have already seen versions of this back-and-forth, inside–outside process numerous times in our journey. We have also implied it all along, through our central tropes of the mirror and the skill of reflexivity. Berger's elegant version is separated into three steps or reflections: (1) externalization; (2) objectification; and (3) internalization.

Externalization is the human activity of building a cultural world through sign, symbol, myth, ritual, and institution, as discussed above: in effect the human species "externalizes" itself in culture; it builds a world. Objectification is a further extension of this process: an independent world of "objects" comes to confront the human being—the subject—as facts outside that subject. The world externalized by humans now takes on material, physical form. It becomes a literal set of objects "out there."[11] Finally, internalization is the reabsorption back into consciousness of this objectified world, in such a way that the structure of the world "out there" comes to determine the subjective structure of consciousness "in here." At this level society functions as the formative agency of individual consciousness, in a process that is normally referred to as "socialization."[12]

It is very important to understand this tripartite process as thoroughly dialectical—as in a circle or mirror, again. Hence internalization does not mean that the individual is some inert subject, passively receiving the world as it is. Rather the individual "is formed in the course of a protracted conversation in which he [or she] is a participant."[13] The individual is actually a co-creator of the social world, which, of course, has been co-created before that individual by countless others. This, we might add, is precisely what the general history of religions *is*: the construction, deconstruction, and reconstruction of countless worlds.

Such "realities" are highly precarious, given their profound dependence on human beings, and hence they are in need of constant maintenance and confirmation. So why construct them in the first place? What are these cultural worlds finally *about*? For Berger, they are fundamentally about meaning, order, and reliability. Social worlds are grand schemes that provide a meaningful order, a *nomos* ("law" or

"order" in ancient Greek) for the discreet experiences of the individual, with the aim of shielding this person from the terror of chaos and constant disruption. This *nomos* is the "sacred canopy" of the book title. Religion is the seemingly safe and reassuring canopy that we create in the very dark and foreboding forest of the real.

The more transcendent, pervasive, and seemingly independent of human agency such constructed canopies appear to be, the more successful they are in creating order and assurance. This is where religion appears in Berger's analysis. Through religion, human beings make sense—or claim to make sense— of the entire realm of existence. They do this by creating fantastic narratives (that is, myths) that pit a "sacred" cosmic order against a "profane" realm of chaos or evil. In this way the human desire and need for order is projected onto the totality of being, in "an audacious attempt to conceive of the entire universe as being humanly significant."[14] Social structures and institutions like kinship, kingship, and religious priesthood serve the same purposes. All ultimately validate our safe status in the cosmos.

Religion requires a social "base" that can continue to project and maintain its validity independently of the attentions (or inattentions) of this or that subject. Berger calls this social base a "plausibility structure." Without such a base, no mythical world can survive. For example, the religious world of pre-Columbian Peru was objectively and subjectively real as long as its plausibility structure, namely pre-Columbian Inca society, remained intact.[15] Once Incan society collapsed, so did the mythical world of the Incas.

In more general terms, we might say not only that such worlds are collectively produced, but also that they remain real by virtue of collective recognition.[16] Their subjective reality "hangs on the thin thread of conversations," as Berger puts it.[17] Disrupt that conversation and the world falls apart. Many a reader might have already experienced such a falling apart through long travel or, much more radically, through immigration. You might have felt that some of the things you were utterly certain about do not make much sense any longer, simply because you have been physically removed from the social "base" that supported them and made them plausible. Previously powerful and utterly controlling ideologies tremble easily, it turns out.

There is a further "catch" here. For Berger, religion is an essentially "alienating" force. That is to say, its proper function is guaranteed only as long as the producer remains alienated from, or ignorant of, this production/projection process. Following a long line of previous thinkers, Berger calls this basic ignorance that makes it all work false consciousness.[18] Astonishingly, religion only works as long as we do not realize that we are behind it. This sociological shocker, of course, is not a new idea. We also find hints of it in various world mythologies, particularly in the very widespread notion—as apparent in ancient European religion as it is in contemporary Confucianism and Hinduism—that God, the gods, or the ancestors demand, need, or require humans' attention, manifested through ritual and sacrifice.

Turns out they do. Without such a ritual base, without such constant attention, the gods die and the ancestors disappear. A stronger sociological re-reader might go further still and suggest that the gods die and disappear when we cease to give them our attention for one simple reason: they were *us* all along. Our attentions give them life, and so our inattentions take that life away. Or back. What really happens, of course, is that life and attention are "reabsorbed" back into human consciousness for future new worlds and future new gods.

We are god-makers.

And god-killers.

Such extreme expressions, it should be pointed out, are more faithful to Nietzsche than to Berger. Whereas Nietzsche advocates a strong version of reductionism, Berger opts for a more moderate version. We will return to him and see why—in our last chapter.

For now, there is another way of putting all of this sociological wisdom. We might observe that human beings classify and compare because they live in social groups; they do not live in social groups because they classify and compare. In other words, it is society that

forms our thoughts and shapes our cognitive processes, and especially the cognitive processes of classification and comparison. Comparison, like Durkheim's totem and Berger's canopy, is finally an expression of society.

•••

These, then, are our two masters of suspicion. Such reductivist readings have hardly ceased, of course. Numerous new theoretical directions have been mapped out since Freud and Durkheim helped pioneer these two ways of re-reading religion. We can outline only three here: postcolonial theory, evolutionary and cognitive psychology, and the present question, so pressing, of religion and violence.

Postcolonial Theory: The Gaze of Empire

A rational re-reading of religion that is very much related to the sociology of knowledge but strongly develops in its own directions is **postcolonial theory**. This discipline is so named because of how the kind of thinking that generated it tracks, describes, and critically analyzes the countless ways in which colonial assumptions and institutions still determine the political practices, cultural productions, economic flows, and interior emotions, anxieties, and desires of people around the planet, even after the colonial period ended—which happened roughly around 1950. The postcolonial, then, as my colleague Elias Bongmba has pointed out, is not simply a matter of European colonialism. It is also a feature of present-day societies, for example in Africa, that were once European colonies and have since internalized and adopted these colonial structures and institutions as their own.

As in all major theories, there are many streams of influence here. One of the most important was Michel Foucault, who advanced a model of knowledge that insists that all forms of knowledge are also forms of power: every form of knowing serves particular political agendas and interests, which is to say particular people.

Orientalism

Taking up this line of thought, the literary critic Edward Said advanced his deeply influential notion of **orientalism**. Historically speaking, before Said an orientalist was a scholar who studied "the orient" (the East), which usually meant some part of the Muslim world or of Asia. This broad notion of "the orient" is still carried in our contemporary expression "the Middle East." In his classic work *Orientalism* (1978), Said observed that western culture's scholarly and artistic interaction with "the orient" took place in the historical context of European colonialism, and that much of this early engagement was defined by underlying assumptions about "the West" and "the East" that consistently rendered the latter inferior to the former, regardless of the positive or negative intentions of any author or thinker.[19] So, whereas the West was commonly coded as masculine, active, and materialist, the East was commonly coded as feminine, passive, and spiritual. The "spiritual East" may *sound* positive, but, once it is placed along the larger historical and literary spectrum, we can see that it is the flipside of the "materialist West," which was consistently framed as the positive, scientific, active, rational pole.

Most of Said's examples were drawn from European representations of Arab cultures (he himself was an American citizen of Palestinian-Lebanese descent)—representations that, he argued, were grossly misleading, false, and self-serving of European and now US imperialistic ambitions. But the basic model has been widely applied to western representations of other non-western contexts. Hence, when a culture, say, like India was being praised or lifted up by both European and Indian authors as a model or as more "spiritual" than "the West" (for instance in expressions like the "mystic East"), Said's rational re-reading would argue that these "orientalist" tropes functioned in ways that advanced the colonial project and privileged the economic and political interests of the European nation-states, even when they appeared to be positive or admiring—or especially then.[20]

Said's work is central to the comparative study of religion because, as we saw in Chapter 2, it is an indubitable fact that the latter arose most recently, through European colonial interactions with these "oriental" cultures and religions and precisely during the colonial period. Many of the field's early and later depictions of Islamic and Asian cultures are very much open to this orientalist critique. And this is before we get to the field's early framing of numerous African, American, and Australian indigenous traditions as "primitive" or "savage"—an unmistakable legacy of colonialism.

Such a bracing critique needs to be answered by the comparativist because, whatever Said's own intentions, his work has been consistently used by others to call into question *any* comparativist practice and to regard it as implicitly colonialist or imperialist. Whereas the psychological and sociological methods discussed above have encouraged and furthered comparativism, Said's orientalist critique has been invoked as part of a broad-based attempt to squash comparativism.

This latter use of Said's critique as a wholesale rejection of comparison needs to be named for what it is: a gross over-simplification. As we have already had multiple occasions to see, all sorts of comparative practices have been performed around the globe for millennia. Moreover, the location of ancient wisdom "in the East" is hardly a European colonial invention. It goes back a full two millennia, and then some—to some of our earliest intellectual and religious sources. There is thus no necessary relationship between European colonialism and the location of special religious knowledge "in the East." Nor is there any necessary connection between comparativism and colonialism, although there *do* seem to be some very deep structural links between radical forms of comparison and mystical forms of thinking.

Moreover, even early scholarship on the orient in the eighteenth and nineteenth centuries was incredibly diverse; key segments of it were advanced in cultures that had no colonies in the East (like Germany) or in former colonies (like the USA); and, perhaps above all, its intense religious interests in the global diversity of humankind and in the ultimate question of human identity or "soul" clearly worked against European ethnocentrism and Christian chauvinism.

Equally problematic and simplistic readings of Said too easily ignore the fact that non-western cultures like those of the Arabic-speaking Muslim societies, India, and China have practiced their own forms of "occidentalism," portraying and representing "the West" in equally distorting and self-serving ways. The other oft-overlooked historical fact here is that in an earlier period Islam itself spread through empire—one that subjected Western Europe and much of the civilized world. In short, Said's bracing criticism cuts both ways.

Or all ways.

We might say, then, that Said was more right than he imagined, as long as we are willing to extend his orientalist critiques into critiques of occidentalism and of every other historical form of empire and projection. That would be most of human history. The history of colonialism and empire, after all, goes far beyond the last few centuries, and much of the histories of both Christianity and Islam are located squarely in the context of imperial and colonial projects. And this is all well after the other empires of history, including China's empires, the Egyptian Empire, the Israelite campaigns in Canaan, the Babylonian Empire, the Persian Empire, the Macedonian Empire of Alexander the Great, the Roman Empire, the Aztec and Mayan Empires, and so on.

The simple truth is that much of recorded human history has been largely determined by imperial history, and that these empires produced any number of positive things alongside all the violence, terror, and military aggression. One thinks here, for example, of ancient Persian, Greek, and Roman cosmopolitanism, or of Roman roads and law, or of ancient Mesoamerican architecture and city building, or, most recently, of western science and technology (think railroads and electricity). This is not to idealize, much less to defend colonial and imperial practices. It is simply to underline the complexity of the issues.

Conversion and Empire

With respect to the comparative study of religion, probably the most significant imperial practice has been that of **conversion**, by which we mean a radical realignment of life and self-understanding around a new religious narrative and set of beliefs. The word itself, derived from the Latin, invokes a certain "turning around," or more literally "turning with," a new set of values and convictions.

Conversion, of course, need not be influenced by or reduced to an imperial project. People also convert to other religions to escape gross economic or social injustice, to assimilate into a new culture, or because of some overwhelming religious experience. Nevertheless, it the case that, in the Christian, Islamic, and European imperial projects, we find numerous examples of manipulated, coerced, or forced conversions, and that much of the world is now Christian or Muslim (and "modern") because of these empires and their colonial conversion campaigns. If you are a Christian or a Muslim or you consider yourself "modern," you likely owe this identity and self-understanding to past colonial and imperial projects.

On Spirit and Spandrels: Cognitive Science, Evolutionary Psychology, and Cultural Evolution

As we have seen already, the main ground on which some of the earliest European intellectuals and anthropologists of religion thought and compared was nourished by the ferment of early evolutionary biology. Such individuals were convinced that Darwin's vision of natural selection would ultimately provide the key to understanding the nature of religion. Given their historical context, it should not surprise us that their early attempts usually ended in some form of colonial ethnocentrism, with the worldview of the European comparativist on top. This is the primary reason why, in the professional study of religion, evolutionary models of religion were more or less abandoned for most of the twentieth century as inescapably problematic, if not actually racist.

Things have changed. A lot. Evolutionary models are now widely celebrated again. Although still young and in their early stages, such models are clearly here to stay, and no responsible mapping of the field can afford to overlook them.

If we look from a wide historical angle, what we can see now is in fact not one, not two, but at least *three* different types of evolutionary models that have spiked at different points over the last century and a half, up to the present day. For the sake of conversation, let us name them theistic models, mystical vitalist models, and cognitive evolutionary psychology models. The first two are not rationalist re-readings in the strict sense, since they take revelation very seriously and incorporate it into the heart of their theorizing. They will not take our attention here, as they are not, strictly speaking, rationalist re-readings. We will only describe them briefly.

Theistic Models

Theistic models are models that posit a personal deity or a god at work behind the natural laws of the universe, especially where evolutionary processes are concerned. These models vary widely and should not be conflated with one another. The nineteenth-century models were theistic in a developmental sense, to the extent that they argued that religion has developed historically from its most "primitive" modes in animism and polytheism up to its fullest flowering in monotheism. So too are the "creationist" arguments of contemporary fundamentalist groups, which themselves vary widely but often end up force-fitting the scientific evidence into some literal reading of the first three chapters of Genesis.

Neither of these comparative practices is acceptable to the vast majority of modern scholars of religion today, as both are clearly based on ethnocentric arrogance (the colonial models) or on a gross denial of the scientific evidence and/or a naïve precritical reading of scriptural texts (the creationist models). Other, more nuanced theistic models are, however, seriously entertained, particularly under that broad banner of "science and religion." These models are generally advanced by believing scientists or theologians and by philosophers trained in the natural sciences. Such authors turn to evidence like the uncanny "fine-tuning" of the four fundamental forces of matter, or the fantastically complicated structure of the cell and its ability to replicate DNA; and they do so in order to posit an intelligence (really a super-intelligence) at work within cosmic history.

Mystical Vitalist Models

Mystical vitalist models move beyond theorizing and claim to intuit, know, or even experience some living force or intelligence within evolutionary processes. Generally this force is experienced as some cosmic spirit or mind gradually coming into fuller and fuller manifestation through cosmological, biological, sociocultural, and now spiritual evolution. Hence the term **vitalism**—*vita* means "life" in Latin—which refers to any philosophical position that posits, at work in the universe, some life force or living energy that is not finally reducible to matter and its mechanisms.

These mystical vitalist models are historically related to the theistic models, but they are also quite different. In the Christian West they go back to ancient convictions about a "soul of the world" (*anima mundi*) and a "spirit of the universe" (*spiritus universi*), or about the natural world being a second book of Revelation. We have seen a few contemporary examples of mystical vitalist models in the mystical experiences of the NASA astronaut Edgar Mitchell and of the comic book writer Grant Morrison. One of the most remarkable examples, however, occurs in the history of Islam. In some of the schools of Sufism in the Ottoman Empire, hundreds of years before Darwin, we find a genre of poetry called *devriyyes* that features the theme of particles of soul "reincarnating" through the mineral world, the vegetable world, the animal world, and the human world until they can all come together in the body of a true saint, realize their own innate divinity, and come to know that everything is one, that everything is God.

Cognitive Evolutionary Models

Cognitive evolutionary models draw on contemporary cognitive science and evolutionary psychology in order to develop a rationalist re-reading of religion that analyzes religious ideation, rituals, beliefs, and institutions as surface functions of deeper neurological systems, which have evolved over millions of years for non-religious, adaptive, and survival purposes. Unlike theistic and mystical vitalist models, cognitive evolutionary ones refrain, in principle, from invoking non-natural or non-material forces. They are truly rationalist re-readings.

Cognitive science is a branch of academic psychology concerned with mapping the internal systems that determine how we all think, feel, and perceive the world. It is interested, we might say, in identifying and testing the deep "operating system" of the brain, which is running all the surface cultural software. It is interested both in the specific shape and structure of religious ideation and in why these beliefs look so remarkably similar across cultures and times. The short answer is this: the human brain produces this deep religious sameness, and local physical and social environments produce the surface differences. **Evolutionary psychology** takes this comparative analysis one step further by arguing that these universal cognitive systems are products of our deep evolutionary past and of the species' adaptive responses to environmental pressures.

Scott Atran explains the comparative robustness of the cognitive evolutionary models through a well-known but often resisted phenomenon: the anthropologist's (or, we would add, the comparativist's) otherwise inexplicable powers to enter any human society and grasp its basic social structures and meanings within a few years. If local difference ruled over global sameness, this would not be possible, or at least it would be extremely difficult and lengthy. But it is possible and it happens all the time—and not just to anthropologists and comparativists, but to

travelers, immigrants, business professionals, even readers. And why not? Both the anthropologist and the "foreign" culture are manifestations of the same evolved neural and biological machinery. Atran emphasizes the latter point: "Even the apparently incommensurable aspects of different cultural groups are only *conceivable* against a rich background of universally commensurable beliefs. If this weren't true, anthropology would be impossible."[21]

Such an evolutionary sameness also implies radical difference, however, since one of the key features of any evolutionary process is diversity. In this case, local social and ecological niches are understood to produce different religious expressions. Hence there are numerous jaguar totems in indigenous South American religions and an elephant-headed god in Hindu India, but there are no jaguar spirits in India or elephant deities in indigenous South America.

That's the simple surface part. The deeper evolutionary argument is more complex. After all, religion demands exorbitant investments of time, energy, and material resources in "counterintuitive beliefs" or "absurd commitments" to "factually impossible worlds." Atran puts the problem this way:

> To take what is materially false to be true (e.g., people think and laugh and cry and hurt and have sex after they die and their bodies disintegrate) and to take what is materially true to be false (e.g., people just die and disintegrate and that's that) does not appear to be a reasonable evolutionary strategy. Imagine another animal that took injury for health, or big for small, or fast for slow, or dead for alive.[22]

Such a species would not survive long.

So what is going on here?

Part of the answer is cognitive. Moderately counterintuitive or factually impossible features of a religious story (as long as they are not *too* counterintuitive) render the myth fantastic, striking, and above all *memorable*, hence it can easily be remembered and transmitted from generation to generation. Moderate strangeness, if you will, is a cognitive feature that selects for survival (read: cultural transmission).

A successful religious representation, then, has to *violate* particular cognitive expectations and *preserve* others at the same time.[23] So we get many monsters in world folklore that display all sorts of human features but are not quite human, whereas we seldom find monsters, or deities for that matter, that are entirely non-human, that, say, look like an amoeba or a jelly fish or an abstract trapezoid.

More of the answer is social. Religions demand public demonstrations of expensive commitments to absurd beliefs from individuals not in order to glorify absurdity but so as to assure these individuals' commitment to the same group. It is, after all, difficult to fake an expensive animal sacrifice or the regular attendance at a weekly or daily religious ritual. By performing such public rituals, individuals perform their own commitments to the social group, whether or not they happen to believe the mythical world they are re-enacting. Moreover, these are extremely important commitments to demand, because every social system contains "representations of false belief and deception."[24] In short, religious worlds are fragile, patently dubious, and so easily questioned. Accordingly they are always under the threat of defection from individuals. The repeated rituals and public acts of commitment prop all of this up and keep it going.

Most of the answer, however, is evolutionary. Thus behind the cognitive and social answers lies a third, even more basic answer as to why religious expressions look the way they do. That evolutionary answer boils down to the primordial pressure to avoid predators and acquire prey and protection. So, for example, the universal tendency to think about the sacred as both positive and negative, as protective and destructive, is rationally re-read as a distant expression of a more basic predator–protector detection system. In consequence, "the evolutionary imperative to detect rapacious agents favors [the] emergence of malevolent deities in every culture."[25] In this way the religious is reduced to the biological.

Not quite. The argument is more sophisticated and more interesting. It is not that religion = biology, full

stop. It is that religion appears within, and well after, a biological system that has evolved under other pressures and for other needs. Religious ideation, practices, and institutions are not biology per se. They are unnecessary "add-ons" of human evolution, which work with the help of and within the well-worn "mental modules" or "templates" that the human brain has developed in order to cope with earlier adaptive, survival, and social challenges.

To employ Atran's metaphor, we might say that religion is like water on an ancient mountain landscape. It flows naturally and goes where the rivulets, canyons, and slopes of the mountainous land take it. Religion follows the "evolutionary landscape" of the evolved brain and the adaptive challenges that the human species has faced over millions of years. Its river can certainly flow or collect elsewhere, and it occasionally does, but it will always tend to "dry up" and wither away if it flows in directions or collects in places that have not been carved out by these millions of years of hominid and now human time.

These cognitive evolutionary models are reductive in both tone and conclusion. They are naturalistic models that accept only material realities and causes. Here, then, even a category like "culture" ceases to be a world to live in—let alone an enchanted set of symbols that might potentially mediate a transcendent reality—and becomes instead "the distributed structure of cognition, that is, the causal networking of ideas and behaviors within and between minds."[26] No particular religious system is understood to point to any ultimate or transcendent truth. Indeed, although religion may well serve reproductive and various socially useful ends (like encouraging people to reproduce, form stable family networks, and cooperate in groups), asking whether a particular revelation is "true" or "false" is a meaningless question. Beliefs, scriptures, and deities are side effects of evolutionary adaptations; but they are not adaptations themselves, and they certainly have nothing to do with any objective or transcendent truth.

As a secular analogue, take the example of American football. Human bipedality evolved so as to increase vision over an African savannah (to detect predators and prey), the human arm evolved its throwing abilities for the hunt, and tribal groups used animals as totems around which to organize their social behavior and competitive inter-tribal warfare. Modern American football uses those same legs, that same ability to throw spears and rocks, and even that same totemic group behavior (hence all those local totemic mascots: the Dallas Cowboys, the Miami Dolphins, the Seattle Seahawks, and so on) for entirely different reasons, but for reasons nevertheless built into the evolutionary architecture of the human body. It would be nonsensical to suggest that evolution "intended" the National Football League, or that American football can tell us something about the cosmos, but it *is* perfectly reasonable to suggest that American football is a by-product or side effect of anatomy, skill sets, and sensibilities that originally evolved around survival, competition, cooperation, predators, and prey.

Evolutionary thinkers sometimes use another metaphor or analogy to transmit the same understanding of religion as an evolutionary add-on or by-product—an analogy drawn this time from architecture. In this analogy, first advanced by evolutionary biologists Stephen Gould and Richard Lewontin in 1979, most products of human cognitive faculties, including language, art, and religious phenomena, are said to be like the spandrels of architecture, those empty places in the right angle of an arch that are filled up with things like sculpted or painted gargoyles, angels, saints, and deities, that is, *with objects of religion and art.* Religion here is not about spirit, for there is no such thing. Religion is about these spandrels.[27] Religion is decorative, but it is decoration that fits into a specific evolved human architecture and meets particular design needs (see Figure 11.2).

Two common focal points of cognitive evolutionary theories of religion can serve to illustrate how these methods are presently forging new explanatory models for our rational understanding of "religion."

Invisible Presences   Religion is famous for positing invisible presences in the environment, from ghosts

Figure 11.2   A spandrel. Saint Pancras Public Baths, London, England. © Philippa Lewis/Edifice/Corbis.

to God. Indeed, "belief in invisible beings" was one of the earliest proposed definitions of religion. From a conventional scientific perspective, such beings are not really there, of course. So how to explain the universal human tendency to believe that they are? Evolutionary psychologists point out that, if we read such beliefs in the light of survival and adaptation needs, we can see quite quickly why these sensibilities would have evolved. The argument goes that it would have been much more costly *not* to detect presences in the environment, some of which (like lions and tigers) would have really been there, than to detect others which (like ghosts and God) were not really there. Nor would this have been simply a defensive posture. It would have been useful, too, for offensive postures—for example in the act of hunting for prey.

In short, we evolved to be super-sensitive to powerful presences in our environment for both protection and our own predatory needs. The religious sensibility to detect invisible presences piggy-backs on this evolved "predator–protector-prey detection schema."[28] Human experiences that involve the detection of things like ghosts and God are, then, "misguided intuitions" built on a real, evolved capacity.[29]

Altruism If the point of adaptation is to ensure survival in order for individuals to reproduce (evolutionary biologists call this fitness), how does one explain the common phenomenon of individuals sacrificing their own welfare, or even life, for others? Clearly such behavior is common and is by no means restricted to human beings. It even occurs *across* species. Ever watch a mother bird lure a cat away from its young by faking an injury? Or watch a dog effortlessly risk its life for its human owner? Evolutionary psychologists have an answer about the ubiquity of this phenomenon. They draw a simple distinction between classical or "Darwinian fitness" and "inclusive fitness." Darwinian fitness concerns the survival of the individual. Inclusive fitness, on the other hand, is concerned with the survival *of the group*. When an individual sacrifices himself or herself for the community, what he or she is really doing, in this view, is protecting the gene pool, including many of his or her own genes, by assuring the stability and security of the social group. Put a bit differently, evolutionary processes do not work toward the survival of individuals, but toward the survival and reproduction of communities and species.

Obviously, these cognitive evolutionary psychological models of religion could not be more different from the theistic or mystical vitalist models. They do not leave any room for the guiding presence or intelligence of deity, not to mention any actual communion with or direct knowledge of the evolutionary impulse itself. They advance a model that is highly abstract, impersonal, computer-like, and, above all, non-**teleological** ("teleology" is a compound the Greek noun *telos*, "end" or "purpose"). In the classic Darwinian model, evolutionary processes possess no meaning and no future goal, end, or purpose. Hence the quip of the theoretical physicist Steven Weinberg: "The more comprehensible the universe becomes, the more it also seems pointless."[30]

Ann Taves and the Building Blocks Approach

One of the most striking features of cognitive and evolutionary models of religion is their almost total lack of attention to actual religious experiences, whose reported details would inevitably reintroduce claims of transcendence and meaning into the discussion. This is partly a natural function of the method's commitment to abstract models such as cognitive templates and cognitive structures, which operate well outside the awareness of the individual. But it is also a reflection of the ways in which rational re-readings of religion have moved further and further away from the category of experience.

One important exception here is the work of Ann Taves, which is designed "to support research on singular experiences across cultures and historical time periods" with the tools of cognitive psychology.[31] This she does through an approach that reframes religious experiences as "experiences deemed religious" or "special." What Taves is most interested in here is how genuinely anomalous experiences become the "building blocks" of religion over time, through people ascribing, either consciously or unconsciously, specialness or sacrality to them, much as Durkheim and the sociology of religion have long argued. She is interested in a "bottom-up" approach to modeling religion instead of a "top-down" approach.

The latter has traditionally worked through complex cultural concepts like "religion" or "God," which are generally not cross-culturally applicable. In contrast, Taves prefers to focus on more basic building blocks, like "play," "nonordinary powers," or "path," which are globally distributed. Indeed, play displays "deep evolutionary roots" and can be observed in the animal kingdom through tail wagging, mock bows, and even, believe it or not, what looks remarkably like laughter, even in rats.[32]

Taves is drawn to the themes of nonordinary powers and nonordinary worlds as particularly useful "building blocks." "Rather than shy away from the idea of an underlying magicoreligious matrix," she writes, "I think we should embrace it."[33] Here she is aligned with scholars like the sociologist of religion Martin Riesbrodt, who, as we saw in Chapter 3, similarly defined religion as a means of dealing with "superhuman powers." She can thus suggest, in the spirit of the toolbox or toolkit again, that what the scholar of religion needs is a "Powers Kit" and an "Alternate Worlds Kit," which "could be used separately or combined to create different effects," that is, different religious worlds.[34]

Her handling of the "Powers Kit" is especially close to my own proposals. She can thus write:

> While theories of the first type [evolutionary psychology models that focus on the detection of threats and resources] argue that religion is a "spandrel" or by-product of evolved capacities with no particular survival benefits, research on the placebo effect suggests that the attribution of nonordinary powers to things may trigger capacities that are otherwise unavailable to people, thus providing an evolutionary advantage.[35]

This, of course, is exactly what we suggested in Chapter 8 under the theme of the truth of the trick.

Taves's handling of William Barnard's self-reported mystical experience (which we treated briefly in Chapter 9) and of his subsequent interpretation of it as evidence for the existence of an immortal self is a good example of her comparative practice. Taves wants to insist both on the felt anomalous, unique, or apparent transcendent nature of such experiences *and* on the attribution processes through which these events are "deemed special" and, in some cases, shaped into religious ideas and (in rare cases) into stable teachings and institutions.

We do not have to accept Barnard's own explanation of his experience, she notes, but we *do* have to take seriously his description of it as special or unique. It is not enough, then, to show how an experience is "constructed." We have to take seriously its genuinely felt or intuited special qualities. In her own words,

> we need a deeper understanding of the ways in which seemingly novel experiences not only inspire individuals to search for alternative meaning systems, as in Barnard's case, but also lead to the generation of new meaning systems that appeal to multitudes of followers, as in the case of Siddhartha Gautama or Joseph Smith [the founders of Buddhism and Mormonism, respectively].[36]

It is both this sensitivity to the nuances of real and extreme religious experiences and this balanced embrace of the special *and* the natural that make the work of Ann Taves a model rational re-reading of religion.

Before we move on, it is worth noting Taves's indebtedness to another important scholar of religion, the philosopher Wayne Proudfoot. It was Proudfoot who initially made the helpful distinction between what he called "descriptive reductionism" and "explanatory reductionism" in his classic study *Religious Experience* (1987).[37] Descriptive reductionism is never appropriate for the student or scholar of religion. It involves describing an individual's religious experiences in terms that are foreign to the subject's own self-understanding and experience. The scholar's first task is to describe a religious experience accurately, *as the experiencer knew and reported it*. After this accurate description, however, the scholar has every right and every need to proceed with an explanation of the religious experience in question, and this explanation in no way needs to correspond to the self-understandings of the subject or to the terms of his or her tradition. There are two different stages in responsible scholarship, then: (1) description; and (2) explanation. The latter can and likely will be reductive. The former, however, should preserve the self-understanding and "feel" of the experience in question. Hence Ann Taves's nuanced treatment of the mystical, immortal experience of William Barnard.

The Study of Religion and Violence before and after 9/11

The events of 9/11 taught the world what scholars of religion already knew all too well: that religion is a complex phenomenon, which can in no way be framed as a simple moral force of good and peace in the world. Much has been written in the last century or so on the subject of religion and violence, largely in response to the historical circumstances and pressing social needs of the authors in question. Debates about "just war" and pacifism were especially common around the two world wars, in the first half of the twentieth century. After the counterculture of the second half, much of the scholarship on religion and violence shifted to the subject of "cults" and "brainwashing." More recently, of course, it has shifted to global terrorism, religious fundamentalism, and the possible links between monotheism and violence. Because of space, we can only touch on the last two subjects here.

The Question of Cults and Brainwashing

In 1978, 918 people committed religious suicide by drinking a cyanide-laced fruit drink in Jonestown, Guyana, under the inspiration of the Christian preacher Jim Jones and his People's Temple movement (see Figure 11.3). In 1993, 76 members of the Branch Davidians (a splinter group of the Seventh-day Adventists), under the leadership of David Koresh in Waco, Texas, died in a fiery holocaust at the end of a 51-day siege by the US government. The details of this event remain highly controversial, including who started the fire and

Figure 11.3   Jonestown, Guyana, November 18, 1978. Bodies belonging to members of the Jonestown community, who committed suicide by drinking cyanide-laced fruit punch. © David Hume Kennerly / Getty Images.

who fired the first shots in the government raid that led to the siege. In 1995, followers of the eclectic Japanese Buddhist–Hindu movement known as Aum Shinrikyo employed a biological weapon, sarin gas, killing 12 and injuring thousands in a Tokyo subway. In 1997, 39 members of a UFO religion called Heaven's Gate committed suicide in the hope of joining a spacecraft that they believed was following the Hale-Bopp comet, which was then approaching the earth's view. They were led to this act by their two charismatic founders, Marshall Applewhite and Bonnie Nettles, who taught that they were, both of them, extraterrestrial "walk-ins," that is, aliens in human form.

One easy explanation commonly offered for these horrific events is that such groups are "cults" and that their members have been "brainwashed." The reality is much more complex. For one thing, the word "cult" (as well as "sect," used more commonly in European countries) has become a loaded prejudicial term, which can too easily justify violence against small religious groups and their members. It is also worth noting that, historically speaking, a "cult" (which comes from the Latin *cultus*) is related to the terms "cultivate" and "culture" and was originally used to describe *any* established religious activity, as in the Catholic "cult of the saints." It carried no negative connotations. Closer to home, "cult" was the term that twentieth-century sociologists used to replace Troeltsch's earlier "mysticism" type. What we have here, then, is yet another "abused" word. Many scholars today use the more neutral phrase "new religious movement."

The term "brainwashing" is similarly unhelpful. The basic problem is that this word assumes that it is psychologically possible for individuals to be forced into actions against their own will and best interests, for long periods of time, in the absence of any physical means of control. Initial public views on brainwashing were based on the anti-American statements made by some American POWs (prisoners of war) during the Korean War (1950–1953). The professional psychological community has since evaluated the evidence and concluded that brainwashing,

as commonly understood, is not psychologically possible, at least not *in the absence of physical restraint or coercion*. This appears to be the key. In some of the cases listed above, such as the Jonestown and the Aum Shinrikyo events, force or restraint was indeed used on some individuals, but in most other cases both affiliation to the group and participation in the violence were voluntary.

As with all other comparative terms, there is a history here. During the 1960s and 1970s, a number of individuals began to use the phrase "coercive persuasion" to explain behavioral changes that took place in the various new religious movements that sprang up in the counterculture. Coercive persuasion came to mean brainwashing without physical restraint. It was said to be achieved through emotional manipulation, hard work, and isolation, supported by chanting, fasting and ascetic practices, all of which were part of a sophisticated system designed to break down the personality of the recruit and assist the leader in remolding it to his or her will. It was alleged that cults used deception, fraud, and even blackmail to retain their members.

Although a few groups did use illegal or unethical tactics, most were simply offering an immersive and high-demand experience that satisfied their members. Furthermore, most of the alleged characteristics of a cult (strange clothes or costumes, strong discipline, specific dietary practices, and distinctive hair cuts) can also be found in more established religions, not to mention the military organizations of almost any nation-state. The comparativist cannot help but notice that the cult label was often applied by Christians to groups with beliefs rooted in Asian religious traditions (more bad comparisons).

Ironically, the emerging "anti-cult" movement justified its own use of coercive or even violent techniques designed to "break" cult indoctrination. These techniques included kidnapping and forced "deprogramming," which basically amounted to holding group members against their will until they agreed to give up their newfound beliefs. One form of coercion had replaced another.

As it turns out, deprogrammings are not very successful, and most recruits to new religious movements leave voluntarily. Individual agency is generally much stronger and more resilient than the language of "brainwashing" suggests (as if we were towels or shirts?). Sociologist Lorne Dawson summarizes the scholarly consensus: "The evidence is weak for assuming that the full and involuntary transformation of identity signified by 'brainwashing' can occur in the absence of physical restraint and abuse."[38] Most scholars today see conversion as a complex process that meets a variety of social, psychological and spiritual needs.

In the end, two conclusions can be drawn from the study of new religious movements and violence. First, violence is rare. As pointed out by Dawson, "even though there have been many world-rejecting apocalyptic groups, few of them have been implicated in any acts of violence, towards themselves or others."[39] Second, violence is usually an interactive process, as it was in the Branch Davidian case. The Branch Davidians were certainly operating with a set of dangerous eschatological beliefs (based on Revelation) and were partly responsible for what happened, but, as Catherine Wessinger observes, "the fire would not have started if tanks had not been inserting a flammable tear gas and demolishing the building."[40]

Most new religious movements do not end violently, even those that experience millennial episodes. As a case in point, consider the several thousand members of Church Universal and Triumphant, a New Age religious movement led by Elizabeth Clare Prophet (mother of Erin). This group constructed a network of underground bomb shelters in Montana and purchased weapons for self-defense in response to Prophet's eschatological predictions of an impending nuclear war. A series of drills were held, but little else transpired. The group members emerged from the shelters peacefully and eventually returned to their homes and jobs. The core group at the church headquarters dwindled over time, and the group renewed its emphasis on peaceful worship. A study of these events reveals the ebb and flow of eschatological themes in response to both a perception of persecution and the fragility of charismatic leadership. It also demonstrates that groups can continue after such near-apocalyptic incidents, weakened for sure, but with a return to non-eschatological teachings and behavior.[41]

In the end we might conclude that beliefs do not and cannot kill people alone; they need people too. Still, if a particular set of beliefs relies on violence for its logic and for the dramatic ending of its story, we have good reason to be concerned.

As we saw on 9/11. The Islamist radicals who hi-jacked those four planes and killed thousands of innocent people murdered and died for religious reasons, "for God." We can argue that these were misguided reasons or reasons not faithful to the real or full teachings of Islam, but we cannot deny the Islamists their own self-understandings and meanings. They were what they were.

"In the Name of God"

Again, it bears repeating: religious terrorism is by no means unique in the historical record. Quite the contrary. People have been killing people for millennia for conscious, well thought out religious reasons, which are always also political, economic, and personal reasons. As the stories go, the tenth and last plague in Exodus involved the god of the Hebrews slaying the (completely innocent) male children of Egyptian mothers and fathers in order to convince the Egyptian leaders to free the Hebrews. How do you think those Egyptian parents felt about the terrorist acts of this foreign murderous god? For centuries, colonizing and missionizing Christians wiped out, sometimes intentionally, through military force, sometimes accidentally, through disease and alcohol, entire indigenous cultures and populations in Africa, Australia, and the Americas. Zen Buddhist priests preached virulent forms of Japanese nationalism and supported the war effort in World War II. Nationalist Hindus carefully planned and organized a nation-wide political movement that led to the destruction of the Muslim Babri mosque in Ayodhya in 1992, which in turn initiated waves of religious violence between Muslims and Hindus that took the lives of thousands of people and opened up an era of politicized Hindu fundamentalism.

How should one respond intellectually, that is, with the tools of clear rational thought, to all of this?

Faith as Prevention, Protection, and Problem

The first thing to say is that we must recognize that religion also, and probably much more often, *prevents* violence to the extent that it suppresses and controls human aggression and instills basic ethical norms in human beings and societies on a daily basis in countless invisible ways. Faith does not just occasionally kill. It also protects and prevents. Numerous writers have commented on the mass massacre that was the twentieth century, and that much of the immeasurable violence was carried out not by religious groups, but by aggressively atheist or secular regimes: Hitler, Stalin, Lenin, Mao, and Pol Pot. In short, it is certainly the case that too much religion can produce real violence, but it is also more than apparent that not enough religion can produce even more. And on an unbelievable scale.

The second thing we can observe is that most of the recent Islamist violence has been directed at the fellow faithful, not at people outside the Islamic world. Although there are no definitive statistics available, it is clearly an understatement to observe that, for every Indian, European, or American who has become a target of violent Islamist attacks, hundreds of Muslims have suffered similar fates at the hands of their fellow Muslims. Islamist radicals, after all, do not simply position themselves against the assumed "godlessness" of modern secular humanism and "the West." They also ferociously oppose the more syncretic understandings of Islam, which often draw upon the mystical elements of the tradition. For an Islamist fundamentalist, all such developments fall into the blank category of "human corruptions," as opposed to the "pure faith" of the founding fathers. This is why radical Islamist groups have been so actively engaged in the destruction of Sufi shrines across the Muslim world.

The third thing we can say is that acts of religious violence make good sense to those who inhabit many traditional forms of religion, which seek to impose their singular vision of humanity, their sameness, on all human beings. These are worldviews that have little sympathy for the modern values of religious liberty, respect for persons, human rights, and cultural and religious pluralism. Indeed, these same values are precisely those that are commonly and openly mocked by fundamentalist leaders and their institutions around the world.

Liberalism and Comparison

These mocked values are all key components of a philosophical orientation and political philosophy called **liberalism**. By "liberalism" we do not mean to refer to any contemporary political campaign or candidate (and we recognize that this term carries very different meanings in different political and national contexts). We mean to refer to a carefully argued philosophical position that has now been developed for centuries by countless political theorists and philosophers, originally and primarily in Europe and in the broader West. Richard Miller, in a cogent study of religion and violence after 9/11,[42] has identified two core principles of liberalism and its specific forms of social criticism, of which the comparative study of religion is clearly one.

The first core principle is that human beings live their lives "from the inside." They are autonomous moral agents. They seek to revise their worlds constantly in the light of new information and of their own decision-making processes. They resist all attempts to have a system of values or norms imposed on them "from the outside." Religious fundamentalists, of course, might say the same, but they would deny that their religious convictions come from the outside, that is, from the accident of birth and the intimate processes of socialization.

The second core principle of liberalism boils down to a set of values that constitute modern liberal democracies, that is, political arrangements built on these same liberal values, namely "the presumption of individual liberty; respect for persons and, with that, the tolerance of different loyalties, communities, and convictions; a commitment to equality; an account of the limited authority of the state; and the organization of political life premised on popular sovereignty," that is, on democratic processes like free elections.

If you value these principles and wish to live in a society that respects them, you are a liberal political thinker and, potentially at least, a liberal social critic who cannot accept the opposite logic of religious conservatism upon which religiously motivated terrorist acts rely for their own logic and support.

Miller's incisive liberal analysis of religious violence is helpful here, since he writes directly against what he calls, quoting another author, the "culture of excuse and apology." This is important to explain, as this culture of excuse and apology is a common one in academic circles. Miller explains:

This is not a culture in which terrorism is openly defended, but one in which the rationales come from oblique and indirect angles. Typically such rationales assume the form of excusing terrorism, including religious terrorism, by assimilating it into a broader critique of political inequality, Western imperialism, or American foreign policy—as if violent zealots were themselves advocating liberal and egalitarian causes.[43]

At the end of the day, what we really have here is two diametrically opposed worldviews of what a human being is and how human societies should organize themselves: one liberal and open-ended; the other conservative and closed. Also two diametrically opposed ways of being religious: one insisting on complete sameness; the other insisting on both sameness (as in human equality and equal rights) and radical difference (as in religious liberty and autonomous moral agency). Put most provocatively, we have here one example of comparison done badly and one example of comparison done well.

The Tough Questions

1   One apparent attraction of functionalism is that such a method appears to avoid or sidestep the tough truth questions: "Is what so-and-so believes true or not?" But does functionalism *really* avoid these questions? Or does it already have an answer? Examine some functionalist treatments of religion in the media and decide for yourself.

2   Where do you stand on the relationship between human evolution and religion? Is it really possible, in the long run, to keep our science and our religion apart?

3   Is there any way to address the problem of religious violence in the modern world without also addressing the problem of religion? Can we really separate the violence from the religious contexts in which it takes place and through which it is expressed?

4   What do you do with the observation that two of the most common professional occupations of fundamentalist leaders around the world have been engineering and computer programming?

Notes

1   For the full poem, "In Memory of Sigmund Freud" (1 September 1939), see *W. H. Auden: Collected Poems*, edited by Edward Mendelson (New York: Vintage, 1991), 273–276.

2   See Carol Delaney, *Abraham on Trial: The Social Legacy of Biblical Myth* (Princeton, NJ: Princeton University Press, 2000).

3   *Saddharma-smrityupasthana Sutra* XXXIV, translated by Arthur Waley. In *Buddhist Texts through the Ages*, edited by Edward Conze, I. B. Horner, D. Snellgrove, and A. Waley (New York: Philosophical Library, 1954), 283.

4   Sigmund Freud, "Three Essays on the Theory of Sexuality." In *The Standard Edition of the Complete Works of Sigmund Freud*, translated by James Strachey in

collaboration with Anna Freud, assisted by Alix Strachey and Alan Tyson, vol. 7 (London: The Hogarth Press and the Institute of Psycho-analysis, 1975), 178.

5   Emile Durkheim, *The Elementary Forms of the Religious Life*, translated by Joseph Ward Swain (New York: The Free Press, 1965), 14.

6   Durkheim, *Elementary Forms*, 19.

7   Durkheim, *Elementary Forms*, 63.

8   Durkheim, *Elementary Forms*, 22.

9   Durkheim, *Elementary Forms*, 29.

10 Peter Berger, *The Sacred Canopy: Elements of a Sociological Theory of Religion* (Garden City, NY: Anchor Books, 1969), 5.

11 Berger, *The Sacred Canopy*, 9.

12 Berger, *The Sacred Canopy*, 15.

13 Berger, *The Sacred Canopy*, 18.

14 Berger, *The Sacred Canopy*, 28.

15 Berger, *The Sacred Canopy*, 45.

16 Berger, *The Sacred Canopy*, 10.

17 Berger, *The Sacred Canopy*, 17.

18 Berger, *The Sacred Canopy*, 85–87.

19 Edward W. Said, *Orientalism* (New York: Vintage, 1978).

20 Richard King, *Orientalism and Religion: Post-colonial Theory, India, and the "Mystic" East* (New York: Routledge, 1999).

21 Scott Atran, *In Gods We Trust: The Evolutionary Landscape of Religion* (New York: Oxford University Press, 2002), 113.

22 Atran, *In Gods We Trust*, 5.

23 Pascal Boyer, *Religion Explained: The Evolutionary Origins of Religious Thought* (New York: Basic Books, 2001), 62.

24 Atran, *In Gods We Trust*, 114.

25 Atran, *In Gods We Trust*, 79.

26 Atran, *In Gods We Trust*, 10.

27 Atran, *In Gods We Trust*, 43.

28 Atran, *In Gods We Trust*, 51.

29 Boyer, *Religion Explained*, 145.

30 See Steven Weinberg, *Dreams of a Final Theory: The Search for the Fundamental Laws of Nature* (New York: Pantheon, 1992), 255 (where he also discusses it).

31 Ann Taves, *Religious Experience Reconsidered: A Building-Block Approach to the Study of Religion and Other Special Things* (Princeton, NJ: Princeton University Press, 2009), 11.

32 Ann Taves, "Building Blocks of Sacralities: A New Basis for Comparison across Cultures and Religions." In *Handbook of Psychology of Religion and Spirituality*, edited by Raymond F. Paloutzian and Crystal Park, 2nd edn. (New York: Guilford Press, 2013), 151. For the notion of animal laughter, I am relying on NPR's Radio Lab episode on laughter, available at http://www.radiolab.org/2008/feb/25/ (last accessed August 30, 2013).

33 Taves, "Building Blocks," 146.

34 Taves, "Building Blocks," 156.

35 Taves, "Building Blocks," 152.

36 Taves, *Religious Experience Reconsidered*, 99.

37 Wayne Proudfoot, *Religious Experience* (Berkeley: University of California Press, 1987).

38 Lorne L. Dawson, *Comprehending Cults: The Sociology of New Religious Movements*, 2nd edn. (New York: Oxford University Press, 2006), 108.

39 Dawson, *Comprehending Cults*, 152.

40 Catherine Wessinger, *How the Millennium Comes Violently: From Jonestown to Heaven's Gate* (New York: Seven Bridges Press, 2000), 20–21.

41 For the details of this particular case, see Erin Prophet, *Prophet's Daughter: My Life with Elizabeth Clare Prophet inside Church Universal and Triumphant* (Guilford, CT: Lyons Press, 2009).

42 Richard B. Miller, *Terror, Religion, and Liberal Thought* (New York: Columbia University Press, 2010).

43 Miller, *Terror, Religion, and Liberal Thought*, 3–4.

The Mage (2001), by Lynn Randolph, 56″ × 51″.

12

Reflexive Re-readings

Looking at the Looker

The god to whom man proves devout,
That is his own soul inside out.

Johann Wolfgang von Goethe (from Anthony Peake, *The Daemon:*
A Guide to Your Extraordinary Secret Self)

We are not human beings having a spiritual experience; we are spiritual beings having
a human experience.

Commonly attributed to Teilhard de Chardin

Instead of looking at the screen, what I want to do is to turn around and look the other
way. When we look the other way what we see is a little hole at the top of the wall with
some light coming out. That's where I want to go. I want to steal the key to the
projectionist's booth, and then, when everybody has gone home, I want to break in.

Jacques Vallee (from Mac Tonnies, *The Cryptoterrestrials*)

Chapter Outline

Comparing Religions: Coming to Terms, First Edition. Jeffrey J. Kripal, Ata Anzali, Andrea R. Jain, and Erin Prophet.
© 2014 Jeffrey J. Kripal. Published 2014 by John Wiley & Sons, Ltd.

We know so little about the true nature of time and, by extension, about what we so easily call "history." Consider the following true story.

I was lecturing at a major research university. Afterwards, as usually happens, really as *always* happens, a colleague asked me if she could tell me a story. She then proceeded to describe the following series of historical events.

A few years before our conversation, she had sent her four-year-old son up to a petting zoo north of the city with their nanny. At 10:06 a.m. she got a sudden "flash" of a picture in her head of her son screaming in his car seat at the back of the car and of the car filling up with what looked like white smoke, which she did not understand. She knew it was a serious car crash, as she could also "feel" the impact in her child's body—viscerally. She immediately called her nanny. They were already at the petting zoo. She instructed the nanny to come home immediately and to drive very slowly. They got home just fine.

The next day the boy wanted to go back to the petting zoo. He had, after all, not been allowed to stay the day before. So the mother decided to drive him up herself this time. On the way there, a car made a sharp turn in front of them on the highway, and a crash ensued. The son was screaming in the back car seat. The airbags deployed and filled the car up with white powder or "smoke." The mother turned around to check on her son: that was when the flash from the day before re-played, like a precise

"video re-run," as she puts it. The man who hit them offered to call the woman's husband after the crash, since the woman could not get to her phone. The emergency call registered on her husband's phone at 10:08 a.m.

Such events should make us think twice about all of those divination practices that we looked at in Chapter 4. It turns out that human beings *can* sometimes see the future, *can* sometimes transcend the normal limitations of linear time. Notice, though, how all bets are off once we step out of time. For example, was this mother seeing into the future? Or was the future, perhaps as her future self, reaching back to her present self? Also note that, by acting on the precognitive vision (and hence by preventing the child from a full visit at the zoo), the mother actually helped cause the future event to happen (since the child now wanted to return). Or did the vision from the future intend a warning, caused her to be more careful and cautious the next day, and this way helped prevent a much more serious event?

The School of the More

What is the historian, who is presumably interested in the full workings of time, supposed to make of such an event? The usual answer to this question is simple: "Nothing." Just ignore it, or, if you have to do something, simply describe it and then call it a "coincidence" or an "anecdote"—anything to get it off the table, so that we may preserve our supposedly perfect and complete understanding of the world. In instances like this, such lazy answers explain exactly nothing, of course, but they do deflect the discussion away from the truly serious, truly embarrassing issues at hand. Deflect and distract long enough, and such matters will go away.

They don't go away, of course. They just keep appearing. Hence the history of religions—humanity's millennia-long encounter and struggle with the anomalous, the powerful, the really, really weird stuff that does *not* fit in, that does *not* make sense.

Is there any way around this dead end?

At first glance, the answer appears to be: "No." The two-hundred-year drama that is the modern study of religion has been driven by a kind of ping-pong movement between faithful re-readings and rational re-readings, that is, between belief and reason. The discussion, moreover, has often proceeded on the assumptions that what we have here is a zero-sum game, an either–or choice that must conclude either on the side of faith and its revealed doctrines or on the side of reason and its materialist and mechanistic conclusions.

A number of thinkers, including myself (and I speak and write in this final chapter as fully myself, relieving my co-writers of any responsibility for what follows), have decided that this is much too simple a picture, that history overflows, mocks, and offends *both* sides. These thinkers take experiences like that of the precog mother extremely seriously. Indeed they take them as keys to a future theory of religion. Accordingly, they have offered ways of looking at religion that I want to name now and bring under the rubric of reflexive re-readings.

Most simply put, a **reflexive re-reading** is that mode of interpretation that combines faithful and rationalist re-readings, even as it moves beyond both. More precisely, reflexive re-readings are those that embrace the most robust rationalist re-readings of religion in order to "reduce" religious phenomena back to human nature and human history, only to find that this nature and history cannot be fully

explained by human reason, that something else or more, and often something truly fantastic, appears to be shining through.

Like extremely precise visions of future car wrecks.

Please note that reflexive re-readings cannot be construed as simply faithful re-readings plus rational re-readings: a little faith here, a little reason there. Quite the contrary, reflexive re-readings constitute a genuinely new or third way of interpreting religion. It is not the case, then, that $1+1=2$ here. Rather, $1+1=3$. That is, we are dealing with yet another "third" or both–and mode of thinking. Robert A. Orsi has recently called this mode of thinking in the study of religion "the tradition of the more."[1] Reflexive re-readings clearly sit in this tradition of thought.

Let us call it "the school of the more."

If one can recognize faithful re-readings by applying the faith test and strong forms of rationalist re-reading by applying the "nothing but" test, we can recognize reflexive re-readings by applying the "more" test. It goes like this: "After a series of reductive or rationalist re-readings, is there some intuited truth or anomalous event, some altered state of energy or knowledge that is not finally explicable in rationalist or materialist terms?" In short: "Is there something more?" Note that this "more" need not be determined or defined, since no faith tradition or set of doctrines is being privileged or required (which is why these reflexive re-readings are not faithful re-readings). All that is required to label a re-reading "reflexive" is for such a "more" to be posited as likely or possible.

The "more" test can be understood better through a discussion of the "cost of admission" into the school of the more. Reflexive re-readings, it turns out, demand some fairly heavy costs of both faithful and rational re-readers.

First, with respect to faithful re-readings, reflexive re-readings are immediately suspicious of the ways in which exclusivism, inclusivism, and even pluralism assume some sort of stable "object" as the topic of theology, belief, and community. That is, the whole realm of comparative theology often implies that there is a single objective truth or, if you prefer, an external "God," which is then revealed by a single tradition (exclusivism), or most fully expressed by a single tradition (inclusivism), or revealed and expressed through multiple cultural lenses and historical experiences (pluralism). Reflexive re-readings suggest in so many words that it is probably more accurate to think of religious truth not as something that is found or discovered, like a treasure buried in the ground, but as a conscious presence continually shaped and re-imagined *by itself*. Put a bit differently, we might say that reflexive re-readings recognize that all religious experience is indeed "constructed," but constructed out of and upon something, which is really not a "thing" at all. It is as if the painter, the paint, and the painting were all different aspects of the same creative process.

As such paradoxical language suggests, there are also real costs related to the rational re-readings. Reflexive re-readings, after all, are those that employ the power of rationalist methods to reduce religious phenomena back to their fundamental base in human nature only to discover that this nature is something quite extraordinary in itself. Hence the "angry ghost" of poltergeist events becomes the "ghost of anger" of parapsychology—still human indeed, but a most extraordinary kind of human, who is clearly violating the way in which the world is supposed to work by reason's rules.

We might recall here our initial definition of the humanities as consciousness studying consciousness in the reflecting mirror of culture. With reflexive re-readings of religion, we are still very much looking into that human mirror, with all the light-bending, mind-bending effects that this act involves, but we are also catching glimpses and clues of the final source of these constantly receding reflections: the looker. The results of this "looking into the looker" can sound utterly outrageous to the faithful believer *and* to the pure rationalist.

Four Exemplars of Reflexive Re-reading

The best way to understand these final reflexive re-readings is not to describe them in the abstract, but to describe how they are performed with specific historical materials by particular members of this school of the more. This is what I will do for the remaining of this chapter, before offering some final concluding personal thoughts.

The Psychological Turn

Freud was a consummate intellectual, as critical of the beliefs of faith as he was of the pretensions of reason. His model of the unconscious was a nuanced system designed to explain and explore how the human really is two. It is certainly true that he thought of the depths of human nature in reductive materialist terms, but he also had his reflexive moments. For example, he was at once conflicted and open-minded about telepathy, as his skeptical (really horrified) friend Ernest Jones has amply documented in his three-volume biography of Freud. Although originally dismissive, Freud became convinced that there was a kernel of truth in such things. More than a kernel, really. He publicly acknowledged this in a 1925 essay and wrote six essays in all on the subject of thought-transference or telepathy.

The most obvious reflexive re-reader in the psychoanalytic tradition, however, is not Freud but his originally chosen successor, Carl Jung. Indeed, it could well be said that the first and most significant crisis in the early psychoanalytic tradition (Jung's break with Freud) was over whether religion should be reductively re-read or reflexively re-read. Freud was adamant that it should be reductively re-read. Jung concluded that the reductive rational re-readings were powerful and true enough within their own range, but that something more was left over; that religious phenomena were indeed projective psychological phenomena, but that these were finally projected from a deeper layer or dimension of psyche that was essentially religious in nature *and was vast*.

Jung went on to argue that an individual psyche possesses its own individual unconscious, but that this personal unconscious is floating, as it were, in a measureless sea of universal mind and being that he called the **collective unconscious**. If the conscious

ego is the tip of an iceberg and the personal unconscious is most of that iceberg lying under the surface
of awareness, then the collective unconscious is the
sea of mind and being out of which the individual
psyche, that is, the person, "freezes" into hard form
and comes into existence, at least for at time, before
it is melted back into the ocean of mind.

Jung, in short, was "reducing" religious myths and
symbols to the psyche, but to a psyche that opens out
onto dimensions that are essentially religious, if not
actually cosmic. He took rational re-readings very
seriously, but he was also deeply concerned about
the ways in which rationalism, mechanism, and
materialism were thwarting human expression,
denying the full range of the psyche, and shutting
human beings off from the paradoxical richness of
existence. For Jung, reality was not contained by
reason and the senses, nor could it ever be.

The Religion of Man

Reflexive re-readings are not restricted to particular
cultural zones. One of the clearest exemplars of such
a comparative practice is the Indian Nobel laureate
and Bengali poet Rabindranath Tagore (1861–1941).
Consider the poet's Oxford lectures, which became
The Religion of Man (1931). At first glance, one might
think that the title of the book is simply an early version of a later "world religions" textbook, Huston
Smith's classic *The Religions of Man* (1958). One
might imagine that here Tagore was after what Smith
would clearly be after, one quarter of a century later,
namely the universal validation of the believer's perspective and an entirely positive view of the world's
religions, which was pioneering for its time.

And one would be wrong. Tagore did not mean
"the religion of man" to refer to the world religions
that human beings have long practiced around the
globe. "Man" here is not the subject, but the proper
object of religion. By "the religion of man" Tagore
means the worship of the human, of the man of the
heart, the supreme person that dwells at the inner
door of each and every human being. Such a vision
hardly affirms the perspective of every believer and

every world religion. Quite the contrary, it requires
a robust critique, even a rejection of just about every
religious tradition on the planet, at least in their
orthodox forms. Hence Tagore can write about how
he left his own tradition, Hinduism, and he can
describe his own Indian culture's "irrational repressions" and "accumulations of dead centuries." He can
also speak of the "ghastly disguise of religion" and, in
a phrase strikingly resonant with the contemporary
"spiritual but not religious" crowd, he can reject religious tradition as "blindly pious but not spiritual."[2]
His conclusion is in fact highly critical of religious
tradition and religious identity across the board:
"The God of humanity," he declares, "has arrived at
the gates of the ruined temple of the tribe."[3]

It will hardly surprise you by now to learn that
Tagore's reflexive comparative practice found its
origin not in any rational process, but in the "sudden
flash" of two mystical experiences, which he relates in
one of his Oxford lectures entitled simply "The
Vision." The first experience, which he compares to
an ancient mist suddenly lifting, occurred when he
was eighteen. It lasted for four days. The second
occurred when he was an adult and was working in
a village: "All things that had seemed like vagrant
waves were revealed to my mind in relation to a
boundless sea." Now he "felt sure that some Being
who comprehended me and my world was seeking
his best expression in all my experiences, uniting
them into an ever-widening individuality which is a
spiritual work of art."[4] The painter who is the painted
and the paint again.

It was such a vision that showed him that "on the
surface of our being we have the ever-changing phases
of the individual self, but in the depth there dwells the
Eternal Spirit of human unity beyond our direct
knowledge."[5] This is what he calls "the surplus in
man," his version of what I have called "the human as
two." In another shift of metaphors, the poet explains
the relationship between difference and sameness: "in
the night we stumble over things and become acutely
conscious of their individual separateness. But the day
reveals the greater unity which embraces them. The
man whose inner vision is bathed in an illumination

of his consciousness at once realizes the spiritual unity reigning supreme over all differences."[6]

Nor will it surprise you that Tagore's initial inspiration for how to articulate his vision was a group of mystics: the Bengali poet-singers called Bauls, who wander to this day the roads, villages, and cities of northeastern India without temple, without scripture, and singing of the secret core of the human being—of what Tagore calls "the divinity of Man."[7] The Bauls are "comparativist" mystics, effortlessly combining teachings of both Hinduism and Islam into their songs and practices.

Significantly, Tagore first chanced upon their songs about the same time he had "given up my connection with our church," after realizing that the religious institutions "represented an artificial average, with its standard of truth at its static minimum."[8] He would now reject all of that and seek "the Supreme Man," who is "infinite in his essence," if "finite in his manifestation in us the individuals."[9] "Religion," he wrote, "is the liberation of our individual personality in the universal Person who is human all the same."[10]

Sociology and the Projector

Durkheim's reduction of religious phenomena to social processes seems complete, even if his respect for the holism and the hidden power of the social system sometimes borders on a kind of reverence or awe. The potential reflexivity of sociological re-readings can best be appreciated in later figures.

Consider again the American sociologist of religion Peter Berger. Toward the very end of *The Sacred Canopy*, Berger makes a most remarkable observation with respect to projection theory and mathematics. Why is it, he asks, that mathematics, which appears to exist only in the minds of human beings, through abstract symbols called "numbers," turns out to reflect and predict, very precisely, the workings of the natural world—the world "out there"? How to explain this unbelievable correspondence between inner and outer? Two and a half millennia ago, Plato had asked the same question. He suggested that the perfect forms of mathematics, which cannot be derived from sensory experience, are not actually learned but are "remembered" by the soul. Math, in short, functions as a sign of the soul's pre-existence, when it had direct contact with the true reality that the perfection of mathematics stands for.

Berger moves in a different theological direction, one more in tune with the Christian notion of human beings made "in the image of God" (another version of the idea of mirror). More specifically, he suggests what he calls an "interesting ploy," which is nothing but a reflexive re-reading of religion: "man projects ultimate meanings into reality because that reality is, indeed, ultimately meaningful, and because his own being (the empirical ground of these projections) contains and intends these same ultimate meanings."[11] In a sequel, his *Rumor of Angels*, Berger puts the matter in even more stark and provocative terms: "If the religious projections of man correspond to a reality that is superhuman and supernatural, then it seems logical to look for traces of this reality in the projector himself."[12] Note, here again, the reflexive cycle in which language about the superhuman is re-read as language about the human, which turns out to be superhuman.

Reflexivity as Modern Mysticism

Finally, consider a contemporary example of a reflexivity so extreme that it becomes, in effect, a mystical experience in its own right. In 1997 American author Erik Davis was in a Zen Buddhist retreat center in northern California; he had gone there to recover from the labors of writing his first book, *Techgnosis*, which dealt with the intersections of technology, magic, and mysticism. Davis was washing vegetables in a garden:

> So I'm rinsing the beets, minding my own business, vaguely enjoying the cool water washing away the moist and pungent mud, when my "I" suddenly rockets like a sci-fi space elevator into the highest, most barren and serene realms of Witness consciousness. I became the *watcher of the watcher of the watcher of the watcher of the watcher of the watcher* … a bootstrapping eensy-weensy spider of observer and observation that shed layers of identification as it flip-flopped up the water spout into even more rarified levels of subjectivity, until there was little left.[13]

Davis resists all "mystic rhetoric" here, because "it sounds like bullshit, and my experience was anything but bullshit, at least to me." The mystic rhetoric, however, is inescapable, and so it appears anyway, if now as a series of subtle allusions to the *vajra*, the "diamond" mind of Tibetan Buddhism and the "grokking" of Robert A. Heinlein's countercultural sci-fi novel *Stranger in a Strange Land*. So Davis continues:

> One thing is for sure: there was nothing particularly human in it. It felt like a being, but it had no attributes I can really name other than awareness and perception. It felt like diamond, like hard serenity, a clear and crystalline meta-mind that was both individual and, in some ungrokkable, transpersonal way, collective. And ever so slightly amused.

Davis calls this level of himself "the bright shards of witnessing angelstuff that lie at the root of my being." This is more than poetic license. Even if this experience was "a neural hiccup," he concludes: "I still know, in the way we know the mad unions of love, that we carry something cosmic within us, that the self is a doorway to another Self, and that death might swallow us in glory after all." In short, Davis had known, directly and dramatically, something astonishing about human nature, something that there was no way to measure or lock down into a system. He had passed through a doorway, or a mirror, to another self—the human as two.

Erik Davis had looked at the looker, who was looking back at him.

The Phenomenology of Religion: What Is versus What Appears

It can be disconcerting to look into the mirror of religion and see yourself looking at yourself, who turns out to be someone else. This is why I kept these methods until the very end of our journey together and why, like all the other re-readings, they are being presented as speculative options for you to take up or set down. Remember: it's a mirror. You don't have to look into it. You can walk away. You are your own authority here. So take responsibility for your choices and for what you are seeing.

And not seeing.

Our eyes pick up about one ten-trillionth of the total light spectrum. That's right. You see one ten-trillionth of what is actually there, right now. Basically, you are totally blind. You do *not* perceive the world as it is. You perceive the world as your evolved biology and its sensory system allow you, force you to perceive it. Even the immediate perceptions you take as accurate photographs of something "out there" are neither immediate nor innocent, objective photographs. Perception is actually memory in the simple sense that what you see, or think you see, has already been processed by your brain into an organized experience. You do not even perceive in the present. You perceive in the just past. Your perceptions are memories shaped into virtual experiences by lightning-quick brain processes. Sensorially speaking, you are living in the past, always. As David Eagleman summarizes the situation: "So the first lesson about trusting your senses is: don't."[14]

This is the present neuroscientific position. It is hardly new. The German philosopher Immanuel Kant (1724–1804) demonstrated the same (minus the math and brain scans) over two hundred years ago. And he was working in a philosophical tradition that goes back at least as far as ancient Greece: thinkers like Plato clearly distinguished between the "divine" world of Forms, which the enlightened philosopher can "know" (even if only indirectly in this life), and the social and sensory world of mere opinion, which is not true knowledge but a mere shadow, a mere ten-trillionth fraction of the real, we might say. Remember Plato's Cave?

For his part, Kant demonstrated that what appears to us and what is out there—the thing-in-itself, as he called the latter—are two *very* different matters. He called what appears to us the **phenomenon** (from the Greek *to phainomenon*, "that which appears/is visible") and the thing-in-itself the **noumenon** (from the Greek *to nooumenon*, "that which is thought"). We can never really get hold of noumenal reality, Kant argued. We can never really know it, and we certainly cannot think it.

We can only perceive and experience the world, he argued, through the already given (today we might say "hard-wired") categories of thinking and perception: space, time, and causality. He called these structures of thinking and perceiving *a priori* **categories**. These precede, shape, and determine thought but are not themselves accessible to view. They may or may not be "out there." They are certainly "in here," however, and they structure and determine everything we think and perceive, everything we *can* think and perceive.

An important branch of the study of religion called the **phenomenology of religion** works on this same philosophical principle. The phenomenology of religion sets aside or "brackets" the truth claims of the religious material it is studying; it seeks instead to describe, as accurately as it can, "what appears" to a person undergoing a particular type of religious experience. Among many other things, this **bracketing** allows the discipline to take seriously the radical pluralism of the religious experience, as this move implicitly recognizes that all religious experience, like all sensory or cultural experience, will be conditioned and shaped, that there is no such thing as a pure religious experience.

One could well argue that no philosophical argument has been simpler, more elegant, and more influential on modern western thought, including the modern study of religion. Indeed *all* of our present methods—from historical criticism, constructivism, and functionalism to evolutionary psychology, cognitive science, and postcolonial theory—come down to a basic conviction that we can never know reality as it is; we can only know reality as it is constructed, shaped, and conditioned by our brains, societies, histories, biologies, politics, cognitive software, and so on.

These assumptions about the human mind and its inability to know reality as it is may not, however, be the final word.

Reflexively Re-reading Miracle: The Man in the Door

New Jersey resident Nina de Santo saw a long-time customer named Michael standing outside her beauty shop one Saturday evening. She met him at the door. Michael was smiling. He was in a hurry and could not stay long. He had been going through a very difficult divorce and had lost custody of his kids. He just wanted to thank Nina for all the times she was there to listen. And then he left. The next day Nina received a phone call from one of her employees. Michael had committed suicide the day before, nine hours before she met him in front of her shop.[15]

A student sent me this story, which was reported by CNN. It reminded me immediately of another set of stories, with which I was very familiar but had not thought about for years: the gospel stories of the resurrected Jesus, whom his mourning disciples encountered on the road to Emmaus and in the breaking of the bread at a meal as a real physical presence, very much like Michael at Nina's beauty shop. I had long assumed that these gospel narratives were socially constructed legends, created in the early Christian communities to express the members' fervent belief in their risen Lord. I am no longer so sure about that. I am beginning to wonder if they are not rather literary transformations of actual historical encounters, much like that of Nina de Santo in New Jersey.[16] My reasoning is simple: if such things can happen in contemporary America, why could they have not happened in the ancient world?

I am by no means the first person to re-read the ancient religious texts in light of reports of contemporary paranormal experiences. Indeed this was a common method in the nineteenth century. Consider the example of an old acquaintance of ours …

David Friedrich Strauss and the Miracle Revisited

Recall that in Chapter 2 we briefly explained how David Friedrich Strauss' *The Life of Jesus Critically Examined* (1835) played a major role in initiating the historical–critical study of the New Testament and, in a broader sense, the modern study of religion. Recall also that much of Strauss' work in that book was about demonstrating in detail how the four gospels cannot be reconciled with one another and why the different miracle and healing stories cannot be taken at face value. What we did not tell you at the beginning of your initiation but can tell you now, at the end of it, is that Strauss later changed his mind about miracles, mostly because he himself had met "the seeress of Provost": a living clairvoyant, medium, and healer named Friederike Hauffe (1801–1829). In her presence Strauss witnessed what he took to be genuinely unexplainable events around the then contemporary phenomena of animal magnetism (see Figure 12.1).

Animal magnetism, also called "Mesmerism"— after the Austrian healer Franz Anton Mesmer (1734–1815), who helped originate and spread the method (this is also the origin of the English word "mesmerized")—was a healing practice that accessed unusual forms of human energy, which Mesmer and the magnetists likened to the invisible force fields of natural magnetism. Indeed they generally thought that these energies *were* a form of natural magnetism. Whatever they were, the literature is filled with dramatic stories about how these energies effected cures and spiritual transformations. "Magnetized" individuals were reported to manifest fantastic abilities, for example the ability to see into bodies (their own or those of others), to diagnose illnesses and suggest treatments, and to manifest clairvoyance. The latter is a French word that means "clear vision" but is normally used in a narrow, specialized sense, to designate the capacity to see things that are otherwise inaccessible, like events happening at a distance.

PHYSIQUE ET CHIMIE POPULAIRES

Liv. 136.   Le Baquet de Mesmur.

Figure 12.1   Mesmer conducting a baquet or group treatment with a "magnetized" tub of water. Mary Evans Picture Library.

It was precisely these kinds of altered states of energy that Strauss was now witnessing close up with the seeress. The great biblical critic realized, with something of a shock, that these abilities, which he could no longer deny, had real implications for how he read the miracle stories of the New Testament, which he had denied. He understood that, if they were happening in his own time, they could have just easily happened in the time of Jesus.

Strauss went further. He read deeply into the Christian mystics. He read authors like the German shoemaker Jacob Boehme, who once saw the meaning of the cosmos in the sunny reflections bouncing off a pewter dish (the mirror again, this time in a form of divination that you might now recognize as lecanomancy). He met the German poet-physician Justinus Kerner, who was working with Hauffe and studying him, and who had come to the conclusion that the traumatic technology of illness was necessary to "open up" a human being to the higher worlds.

All of this would have a profound effect on Strauss' famous book. As his modern editor Peter C. Hodgson explains, Strauss' discussion of miracles in the first two editions revolved around a rationalist re-reading of two types: the miracle as literal truth involving supernatural intervention (which he rejected), and the miracle as a misidentified power of nature, what we would today call suggestion or psychosomatic healing (which he accepted). However, in the 1838 third edition of the book, Strauss felt it necessary to introduce a *third* type: the miracle as a real and highly unusual phenomenon of nature (what would later be called "the paranormal"). "These cures," Hodgson explains,

> can still be explained on the basis of nature, as with the second type, but they display uncommon or extraordinary powers, similar to the absolute miracles of the first type. Strauss has in mind cures involving touch, cures based on the hypnotic power of will or on clairvoyance, and cures at a distance (mental telepathy).[17]

In short, Strauss had in mind the seeress of Provost.

Ioan Couliano's Toolkit for the Fourth Dimension

Ioan Couliano was a historian of religions who worked with Mircea Eliade (both were Romanians) at the University of Chicago and taught there himself. He was an early advocate of the cognitive approach to the study of religion. He argued that the obvious similarities in religious belief across immense stretches of time can be best explained by positing "a simple set of rules" that "would generate similar results in the minds of human beings for a virtually infinite period of time." These rules might be things like "there is another world" or "there is a soul that separates from the body when a person dies." The fact that the cultural transmission of these simple rules—whose limited variants and interactions he compared to the features of rules in a game—is never perfect helps explain both the sameness and the differences that we find in the general history of religions. All human traditions developed in parallel "from analogous premises, although beliefs inevitably interacted and coalesced. The result is a surprising unity in the variety."[18]

The question remained, however: just what kind of mind was playing with all these rules? It was here that he entertained some most remarkable ideas, which went far beyond anything that cognitive science has so far imagined (so it seems appropriate that he named a journal he founded *Incognita*, that is, "things un-cognized" or "unknown"). One of these ideas was that historians should stop thinking about history as if it worked like a straight line on a flat pool table. After Einstein, he pointed out, we know that space and time are not like that. At all.

Couliano was especially fascinated by Einstein's theory of relativity and by the legacy of earlier nineteenth-century authors of the "fourth dimension," particularly Charles Howard Hinton (1853–1907) and Edward Abbot (1838–1926), to which relativity theory was itself indebted. Hinton was a mathematician, bigamist, defender of women's rights, and the inventor of the automatic baseball pitching machine. He authored books like *The Fourth Dimension* (1904) and a collection of *Scientific Romances* (1884–1886),

Figure 12.2   Peering into the secret structure of the cosmos. Sixteenth-century illustration for Nicolas Camille Flammarion, *L'atmosphère: Météorologie populaire* (Paris, 1888). © Stefano Bianchetti/Corbis.

a kind of early science fiction that Couliano describes as "mystic–scientific fantasies." For his part, Abbot authored the classic *Flatland* (1883), a little book that influenced Einstein (and a whole lot of science fiction).

Drawing on Abbot's *Flatland* and on Hinton's insistence that certain inexplicable experiences (namely experiences that we, today, would call "paranormal") are in fact real experiences of a fourth spatial dimension, Couliano pointed out that most of the "miraculous" abilities reported in ecstatic states, otherworldly journeys, and parallel universes would be easily understandable if we simply imagined them as functions of a "mind space" that exists in four spatial dimensions and relates to our three-dimensional world much as our three-dimensional nature might relate to a being restricted to a two-dimensional world—just like in Abbot's Flatland.

Imagine our relationship to a community of beings restricted to a tabletop. Such beings cannot move vertically, nor can they perceive anything that is not on the tabletop. They can only move or perceive on that flat surface: "In relation to them," Couliano observed,

> we can act like gods: we can make objects appear and disappear from the most recondite recesses (such as bank safes), we can take them instantly from one point of their space to another (an experience that they would probably interpret in mystical terms), and we can even flip them around through the third dimension so that their right side becomes left and their left side right. We can observe them at every moment and remain unnoticed.[19]

To the 2-D Flatlander, any 3-D being would seem omniscient and omnipotent, not to mention miraculous and completely invisible.[20] Something similar (if more extreme), of course, would be true of a 4-D intervention into a 3-D world. Hence the paranormal: the normal just "beyond" (*para*) the normal.

Note here that one needs no particular belief, deity, or religious identity to perform this re-reading of miracle "from the fourth dimension." There is no "supernatural" here. All one needs is a mathematical modeling of multiple dimensions and an ability to imagine ourselves outside our three-dimensional box (or cave). Hence Couliano's provocative observation that "physics and mathematics are to be held responsible to a large extent for the return of interest in mystical ways of knowledge."[21] After all, in light of modern physics and mathematics, "we are entitled to believe that our mind space has amazing properties, the most remarkable of which is that it is not limited to three dimensions."[22] (See Figure 12.2.)

Couliano turns to the history of otherworldly journeys or flights of the soul from ancient Greece to the modern literatures on the near-death experience (NDE) for confirmation of his most remarkable suggestion. These accounts, after all, describe—if usually in exaggerated mythical language—exactly the kinds of things one would expect if a mind space were to enter a hyper-dimensional state. They thus speak of "being turned around" (we find this phrase as early as in the Greek philosopher Plotinus and as late as in the comic book writer Grant Morrison), of being able to see in all directions at once, of being present at all places and times, of being able to see inside reality, and of turning into their own mirror image, "not unlike," Couliano points out, Alice when she "stepped through the looking glass into a reversed world."[23]

Couliano calls this re-reading of miracle through physics and mathematics "a historian's kit for the fourth dimension." Such a kit is a reflexive re-reading of religion, since it reduces the seemingly miraculous religious event to something natural, in this case the hyper-dimensional structures of space–time, only to discover that miracles are real and that the natural is better framed, particularly from our limited 3-D perspective, as the super natural.

There are many very real pay-offs here for the student of religion. One of them is that Couliano's kit helps us explain, almost effortlessly, why the ancients imagined the heavens to be "up," *and* why we can no longer do so. All human beings who lived before the last hundred years or so could not physically move up into the sky. They were stuck tight to the more or less flat two-dimensional surface of the earth. Practically speaking, they lived in a kind of Flatland. They thus naturally imagined their spiritual flights in three dimensions, that is, as moving "up." But we can now go up into the sky quite easily. Little wonder, then, that the religious imagination has moved on to four and five dimensions (since, after Einstein, we now understand time to be the "fourth dimension"). Remember Grant Morrison's alien contact experience, in which he was turned around, "rotated through a plane I could not now point to," and "twisted off the surface of the universe into the fifth dimension"? Ioan Couliano would have appreciated that.

Synchronicity and the Pauli Effect

Another most remarkable twentieth-century example of a reflexive re-reading of miracle and magic involved physics again, this time in the person of one of the early pioneers of quantum physics. The story also features two famous psychologists and a poltergeist of sorts. It goes like this.

We have already met the poltergeist—the "angry ghost." Recall that researchers have consistently noticed that poltergeist events tend to happen around very distraught pubescent boys and girls. It is as if these young men and women, all pent-up and conflicted inside, can no longer contain their emotions, and so they "let them out." Pictures fall off the wall. Things break and fly. But, interestingly, it is extremely rare that anyone is ever reported hurt or injured. It is as if such things are ultimately performances designed to attract attention, but not to do actual harm. Researchers, feeling indebted to Freud, have called this the "projected repression hypothesis."

Still in a Freudian mode, other thinkers have noticed that the emotional conflict is sometimes also sexual. They have speculated that rare types of sexual energy are sometimes being deployed in such events. In one reported case, for example, poltergeist phenomena, including moving furniture and floating school desks, spiked around an eleven-year-old Irish girl named Virginia Campbell on a twenty-eight-day cycle.[24] Human sexuality—the menstrual cycle, to be precise—has become here a kind of unconscious superpower.

It is by no means always the kids who are distraught, though. Poltergeist-like events have also played important roles in both the history of the study of religion and, believe it or not, the history of science. They marked, for example, one of the most significant breaks in the history of modern psychology: that between Sigmund Freud and his chosen heir, C. G. Jung. As Jung tells the story in his famous memoir, *Memories, Dreams, and Reflections*, 1909 was the turning point. The two men were in Freud's study arguing about the reality of precognition and other similar phenomena. Freud was rejecting it all as nonsensical, out of his own materialistic convictions (it would be years, Jung explains, before Freud "acknowledged the factuality of 'occult' phenomena"). And here is, according to Jung, what happened next:

> While Freud was going on this way, I had a curious sensation. It was as if my diaphragm were made of iron and were becoming red-hot—a glowing vault. And at that moment there was such a loud report in the bookcase, which stood right next to us, that we both started up in alarm, fearing the thing was going to topple over on us. I said to Freud: "There, that is an example of a so-called catalytic exteriorization phenomenon." "Oh come," he exclaimed. "That is sheer bosh." "It is not," I replied. You are mistaken, Herr Professor. And to prove my point I now predict that in a movement there will be another such loud report!" Sure enough, no sooner had I said the words than the same detonation went off in the bookcase.[25]

Such events were common in Jung's life and often marked significant moments of creativity or insight.

Indeed Jung thought and wrote about the paranormal for his entire career. His dissertation was on occultism (more precisely, on a medium who happened to be his own cousin). His house was haunted by poltergeist effects around his break with Freud—a series of events that ended only when he allowed himself to channel a new gnostic scripture entitled "Seven Sermons to the Dead." Moreover, late in life he wrote a quite prescient little book on UFOs that is still relevant and germane to the topic. Clearly and most remarkably, Jung had "come to terms" with the paranormal.

Partly this coming to terms happened through another new term: **synchronicity**. By it Jung meant to refer to those fantastic coincidences in our lives that seem to point to something more. He eventually concluded that at least some of these are not really coincidences at all; nor are they exactly "caused." Rather they show every evidence of being organized around meaning and metaphor, like, say, a poem or a symbol—something very much akin to what Charles Fort meant when he insisted that anomalous events are "expressions," or to what Mark Twain meant when he wrote that history may not repeat itself, but that it rhymes.

What Jung intended to express with his notion of synchronicity was the fact that sometimes what is going on *inside* the subject corresponds in a profound way to what is going on *outside* the subject, as if the mental and material dimensions of those special moments had "split off" from some deeper one single thing. We might say, then, that the mental and material dimensions of our experience sometimes "correspond" or "coincide" (remember our discussion about the symbol?) precisely because they have split off a common source that is neither mental nor material. Jung in fact speculated that this was precisely the case and referred to the deeper super-reality as the *unus mundus*, that is, "the one world" or "the unitary world."

What we have here, of course, is a modern updating of "magic," now re-read reflexively: not as a supernatural force attributed to a deity or demon, but as a manifestation of the deepest levels of the real world, of which the human being would be a double expression (material and mental).

There is a funny but important back-story here that involves the history of science. Jung developed his original concept of synchronicity out of a decades-long correspondence and friendship with the Nobel prize-wining quantum physicist Wolfgang Pauli (1900–1958). Pauli was quite conflicted about his emotional and sexual life. Indeed he first approached Jung when he was in pain, for help. Pauli, a famously explosive personality, was well known among his physics colleagues for a rather unique ability: they called it "the Pauli effect." The Pauli effect boiled down to the strange fact that, whenever Pauli would walk into a physics laboratory, an apparatus would inevitably fall, break, shatter, or burn. Pauli, who was very proud of the effect, clearly believed in its reality. He also noted in his correspondence that, whenever "it" happened, he would feel relief from his inner tension. It is difficult to avoid the conclusion: Wolfgang Pauli was a walking poltergeist (see Figure 12.3).

The physicists, of course, avoided such religiously loaded language. Hence their safe and sterile coinage: the Pauli effect. They hardly avoided the topic, though. In his history of quantum physics, theoretical physicist and cosmologist George Gamow explained that "something would usually break in the lab whenever he merely stepped across the threshold." Gamow goes on to describe one of the most famous—and most humorous—cases in the lore of physics:

> A mysterious event that did not seem at first to be connected with Pauli's presence once occurred in Professor J. Franck's lab in Göttingen. Early one afternoon, without apparent cause, a complicated apparatus for the study of atomic phenomena collapsed. Franck wrote humorously about this to Pauli at his Zurich address and, after some delay, received an answer in an envelope with a Danish stamp. Pauli wrote that he had gone to visit Bohr, and at the time of the mishap in Franck's laboratory his train was stopped for a few minutes at the Göttingen railroad station.[26]

Figure 12.3 *Jung–Pauli Dialog* (1995), by Juergen Jaumann, acrylic on canvas, 150 × 100 cm. Private collection of Harald Atmanspacher.

And the lore goes on. Pauli's friend, Otto Stern, actually banned Pauli from his own laboratory in Hamburg because of the same effect. And when I once spoke about Pauli in a Unitarian church service in Houston, an elderly man approached me afterwards to tell me about the time he was with Pauli at a physics conference in Jerusalem. It was a very hot day. The organizers made Pauli sit on the side of the room opposite the air conditioner. Sometimes practical concerns trump everything else.

The Filter Thesis: The Door in the Man

There are still other ways to re-read religion reflexively. One of the most common and useful is the **filter thesis**. Put simply, the filter (or transmission) thesis suggests that consciousness (as opposed to social identity, cognition, culture, or ego) is filtered, reduced, or transmitted through the brain but not produced by it.

The Myers–James Filter Thesis

Until the very end of his life, William James struggled with religious experience at its most extreme. He worked closely with mediums and witnessed psychical phenomena up close. He never claimed to understand what he had witnessed, but he did have a set of working theses, which appeared in *The Varieties* as the notion of a "door" in the subconscious and, in a late essay on the baffling nature of psychical research, as a "mother-sea" of consciousness in which we are all floating.

The door imagery appears in *The Varieties* as James's Lecture X on the subject of conversion. James is discussing the notion of a "subliminal self," which he borrowed from his close friend and colleague Frederic Myers. Myers' **subliminal self** was meant to refer to that vast region of the human personality that exists and works "below" (*sub*) the "threshold" (*limen*) of normal consciousness (another kind of "liminal" region), and that may be responsible for extraordinary capacities like telepathy

and clairvoyance. Myers would often capitalize this subliminal "Self," to signal its astonishing reach and cosmic implications. This was the Superman to the ego's Clark Kent.

In his own use of the subliminal self, James discussed how dramatic conversion experiences—in which a person suddenly changes character overnight, even instantly—appear to require some sort of "leaky or pervious margin." By this he means to suggest that in some individuals the conscious sense of self is porous and open to "external" influences, which may in fact be "internal." The human as two again.

This is a very old theme, of course. And a gendered one. In her *The Hammer and the Flute* (2005), historian of religions Mary Keller has pointed out that such a porous nature has traditionally been framed in primarily negative terms and related to the female gender. Noting that women are often more likely than men to be possessed by deities or spirits, numerous (male) commentators have suggested that this is because women are naturally more "passive" or "penetrable" (and the sexual connotations were often duly noted).[27] Myers and James were developing a similar notion, but for them this porous nature was not restricted to one of the genders. Moreover—and this was their real originality—they considered such an openness eminently positive. This, after all, was what makes a great writer, a great thinker, or a religious prodigy. This is what makes a *genius*. Hence lines like these: "The hubbub of the waking life might close a door which in the dreamy Subliminal might remain ajar or open … If there be higher powers able to impress us, they may beg access to us only through the subliminal door."[28]

Perhaps nowhere was James more clear on this than in his "Final Impressions of a Psychical Researcher" (1909), published less than a year before his death. James had finally concluded what his old friend Fred Myers had concluded: that we are not who we think we are. Here is how he put it:

> Out of my experience such as it is (and it is limited enough) one fixed conclusion dogmatically emerges,

and it is this, that we with our lives are like islands in the sea … there is a continuum of cosmic consciousness, against which our individuality builds but accidental fences, and into which our several minds plunge as into a mother-sea or reservoir. Our "normal" consciousness is circumscribed for adaptation to our external earthly environment, but the fence is weak in spots, and fitful influences from beyond leak in, showing the otherwise unverifiable common connection.[29]

James called this a "panpsychic" view of the universe, where people "individuate" out of a psychophysical sea—again, not unlike floating icebergs freezing into shape and then melting away in the endless waves of an ocean that is at once mental and material. Hence his speculations about "subtler forms of matter" in this "psychic sea."[30] Recall that panpsychism is a modern term resonant with many ancient worldviews in which "everything (*to pan*) is soul (*psuchē*)," in which everything, including what we think of as "dead" matter, is actually alive. In a figure like William James we can now see that such a position can also become a reflexive position in which everything is understood to be matter, but this matter, it turns out, is minded—another reflexive "flip" or reversal.

The filter or transmission thesis, it should be said, is not really new. Something very similar appears to be implied by Plato's famous parable of the Cave, with its primitive "projection technology" (our two-dimensional shadow senses are projected from a richer three-dimensional space, which itself is finally transcended by a hyper-dimensional world "outside"). Paul Marshall has also noted that the Hindu Tantric *kundalini yoga* system seems to assume something similar, through a series of increasingly dense filters (the *chakras*) "stepping down" consciousness, from outside the body "down" into the brain and the various neurological functions of the spinal system.[31]

As for the filter thesis itself, it would have a long rich history in the twentieth century. After Myers and James, it was taken up and developed further by the French philosopher Henri Bergson, by the English philosopher C. D. Broad, and by the novelist Aldous Huxley. Most recently, it has appeared among a number of contemporary neuroscientists and medical professionals as either a possible solution to the "hard problem" of consciousness, or, as we will see in a moment, as a cosmic truth known directly in stroke and coma.

Aldous Huxley and Mind at Large

Huxley was especially influential in the cultural life of the filter thesis. But his thinking was not just thinking. It was a direct and immediate mystical experience turned into thinking and then into a most remarkable little book: *The Doors of Perception* (1954). This slim volume is easily one of the most influential essays on an individual religious experience published in the twentieth century. In it, Huxley drew on both Asian religious and western poetic and philosophical sources in order to describe what he had known during an eight-hour "trip" on four tenths of a gram of mescaline, swished down in a simple half-glass of water. Those few historical gulps took place on May 4, 1953, in the hills of Los Angeles, under the supervision of a British psychiatrist named Humphrey Osmond. Huxley had written to Osmond the year before and proposed just such an experiment.

The problems Huxley faced in explaining to the public what happened to him on that special day were considerable, but they were not what one might first imagine. The problems were not legal ones, as there were no laws at this point against taking mescaline, or LSD for that matter (the journalist and writer Don Lattin once showed me a television clip from the 1950s in which an American housewife was given LSD *on the program*). The problems were rather theological, ethical, and philosophical. The theological and ethical problems all boiled down to the strange fact that a person, theoretically *any* person, could come to know something of what the mystics, mediums, and saints of the world's religions had known, *without* their beliefs, *without* their rituals, or, most shocking of all, *without* their moral development. All one needed was the right chemical trigger.

The philosophical problem boiled down to the question of whether such states were simply a matter of brain chemistry, that is, of the "drug." Huxley did not think so. For one thing, his own experience on mescaline produced no trippy visions. He clearly was not hallucinating. Quite the contrary, as he put it, "the great change was in the realm of objective fact."[32] What he meant by this was that the mescaline somehow opened him up to a direct encounter not with another symbol or representation, but with reality *as it really is.*

This, Huxley thought, was a true glimpse of what the Hindus call enlightenment and the Buddhists call emptiness or "the void." It certainly was *not* Immanuel Kant, who had staked his entire philosophical project on the claim that such a moment could never ever happen.

It did to Aldous Huxley.

To explain it, Huxley adapted the filter thesis and then used it to explain how psychedelic substances might well be necessary catalysts of such mind manifestations without ever causing them. He speculated that the main function of such chemicals is not to produce or cause something, but to *suppress*, *inhibit*, or *stop* something, namely the brain's basic utilitarian function as a filter or "reducing valve" of consciousness. By doing so, such chemicals allow other forms of mind, which are probably always present, to rush in. The mescaline, then, is no biochemical cause. It is a trigger. It is *a door.*

This idea is precisely what lies behind the new and soon to be famous word that Osmond would coin in correspondence with Huxley: "psyche-delic" or "mind-revealing." The paramount example of this revealed mind is what Huxley called "Mind at Large." What he meant by Mind at Large was what his beloved mystics had meant. For him, Mind at Large is more or less equivalent to what the Hindu tradition calls *brahman* and what the Chinese and Tibetan Buddhist traditions call "Buddha nature" or "the mind of clear light." Mind at large is who we really are beyond our superficial surface selves, religious identities, and limiting physical senses. It is that form of consciousness that perceives reality directly and

immediately, without all the utilitarian filters of survival, measurement, and language. Hence Huxley's famous quoting of the English poet William Blake: "If the doors of perception were cleansed, everything would appear as it is: infinite." This is a line from Blake's *The Marriage of Heaven and Hell* that inspired the title of Huxley's own book (see Figure 12.4).

It did to Aldous Huxley.

In this model at least, mind is not the brain, but mind is indeed filtered through the brain with all its mind-boggling evolutionary, neurological, cultural, linguistic, emotional, political, and historical complexities. We are local context and construction, *and* we share a kind of cosmic consciousness that is universal and irreducible to any local context or construction. In short, the filter thesis is a comparative practice that effectively combines radical difference with radical sameness.

It should be stressed at this point that all those who proposed the filter thesis did so not because they "believed" anything (including the crude 3-D metaphor of a filter), but because they understood quite keenly that the materialist models simply cannot recognize the existence of the full sweep of the historical data, much less explain it. Today we might say that they understood that something like the filter thesis has the advantage of being capable of embracing both the findings of modern psychology, neuroscience, and cognitive science (as applicable to the brain and the socially constructed ego) and some of the most astonishing moments in the general history of religions (as applicable to a multi-dimensional mind space or Mind at Large).

How? In these models, mind is not simply a product of brain or culture. It exists in its own dimensions and on its own terms. To employ a much maligned expression in the study of religion, consciousness here is a thing "unto itself" or "of its own kind" (*sui generis*), finally determined *neither* by the three dimensions of space *nor* by time (which is to say history). Once we make such a move, that is, once we stop thinking crudely, in three dimensions, about a "ghost in a machine" or some kind of separable soul "inside a box" (of the skull), much that was

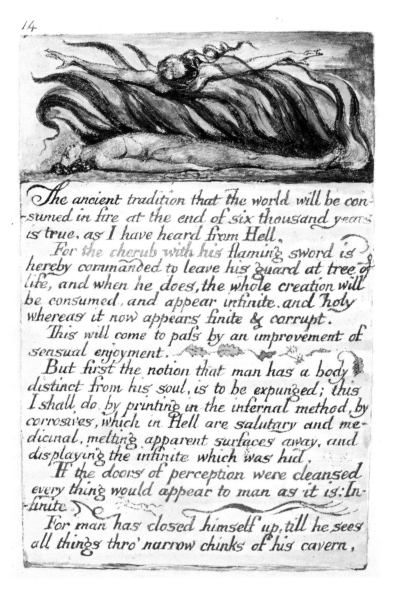

Figure 12.4   Plate 14 from *The Marriage of Heaven and Hell* (c. 1808) by William Blake, hand-colored etching. Fitzwilliam Museum, University of Cambridge, UK/The Bridgeman Art Library.

previously puzzling and impossible becomes immediately understandable and possible.

Such models have no problem explaining how, for example, the precog mother in our opening story "saw" in perfect detail a quick series of events that would take place miles away and exactly twenty-four hours in the future, or how Mark Twain had a

precognitive dream of his brother's death, both up the river and up the calendar. Such feats, after all, are only impossible if we understand mind as something produced by a local brain contained in a three-dimensional box. If, on the other hand, we understand consciousness as a multidimensional mind space that is "filtered" or transmitted into and through a particular 3-D brain-box and further into history, but never completely localized in either, then there is nothing in principle to prevent such a mind space from knowing about an event beforehand or hundreds of miles away. Indeed, we would expect *exactly* these sorts of events. The theory, in other words, predicts precisely what we find.

We simply have to shift our mind space. We have to move out of Flatland.

John Hick on Religion as Filter

Few scholars have taken the filter thesis more seriously than the comparative theologian John Hick, whom we met in Chapter 10. Indeed, for Hick, it is not just the brain that is a "filter." So too is religion. This basic metaphor of religion as filter allows Hick to acknowledge *both* the constructed nature of all religion (the rightful concern and focus of the rational re-readings) *and* its likely transcendent referent or source (the rightful concern and focus of the faithful re-readings). Hick, in other words, insists that human beings do have access to the *real*, and that this divine reality communicates with human beings through the medium of the religious imagination.

In *God Has Many Names* (1982) he compared such communications to the spiritualist communications of nineteenth-century séances, which featured different spirit personalities manifesting in and through the psyche of the medium. Empirical and objectively true information often came through in these telepathic events, but always and only through the personality or "filter" of the medium's psyche.[33] That is, after all, why they were called *mediums*.

Hick extended these filter readings in his later work. In the most recent edition of *An Interpretation of Religion* (2004), for example, he consistently employed parapsychology and the category of telepathy to describe the direct or extra-sensory information transfer that is commonly reported in mystical experiences.[34] He also, once again, described religions as "filters" through which "the real" is communicated and experienced by different historical communities as both personal and impersonal.[35] "In

terms of information theory," he writes on the last point, "we are speaking of the transmission of information from a transcendent source to the human mind/brain and its transformation by the mind/brain into conscious experience."[36] He compares this mind-to-mind information transfer to extrasensory perception (ESP). Because the brain's main function is to limit or select incoming information, there is always distortion; and yet something is indeed coming through. This is why religions are at once fallible and fantastic, at once false and true.

Hick also describes religions as "resistances," in the electronic or electrical sense of the term ("resistance" is a measure of how much a particular material or object blocks or obstructs the free passage of electrons through it). This second metaphor allows him to explain how religions, like individual brains, "step down" the energy or power and so preserve the autonomy and "finite freedom" of individuals and communities.[37] In short, brains and religions do not only filter the real; they also *protect us from it*. The sacred as a kind of dangerous energy again.

Obviously, in a figure like John Hick, the filter thesis is not just a method for integrating mystical states and modern brain science. It has become the privileged model for balancing sameness and difference and for doing comparative theology across the entire history of religions.

Neuroscientists at the Cusp

But all of this, to put it mildly, is a hard sell. It is pure heresy within contemporary neuroscience, which continues to insist that mind is a purely local, material process that blips out when the brain blips out. Oddly, scholars of religion, who one would think might have some serious questions here, have largely followed suit, insisting that all human experiences are products of local historical, social, and biological events. Any true transcendence of spatial or temporal boundaries (that is, of history) has become, in principle, impossible. We are back to a form of the traumatic secret, which really boils down to honest intellectual differences between those who have been "split into two" and those who have not.

But what happens when a previously doubting neuroscientist or medical professional *is* split into two? What then? It is a most striking fact that the filter thesis has recently returned in a number of practicing brain scientists and medical professionals, who often come to a very similar conclusion through their own extraordinary experiences. Moreover, very much unlike the humanists and the forgotten philosophers, these scientists are given immense authority in our present culture. Hence their voices can be heard in a different way.

What do they say? Pretty much exactly what the humanists and the forgotten philosophers have said: that there are other ways of knowing; that the forms of knowledge that these others ways generate do not need to be pitted against science; and that the brain may well be a wondrously evolved piece of biological electronics for picking up something not really "in" the brain.

Jill Bolte Taylor's Stroke of Insight

Consider first the Harvard-trained brain anatomist Jill Bolte Taylor. On the morning of December 10, 1996 Taylor experienced a massive stroke that shut down the left hemisphere of her brain. As a neuro-anatomist, she knew exactly what was happening as it happened. She watched her linguistic, memory, and identity processing disappear like cotton candy on a tongue. Deprived of its neurological base, it just all melted away. But, as these cognitive and ego-related capacities in the left hemisphere blipped out, something else, shining through the right hemisphere, blipped in. The sun of the rational mind was temporarily blocked out by a total neurological eclipse of sorts—the stroke. Night fell, and the vastness, peace, and infinity of an inner outer space could suddenly be "seen."

Those are my words. In her own neuroanatomical (and Buddhist) language, as her left side gradually came back online over the next eight months, Taylor found herself alternating "between two distinct and opposite realities: the euphoric *nirvana* of the intuitive and kinesthetic right brain, in which she felt a sense of complete well-being and peace, and the logical, sequential left brain."[38] Consciousness and culture were gradually coming back together, and with them her sense of social reality and personal identity.

This still sounds more than a bit like the reduction of mind to brain, even if it is to two brains now. But there was more, and Taylor seems to find religious language the only really adequate means to express it. "By the end of that morning, my consciousness shifted into a perception that I was at *one* with the universe. Since that time, I have come to understand how it is that we are capable of having a 'mystical' or 'metaphysical' experience—relative to our brain anatomy."[39] Obviously, her language is very careful here: "a perception," "relative to our brain anatomy." Those scare-quotes around "mystical" and "metaphysical" are guarded and ambiguous. But then there is that italicized word: "I was at *one* with the universe." Like her double-sided brain, Jill Bolte Taylor is alternating between two different worlds of meaning, two different possibilities: a rational one and a reflexive one.

Like a good brain scientist she was "reducing" it all to the brain, but this brain was looking more and more like a, well, *like a door.* The human being now appeared to her as "an electrical being; an apparition of energy smoldering around an organic lump."[40] She now knew the brain-body much as Ioan Couliano imagined it, that is, as a "a portal through which the energy of who I am can be beamed into a three-dimensional external space." The body, she could see now, is "a marvelous temporary home." She marveled at how she could have spent so many years unaware of this, never really understanding "that I was just visiting there."[41]

She turns to one of the traditional symbolisms of the soul: as a living force or cosmic energy. Like Myers and James before her, she concludes that we are not who we think we are:

> I shuddered at the awareness that I was no longer a normal human being. How on earth would I exist as a

member of the human race with this heightened perception that we are each a part of it all, and that the life force energy within each of us contains the power of the universe? How could I fit in with our society when I walk the earth with no fear?[42]

An eccentric comparative side note. As Taylor's left brain shut down during the stroke, she reports perceiving her body as if it were a strange creature; she now perceived her hands, for example, to be long and claw-like. Although she does not put it this way (this is my sin, not hers), we might go so far as to suggest that Taylor was "splitting" into two and perceiving herself as an alien or "other." Or is it just an accident that long, claw-like hands are commonly reported in the alien encounter literature?

Being in one's "right mind" certainly took on new meaning. To our right mind, Taylor explains, "the moment of *now* is timeless and abundant." Time, history, and the clock are no more. It is this same "right mind" that is the source of some of our deepest ethical sensibilities and political dreams: "The present moment is a time when everything and everyone are connected together as one. As a result, our right mind perceives each of us as equal members of the human family."[43]

Sameness.

Not so the left mind. It is analytic and thinks in units of linear time. It divides, dissects, analyzes, and insists on "details, details, and more details about those details."[44] It also goes on and on (and on) about "the insignificant affairs of society."[45] It chatters to us constantly in order to shore up the social ego with all its ethnic, racial, national, cultural, and religious convictions.

Difference.

But it is the sameness that is finally deeper than the differences within the human as two. Thus Taylor marvels at how she finally realized that "I really had been a figment of my own imagination!" In short, the ego was revealed for what it is—a social construction, a relative, temporary point of view on the space–time grid. And consciousness was revealed for what it is—a presence of mythological proportions, beyond space and time, which is filtered through the brain and body but is in fact neither. In Taylor's own words: "I was simply a being of light radiating life into the world."[46]

Sameness and difference.

Eben Alexander's Cosmic Coma

Consider a second example: the neurosurgeon Eben Alexander, III and his *Proof of Heaven: A Neurosurgeon's Journey into the Afterlife.*[47] Alexander completed his MD at Duke Medical School and spent fifteen years on the faculty of Harvard Medical School. He shared the usual medical reductive convictions about the material nature of mind: mind is brain and nothing more. That was before November 10, 2008, when, at the age of 54, Alexander began experiencing intense pain in his back and head and collapsed for seven days into a deep coma, brought on by an extremely rare case of e-coli meningitis.

Within the coma, Alexander encountered, in his own emphasis, "a world of consciousness that existed *completely free of the limitations of my physical brain.*" This world may or may not have been independent of the brain, but it was certainly formed around some classical religious themes—particularly flight, energy, light, music, unity, and love. This was also a world organized around some vivid visionary stages, to which he gives capitalized names: the Realm of the Earthworm's-Eye View, the Spinning Melody, the Gateway, the Girl on the Butterfly Wing (who is also encountered as an Orb of Light), and, finally, the Core.

As we have seen throughout these pages, modern mystical experiences often take place within an evolutionary framework. Alexander's fits into this pattern. While in the Realm of the Earthworm-Eye's View, he describes how he was in a "primordial" state. It was "as if I had regressed back to some state of being from the very beginnings of life." He felt like a mole or a worm. "I wasn't human while I was in this place. I wasn't even animal. I was something before, and below, all that."[48]

It was the Spinning Melody that rescued him from this muddy, earthy world—a beautiful white musical light that spun slowly, casting out golden filaments, as it called to him. It is not clear how, but the Spinning Melody acted as the means through which he entered what he calls the Gateway (the theme of the door or portal again), a paradisiac natural landscape that he experienced as "completely real" or "hyper-real." This world featured millions of butterflies, gorgeous valleys, streams, waterfalls, people, dogs, and, high above the clouds, "flocks of transparent orbs" or "shimmering beings" that resembled birds or angels but that were "more advanced. *Higher*."[49] He was riding one such butterfly, accompanied by a girl in a powder blue and indigo dress. Alexander communicated with the beings there directly, without language. He understood instantly things that, here, would have taken him years to process and understand.

He then entered "an immense void, completely dark, infinitive in size, yet also infinitely comforting." This was the Core. The Core was God as "mother" or "giant cosmic womb." Alexander remembers one particular sound associated with the Core: "Om" (which the student of religion recognizes immediately as the most famous of all Hindu mantras and the modern icon for Hinduism as a world religion). Om taught him that there are "countless higher dimensions" from which one can enter our world at any place or time.[50] Most of all, he learned that love is "the basis of everything."[51]

Alexander invokes the now familiar filter thesis and the bilateral brain to explain why we normally cannot access such truths. Indeed he explicitly cites the most extensive contemporary work on the filter thesis, *Irreducible Mind* (2007), edited by neuroscientist Edward Kelly and his colleagues.[52] In his own words, our "brain blocks out, or veils, that larger cosmic background."[53] In an interview with National Public Radio (NPR) host Steve Paulson, he expands on this idea. There he explains how we are being "dumbed down" by our bodies. He speaks of the "shackles" of our brain and body and of how "we are conscious in spite of our brain," not because of it. All of this is necessary, he speculates, since, if we were in constant touch with what he was in touch with in that world, we would not be able to survive as mammals

in this one. He even refers to our individual forms of mind as a "divine spark" and the brain as a kind "reducing valve" actively reducing our access to and awareness of this spark of divinity.

Alexander believes that he was given a "foretaste" of our evolutionary future. He has little practical hope of explaining all of this to us here and now, though. His experience, after all, was

> rather like being a chimpanzee, becoming human for a single day to experience all of the wonders of human knowledge, and then returning to one's chimp friends and trying to tell them what it was like knowing several different Romance languages, the calculus, and the immense scale of the universe.[54]

This, of course, is an evolutionary updating of Plato's Cave.

His takeaway? That "conscious awareness can exist entirely independent of the brain," and that only a fraction of what consciousness is can be captured in language and communicated to those who have not "been there." Alexander now knows many things that his peers and medical colleagues, who have not "been there," do not. Foremost among these things is that the materialist model upon which conventional science is based is "fundamentally flawed." "At its core," the neurosurgeon writes, this materialism "intentionally ignores what I believe is the fundament of all existence — the nature of consciousness."[55] Accordingly, we will never make sense of consciousness working from below up. It makes infinite more sense to come down "from the other side."[56]

There has been much debate about Dr. Alexander's book. Whenever an elite cultural figure (like a neurosurgeon) stands up against the reigning materialist paradigm, he or she is likely to get some serious push back. As we noted in Chapter 8, the social system cannot tolerate such open challenges to its (always false) claims to represent all of reality. What is there to say, then? A reflexive re-reader of religion (this one, anyway) would be deeply sympathetic to Alexander's most basic takeaways: that mind is not brain, and that trauma is necessary to break open the healthy brain filter. Such a reader, however, would also note that the neurosurgeon lacks an adequate theory of the image and the imagination. Hence he appears to interpret his visions in a very literal manner, that is, as a light *not* filtered and shaped by the stained glass windows of the religious imagination.

Moreover, both Dr. Alexander *and* his critics seem unable to think in both–and terms, that is, in ways that can appreciate both the constructed, imagined nature of the visionary event (the stained glass window) and the potential cosmic truths that appear to be "coming through" that glass (the light). To stick to our analogy, Alexander himself appears to identify the stories told in the stained glass window with the light itself, while his critics cannot seem to recognize that there may be real light coming through the window of his brain. In both cases, the both–and has collapsed into a simple either–or.

Sam Harris on Telepathy and Panpsychism

Along with evolutionary biologist Richard Dawkins and the late journalist Christopher Hitchens, neuroscientist Sam Harris is one of a handful of intellectuals who have carved out a public voice sometimes called the New Atheism. New Atheism is a movement concerned to establish Enlightenment reason, particularly as it is enshrined in modern science, as the only legitimate mode of knowing the world and ourselves. These authors have taken an extreme polemical stance toward religion, more or less equating it with its most literalist, fundamentalist, and exclusivist forms. Harris's *The End of Faith* (2004) is a good example of this polemical writing.

There is much that could be said about the New Atheists, from the obvious post-9/11 moral concerns around religious intolerance, which animate their project, through their general lack of training in the humanities, to the simplistic and frankly naïve pictures that they paint of religious people. They appear to share the assumption that being a scientist somehow makes one an authority on everything, even on things that one quite obviously knows very

little about. A single feature of the New Atheism will concern us here, namely that which sets apart Harris from the other voices: his transparent openness to psychical phenomena and his willingness to entertain panpsychism as a plausible option for modeling the relationship between mind and matter.

In his books, blog, and interviews, Harris has made it clear that he considers the data on psychical phenomena, including telepathy and the CORT literature, to be worthy of consideration.[57] In an interview with NPR host Steve Paulson, he spoke casually of experiencing minor instances of telepathy (for example, knowing that someone was going to call on the phone before the phone rang). Very much unlike his atheist colleagues, Harris is willing both to admit that such things are quite common and then to observe that such phenomena may well have something profound to teach us about the world and the mind's relationship to it.

Harris is deeply skeptical that egos survive death, so he is hardly arguing for something like "the immortality of the soul." But he is open to the possibility that some other, impersonal form of consciousness is fundamental to the nature of the cosmos. He said this to Paulson:

> So the idea that a brain can die and a soul that still speaks English and recognizes Granny is going to float away into the afterlife, that seems to be profoundly implausible. And yet we do not know what the relationship between subjectivity and objectivity ultimately is. For instance, we could be living in a universe where consciousness goes all the way down to the bedrock so that there is some interior subjective dimension to an electron.[58]

Recall that we have seen this possible solution already in a figure like William James, who imagined "subtler forms of matter" and a sea of cosmic consciousness out of which all subjects and objects arise.

For his own part, Harris explains that he is "quite skeptical" of science ever being able to solve this. I can only add: and well he should be. The scientific method, at least as it is presently conceived, only works once one has separated the subject *from* the object being studied, indeed removed subjectivity altogether. It seems extremely doubtful that one could ever establish the subjective nature of a minded cosmos by removing subjectivity from one's mode of knowing and then insisting that this purely objectivist form of knowledge is the only way to know the universe.

David Eagleman, the Broken Watch, and the Parable of the Radio

Finally, consider again the neuroscientist David Eagleman. Eagleman intentionally wears a broken Russian watch to his lab, as a sign that "we're all wearing broken watches." What he means by this is that linear history or clock time is "at best a convenient fiction." Watches (and historians, I would add) assume that "time ticks steadily, predictably forward, when our experience shows that it often does the opposite: it stretches and compresses, skips a beat and doubles back."[59] It also sometimes stops, or just ceases to be, as we have seen numerous times in our journey together, from Meister Eckhart and Anita Moorjani to Jill Bolte Taylor.

As one would expect by now, Eagleman's radical thinking about time possesses its own anomalous origins. Indeed he credits his eventual turn to neuroscience to a most unusual event of his boyhood: yet another secret revealed in the midst of a trauma. Eagleman was eight when he stepped out onto a roof on a construction site that turned out to be no roof at all but a sheet of tar paper. Here is how *The New Yorker* columnist Burkhard Bilger describes what happened next:

> His body stumbles forward as the tar paper tears free at his feet. His hands stretch toward the ledge, but it's out of reach. The brick floor floats upward—some shiny nails are scattered across it—as his body rotates weightlessly above the ground. It's a moment of absolute calm and eerie mental acuity. But the thing he remembers best is the thought that struck him in midair: this must be how Alice felt when she was tumbling down the rabbit hole.[60]

Eagleman has been venturing down that rabbit hole ever since. He calls himself a "possibilian," by which he means that he is open to considering things that are now considered to be impossible by our best science.

Including, it turns out, the filter thesis. At the very end of his book, *Incognito* (2011), he turns to the question of the soul. Here he advances a critique of reductionism, that is, of the idea that we can understand something like mind by reducing it to its constituent parts, like neurons and chemicals. Probably not, Eagleman concludes. He also expresses some serious reservations around **promissory materialism**—the commonly heard claim that, although we do not yet know how to explain mind through material processes, we eventually will. Indeed *everything* will eventually be explained in a materialist framework because everything is finally only matter.

Maybe, Eagleman concludes; maybe not. It is extremely unlikely that we just happen to be living at the moment when all things will soon be explained, he points out. Previous generations claimed the same, and they were all very wrong. The much more likely scenario, Eagleman observes, is that the more we learn about the brain and consciousness, the more strange, not simple, things will get. Here is where his final thought experiment comes in. A parable:

> Imagine that you are a Kalahari Bushman and that you stumble upon a transistor radio in the sand. You might pick it up, twiddle the knobs, and suddenly, to your surprise, hear voices streaming out of this strange little box … Now let's say you begin a careful, scientific study of what causes the voices. You notice that each time you pull out the green wire, the voices stop. When you put the wire back on its contact, the voices begin again … you come to a clear conclusion: the voices depend entirely on the integrity of the circuitry. At some point, a young person asks you how some simple loops of electrical signals can engender music and conversations, and you admit that you don't know—but you insist that your science is about to crack that problem at any moment.

Assuming that you are truly isolated, what you do not know is pretty much everything that you need to know: radio waves, electromagnetism, distant cities, radio stations, and modern civilization. You would not even have the capacity to *imagine* such things. And, even if you could, "you have no technology to demonstrate the existence of the waves, and everyone justifiably points out that the onus is on you to convince them." You could convince almost no one, and you yourself would probably reject the existence of such mysterious, spirit-like waves. You would become a "radio materialist."

"I'm not asserting that the brain is like a radio," Eagleman points out at the end of his book, "but I *am* pointing out that it *could* be true. There is nothing in our current science that rules this out."[61] This is where the historian of religions steps in. There are, after all, numerous clues in the general history of religions that rule the radio theory in, and that suggest—though hardly prove—that the human brain may well be a kind of transmitter or receiver of consciousness. The historian of religions, this one anyway, says to the open-minded neuroscientist: "Looker, look *here*."

Concluding Thoughts: Culture, Cognition, and Consciousness

I am often asked by my students what I think about all of this. I just tell them. Why not? I ask them to tell me what they think. Why should I not answer their questions about what I think? As you have probably guessed by now (I have hardly hidden the fact), my answers stumble through and around these last reflexive re-readings.

Much of this goes back to my dad's advice about mechanical systems: you can best understand a system by *taking it apart* and by noticing, very carefully, when it misfires or does *not* work the way you expected. We saw this truth, of course, in the mythical figure of the trickster very early on in our journey together, in Chapter 4. We encountered it again, in Chapter 6, with the subject of purity systems and

sexual–spiritual transgression, and once again in Chapter 8, with the anomalous nature of robust paranormal events. Here we are again, addressing completely outrageous things, like a precog mother, clairvoyant death dreams, a modern resurrection apparition, the fourth dimension, poltergeist physics, and neuroscience mystics.

And why not? Are not these exactly the kinds of things that my dad told me to look for? They certainly look like "glitches" in the consensual fabric of our social reality. Remember Neo in *The Matrix* seeing what he thinks is the same black cat walk by twice? The character named Trinity explains that such déjà vu moments "happen when they change something," that is, when the illusion of social reality is being tinkered with or recalibrated. That is very close to how I understand extreme religious experiences. These are moments when the social, psychological, and spiritual fabric of reality *can* be changed, rewritten, coded anew. Whether this fabric is changed or not depends upon a community's response to them. It is by no means automatic.

Not that I "believe" such things. Actually I do not believe in beliefs at all (although I do believe in belief). But I am most intrigued by the "written" or "authored" qualities of these moments in our lives. Hence two of the most common modern descriptors: "It was as if I were caught in a novel," or "It was as if I were a character in a movie." I think such phrases are more or less accurate descriptions of what is actually happening, not just in a robust paranormal event (when this is made patently obvious), but in every moment of our normal day-to-day lives (when it is not obvious at all). We *are* caught in a type of novel or movie (called a culture or religion), which we ourselves have written and performed in all the ways we have explored together.

But here is the "flip." Here is why we opened with Rob Beschizza's wonderful image of *The Reader*. If our cultural and religious worlds are authored by us (and they are), and if we are caught in them as if in a novel or a movie (and we are), it naturally and inevitably follows that we can re-read ourselves and so author new novels and movies in which to live. The process can be reversed. The very fabric of our lives can be re-read, and hence, eventually, re-written. *You* (both of you) have this extraordinary power to help re-read the human past and hence re-write the human future.

Granted, we do not really understand our individual roles in these reading and writing processes. It is difficult to detect the glow of our own eyes (a Hindu or Buddhist adept might say, "to know when the 'divine eye' or third eye opens"), that is, to know when we are re-reading and hence also re-writing our cultural script, and when we are just being read by it. Maybe both processes (the psychological and the social) are always in play. Maybe we always possess three eyes, even if the third visionary eye is usually closed. Obviously, then, I do not offer anything here as the last word on religion. I too am written, am read, am a character in someone else's novel. I have not stepped off the page or out of the movie screen.

But others have. This is why I think we have so much to learn from the spectacles of Taylor's stroke of insight, Alexander's cosmic coma, and Eagleman's fall off the roof into the rabbit hole. To be perfectly frank, I think that the future of "comparing religions" lies precisely in these sorts of extreme events and what they can teach us about the human brain and the deeper nature of consciousness—which we might think of here as the ultimate C behind, below, and above all the other Cs of our previous comparative practices.

Consciousness is not only the ground of all comparative grounds, of all our previous Cs. It is also the ground of *all* science, *all* rationalism, *all* reductionism, *all* religious experience, indeed *all* human knowledge and experience. Moreover, as far as we can tell at the moment, this final C is entirely *sui generis*. It is its own thing. We know of nothing else like it in the universe, and anything we would know later we would only know in, through, and because of this same consciousness. Many today, of course, want to claim the exact opposite, namely that consciousness is not its own thing, is reducible to warm wet tissue and brainhood. But to this day no one has come even close to showing how this might work.

Probably because it doesn't.

Let me frame the situation in neuroanatomical terms. An author like Jill Bolte Taylor shows us that the human as two is not just an ancient mystical doctrine, as we saw in Chapter 9. *The human as two is a universal neuroanatomical fact.* This is not a truth that you are free to accept or deny, as if denying it would suddenly turn your two brain hemispheres into one hemisphere. You cannot deny what you secretly are behind that thick skull of yours. In essence, we all have two brains. We are different *from ourselves.* There is an alien or Other *inside us.*

No one has shown us this more clearly and elegantly than the British psychiatrist Iain McGilchrist. His massive work on the bilateral brain, *The Master and His Emissary* (2009), demonstrates that, although imagination and reason are "global" functions of *both* brains, each hemisphere does indeed specialize in different functions, as we saw already above with Jill Bolte Taylor. But here is the twist. For McGilchrist, it is the right brain, with its focus on broad patterns, interconnectedness, implicit meaning, and wholeness, that is the "Master," that is more fundamental to our being in the world, whereas the left brain, with its focus on detail, abstraction, and precision, is the "emissary" of this Master. In the language of Albert Einstein, the intuitive mind is "a sacred gift," and reason is "a faithful servant."[62]

McGilchrist has summed up his ideas in a brief animated lecture.[63] There, as in the book, he points out that western culture has seen an increasing "take over" by the left brain. The servant now claims to *be* the Master. It is all about the left brain's way of seeing the world. It is all about more and more "information" and less and less "understanding." It is all about the "closed system" of reason, science, abstraction, and a mechanical perfection in which everything can be explained. But this closed system is perfect and complete only because it has expelled everything that does not fit into it.

Sound familiar?

It is probably no accident that McGilchrist, as an advocate of balance and wisdom, tends toward the filter thesis. He writes: "I believe it may be that consciousness does not depend on a brain for its existence: just, in the absence of a brain, it is deprived of its expression as that particular mind." To illustrate what he means, the psychiatrist invokes an analogy that is common among filter theorists. He compares the brain to a television set. He observes: "the TV set is only mediative. It does not give rise to the programme you watch. And you couldn't tell which it does—originate the programme or transmit it—by inspecting the workings: the TV set would look much the same whichever."[64] This, of course, is exactly what Eagleman suggested with his parable of the radio. It would *look* like the voices are coming from the box. But they are not.

We can go further. The fact that a particular TV is unplugged, malfunctioning, or completely destroyed does not mean that the little people who once appeared in it are no more. It simply means that the signals that are beaming them into this three-dimensional box cannot be received, translated, and projected any longer. This would also explain all those reports that compare soul-states to energy-states, to "light," "radiance," "power," "magnetism," "electricity," or now "plasma." Maybe they are. Maybe that is what is running the human television set.

We can also note that the analogy, like all analogies, is flawed, since it is extremely doubtful that what we call a "person" is independent of the body brain, as an actor or actress is independent of your TV set. It seems more likely that the human personality is created from the *interaction* of the energy of consciousness and the biological TV that is a human being. It is as if the cosmos evolved a biological organism to broadcast and watch itself.

Such a thought experiment, of course, does not prove anything. But at least it gives us an idea of how something like a soul that is "in" but not entirely "of" the body *could* be the case. Such a thought experiment enables us to imagine the impossible as possible.

What does all of this bilateral brain talk have to do with the study of religion? Pretty much everything. Are not *all* the rational re-readings that we have examined and performed here—all those historical, contextual, psychological, sociological, postcolonial, and cognitive

methods—left brain methods? They emphasize difference and division, not sameness and equality. They only recognize the clock time of the calendar or the cognitive computer-like processing of the brain. They know nothing of what Eckhart, Moorjani, Huxley, and Taylor call the *now* of consciousness. Similarly, they are all comfortable enough with talk of mechanical or machine-like "metaphors," but they reject, in principle, the possibility of any living "symbol" manifesting something outside the brain-box.

This is hardly a new story. Once we understand the bilateral brain, we can easily see that the left brain (which controls the right side of the body) has long demeaned and even demonized the right brain (which controls the left side of the body). Hence all those cultural examples of the "left" side being associated with impurity, negative moral judgments, indeed evil itself (the Latin word for "left" is *sinister*). Jesus, after all, does not sit at the left hand of God, and when Er saw souls judged negatively, he saw them going to the left and down. Closer to home, when my father was in Catholic grade school in the 1940s, the nuns literally hit his "bad" left hand with a ruler whenever he tried to write with it. The result: he learned to write with his "right" hand.

Alas, much too often, rational re-readers behave more or less like those misguided nuns. They whack the left hand and so scold the right brain as *bad*. They focus—admittedly, exquisitely—on culture and cognition, that is, on all those cultural grids, mental modules, metaphors, and processes of the computer-brain that so effectively delimit, particularize, and personalize consciousness. But they make fun of any intuited whole, any grand comparison. And they adamantly deny consciousness as consciousness, that is, the Sun outside Plato's Cave. Although they should be celebrated as major intellectual accomplishments, we can now see that the left brain rational re-readings represent only half of the picture.

I am not, of course, proposing that we simply move now from the methods of the left to those of the right. That would be disastrous, and dangerous. I am proposing rather that we learn *to move back and forth*, that we acknowledge both the colorful stain of the man-made windows and the light streaming through. Such a reflexive model, I hasten to add, need not imply that mind is often, or even ever, experienced in a completely unmediated form, or that it is distinct from the material cosmos. Hence my "interaction" comments on the flawed TV analogy. As the scholarship has long argued, it appears that mind as we know it is always mediated, filtered, reduced, embodied. As egos, we *are* those socialized fleshy filters, and if we know anything as egos, it must, *by definition*, be mediated.[65] Hence that lovely line that Philip K. Dick heard in a dream after he was radiated by Valis and came to understand the human as two: "'One day the masks will come off, and you will understand all.' It came to pass—and *I* was one of the masks …"[66]

Do we *really* think that we can explain what Jill Bolte Taylor refers to as a species-wide, mutating life force beaming through the portal of the right brain with the local cultural, ego-related, and linguistic equipment of the left brain? Can more and more reason and computer metaphors *really* get us there? Can the mask explain the masked?

Probably not.

We might finally observe that the reflexive re-reader, the student in the school of the more, "wants it both ways" not because he or she is confused or is trying to be diplomatic, *but because the human being really is both ways*. If one were to take this doubleness to its end, one might find that reflexivity—the key skill that we have practiced throughout this book—eventually leads to a most profound comparative practice. We might imagine this double vision as a yet more acute awareness of our biological, historical, social, and economic conditionings, but also as a future mind space that has yet to take any stable institutional form. In terms of the latter, we might imagine a future form of consciousness becoming aware not of just more and more culture and more and more cognition, but of *consciousness itself*. That is, we might imagine "turning around" from all those entrancing movies on the screen to the projector behind us doing all that projecting. We might gaze at the light coming through the hole in the wall and look at the looker looking back at us.

The Tough Questions

1 Watch Jill Bolte Taylor's TED talk at http://www.ted.com/talks/jill_bolte_taylor_s_powerful_stroke_of_insight.html and comment on her use of Buddhist language to describe the felt experience of what she knew. Do you think this would have worked with theistic language about "God"?

2 What do you think this sentence means? "I don't believe in beliefs (although I do believe in belief)." How is this an example of a reflexive re-reading of religion?

3 As we have seen in this last chapter, scientists, like everyone else, often have profound religious experiences that shatter their worldviews and remake them. Why do you think that these reports carry so much authority in our present culture, when they are saying much the same things that other writers have said for millennia?

Notes

1 Robert A. Orsi, "The Problem of the Holy," in *The Cambridge Companion to Religious Studies*, edited by Robert A. Orsi (Cambridge: Cambridge University Press, 2012), 99.

2 Rabindranath Tagore, *The Religion of Man* (London: Unwin Books, 1970), 76.

3 Tagore, *The Religion of Man*, 101.

4 Tagore, *The Religion of Man*, 58–59.

5   Tagore, *The Religion of Man*, 11.

6   Tagore, *The Religion of Man*, 67.

7   Tagore, *The Religion of Man*, 12.

8   Tagore, *The Religion of Man*, 68.

9   Tagore, *The Religion of Man*, 74

10 Tagore, *The Religion of Man*, 120.

11 Peter Berger, *The Sacred Canopy: Elements of a Sociological Theory of Religion* (Garden City, NY: Anchor Books, 1969), 180.

12 Peter Berger, *A Rumor Angels: Modern Society and the Rediscovery of the Supernatural* (New York: Anchor Books, 1970), 47.

13 Erik Davis, *Nomad Codes: Adventures in Modern Esoterica* (Portland, OR: Yeti Publishing, 2010) 196–199.

14 David Eagleman, *Incognito: The Secret Lives of the Brain* (New York: Pantheon Books, 2011), 53, 77.

15 John Blake, "Do Loved Ones Bid Farewell from Beyond the Grave?" at http://www.cnn.com/2011/09/23/living/crisis-apparitions/index.html?hpt=hp_c1 (accessed August 24, 2013).

16 For a New Testament critic who insists on similar comparisons between the ancient material and the modern parapsychological cases, see Dale C. Allison, *Resurrecting Jesus: The Earliest Christian Tradition and Its Interpreters* (New York: T & T Clark, 2005).

17 Editor's Introduction to David Friedrich Strauss, *The Life of Jesus Critically Examined* (Ramsey, NJ: Sigler Press, 1994), xliii.

18 I. P. Couliano, *Out of this World: Otherworldly Journeys from Gilgamesh to Albert Einstein* (Boston, MA: Shambalah, 1991), 233.

19 Couliano, *Out of this World*, 18.

20 For a simple and effective animated illustration of this same thought experiment, watch this clip from "What the Bleep Do We Know!?" at http://www.youtube.com/watch?v=BWyTxCsIXE4 (accessed August 24, 2013).

21 Couliano, *Out of this World*, 12.

22 Couliano, *Out of this World*, 3–4.

23 Couliano, *Out of this World*, 28.

24 Michael Clarkson, *Poltergeists: Examining Mysteries of the Paranormal* (Buffalo, NY: Firefly Books, 2006), 143–152.

25 C. G. Jung, *Memories, Dreams, Reflections*, recorded and edited by Aniela Jaffé (New York: Vintage Books, 1989).

26 George Gamow, *Thirty Years that Shook Physics: The Story of Quantum Theory* (New York: Dover, 1985), 64.

27 Mary Keller, *The Hammer and the Flute: Women, Power, and Spirit Possession* (Baltimore, MD: Johns Hopkins University Press, 2002).

28 William James, *The Varieties of Religious Experience: A Study in Human Nature* (New York: The Modern Library, n.d.), 237–238; see also 506.

29 William James, "Final Impressions of a Psychical Researcher." In *William James on Psychical Research*, edited by Gardner Murphy and Robert O. Ballou (New York: The Viking Press, 1960), 324.

30 James, "Final Impressions."

31 Paul Marshall, "The Psychical and the Mystical: Boundaries, Connections, Common Origins." *Journal of the Society for Psychical Research*, vol. 75.1, number 902 (January 2011), 1–13.

32 Aldous Huxley, *The Doors of Perception* (London: Chatto & Windus, 1954), 16.

33 John Hick, *God Has Many Names* (Philadelphia, PA: The Westminster Press, 1982), 99–100.

34 John Hick, *An Interpretation of Religion: Human Responses to the Transcendent* (New Haven, CT: Yale University Press, 2004), 154, 165, 167.

35 Hick, *An Interpretation of Religion*, 163.

36 Hick, *An Interpretation of Religion*, 244.

37 Hick, *An Interpretation of Religion*, 162.

38 Jill Bolte Taylor, *My Stroke of Insight: A Brain Scientist's Personal Journey* (New York: Viking, 2008), cover flap.

39 Taylor, *My Stroke of Insight*, 3.

40 Taylor, *My Stroke of Insight*, 66.

41 Taylor, *My Stroke of Insight*, 45–46.

42 Taylor, *My Stroke of Insight*, 45.

43 Taylor, *My Stroke of Insight*, 30.

44 Taylor, *My Stroke of Insight*, 31.

45 Taylor, *My Stroke of Insight*, 43.

46 Taylor, *My Stroke of Insight*, 70–71.

47 I am relying on three sources: (1) Eben Alexander, III, "My Experience in Coma." *AAANS Neurosurgeon*, 21.2 (2012), at http://www.aansneurosurgeon.org/210212/6/1611 (accessed August 24, 2013); the Steve Paulson interview, at http://www.btci.org/bioethics/2012/videos2012/vid3.html (accessed August 24, 2013); and Eben Alexander's book *Proof of Heaven: A Neurosurgeon's Journey into the Afterlife* (New York: Simon & Schuster, 2012).

48 Alexander, *Proof of Heaven*, 29, 31.

49   Alexander, *Proof of Heaven*, 45.

50   Alexander, *Proof of Heaven*, 47–49.

51   Alexander, *Proof of Heaven*, 71.

52   Edward F. Kelly, Emily Williams Kelly, Adam Crabtree, Alan Gauld, Michael Grosso, and Bruce Greyson, eds., *Irreducible Mind: Toward a Psychology for the 21st Century* (Lanham, MD: Rowman & Littlefield, 2007).

53   Alexander, *Proof of Heaven*, 71–72.

54   Alexander, *Proof of Heaven*, 82–83.

55   This material is from Alexander, "My Experience in Coma."

56   Quoted from the Paulson interview.

57   Sam Harris, *The End of Faith: Religion, Terror, and the Future of Religion* (New York: W. W. Norton, 2004).

58   Steve Paulson, *Atoms and Eden: Conversations on Religion and Science* (New York: Oxford University Press, 2010), 57–58.

59   As quoted in Burkhard Bilger, "The Possibilian: What a Brush with Death Taught David Eagleman about the Mysteries of Time and the Brain." *The New Yorker*, April 25, 2011: 1. At http://www.newyorker.com/reporting/ 2011/04/25/110425fa_fact_bilger (last accessed on August 30, 2013).

60   Bilger, "The Possibilian," 1.

61   David Eagleman, *Incognito: The Secret Lives of the Brain* (New York: Pantheon, 2011), 221–222.

62   Iain McGilchrist, "The Divided Brain and the Making of the Western World." At http://www.youtube.com/ watch?v=dFs9WO2B8uI (accessed August 24, 2013).

63   McGilchrist, "The Divided Brain." This lecture also addresses the simplifications of the bilateral model that were popularized in the 1960s and 1970s, which we now know to be false or, in the language of the present book, too "either–or."

64   Ian McGilchrist, *The Master and His Emissary: The Divided Brain and the Making of the Western World* (New Haven, CT: Yale University Press, 2009), 465, n. 15.

65   I am indebted here to Chad Pevateaux.

66   *The Exegesis of Philip K. Dick*, edited by Pamela Jackson and Jonathan Lethem, annotations editor, Erik Davis (Boston, MA: Houghton Mifflin Harcourt, 2011), 384.

Earth Rise. © Digital Vision/Getty Images.

… and Cosmos

Epilogue from Houston

What happens when people have to face up to the fact that their understandings of what is "real" are dependent on a particular, and ultimately contingent narration of what life is like? And how do they, once they are lucid about the contingency of their reality definitions, produce a sense of the really real?

Mattijs van de Port, *Ecstatic Encounters*

One always ends where one is. Where else could one end? Accordingly, I would like to close with a story very much connected to Houston, the hometown of my own academic home, Rice University.

Rice University is very proud of the fact that it was here, in our football stadium, in September of 1962, that President Kennedy announced the nation's intentions "to go to the moon in this decade." Houstonians are very proud of the fact that "Houston" was the first word spoken on the surface of the moon, still in that decade, on July 20, 1969. It was Neil Armstrong of the Apollo 11 mission who would say then: "Houston, Tranquility Base here. The Eagle has landed." This little sentence, it turns out, is part of a much larger story that can easily function as a parable of sorts, and one particularly worthy of the comparative practices that we have engaged in here, in an effort to see and understand something of "the big picture."

And talk about a big picture. From the moon, of course, one can see the earth as a whole from a perspective that is not of this earth. One can also see that in reality there are no such things as borders. Political borders and nation-states—much like religions—are imaginary lines drawn on maps to mark the temporary results of the ongoing debates, compromises, and violences of human history. No such borders, and no such religions, can be seen from space. It's all one blue planet floating in the seeming infinity of space–time.

We too, in a much more humble way, have launched ourselves into space above and beyond these same local borders and temporal boundaries: theory as visionary journey and time travel again. And what have we seen? What do we take back with us as we land, with a splash (or a crash), in our home cultures, communities, and religions? Perhaps another famous NASA/Houston line is most appropriate at this point: "Houston, we have a problem."

Our journey began with a simple ethical gesture: the gesture of granting integrity, sincerity, and goodwill to other human beings and their cultural creations. We traveled in our minds and our imaginations

Comparing Religions: Coming to Terms, First Edition. Jeffrey J. Kripal, Ata Anzali, Andrea R. Jain, and Erin Prophet.
© 2014 Jeffrey J. Kripal. Published 2014 by John Wiley & Sons, Ltd.

through many such worlds. Our initiation ended with a return to our own beliefs, now renewed, rejected, or revised in the light of these shared travels and transformations.

There are many possible paths from here. Perhaps one will feel moved to learn another language, live in another culture, even convert to another worldview and way of life. One could then employ this new worldview to "step out" of one's birth culture. Later one could just as easily employ the culture one was born in to "step out" of this newly adopted culture. Back and forth. Back and forth. One may then choose to learn a third worldview, hoping that it will resolve the dilemmas and questions the first two could not. And then perhaps a fourth, to answer the questions that the first three could not. And a fifth …

And then what? At what point does one realize that *all* cultures are conditioned and constructed, that each has its strengths and weaknesses, that we do not live in reality as it is, but in our own, always limited social and symbolic webs of meaning and story? Comparison, it turns out, finally reveals the limited nature of our most basic beliefs. All of them. We really are floating in outer space now, as we have always been.

Such a stunning realization has led many thinking human beings to absolute relativism or honest atheism, which are perfectly rational and reasonable positions. In the end, the radical act of entertaining the possibility that all religious systems contain much truth leads to the realization that none of them is true in any objective or universal sense. Radical openness leads to radical skepticism.

But, as we have also seen, relativism and atheism are not the only reasonable conclusions. We have met many a religious thinker who has adopted some form of exclusivism, inclusivism, or pluralism to answer the problems that our travels have produced. We have also met many a figure who, like the Dutch anthropologist Mattjis van de Port, was shocked into the understanding that, yes, of course, culture is constructed. But it is also enchanted. The body is now not just a meat factory, or yet another means for society to write itself into the deepest crevices of the psyche. It is also a potential portal or star-gate. And everything—from elaborate ritual cycles and kitschy religious statues to possession states and magical coincidences—can be re-read both as historically conditioned *and* as pointing beyond itself, to what van de Port hymns as "the-rest-of-what-is."

It turns out that there are ways of knowing other than the way of words, numbers, and egos. Deeper ways. We are more than our left brains. Way more.

Not that such ways will solve all the burning questions about religion in our modern world. They will not. But at least they might help us to ask these questions in new, more radical and effective ways. And, together with the faithful and rational re-readings (without which there would be no reflexive re-readings), at least we can now see that these *are* problems, if not actual crises, and that it is crucial to our long-term survival as a species to turn around, look in the mirror, and ask the tough questions. The question of women. The question of race. The question of class, of social and economic justice. The question of sexual orientation. The question of population control and environmental sustainability. The question of religious violence. The question of cultural and religious pluralism. The question of democracy and freedom. The question of human rights (*all* of them). And the question of old, worn-out religious scriptures and myths.

Thanks to the hard intellectual labor and moral courage of many previous generations, all of these questions are being asked today, although none of them is really resolved at a global level. We have not "come to terms." Yet.

I hope it goes without saying that the study of religion will be, *must be* an integral part of this coming to terms and of any sustainable human future on this planet. That future will depend partly, maybe largely, on whether you and your children can step back and out of your own ethnic, religious, and cultural identities and learn to live in a world that is irreducibly plural and irreducibly the same. We might never be able to see—literally, like the astronauts in outer space—this planet as a single whole; but our futures, *your* futures, will almost certainly depend on whether this planet's people can embody such a cosmic perspective in their personal, social, political, professional, and religious lives.

It is up to you and your generations now …

Moon through the Trees (2002), by Lynn Randolph, 8″ × 6″.

Glossary

Part of "coming to terms" with the comparative study of religion is actually and literally "coming to terms," that is, defining and using a set of technical terms in precise and nuanced ways. The following definitions will help you do just this. We have striven for both brevity and clarity here. We have also restricted our definitions to the specific uses of these terms in the professional study of religion. Some of them, of course, may have other meanings in other contexts.

a priori **categories** structures of thought like space, time, and causality, which are regarded as innate (hence *a priori* or "from before") and shape the way we think and perceive, usually without us realizing it

abolition movement the movement to abolish the practice of slavery in the USA

agnosticism position claiming that we cannot know the truth about religious matters; it is often combined with the conviction that science is the only reliable means of knowing

agricultural pattern a widely distributed comparative pattern through which sexuality is rendered analogous to agriculture, the male being viewed as planter of the "seed" in the female "soil"

alchemy a practice that combines chemical and spiritual techniques to transform matter into gold and/or the human being into spirit

altered states of consciousness forms of mind, often of an extreme religious nature, that are experienced as radically other than the social ego

ancestor worship or veneration praying to, piously remembering, or religiously honoring one's deceased family members

ancient wisdom narrative an imagined history of religious truth that posits a line of inspired teachers who passed on a specific revelation

angelology the study, interpretation, and classification of angels

animism the belief that all things possess soul (*anima*) or spiritual intelligence

anomaly any figure, event, or thing that does not fit into an explanatory system

anthropocentrism tendency to think of human beings as the most valuable species on earth

anthropogony myth about how human beings came to be

Comparing Religions: Coming to Terms, First Edition. Jeffrey J. Kripal, Ata Anzali, Andrea R. Jain, and Erin Prophet.
© 2014 Jeffrey J. Kripal. Published 2014 by John Wiley & Sons, Ltd.

anthropomorphism   tendency to attribute human form to non-human entities like gods

apocalypse   term of Greek origin designating the "uncovering" or "revelation" of a secret such as the end of the world

apologetics   the discipline of defending through argument one's own religious system or philosophical position

asceticism   a religious lifestyle of discipline and denial of bodily pleasures for spiritual ends

auditions   "hearing" a spirit or deity speak

Axial Age   that period of time, roughly between 800 and 200 BCE, during which human civilizations around the world developed radically new religious orientations

belief   implicit or explicit intellectual assent to the truth of a given proposition or claim

binary   any set of opposites (self/other, subject/object, mental/material, inside/outside) within a cultural or cognitive system that structures thought, feeling, and behavior within that system

black theology   a way of thinking and speaking of God from the perspective of the historical experience of African Americans

blood sacrifice   a sacrifice that involves killing an animal or a human being

both–and   the paradoxical cognitive structure that robust comparison often produces

bracketing   the act of setting aside questions about the source, object, or truth of religious experience for the sake of careful description, classification, and comparison

bridge–bonding dilemma   the tension that arises between a community's need to form stable social bonds among its own members and to secure workable connections to outgroups within the broader society

canon formation   the process whereby a tradition defines the scope and content of its scriptures by choosing certain texts as authoritative or revealed and rejecting others

cases of the reincarnation type (CORT)   cases involving individuals, often very young, who remember the details of their previous lives

celibacy   a religious state defined by the commitment not to engage in any sexual activity for the sake of some religious end

channeling   the modern phenomenon of an individual acting as a "channel" for some textual revelation or for contact with a living soul or a deceased spirit

chaos   state of complete disorder and non-meaning

charisma   a special power attributed to or experienced in the presence of a religious figure who, by virtue of this power, is set apart as sacred or superhuman

Christ of faith   the theological understanding of Jesus of Nazareth as the Messiah or Son of God, within a Christian community or belief system

church   a religious organization closely aligned with the political polity, which seeks to instill a comprehensive and singular worldview in which people participate more or less automatically

circumcision   the cutting of the tip of the foreskin as a mark of religious identity

civil religion rituals   public ceremonies that draw on religious structures for political purposes, thus imbuing the city or nation-state with sacred values

civil rights movement   a widespread social movement in the USA that sought to overturn an array of discriminatory and violent racist laws and attitudes

clairaudience   the ability to hear a voice or voices speaking, usually on an issue at hand

clairvoyance   "clear seeing," French word used to refer to the ability to see things at a distance (in space and/or time)

class   the place of an individual or group in a hierarchical social system, usually determined by birth, wealth, education, and/or political power

cognitive science   branch of psychology concerned with mapping the internal "operating systems" that determine how we all think, feel, and perceive the world

collective unconscious   a posited level of the psyche that is shared by all human beings and results in striking similarities across world mythologies and religious experiences

commensality the required practice of eating with one's own social class or subgroup

commentarial tradition a body of readings and interpretive techniques that relate a revelation to the questions, needs, and forms of knowledge of succeeding generations

comparative practices of popular culture the often implicit comparative methods at work in genres like film, television, literature, and the Internet

comparative theology a practice that draws on tradition, reason, and intuition to address the challenge of religious pluralism for a particular faith community

comparison the intellectual act of negotiating sameness and difference in a set of observations

constructivism position claiming that all forms of human experience, including religious forms, are best explained as "constructed" through local processes

contagion the belief that an attribute of a social nature (like pollution or impurity) can be transmitted through touch or physical contact

contemplative prayer communing or becoming one with a deity or ultimate state, often through some advanced spiritual technique and a breakdown of the subject/object split

contextualism position claiming that human behavior and experience are best explained as the product of local linguistic, social, and political processes that cannot be universalized

conversion the realignment of an individual's life and worldview around a new religious narrative and set of beliefs

cosmogony myth about the genesis of the universe

cosmology the study of the origin, evolution, and structure of the physical universe

cosmos state of order and meaningful structure

cosmotheism a religious system that understands the physical universe to be a God and posits local gods as partial manifestations of this cosmic God

counterculture a youth movement, roughly from 1960 to 1975, that aimed to "counter" established society and to embrace alternative forms of consciousness and culture

creation myths sacred stories about how the world came into being

cultural anthropology the study of human nature through the analysis of social practices, symbols, myths, rituals, and so on

culture the entire network of institutions, laws, customs, symbols, technologies, and arts that constitute the life of a particular society

deep ecology a broad environmental movement that seeks to awaken human beings to the biological fact that they are intimate parts of a larger ecosystem, which *is* their bigger body

defense mechanism an attempt on the part of the psyche to protect itself from difficult material that would expose its own illusions or false assumptions

deism natural theology that views the universe as a kind of machine assembled by a God who "steps back" after creation, leaving the world to its own mechanisms

demonology the study, interpretation, and classification of demons

denomination modern sect that no longer takes a contentious position vis-à-vis the world and other religious communities but has become respectable and gone mainstream

difference describes the fact that a set of observations do not resemble one another but seem distinct

diffusion theory the hypothesis that the religious complex found in one place came from another place through migration, trade, war, or other forms of travel

divination any practice, formal or spontaneous, that attempts to intuit, predict, or fathom the future, usually toward some practical end (such as deciding on a course of action)

divinization the process of becoming a god or goddess

doctrine specific teaching or system of beliefs

Draper–White thesis a model of the interaction of religion and science that emphasizes conflict and the attempted suppression of science by religious authorities

ecology of religion the study of religions as expressions of their natural local environments

ego   one's conscious sense of self or personality coded in one's given name

empowered religious imagination   the temporary "supercharging" of the imagination toward the mediation of empirical or transcendent truths via image, symbol, and myth

endogamy   practice of marrying strictly within one's close social subgroup

entheogen   "generating a god within," a modern name given to sacred plants and substances that can catalyze extreme religious states

erotic   describes a sexual event that also functions as an opening or trigger to a religious experience

eschatology   a religion's "teachings about the end," that is, its understanding of the ultimate goal or final state of the individual and/or the world

Euhemerism   the theory that the gods had originally been human beings who were worshipped in their own lives for their accomplishments and were later divinized as local gods

evolutionary monotheism   the historical phenomenon of polytheistic systems developing into an accompanying monotheistic system

evolutionary psychology   branch of psychology that is interested in finding out how human cognitive, emotional, and perceptual structures are distant products of our deep evolutionary past

exclusivism   the rejection of other religious worldviews on the basis of one's own religious categories and worldview

experience   a subjectively felt, perceived, or cognized event that is self-evident to the person "having" it

explicit theology   a model of the nature of God (or the gods) that is spelled out systematically

faithful re-reading   the comparison and analysis of religions from a perspective informed by and committed to a particular faith tradition

false consciousness   any form of awareness that relies for its stability on the person remaining ignorant about the true nature, dynamics, and/or origin of his or her ideas and beliefs

feminist theology   a way of thinking and speaking of God from the perspective of women, toward a more just inclusion of female identities, values, and forms of knowledge

filter thesis   the hypothesis that consciousness is filtered, translated, reduced, or transmitted through the brain but not ultimately produced by it

fitness   the individual organism's ability to reproduce

Fortean   "in the spirit of Charles Fort," an epithet usually applied to bizarre, weird, or humorous occurrences that cannot be explained scientifically or religiously

founding myth   sacred story about the founding figure of a religion

functionalism   a method that examines the psychological and social uses of the religions and generally avoids any normative discussion of their truth claims

fundamentalism   a modern way of being religious that relies on highly selective literalist readings of an inerrant scripture and on a return to fundamentals— the postulated original truths of the faith

funerary rituals   religious practices around death and the handling of corpses

Gaia theory   the hypothesis that the earth is a self-regulating system

gender   the "standard" model of what it means to be a man, a woman, or some third gender in a particular culture

gender equity   the ethical principle that the genders should be treated as equal

general history of religions   the full historical sweep of humanity's religious experience, from prehistory to the present day

gift model of sacrifice   the implicit or explicit understanding that a sacrificial offering is a "gift" to the deity for which something is expected in return

gnostics   Jewish and Christian communities of the first centuries CE who emphasized a direct mystical knowing (*gnōsis*) over literalist belief

hagiography   an idealized story of a saint or founder that expresses the self-understanding and values of the tradition in question

heretics   people who, instead of submitting to the authority of tradition, follow their own opinion and choose to believe something else

hermeneutics   the art, practice, and method of interpretation

hero or quest myths   a type of myth that works through the staged tropes of departure, adventure in a foreign land, temptation, battle, discovery or victory, and return

heterodoxy   any religious system believed to be "other" than/at variance with the official (orthodox) position, hence incorrect, and hence not authoritative

hierarchy   any system that subordinates "lower" classes of people to "higher" classes of people within an idealized social whole

hierophany   a "manifestation of the sacred" through the medium of a natural object or event, for instance a tree, a rock, a place, an image, or a celestial phenomenon

historical consciousness   consciousness or awareness of the fact that every perspective, including one's own, is limited by and relative to a particular place and time

historical Jesus   the historical figure of Jesus of Nazareth, as best we can approximate his life and teachings through academic methods

historical–critical method   contextualizing a text by treating it as a human product written at a particular time, in a particular place, for a specific audience, and with a specific purpose

history of religions   branch of the study of religion that emphasizes the comparison of religious forms, often of an extreme nature, across large stretches of space and time

Holocaust   the systematic murdering of approximately ten million people, mostly Jews, in the labor prisons of the Nazi concentration camps

humanities   the study of consciousness coded in culture

id   the largely unconscious mental realm of instinctual drives, primarily of a sexual and aggressive nature

ideal type   an abstract pattern (for example social) that cannot be found in the real world in pure form but can nevertheless be used as a comparative device

idealism   a philosophical position that understands mind as the ultimate nature and source of reality

imaginal   the content of the empowered religious imagination and its mediation of empirical events (as in telepathy) or transcendent realities (as in revelation)

immanence   being present in (or coextensive with) the natural or the physical world

implicit theology   a model of the nature of God or the gods that is not spelled out systematically but assumed in mythology or ritual

inclusivism   the acceptance of other religious worldviews on the basis of one's own religious worldview and its categories

ingroup   the community one belongs to and identifies with

initiation   a set of formalized activities and teachings through which a person's social or religious identity is transformed

insider–outsider problem   the question of who makes a better scholar of religion: the "inside" believer or the "outside" analyst

institutionalization of charisma   the social process whereby the special power or "charge" of a religious figure is preserved, maintained, and passed on after his or her death

kosher laws   dietary rules prominent in many forms of Judaism

LGBT theology   a way of thinking and speaking of God from the perspective of those with marginalized sexualities—lesbian, gay, bisexual, or transgendered

libation rituals   religious practices of spilling a liquid, often over or before the image of a deity, and often in commemoration of the dead or chthonic deities

liberalism   a philosophical position that emphasizes individuals as autonomous moral agents who seek to constantly revise their world and the democratic arrangements that protect it

liberation theology a way of thinking and speaking of God that understands God as identifying with the poor, the marginalized, and the oppressed

libido the life energy of the body that is closely aligned with the biology of sexuality but can be redeployed for all kinds of nonsexual, creative, and cultural ends

life-cycle rituals religious practices around a biological event or a social transformation related to a biological event (such as birth, puberty, marriage, death)

liminal state the middle or "in-between" phase of an initiation in which the person's old identity is deconstructed

linguistics the study of languages—sometimes pursued from a comparativist angle and aimed toward modeling the universal structures of languages

liturgical prayer communal praise of a deity, often of a highly ritualized and formal nature

liturgical rituals religious practices designed to honor, worship, or praise a deity

magic ritual practice in which an assumed correspondence between a mental state and some aspect of the physical world allows the former to influence the latter

male : female :: spirit : nature a widely distributed comparative pattern in which the male is associated with the spiritual/transcendent world and the female with the natural/immanent world

male androgyne a mythical figure, often symbolizing wholeness or divinity, who is both male and female but whose maleness is privileged as a primary feature

martyr someone who becomes—usually through death and dramatic suffering—a "witness" to a particular truth, especially that of a religious creed

Marxism the philosophical doctrine of Karl Marx—a form of dialectical materialism positing that all the forms of human consciousness, social behavior, political order, culture, art, and ideology ("the superstructure") are produced by their corresponding economic systems ("the base")

material religion an umbrella term for all of those physical objects or things that enable a community to imagine, express, and perform its respective religious creed

materialism a position according to which matter is the primordial factor or "existent" in the universe

materialization the reported capacity of the empowered religious imagination to express in material or quasi-material form its content

meditation general description of a kind of mental discipline that often involves extreme forms of concentration pursued for religious ends

medium a person who acts as a mediator between the living and the dead

Merton thesis a model of the interaction between religion and science that emphasizes resonance and religion's influence on the development of science

metaphor classical figure of speech essential to poetry, which links two things for the sake of describing one through the other but, unlike comparison and analogy, leaves the correspondence between them unstated or implicit

metaphysical religion a phrase used to describe those alternative movements in modernity that emphasize mind, magical powers, energy, and healing "beyond the physical"

miracle an anomalous, wondrous, or even simply uncommon event that functions as a "sign" for the truth of a particular religious tradition

moderate forms of reductive inquiry methods that employ reductive models but either leave the door open to transcendent influences or avoid addressing this question

modernity a period characterized by a very broad and influential style of thought and practice, which emphasizes scientific progress, reason, and universalism

monasticism the practice of living in celibacy, within a same-sex community, for the sake of religious principles or belief

monotheism any religious system that holds that there is only one God

monster figure of the religious imagination that can function as a sign or omen in the revelation of the "left" side or negative mode of the sacred

moral relativism position in ethics claiming that it is impossible to judge fairly between different value systems on moral matters, since each system is internally consistent and self-justifying

mystical dimension of a religious system that emphasizes an element of "secret" communion, connection, or identity between human nature and the divine or the "really Real"

mysticism a highly individualistic type of religious orientation, which focuses on the direct experience of inner spiritual realties and hence is very difficult to organize socially

myth a sacred story that founds or grounds a particular religious world

mythology the systematic study of myths and sacred stories

natural theology a way of thinking about God that relies on the study of the natural world as an expression of God's nature, wisdom, and intentions

Neoplatonism Middle Platonism, a continuation of the Platonic tradition in Alexandria after the closure of Plato's Old Academy in Athens, became "Neoplatonism" from Plotinus on (third century CE)

nocebo effect *nocebo* means "I will harm," and the whole phrase applies to the phenomenon of a fake substance harming individuals when they believe that it is real

nonlocal self the phenomenon of recognizing one's self most accurately reflected not in the culture and religion one was born in, but in a "foreign" framework

noumenon in Kant's philosophy, that which exists independently of one's perception of it—the thing-in-itself

Oedipus complex a universal pattern postulated by Freud, whereby a young son's sense of self emerges gradually from his infantile love of the mother and his aggressive competitive stance toward the father

omens signs that occur either spontaneously in nature or in a formal ritual context and indicate that something—often something of a bad nature—is about to happen

oracles prophecies or ecstatic and enigmatic utterances given by a professional medium at a client's request

orientalism a model of human civilizations that posits, often for political purposes, an inferior "East"—spiritual, feminine, or passive—set against a superior "West"—rational, masculine, or active

orthodoxy an ideological system, especially religious—usually the one in authority—believed to be "straight" (*orthos*), in other words correct

outgroup a community, often framed as other, foreign, dangerous, or impure, to which one does not belong and against which members of the ingroup identify themselves

pagans people (originally from the countryside) who do not accept Christianity

panentheism position claiming that the physical universe is within God or is a part of God's body, but that God also transcends it

panpsychism like animism, the belief that "everything" or "the whole" (*to pan*) possesses soul or spiritual intelligence (*psuchē*)

pantheism position claiming that everything is God and God is identical with the physical/natural universe

paranormal a term referring to mind-over-matter events that are thought to be natural but still beyond the modeling of contemporary science

parapsychology branch of modern psychology that studies mind–matter interactions that are beyond our present scientific models

particularity manner in which a tradition emphasizes the specific cultural and historical expressions of its revelation or sacred truths

paternity–patriarchy principle a mode of comparison that follows issues of "correct" family line, inheritance, and the privileging of male authority

patriarchy "rule by the father"—a term that characterizes societies and cultures heavily dominated by male interests, perspectives, and authority; a very stable, nearly universal feature in traditional social systems of the past

perennialism   position claiming that the different major religions all possess a single mystical truth or a common core

petitionary prayer   prayer in which one asks for something from a god

phenomenology of religion   the study of religion through a close description and analysis of how it "appears" within individual experience

phenomenon   in Kant's philosophy, that which appears, that is, how a thing is perceived by a subject or its subjective appearance/representation

pilgrimage rituals   ritual acts of traveling, for a religious purpose, to a place held to be sacred

placebo effect   *placebo* means "I will please," and the whole phrase captures the phenomenon of a fake substance helping individuals when they are convinced that it is real

Platonic orientalism   the ancient tendency to locate in the orient ("the East") revelation and wisdom, thought to resemble or prefigure the teachings of Plato

plausibility   the degree to which an idea is accepted or rejected within a particular cultural context, very often irrespectively of its objective truth or falsehood

pluralism   openness to or potential acceptance of all religious worldviews, regarded as cultural approximations or partial actualizations of an underlying reality or truth, which is understood to transcend them all

polemics   the art or practice of arguing against an alien philosophical position or religious belief

poltergeist   in parapsychology, the "angry ghost" generally believed to materialize from the extreme emotional states of a focal agent, often in adolescence

polytheism   any religious system that holds that there are many gods

postcolonial theory   a means of interpreting modern historical phenomena as deeply intertwined with the previous colonial era and its political, economic, and imperial injustices

preferential option for the poor   the principle that the Bible should be read, and Christian life should

be lived, in ways that express God's primary identification with the poor

priest   a religious figure who mediates the charisma of the tradition through an official role or recognized office and whose authority does not rely on personal charismatic powers

primal scene   the infant's or the child's witnessing of parental sex

principle of extremity   the hypothesis that the dynamics of religion can best be seen in extreme forms of religious experience, where they are magnified and therefore rendered visible

profane   that which is ordinary, banal, or mundane

projection theory   a model of religion that posits that the gods and other religious phenomena are expressions of human nature rendered "objective" or external to human beings

promissory materialism   position claiming that, although we do not yet know how to explain some phenomena through materialist models, we eventually will

prophecy   the use of altered states of consciousness to predict the future or to criticize a political or religious authority

prophet   a religious prodigy—an individual endowed with superhuman gifts—who speaks for a god to a particular community or individual

psi   technical term in parapsychology that refers to postulated but unknown mechanisms of psychical phenomena

psychical   a term referring to the alleged powers of the human mind to know things outside the normal sense channels and beyond the ordinary parameters of space–time

psychology of religion   branch of the study of religion that focuses on the internal, subjective, or experiential dimensions of religions

purity codes   a set of rules and attending moods and assumptions that structure a particular community around the binaries of "purity" and "pollution"

queer criticism   an approach to interpreting human sexuality and its expressions that emphasizes the fluid and morphing nature of sexual desire and gender identity

queer theology thinking and speaking of God from the perspective of queer individuals, who understand sexual identities as socially invented, and often in unjust ways

race a person's or a group's identity, as constructed on the basis of skin color or presumed physical features

rational re-reading the comparison and analysis of religions within the parameters of human reason, human cognition, and sensory data

reason human faculty guided and limited by information derived from the senses, which it processes according to standardized forms of logic and the structures of human cognition

reductionism the explanation of religious and other phenomena as effects of some deeper, underlying, and hence more basic causes, processes, or mechanisms of a different, non-religious nature

reflexive re-reading comparison and analysis of religions that rationally reduces religious phenomena to human nature, only to discover that this nature overflows the reach of the original rationalist models

reflexivity capacity to think about thinking, become aware of awareness, and hence free consciousness temporarily from the parameters of society and ego

relics remains of human bodies considered to be holy and used ritually, as if they contained a power akin to electricity or contagion

religion any set of established stories, rituals, mental and bodily practices, and institutions that have built up around extreme encounters with some anomalous presence, power, or hidden order

religious freedom citizens' right to choose and practice their own religions, as long as these do not negatively and unduly impact the freedoms and wellbeing of others

religious primacy the belief or assumption, usually displayed by the dominant religious group, that "religious freedom" means that one's own beliefs and rituals should control civic spaces

religious question any question that attempts to address matters of ultimate concern, such as the nature of reality, the meaning of life, or the purpose of suffering

religious tolerance the civic virtue or public policy of not attempting to eliminate, suppress, or otherwise discriminate against religious beliefs and practices outside the society's dominant worldview

revelation set of claims about ultimate matters that do not derive from anything available to the senses or to human reason but are given to a community, often through a single individual, within an extreme religious event or experience

revolutionary monotheism a type of monotheism that denies the existence of other gods rather than seeing them as expressions of its own cosmic god

ritual the re-enactment of a myth through repeated scripted actions, usually in a culturally prescribed space and time by a religious specialist

romantic reversal an employment of projection theory during the romantic movement that suggested that the human projector may in fact be divine

sacred that which is special or set apart from the ordinary and is often experienced as a power or presence at once terrifying and attractive

sacrifice a ritual in which some vegetable, fluid, animal, or human being is offered to a deity, sometimes through violence and usually in hopes that the deity will give something in return

saint a religious prodigy considered to be especially representative of the values and worldview of a particular religious community

sameness describes the fact that a set of observations resemble one another or seem related

scapegoat model of sacrifice model that works on the implicit or explicit assumption that the sacrificial offering is a replacement or stand-in for the community

scripture any set of writings believed to be revealed or divinely inspired

sect a community that has become disillusioned with the public church and has broken away from it in order to reconstruct religious life around some key doctrinal or ritual point

secularism   any system of thought or practice that does not invoke a religious principle and does not rely on explicitly religious values

separable soul   widespread belief that the essence of the human being is not the body and in consequence can be separated from it —in dreams, trance, ecstasy, and death

sexual orientation   the specific (but often quite fluid) ways in which a person's sexual desires are oriented toward an object or objects of a particular gender

sexual trauma   condition in which the psyche has been wounded, cracked open, or otherwise compromised by some previous sexual violation or negative experience

sexuality   a biologically driven instinct that, although genetically determined to varying degrees, is nevertheless open to cultural shaping

shaman   a religious specialist found in many indigenous cultures, who specializes in trance states, ecstatic journeys, healing, magical powers and battle, music, and mythical lore

Shoah   the preferred Hebrew word for the Holocaust

sky god   a deity, generally male, believed to reside in the sky

social gospel movement   a faithful re-reading of the "kingdom of God" as a call for social justice and as a subsequent program working for broad-based structural changes in society

social justice   the moral insistence on being treated the same

sociology of knowledge   discipline that explores the theory that truth and knowledge are not simply "out there" and discovered, but are largely constructed through historical processes and social institutions

sociology of religion   branch of the study of religion that focuses on the external, objective, or institutional dimensions of religions

spirit possession   state of being taken over by the spirit of a god, demon, or deceased person

spirituality   term used to signal a personal way of relating to the divine or the underlying reality, a way that is more or less independent of religious authority and its social institutions

strong forms of reductive inquiry   methods that reduce religious events and experiences, entirely and without remainder, to natural or materialist mechanisms and explanations

structuralism   method within anthropology that understands particular social phenomena as meaningful parts of a larger metasystem, whole, or "structure"

sublimation   process whereby libidinal energies are diverted from their original sexual aims and converted into cultural accomplishments such as those of art, literature, and religion

subliminal self   a region of the mind that exists "below the threshold" (*sub limine*) of normal awareness and is considered responsible for extraordinary capacities like telepathy, clairvoyance, or what makes a genius

substantive comparative practices   practices illustrating an approach to religions that is concerned with these religions' truth claims about ultimate matters

suffrage   the right to vote

super sexualities   altered states of energy and consciousness commonly experienced both as sexual and as the means of divinization, transcendence, and/or religious transmutation

superego   the psychological realm of the conscience, which derives from social interactions with the parents and later on with other social actors and institutions

supernormal   the immediate predecessor of the paranormal; it has the connotation that psychical capacities are linked to evolutionary processes and signal future powers of the species

symbol   an image, often spontaneous and enigmatic in nature, that shares in the essence of that which it signifies

synchronicity   in Jung's usage, co-occurrence or simultaneous occurrence of a mental and a material event that have no (discernible) causal connection yet are experienced as being meaningfully (and sometimes uncannily) related

Tantra an umbrella term covering a set of Asian traditions that emphasize the unity between the divine and the human nature, particularly as this unity is manifested in the human body and its erotic energies

teleological possessing an end, goal, or purpose

telepathy "pathos at a distance," communication outside the normal sense channels, usually between loved ones in extreme emotional, traumatic, or deadly states

theodicy word that means "god's justice" and names various theological–philosophical attempts to reconcile the problem of suffering and evil with God's goodness and omnipotence

theology intellectual domain consisting in attempts to relate human reason to a revelation, particularly around the nature of God, in the traditions of a given community of believers

theōria "sight," "spectacle," "contemplation"—the Greek word from which "theory" originates; originally it referred to what "was seen," either on a pilgrimage to another land or within a direct vision of philosophical truth

third gender general phrase for all those mixed genders, alternative sexualities, bisexualities, or transsexualities that do not follow the traditional binary logic of male/female

totem an animal or an object that serves to represent or symbolize a particular group of people

tradition the result of passing on or transmitting anything—for instance a religious system—from one generation to another

trance capacity of human beings to enter altered states of consciousness, often in order to facilitate contact with deities and the dead

transcendence state of being above, beyond, or outside the natural–physical world

transgression ritual act of subverting a purity code system toward some religious end

transhuman "beyond what is human," an attribute based on the idea that the human being or the soul can take on forms that are beyond human nature in its present condition

trickster a mythical figure who, through various comedic, deceitful, and offensive behaviors upsets the established order in order to mock, renew, or reform the world

unconscious mental realm inaccessible to the conscious self, which nevertheless influences (if not determines) much of one's thinking, feeling, and behavior

universality all-inclusive manner in which a revelation makes claims on human beings, irrespective of their historical or cultural context

vitalism position claiming that there is a life force or living energy at work in the universe that is not reducible to matter and its mechanisms

world religion a religious tradition that has expanded beyond its original cultural context, to reach a global audience

Index

Page references for illustrations are given in italics, e.g. *121*. Title entries for films and books are given as, for example, *Close Encounters of the Third Kind* (1977); *Communion* (Strieber).

Comparing Religions: Coming to Terms, First Edition. Jeffrey J. Kripal, Ata Anzali, Andrea R. Jain, and Erin Prophet.
© 2014 Jeffrey J. Kripal. Published 2014 by John Wiley & Sons, Ltd.